# BUDDHISM IN CHINA
## A HISTORICAL SURVEY

# BUDDHISM
# IN CHINA

## A HISTORICAL SURVEY

BY KENNETH K. S. CH'EN

PRINCETON UNIVERSITY PRESS
PRINCETON, NEW JERSEY

To the Memory of my *Guru,*
Professor Walter Eugene Clark,
who is now in nirvana

## THE VIRGINIA AND RICHARD STEWART
## MEMORIAL LECTURES

Professor Ch'en's study of the history of Buddhism in China is the first fruit of a generous bequest by Miss Marie Stewart to the Council of the Humanities of Princeton University to establish a series of lectures and seminars in honor of her mother and father. The Virginia and Richard Stewart Memorial Lectures are designed to bring leading scholars of the religions of the world to the Princeton campus for a period of research, during which time, through public lectures and seminar discussions, they share with students and faculty the results of their studies.

This volume, the first in a series to be known as the "Princeton Studies in the History of Religions," is an attempt to share with an even wider audience knowledge of contemporary research into the history, beliefs, and practices of the varied religions of the world. It was Miss Stewart's hope that "these lectures will be made available for the widest possible public dissemination by every means in order that their influence upon all people may be more effective and enduring."

Philip H. Ashby
Department of Religion
Princeton University

# PREFACE

BUDDHISM, one of the most important religions in the history of East Asia, began in a tiny kingdom at the foot of the Himalayas. As it developed, it spread into East and Southeast Asia, influencing the lives and thoughts of this vast segment of the world's population. This book is concerned with only one of these regions—China.

There is a wealth of information concerning Buddhism in China that is written in Chinese or Japanese or has been published in learned journals not readily available. The author, by extensive research over a long period of years, has uncovered much of this material and hence is able to give a comprehensive historical survey of Buddhism in China for those who do not have the time or the linguistic equipment to read the research literature.

This book is written primarily for those people who already have a general acquaintance with the history and religions of the Far East, with some particular interest in Chinese history and civilization, and who desire to know more about the development of Buddhism in China. It will serve also as a useful source of collateral readings for courses dealing with the history and culture of China and East Asia.

For those who desire to pursue further some of the topics discussed in the text, there is a selected bibliography of references written in European and Oriental languages, together with some comments. It is possible to check on the authority of any statement or quotation in the text by referring to this bibliography.

The following publishers have graciously permitted me to quote from their published works: The Clarendon Press, Oxford, from the *Sacred Books of the East*, Vol. 21 and 49, and from J. Legge, *The Texts of Taoism*; The Ronald Press Company of New York, from *Ennin's Diary, The Record of a Pilgrimage to China in Search of the Law*, translated by Edwin O. Reischauer, and from Edwin O. Reischauer, *Ennin's Travels in T'ang China*; Cambridge University Press, from J. Needham, *Science and Civilization in China*, Vol. 3; Sheed and Ward Inc., from H. de Lubac, *Aspects of Buddhism*; George Allen and Unwin, Ltd., from A. Waley, *The Real Tripitaka*; Harper and Row, from C. C. Chang, *The*

*Practice of Zen*; Luzac and Company, from D. T. Suzuki, *Outlines of Mahayana Buddhism*; G. Routledge and Kegan Paul, from A. Waley, *Travels of an Alchemist*; Alfred A. Knopf, Inc., from R. Grousset, *Civilizations of the East*, Vol. 3; Istituto Poligrafico Dello Stato, from G. Tucci, *Tibetan Painted Scrolls*, Vol. 1; Statens Etnografiska Museum, from F. Lessing, *Yung Ho Kung*; E. J. Brill, from E. Zürcher, *The Buddhist Conquest of China*.

In the process of writing this book, the author received financial assistance from the American Council of Learned Societies, the Research Committee of the University of California at Los Angeles, and the University Research Fund of Princeton University. This financial assistance is gratefully acknowledged here. He wishes also to acknowledge his indebtedness to a host of individual friends who have offered assistance and criticism in one form or another, but especially the following people: Professors Lien-sheng Yang and William Hung of Harvard University; Professor W.-T. Chan of Dartmouth College; Dr. Alfred Chiu, librarian of the Chinese Japanese Library of the Harvard Yenching Institute; Mrs. P. K. Mok, librarian of the Oriental Library at the University of California at Los Angeles; Mr. Tung Shih-kang, curator of the Gest Oriental Library at Princeton University; and his colleagues Professors Philip Ashby, Paul Ramsey, and Marius Jansen, all of Princeton University. In the final stages of preparation valuable editorial assistance was given by Professor Kenneth Morgan of Colgate University, Mrs. Dorothy Sickels, Mrs. Mary Tozer, and Mrs. Polly Hanford. For this the author is grateful. He wishes to acknowledge also the contributions of Mrs. Clarence Shangraw, Mrs. Lester Vetter, and Mr. Leighton Ch'en, who typed different portions of the manuscript when it was under preparation. Finally, but not least, one vote of thanks for all the assistance rendered unstintingly throughout the years by Willow Ch'en.

KENNETH CH'EN

Princeton University
December 1963

# CONTENTS

[ xi ]

CONTENTS

# INTRODUCTION

# TABLE OF CHINESE DYNASTIES

| | | | |
|---|---|---|---|
| Shang | ca.1766-ca.1125 B.C. | | |
| Chou | 1122-256 B.C. | | |
| Ch'in | 221-206 B.C. | | |
| Han | 206 B.C.-A.D. 220 | | |
| Wu 222-280 | Wei 220-265 | Shu 221-263 | |
| Western Chin | 265-316 | | |
| Eastern Chin | 317-420 | Hou Chao | 328-352 |
| | | Ch'ien Liang | 313-376 |
| | | Ch'ien Ch'in | 351-394 |
| | | Hou Ch'in | 384-417 |
| | | Pei Liang | 397-439 |
| Liu Sung | 420-479 | Northern Wei | 386-534 |
| Ch'i | 479-502 | | |
| Liang | 502-557 | Northern Ch'i | 550-557 |
| Ch'en | 557-589 | Northern Chou | 557-581 |
| Sui | 581-618 | | |
| T'ang | 618-907 | | |
| Wu-tai | 907-960 | | |
| Sung (North) | 960-1127 | | |
| (South) | 1127-1279 | Liao | 907-1124 |
| | | Chin | 1115-1234 |
| Yüan | 1280-1368 | | |
| Ming | 1368-1644 | | |
| Ch'ing | 1644-1912 | | |

# CHAPTER I

# BACKGROUND

THE study of Buddhism in China is of importance to the world because of its influence on the Chinese way of life throughout history. The decline of Buddhism in China during the last few centuries should not obscure the fact that when the religion was enjoying prestige and popularity, it influenced Chinese culture in many ways and left lasting impressions on Chinese life. Neo-Confucianism was stimulated in its development by a number of Buddhist ideas. Certain features of Taoism, such as its canon and pantheon, were taken over from Buddhism. Words and phrases in the Chinese language owe their origin to terms introduced by Buddhism, while in astronomical, calendrical, and medical studies the Chinese benefited from information introduced by Indian Buddhist monks. Finally, and most important of all, the religious life of the Chinese was affected profoundly by the doctrines and practices, pantheon and ceremonies brought in by the Indian religion. Before we begin our account of the introduction and spread of Buddhism in China, however, we shall turn briefly to the origin and development of the religion in India.

## ORIGIN OF BUDDHISM IN INDIA

Buddhism was founded by an Indian prince, Gautama Śākyamuni, who lived during the sixth and fifth centuries B.C. He was the son of the king of a tiny state at the foot of the Himalayas and was brought up amidst the luxuries and pleasures befitting one of his birth and class. However, unlike other Indian princes, Śākyamuni soon became disenchanted with the life of sensual pleasures he was leading, and left the sheltered, comfortable, and luxurious life of the home to become a religious mendicant. After years of religious striving he attained enlightenment at the age of thirty-five and thenceforth was known as the Buddha. The next forty-five years of his life were spent in preaching his message to his fellow men; at the age of eighty he died.

The Indians at the time of the Buddha were already a highly

civilized race with sophisticated ideas of religion and salvation. Some Indian sages maintained that salvation could be attained by the scrupulous observance of the rituals prescribed in the Vedas or the sacred literature of the Hindus, as such a performance generated so much magic power that it could induce even the gods to do the will of man. Others advocated emancipation by intellectual means. For these, the quest was for a unity of the impersonal Brahma, the cosmic principle pervading the entire universe, with the atman, the psychic principle or inner essence of man. This was the main teaching of that body of Vedic literature known as the Upanishads. Once this unity was achieved by the seer sitting in the forest immersed in speculations, he was said to have reached enlightenment or release from *saṁsāra*, the endless round of rebirths. Still other teachers taught that the way to salvation consisted of self-mortification: torture of the body for long periods of time by taking no food or by sitting on thorns or on burning cinders.

Amidst such a welter of contending beliefs, Śākyamuni established a system that repudiated the Brahmanical claim of the Vedas to be the divine and infallible source of spiritual truth, rejected the rituals as the sole means to salvation, and disapproved of the intellectual approach of the Upanishads. He welcomed into his community of followers not only the high-caste Brahmans and warriors but also the traders, merchants, artisans, women, and even outcasts. His way to salvation was based on a rigorous code of personal spiritual behavior with the emphasis on conduct as the chief means to salvation. Because he steered a middle course between austerities on the one hand and gratification of the senses on the other, he called his teachings the middle path.

## THE TEACHINGS OF THE BUDDHA

Though the Buddha did not accept many of the ideas current in the Indian religions of his time, he did incorporate into his system the prevailing doctrines of karma and rebirth. The word "karma" means deed or act. Every act produces a result or fruit; a good deed produces a good fruit; an evil deed, an evil fruit. The process operates automatically without any supernatural agent sitting in judgment to render a decision. "Karma" to the Indians means the deed performed and the results that arise from it. To this conception of karma the Buddha made a significant addition. He taught that karma involved not just the deed and the reward but also the intention behind the deed. For karma to be generated there must be intention, and he considered this intention to be much more important than the deed. If the deed is unintentional, he said, no karma is generated, but if intention is present, then karma is produced even though the deed itself is not actually performed. The Buddhist definition of "karma" is therefore "intention plus the bodily action that follows the intention."

According to the karma of the past, a living being will undergo repeated rebirths in the cycle of existence and assume a different form in each rebirth. To the Buddhist the life of an individual started from a beginningless past and will extend into the endless future. When a living being dies, he believes, the karma that he has accumulated in the past will determine the nature of the next rebirth. In Buddhism there are five states of existence: deity, man, animal, hungry ghost,[1] and denizen of hell. The first two are considered to be good states; the last three, evil.

One of the fundamental beliefs of Buddhism is that so long as we are revolving in this endless cycle of rebirths, we are continually subject to suffering and misery. In the very first sermon that the Buddha preached he said that birth is suffering, old age is suffering, death is suffering, separation from beloved ones is suffering, not getting what one wishes is suffering. If we wish to get rid of suffering, we must get outside the round of existence. The aim of Buddhism, as with all Indian religions, is to break the cycle of rebirth at some point, so that the living being no longer continues to suffer repeated rebirths. When the living being stops transmigrating, he attains salvation.

How does the Buddhist achieve this salvation? The classical formulation of the Buddhist doctrine of salvation was given by the Buddha in his first sermon, in which he enunciated the four noble truths: life is suffering; this suffering has a cause, which is craving for existence and sensual pleasures; this suffering can be

---

[1] The term "hungry ghost" denotes a class of beings with tiny pin-sized heads and huge stomachs, so that, no matter how much they eat, they are in perpetual hunger. The All Souls' Feast, celebrated by the Buddhists on the night of the fifteenth day of the seventh month, was for the purpose of appeasing these hungry ghosts by providing food and clothing for them.

suppressed; the way to suppress suffering is the practice of the noble eightfold path, which consists of right views, right intentions, right speech, right action, right livelihood, right effort, right mindfulness, and right concentration.

This eightfold path is usually divided into three categories that comprise the whole range of Buddhist discipline: morality or moral conduct (right speech, right action, and right livelihood); mental discipline (right effort, right mindfulness, and right concentration); intuitive insight or wisdom (right views, right intentions).

The kernel of the Buddhist moral discipline is contained in the following words of the Buddha: "Not to commit any evil, to do good, and to purify one's own mind." As to what constituted evil, he said that any act that is harmful to oneself or to another is evil. "When you wish to perform an action, consider whether it is going to be harmful to others, harmful to yourself, harmful to yourself and others; if it is, do not perform it, for it is an evil action whose fruit will be suffering." Right speech means refraining from falsehood, malicious talk, and abusive language. Right action means refraining from stealing, killing, and unchastity; and right livelihood means abstaining from earning a living by improper means, such as killing living beings, making astrological forecasts, or practicing fortune-telling. However, moral conduct also embraces such virtues as loving friendship, compassion, sympathetic joy, and equanimity.

The second of the tripod, mental discipline, has as its objective the control of the mind. To the Buddhist the root of all evil is craving, craving for sensual pleasures and craving for material possessions. Such cravings require two elements, the organs of sense and external objects. External objects are too numerous to be ignored or annihilated, and they impinge on our senses on all sides. Moreover, Buddhism does not encourage the practice of austerities that aim at torturing the senses. However, the Buddha said, we can control the mind and discipline it in such a way that it will not make the mistake of looking upon unpleasant, impure, and impermanent things as pleasant, pure, and permanent. This control of the mind is achieved through mental discipline. Mental discipline means bringing the mind to one single point and holding it steady on that point, so that there is no wavering or wandering. The Buddhists claim that when the mind is not disturbed by external elements, it can attain stages of bliss and ecstasy not otherwise obtainable, and that it will promote spiritual development, diminish the impact of suffering, and deepen the virtues of compassion and gentleness.

In a famous passage the Buddha declared that he who practices mental discipline will see things as they really are. In this manner the Blessed One indicated the relationship between the second and the third leg of the tripod, intuitive insight or wisdom, the seeing of things as they really are. This category presupposes that there is a surface and a depth of things, and that it is necessary to penetrate beyond external appearances to get at true reality.

Intuitive wisdom consists of taking the right view of things, namely, holding to the truths that all existence is suffering, that all existence is impermanent, and that there is no permanent self or soul in man. The first of these truths has already been mentioned. The Buddha once said that the tears shed by man over the loss of his beloved ones during the course of interminable existence are more voluminous than the waters of the ocean. Once a woman came to the Buddha and asked him to restore to life her child who had just died. The Buddha consented, on condition that she obtain a mustard seed from a family which had not endured the suffering of death. The woman went out feeling hopeful, but as she went from family to family, she found that they all had experienced such suffering at one time or another. The universality of suffering now dawned upon her, whereupon she returned to the Blessed One and asked to be taken into the order of nuns.

Concerning the truth of impermanence, the last words of the Buddha were, "Subject to decay are all compound things." He often said that in his teachings he sought to avoid the two extremes of materialism, that everything is, and nihilism, that everything is not. Instead, he taught the middle path, that everything is a becoming. There is no static moment in life, only an eternal flux without beginning or end. We are constantly changing and becoming something else every moment. Even the most durable things are undergoing a process of change.

The third basic truth is the doctrine of no permanent self or soul. The prevailing Indian idea at the time of the Buddha was that there exists in each individual a permanent self which when merged with the universal self meant emancipation from the cycle of rebirth. The Indian clung dearly to this concept of a permanent self. To the Buddha, however, such a belief in the existence of a permanent self was one of the most pernicious of errors, the most deceitful of illusions, which must be destroyed before one could enter the path of salvation. Belief in a permanent self, he declared, breeds attachment, attachment breeds egoism, and egoism breeds craving for existence, pleasure, fame, and fortune, all of which keep one tied to the round of existence. To counteract this pernicious belief the Buddha boldly enunciated the doctrine of no permanent self or soul. He said he looked everywhere for this permanent self but could not find any; instead, he found only a conglomeration of the five aggregates: material body, sensation, perception, predisposition, and consciousness. At any one moment we are but a momentary collection of these five aggregates, a combination of physical matter and mental energies or forces. As these change every moment, so does the composition. We are but a continuous living entity which does not remain the same for two consecutive moments, which comes into being and disappears as soon as it arises. Once we deny the existence of a permanent self, we destroy all our selfish desires and self-interests, we give up our egoistic pursuits, and we abandon the quest for personal pleasures and gains.

Inevitably the question arises, If there is no permanent self and only a momentary combination of the five aggregates, then what is it that is reborn, what is it that stores up karma and expends it? The action performed one moment would have no reward, for the agent of the act would have disappeared the next moment.

In answer to this problem the Buddha taught that when a living being dies, the five aggregates disintegrate, but because of the karma of the past, there must be fruition. A new being that inherits the karma of the past comes into existence, not the same as the one just passed away, but not different either. He said there is a life stream that connects the different rebirths, and he tried to elucidate this concept by numerous examples. A favorite one is that of the river which maintains one constant form, one seeming entity, though not a single drop of water remains today of the volume which composed the river yesterday. Another example is that of the candle. If we light one candle with another, the transmitted flame is one and the same, but the candles are not. In a child, the physical, mental, and moral faculties are young and weak, while in a grown man they are strong and tough. Obviously the man is not the same as the child, but he is not different either, for the man sprang from the child, and the life stream is the same. When a living being dies, it is not the end of the life stream; it is merely the dissolution of one composition of the five aggregates, to be followed immediately by the appearance of another combination.

To sum up, the Buddhist doctrine of nonself means that there is no permanent self or soul in the individual, that there is only a living complex of physical and mental elements living on the fruits of the individual's acts. It can exert efforts to acquire meritorious karma and eventually attain salvation.

Right view to the Buddhist also includes a correct understanding of the formula of dependent origination or the chain of causation. This formula, which consists of twelve members, is stated in the following manner: with ignorance as cause, predisposition arises; with predisposition as cause, consciousness arises; with consciousness as cause, name and form arise; with name and form as cause, the six senses arise; with the six senses as cause, sensation arises; with sensation as cause, contact arises; with contact as cause, craving arises; with craving as cause, grasping arises; with grasping as cause, becoming arises; with becoming as cause, birth arises; with birth as cause, old age and death arise. The formula is not intended to show the origin of the world but is just an early attempt to formulate a law of causation, recognizing that events are not caused by the arbitrary will of some outside power, but that each event arises out of some previous cause.

For the Buddhist who practices the eightfold path, salvation consists of escape from the endless cycle of rebirths and the realization of nirvāna. As the chief characteristic of the round of existence is suffering, then nirvāna would be the cessation of suffering. By practicing the discipline described in the foregoing, the individual puts an end to craving. When craving is extinguished, no more karma is generated and there is no further rebirth. When rebirth is terminated, the individual realizes nirvāna.

If one would ask a Buddhist, "What is this nirvāna?" he would have the greatest difficulty in answering. If pressed, he would say that nirvāna could not be defined or described with words, for words are finite and can only describe finite things, whereas nirvāna is infinite and transcendental and cannot be described with finite words. As one reads the Buddhist scriptures, however, he will find two kinds of nirvāna—nirvāna with residue and nirvāna without residue. The first denotes the nirvāna attained by the perfect saint here and now, with the five aggregates still present, although the cravings that bind one to existence are at an end. This is the nirvāna attained by the Buddha at the age of thirty-five. In the second there is cessation of all existence, as in the case of the death of a Buddha.

Concerning nirvāna with a residue, the Buddha sometimes resorted to negative terms to refer to it—unconditioned, uncompounded, cessation of cravings, abandonment of all defilements, the extinction of hatred and illusion. At other times he referred to it as a state full of confidence, tranquility, bliss, and purity, and said that a person realizing it is the happiest person on earth, for he is free from anxieties, obsessions, worries, and troubles. Living fully in the present, such a person does not regret the past or brood over the future.

On the nature of nirvāna without a residue, or final nirvāna, the scriptures do not throw much light. In fact, the Buddha refused to elucidate on this problem. On one occasion a monk went up to him and asked a series of questions, one of which was whether the saint does or does not exist after death. The monk said that he did not receive a satisfactory answer and challenged the Buddha to provide an answer or admit that he did not know. The Buddha did not answer the question directly, nor did he say that he did not know. Instead, he answered that the question did not tend to edification, that the religious life did not depend on the dogma as to whether the saint does or does not exist after death. Any attempt to answer such a question, he said, would be like entering a jungle or wilderness, for the result would be misery and despair rather than absence of craving, quiescence, wisdom, and nirvāna. Consequently, he refused to answer the question posed.

By his silence the Buddha took the position that final nirvāna was not a matter for empirical observation; by so doing, he was merely following the Upanishadic tradition of not applying the categories of the phenomenal world to the ultimate reality. When pressed, he answered that it was profound, indescribable, hard to comprehend, and beyond the sphere of reasoning. He urged his followers not to be entangled in metaphysical arguments but to devote themselves to the religious life and the way leading to the truth, and to strive for nirvāna here and now. He set himself up as an example of one who had practiced the way and attained nirvāna, and he assured his followers that they too, by following the path he had discovered, would reach the goal he had set before them.

## THERAVĀDA AND MAHĀYĀNA BUDDHISM

The aspect of Buddhism which we have been describing is called Theravāda Buddhism. The word itself means doctrine of the elders. The question as to whether or not Theravāda Buddhism represents the original teachings of the Buddha is one which has occupied the attention of Buddhist scholars for a long time. We derive our knowledge about Theravāda Buddhism from the Pali canon (Pali being an ancient Indian literary language) which was committed to writing during the first century B.C. In view of the lapse of some four centuries between the death of the Buddha and the composition of the canon, scholars contend that what is taught in the Pali canon does not constitute the original teaching of the Blessed One but represents the views of the monastic community during the first century B.C. They call this original teaching, pre-canonical or primitive Buddhism, in contrast to the canonical or monastic Buddhism presented in the Pali canon. However, in spite of decades of controversy, there is still no general agreement as to the contents of precanonical Buddhism.

Theravāda or canonical Buddhism is essentially a discipline for personal salvation by the individual for himself. Moreover, this salvation is possible only for those who join the monastic order to become monks or nuns. The monk is intent on the accumulation of meritorious karma for his own salvation and these merits cannot be transferred to others. After entry into the order, the monk strives to become an arhat or perfect saint. This arhat is a cold, severe, passionless being who has put an end to his cravings and who holds himself aloof from society to practice the religious life by himself for himself.

As the religion developed in India, dissatisfaction arose over what were considered to be shortcomings in the Theravāda tradition. It was criticized as being too spiritually narrow and individualistic because it was concerned primarily with individual salvation. It was also criticized as being conservative and literal-minded, clinging to the letter rather than to the spirit of the master's teachings. Out of this dissatisfaction arose the second aspect of Buddhism, called the Mahāyāna or the Great Vehicle. Its sacred literature is written in Sanskrit, and its followers coined and applied the term "Hīnayāna," or the Lesser Vehicle, to the Theravāda.[2]

In contrast to the Theravāda, the Mahāyāna offers salvation not to the select few but to all sentient beings. This is the consequence of a remarkable doctrine developed by the Mahāyāna— that all sentient beings possess the Buddha-nature in them and hence have the potentiality of being enlightened. Instead of the strenuous discipline advocated by the Theravāda, the Mahāyāna emphasizes that enlightenment is to be achieved mainly by faith and devotion to the Buddha and love for all fellow men, mani-

---

[2] The term "Hīnayāna" requires some clarification. As now used, it is applied chiefly to the Theravāda School, but when first used it had a much wider scope. In Buddhist history the first schism in the original community of monks took place at the Council of Vēsalī, held in ca.383 B.C. At this council two rival groups representing the liberal and conservative elements in the community argued over the interpretation of the rules of discipline and the qualities of the arhat. After being outvoted, the liberal faction bolted the council and formed a dissident group called the Mahāsanghika, or members of the great council, while the conservative element became known as the Theravāda. In opposition to the Theravāda, the Mahāsanghika School contended that the arhat is not perfect and is still subject to karma, but its main contribution to Buddhist doctrine was its concept of a transcendental Buddha who is omnipresent and omnipotent, who manifests himself in an earthly form to conform to the needs of man.

After this initial schism further fragmentation of the Theravāda School occurred; this gave rise to several groups, the most important of which was the Sarvāstivāda (the doctrine that all exists) School. This school analyzed the world into seventy-five dharmas or elements of existence, and contended that these elements exist in some form or another through the three periods of time—past, present, and future.

When the term "Hīnayāna" was first used, it embraced all these schools of early Buddhism, but in current usage it refers primarily to the Theravāda School, which is the only one active at present.

fested by compassion, charity, and altruism. The religious ideal is the bodhisattva, or a being destined for enlightenment, who is the epitome of all the Mahāyāna virtues. Though qualified to enter nirvāna as a result of merits accumulated in the past, the bodhisattva delays his final entry and chooses to remain in the world until he has brought every sentient being across the sea of misery to the calm shores of enlightenment. He is able to do this by transferring some of his inexhaustible stock of merits to less fortunate creatures so that they too may share in the rewards of those merits. He vows to do anything, even to the extent of sacrificing himself, if this is of assistance to others. Universal compassion, manifested by perfect self-sacrifice, is the chief characteristic of the Mahāyāna bodhisattva in contrast to the narrow spiritual individualism of the Theravāda arhat.

The bodhisattva is considered to be the personification of a particular trait of the Buddha's personality, and as there are a number of such traits, so there are different bodhisattvas. Mañjuśrī represents wisdom, while Avalokiteśvara represents the compassion of the Buddha. The master is often described as being excellent in all ways, and this is symbolized by the bodhisattva Samantabhadra. Of these, Avalokiteśvara occupies the preeminent position. He is able to abrogate the law of karma, he visits the numerous hells to lighten the miseries of unfortunate creatures, and he is especially on the lookout for people facing the dangers of water, fire, demons, sword, and enemies. In iconography he is often shown with a thousand eyes and a thousand arms, the better able to see and help the suffering.

The notion of the Buddha in Mahāyāna Buddhism is also different from that held by the Theravāda Buddhists. To the latter, the Buddha is regarded as a human teacher who lived on earth, carried out his mission, and then passed into nirvāna. In the Mahāyāna, the Buddha is regarded as an eternal being who is the embodiment of universal and cosmic truth, who is neither born nor dies, but lives from eternity to eternity. To save errant mankind from evil, this eternal Buddha became incarnated as the historical Śākyamuni, the son of Māyā. The eternal Buddha has created such phantom appearances on earth countless times in the past and will continue to do so in the future. As the earthly Śākyamuni is considered to be just an illusory being, an apparitional creation of the eternal Buddha, the facts of his life are no longer of importance; what matters are the metaphysical speculations about the eternal Buddha. Out of such speculations emerged the doctrine of the triple body of the Buddha, the *dharmakāya* or body of essence, *sambhogakāya* or body of communal enjoyment, and *nirmānakāya* or body of transformation.

The body of essence is the only real body of the Buddha; this body connects and unites all the Buddhas of the past with those of the future. Though there are many Buddhas, there is only one body of essence.[3] When the body of essence is called upon to fulfill the spiritual needs of the bodhisattvas, it then appears in the second form, the body of communal enjoyment. It is the privilege of the bodhisattvas to perceive this body, a marvelous symphony of light and sound, with light emanating from every pore, illuminating the entire universe, and with his voice preaching the Mahāyāna sutras to multitudes of people gathered on Vulture Peak. Lastly, to explain the appearance of a Buddha like Śākyamuni among mankind, there is the body of transformation. The eternal body of essence creates a fictitious phantom of himself and causes this to appear among ignorant and wicked mankind in order to convert it. Śākyamuni was such a phantom; he took on all the characteristics of man; he lived and followed the ways of the world; he lived, preached, and then entered into nirvāna. The eternal Buddha has done this not once but countless times, but these creations are only illusions and appearances.

[3] Though the Mahāyāna writers consider the *dharmakāya*, or the body of essence, to be eternal and unknowable, they still attempt to describe it so far as language permits. This is how the *Avataṁsakasūtra* (*Garland Sutra*) describes it: "It is not an individual entity, it is not a false existence, but it is universal and pure. It comes from nowhere, it goes to nowhere, it does not assert itself, nor is it subject to annihilation. It is forever serene and eternal. It is the One devoid of all determinations. This Body of Dharma has no boundary, no quarters, but is embodied in all bodies. Its freedom or spontaneity is incomprehensible, its spiritual presence in things corporeal is incomprehensible. All forms of corporeality are involved therein, it is able to create all things. Assuming any concrete material body as required by the nature and condition of karma, it illumines all creation. Though it is the treasure of intelligence, it is void of particularity. There is no place in the universe where this body does not prevail. The universe becomes, but this body remains forever. It is free from all opposites and contraries, yet it is working in all things to lead them to nirvāna. . . . It presents itself in all places, in all directions, in all dharmas, and in all beings; yet the Dharmakāya has not been particularized." See D. T. Suzuki, *Outlines of Mahāyāna Buddhism*, London, 1907, 223-224.

# FORCES RESPONSIBLE FOR CHANGE

The origin of Mahāyāna Buddhism is still one of the puzzling problems in the history of the religion. When and where did it take place? What forces were at work to bring it about? We cannot give adequate answers to these questions because of the lack of historical records in India. It appears likely, however, that this new aspect of Buddhism developed during the two centuries immediately preceding the Christian era. As for the forces responsible for the far-reaching changes, there is little unanimity of opinion. Some believe that the passionate, emotional element so prominent in Mahāyāna Buddhism, especially concerning the bodhisattva, was a purely Buddhist development, being an evolution from the idea of *saddhā* or faith in the Buddha found in the Theravāda canon. Others argue, however, that it was borrowed from Hinduism. It is pointed out that the concept of Krishna as a personal god who could help his worshipers developed in the centuries before the Christian era. The moral principle taught in the *Bhagavad-gītā* (*The Song of God*), where Krishna is the voice of God, is similar to that advocated for the bodhisattva, namely, that action is superior to inaction, but that such action should be entirely disinterested and not directed toward any selfish purpose. Then there is the idea that those who thought of Krishna when dying went to Krishna; this has its counterpart in the teaching of the *Pure Land Sutra* of Mahāyāna Buddhism.

# IRANIAN INFLUENCES

Mention of the *Pure Land Sutra* brings us to a consideration of possible Iranian influences on Mahāyāna Buddhism, especially the Amitābha cult based on that sutra. There are some reasons to believe that the sun-worship of the Zoroastrians had influenced Mahāyāna Buddhism. The word "Amitābha" means infinite light. The Buddha Amitābha presides over a paradise of light inhabited by pure, stainless beings who are reborn there after invoking the name of Amitābha. In Zoroastrianism there is the heaven of boundless light presided over by Ahuramazda, described as full of light and brilliance. Such Mahāyāna Buddhas as Vairocana, the Brilliant One, and Dīpankara, Light Maker, also may be indicative of sun worship. Amitābha also bears the name Amitāyus, Infinite Life. An Iranian deity, Zurvan Akaranak, also has the connotation of infinite time and space. Some scholars suggest a connection between the Pure Land triad of Amitābha, Avalokiteśvara (representing light), Mahāsthāma (representing force) and an Iranian trinity, in which Zurvan is the supreme deity, Mithras the luminous element, and Vṛthragna, force and wisdom. As further support of this line of reasoning, it is pointed out that these ideas in Buddhism developed not in India proper but in those areas in northwest India and beyond where the Kushan Dynasty was dominant and where Iranian influences were uppermost. Moreover, the first monk to introduce and translate a *Pure Land Sutra* in China was An Shih-kao, a Parthian; he was followed by other monks from Central Asia, Chih Ch'ien, whose ancestors were from the Yüeh-chih (Scythia), and K'ang Seng-hui, a Sogdian. Taken singly, these points may not have very much significance, but taken as a whole, they provide strong reasons to believe that the Mahāyāna development was influenced by Iranian elements.

## THE SPREAD OF BUDDHISM

During the first two centuries of its existence Buddhism was confined to the Ganges Valley. In the middle of the third century B.C. it began to expand in all directions, southward across the sea to Ceylon, and northwestward into Gandhāra and Kashmir in northwest India. The propelling force behind this sudden development was provided by the third ruler of the Mauryan Dynasty, the great Indian monarch Aśoka, who ruled from ca.274 to ca.236 B.C. After an early period of warfare and bloodshed Aśoka became converted to Buddhism and thereafter decided to use Buddhism as the ideology needed to unify his domain. To this end he dispatched missionaries to the neighboring countries in four directions; he appointed ministers of the law to propagate the Buddhist teachings among his subjects. As a display of his own religious zeal he visited the sacred places connected with the life of the Blessed One, and at Lumbini Grove had a pillar erected commemorating the birthplace of the master. In order to record for posterity the various deeds he performed for the dharma or teachings of the

Buddha, he had edicts inscribed on rocks and on pillars, many of which have been discovered and deciphered, furnishing us with valuable information about his reign and activities. Due mainly to his efforts Buddhism burst out of the confines of India to take its place in the main stream of world culture. From Gandhāra and Kashmir, where the religion had reached during Aśokan times, it spread into Central Asia and eventually to China and Japan; from Ceylon and southern India the religion leaped across the ocean in later centuries to what is now Burma, Indonesia, Thailand, and Indo-China.

Across the border of Gandhāra in northwestern India was the Greek state of Bactria, founded by Ionian Greeks who had settled there after Alexander's campaigns. The rise of the Parthians in Persia cut off these Greeks from their Hellenistic homelands; hence they turned their faces toward the centers of Indian culture. With the disintegration of the Mauryan Dynasty in India at the beginning of the second century B.C., the Greeks began to invade northern India. At the height of their invasions they extended their sway over the whole of the Indus Valley in northwest India and the western parts of the United Provinces. The most famous of these Greek kings was Menander, who ruled during the second century B.C. Coins have been unearthed bearing the name and image of Menander on one side and the Buddhist wheel, the emblem of the preaching of the law, on the other. However, Menander is remembered in India not as a conqueror but as the philosopher who engaged in the celebrated dialogue with the Buddhist monk Nagasena. Plutarch has preserved a tradition that Indian cities vied with one another for a portion of Menander's ashes after his death. All these items point to the conclusion that in the second century B.C. Buddhism had already been introduced into Bactria and had gained a foothold there.

The kingdom of Bactria was in turn conquered by a race of people known as the Yüeh-chih, or Scythians, who originally had their homes in northwestern China but had been driven out from that area by some Turkic tribes known as the Hsiung-nu, to start their migrations across Central Asia in ca.175 B.C. After subjugating Bactria in ca.130 B.C., the Scythians settled down and within a century had established an empire powerful enough to conquer the entire Indus Valley, northern India, and central India down to Mathura and Benares. Of the Scythian kings who ruled over this vast empire, the most famous was King Kanishka of the Kushan Dynasty, who ascended the throne in either ca. A.D. 78 or ca.144. Both epigraphic and numismatic evidences give proof that he was converted to Buddhism. Coins of his reign bear the image of the Buddha with the inscription "Boddo."

Under the patronage of this powerful ruler Buddhism spread rapidly over the vast Scythian kingdom. One of the most important events connected with Buddhism during Kanishka's reign was the convocation of a council which met in Kashmir to collect the available Buddhist manuscripts and to compose commentaries on them. The selection of Kashmir as the scene of this Kanishkan council pointed to the importance of that region as a Buddhist center.

With Buddhism firmly established in Gandhāra and Kashmir, the Buddhist missionaries during the first centuries B.C. and A.D. began to use these areas as bases to spread their religion to such regions as Parthia, Sogdia, Khotan, and Kucha in Central Asia. Of these, Khotan and Kucha were the most important, for they were located at strategic points along the land routes across Central Asia to the Far East.

## BUDDHISM SPREADS INTO CHINA

A traveler venturing forth for the overland trip from India to China at this time usually started from northwest India. He would first journey to Bamiyan in Afghanistan, then across the Hindukush Mountains to Balkh. From Balkh his route would take him across the Pamirs to Kashgar. This stopping place with its numerous Buddhist monasteries provided a welcome haven for the tired travelers who had been climbing over dangerous mountain passes and cliffs since leaving India. As the traveler left Kashgar, he had to decide whether to take the northern route, which followed the northern fringe of the Takla-makan Desert, or the southern route, which skirted the southern fringe. Should he follow the southern route, he would then pass through a series of oasis centers of which Khotan was by far the most important. If he were to follow the northern route, his journey would take him through Kucha, Karashar, and Turfan. The two routes then converged in Tun-huang on the Chinese northwest frontier. Because of its focal location, Tun-huang was an important Buddhist center in China. To provide havens for the travel-weary monks, caves were dug out of the nearby hills, and in these grottoes monks from the entire known Buddhist world of Central Asia gathered to hold religious discussions, to translate the sacred scriptures, and to promote the development of Buddhist art and sculpture.

Buddhist pilgrims were not the only travelers to be encountered on this overland route. Even before the monks started to travel, merchants and traders and diplomatic envoys had already left their footprints on these same roads. It was indeed the great international highway for over a thousand years, beginning with Chang Ch'ien, the Chinese envoy to the Yüeh-chih during the second century B.C. on to Marco Polo, the Venetian traveler during the time of the Mongols.

If one judges from the testimony left behind by these travelers, it is clear that Central Asia was much more inhabitable during the first millennium of the Christian era than it is now. All accounts spoke of flourishing towns and cities with a high level of civilization. Rivers and oases were much more abundant. Such centers are now covered by desert sands or are reduced to mere shadows of their former glory. One school of thought, led by Ellsworth Huntington, the American geographer, attributes this decline to climatic changes: that the climate now is dryer and warmer than it was formerly, and that the subsequent drying up of rivers and lakes caused the centers of civilization to die. Another school, led by Aurel Stein, the English archeologist, argues that the drying up of the region was not due to less rainfall but to the diminution of the glacial cap. During the first millennium the melting of this glacial cap in the high mountains and plateaus still provided enough water for the rivers and lakes, but in the second millennium these glaciers were gradually disappearing.

Besides the Central Asiatic highway, there were two other land routes, but these were seldom used by monks. One was by way of Assam through upper Burma into Yunnan in southwest China. The other passed through Nepal and Tibet. For a brief period during the T'ang Dynasty this route was used by Chinese monks journeying to India.

It was also possible to go from India to China by the sea route. The main ports of debarkation on the Bay of Bengal were Kaveripattanam at the mouth of the Cauvery River and Tamralipti at the mouth of the Ganges. At times ships sailed for China from Bharukaccha (modern Broach) on the western coast of India. After leaving these ports, the ships could sail directly to Java or follow the coast line around the Malay Peninsula until they reached Tonkin or Canton in south China. Beginning with the latter half of the seventh century, when Chinese power was no longer dominant in Central Asia, more and more monks turned to the sea route as a means of travel between India and China. I-tsing, the Chinese pilgrim who left China in 671 and returned in 695, has left behind a useful and informative account of countries along this sea route.

By the first century B.C. Buddhism had already been established in Central Asia and was poised for the leap across the desert sands to the populous and civilized centers of China. The time was ready. In China the mighty and expanding Han empire was in power, while at the western end of the trans-Asiatic highway the Scythians were consolidating their domain in areas where Buddhism had already taken root. Commercial travelers had already made the journey between the two centers of civilization. At the beginning of the Christian era some Buddhist missionaries also made the trip. Without knowing it, the first Buddhist missionary to negotiate the distance initiated one of the greatest cultural movements in history.

# CHAPTER II

# INTRODUCTION AND EARLY
# DEVELOPMENT: HAN DYNASTY

BEFORE we discuss Buddhism in China during the Han Dynasty, we shall devote some attention to the religious conditions existing during this period. Such a discussion will provide a rough picture of the ideas and practices which the Buddhist missionaries had to cope with when they arrived to propagate their religion.

## CONFUCIANISM

As soon as the Buddhist monk made his appearance on the Chinese scene in the Han Dynasty, he was confronted with a politico-religious system known as Confucianism. At the apex of this system was the emperor, who maintained his rule over the empire in accordance with a remarkable theory known as the mandate of heaven. According to this theory the ruler was the Son of Heaven, appointed by heaven to rule over the world for the welfare of mankind. So long as he fulfilled this objective, so that the people under him enjoyed peace, prosperity, order, and justice, he was said to be ruling faithfully in accordance with the mandate of heaven, and his person was sacred and inviolate. As soon as he failed to rule for the welfare of the people, as soon as he departed from the accepted norms of virtue and proper conduct, he was said to have lost the heavenly mandate; he ceased to be the rightful ruler, and the people were then justified in rising up against him and installing another ruler in his place. No question of voting was involved, but it was firmly believed that heaven decided as the people decided, and if a rebel leader succeeded in deposing the ruler and occupied the throne himself, it was a sign of heaven's favor. The success of the revolution constituted its justification and sanctification.

To assist the ruler in his administration and to advise him on what constituted virtue and proper conduct according to the Confucian pattern, it was necessary to have a class of officials learned in the Confucian classics and recruited through a system of examinations based on those classics. These scholar-officials were the technical experts on the rituals which the ruler had to perform on stated occasions during the year, and on the rules of proper conduct which were to serve as examples for the masses of people to follow. These scholar-officials together with the ruler constituted the ruling class, which held a monopoly of all the power, prestige, education, and culture in the realm. The Confucian ideology which they upheld promoted order, stability, and harmony in government and society, with each member performing correctly the functions that pertained to his status. Confucius once said that orderly government would prevail when the ruling prince ruled, the ministers ministered, the fathers behaved as fathers should, and sons conducted themselves as sons should. It was the function of the ruler and the scholar-officials to rule and to minister, and that of the masses of people to obey and to follow the examples of their rulers. By their words and actions the scholar-officials and the ruler indicated to the masses what to believe and how to behave.

Under the Han Dynasty certain innovations were added to the system as the result of influences emanating from Taoism and the prevalent occultism and superstition brought into the centers of Chinese culture from the outlying regions. As formulated by the Confucian scholars of the dynasty, Han Confucianism consisted of the following features:

1. Belief in heaven or a personal god who watches over the conduct of man and government;

2. Belief that man is the noblest creature created by the essence of heaven and earth, and is favored by heaven;

3. Belief in rewards and punishment for good and evil;

4. Belief that there is a reciprocal relationship between heaven and the conduct of man, so that good deeds bring forth propitious omens and evil deeds, warnings and penalties;

5. Belief in astrology as the means of predicting events and interpreting the meaning of heavenly phenomena.

All these elements were woven into a comprehensive system of politico-religious philosophy under the guise of Confucianism. Tung Chung-shu (179-104 B.C.), the greatest Confucian scholar of the age, expressed the central idea best when he wrote that the action of man flows into the universal course of heaven and earth and causes reciprocal reverberations in their manifestations. Since there was this close relationship between heaven and man, the Han Confucianists believed that abnormal events in the human world caused heaven to manifest abnormal phenomena in the natural world. These abnormal phenomena were known as catastrophes and anomalies. Catastrophes represented the warnings of heaven to errant man. Such warnings might be in the form of floods, famines, landslides, or earthquakes. If man persisted in his evil ways despite these warnings, then heaven caused strange anomalies to arise in the form of eclipses of the sun or moon, unusual movements of the stars, growth of beards on women, or birth of babies with two heads. If man still persisted in evil, unmindful of these signs from heaven, then he was doomed to ruin. On the other hand, if man acted correctly, then the world system would be harmonious and well governed.

This imposing structure of Han Confucianism did not go unchallenged. The most outspoken critic was Wang Ch'ung (ca. A.D. 27-100), whose views were set forth in his *Essays of Criticism*. He directed his attack mainly against the Confucian idea of a reciprocal relationship between the activities of man and heavenly phenomena. Eclipses of the sun and moon, he contended, are regular astronomical occurrences and have nothing to do with the political actions of rulers on earth. He ridiculed the notion that man could influence the operation of heavenly will, and likened man's place in the universe to that of a flea under the clothing or an ant in its underground cave. The flea and the ant may move about, but such movements never affect the atmosphere of their hiding places. Since heaven is so vast and man so tiny, how can man hope to affect the air of heaven with his tiny body? Wang Ch'ung also branded as false the Confucian idea that heaven purposely created man. How do we know that heaven did not purposely create man? Because, he contended, if it did, it would have created man to love his fellow man and not to hate him. Nor did heaven purposely create grains to feed and silkworms to clothe man, just as it did not cause catastrophes and anomalies to warn man. Such things are born of themselves, and man merely makes use of them to feed and to clothe himself. Man eats the food of insects, and insects eat the food of man. Man regards insects as a plague, but if insects had intelligence, they would accuse man of being a calamity to them.

There was yet another aspect of this Han Confucianism that operated to its disadvantage. In this system man is not considered as an individual but as a collective being or as the people, symbolized by the emperor and his functionaries. The well-being that results from meritorious efforts is not shared by the individual man but by the abstract concept of society or the collection of people. The aspirations and anxieties of the individual man, his desire for longevity, justice, compassion, immortality, all these are neglected by the Han Confucianists. It was to satisfy these aspects of his life that the individual turned to another religion, Taoism, a personal religion which arose as a protest against the collective religion then in vogue.

## TAOISM

The important names in Taoism are Lao-tzu and Chuang-tzu. They refer to persons as well as to texts. The person named Lao-tzu is of doubtful historicity, but the text by the same name, also known as the *Tao-te-ching* (*The Way and Its Power*) and compiled by more than one person, is still extant and is one of the basic texts of Taoism. As for the man Chuang-tzu, there is no question but that he lived ca.300 B.C., but whether or not the text *Chuang-tzu* was written entirely by him is another matter. The consensus is that more than one writer was involved.

Taoism, as represented by these works, is a sort of nature mysticism. The Taoists discovered nature, expressed their joy and amazement over it, and sought to be identified with this nature, which they also called the tao. Because they were preoccupied with this tao, they are called Taoists. The Confucian tao is the right way of action, moral, social, and political. The tao of the Taoist is metaphysical; it is the natural law of the universe. To him the tao brings all things into existence and governs their every action. The guiding aim of the Taoist is to achieve union with this tao through identification. Since the tao is conceived to be eternal, everlasting, and unchanging, the individual achieving unity with it is also considered to have achieved eternity. To distinguish this aspect of Taoism from another development, this form is called philosophical Taoism.

About the same time that philosophical Taoism was taking shape in the third century B.C., there developed another movement which was primarily a religion of salvation, having as its primary aim the attainment of immortal life by the individual. This movement became prevalent about the beginning of the Christian era and represented an amalgamation of all the popular ideas and superstitions rampant in Chinese society at the time. It is held that the cult called itself Taoism during the Han Dynasty in order to acquire some respectability, since the contents of the text *Lao-tzu* were vague and ambiguous enough to accommodate its views. In the following discussion, whenever we use the term "Taoism," it is this group that is referred to, not the philosophical Taoists.

In this religion of salvation the ambition of the Taoist is to acquire material immortality. To the Taoist, man is not formed with a spiritual soul and a material body; man is entirely material, consisting of constituent elements that disperse at death. Immortality is achieved by conquering these constituent elements that compose the body and by preventing them from dispersing.

In order to obtain immortal life certain obligations are necessary. First, the body has to be nourished in order to suppress the causes of decrepitude and to create an embryo endowed with immortality. Second, the spirit has to be nourished, and this involves meditation and concentration. Even during the centuries before the Christian era the Taoists were already practicing these activities. In *Chuang-tzu* there is an allusion to practices conducive to everlasting life, such as abstention from the five cereals, respiratory exercises, and meditation. Wang Ch'ung also left behind glimpses of such Taoist practices during his time. He wrote that the Taoist adept absorbs the essence of gold or jade to make the body immortal (alchemy), abstains from cereals, controls the breath, and nourishes the vital principle.

For the Taoist, alchemy consists primarily of the preparation and absorption of the cinnabar, a mercuric sulphide, which is supposed to contribute to the formation of the immortal body. Dietary practices are important because the Taoists believe that cereals are responsible for the breeding of certain maggots in the body which sap the vitality of the individual and thus bring about decrepitude. These maggots are not ordinary creatures, but are evil species, developed by long practice of cereal eating; the way to kill them is to cease eating cereals. Respiratory exercises play a much more important role because of the Taoist notion that man is created and animated by air or breath. At the origin of the world, the Taoist believes, there were nine breaths mixed together to form chaos. When this primeval chaos dispersed, the breaths also scattered. The pure and subtle breaths ascended to form heaven, while the gross and impure breaths descended to form earth. The twisting motions of the breaths created the gods. Later one of the gods created man. He did so by setting up four statues of earth at each of the four cardinal directions and exposing them to the breaths for three hundred years. When they were impregnated with air, they were able to move and talk. The body of man is thus made of the impure breath of earth, but the vital breath which animates him is the pure air between heaven and earth. In order to become immortal, it is necessary for man to discharge the impure air within him and fill himself with pure air. To do this, breathing exercises are necessary. In these exercises the Taoist attempts to get as much pure air as possible into his system. When the body becomes filled with pure air, with all the impure air expelled, it is transformed from a gross heavy body into one that is light and subtle.

If Taoism had been merely concerned with drugs, diets, and breathing techniques, it would have been merely a system for nourishing the body and would have been nothing more than a system of hygiene. However, it was as a religion that Taoism was known during these centuries at the beginning of the Christian era, and this meant that there were other practices besides nourishing the body. Here we come to the second aspect of Taoism—nourishing the spirit. This meant getting in touch with spirits and deities that could aid in the quest for immortality.

Where is the adept to find these deities? He might find them in the celestial palaces, but such palaces are inaccessible. Happily, such spirits have a habit of descending from their celestial palaces to live in famous mountains and grottoes. The adept might visit these places in the hope of finding the deities there. However, such deities do not show themselves to anyone who comes to search for them, and the adept might search in vain for years.

Fortunately, there is still another method. The Taoists believe that such deities are right within us. Our bodies are filled with these deities, which are the same as those in the external world. This is one of the consequences of the Taoist belief that the human body is identical with the world, a microcosm within the macrocosm.

The Taoist seeks to establish relations with these deities to get their advice on immortality and to gain their assurance that they will not leave the body. The procedure to establish this relationship is called *shou-i*, guarding the one, or meditation. By meditation and concentration, and by cultivating the inner vision, the adept can see all the deities within his body and obtain from them the assurance that they will remain there. If he has already achieved success in his other endeavors, such as controlling the breath or abstention from cereals, he becomes an immortal. This does not mean that he will live indefinitely in the house of his senses. His body is now subtle and light enough to enable him to fly. In order not to trouble mankind, to whom death is normal, he pretends to die, leaving a sword or stick to which is given the appearance of a corpse, while flying away to the celestial sphere.

In the vocabulary of the Taoists of the Han Dynasty there is frequent reference to the compound word Huang-Lao. This refers to Huang-ti, the Yellow Emperor, and Lao-tzu. The Taoists claimed that such practices as sacrifices to and worship of spirits, the eating of potions, and yogic exercises originated with the Yellow Emperor and Lao-tzu, hence they acknowledge these two as their ancestors. We read in the contemporary records that Emperor Huan (147-167) of the Han Dynasty followed the practices of Huang-Lao and established an altar dedicated to them in the imperial palace. To the emperor, Huang-Lao were the deities of a religion in which men were striving for immortality through dietetics, respiratory exercises, alchemy, and concentration.

This was the religious setting in China during the Han Dynasty when the new religion, Buddhism, was brought over mountains and deserts into the country from India.

## VARIOUS LEGENDS

One legend concerning the introduction of Buddhism into China says that Confucius knew about the existence of Buddha. The source for this statement is the *Lieh-tzu*, which is generally regarded by Chinese scholars as a forgery of the third century A.D. or later. Another account tells us that the religion was already known in 317 B.C. when a foreign magician carrying a staff and begging bowl visited the court of Prince Chao of Yen and created a stupa three feet high on his finger tips. Quite apart from any reference to the magic feat, this story is groundless and unreliable, for at the date mentioned Buddhism had not yet left the confines of India. There are a number of Buddhist works that attempt to connect the introduction of the religion with the evangelical activities of King Aśoka during the third century B.C. Among the 84,000 stupas erected by Aśoka, some were said to have been discovered in China, and relic bones of the Buddha were said to have been unearthed from one of them. Likewise, it is thought that the foreign monk Shih Li-fang, who reportedly arrived carrying Buddhist sutras into China during the reign of Ch'in Shih-huang (221-210 B.C.), was one of the missionaries dispatched by Aśoka. These attempts by the Chinese Buddhists to find some connections with Aśoka are understandable, but there is nothing in the Aśokan inscriptions nor in the Ceylonese chronicles to indicate the slightest hint of Aśoka's having propagated the religion in China.

Other accounts would place the introduction during the reign of Emperor Wu (140-87 B.C.). When a lake was being dug during his reign, some black ashes allegedly found at the bottom were said to be the ashes left by the fires that consumed the world at the end of an aeon. The writers of these accounts contend that such an explanation would have been possible only after the introduction of Buddhism.

Some Buddhist writers also argued that Chang Ch'ien, the Chinese envoy who traveled across Central Asia to Bactria in the second century B.C., heard about the Buddhist faith in his travels abroad and brought back to China some information concerning it. But only in Buddhist records of the T'ang Dynasty was it indicated that Chang Ch'ien brought back such information. In the earlier sources there is no record of his having mentioned the Buddha.

When the Han general Ho Ch'ü-ping vanquished the Hsiung-nu in the northern frontiers in 120 B.C., he found some golden statues of human forms, to which no sacrifices were offered, only the burning of incense and ceremonial bowing. These golden statues were once considered to be images of the Buddha, and their introduction was said to mark the beginning of the spread of Buddhism in China. However, it is now well established that these golden statues were not images of the Buddha but were symbols of some local Hsiung-nu deities. We must conclude that all these accounts concerning the introduction are legendary or unreliable or are due to the religious zeal of Buddhist writers.

After Buddhism has been introduced and established in China, Chinese critics often charged that the religion tended to shorten the duration of the ruling houses supporting it. As evidence of this, they pointed to the short-lived dynasties of Later Ch'in, Later Chao, Sung, and Ch'i, which lasted only 33, 24, 59, and 23 years respectively. To counteract these criticisms, the Buddhists forged texts purporting to show that the religion was introduced into China during the early years of the Chou Dynasty (ca.1100-256 B.C.). The motive for assigning the date of introduction to the early Chou Dynasty is very clear, for the Chou lasted over eight hundred years and provided just the answer needed to refute the anti-Buddhist critics. As fitting accompaniments to the birth and death of such a famous sage as the Buddha, many anomalies and unnatural events, such as earthquakes, violent winds, and a rainbow with twelve color bands which did not vanish even at night, were listed in the forged texts and were said to have been observed by the Chou ruler.

## THE DREAM OF EMPEROR MING

The dream of Emperor Ming (A.D. 58-75) of the Han Dynasty has often been connected with the introduction of Buddhism into China. Briefly, the episode is as follows. One night in a dream Emperor Ming saw a golden deity flying in front of his palace. On the morrow he asked his ministers to explain the identity of this deity. One of them, Fu Yi, replied that he heard there was a sage in India who had attained salvation and was designated the Buddha, who was able to fly, and whose body was of a golden hue. He went on to say that the deity seen in the dream was this Buddha. The ruler accepted his explanation and dispatched envoys abroad to learn more about this sage and his teachings. The envoys returned bringing back with them the *Sutra in Forty-two Sections*, which was received by the emperor and deposited in a temple constructed outside the walls of the capital, Lo-yang.

An anachronism is inherent in this story. If this purports to be the first introduction of Buddhism into China, where, how, and when did the minister, Fu Yi, obtain his remarkably accurate description of the Buddha? To make the problem more complicated, the various Chinese sources describing this episode do not agree on significant details. The date of departure of the mission ranges from 64 to 68, while the return date varies from 64 to 75. The names of the envoys also are not uniform. In one source Chang Ch'ien, who journeyed to Bactria in the second century B.C., appears as one of the envoys, but this historical anachronism is too glaring and in a later source his name is withdrawn. The destination of the mission is Scythia in some accounts, India in others. At first no mention is made of foreign missionaries returning with the mission, but in a fifth-century version one Indian monk is mentioned, while in a sixth-century work two such monks appear.

This version of the introduction of Buddhism into China cannot be accepted as authentic and reliable. It is improbable that so important an event as the dispatch of envoys occurred as the result of a dream. The lack of unanimity in the different sources concerning such important items as the date of the mission, the destination, names of the envoys, and the foreign monks accompanying the return mission is a compelling argument against the reliability of the story. It appears that the episode became more and more embellished with details as time passed, so that by the fifth century it had become fully crystallized. At that time we are told that not only an Indian monk returned with the Chinese envoys, but that they also brought back Buddhist scriptures and images of the Buddha. These images were welcomed by the emperor since they resembled in appearance the deity he had seen in his dream. Paintings were also made of these images, we are told, and placed in the imperial palace.

It was once thought that the mission could not have taken place because Chinese historical records indicated that relations between China and Central Asia had terminated for sixty-five years prior to A.D. 73. This view is not correct, for it was based on an erroneous interpretation of the records. What was terminated was mainly the relationship of vassal to master; the countries in Central Asia no longer acknowledged China's suzerainty. During those sixty-five years communications were still carried on. In A.D. 38 Yarkand and Shan-shan sent envoys to the Chinese court; in A.D. 60 some Chinese went to Khotan to help set up the Khotanese ruler. Such communications continued even during the reign of Emperor Ming. Consequently, it is no longer tenable to argue against Emperor Ming's mission on the grounds that relations did not exist between China and the western regions.

If the story of Emperor Ming's dream and the subsequent mission lacks firm historical basis, then how did the legend arise? The following hypothesis has been advanced. During the Han Dynasty there were other centers of Buddhism in China besides the Lo-yang community, some of which antedated the Lo-yang group in origin. The members of the Lo-yang center, in their desire to acquire prestige and authority, sometime during the second half of the second century A.D., fabricated the story of the dream in order to claim priority over the others in the establishment of their church. However, this theory brings in its wake another question not so easily answerable. If the legend originated in Lo-yang, how can we account for its early inclusion in the *Mou-tzu*, a text composed in south China at the end of the second century by a Chinese Buddhist convert who had never been to Lo-yang? (The *Mou-tzu* will be discussed in detail later in this chapter.)

The most telling argument against this version of the introduction of Buddhism under Emperor Ming lies in the fact that Buddhism was already introduced into the country at the time of the purported dream.

## THE WEI-LÜEH

During the period 239-265 a certain Yü Huan compiled a work entitled *Wei-Lüeh* (*A Brief Account of the Wei Dynasty*), which is no longer extant but which is quoted extensively in the commentary to the *San Kuo Chih* (*Record of the Three Kingdoms*) by P'ei Sung-chih. One portion of this *Wei-Lüeh* describes Scythia. It is recorded that Kipin, Bactria, and India were all under the control of Scythia. One of the kingdoms in India was Lin-erh (Lumbini), where the ruling prince had a son named Buddha. The father of the Buddha was Śuddhodana; the mother, Māyā. Māyā conceived when she dreamt about a white elephant. The child issued forth from her left side and he immediately took seven steps. Then comes a significant passage in the record: "Formerly, in the first year of the Yüan-shou era (2 B.C.) under the reign of Han Ai-ti, the Po-shih-ti-tzu Ching-lu received from Yi-ts'un, ambassador of the King of Yüeh-chih, the oral transmission of the Buddhist scriptures."

Did Ching-lu receive the oral transmission of the law in China or in Scythia? Unfortunately, the *Wei-Lüeh* is not clear on this point. No other reference to this exchange between Ching-lu and Yi-ts'un has been found. However, the tenor of the passage is such that it begets confidence in the composer, Yü Huan. He pin-points the place where the Buddha was born; he relates correctly some details in the biography of the Buddha, and he mentions some technical terms connected with the order, such as *upāsaka* (layman), *śramana* (recluse), and *bhikshu* (monk). All these details indicate that he had access to some authentic Buddhist materials.

The contemporary historical scene made such an exchange extremely probable. As a result of Chang Ch'ien's travels the Han empire had pushed its diplomatic and military arms into Central Asia, and in the succeeding years countries like Bactria, Ferghana, Parthia, and Scythia all sent envoys to the Chinese court. At the time in question the Scythians were dominant in northwest and northern India and were already converted to Buddhism. In the wake of these diplomatic missions came merchants carrying jade from Khotan and tapestry from Parthia. In due time Buddhist monks must have come also. Moreover, we know that the oral transmission of the law was the chief method of spreading the dharma during this early period of Buddhism. Taking all these points into consideration, we are justified in accepting the *Wei-Lüeh* account as trustworthy. This would push the recorded introduction of the religion back to the beginning of the Christian era.

# THE BIOGRAPHY OF PRINCE YING

There is yet another body of evidence attesting to the existence of Buddhism under the Han before Emperor Ming's dream. This is the biography of Prince Ying of Ch'u. Ying was a half brother of Emperor Ming, was made a duke in A.D. 39, and then a prince in 41. At first he remained in the capital, but in 52 he went to live in P'eng-ch'eng, capital of his kingdom of Ch'u in northern Kiangsu. In 65 Emperor Ming issued an edict authorizing those who had been condemned to death to ransom themselves by payment of a certain number of rolls of silk. Apparently, because he had committed some offense and had a guilty conscience, Ying took advantage of this offer of amnesty to present thirty rolls of silk to the throne. The emperor did not consider Ying guilty and, in addition to refusing to accept the ransom, declared that Ying esteemed highly the profound sayings of the Yellow Emperor and Lao-tzu and the virtuous deeds of the Buddha. Ying expressed repentance for his former deeds, and then used the ransom money to prepare a sumptuous vegetarian feast for the pious laymen and monks living in his kingdom.

This last sentence contains a very significant piece of information. Here is the earliest mention (A.D. 65) of a Buddhist community in China. What is more, this community that consisted of monks and pious laymen was not in Lo-yang, the capital, but in an outlying area in what is now Kiangsu and Shantung. We do not know whether these monks were Chinese or non-Chinese; very likely they were foreign, while the laymen were Chinese. It is interesting to note that this Buddhist community was already observing the practice of fasting. Ying himself must have been a convert and a patron of the new faith—a fact which indicates that the religion had already won some converts among the royal family. The presence of Buddhist monks and laymen would imply that the community had already existed for some time prior to 65. Where these monks came from, if they were not Chinese, we do not know. If the initial transmission between the Scythians and Chinese in 2 B.C. had been continued and extended, that would provide over half a century for Buddhist missionaries to spread the law in China. Unfortunately, the Chinese historical records were compiled by orthodox Confucian scholars who disdained to notice the presence of a few insignificant foreign monks; hence their names and their activities are not preserved in the Chinese records and are lost forever.

## THE SUTRA IN FORTY-TWO SECTIONS

According to the version of Emperor Ming's dream as found in the *Mou-tzu*, the Chinese envoys went to Scythia and copied a *Sutra in Forty-two Sections* which they brought back. This would make the *Sutra* the earliest piece of Buddhist literature in China. In some versions, however, an Indian monk named Kāśyapa Matanga was the translator; in others the translators were said to be Matanga and another Indian monk named Chu Fa-lan.

Nor is there any unanimity of opinion as to whether or not the *Sutra* is a product of the Han Dynasty. Some scholars[1] argue that the *Sutra* belongs to the fourth century, while others[2] advocate that it is a product of the fifth century.

Again, there is a difference of opinion as to whether the *Sutra* is a translation or a compilation of essential points in the religion. The contents of the work indicate strongly that it is a summary of different works. For example, there is one section which reads: "The Buddha said to the monks, 'You must be careful and not look at women. If you meet them, act as if you do not see them. Be careful not to talk with them. If they should speak to you, then be mindful and upright.'" This section is identical with a passage in the Pali *Mahāparinibbanasutta* (*Discourse on the*

---

[1] One of these scholars was Liang Ch'i-ch'ao, who based his dating of the sutra primarily on the style. His views may be found in *Liang Jen-kung chin-chu ti-i-chi*, 2,10-13, Shanghai, 1925-1926.

[2] The Japanese scholar Sakaino Kōyō held that the sutra was compiled in the fifth century and that it contained passages taken from the following sources: *Jui-ying pen-ch'i ching*, translated in 222-228; *Ch'u-yao ching*, translated in 383; *Tseng-i a-han ching*, translated in 397; *Chung a-han ching*, translated in 397; *Ta-chih-tu lun*, translated in 405. See his *Shina bukkyō seishi*, 36-57, Tokyo, 1935.

Matsumoto Bunzaburō, in his article "Shijunishōkyō seiritsu nendai kō," *Tōhō Gakuhō*, Kyoto, 14 (1943), 1-38, likewise held that the sutra should be dated the fifth century. He thought that the sutra was not given its present title until sometime during the Eastern Chin Dynasty (317-420). As for the preface of the sutra, which some scholars accept as a Han product, he held that it was based on the account in *Mou-tzu* concerning Emperor Ming's dream, and would assign it to a period after 473-493, the date he proposed for *Mou-tzu*. The preface and the text were then put together to give us the sutra in its present form.

*Great Decease*). We also note that the contents of the *Sutra* are mainly Hīnayāna in nature.

Though there are still these puzzling and unsolved problems concerning the work, scholars are now fairly convinced that there existed a *Sutra in Forty-two Sections* in some form during the Han Dynasty. The best evidence for this belief lies in the memorial presented by Hsiang K'ai in 166 to Emperor Huan: "I have also heard that in the palace there are established altars to Huang-Lao and the Buddha. This doctrine is one of purity and emptiness, it reveres *wu-wei* (nonactivity), it values life and hates killing, it diminishes the desires and destroys excesses. Now Your Majesty does not extirpate your desires and excesses, your executions and penalties exceed reason. Since Your Majesty has deviated from this doctrine, how can you hope to obtain rewards which adherence would bring? Some have said that Lao-tzu entered the land of the barbarians to become the Buddha. The Buddha did not pass three successive nights under the mulberry tree: he did not wish to remain there long, for this would give rise to attachment and liking (for the place); that was the extreme of refinement. The gods sent beautiful maidens to tempt him, but he said, 'These are nothing but sacks of skin containing blood,' and he paid no further attention to them. His concentration was like this, and so he attained illumination. Now the courtesans that Your Majesty keeps are the most sensuous and beautiful on earth, the tenderness of the meats and the excellence of the wine on your table are unique here in this world; how can you hope to be the equal of Huang-Lao?"[3]

In this memorial two passages appear to be taken from the *Sutra in Forty-two Sections*. The first, "The Buddha did not pass three successive nights under the mulberry tree," is but a rephrasing of the following passage in the *Sutra*: "One meal a day, one lodging under the tree, and neither should be repeated." The second passage concerns Buddha's disdain for the maidens sent by Māra. In the *Sutra* the section reads: "The Lord of Heaven offered a beautiful maiden to the Buddha, desiring to test the Buddha's intentions and teachings. The Buddha replied, 'You are but a leather bag filled with filth, why do you come?'" These

[3] *Hou-Han shu*, 60b,23a.

passages indicate that some version of the *Sutra in Forty-two Sections* was already in existence in 166, when Hsiang K'ai composed his memorial. They are the earliest traces of the contents of the *Sutra*. Hsiang, incidentally, was a native of east China, an area where Buddhists were already known to be present in 65; this might imply that the *Sutra* was already popular in that region. One other point needs to be emphasized here. This memorial of Hsiang K'ai, mentioning as it does the worship of Buddha within the palace, definitely indicates that the Indian religion was practiced in Lo-yang, and had won converts within the imperial family.

During its long history this earliest piece of Buddhist literature in China has undergone numerous changes, so that the version as preserved in the present Chinese canon differs in many places from that current during the T'ang era. The wording of passages has been changed; some portions of the T'ang version are not found in the Sung editions. More serious are changes which added new ideas to the *Sutra*, changes which were apparently made by followers of the Ch'an School. For example, T'ang versions of the *Sutra* make no mention of *bodhi* (enlightenment) or *bodhicitta* (thought of enlightenment); yet these terms are found in Sung versions. Again, the Sung edition has a remarkable passage: "Buddha said, 'My doctrine is to think the thought that is unthinkable, to practice the deed that is not performable, to speak the speech that is inexpressible, and to be trained in the discipline that is beyond discipline. . . .'" Such a passage bears the mark of later Mahāyāna sutras, and appears to be out of harmony with the rest of the *Sutra*. In the version as found in the Korean edition of the Chinese Tripitaka, the reading is only: "What should I think about? The Way. What should I practice? The Way. What should I speak about? The Way."

## MOU-TZU LI-HUO-LUN

Besides the *Sutra in Forty-two Sections*, there is another work, the *Mou-tzu Li-huo-lun* (*Mou-tzu on the Settling of Doubts*), which is an important source of information for students of early Chinese Buddhism. As in the case of the *Sutra*, a good deal of controversy has arisen over the date and authenticity of this text.

The text of *Mou-tzu* is preserved in a Buddhist collection entitled *Hung-ming-chi* (*Collected Essays on Buddhism*), compiled by Seng-yu in ca.518. It contains a preface filled with detailed historical data that have provided the basis for a number of scholars like Paul Pelliot and Hu Shih to date the entire treatise at the end of the second century. Henri Maspero, while accepting the authenticity and trustworthiness of the preface, is in favor of a later date, 225-250, because the body of the text contains passages which are strikingly similar to portions of a biography of the Buddha translated in 222-228. Maspero finds some support in the conclusions of Fukui Kojun, who favors ca.250 as the date. However, there is another group, which includes Liang Ch'i-ch'ao and Matsumoto Bunzaburō, who contend that the date of the composition should not be determined by the contents of the preface but by the nature of the text, and their conclusion is that the text should be dated in the fifth century.[4] Both groups probably are right in some instances and wrong in others. Instead of adopting the view that the entire work was compiled at one time, either at the end of the Han Dynasty or during the fifth century, it is more reasonable to suppose that the treatise, as we have it now, was in process of composition for a long time. The earliest parts of the text very likely were composed during the end of the Han Dynasty, but there were also later accretions. The preface should not pose any problem, for the historical data in it all point to the end of the Han Dynasty. In the main text there also occur terms, expressions, and allusions used prevalently during the Later Han (A.D. 25-220) by writers of apocryphal literature. Portions containing these materials belong to the same period as the preface. However, in portions of the text that mention rules of discipline, the voluminous mass of Buddhist literature in China,

---

[4] Matsumoto's arguments may be found in his article "Bōshi riwaku no jutsusaku nendai kō," *Tōhō Gakuhō*, Kyoto, 12 (1941), 1-33. In it he adduces three points of evidence to substantiate his opinion:

*a*) *Mou-tzu* has passages taken from the *Jui-ying pen-ch'i ching*, translated in 222-228, and the *Liu-tu chi ching*, translated in 251.

*b*) In *Mou-tzu* it is said that the Buddha entered nirvāna on the fifteenth day of the second month. This is the view held by the Mahāyāna, not the Hīnayāna, and it must have arisen after the translation of the Sanskrit *Mahāparinirvānasūtra* by Fa-hsien in 418.

*c*) The items discussed in the text indicate that the treatise was written after the appearance of the *I-hsia-lun* (*Treatise on the Barbarians and Chinese*), by Ku Huan, who died in the latter part of the fifth century.

and details concerning the biography of the Buddha, there are elements that point to a later period and these portions must have been added later, possibly during the fourth and fifth centuries.

The first point we learn from the preface of *Mou-tzu* is that, in addition to the Buddhist centers in east China and Lo-yang, there existed a flourishing Buddhist community in south China during the Han Dynasty. The origins and early development of this community are shrouded in mystery. We do know that Indian traders were already making the trip by sea to ports in south China during the Han Dynasty. Even merchants from the Roman Empire appear to have participated in this trade, for in 166 an individual who claimed to be an envoy of the Roman ruler An-tun (Marcus Aurelius Antoninus) arrived in China by sea. Among the Indian traders undoubtedly were Buddhist converts. Buddhist monks must have been present also, for we find them described in *Mou-tzu* as shaving their heads, wearing saffron-colored robes, eating one meal a day, controlling the six senses, leaving the household life and abandoning their wives and children. K'ang Seng-hui, who arrived in Nanking in 247, was said to have been descended from a Sogdian family who had moved to Tonkin for commercial reasons after having lived in India for a number of generations.

The *Mou-tzu* was written as a sort of defense of Buddhism, supposedly by an author bearing the same name, to explain why he was converted. The main body of the treatise is in the form of questions and answers. Some of the questions asked are: (1) What does the term "Buddha" mean? (2) If the teaching of the Buddha is so venerable and grand, then why is it that the ancient Chinese sages Yao, Shun, Duke Chou, or Confucius did not practice it? (3) By shaving their heads, are not the Buddhist monks being unfilial to their ancestors? (4) How can the Buddhist say that when a person dies, he becomes reborn in another life?

In these questions, and in the answers supplied by Mou-tzu, are to be found some interesting data concerning Buddhism. For instance, reference is made to some biographical details in the life of the Buddha, to the voluminous body of Buddhist literature, and to some of the moral precepts that regulate the life of a monk, such as abstinence from intoxicating liquor and meat, and celibacy. "The Buddha" is explained by Mou-tzu as one who is awakened, endowed with supernatural powers, and untouched by fire, weapons, or impurities, while "the way" is interpreted as that which guides man to the realm of inactivity, or *wu wei*, the term used for nirvāna at the time.

In answer to the second question Mou-tzu wrote: "Books are not necessarily the words of Confucius; a remedy is not necessarily prepared by Pien-ch'iao [a doctor of the fifth century B.C.]. If a book is in accord with what is just, one follows it. If a medicine cures, it is good. The superior man accepts all that is good to sustain his body. . . . Yao rendered homage to Yin Chou, Shun to Wu Ch'eng, Chou-kung to Lü Wang and Confucius to Lao Tan. But none of these is mentioned in the seven classics. Now these masters are all sages, but comparing them with the Buddha is like comparing a white deer to a unicorn, a swallow to a phoenix. If Yao, Shun, Duke Chou, and Confucius accepted these as masters, how much more should they accept and not reject as master the Buddha with his major and minor marks, gift of metamorphosis, and his supernatural powers without limit? The five classics render homage to justice, but there are things not found there. If the Buddha is not found there, is that ground for suspicion?"[5]

In answering the charge of unfilial conduct, Mou-tzu tells a story of the father and son of Ch'i who crossed a river by boat. Midway the father fell into the water. The son pulled him aboard the boat, then turned him upside down to get the water out through his mouth. By so doing he saved his father. Yet there is nothing more unfilial, Mou-tzu contends, than a son seizing his father and turning him upside down. But he did it to save his father. If the son had insisted on observing filial piety, the father would have drowned. This, Mou-tzu concludes, was what Confucius means by adjusting oneself to circumstances.

As for the last question about rebirth after death, Mou-tzu explains that in death only the material body perishes, but a soul or spirit remains to live on and on. The body is like the leaves and roots of plants, while the soul is like the seed. The leaves and roots may wither and perish, but the seeds will continue to live forever, producing new plants again and again.

[5] *Hung-ming-chi*, 1; *Taishō*, 52,2bc.

The text *Mou-tzu* is important not only for the information it presents about Buddhism in China, but also because of the distinction it enjoys as the first treatise on Buddhism to be written by a Chinese convert. By defending Buddhism and criticizing the ideas and practices of native cults and superstitions, the text may be said to exemplify the spirit of independence developing within Chinese Buddhism. If we assume that parts of it stem from the third century, it also mirrors the transition that was taking place in Chinese thought. During the Han Dynasty interest in the teachings and practices of Huang-Lao was still very much in vogue, but during the following period interest shifted to the teachings of Lao-Chuang. In *Mou-tzu* we find the beginnings of this shift in the numerous quotations taken from *Lao-tzu* to reinforce the teachings of the Buddha. The text thus fills a strategic role not only in Chinese Buddhism but also in Chinese thought.

## HAN CENTERS OF BUDDHISM

On the basis of the foregoing discussion, we may conclude that there were at least three centers of Buddhism during the Han Dynasty: P'eng-ch'eng or the Lower Yangtze region in east China, Lo-yang, and Tonkin in south China (now in Vietnam). The Tonkin center was primarily started by monks arriving by sea. One can only guess how and when the P'eng-ch'eng center was started. Hu Shih has suggested that there might have been some links between the south and east China centers. He thought it possible for some monks to have made the trip overland from Tonkin to Wu-chou in Kwangsi, thence to Canton, then northward over the mountains into the lower Yangtze Valley. Han records mention some sea voyages between the Yangtze River and Tonkin, which would have provided another avenue for monks to get to the north.

The P'eng-ch'eng center is mentioned once more in the Han records, this time with Chai Jung as the central character. In the last decade of the second century Chai was placed in charge of grain transport in the lower Yangtze Valley. He soon rebelled and intercepted for his own use the grains which were in transit within the area under his control. His next move was to construct a large Buddhist temple, in which he erected a statue of the Buddha in bronze coated with gold. In the vicinity of the temple he then put up a building large enough to accommodate three thousand people. With these preparations finished, he ordered that Buddhist sutras be recited within the temple, and he also invited all the Buddhist devotees in the surrounding area to assemble and listen to the discourses on the law. More than five thousand people

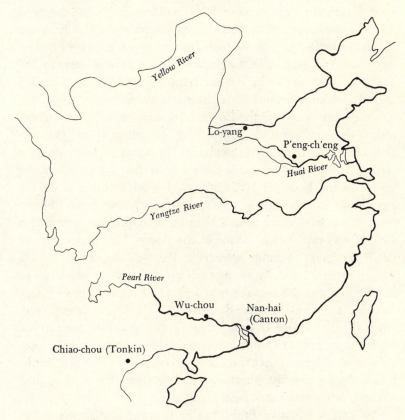

*Spread of Buddhism in the Han Dynasty (1st–2d century A.D.)*

would gather for these assemblies. Every day the image of the Buddha was bathed; food and wine were served to the assembly. Apparently the buildings were not sufficient to accommodate the multitudes who came from far and near, exceeding ten thousand in number, for it was said that food was even spread over the open roads.

This passage is of great historical value, for it is the first mention of a Buddhist image in the Chinese historical records. It is also the earliest description of a Buddhist temple in China, and, furthermore, it provides the first glimpse of the impact of Buddhism upon the common masses.

Of greater importance was the center at Lo-yang. The influence of this center penetrated even into the court. Hsiang K'ai's memorial, presented in 166, contains a passage pointing to the presence of worshipers of the Buddha in the palace under Emperor Huan. According to this, the emperor set up an altar where he sacrificed to Huang-Lao and the Buddha. There were at least two havens for Buddhist monks, Pai-ma Temple (White Horse Temple) and Hsü-ch'ang Temple. This latter temple may offer some clue about the beginnings of the Lo-yang community, for it was named after a maternal cousin of Prince Ying. According to one explanation, after Ying committed suicide in 71, some of his followers who were Buddhist converts made their way to the capital and sought refuge in the house of Hsü Ch'ang. Hsü felt obliged to offer a portion of his residence as a haven to these converts, and before long it was converted into a temple, to which the name Hsü Ch'ang was attached in honor of the donor. This connection of the Hsü Ch'ang community with the P'eng-ch'eng center of Ying would also explain why Emperor Huan in Lo-yang sacrificed to Huang-Lao and the Buddha in the palace. Ying's group in P'eng-ch'eng was closely associated with the Taoists of that area, and when they moved to Lo-yang, they probably carried over to the capital some of that Taoist influence. If this explanation is acceptable, it would mean that the Lo-yang community was first established during the last quarter of the first century by Buddhist converts who went there from P'eng-ch'eng.

The first mention of Buddhism in Lo-yang in Chinese *belle-lettres* may be found in the *Hsi-ching-fu* (*Ode to the Western Capital*) by Chang Heng (A.D. 78-130), who, in describing the seductive charms of the women of Ch'ang-an, wrote, "Even the virtuous Chan Chi or a *śramana*—who could not be captivated by them?" The important point here is the use of the word *śramana*. Chang finished his poem in Lo-yang ca. A.D. 100, and probably became acquainted with the Buddhist term while he was living in that city.

## EARLY FOREIGN MONKS

In Lo-yang there was a translation center organized by foreign monks. Of these foreign monks living and working in Lo-yang, the most famous was also the earliest arrival in that center, An Shih-kao. An was a Parthian of royal lineage, his family bearing the name Arsacide or Arsakes, from which the Chinese designation for Parthia, An-hsi, was derived. It is significant that the first important known Buddhist translator in China was a Parthian, not an Indian. He is described as one who understood the language of birds and animals and was well versed in astronomy and medicine. He was due to succeed to the throne when his father, who had been the ruling prince, died, but, instead, he abandoned the throne in favor of an uncle and retired into a Buddhist monastery. Arriving in Lo-yang during the reign of Emperor Huan (the date of arrival is usually given as 148), he was to spend more than twenty years in China, carrying on his translating and his propagation of the religion. The center that he founded in Lo-yang included a fellow countryman from Parthia, An Hsüan, and a Chinese, Yen Fou-t'iao. The picture of his translation activities is somewhat complicated. The *Ch'u San-tsang chi-chi* (*A Collection of Records Concerning the Tripitaka*), compiled by Seng-Yu ca.518, listed thirty-five titles; a Sui Dynasty catalogue by Fei Ch'ang-fang raised the number to one hundred and seventy-six, while the *K'ai-Yüan Lu* (*Catalogue of the Kai-yüan Era*) of 730 counted ninety works. Such great disparity in the figures would naturally cause one to be cautious about the validity of later numbers; undoubtedly many works ascribed to An Shih-kao were not actually translated by him.

The sutras translated by An Shih-kao were concerned primarily with *dhyāna* practices such as concentration and meditation, techniques of breath control, and so forth. He also had a penchant for categories and numbers. The Buddhists like to divide their teachings into categories such as the three impurities, the four truths, the eightfold path, the five hindrances. The *Anguttara-nikāya* (*Gradual Sayings Arranged in Ascending Numerical Order*), for instance, consists of eleven sections; section one treats of things of which there are one; section two, two; and so on until the last. This same division into categories is also a feature of the Abhidharma literature.

Among the foreign coworkers of An Shih-kao, we have already mentioned An Hsüan, who had arrived in Lo-yang as a trader but later became so much interested in Buddhism that he decided to devote more time and energy to propagating this religion. Another was Chih Lou-chia-ch'an, often shortened to Chih-ch'an, a Scythian who arrived in Lo-yang ca.167, and whose primary interest, in contrast to that of An Shih-kao, was in the *Prajñāpāramitā* texts. The only Indian in the Lo-yang center that we hear of was Chu Shuo-fo. Still another Central Asiatic country, Sogdiana, was represented by two individuals, K'ang Meng-hsiang and K'ang Chü. The peculiar practice of naming foreign monks after the names of their countries of origin now becomes apparent. For example, the Parthians An Shih-kao and An Hsüan have An as their surname, derived from An-hsi. Monks from Scythia (Yüeh-chih) usually had Chih in their names; those from India (T'ien-chu) had Chu, while the K'ang in K'ang-chü (Sogdiana) was responsible for the surname K'ang among the Sogdians.

## EARLY CHINESE CONVERTS

Since there were about half a dozen known foreign monks working in Lo-yang during the second half of the second century (undoubtedly there must have been others whose names have not been preserved), it would be interesting to find out what sort of response the newly introduced religion received from the Chinese. Unfortunately, there is no mention of this in the official histories other than the notices referring to Emperor Huan's performance of sacrifices in the palace to Buddhist and Taoist deities. In the Buddhist records there are some further bits of information. Two Chinese, Meng Fu and Chang Lien, were mentioned as copyists for Chih-ch'an. Among the followers of An Shih-kao appear three names, Ch'en Hui, Han Lin, and P'i Yeh. These Chinese were lay adherents, men who had been attracted by the new faith and volunteered their services, either as copyists to write down the translations or as assistants in the evangelical efforts of the monks. Were there any Chinese who joined the order?

According to the generally accepted story, there were no Chinese monks in China until the fourth century. The basis for such a belief is the memorial presented by Wang Tu in 335 to Shih Hu (who ruled from 334 to 349), ruler of the kingdom Later Chao in northern China. In this memorial Wang declares that although Buddhism was introduced during the Han Dynasty, the Han emperors permitted only foreigners to build monasteries and to enter the new religion. This practice was followed by the Wei rulers. Now that the Chao Dynasty had received the mandate from heaven, it should follow the ancient rules and prohibit Chinese from joining the religion, especially since the Buddha was a foreign deity and therefore had nothing in common with the Chinese. Shih Hu in reply retorts that he was a barbarian before he entered China, and sees no reason for any ban on the barbarian deity. He thereupon authorized all those who desire to do so to enter the religion.

Wang Tu to the contrary, there is some evidence that during the Han Dynasty, at least one Chinese did leave the household life to join the order of monks. We can disregard the tradition that the first to do so was Liu Chun, Marquis of Yang-ch'eng, during the reign of Emperor Ming (56-75), because the ordination ceremonies, as a rule, required the presence of a minimum number of ordained monks (ten) and the observance of the rules governing the conduct of monks, called the *Pātimokkha* rules. It is extremely unlikely that these requirements could be met under Emperor Ming. During the latter part of the second century conditions were ready. A sufficient number of ordained foreign monks were known to be in Lo-yang; moreover, the *Pātimokkha* rules were being circulated by oral transmission, if not in writing. The ten cardinal precepts governing the conduct of monks were mentioned before in the *Sutra in Forty-two Sections* and *Mou-tzu*. It was no mere coincidence that at the end of the second century a Chinese emerged who not only helped the foreign monks with their translating, but did some translating of his own. His name was Yen Fou-t'iao, a convert of An Shih-kao. He also had to his credit an original work, a book of instructions entitled *Sha-mi-shih-hui* (*Ten Wise Rules for the Novice*). This work is now lost, but his preface to it is still preserved, and here he is designated as an *ācārya* or teacher. Other sources say definitely that he was a monk. In all probability Yen was the first Chinese monk, and since he assisted the foreign monks in their translations, he was very likely the first Chinese to understand the foreign Buddhist texts.

## BUDDHIST TEACHINGS OF THE HAN PERIOD

During the Han period the main tenets of Buddhism were the indestructibility of the soul and the cycle of rebirth and karma. At first glance the idea of the indestructibility of the soul would appear to be contrary to the cardinal Buddhist doctrine of *anatta* or nonself. In the beginning the Chinese Buddhists had difficulty understanding the idea of repeated rebirths without some abiding entity linking together the different stages of rebirth. To overcome this difficulty they evolved the concept of *shen-ling* or an indestructible soul that is transmitted through successive rebirths. Man consists of a material body and a spiritual soul. The body comes into being at birth and disintegrates at death, but the soul is eternal and indestructible. Due to the effects of karma, this soul is forever bound to the cycle of rebirths. The *Hou Han Chi* (*Annals of the Later Han*) of Yüan Hung (328-376) summarizes this Buddhist view succinctly: The Buddhists "also teach that when a person dies, his soul does not perish, but would become reborn and assume another form. The meritorious and evil deeds performed during the lifetime would all have their rewards and punishments. Therefore they value the practice of meritorious deeds and the cultivation of the way, so as to discipline the soul. By so doing they would attain to nirvāna and become a Buddha."[6] In answer to a question, "Since a person who follows the way and one who does not both die, what is the difference?" Mou-tzu replied, "When those who follow the way die, their souls go to paradise, but when those who are evil die, their souls certainly go to disaster."

This idea of the Buddhist that a soul lives forever in accordance with karma fitted in with prevalent Later Han Taoist beliefs, namely, that a man upon death becomes a spirit with knowledge and feeling, and can assume human shape to harm people. Fol-

---

[6] Yüan Hung, *Hou-Han-chi*, 10,5a (*Ssu-pu ts'ung-k'an* edition).

lowers of the Confucian tradition also shared in this belief of a spirit's surviving after death, as indicated by their practice of mounting the roof top and calling the name of a person who had just died. Such a practice was known as Recall of the Departed Spirit. Wang Ch'ung had a chapter in his *Essays of Criticism* attacking such beliefs.

As for the cultivation of the way, the Han Buddhists emphasized the suppression of the passions. There are numerous passages in the *Sutra in Forty-two Sections* stressing the evils of unrestrained passions. "Those who are addicted to the passions are like the torchbearers running against the wind; their hands are sure to be burned." "From the passions arises worry, and from worry arises fear. Away with the passions, and no fear, no worry." "People cleave to their worldly possessions and selfish passions so blindly as to sacrifice their own lives for them. They are like a child who tries to eat a little honey smeared on the edge of a knife." Because wealth and sensual pleasures were considered to be the roots of passions, the monks were commanded to withdraw from society and to abandon all wealth.

This Buddhist teaching of suppressing the passions was something new to the Chinese and not found in Taoist practices. Two methods of suppression were taught by the Buddhists: concentration and observance of the rules of conduct, namely, the two hundred and fifty *Pātimokkha* rules. Numerous translations were made during the Han Dynasty to popularize concentration techniques. One could extirpate lust, for instance, by going to the cemetery and meditating on a corpse in various stages of decay. The Chinese were offended by the gruesomeness of such a practice, and they emphasized, instead, breathing exercises or control of the breath. The most influential and popular sutra teaching this method was the *An-pan-shou-i-ching* (*Sutra on Concentration by Practicing Respiratory Exercises*), translated by An Shih-kao. The Chinese characters *an-pan* represent the Sanskrit term *anāpāna* for inhalation and exhalation. Breathing exercises were adopted and emphasized by the Buddhists because of their affinity to the Taoist practices, which had already been in vogue among Taoist circles since the late Chou period.

Besides emphasizing suppression of the passions, the Buddhists also stressed charity and compassion. By encouraging the donation of earthly belongings such as money, goods, and food to the monastic community, the religion sought to eliminate avariciousness. In order to destroy malice and to propagate love and friendship, the feeling of compassion for fellow beings was stressed. Compassion also entails the injunction not to kill living creatures. As this feature is mentioned by a number of Han writers, it must have attracted the attention of the Chinese. Hsiang K'ai describes the religion as being opposed to killing, as does Yüan Hung, author of the *Hou Han Chi*.

After a period of training, in which the individual has adhered faithfully to the rules of discipline, extirpated his desires and passions, fostered the development of charity, compassion, and liberality, and practiced concentration, he attains arhatship, and can fly, assume any shape, shake the world, and live an eternal life. Any individual attaining this stage of arhatship is no longer in the sea of misery, but is emancipated. Because the Buddha was such an emancipated figure living an eternal life, he was considered to be an unchanging and immortal deity, and hence was a proper object of worship. This would explain why Emperor Huan erected altars in the palace to worship the Buddha. It was also believed that the Buddha could save all sentient beings from misery, so that worship of him would enable one to acquire blessings.

## BUDDHIST-TAOIST MIXTURES

In the eyes of Emperor Huan and other Chinese this Buddha was closely linked to Taoist deities. The best piece of evidence to support this was the memorial of Hsiang K'ai, who used the term "this doctrine" in referring to both Huang-Lao and the Buddha. During the hundred years from the time of Prince Ying to Emperor Huan the two systems were intermingled to a considerable extent, with the newly introduced Buddhist faith's being accepted as part of the Taoist system. This might be the reason why Buddhism was not mentioned separately in the dynastic history during those years.

Several factors were responsible for the Buddhist-Taoist mixture. First, there were certain external similarities that hid the doctrinal differences between the two. In their public ceremonies both systems practiced worship without sacrifices. In their private practices both emphasized concentration and meditation, control of respiration, and abstinence from certain kinds of food. The religious tenets of the Buddhist aimed at purity of thought and action, the suppression of passions, and the avoidance of luxury. Though some Han Taoists practiced the "arts of the inner chambers," others followed the Buddhist in favoring control of the passions. The Buddhist taught the indestructibility of the soul and rebirth in the Brahma heavens; the Taoists believed in the land of the immortals in the Eastern Seas, or sought immortality in the Heaven of Grand Purity. Because of these numerous elements of apparent similarity between the two, the Buddhists and the Taoists joined forces. For the Buddhists this union was an advantage because it enabled them to gain a hearing among the Chinese; by presenting their religion as one aspect of the native Taoist system, they were able to overcome some of the prejudice against a foreign faith.

Another factor that tended to draw the two systems together was that the Chinese who assisted in the early Buddhist translations were usually drawn from among the Taoists. This can be seen in the choice of texts translated and in the terminology used.

If we examine the Han translations, we are confronted with a curious situation. Not many of the translations are concerned with the fundamental doctrines of Buddhism: the four truths, chain of causation, nirvāna, nonself, transitoriness, and so forth. Rather, most of them are concerned with concentration practices and breath control, subjects of interest to the Taoists. It appears that the foreign missionaries did not choose these texts for presentation to the Chinese; rather, it was the Chinese followers, often influenced by Taoism, who determined the choice, since such texts were the ones that interested them. Or perhaps the foreign monks chose to translate only those texts because they were the ones of interest to the Chinese.

One example of such a translation by An Shih-kao is the *Chiu-heng-ching* (*Sutra on the Nine Causes of Unexpected Death, Taishō Tripitaka*, 880, 883). In this sutra the Buddhist teaches that there are nine causes which prevent life from being successfully completed: (1) eating what should not be eaten, (2) eating to excess, (3) eating unaccustomed food, (4) not vomiting when having eaten too much, (5) having indigestion, (6) not observing the moral precepts, (7) approaching evil without knowing it, (8) entering a village at an inopportune time, (9) not evicting what should be evicted. The wise man recognizes these nine causes and avoids them. By avoiding them, he obtains longevity and an opportunity to hear the word of the teacher. There is nothing in such a teaching that is particularly Buddhistic.

With reference to the terminology used in the translation, we must bear in mind that An Shih-kao and others during the Han Dynasty were not addressing themselves to people who were already prepared for the Buddhist message. Consequently, they had to use terms which the listeners and readers could understand. Nor were their Chinese collaborators acquainted with any foreign language, and, as in many instances they were either Taoists or influenced by Taoism, they very naturally fell back upon Taoist terms to express Buddhist ideas.

In the eyes of the Han Chinese, Buddhism was but another aspect of Taoism, since its practices and tenets were akin to those of the Taoists. To the Taoists, Buddhism was a new method of obtaining immortality. They felt that the Buddhist nirvāna was no different from the Taoist salvation, the arhat like the Taoist *chen-jen*, or pure man. True, the Buddhist discipline was stricter and more reasonable; its doctrines were more profound and did not include the practice of alchemy. But, on the whole, the points of similarity were so numerous that the Chinese overlooked the differences and considered Buddhism as but another sect of Taoism.

Yet how was it that the Chinese could have accepted a foreign deity from a foreign country and worshiped it as equal with Huang-Lao? The explanation for this is to be sought in a remarkable doctrine developed by the Taoists—that of *hua-hu*, the conversion of the barbarians. According to this doctrine, Lao-tzu, after disappearing in the west, went all the way to India, where he converted the barbarians and became the Buddha. Therefore the founders of Buddhism and Taoism were one and the same person, for the Buddha was but an incarnation of Lao-tzu. Since the two religions originated from the same source, there was no difference between them, so that it was quite proper for the deities Buddha and Huang-Lao to be worshiped on the same altar.

This doctrine probably developed at first in the area where Buddhists and Taoists were thrown together, namely, in the east China region, where present-day Kiangsu and Shantung meet. This was the region where the community led by Prince Ying of Ch'u was centered. Hsiang K'ai was the first to refer to this doctrine. In his memorial of 166 he wrote, "Some have said that Lao-tzu entered the land of the barbarians to become the Buddha." Yü Huan, in his *Wei-lüeh*, also referred to this tradition concerning Lao-tzu. The passage here reads: "The Buddhist sutras are on the whole similar to the Canon of Lao-tzu in content. This is because when Lao-tzu left the passes in the west, he traversed the Western Regions and reached India, where he converted the barbarians into Buddhists." Yü Huan's account shows an advance over that of Hsiang K'ai, for it speaks of Lao-tzu's converting the barbarians. Tradition has it that the *Hua-hu-ching* (*Sutra on the Conversion of the Barbarians*) was composed by Wang Fu of the Western Chin Dynasty (265-316). What Wang Fu did was to gather together all the old traditions concerning Lao-tzu and his sojourn in the west and incorporate them into his work.

The region which gave birth to the *hua-hu* doctrine also witnessed the appearance of the *T'ai-p'ing-ching* (*Sutra on the Great Peace*), a Taoist work that had something to do with Buddhism. Taoist traditions say that during the reign of Emperor Shun (126-144) the Taoist Kung Ch'ung revealed this work of his master Yü Chi. This work originated and was popular in the east China region, where Buddhism was already established, and it is clear that the compiler knew about the new religion, for he attacked it on four counts. First, Buddhism is unfilial, as it encourages abandonment of parents. Second, it results in the neglect of wives and children; it encourages celibacy and no offspring. Third, it permits eating of impurities. Fourth, it promotes begging for alms. The first two criticisms might be taken to indicate the presence of Buddhist monks and converts in the area. The third point referred to the practice by the Buddhist of taking urine as medicine. (Wang Ch'ung once noted that Prince Ying ate impurities.) As for begging, the indigenous religions in China never engaged in this; consequently, begging was considered unnatural in the *T'ai-p'ing-ching*. From this it would appear that during Han times there was some begging for alms among the Buddhists, but, later, customs and conditions in China did not encourage the practice; hence the polemical literature against Buddhism during the Period of Division (fifth and sixth centuries) makes no mention of it.

Although the *T'ai-p'ing-ching* attacked Buddhism severely, it also exhibited some borrowings from the foreign religion. The compiler wrote that he drew his materials from the writings of sages past and present, native and foreign, from the terminology of the common people as well as of slaves. Some Buddhist terms are evident: *pen-ch'i* meaning *jātaka*, or birth story, and *san-chieh* meaning the three worlds. In the description of Lao-tzu's birth we find the story of the nine dragons spitting water. Such virtues as liberality, compassion, and kindness to living creatures were encouraged. There is no mention of karma or rebirth, though there is the concept of *ch'eng-fu* (transmission of burden). According to this notion, whatever good or evil had been performed by ancestors influenced the destiny of the descendants. Ancestral sins would be rewarded by calamity to posterity. Such influence in the case of kings would last thirty thousand years; ministers, three thousand years; ordinary people, three hundred years. The most severe retribution of ancestral sins was to have no offspring or descendants. This concept accounts for such an apparent case of injustice as the death without children of Yen Yüan, the gifted disciple of Confucius. Obviously, this doctrine is not the same as the Buddhist karma. The Buddhist idea is that rewards and retributions are experienced in one's own later rebirths, not by one's descendants. The object receiving the rewards or punishment is not the same, but the idea of transmission is present. Since the *T'ai-p'ing-ching* mentioned the concept of *ch'eng-fu* several times, was it influenced by the Buddhist doctrine of karma?

In two places in the *T'ai-p'ing-ching* there is a reference to the heavenly deity's dispatching beautiful maidens to test the neophyte cultivating the tao. This was borrowed from the episode of the *Sutra in Forty-two Sections*, where Māra sent his daughters to tempt the Buddha. Thus Yü Chi, like Hsiang K'ai, used the reference in the *Sutra in Forty-two Sections*.[7]

[7] In a previous passage it was stated that the *Sutra in Forty-two Sections* was popular in the east China region where Hsiang K'ai lived. The fact that the *T'ai-p'ing ching* borrowed from the sutra also points to east China as a possible place where the sutra originated.

We have described this close relationship between the Buddhist and the Taoist under the Han Dynasty at some length so that we can understand the nature of Han Buddhism and the subsequent history of Buddhist-Taoist relations. As a result of this alliance, the Han emperors placed deities of both religions on the same altar and worshiped them together. Ministers and the common people also regarded the two systems as one. Maspero has suggested that if contacts with India had ceased at the end of the Han Dynasty, Buddhism might have become absorbed into Taoism and disappeared from the scene.

This did not happen. More and more Buddhist missionaries arrived in China, making new converts and translating new texts. By the end of the Han Dynasty a new spirit of independence was developing within Buddhism; it no longer accepted the close connection with Taoism. Probably the first step toward independence was the appearance of the work *Mou-tzu,* which took a definite stand against Taoist doctrines and occultism, and asserted that Buddhism was ready to stand on its own feet in China. On the part of the Taoist, the renunciation of relations did not occur so early. For a long time the Taoists insisted that Lao-tzu went west to convert the barbarians and to become the Buddha. This insistence was to lead to a series of Buddhist-Taoist debates lasting over a thousand years, to be settled finally by the Mongol emperors in favor of the Buddhists.

# GROWTH AND DOMESTICATION

# CHAPTER III

## INITIAL CONTACT AND RESPONSE: BUDDHISM UNDER THE EASTERN CHIN DYNASTY

WITH the downfall of the Han Dynasty in 220 China entered a period of travail and disunity that did not end until 589. Throughout the third century short-lived and weak Chinese dynasties still managed to maintain a foothold in north China, but, beginning with 311, the fortunes of the Chinese began to decline. In that year the Hsiung-nu, or the Huns, captured the city of Loyang, and in 316 Ch'ang-an also fell. This marked the end of Chinese control of the north for almost three hundred years. With the fall of these two centers of Chinese civilization there began an exodus of the literati, officials, and learned monks from the north to the south, where they finally settled in Chien-k'ang, near the present Nanking. There they assisted in the establishment of the Eastern Chin Dynasty and, as life became more settled in the south, began to play a dominant role in the intellectual life of the area. In conjunction with the learned Buddhist monks of the region they developed what is sometimes called Buddhism of the upper classes, or gentry Buddhism.

The Eastern Chin Dynasty and their gentry supporters regarded themselves as the true heirs and preservers of Chinese culture, and looked forward to the time when they could recapture north China and reassert the supremacy of Chinese culture over the whole country. However, while professing to be supporters of the traditional Chinese way of life, they must have been struck by some moments of doubt. The loss of the heartland of Chinese culture raised some question as to whether the traditional ideology was sufficient as a rallying force to strengthen them for the recovery of the north. In this mood they turned to Buddhism. The type of gentry Buddhism, therefore, which they and the Buddhist monks developed in the south emphasized both Buddhist and Chinese learning, philosophical discussions, literary activities, a mixture of Taoist and Buddhist ideas, and congenial association between monks and the cultured elite of Chinese society. Since the imperial house was generally weak, the monastic community was able to assert its independence of secular authority and to maintain what amounted to an empire within an empire.

In the north, however, due to the presence of non-Chinese rulers and a large non-Chinese population, the religion developed along lines markedly different from those in the south. For one thing, it was very much under the control of the state and served the purposes of the state, so much so that it was sometimes looked upon as a state religion. Again, the monks who were prominent in north China, unlike their brethren in the south who were inclined toward literature and philosophy, were often those who were skilled in political and military counsel or in the exercise of magical powers. The first feature was to play an important role in determining the nature of Buddhism after the unification in 589. Of more immediate importance, however, was the development of the religion in the south between the third and fifth centuries.

At the end of the Han Dynasty two different trends had already developed in Buddhism. One was the Dhyāna School, with its emphasis on control of the mind, concentration, and suppression of the passions. This school was based mainly on the translations of An Shih-kao and was Hīnayāna in nature. Opposed to this was the Prajñā School, based largely on the translations of Chih-ch'an and inclined toward Mahāyāna in spirit. It was more interested in probing into the nature of the Buddha and the ultimate reality behind the external appearance of things. Beginning with the middle of the third century this aspect of Buddhism was to grow and develop until it became the dominant tendency within Buddhism in the south. The popularity of the Prajñā School brought about two results: first, the spread of Mahāyāna sutras in China, and, second, the development of closer relations between the Buddhist monks and the Chinese literati who embraced the Lao-Chuang school of thought.

## PRAJÑĀ SUTRAS

The Prajñā sutras comprised an important and voluminous section of Mahāyāna literature. The earliest of these sutras was probably the *Aṣṭasāhasrikā* or the *Perfection of Wisdom in 8,000 Lines.* This basic text, which probably dates back to the first century B.C., was either expanded into longer works or condensed into shorter pieces. During the first two centuries of the Christian era it was expanded largely by endless repetitions into the *Perfection of Wisdom in 100,000 Lines,* the *Perfection of Wisdom in 25,000 Lines,* and the *Perfection of Wisdom in 18,000 Lines.* The very bulkiness of these works proved to be disadvantageous, and soon condensed summaries of the text began to appear. Of these shorter versions, the two earliest, finished during the fourth century, were the *Heart Sutra* and the *Diamond Cutter Sutra.* Other condensations were the *Perfection of Wisdom in 2,500 Lines* and the *Perfection of Wisdom in 700 Lines.* This process was pursued still farther in the form of mantras and dhāraṇīs (mystic formulas), and in the Tibetan canon there is a *Perfection of Wisdom in One Letter,* in which the letter *A* is said to represent the epitome of all the Prajñā literature.

Early Buddhist thought conceived of the world as composed of an unceasing flow of dharmas, or ultimate facts of reality. These dharmas were divided into two categories: *asaṁskṛita* or unconditioned and *saṁskṛita* or conditioned. The unconditioned dharmas, such as nirvāna and space, were considered to be permanent, while the conditioned dharmas were conceived to be impermanent, to be caused by something else, to last only a moment, and to perish as soon as they were born. These conditioned dharmas belonged to the world of sense desires, the world of form, and the formless world. The first step for the Buddhist was to see these conditioned dharmas as they really were, to see their *sva-bhāva,* own-being or self-nature, so to speak. The *sva-bhāva* was the essential feature of a dharma. The principal teaching of the Prajñā sutras, from the shortest to the longest, was that the nature of the dharma was *śūnya* (void or empty). The Mahāyāna thinkers conceived of *śūnyatā* (emptiness) as meaning that the dharmas did not possess their own self-nature, were not ultimate facts by their own right, but were merely imagined, or came into existence depending on something else. All *saṁskṛita* dharmas were tied to conditions and were the results of many causes; they did not exist by themselves, and were said to be empty. This lesson the Prajñā sutras repeat endlessly. To attain this view was to attain *prajñā* or wisdom.

If the separate dharmas were void or nonexistent, then there was no individual to realize or obtain anything, nor was there any entity to be obtained. The attitude of the enlightened one, therefore, was one of nonassertion. He did not assert his self in any way, for there was no self in the first place, and there was no belief in a separate entity. This led to the doctrine that assumption of any duality was erroneous—a doctrine that is fundamental in the Prajñā literature—no dualism between subject and object, affirmation and negation, *saṁsāra* and nirvāna.

As early as the Han Dynasty a translation of the *Perfection of Wisdom in 8,000 Lines* was made by Chih-ch'an. Toward the end of the third century two translations of the *Perfection of Wisdom in 25,000 Lines* were completed, one by Dharmaraksha in 286 and one by Mokshala in 291.

All through the fourth century this Prajñā School was dominant in China. Translations of the Prajñā sutras were read, studied, and discussed by Buddhist monks and the literati of the age. One of the figures instrumental in promoting the popularity of this school was Tao-an (312-385), who personally taught and commented on the sutras and encouraged his disciples to do likewise. So prevalent were the discussions on these sutras that different groups arose, known as the Six Houses and the Seven Schools, each one adhering to some special doctrine. The names of the Seven Schools give some indication of the wide range of subjects speculated upon: the School of Original Nonbeing, the Variant School of Nonbeing, the School of Stored Impressions, the School of Matter as Such, the School of Phenomenal Illusions, the School of Nonbeing of Mind, the School of Causal Combinations. However, the information given about these schools is so cryptic and meager that very little can be made out as to what their doctrines were and how they differed from one another.

To understand what was responsible for this widespread interest in the Prajñā sutras, a few words about the intellectual climate of the period is necessary.

# NEO-TAOISM

As a result of the vicissitudes which followed in the wake of the breakdown of Han imperial authority, scholars and literati who normally sought and found service in the governmental bureaucracy no longer had such opportunities for officialdom open to them, and so they turned away from practical politics and human events to take refuge in poetry, wine, and the quietism and nonactivity of Taoism. Because of this, they were sometimes called Neo-Taoists. In this quietistic atmosphere of Taoism they found consolation and solace in a fundamental idea which the Taoists developed, that of *tzu-jan* (naturalness or spontaneity). In the realm of human activities naturalness was associated with the full freedom of the individual to act and talk as he pleased, unrestrained by the conventions of society. In the realm of nature it was pointed out that although no one did anything, everything was produced continually and naturally. In this sense naturalness was equated with nonactivity.

This interest in naturalness took two different forms. In one the followers strove to develop the art of conversation to the highest intellectual level, such conversations to be in the form of philosophical dialogues or subtle repartee and to be expressed in the most elegant language and precise phrases. Conversations were usually held between friends of comparable tastes and intellectual attainments. At times the participants understood each other so well that they just remained silent. The best examples of such conduct were the lives of the Seven Sages of the Bamboo Grove, who "all revered and exalted the void and non-action, and disdained the affairs of the world."

The other form which this interest in naturalness took was the contemplation of the mystery behind all mysteries, the ultimate truth that is behind the phenomenal world. As these men contemplated the natural order of the universe, the regularity of the seasons, the orderliness of the animal and vegetable kingdoms, they speculated that there must be some absolute principle that is the origin of it all, some ultimate reality that brings about this universal harmony. Out of such speculation arose the concept of *wu* or nonbeing that is the basis of all things. "Though Heaven and Earth, in their greatness, are richly endowed with the myriad things; though their thunder moves and their winds circulate; though through their revolving operations the myriad transformations come to be—yet it is the silent and supreme non-being that is their origin."[1] This nonbeing can function only in being, and is made manifest in being. Nonbeing itself is without substance or tangible appearance, but it can be manifested in the functioning of being.

In its definition of the sage the Neo-Taoists contended that he is one who is completely identified with nonbeing. He is also satisfied with what is natural. In this state of sagehood all distinctions between the self and others, life and death, right and wrong, are forgotten. By forgetting such distinctions he becomes identified with the universe, and since the universe continues indefinitely, he also continues indefinitely.

## BUDDHIST-TAOIST RAPPROCHEMENT

This Neo-Taoist School represented the dominant trend of thought among literary circles in south China during the fourth century, at the very time that the Prajñā School was gaining supremacy in Buddhist circles. When the two schools confronted each other it was soon discovered that they held to a number of ideas in common. The Buddhists held that all things were by nature empty or void, while the Neo-Taoists maintained that the myriad things had their origin in nonbeing. Emptiness was equated with nonbeing and both were considered as ultimate truths. Just as the sage of Neo-Taoism was said to be identified with nonbeing, so was the Buddha said to be identified with *śūnyatā* or emptiness. In such a state of identification, all dualisms, all distinctions disappeared. The Taoist sage, once united with the supreme tao or nonbeing, became eternal and could assume any shape or size, just as the Buddha was eternal and could manifest himself in any form and in any place. Once this affinity between the two groups was discovered, the stage was set for a period of close relationship and interplay of ideas between the two groups. Such an interchange was carried on chiefly in the southern capital, Chien-k'ang, and in K'uai-chi in east China, near modern Hang-chou.

[1] Fung Yu-lan, *History of Chinese Philosophy*, Princeton, 1953, 2,181.

The Neo-Taoists, indulging in their pure conversations, began to play with Prajñā ideas, while the Buddhist monks also began looking into the various aspects of Lao-Chuang philosophy. Since this was the prevailing mood among the intellectual circles of the times, it is no wonder that the study of the transcendental wisdom of the Prajñā sutras became more and more widespread. By their interest in the philosophical ideas of Lao-Chuang the Buddhist monks during this period, beginning with the Western Chin (265-316), were able for the first time to establish friendly relations with the famous literary men and gentry of the age.

Since both the Neo-Taoists and the Buddhists were interested in the problem of ontology, their discussions were mainly concerned with *pen-t'i* or the essence of things in the abstract. Nonbeing or emptiness was considered to be the *pen*, the base or foundation of all things, the ultimate reality or the transcendental truth, while the *t'i* or outward manifestations of this ultimate reality in the phenomenal world were taken as the relative truth. Among both Neo-Taoists and Buddhists the tendency was to value nonbeing and to deprecate the phenomenal world.

In discussing *pen-t'i*, Chinese thinkers never departed from considerations of human life; therefore primary concern was given to the realization of the original nature of a human being. When one became identified with his original nature of nonbeing, as in the case of the sage, he was said to have *fan-pen* or to have reverted to the original.

Buddhism was a way of salvation for living beings. In Chinese Buddhism the idea of an indestructible soul was developed at an early time; this soul was forever transmigrating in the sea of misery because of its attachment to the myriad things in the world. In order to attain the goal of nirvāna all attachments to existing things had to be eradicated. The key to eradication of such attachments was the attainment of wisdom, or the understanding that the myriad things were illusory and nonexistent. When this wisdom was attained, one realized his Buddha-nature. To become the Buddha meant not being attached to the myriad things, just as the sage or the perfect man of the Neo-Taoists had no desires and was not ensnared by things of the world.

As a result of this community of interests the conduct of the Buddhist monks in the south, the books they studied, the terms used, and the concepts held were the same as those of Neo-Taoism. The Neo-Taoists themselves failed to see the differences between Buddhism and Lao-Chuang. Thus Liu Ch'iu (438-495) wrote: "From the K'un-lun Mountain eastward the term 'Great Oneness' is used. From Kashmir westward the term *sambodhi* (omniscience of the Buddha) is used. Whether one looks longingly toward 'non-being' or cultivates 'emptiness,' the principle involved is the same." Fan Yeh (398-445) also had the same idea in the *Hou-Han shu*: "If we examine closely its (Buddhist) teachings about purifying the mind and gaining release from the ties of life, and its emphasis upon casting aside both 'emptiness' and 'being,' we see that it belongs to the same current as do the Taoist writings."[2]

This close relationship between the Buddhists and Neo-Taoists was based also on the fact that some of the monks arose out of the same social class, the gentry and aristocracy, as did their counterparts. The most powerful gentry clan in Chien-k'ang during the early part of the Eastern Chin Dynasty was the Wang family. The head of this clan, Wang Tao (276-339), was prime minister and a faithful patron of Buddhism. Together with his cousin, Wang Tun (266-324), who was commander in chief of the army, he regulated the affairs of the Chin state in the south. Two members of the Wang clan forsook their lives as scholarly gentlemen to join the Buddhist order. One was Chu Tao-ch'ien (286-374), younger brother of Wang Tun, who became the most prominent monk in the Chin court and the respected adviser of successive Chin emperors. When he died in 374, the Chin emperor donated 100,-000 cash for his funeral expenses. The other was Shih Tao-pao (fourth century), younger brother of Wang Tao. Other monks who came from cultured families were Chu Fa-i (307-380), K'ang Fa-ch'ang (fourth century), and Chih Min-tu (fourth century).

Among the foreign monks who participated in these discussions in Chien-k'ang, the most prominent was K'ang Seng-yüan, whose forebears probably came from Sogdia in Central Asia; he himself was born in China. He had become so Sinicized that he was said to be "foreign in appearance but Chinese in speech." His Chinese friends twitted him about his deep-set eyes and high nose, where-

---

[2] *Ibid.*, 2,240.

upon he replied with a statement that has been regarded as a classical example of pure wit: "The nose comprises the mountain of the face, while the eyes are its springs. If a mountain is not high, it will not be famous, if a spring is not deep, its waters will not be clear."

## CHIH TUN

The Buddhist monk who best represented this conjunction of Prajñā and Neo-Taoist thought was Chih Tun (314-366), also known as Chih Tao-lin. Tun was a native of Ch'en-liu (modern K'ai-feng) and came from a family which had been Buddhist for generations. Soon after his ordination, which took place when he was twenty-five, he went to the capital at Chien-k'ang, where immediately he surrounded himself with kindred souls who delighted in pure conversations. Apparently one such discussion took place in the White Horse Temple in the capital, where the topic of conversation was the "Chapter on the Happy Excursion" in *Chuang-tzu*. The standard commentaries on this chapter say that happiness consists of everyone's following his own nature and living in accordance with the capacity and quality which have been allotted him. If he tries to be other than what he is destined to be, he is unhappy.

According to his biography Chih Tun objected to this view, saying that the "nature of the tyrants Chieh (last ruler of the Hsia Dynasty) and Chou (last ruler of the Shang Dynasty) was to do destructive harm, so that if achievement of happiness simply consists in following one's nature, they too enjoyed perfect happiness. Thereupon he withdrew and wrote a commentary on 'The Happy Excursion' which all the old time scholars admired and followed."[3]

Although this commentary is no longer preserved, some of its contents may be gleaned from quotations preserved in other sources. According to these, Tun's ideal was the perfect man who, like the giant bird, "avails himself of the right course of Heaven triumphantly, and roams around endlessly in perfect freedom."[4] Such a perfect man is superior to the ideal described by the

[3] *Kao-seng-chuan*, 4; *Taishō*, 50,348b, translated in Fung, *op.cit.*, 2,250.
[4] *Shih-shuo hsin-yü, Wen-hsüeh-p'ien chu*, translated in Zürcher, *Buddhist Conquest*, Leiden, 1959, 1,129.

Taoists in their commentaries, who is satisfied with achieving an inferior grade of happiness by following his own nature.

If Chih Tun's Buddhist background were considered, then his views on this matter become understandable. When the Taoists argued that a man is justified in leading any sort of life so long as it is in accordance with his natural share and talent, they were taking a position contrary to the Buddhist world view governed by moral law, and Tun felt obliged to refute them. He also viewed the fatalism of the Taoists—that a man can be only what he is destined to be—as being opposed to the doctrine of karma, whereby he can improve his destiny by his own efforts.

Chih Tun's first stay in the capital lasted only a few years. Then he moved eastward to K'uai-chi, near present-day Hang-chou, where he continued his close contacts with the aristocrats and Neo-Taoist scholars of the area. Within these circles the conversations might be chapters in the *Chuang-tzu* or the Prajñā sutras. Because of his original ideas expressed in his commentary on *Chuang-tzu*, the famous Neo-Taoists of the age vied with one another to include him among their friends.

It was Chih Tun who was responsible for a change in the meaning of the very important Chinese concept of li. According to Chinese classical thought this li refers to the natural order of the universe or reason. Under the influence of Prajñā philosophy Chih Tun invested this term with a new metaphysical meaning, and interpreted it as the transcendental absolute principle, a concept unknown to the Chinese until then. In the writings of the Buddhists from the fourth to the tenth centuries, li as the absolute was regularly opposed by shih, mundane events or facts of empirical experience. Later on, the Neo-Confucians took over this pair, keeping li in the sense of the absolute truth, but opposing it with ch'i, vital energy or matter.

In appearance Tun was said to have been ugly, so that people remarked that they liked to hear his words but hated to see his face. He was brilliant and subtle in conversation, fond of raising hawks and horses, and appreciative of mountain scenes. He also seemed to be the possessor of a waspish tongue. Once when friends asked his opinion about two persons he had just seen, he replied, "I have only seen a swarm of whitenecked crows, and heard their noisy cawing."[5]

[5] Zürcher, *op.cit.*, 1,119.

In his old age he was summoned by the Chin emperor to the capital to lecture on the Prajñā sutras. His success in these lectures prompted the Neo-Taoist Hsi Ch'ao to write that in the past few centuries only Chih Tun had succeeded in clarifying the great law so that the truth might continue without interruption.

## BUDDHIST LAYMEN AMONG THE GENTRY

Who were some of the gentry leaders and literary men who participated in these philosophical discussions with the cultured Buddhist monks? Among the lay followers of Chih Tun a long list of such people is mentioned. The most prominent was Hsi Ch'ao (336-377), who came from a Taoist family with strong Buddhist connections. Ch'ao must have been a diligent student, for he wrote a treatise entitled *Feng-fa-yao* (*Essentials of the Dharma*), presenting his knowledge of the religion. Besides dabbling in Buddhism, Ch'ao was also active in the court intrigues of the period, and was a close collaborator of the Chin general Huan Wen, who attempted to seize the imperial throne in 371 but failed.

Another prominent layman was Yin Hao (d. 356), a rival of Huan Wen, who suffered a disastrous defeat when he led a campaign against the Former Ch'in state in 353. As a result of this defeat he was reduced to a commoner and banished to Chekiang, where he died in 356. It was during these years that he began to study the Prajñā sutras and to discuss with the Buddhist monks the obscure problems he found there.

Mention must also be made of Sun Cho (ca.300-380), one of the best-known literary figures of the age. One of his works, *Tao-hsien-lun* (*Treatise on Monks and Worthies*), is a comparison of some famous monks and literati. Another of his works, the *Yü-tao-lun* (*Treatise Illustrating the Tao*), is an attempt to reconcile the other-worldly creed of Buddhism with this-worldly social virtues of Confucianism. According to him the difference between the two is mainly one of expediency; Buddhism, he said, represents the inner teaching and Confucianism the outer. The difference may be accounted for by the divergences in circumstances, but as to their inner nature, they are the same. He wrote that "the Duke of Chou and Confucius are identical with the Buddha; the Buddha is identical with the Duke of Chou and Confucius." His Neo-Taoist influence may be seen in his definition of the Buddha as "the one who does nothing and yet there is nothing that he does not do."[6]

Others in this group of cultured laymen and friends include Wang Ch'ia (325-358), son of Wang Tao and governor of Wu-hsing in Chekiang; Hsü Hsün (fourth century); Hsieh An (320-385); and Wang Hsi-chih (321-379). Ch'ia carried on some correspondence with Tun on problems concerning nonbeing and asked the master to furnish him with some scriptural corroboration. Hsü Hsun was a famous poet and connoisseur of pure talk who turned to Buddhism after his retirement to the mountains in the Hang-chou area. Such pure conversations were often held in the mansion of Wang Meng (ca.309-347), a friend of Chih Tun. Hsieh An, a general of the Chin Dynasty, was one of the chief figures in the decisive battle of Fei-shui in 383, when the armies of the non-Chinese dynasty, Former Ch'in, were disastrously defeated. Wang Hsi-chih was one of the well-known calligraphers of the age, as were also Wang Ch'ia, Hsieh An, and Wang Meng. We can still catch the flavor of the animated discussions carried on by this group, preserved in the *Shih-shuo hsin-yü* (*New Discourses on Contemporary Conversations*), written by Liu I-ch'ing (403-444).

## KE-YI, OR MATCHING THE MEANING

Since the Buddhists of this period were familiar with the external or Taoist literature, it is not surprising to find them having recourse to Taoist texts for words and phrases to use in their translations. This practice of the Buddhists of searching through Chinese literature, mainly Taoist, for expressions to explain their own ideas is known as *ke-yi*, or the method of matching the meaning. This method was used especially by the translators of the Prajñā sutras for the purpose of making Buddhist thought more easily understood by the Chinese.

The founder of this method was said to be Chu Fa-ya (fourth century). According to his biography, "As a youth, he was skilled in external (non-Buddhist) studies, but as he grew up, he came

[6] *Taishō*, 52,16b, 17a.

to comprehend the concepts of Buddhism. . . . At this time his disciples were only versed in the non-Buddhist writings, but not in Buddhist principles. So Ya, with K'ang Fa-lang and others, equated the numerical categories of the sutras with the external writings, in order to establish examples that would create understanding. This was called the method of analogy. . . . In this way external writings and Buddhist sutras were mutually transmitted, each being expounded in terms of the other."[7] Since the ideas of Lao-Chuang were considered closely akin to the Prajñā doctrines, they were used by many. The most famous example is that of Hui-yüan (334-416), who was well versed in both Confucian and Taoist literature. Concerning one of his lectures it is said: "Once some guests listened to his lectures, and questioned him about his theory of reality. Though the discussion continued back and forth for some time, they (the attendants) became increasingly doubtful and bewildered. Thereupon Yüan quoted ideas from *Chuang-tzu* that belonged to the same category, and in this way the skeptics came to understand."[8]

From the above it would seem that the method was sometimes used to teach students. Original Chinese ideas were used and compared with those of Buddhism, so that a student already familiar with Chinese concepts gained an understanding of the newly introduced Buddhist ideas. It was said of Chu Fa-ya, "Each time he, together with Tao-an and Fa-t'ai, unravelled the knots of perplexity and resolved doubts, they jointly exhausted the essential purport of the scriptures."[9] Nevertheless, it seems that the method was used mostly in the translation of the Prajñā sutras. In spite of its usefulness, it was criticized as being contrary to reason, pedantic, and divergent from the original text. After Kumārajīva arrived in 401 to present the authoritative interpretation of Buddhist thought and translated the Buddhist texts correctly, the *ke-yi* method was no longer used.

## THE FENG-FA-YAO (ESSENTIALS OF THE DHARMA)

In view of the numerous contacts and discussions between the Buddhists and the literary men and aristocrats of the age, what

[7] Fung, *op.cit.*, 2,241-242, with some changes.
[8] *Ibid.*, with some changes.
[9] T'ang Yung-t'ung, "On Ko-yi," *Radhakrishnan: Comparative Studies in Philosophy*, 1950, 277.

sort of understanding of Buddhism did the latter group attain? The best way to answer this question would be to refer to the contents of the *Feng-fa-yao* by Hsi Ch'ao (336-377). Ch'ao came from a Taoist family but he himself was a fervent admirer of Buddhism. His circle of friends included some of the leading Buddhist monks of the Prajñā School. His work, the *Feng-fa-yao*, is preserved in the Buddhist collection *Hung-ming-chi*, compiled by Seng-yu in the early part of the sixth century.

The first part of the treatise is taken up with a discussion of the three jewels, the five cardinal precepts, the observances of the fast, the four sublime states (friendship, compassion, joy, and equanimity), the six bases of mindfulness (Buddha, dharma, community of monks, charity, moral precepts, and deities), the ten meritorious deeds, the five modes of existence (deity, man, animal, hungry ghost, and denizen of hell), the five aggregates, the five hindrances, and the six feelings. The sources of these Buddhist concepts were the early translations of An Shih-kao, Chih Ch'ien, Chih Yao, Fa-hu, and others. It must be pointed out here that Ch'ao makes no mention of such fundamental ideas as the four noble truths, the eightfold path, or the chain of causation. Following this, Ch'ao takes up the concept of karma. He stresses clearly the idea that the effects of karma are borne by the individual alone and quoted approvingly the statement: "If the father performs some evil deed, the son does not suffer the consequences for him; if the son performs some evil deed, the father does not suffer the consequences for him. A good deed naturally brings about its own blessings, an evil deed its own calamity." In this instance Ch'ao understood very well the Buddhist concept of karma and realized how different it was from the Confucian concept of collective responsibility or the Taoist idea of *ch'eng-fu* or transmission of burden, which meant that the good or evil performed by the ancestors would influence the destiny of the descendants. He also indicated that he recognized the role performed by the mind or will in the operation of karma, for we read in his treatise:

"It is said in the scriptures, the mind makes one a deity, the mind makes one a human being, or an inhabitant of hell or a domestic animal, even the state of one who has gained the way is the result of the mind.

"Each and every thought that springs from the mind is subject to retribution; even if the fact or act has not been realized, the hidden response of karma has been built up in the dark. Now feelings and thoughts are swiftly moving about; suddenly and abruptly they appear one after another in a continuous succession, and stimulated by an insignificant motive they at once expand throughout the universe. Future punishment and happiness, bodily form and destination, there is none that does not spring from them; fortune or disaster, shame and regret are decided in a single moment. That is why he who practices the way is always 'careful of himself when being alone.' In his mind, he should beware of the beginnings of the slightest evil thought. Using the perfect principle of the doctrine as his bulwark, he always remains in control of what is fundamental in order to restrain what is secondary. He does not rashly form thoughts because matters have not yet taken shape. . . .

" 'All dharmas are born from and are shaped by thought.' Hence when the first signs become active in the mind, the acts will follow as a response. When ideas arise there is worry, when they cease there is none. Once the thoughts are appeased, our ways will be smooth whatever happens, and once the emotions are obstructed, we shall be impeded wherever we go. It follows that the smooth or interrupted flow of the emotions lies in ourselves and not in the outer world. For when fear arises in the heart, then the hostile forces from without will take advantage of our weakness, and when this happens, the inner fear will accumulate more and more. For if one is afraid to lose, one is capable of doing anything. That is why the scripture says that 'if a strong man is afraid, then the demons will take advantage of him.' But if one is really able to restrain one's mind by reason, so that the natural bastion is made strong inside, then man and demons will find no crevice to get in by, and the process of causation would cease by itself. The myriad phenomena of existence will have no power to bind; all evil will be unable to attack."[10]

Following this, Ch'ao took up the basic Buddhist concepts of misery, impermanence, nonself, and emptiness. "The four aspects of what is not permanent are the following: impermanence, suffering, emptiness and non-self. That forms change from young to

[10] Zürcher, *op.cit.*, 1,167-172, with some changes.

old, and that hills become valleys and valleys hills, is called impermanence. Prosperity and decline succeed one another, joy inevitably gives rise to sorrow, this is suffering. All existing things in the end go to nothingness, this is emptiness. The soul has no constant abode, it moves and changes without cease, this is nonself. The scripture says that when one dwells in a place of delusive joy, one should be conscious of the inevitableness of misery. For one can see this affirmed in the shifting phases in the cycle of life and in the fact that when joy disappears, sorrow arises. Therefore, though one lives in peace, he should worry about danger; though he enjoys glory, he should be vigilant at night. If one is profoundly aware of misery, then one is said to have attained the truth. To have conscious thought means to have obstructions; whenever there are such obstructions there is misery. Even if one belongs to the highest nobility among men and gods, and is in a position both high and venerable, yet the greater his authority and display of power, the more painful in principle are the pleasures in which his senses delight. Therefore the scripture says, 'the triple world is all suffering, there is nothing enjoyable about it.' 'All beings in the five modes of existences are together in one vast prison.' When the mind is fettered with existence, then punishment and bliss are intimately connected, therefore the triple world as a whole is called one vast prison. The Buddha once asked his disciples, "What is meant by impermanence?" One of them answered, 'That which cannot be preserved even for the duration of one day, that is impermanence.' The Buddha said, 'You are not my disciple.' Another said, 'That which cannot be preserved even for the duration of one meal, that is impermanence.' The Buddha said, 'You are not my disciple.' Another said, 'That after a single exhalation without response, one has already passed into the next generation, that is impermanence.' The Buddha replied, 'You are truly my disciple.' "[11]

Finally comes the discussion on nirvāna. This state is described as one in which existence is forgotten, the operation of karma ceases, and rebirth is discontinued. In nirvāna one is troubled neither by being nor nonbeing; one possesses intuitive understanding and is not conditioned by anything. It is one immeasurable,

[11] *Ibid.*, 1,172-173, with numerous changes.

mysterious abandon, and Hsi Ch'ao designates it by the Taoist term *wu-wei.*

Such are the main points stressed by Hsi Ch'ao. In fairness to him it must be admitted that his treatise manifests a high degree of understanding, superior in many respects to the work of Mou-tzu. If Hsi Ch'ao is guilty of any mistake or misunderstanding, as in his explanation of emptiness and nonself, he is not alone, for such shortcomings are shared by his compatriots, including even the Chinese Buddhists. The advancement achieved by the Chinese in the understanding of Buddhism becomes self-evident when the content of this work is compared with that of the *Mou-tzu li-huo-lun.*

## BUDDHISM AT THE SOUTHERN COURT

Not only were the Buddhist monks during the Chin Dynasty on friendly terms with the aristocracy and men of letters, but they also enjoyed cordial relations with members of the ruling hierarchy and imperial household. This is not surprising, considering the fact that some of the monks themselves were originally members of the aristocracy. Early in the dynasty there was the Wang clan, led by Wang Tao and Wang Tun, which was the pillar of the Buddhist community in the capital. In the middle of the fourth century it was the turn of the Ho clan, led by Ho Ch'ung (292-346), to become patrons of the religion at the court. Ho had been a protégé of Wang Tao, and in 345 became regent. In this capacity he began to promote Buddhism within the court circles. Being on good terms with such famous monks as Chu Tao-ch'ien and Chih Tun, he took his study of Buddhism seriously and spent an enormous amount of money building monasteries and entertaining monks. It was Ho who first built a nunnery in the southern capital shortly before his death in 346.

As a result of Ho Ch'ung's activities Buddhism began to play an increasingly important role at the court in Chien-k'ang. Famous Buddhist monks like the two mentioned above were invited by the emperor to lecture on the sacred scriptures, and some of these lectures were personally attended by the emperor himself. It was under the reign of Emperor Chien-wen (371-373) that there occurred the first recorded case of a Chinese emperor resorting to the magic power of a Buddhist monk to exorcise the baleful influence of an evil star. Buddhism was to achieve its greatest success during this period under the next emperor, Hsiao-wu (373-396). In 381 he formally accepted the Buddhist doctrine and became a devoted layman. Immediately after this he built a sanctuary within the imperial precincts and invited monks to live within it. The establishment of this sanctuary probably led to the introduction of sixteen rolls of Buddhist scriptures into the imperial library.

Under these favorable conditions Buddhism began to make progress. It is estimated that in the region controlled by the Eastern Chin there were 1,786 temples and 24,000 monks and nuns. In the capital, Chien-k'ang, the names of 37 temples have been preserved. The most famous of these are the Wa-kuan Temple, completed in 363/364, and the An-lo Temple. As the religion gained in popularity, it became the target of criticisms directed against its moral laxity and its extravagance. It was charged that huge amounts of wealth were spent in constructing and decorating the monasteries, but that in spite of this there was no corresponding increase in the beneficial effects to the ruling house, the prosperity of the country, or the health of the people.

The strongest attack was directed against clerical meddling in the affairs of the state, especially during the closing years of the dynasty. Emperor Hsiao-wu was only ten years of age when he ascended the throne, and power rested in the hands of his mother, the empress dowager. Both the emperor and the empress dowager were followers of Buddhism. As the emperor grew up, he and his administrator, Ssu-ma Tao-tzu, began to neglect affairs of state for a gayer life, and entrusted governmental business to monks and nuns. These conditions continued during the early years of the next emperor, An, who ruled from 397 to 418. Graft and corruption and miscarriage of justice soon became rampant —a fact which gave rise to memorials criticizing the excesses of the emperor and the monks. One by Hsü Jung presented in 389 read: "Monks, nuns and wet nurses are vying with each other to enter into the cliques and parties. . . . I have heard that the Buddha is a spirit of purity, far-reaching intelligence, and mysterious emptiness. He has based his doctrines upon the five lay commandments such as those prohibiting intoxicating drinks and debauchery. But nowadays the devotees are vile, rude, servile, and addicted to wine and women."[12]

The influence of nuns began to emerge during this period. The nunneries established in the capital by Ho Ch'ung and his niece, the Empress Ho, maintained close relationship with the female members of the imperial family, and this led to court intrigues by the nuns. One of the most powerful of these nuns was Chih Miao-yin, a favorite of Emperor Hsiao-wu. A temple was established by Ssu-ma Tao-tzu with Miao-yin as abbess. So powerful was her influence that people flocked to the temple to seek her favor and hundreds of carriages were parked at her gates daily. Such meddling in state affairs by monks and nuns sealed the fate of the dynasty.

One of the interesting problems that arose during the Chin Dynasty was that of the relations between the sangha or Buddhist community and the head of the state. In India the community of monks considered itself to be an autonomous body governed by its own laws, above and beyond the jurisdiction of the civil authorities. According to time-honored custom it was the ruling prince who showed respect to the monk, even though the latter might formerly have been an outcast. When this idea of an autonomous clerical body existing side by side with the imperial state was carried over to China, it immediately ran into opposition from the imperial bureaucracy motivated by Confucian ideology. Such an ideology regarded the emperor as the supreme ruler who regulated the social and political behavior of all his subjects. He was invested with a religious aura as the Son of Heaven, whose task it was to regulate the affairs of man in accordance with the processes of heaven. Into such a society the intrusion of an organization such as the Buddhist clerical order, claiming extraterritorial privileges for itself, was certain to arouse suspicion and opposition.

During the Chin Dynasty this problem of sangha-state relationship arose out of the specific question as to whether or not the monks should render homage to the ruler. In China, where the prevailing practice was for the subjects to prostrate themselves before the emperor, the Buddhist monks claimed exemption on the ground that the rules of discipline did not countenance a

[12] *Chin-shu*, 64,14b, translated in *ibid.*, 1,153.

monk's showing reverence to a householder. The question first arose in 340 when Yü Ping, regent during the reign of Emperor Ch'eng, proposed that monks should show the proper respect to the ruler just as any other subject. He argued that the Confucian system, which called for such respect, was the basis of government, and that if certain rules in that system were not enforced, the whole system would be undermined. He further argued that if the Buddhist sangha should occupy a position equal to and independent of the state, there would be confusion within the land. For the sake of order and harmony, therefore, the ruler should be superior and the monks inferior in position.

Yü Ping's position was opposed by Ho Ch'ung, the powerful Buddhist layman in the Chin court. He contended that as the monks were observing the five cardinal precepts of abstaining from killing, lying, stealing, unchastity, and intoxicating liquor, they were actually aiding the state in enforcing its laws. Moreover, whenever monks burned incense or uttered their earnest wishes, they prayed for the welfare and prosperity of the land and the well-being of the ruler, and thus indicated that they were not disloyal to the throne. On this initial occasion the Buddhist viewpoint prevailed, and Yü Ping's suggestion was not followed. While this controversy on the surface appears to be between the sangha and state, there is reason to believe that underlying it was a conflict between the two rival gentry clans, Yü and Ho, for leadership in the political sphere.

In 403 the usurper to the Chin throne, Huan Hsüan, once more raised the demand that monks should pay proper respect to the ruler. He was answered by the famous Chinese monk Hui-yüan, who wrote that Buddhism was divided into two levels—the laity who followed the teachings of the Buddha but remained in society, and the monks who withdrew from society and lived the religious way of life. There was no question concerning the conduct of the first group; its members paid homage to the ruler, respected their parents, practiced filial piety, and were loyal just as any other subject in the empire. On the other hand, those who had left the household life to become monks had transcended society and had no concern with worldly affairs. Such people should not be judged by the ordinary rules of society. It appeared that Huan was convinced by Hui-yüan's reply, for the monks were not called upon to pay the usual respect to the emperor.

On another occasion the same Huan Hsüan became upset by the extravagant and dissolute conduct of some monks and proposed to eliminate the undesirable elements from the monastic order. He felt that only those monks who could read and explain clearly the meaning of the sutras, who practiced diligently the moral precepts, and who lived in retirement in the hermitages should be permitted to continue as members of the monastic community. All others should be defrocked. Hui-yüan protested vigorously against this proposal too. He claimed that there were meritorious monks who did not live in the hermitages, that there were learned monks who were not eloquent, that there were some too advanced in age to perform meritorious deeds or to study diligently; such monks would be unjustifiably defrocked, he contended. In areas far from the capital it would be very difficult to ascertain who were pious or impious monks. This protest by Hui-yüan again seemed to have had the desired effect in stopping Huan from carrying out his proposal.

In these two instances we see the Buddhist sangha in the south courageously asserting its independent status. Its action enabled it to enjoy what amounted to extraterritorial rights within the empire, for in the monasteries the monks were governed by their own monastic laws, were exempted from taxation, and paid no reverence to the secular rulers. Undoubtedly the support which the Buddhist sangha received from the prominent official and aristocratic families of the times contributed to this favorable status.

## BUDDHISM IN NORTH CHINA DURING THE EASTERN CHIN DYNASTY

While south China under the Eastern Chin enjoyed some measure of peace during the fourth century, north China was in the throes of constant fighting among the various non-Chinese tribes vying for supremacy. Ethnically these tribes were mainly of Turkic or Tibetan origin who had migrated into north China. In a document dated 299 it was recorded that such non-Chinese groups living in the Ch'ang-an area numbered over half a million—more than one half the population of the region. It was the Hsiung-nu, a Turkic tribe, who first exerted pressure on the Chinese rulers in the north by capturing Lo-yang in 311 and Ch'ang-an in 316. From this period on, north China was under the sway of non-Chinese rulers. This fact had a profound effect on the progress of Buddhism and the type of Buddhism developed in that area.

Among the non-Chinese rulers in the north during the fourth and early fifth centuries the following deserve mention because of their connections with Buddhism: Later Chao, 328-352, under the Shih family of Hsiung-nu origin; the Former Ch'in, 351-394, under the Fu family of Tibetan origin; the Later Ch'in, 384-417, under the Yao family, also of Tibetan origin; and the Pei Liang, 412-439, under the Chü-ch'ü family of Hsiung-nu origin.

Amidst the constant struggles between these non-Chinese peoples life and property were at a premium. In order to spread their religion Buddhist monks had to move among the populace, but when disorders and strife were rampant, this was a dangerous undertaking. Leaders of the Buddhist church decided that in order to propagate their faith they must attach themselves closely to the ruling prince and depend on whatever support and protection they could gain from him. Tao-an (312-385) gave vocal expression to this idea when he said, "We are now meeting with evil times, and if we do not rely on the ruling prince, the affairs of the religion will be hard to establish." In north China, therefore, the religion became a vehicle of the state to serve the purposes of the state.

To gain the support of the non-Chinese rulers in the north the Buddhist monks offered their services as political, diplomatic, and military advisers. In a period when struggles for political or military paramountcy were the order of the day, such skills as the ability to prophesy the outcome of battles, the success of projected expeditions, the rise and fall of empires, the loyalty of subordinates and allies were especially valuable. A number of monks possessing such skills were available in north China, and by offering their technical services to the rulers, they were able to persuade them to become staunch supporters of Buddhism.

In a society plagued by constant warfare the livelihood of the people was bound to suffer from the attendant insecurity. The rich and the powerful could be reduced to poverty in a twinkling;

the poor could rise to eminence and munificence in one stroke. With life so uncertain, people were inclined to place more reliance on fate and luck, and to grant a hearing to those who claimed to be able to foretell the future or to perform feats of magic. In the Buddhist scriptures there is a meaningful statement, "Ordinary people are quickly converted by the manifestation of magic." It would be straining credulity too much to accept all of these tales concerning the magical prowess of monks; these were undoubtedly embellishments added by pious biographers later on, not with the deliberate intent to deceive, but rather to glorify the mysterious powers of the Buddha, who was able to endow his followers with such extraordinary faculties. Discounting these embellishments, one is still inclined to believe that Buddhist monks like Fo-t'u-teng and Dharmakshema were able to perform magical feats which assisted them in the task of winning converts.

## FO-T'U-TENG

Fo-t'u-teng was a monk of Central Asiatic origin who arrived in north China ca.310 for the purpose of establishing a religious center in Lo-yang. The time of his arrival coincided with the period of warfare raging in the north, which prevented him from carrying out his original project. By his display of magic, such as using spirits as his messengers, producing a lotus out of a bowl of water, and drawing water from dried-up wells with toothpicks, he gained the confidence of Shih Lo of the Later Chao Dynasty, and served him for more than two decades as imperial adviser. In this capacity his occult powers enabled him to make notable contributions in diverse fields. His ability to produce rain was a boon to the agricultural people of the north, and his power of prognostication was extremely useful in military strategy and tactics. It was he who initiated the policy of monks' participating in the affairs of state, for he felt that such connections would be beneficial to the religion.

Shih Hu, another ruler of the Later Chao Dynasty, once asked Teng what the Buddhist dharma consisted of, and Teng replied that it consisted of a precept against killing. Hu declared that since he was the ruler, he must resort to killing and execution to pacify the realm. Since he had broken the precept against killing, could he attain merits by following the way of the Buddha? Teng told him that those who were guilty should be punished and, if necessary, executed. But if the ruler should become tyrannical and kill those who were innocent, then he would reap inevitable calamities and misfortunes even though he followed the dharma. By thus stressing the cardinal doctrine against killing Teng exercised some civilizing influence on the conduct of the barbarian ruler. It was also Teng who insisted that the ruler should rule with compassion and love.

The growing popularity of Buddhism prompted a minister, Wang Tu, serving under Shih Hu, to present a memorial in 335 in which he argued that since Buddha was a foreign deity, he was not a proper object of worship for the ruler and the people. He called upon the ruler to forbid the people of Chao to worship the Buddha, to punish those who should transgress this prohibition, and to return to the laity those who had become monks. Shih Hu retorted that since the ruler and the people of Later Chao were foreign in origin, the Buddha who was a foreign deity should be the very one that they should worship. He then granted permission to all those who took pleasure in worshiping the Buddha to become converted to Buddhism.

## THE FORMER CH'IN AND LATER CH'IN KINGDOMS

The Later Chao kingdom was soon superseded by another, the former Ch'in (351-394), founded by a Tibetan clan named Fu. The most powerful ruler of this kingdom was Fu Chien, who extended his dominion over all of north China. Being overly ambitious, he tried to conquer the Eastern Chin also, but was defeated in the famous battle of Fei-shui in 383. Due to the encouragement given Buddhism by Fu Chien, monks from Kashmir, such as Sanghabhuti, Dharmanandi, and Sanghadeva, began to arrive in Ch'ang-an, both to translate the Sarvāstivādin canon into Chinese[13] and to gather and train a corps of Chinese monks as

---

[13] The Sarvāstivāda School is considered to be Hīnayāna, as it is an offshoot of the Theravāda School. It has a complete canon of its own written in Sanskrit. Like the Pali canon, it consists of three parts, the *Vinaya* or Rules of Discipline, *Sutras* or the Discourses of the Buddha, and *Abhidharma*, the Higher Discourses. The main center of the school was in Kashmir, and

translators. The most important Chinese monk at this time was Chu Fo-nien, who performed meritorious service in the translation work. Later on, this corps of trained Chinese monks was to be of great assistance in the large-scale translation bureau organized in Ch'ang-an.

After the defeat at Fei-shui the fortunes of the Fu family declined rapidly, and in 385 it was overthrown by Yao Ch'ang, who established the Later Ch'in kingdom. The capital remained at Ch'ang-an, and the Yao family continued the Buddhist activities started by Fu Chien. Under Yao Hsing, who ruled from 393 to 415, Buddhism was to enjoy a period of imperial patronage and favor seldom equalled in Chinese history. Buddhist records speak of Yao Hsing's sustaining three thousand monks through his donations, so intense was his zeal for the dharma. Monks entered the imperial palaces at will. Of the foreign monks in the capital at this time the most famous was Kumārajīva (344-413, var. 409).

## KUMĀRAJĪVA

Kumārajīva was born in Kucha of a Brahman father and a Kuchean princess. After the birth his mother wanted to become a nun, but her husband refused to permit this until another son had been born. At the age of seven, Kumārajīva followed his mother into the Buddhist order, and together the two traveled to Kashmir to study the sacred texts there for three years under one of the most famous masters of the land, Bandhudatta. It was said that while in Kashmir, Kumārajīva once refuted the arguments of some heretical teachers who became careless in a debate against him when they saw his youthfulness. After their sojourn in Kashmir, mother and son went to Kashgar, where they stayed for one year.

Up to this time Kumārajīva had been concentrating on the Hīnayāna sutras, especially the canon of the Sarvāstivādin School, but in Kashgar a change began to take place. Besides studying the sutras, he applied himself to the Vedas and books on astronomy, mathematics, and the occult sciences. As a result he became conversant with the whole field of Indian literature. More im-

it was from that area that the school was introduced into China. This helps to explain the fact that the translators of the Sarvāstivādin canon in China were mainly Kashmirians.

portant than this was his introduction to Mahāyāna literature. After he had been initiated into this new field of ideas by Sutyasoma, a royal prince from Yarkand, he confessed that formerly, when he studied the Hīnayāna texts, he was like one who did not recognize gold and considered stone to be a wonderful object.

After this one year in Kashgar, Kumārajīva returned to Kucha and received the full ordination in the king's palace when he became twenty. Now began a period of about twenty years in Kucha, during which time he concentrated on the Mahāyāna sutras. Having been converted to the Great Vehicle, he now hoped to win over his former teacher Bandhudatta, whom he invited to come to Kucha from Kashmir. Kumārajīva explained to Bandhudatta the profundities of the Mahāyāna doctrines, emphasizing especially the concept of *śūnyatā*, that all elements are void and have no self-existence. Bandhudatta, upon hearing this, replied that this doctrine of everything's being void was just empty talk and was to be ignored. Then to illustrate his point, he told a story. A madman asked a weaver to weave as fine a thread as possible. The weaver did so, but the madman complained it was still too coarse. The weaver tried again, and still could not please the madman. Now the weaver became angry, and when the madman came a third time, he pointed to the air and said, "Here is your thread." The madman protested he could not see the thread, whereupon the weaver said it was so fine no human eye could see it. The madman was now satisfied, paid the weaver, and presented the invisible thread to the king. In reality, said Bandhudatta, there was no such thread, just as there was no substance to the Mahāyāna doctrine of *śūnyatā*. However, Kumārajīva eventually succeeded in converting Bandhudatta.

In 379 the fame of Kumārajīva reached China through the report of a Chinese monk, Seng-ch'un, who had traveled to Kucha. Immediately efforts were made by Fu Chien, ruler of the Former Ch'in Dynasty, to get Kumārajīva to the capital in Ch'ang-an. These efforts were to be frustrated for almost two decades, mainly because of the activities of one Lü Kuang, the general sent by Fu Chien to subdue the Kucha kingdom. Being a non-Buddhist, Lü Kuang treated Kumārajīva with all kinds of indignities, and kept him in Liang-chou in northwestern China for seventeen years, in spite of repeated pleas from the Yao family in Ch'ang-an to send him east. Finally in exasperation Yao Hsing dispatched armies to Liang-chou to defeat Lü and to bring Kumārajīva to Ch'ang-an in 401.

Ch'ang-an, under the patronage of the ruling Yao family, was a flourishing center of Buddhist activities, with the famous monks of the realm congregated there. The Hsiao-yao Garden was placed at the disposal of Kumārajīva and his fellow monks, and here, with a thousand monks sitting in daily sessions, Kumārajīva carried on his translation activities. Sometimes the ruler, Yao Hsing, personally participated in these proceedings by holding the old translations which were used by Kumārajīva as the basis for comparison. During his long sojourn in Liang-chou, Kumārajīva had undoubtedly learned Chinese very well, so that as soon as he arrived in Ch'ang-an he was able to plunge into his work. He was honored with the title *Kuo-shih* (National Preceptor) and from 402 to his death in 413 he and his colleagues poured forth a steady stream of translations, which included some of the most important items in the Chinese canon.[14]

Contemporary Chinese records speak of Kumārajīva as honest, loyal, humane, tolerant, skillful in adapting himself to circumstances, hard-working, and self-sacrificing. Yao Hsing once came up with what he thought was a brilliant eugenic experiment. He felt that Kumārajīva's extraordinary brilliance and understanding should be transmitted to offspring, so he assigned ten girls to live with Kumārajīva and installed them in separate quarters. Kumārajīva complied with the ruler's wishes, but he realized his own shortcomings, for it is recorded that when he preached he warned his audience to take only the lotus that grew out of the mud and to leave the mud alone. Later records speak of sons and grandsons of Kumārajīva, but none of them lived up to the high hopes held by Yao Hsing.

[14] The *Amitābhasutra*, basic text of the Pure Land School in China, was translated in 402. The next year Kumārajīva started on the *Perfection of Wisdom in 25,000 Lines* and completed it in 404. In this year the *Treatise in One Hundred Verses* was also completed; this work, together with the *Treatise on the Middle* and the *Treatise on the Twelve Gates* finished in 409, constituted the basic texts of the San-lun School in China. In 405 he completed a massive work in 100 *chüan*, *Treatise on the Great Perfection of Wisdom*; in the following year he finished two important Mahāyāna sutras, the *Lotus of the Good Law* and the *Sutra Spoken by Vimalakīrti*. In 410 appeared the translation of the *Sutras on the Ten Stages*, and in 412 the *Treatise on the Completion of Truth*.

# THE MĀDHYAMIKA SCHOOL
# AND SENG-CHAO

Through his translations Kumārajīva was responsible for the establishment of an important Mahāyāna School in China, the San-lun or School of the Three Treatises.

The three treatises, all translated by Kumārajīva, which form the basis of this school are the *Chung-lun* (*Treatise on the Middle*), the *Po-lun* (*Treatise in One Hundred Verses*), and the *Shiherh-men lun* (*Treatise on the Twelve Gates*). The founder of this school in India was Nāgārjuna (second century A.D.), who composed the *Mādhyamika-kārikā* (*Stanzas on the Middle Path*) and with his disciple Āryadeva consolidated the position of the school. In the fifth century the second phase of the school developed with its splitting into two rival camps, one led by Bhavaviveka and one by Buddhapalita. The latter took the position that the sole purpose of the school was to reduce to absurdity the arguments of its opponents, while the former contended that the school should hold onto a philosophical position. In the third phase Candrakīrti (seventh century) was the dominant figure, and it was he who finally gave the school its orthodox form by supporting the position of Buddhapalita.

The term "Mādhyamika" means the doctrine of the Middle Path, that is, the middle between the two extremes of existence and nonexistence, affirmation and negation, pleasure and pain. Nāgārjuna related this Middle Path to the doctrine of dependent origination, which he paraphrased by means of the eightfold negation: "Nothing comes into being, nor does anything disappear. Nothing is eternal, nor has anything an end. Nothing is identical, or differentiated, nothing moves hither, nor moves anything thither." By means of this eightfold negation he sought to explain the truth of *śūnyatā*, or emptiness, or the unreality of all the elements of existence.

The Hīnayāna doctrine of dependent origination, that all things depend on causes and conditions for their origination, provides the starting point for the Mādhyamika viewpoint that "what is produced by causes is not produced in itself, and does not exist in itself." Because all things are produced by causes and conditions, they do not have any independent reality; they do not possess any self-nature. When these causes and conditions disappear, these things also disappear. Hence they are said to be *śūnya* or empty.

The word *śūnya* is also interpreted as relative. A thing is *śūnya* in that it can be identified only by mentioning its relation to something else; it becomes meaningless without these relations. The Mādhyamika School admits that relations and dependence constitute the phenomenal world, but it teaches that one is unable to explain these relations satisfactorily and intelligibly. In the *Mādhyamika-kārikā*, Nāgārjuna employs a merciless logic to demonstrate that all such relationships are false and erroneous; he insists that any contradiction is an infallible proof of error, and proceeds to find contradictions in every concept. With such logic Nāgārjuna demonstrates that the whole phenomenal world is unreal because it is based on relations the nature of which we do not understand and which cannot be explained.

Thorough comprehension of the empty, unreal, or relative nature of all phenomena leads to *prajñā* (intuitive wisdom or nondual knowledge). When we achieve *prajñā*, we reach the state of absolute truth which is beyond thought and conception, unconditioned, indeterminate. This absolute truth cannot be preached in words, but, in order to indicate it, it is called *śūnyatā*. "*Śūnyatā* is the synonym of that which has no cause, that which is beyond thought or conception, that which is not produced, that which is not born, that which is without measure."[15] This absolute truth contains nothing concrete or individual that can make it an object of particularization.

Nāgārjuna is careful to point out, however, that this absolute truth can be realized only by going through a relative or worldly level of truth. Here we have the double level of truth of the Mādhyamika. The relative level consists of man's reasoning and its products. It causes man to see the universe and its manifold phenomena, and to consider them as real. He cannot dispose of this relative truth by his arguments, just as a person in a dream cannot deny his dream by any argument. Only when he wakens can he prove the falsity of the objects in the dream. In this relative level one sees the distinctions between subject and object, truth and error, *saṁsāra* and nirvāna. This relative level is necessary,

[15] H. Zimmer, *Philosophies of India*, New York, 1951, 522.

according to Nāgārjuna, because the absolute level can be under-stood and realized negatively only by the removal of relative truths. The removal of the relative truths must therefore precede the realization of the absolute truth. The truths attained through reasoning and the intellect are not to be discarded even though they are not final. Consequently, acceptance of the doctrine of *śūnyatā*, or the unreality of all phenomena, does not mean that we have to devaluate all human experience. Before attaining the final absolute truth, beings still have to move in the world of phenomenal appearances, where the laws of karma and empirical understanding are applicable.

Inevitably the question arises as to how finite beings can gain access to the absolute truth that transcends all phenomena. The Mādhyamika teaches that this process is accomplished through an intermediary, the Buddha, who by his enlightenment gained a direct intuition of the truth. Because of this, the Buddha is the embodiment of the absolute, and though he lives in the phenom-enal world, he is free from all phenomena. "A Buddha, therefore, is able to teach and lead others to the truth. Thus in him imper-sonal truth becomes personalized."[16]

Among the disciples of Kumārajīva, Seng-chao was said to be the outstanding master of the Mādhyamika system. The latest study by the Japanese scholar Tsukamoto Zenryū puts his date at 374-414. His biography states that he came from a poor family and had to earn his living as a copyist. This task enabled him to gain a thorough acquaintance with the classics and history. Being mystical in nature, he was at first attracted to the Lao-Chuang philosophy, but after reading the *Vimalakīrti* he found his pole-star, and became converted to Buddhism. By the time he was twenty he had already achieved an enviable reputation in Ch'ang-an, where he mingled with the leading literary men of the age. When he heard that Kumārajīva was at Ku-tsang in northwest China, he hastened there to become his disciple, and then followed the master to Ch'ang-an. Together with Kumārajīva, he stayed in the Park of Perfect Happiness, where he rendered valuable as-sistance in explaining and collating the sutras. Not long after Kumārajīva died, he too passed away in the year 414.

[16] C. H. Hamilton, "Encounter with Reality in Buddhist Mādhyamika Philosophy," *Journal of Bible and Religion*, January 1958, 17.

The fame of Seng-chao as a writer and thinker rests on three treatises: (1) *The Immutability of Things*; (2) *The Emptiness of the Unreal*; (3) *Prajñā is not Knowledge*. The philosophical controversy of the age was centered mostly on what the Chinese called *t'i* (unity, noumenon, substance, or foundation) and *yung* (diversity, phenomenon, function, or appearance). The gist of Seng-chao's writings is that *t'i* and *yung* are not opposed but are the same. He thus sought to synthesize the extremes; this was his middle path. His idea is that it is not from an unchanging base or foundation that the multitude of appearances or phenomena arise; for him foundation and appearances are inseparable. Written in beautiful prose, these essays constitute an effective synthesis of Indian and Chinese thought.

In the first essay on *The Immutability of Things* Seng-chao wrote that there are two assumptions about events or things. One is that they are quiescent, so that things of the past are identical with those of the present. The other is that they move, so that things of the past, though not identical with those of the present, have evolved to become those of the present. Thus one gets the dualism of quiescence and movement. Seng-chao declared that this is wrong, that in the fundamental sense things are immutable because there is neither quiescence nor movement.

In the second essay, *The Emptiness of the Unreal*, Seng-chao sought to elucidate his concept of *śūnyatā* or emptiness. All things come into being through a combination of causes and perish when the causes disappear. They resemble a man created by magic and in this respect are nonexistent. Yet a magic man, though not real, does exist as a magic man; hence he is not unreal. By extending this principle to all things Seng-chao arrived at his middle path— that things both exist and do not exist.

In the third essay Seng-chao discussed the nature of *prajñā*. *Prajñā* is defined as sage wisdom, which is not the same as ordinary knowledge. Ordinary knowledge has an object of knowledge, whereas sage wisdom has as its object the absolute truth, which cannot be an object of knowledge, since it is empty and without phenomenal qualities. This absolute truth, however, is not isolated from events and things. The sage endowed with *prajñā* thus has a double nature. He abides in the realm of emptiness and nonactivity, but he also moves in the realm of activity. Here again is Seng-chao's idea of the middle path.

## BUDDHISM IN LIANG-CHOU AND DHARMAKSHEMA

While Kumārajīva and his followers were carrying on their prodigious translation activities in Ch'ang-an, another non-Chinese ruler in northwest China was also being attracted to the religion. This was Chü-ch'ü Meng-hsün, who established the Pei Liang kingdom in Liang-chou at the beginning of the fifth century, and took control of the region through which Buddhism entered China via the overland route. Meng-hsün became an active Buddhist who devoted much time and energy to the propagation of the religion. Among the pious deeds attributed to him was the construction of a sixteen-foot Buddha in honor of his mother. His successor, as well as his cousins, was also a devout follower of Buddhism.

The most famous Buddhist monk in Liang-chou at this time was Dharmakshema, who served as royal adviser to Meng-hsün. Dharmakshema was said to be endowed with remarkable occult powers, such as the ability to produce rain or to prophesy the outcome of political events or military campaigns, powers which caused him to be highly valued by Meng-hsün. His greatest contribution was the translation of the Sanskrit version of the *Mahāparinirvānasūtra*, a text on which the Nirvāna School in China based its doctrines. The fame of Dharmakshema as a royal adviser and Buddhist monk was so great that the T'o-pa Wei rulers made repeated attempts to lure him away from Liang-chou. Meng-hsün steadfastly refused to part with him, however, for he feared that the departure of the monk to an unfriendly state would give that state too great an advantage. When Dharmakshema did leave Liang-chou to go to Central Asia to search for more versions of the *Mahāparinirvānasūtra*, Meng-hsün thought that he was going to take the opportunity to escape to another state and so sent agents to assassinate the illustrious cleric.

## TUN-HUANG

In another part of Meng-hsün's kingdom was Tun-huang, a strategic point in northwest China where the northern and southern routes across Central Asia converged. Monks and commercial travelers after the long arduous journey welcomed the respite at this oasis on the borders of Chinese territory. For accommodations they dug cave temples in the hillsides, the earliest dated one, built by a monk named Lo-tsun, going back to 366. In the Cave of the Thousand Buddhas, the most famous of such caves, there is a wall painting executed in 344.

At the end of the third century there was already a flourishing colony of monks in Tun-huang, attested by the presence of Dharmaraksha, one of the most important monks and translators during the formative period of Chinese Buddhism. Dharmaraksha was of Yüeh-chih ancestry but was born in China. Since he was proficient in Chinese and Central Asiatic as well as Indian languages, he was able to translate a prodigious number of sutras. The catalogue of Seng-yu in the early sixth century attributed one hundred and fifty-four items to him, the most important being the *Lotus Sutra* and the *Lalitavistara* (*Detailed Narration of the Sport of the Buddha*). Through his translations and his religious activities he played an instrumental role in the spread of Buddhism in north China. During the fourth century numerous monks fled to Tun-huang to escape from the political and military disturbances in the rest of north China, and their literary and religious activities there enhanced further the reputation of Tun-huang as a Buddhist center.

The most famous treasures of Tun-huang are the murals painted on the walls of the caves. The dry climate of the region has preserved these murals in remarkably good condition. Covering as they do a thousand years of Chinese history, from the fourth century down to the end of the Sung Dynasty, these murals provide an invaluable record of the history of Chinese art, especially so since so few if any of T'ang paintings are still preserved today.

## FA-HSIEN

It was while Yao Hsing was ruling in north China that the first important Chinese pilgrim, Fa-hsien, left China for India in 399 in search of the holy law. The success of his pilgrimage inaugurated a movement in which a considerable number of Chinese monks participated after him. A variety of motives were at work impelling these intrepid and pious monks to take up their walking sticks and go to the holy land of Buddhism. For some it was to search for the sacred texts. For others it was to seek for some famous Indian masters who could teach them more about the religion they loved so much. For some, also, it was to visit the holy sites of Buddhism: Lumbini Grove, the birthplace of the Buddha; Bodhgaya, the scene of enlightenment; Benares, where the wheel of the law was first turned; and Kusinara, where the Buddha passed away. Such visits were often made as the fulfillment of vows. For still others it was to search for Indian teachers and invite them to come to China to preach the law. Some went singly; other traveled in groups. Many started, but few reached their destinations and accomplished their objectives; even fewer returned to China.

Prior to Fa-hsien's departure there had been some earlier Chinese pilgrims who had attempted the journey. However, these either stopped in Central Asia and never ventured as far as India, or if they did arrive in India, they never returned to China. The importance of Fa-hsien in the history of Sino-Indian relations lies in the fact that he was the first Chinese monk actually to arrive in India, study there for a lengthy period, and then return to China with the sacred scriptures. He also made significant contributions to the knowledge of Indian history and geography. The Indians as a people do not appear to possess as keen a sense of history as do their neighbors the Chinese. For them, accurate historical records were of little import; what mattered was the philosophical and religious literature preserving the wisdom of their sages. For scholars trying to reconstruct the history of India a coin dug out from the earth, or a stray remark by some Greek mariner or Chinese traveler, was more important than the mass of metaphysical speculations so prized by the Indians. Fortunately for later historians and archaeologists, Chinese travelers to India and Central Asia have left behind fairly detailed records of their journeys. Fa-hsien was the earliest of such Chinese pilgrims to do so.

Up to the time that Fa-hsien left China in 399 on his historic journey, there was yet no translation of the entire *Vinaya* or the *Rules of Discipline* in Chinese. Being a very pious monk, Fa-hsien felt deeply the need for such a translation, and his main purpose in going to India was to obtain an original version of the *Vinaya* and bring it back to China to be translated. Had he delayed his departure for two years, he would have heard of the arrival of Kumārajīva in Ch'ang-an in 401—Kumārajīva who was to be instrumental in translating the *Vinaya* of the Sarvāstivādin School. Would Fa-hsien still have gone to India had he known that the entire *Vinaya* had been translated? An unanswerable question, indeed. But the Buddhist community in China would have been the poorer if he had not gone.

On this trip Fa-hsien first proceeded as if he were going by the northern route to Central Asia, but instead he crossed the desert, which he described as being filled with evil spirits and howling winds, and with tracks marked only by the bones of the dead, to arrive at Khotan. From Khotan he followed the southern route across the snowy mountains into northwestern India. Among the places he visited in that part of India were Udyāna, Gandhāra, Peshawar, and Taxila. After this he proceeded to the holy land of Buddhism in eastern India and visited all the sacred spots. At Pātaliputra he found what he came for and worked hard in studying the Indian language and in copying the *Vinaya* of the Mahāsanghika School. He was also able to obtain the text of the Sarvāstivāda *Vinaya* and the *Mahāparinirvānasūtra*. Now that he had attained his objectives, he decided to return to China; so he went to Tamralipti to make the trip by sea. He first went to Ceylon, however, where he spent two fruitful years, and there he secured the texts of the Mahiçasaka *Vinaya* and portions of the Sarvāstivāda canon. From Ceylon he set sail for his homeland, but a storm first drove his ship to an island that is probably Java, where he transferred to another trading vessel destined for Canton. Again a storm blew the ship off course, and, instead of arriving at the south China port, it finally stopped at a port on the Shantung peninsula sometime in 414. In all he was on the sea for more than two hundred days. After his return to China he devoted the rest of his life to the task of translating the sutras which he had brought back.[17]

Though we are now separated by over fifteen hundred years

[17] To his credit are the translations of the *Mahāparinirvānasūtra*, the *Vinaya* of the Mahāsanghika School, and his book entitled *Record of Buddhistic Kingdoms*.

from this pioneering pilgrim, we can still share with him his fears, hardships, and dangers through the writings which he left behind. Deep and profound indeed must have been his faith as he ventured forth to face the terrors of sand and snow and the perils of the sea. This is how he described his journey across the desert:

"In the desert were numerous evil spirits and scorching winds, causing death to anyone who would meet them. Above there were no birds, while on the ground there were no animals. One looked as far as one could in all directions for a path to cross, but there was none to choose. Only the dried bones of the dead served as indications."[18] On crossing the Pamirs he wrote: "The path was difficult and rocky and ran along a cliff extremely steep. The mountain itself was just one sheer wall of rock 8,000 feet high, and as one approached it, one became dizzy. If one wished to advance, there was no place for him to place his feet. Below was the Indus River. In former times people had chiselled a path out of the rocks and distributed on the face of the cliff over 700 ladders for the descent."[19]

In spite of these dangers and hardships in succeeding centuries many other Chinese pilgrims were to follow in the wake of Fa-hsien across the trackless wastes of Central Asia to India, there to drink deeply of the wisdom of the Indians, returning to China to transmit it to their fellow Chinese.

In view of what has been said in this chapter, it is safe to conclude that this period between the third and early fifth centuries was one of preparation in the history of Buddhism. In the beginning only a limited number of sutras were available, and there was no outstanding Chinese monk to speak of. By the end of the Eastern Chin in 420, some of the most eminent monks had performed their work, and had made available to the Chinese such important Mahāyāna texts as the *Lotus Sutra, Vimalakīrti,* and the *Nirvāna Sutra*. The *Vinayas* of the important schools had also been translated and available for the regulation of the monastic community. More important was the fact that this period witnessed the religion developing along two divergent lines in the north and south. In the south the emphasis of the Buddhist monk was upon philosophical discussions with the Chinese literati, but

---

[18] *Fa-hsien-chuan; Taishō*, 51,857c.
[19] *Taishō*, 51,858a.

in the north the emphasis was upon rendering service in the form of military and diplomatic counsel to the non-Chinese rulers of the area. This feature of the sangha working in the interests of the state paved the way for the closer supervision of the monastic community that was to develop at a later date. The missionary work which the educated monks in the south carried on among the cultured Chinese gentlemen enabled them to start working for a wider base of support in the next era of Chinese history, not only among the leaders of Chinese society but among the great masses of people.

# CHAPTER IV

# EMINENT MONKS UNDER THE EASTERN CHIN DYNASTY

I N addition to Chien-k'ang and K'uai-chi, during the Eastern Chin Hsiang-yang in Hupei and Lu-shan in Kiangsi were important localities in south China that figured prominently in the development of Buddhism. Attached to these centers were two of the most illustrious names in Chinese Buddhism, Tao-an in Hsiang-yang and Hui-yüan in Lu-shan. Associated with Hui-yüan for a time in Lu-shan was Tao-sheng, one of the most original Chinese Buddhist thinkers. So important are the roles of these clerics that this chapter is devoted primarily to their lives and activities.

## TAO-AN

Hui-chiao, compiler of the *Kao-seng-chuan* (*Biographies of Eminent Monks*) wrote in his preface: "If a man of solid achievement keeps his brilliance under cover, then he is eminent but not famous. If a man of slight virtue happens to be in accord with his times, then he is famous but not eminent."[1] This distinction drawn by Hui-chiao between an eminent monk and a famous one is important. A famous monk might be able to glorify his religion during his lifetime, but an eminent monk was one who was able to stand above the host of clerics, and by his learning and example open new vistas and herald a new age for Buddhism. Such monks were rare in Buddhist history, but during the Chin period there arose just such a personality, Tao-an (312-385). In an age characterized by incessant strife and insecurity Tao-an carried on his evangelical activities north of the Yangtze River, and, more than anyone else of his age, he exemplified the spirit of the Tathāgata, to teach and propagate the religion in spite of hardships. Tao-an thus differed from his fellow monks in the south who were adept in the art of pure conversation or who engaged in soaring flights of the imagination, but were somewhat lacking in the depth of their devotional religious zeal.

[1] *Taishō*, 50,419a.

EARLY YEARS IN NORTH CHINA

Tao-an, originally surnamed Wei, was born in north China in what is now the province of Hopei. His parents were good Confucianists, but he left home to become a novice at the early age of twelve. Although he was a keen and brilliant student, his ugly features did not endear him to his master, who forced him to work in the fields for three years instead of studying. Yet the boy showed no anger. After three years he asked his master for a sutra. The teacher gave him a text, the *Pien-i-ching* (*Sutra on the Discussion of Will*), consisting of about five thousand characters, which he took with him to the fields to read during his rest period. In the evening he returned and asked his master for another text. The teacher said he had given him one in the morning and wondered why he should ask for another. Tao-an replied that he had already finished it, and recited the entire text just to prove it. The master, somewhat surprised, gave him a text consisting of over ten thousand characters, the *Ch'eng-chü-kuang-ming-ching* (*Sutra on Complete Illumination*), translated by Chih-yao of the Han Dynasty. An did the same thing the next day, and in the evening he recited the entire sutra. The master was now amazed by this young fellow and began to treat him with respect. He ordained Tao-an and urged him to travel and study under more famous teachers.

Tao-an followed this advice and went to Yeh (in present Honan) to study under Fo-t'u-teng. It was stated that the first meeting between the two lasted the entire day, and when some of the other monks present expressed surprise that the master was willing to devote so much time to this one ugly person, Teng replied that Tao-an was so advanced in knowledge that he was not to be compared to others. Now began a period of intensive study of the *Prajñā* texts and the sutras on *dhyāna* exercises. The results of this study are embodied in a series of commentaries on the *dhyāna* sutras translated by An Shih-kao.[2] These commentaries increased Tao-an's reputation as a teacher and also the number of his disciples. Officials and ruling princes began to vie

[2] These included such sutras as the *An-pan shou-i-ching, Yin-ch'ih-ju-ching* (*Sutra on the Aggregates*), *Tao-ti-ching* (*Sutra on the Way and Stages*), and *Jen-pen-yü-sheng ching* (*Sutra on Man's Origin, Desires, and Modes of Existences*).

with one another to invite him to lecture. The constant warfare in the north, however, caused him to change residence nine times. In spite of this unsettled mode of life he continued his studies and commentaries, in marked contrast to the conduct of monks in the south who withdrew from society to study by themselves.

When Tao-an was about forty years old, a new trend developed in his thinking. He became dissatisfied with the method of *ke-yi*; he felt that in spreading the religion one should not depend on non-Buddhist works; he wanted an independent Buddhist system not leaning on another for its terminology or concepts.

The peripatetic life in the north finally caused him, at the age of fifty-three, to leave in 365 for Hsiang-yang (in present Hupei). In this flight he scattered his disciples, said to number more than four hundred in all, and exhorted them to go forth to spread the religion. Some of these disciples, like Chu Fa-t'ai and Fa-ho, were instrumental in spreading the religion in the Yang-chou and Szechuan areas respectively. Tao-an arrived in Hsiang-yang the same year, and remained there for fifteen years, gathering around him another group of disciples. In 379 Fu Chien of the Former Ch'in Dynasty, having consolidated the north, dispatched Fu Pei to attack Hsiang-yang and to capture the city. Tao-an again scattered his disciples. Among those who crossed the Yangtze into south China was Hui-yüan, who established the famous Buddhist center of Lu-shan in Kiangsi.

### THE YEARS AT HSIANG-YANG IN SOUTH CHINA

During these fifteen years in Hsiang-yang, Tao-an was able to enjoy some measure of peace, so he spent the time putting the sutras in order, compiling his catalogue, writing commentaries, constructing stupas, and erecting statues. As a result of these activities his reputation spread even more, and rulers such as Fu Chien and Emperor Hsiao-wu of the Chin Dynasty sent him presents. One of the leading men of letters in Hsiang-yang, Hsi Tso-ch'ih, befriended him and described him as an unusual monk who had several hundred disciples, who fasted and lectured on the sutras without fatigue, who did not resort to magical tricks to deceive people, did not depend on authority but only on the gravity of mien to win the response of his disciples, and was not only versed in Buddhist subtleties but also in secular literature, *yin-yang*, and mathematics.

As for Tao-an's activities, his first task was to put the sutras in order. This consisted of correcting wrong translations and terminology, and of providing the proper meaning to passages through commentaries. The early translators often made mistakes, as some of them were not familiar with the meaning of the original. Since the foreign monk often did not know Chinese well, and the Chinese collaborator was ignorant of the foreign tongue, chances for misunderstanding and mistakes were present at every turn.

The difficulties of translation were increased, according to Tao-an, by the nature of the foreign language. Very often abbreviations occurred in the original text, so that when such abbreviated passages were translated, they were difficult to understand. Secondly, the foreign terminology was at times vague and ambiguous, and it was difficult to find the precise Chinese characters or phrases to convey the finer shades of meaning. In the third place, the involved, complicated passages in some sutras, with sentences and phrases piled one upon another, might appear to be repetitious, but in reality they contained well-developed ideas which were lost because translators left out some portions. Finally, according to Tao-an, the syntax in the foreign language was often the reverse of the Chinese, and the translator had first to straighten out the order of the words in the Chinese translation if the meaning of the sentence were to be made clear. Through his wide reading and study Tao-an was able to penetrate deeply into the profound subtleties of the troublesome passages, and to clarify their meanings through his commentaries, which were praised even by Kumārajīva.

CATALOGUE OF SUTRAS

Since Tao-an aimed at a wide knowledge of the sutras, he strove to collect as many of them as possible. Wherever he went in his travels, he had sutras copied for him; he also received them from a wide circle of friends. This search for sutras led him to compile a catalogue of all translations made from the Han Dynasty to 374, entitled *Tsung-li chung-ching mu-lu* (*Comprehensive Cata-*

*logue of Sutras*), abbreviated often to *An-lu* (*An's Catalogue*). This was really a pioneer effort, for there was no previous catalogue for him to follow. He literally examined every sutra himself. His main problem was to find out the names of the translators, for the ancient copyists often neglected to include this information in the sutra. He resorted to two methods to find out the names. One was to search for as many manuscripts as possible of the same sutra. Thus, while one manuscript might lack the name, another might show it. This wide selection of manuscripts might also furnish some data on the time, place, and circumstances of the translation.

If all the manuscripts lacked the necessary data, then Tao-an resorted to his second method. He studied carefully the entire sutra, noting especially the style, phraseology, use of words, and so forth, in the hope that these might furnish clues as to the identity of the translator. If, after such an exhaustive study, he still could not determine the name of the translator, then he listed such sutras in a section entitled *shih-i* (names of translators lost). His careful study of the sutras also led him to decide that some translations were forgeries, and these were placed in a category entitled *i-ching-lu* (spurious sutras). In some cases he found that the same sutra had undergone several translations. He then listed all the translations and names of translators, and if no names existed, he gave the opening sentence of that version, in the manner of present-day Christian hymnals. This approach permitted students to distinguish among the various versions.[3]

Tao-an's catalogue was valuable in that (1) it was a pioneer effort, breaking new ground for later compilers of the Buddhist catalogues; (2) whenever possible, it provided the titles, names of translators, and dates of translation. Such data proved to be extremely valuable for later generations of Buddhist scholars and writers.

During his sojourn in Hsiang-yang, Tao-an appears to have

[3] In all, the *An-lu* mentioned 611 titles, of which 244 were made by translators whose names have been preserved. An Shih-kao has 35 items listed after his name; Dharmaraksha has 154. Compare these figures with those given in the *Catalogue of the K'ai-yüan Era*, 95 for An Shih-kao and 175 for Dharmaraksha, and one would conclude that either Tao-an was not complete in his catalogue or the later compilers attributed more translations to these individuals than was warranted.

devoted a good deal of time and attention to the *Prajñā* sutras. The results of such study are indicated in the numerous commentaries and prefaces that he wrote on different versions of these sutras, and in the establishment of a special exegetical school attributed to him, called the School of Original Nonbeing. It was his practice to go over the entire text of the *Fang-kuang-ching* (Mokshala's translation of the *Prajñā-pāramitā in 25,000 Lines*) twice each year—a practice which he started in Hsiang-yang and later carried over into Ch'ang-an. This preoccupation with the *Prajñā* sutras undoubtedly led Tao-an to acquaint himself with the speculations carried on in Chien-k'ang and K'uai-chi by the Neo-Taoists and the *Prajñā* scholars there.

## RULES OF DISCIPLINE

While Tao-an was in Hsiang-yang, he realized the insufficiency of the *Vinaya* rules, or the rules of discipline that govern the conduct of monks. It was said that his followers there numbered up to three hundred, and with such a large community gathered in one place the absence of *Vinaya* rules to govern the conduct of the monks was a grave handicap. This deficiency had led Fa-hsien to undertake a trip to India in 399 to obtain a complete text of the *Vinaya*. Faced with this problem, Tao-an did two things: (1) He established his own rules. These rules were divided into three categories. The first concerned the offering of incense as an indication to the Buddha of faith, and the method of ascending the platform to lecture on the sutras. The second concerned the manner of worshiping the image of the Buddha and also of eating. Six times a day (morning, noon, evening, the first, second, and third watches of the night) the circumambulation, or circling, of the Buddha figure was to be performed, always with the figure at the right. Meals were to be eaten only at the noonday hour. The third category concerned the *uposatha* or fortnightly ceremony. (2) He also encouraged translations of the *Vinaya*. In Hsiang-yang he wrote: "It is said there are five hundred *Vinaya* rules, but I do not know why they are not complete here. The introduction of these rules is the most pressing business at hand. As long as the four congregations are not complete, there is something lacking on the work of conversion."

Tao-an translated a *Pi-nai-yeh-lü*, based on a portion of the Sarvāstivādin *Vinaya*, and it was he who first suggested that Kumārajīva be invited to China. By so doing he played a role in overcoming the absence of the *Vinaya* rules, for not long after arriving in China Kumārajīva and a few other collaborators translated the entire *Vinaya* of the Sarvāstivādin School, entitled the *Shih-sung-lü*. With this translation available it is likely that the rules established by Tao-an in Hsiang-yang were no longer followed by the Buddhist community. However, there was one rule formulated by Tao-an that has persisted through the ages. In the early history of the Buddhist community in China the disciples upon ordination followed the surnames of their masters. Tao-an felt that since Śākyamuni was the primary teacher of all monks, everyone who was ordained should take the surname Shih—a suggestion that was followed. Afterward Tao-an found that his idea was supported in the *Ekottarāgama*, where it was said that all rivers empty into the ocean to lose their names; so do all monks become Shih after they are converted.

## MAITREYA CULT

While Tao-an was in Hsiang-yang, he helped organize a cult to Maitreya. With eight of his disciples he appeared before an image of Maitreya and uttered the earnest wish to be reborn in the Tushita heaven, which was the abode of the future Buddha. The Buddhists believed that Maitreya was residing there in his abode, waiting for the opportune time to descend to earth to remove all doubts concerning the dharma among the people. Tao-an felt that his mission was the same. That Tao-an was actively associated with the cult was also indicated by the fact that Fu Chien sent him an image of Maitreya. At least two sutras on Maitreya already existed at the time of Tao-an, translated by Dharmaraksha, entitled *Mi-le ch'eng-fo ching* (*Sutra on Maitreya Becoming the Buddha*) and *Mi-le-p'u-sa pen-yüan ching* (*Sutra on the Vow of the Bodhisattva Maitreya*).

In the biography of Tao-an it was recorded that once he dreamt of seeing an old Indian monk, with white hair and long eyebrows, who told him that his commentaries were all good, that he (the old man) could not enter nirvāna but must wander about the earth protecting and propagating the religion. Finally he asked Tao-an to prepare some food for him. After Tao-an awoke, he realized that the old man was Pindola, the arhat who because of his unwise exhibition of his extraordinary faculties was sentenced by the Buddha to remain on earth so long as the dharma lasted in order to protect it. Tao-an prepared the food as asked, and presented it on the altar to Pindola. This practice gave rise to yet another aspect of Buddhism in China—the installation of Pindola as patron saint of the refectory.

## LAST YEARS IN CH'ANG-AN

This productive period of some fifteen years in Hsiang-yang came to an end in 379, when Fu Chien attacked and captured the city. Fu then asked Tao-an and his literary friend Hsi Tso-ch'ih to return with him to Ch'ang-an, and was reported to have said, "We captured Hsiang-yang with 100,000 soldiers, but we only obtained a man and a half." Tao-an therefore spent the last years of his life in Ch'ang-an under the patronage of Fu Chien, where he attracted a wide following among the nobles and aristocracy. He was honored as the imperial adviser, but on one important occasion his advice to Chien not to attack the Eastern Chin was not heeded, with the result that Fu's armies suffered a disastrous defeat at Fei-shui in 383. This battle has been considered as one of the decisive battles in world history, for had the armies of Fu Chien been successful against the Eastern Chin, that citadel of Chinese culture during this period of disunity would have been destroyed, and one can only guess what the later history of Chinese culture would have been.

While in Ch'ang-an, Tao-an was instrumental in getting the Sarvāstivādin literature translated into Chinese. It was at this time that monks from Kashmir began to enter China in large numbers and these monks brought the texts of the dominant Sarvāstivādin School of their homeland, which they then translated into Chinese.[4] Of the Chinese monks who assisted in these

[4] Among these Kashmirian monks were Sanghabhuti, who translated the *Abhidharmavibhāsha* (*Commentary on the Abhidharma*), and Sanghadeva, who translated the *Madhyamāgama* (*Middle Length Scriptures*), the *Ekottarāgama* (*Gradual Length Scriptures*), and the *Jñānaprasthāna* (*On the Source of Knowledge*). The Sarvāstivādin *Prātimoksha* for monks and nuns were also translated at this time.

translations, one of the most prominent was Chu Fo-nien. This monk was a native of Liang-chou, and since his family lived in an area where foreign monks congregated after making the overland journey, he acquired a knowledge of foreign languages from them, and put this knowledge to good use in his translations. It was mainly due to his efforts that Ch'ang-an was one of the important centers of translation at this time. To carry on the intensive translation activities in Ch'ang-an, Tao-an assembled many workers to assist the foreign monks, providing a pool of trained talent in the city that was to prove extremely valuable and useful to Kumārajīva when the latter began his large-scale translations.

The life of Tao-an can be divided into four stages:

*a*) The period of study and preparation in Hopei under Fo-t'u-teng. Some of his fellow students of this period were Fa-ho, Chu Fa-t'ai, and Fa-ya, all of whom were versed in Buddhist and non-Buddhist literature. Fa-ya, as has been said, originated the *ke-yi* method, which Tao-an resorted to also at this time.

*b*) Period of instruction in Hopei. During this period he concentrated on the *dhyāna* sutras translated by An Shih-kao, such as the *Yin ch'ih-ju-ching* (*Sutra on the Aggregates*), *Tao-ti-ching* (*Sutra on the Way and Stages*), and *Ta-shih-erh-men-ching* (*The Major Sutra on the Twelve Gates*). His interest in *Prajñā* philosophy was also beginning to emerge at this time, and it appears that he forsook the method of *ke-yi* then.

*c*) Period of concentration on *Prajñā* thought in Hsiang-yang. This emphasis is reflected in the fourteen works which he wrote on *Prajñā* literature.

*d*) Period of encouraging the translation of the Sarvāstivādin literature in Ch'ang-an.

Any summary must assign to Tao-an his proper place in the development of Buddhism in China. Professor T'ang in his book on the history of Buddhism has stated the case better than anyone else. Since the Han Dynasty, he wrote, there had been two main streams in the religion, the *dhyāna* and *Prajñā* aspects. Both of these streams were united in Tao-an. Again, during the Wei and Chin Dynasties there were three fundamental developments within the religion. First, there was the coalescing of interests between the Neo-Taoist and the Prajñā School. Tao-an was well versed in the literature of both these schools, so that once again in the person of Tao-an we have the convergence of both traditions. In the second place, while Tao-an was in Ch'ang-an during the twilight of his life, he was instrumental in getting the literature of the Sarvāstivādin School translated into Chinese. After him, Hui-yüan continued this emphasis on the Sarvāstivādin in Lushan. As a result of the attention of these two men, master and disciple, the literature of this school became the subject of widespread discussion during this period. In the third place, as we have seen, it was Tao-an who initiated steps to invite Kumārajīva to China. The latter monk, on his part, considered Tao-an the sage of the east. The talent collected and trained by Tao-an in Ch'ang-an proved extremely helpful to Kumārajīva when the latter began his translations, which were to open up entirely new vistas to the eyes of the Chinese. Tao-an was therefore the pivotal figure in all the main developments within Buddhism during his age. It was because of this that he was acclaimed as one of the most eminent of Chinese Buddhist monks.

## HUI-YÜAN

Of the disciples of Tao-an who crossed the great river to the south after the fall of Hsiang-yang, the most famous was Hui-yüan (344-416). Even more than his master, he was intimately connected with the metaphysical speculations carried on in Chien-k'ang and K'uai-chi on Lao-Chuang and *Prajñā* philosophy. He was also connected with two important movements in south China, the translation and propagation of *dhyāna* exercises by Buddhabhadra. Finally he is remembered for the purity of monastic discipline in his center at Lu-shan.

Hui-yüan was born in Shansi and was originally surnamed Chia. As a youth he devoted himself to an intensive study of the Confucian classics and Lao-Chuang philosophy. When he was about twenty-one, he heard of the great reputation of Tao-an as a teacher and went to listen to him. After he had heard the master explain the meaning of the *Prajñā* sutras, he realized that he had found the truth, and exclaimed that the teachings of Confucius, Lao-tzu, and others were nothing but external superficialities. Years later, in his old age, he referred again to this period of his life by writing that at first he felt that the Confucian classics contained the flower of Chinese thought. Later on, when he came into contact with Taoism, he realized that all religions were but empty talk. But finally, after having studied Buddhism, he acknowledged it to be the leader in showing the way to the profound mystery.

He joined the monastic order after meeting Tao-an, and from then on devoted all his time, day and night, to the study of the Buddhist scriptures. Before long he himself was qualified to teach the *Prajñā* sutras. It was said that at times his audience was unable to comprehend the meaning of these sutras, whereupon he resorted to passages and concepts in the Lao-Chuang writings to make the meaning clear. He followed Tao-an to Hsiang-yang and remained there until 378, when the armies of Fu Pei began attacking the city. Yüan now parted from his master, and the two never saw each other again. At this second scattering of his disciples Tao-an gave instructions to all but Hui-yüan, whereupon the latter knelt before his master and said: "I alone have not received any instructions. I fear that I am not as worthy as the others." To this, Tao-an replied, "Is there any need for anxiety toward such a one as you?"

THE COMMUNITY AT LU-SHAN

At first Yüan planned to go as far south as the Lo-fou Mountains in what is now Kwangtung, but on his way south his path took him to Lu-shan in Kiangsi, where he was so attracted by the natural scenery of the locality that he decided to remain right there. It happened that one of Yüan's fellow monks in Hsiang-yang, Hui-yung, had already established himself at Lu-shan and invited Yüan to stay with him. Yung then asked the authorities to set up quarters for Yüan and his followers. The authorities agreed, and a monastery was built on the eastern slopes of the mountain, called the Tung-lin-ssu (Monastery of the Eastern Grove). This monastery was to serve as Yüan's home for the rest of his life. It was finished in ca.386. The location was a perfect setting for a monastery, for the buildings were put up amidst caves, waterfalls, rock formations, mountain springs, and floating clouds. After his quarters were finished, it was said that Yüan did not leave the mountains for thirty years. His biography recorded that "his shadow never left the mountain, his footprints never entered the secular world. When he bade farewell to his guests, he went only as far as the Tiger Creek." His fame, however, was truly far-reaching, for monks, laymen, and famous literary figures converged on Lu-shan from all directions. When Huan Hsüan wanted to purge the monastic community of undesirable elements, he specifically exempted Lu-shan from the scope of the purge, saying that the community at Lu-shan was a model of religious discipline. It was also Yüan who was able to dissuade the ruler from requiring monks to render the proper obeisance to him. These acts were indications of the enormous prestige that Yüan enjoyed during this period.

Of the Kashmirian monks in China at this time none was more active than Sanghadeva, who was the first to translate the *Sarvāstivādin* literature into Chinese. Of this literature the *Jñānaprasthāna* (*On the Source of Knowledge, Fa-chih-lun*) was the most important. Sanghadeva first worked in Ch'ang-an, then moved to Lo-yang, and finally to Lu-shan, where he became active in propagating the Sarvāstivādin doctrines. The rise in the popularity of this school was due primarily to his efforts, with the effective assistance from Hui-yüan and his fellow monks in Lu-shan.

## CORRESPONDENCE WITH KUMĀRAJĪVA

During this period the Eastern Chin was established south of the Yangtze, while the Yao Ch'in Dynasty was paramount in the north. In 404 the Eastern Chin ruler dispatched a mission to Ch'ang-an, seeking to establish friendly relations with the Yao Ch'in kingdom. Yao Hsing, the ruler in the north, agreed to this amicable exchange between the two regions, and for a number of years monks traveled back and forth between the two areas. Many monks from the south journeyed to Ch'ang-an to study under Kumārajīva, among them Tao-sheng and Hui-kuan. Hui-yüan also heard of the reputation of Kumārajīva and initiated some correspondence with him. Kumārajīva in one letter called Hui-yüan the bodhisattva-protector of the law in the east, and added: "Treasures consist of the five perfections, blessings, moral precepts, extensive learning, readiness of wit, and profound wisdom. When these five perfections are present, the law flourishes, but when they are lacking, then doubts arise to impede progress. In you, these five perfections are complete." Later on, when some emissaries from the north reported that Kumārajīva was thinking about returning to the west, Hui-yüan wrote immediately, urging him to remain, and initiated a series of letters touching on points of the dharma. These letters, eighteen in all, together with Kumārajīva's answers, are preserved in the *Ta-ch'eng ta-i-chang* (*Chapter on the Grand Meaning of the Mahāyāna*). Ten of these eighteen letters raise questions about the *dharmakāya*, and this emphasis may be construed as an indication of Hui-yüan's preoccupation with this subject. In these letters he asks whether the *dharmakāya* is visible or audible, how it comes into being if all causation is ended, whether the thirty-two marks of the Buddha appear in the *dharmakāya*, whether or not it has a material base to manifest its supernatural faculties, and how the life duration of the *dharmakāya* is to be interpreted, in terms of being or nonbeing. From these questions one can see that Hui-yüan was not satisfied with the abstract ideas about this Body of Essence, and was groping around for some concrete image, endowed with sensory faculties, that he could grasp. In his replies Kumārajīva resorted to a great mass of quotations, chiefly from the *Ta-chih-tu-lun* (*Treatise on the Great Perfection of Wisdom*) of Nāgārjuna. In the other letters Hui-yüan asked about the differences between a bodhisattva and an arhat, about the future Buddhahood of the arhats (which he thought was impossible, since the arhat had already destroyed all karma), how the theory of the elements of existence can be harmonized with the doctrine of emptiness, how one can reach nonexistence by the division of existing things, and how it is possible to remember anything if one accepts the theory of momentariness.

## AMITĀBHA CULT

According to his biography Hui-yüan in 402 assembled a group of one hundred and twenty-three of his followers before a statue of Amitābha and made a collective vow to be reborn in the Western Paradise. Among those who participated in this ceremony were some of the cultured laymen who were followers and admirers of Hui-yüan: Liu Ch'eng-chih (354-410), Lei Tz'u-tsung

(386-448), Chou Hsü-chih (377-423), and Tsung Ping (375-443). According to traditions prevalent after the middle T'ang period this group of one hundred and twenty-three was said to have formed a White Lotus Society on this occasion. On the basis of such traditions Hui-yüan is regarded as the founder of the Pure Land School and its first patriarch. The names of some of the one hundred and twenty-three followers, especially the eighteen who were said to be worthies, are also given.[5] These traditions deserve to be examined more closely.

There are a number of points open to question here—first, with reference to the name of the society. In the original vow as composed by Liu I-min there is no mention of lotus; it is only after the middle T'ang period that the term "Lotus Society" appears. In the Sung Dynasty there were still various explanations concerning the origin of the term "Lotus Society." One version says that the name was used because of the abundance of lotus in the Tung-lin Temple area. A second version explains that the term was used because Amitābha divided the people that he welcomed into his paradise in accordance with the nine grades of lotus. A third explains that it was because those who joined the society were not contaminated by fame and gain, just as the lotus is not tainted by the mud from which it arises. A fourth says the name derives from a wooden lotus flower with twelve petals constructed by a monk. This wooden flower was said to be equipped with a mechanism which, when put in water, pealed off one petal at each hour.

The most glaring discrepancies occur in the list of members of the society. Among the list were included the foreign monks Buddhayaśas and Buddhabhadra. There is no record that Buddhayaśas, who arrived in Ch'ang-an in 408, ever went to the south. Buddhabhadra did not go south until 410 or 411, and so could not have been present at a ceremony which occurred in 402. Among the worthies listed as members we find one Hui-ch'ih, who had already left Hui-yüan in 399 to go to Szechuan. Equally erroneous was the case of Lu Hsiu-ching, who did visit Lu-shan, but after Hui-yüan's death. Lu died in 477, at the age of seventy-two, so that his date of birth would have been 405; in other words, he was not even born when the society was said to be organized.

[5] *Taishō*, 49,265.

Another equally erroneous case was that of Ch'üeh Kung-tse, who died during the period 265-274 and was probably already in the Western Paradise in 402. Some lists include the well-known literatus Hsieh Ling-yun, while others said that though Hsieh was present, he was refused admittance because his mind was too fickle and not yet ready for steady concentration.

In view of the above, all one can say is that Hui-yüan and a group of followers (not called the White Lotus Society) made a vow before an image of Amitābha and offered incense and flowers as part of the ceremony. This emphasis on the devotional aspect of Buddhism, with a visual object as the basis, was probably due to the presence of a large number of lay followers in the community at Lu-shan who needed some practical and simple approach to the religious life. As for the tradition that this group formed a White Lotus Society, we must conclude that it was of late origin and did not rest on any historical basis.

One would expect that such a group led by Hui-yüan would be active in spreading the Pure Land doctrine. However, the contrary was true. The group consisted mainly of recluses and hermits, interested in the Pure Land mainly as an escape from the mundane world. It was not a society with a strong missionary zeal to convert sentient beings. With the passing of Hui-yüan the group was heard of no more. Though the group itself exerted little influence during its existence, the idea of Hui-yüan and his society served as an inspiration and model for later groups. Hui-yüan's virtues, his learning, his strict code of discipline were examples to be emulated, and his group was a forerunner of many societies of recluses and hermits who retired to the seclusion of the mountains to lead their quiet lives. Even after many centuries, when the society founded by Hui-yüan no longer existed, the memory of that society still excited the imagination and admiration of monks. This memory caused not a few monks to make the vow for the Pure Land, and might be the reason why Yüan is sometimes regarded as the first patriarch of the Pure Land sect.

### DHYĀNA PRACTICES

Another of Hui-yüan's contributions was his encouragement of *dhyāna* practices in the south. Yüan's master, Tao-an, had been an active promoter of *dhyāna* exercises, and Yüan himself was also interested in this aspect of the Buddhist discipline, so much so that he dispatched two clerical emissaries to Central Asia to obtain sutras and instructions bearing on it. Through these emissaries and the translation activities of Buddhabhadra, the teachings of one of the most famous masters of *dhyāna*, Buddhasena, were introduced to the Chinese. Buddhabhadra, a clansman of the Buddha, met the Chinese monk Chih-yen in Kashmir while the latter was studying under Buddhasena, and was persuaded to go to China after that meeting. He first arrived in Ch'ang-an ca.408, when Kumārajīva was still the arbiter of all things Buddhist. Disagreement apparently arose between the two over some aspects of discipline. Kumārajīva was provided with royal quarters in Ch'ang-an, and also with the pleasures of the inner apartments —conduct that a strict disciplinarian like Buddhabhadra must have looked upon with disfavor. At any rate the followers of Kumārajīva fabricated charges against Buddhabhadra and compelled him to leave Ch'ang-an. It appears that doctrinal differences also (since Buddhabhadra was a Sarvāstivāda adherent) were responsible in part for this lack of friendship between the two Buddhist masters. Buddhabhadra first went to Lu-shan, where he was welcomed warmly by Hui-yüan, who long ago had heard of his reputation as a *dhyāna* master. Through the efforts of Buddhabhadra the *dhyāna* teachings of Buddhasena were proclaimed throughout the region south of the Yangtze.

In his youth Hui-yüan had delved into the Confucian classics and had acquired such a mastery of texts like the *Book of Poetry*, the *Book of Changes*, and the *Book of Rites* that even scholars as well known as Chou Hsü-chih and Lei Tz'u-tsung frequently visited Lu-shan in later years to consult with him on literary and philosophical subjects. However, the prevailing tendency of his age was Neo-Taoism and *Prajñā* philosophy, and he could not escape from these systems of thought. His biography informs us that when he was young he became proficient in Lao-Chuang philosophy, the terminology of which he sometimes used in his lectures as aids to his students in grasping the meaning of Buddhist ideas. In his writings, likewise, he had frequent recourse to Taoist terms. Though he aimed at establishing an independent tradition for Buddhism, still in discussing Buddhist principles he often relied on Neo-Taoist expressions. He believed that Buddhist and non-Buddhist learning could be fused into one system for the extensive proclamation of the dharma. In Buddhism his main interest while at Lu-shan was on the *Prajñā* thought, and his reputation in this field was such that Yao Hsing asked him to compose a preface to the *Ta-chih-tu-lun* of Kumārajīva, which he did, though unfortunately the preface is now lost. He also made an abbreviated version of the same work as an aid to beginners, but this is also lost at present.

Although Hui-yüan's biography noted that once he entered Lu-shan, his footprints never reentered the secular world, the secular world made its way to him. Visitors to the mountain retreat included emissaries from the non-Chinese courts in north China as well as from the Chinese courts in Chien-k'ang. Much more important were the members of the cultured class who came to Lu-shan and stayed as lay followers. One of these was Liu Ch'eng-chih, who had once been a prefect in Hupei. Another was Lei Tz'u-tsung, a young scholar who became an expert on the Confucian rites through his studies at Lu-shan. Chou Hsü-chih was another scholar widely read in the Confucian and Taoist classics who was particularly attracted by the pure monastic ideal of Lu-shan, so much so that he observed celibacy, wore simple clothes, and followed a vegetarian diet. Finally there was Tsung Ping, scholar, calligrapher, painter, and musician, who became one of the stoutest defenders of the religion in the anti-Buddhist debates of the period.

WRITINGS

A good deal of Hui-yüan's works has been preserved, and the following are excerpts from some of them. The doctrine of karma was one of the controversial issues of the day. Because so many of his contemporaries doubted that such a principle operated in the universe, Hui-yüan wrote a strong defense of the doctrine, entitled *San-pao-lun* (*Treatise on the Three Rewards*), which contained the following passages:

"The sutra says that karma has three kinds of response: first, in the present life; second, in the next life; and the third, in later lives. In the first, good and bad deeds originate in this present life and are rewarded in this life. In the second, the deeds are rewarded in the next life, while in the third, the deeds are rewarded in the 2nd, 3rd, 100th, or 1,000th life afterwards. The retribution is not its master, it must arise from the mind. The mind is under no definite control, it responds as it is influenced by external factors. The response might be fast or slow, so the retributions may be early or late. Although there is this difference of being early or late, all the retributions must correspond with the nature of the deed, being forceful or weak as the cause may be; therefore there is the difference between light and heavy retribution. These are the rewards and punishments of nature, and represent the general idea of the three retributions. . . .

"Again, although the three types of karma are different in nature, they are similar in that they ripen at a definite amount. When the retribution has been settled upon, then it must be received; it cannot be changed by prayer or avoided by the exercise of intelligence. . . . In this world there are people who have good karma and yet collect disaster. Perhaps there are cruel and evil ones who arrive at good fortune. This is all because the karma that should be rewarded in the present life are not yet manifested, while those of former lives are bearing fruit. Therefore it is said, 'An auspicious omen meets with misfortune, an ill omen encounters blessings.' . . . The reason why such views arise lies in the fact that the literature of the world considers one existence as the limit, and does not understand what is outside that one existence. Thus those who seek the truth confine themselves to what can be seen or heard."[6]

Writing on nirvāna, Hui-yüan noted, "Nirvāna does not change, it makes the end as its abode, while the Three Worlds, which are continually in flux, take evil and suffering as their stage. When the transformations end, then the operation of cause and effect comes to eternal rest, while the movement in the Three Worlds brings endless suffering."[7]

On the indestructibility of the soul, one of the central contentions of the Chinese Buddhists, this is what Hui-yüan had to say: "As for the soul, it responds perfectly and has no master, it is extremely mysterious and nameless. It moves in response to things, and it functions in individual destinies. Though it responds to things, it is not a thing; therefore the thing may change but it does not perish. It is attached to individual destinies but it is not

[6] *Ibid.*, 52,34bc.          [7] *Ibid.*, 52,30c.

bound to them, so that it is not exhausted when the destiny is terminated. Because it has feelings, it can be encumbered by things; because it has intelligence, it may seek an individual destiny. Since there are fine and coarse destinies, their natures are different, and since there are bright and dull intelligence, their light are not the same.

"From this we reason that the transformations are stimulated by the feelings, and that the soul is transmitted by change. The feelings are the mother of change, and soul is the root of feeling. The feelings have a way of uniting with things, while the soul has the power of moving subtly. . . .

"May I prove this for the sake of my opponent. The transmission of fire to firewood is like that of the soul to the body. The transmission of fire to another firewood is like that of the soul to another new body. . . . The former body is not the latter body, and we therefore know that the interaction between feelings and destiny is profound. A deluded person, seeing the body destroyed in one life, assumes that the soul and feelings also perished with it, as if fire would be exhausted for all time when a piece of wood is burned."[8]

In any attempt to assess Hui-yüan's place in Buddhist history, emphasis must be given to him as leader of the Lu-shan community, where Neo-Taoist metaphysical speculations mixed with *Prajñā* thought, and where the monastic ideal attracted the attention of the Confucian literati. He may be said to epitomize the Buddhism of south China, or gentry Buddhism in its fullest form. By his defense of the monastic ideal he established the independent status of the Buddhist community of monks on a firm basis in south China. Lastly, he gave a new orientation to Buddhist thought in the south by his efforts in introducing the new sutras translated by the Kashmirian monks and Kumārajīva in Ch'ang-an, especially those of the Sarvāstivādin and Mādhyamika Schools.

## TAO-SHENG

Among the disciples of Hui-yüan there was one who served as a bridge between the Buddhist centers at Lu-shan and Ch'ang-an,

[8] *Ibid.*, 52,31c-32a.

and made significant contributions to the development of Buddhist thought in China, especially with reference to the Nirvāna School. This was Tao-sheng, who died in 434.

The date of birth of Tao-sheng, whose lay surname was Wei, is not known, although it is believed to be ca.360. In his youth he was a gifted child who understood easily what was taught him. He became converted after meeting Chu Fa-t'ai and when ordained was already a well-known teacher. It was in ca.397 that he arrived in Lu-shan, where he met Hui-yüan and Sanghadeva, and under the tutelage of the latter commenced his studies of the Sarvāstivāda *Abhidharma* literature. About 405 or 406 he moved to Ch'ang-an to join the inner circle surrounding Kumārajīva where he probably participated in the translation of the *Vimalakīrtinirdeśa* (*Sutra Spoken by Vimalakīrti*) and the *Lotus Sutra.* He did not stay long in Ch'ang-an, however, for he left, probably in 408, for Lu-shan and Chien-k'ang in the south, taking with him Seng-chao's treatise, *Prajñā is not Knowledge*, which attracted the attention of Hui-yüan. It was during this period of his life that he concentrated on the *Nirvānasūtra.*

While he was in the capital Chien-k'ang, the following incident was reported to have taken place. Emperor Wen of the Liu Sung Dynasty was having a meal with Tao-sheng and a number of monks. The food was served rather late, and the monks were hesitant about partaking of it after the appointed noonday hour. The emperor noticed this and said, "It is just the beginning of midday now," whereupon Tao-sheng immediately replied, "The sun is attached to Heaven, and since Heaven says it is noon, it must be so."[9] With this remark he took up his bowl to eat, to be followed by the rest of the monks. His presence of mind impressed everyone.

## THE NIRVĀNASŪTRA

Since Tao-sheng's interest during the latter part of his life was concentrated on the *Nirvānasūtra*, some attention to the Chinese translations of this important sutra is in order. In the Pali canon the sixteenth sutra in the *Dīghanikāya* is the *Mahāparinibbana-*

[9] *Ibid.*, 50,366c.

*sutta*, of which three Chinese translations exist.[10] The Mahāyāna version of the same sutra was first translated by Fa-hsien in collaboration with Buddhabhadra, and entitled *Ta-pan ni-yüan-ching*. The second and standard translation entitled *Ta-pan nieh-pan-ching*, was made by Dharmakshema in Pei-Liang in 421. After it was introduced into the south during the middle of the Yüan-chia era (424-453), a group of Chinese Buddhists in Chien-k'ang, consisting of Hui-yen, Hui-kuan, and Hsieh Ling-yun, sought to improve it by making alterations in the sectional divisions. This altered version is commonly referred to as the *Southern Text*, while Dharmakshema's translation is designated as the *Northern Text*.

During the Eastern Chin period the Chinese Buddhists were mainly interested in Lao-Chuang and *Prajñā* philosophy, with the emphasis on *śūnyatā*. During the next period, under the Northern and Southern Dynasties, the Mahāyāna *Nirvānasūtra* as translated by Dharmakshema and Fa-hsien came to the fore. According to the Theravādin tradition the monk attains nirvāna when he is released from the miseries of phenomenal existence. In such a state karma ceases and the elements of existence come to rest. Some Mahāyāna works, such as the *Lotus* and the *Mādhyamika-śāstra*, taught that this nirvānic state consists of the thorough comprehension of *śūnyatā*, or the unreality of all the elements of existence. Instead of stressing unsubstantiality, the *Nirvānasūtra*, emphasizing the eternal, joyous, personal, and pure nature of nirvāna, says that all sentient beings can attain Buddhahood since they all possess the Buddha-nature within them. In the second *chüan* of the Dharmakshema translation we read: "That which is without self is life and death; but it is the self that is the Tathāgata. Finite is the *śrāvaka* (hearers, or Hīnayāna fol-

---

[10] These are the *Yu-hsing-ching*, the second sutra in the *Ch'ang-a-han*; the *Fo-pan ni-yüan-ching*, by Po Fa-tsu, made in 296-306; and the *Pan ni-yüan-ching*, translator unknown. The contents of the latter two translations follow in general the Pali version, although it is likely that they were not made from that text. One very significant difference between the Pali and the above two versions is the narrative concerning the Council of Rājagaha. In the Pali *Mahāparinibbanasutta* no mention is made of this council after the death of the Buddha: it is in the *Cullavagga* of the *Vinaya* that we find the council described. In the above two Chinese translations, however, the account of the council follows immediately after the death of the Buddha. There is still another translation of the Hīnayāna version, entitled *Ta-pan nieh-pan-ching*, attributed to Fa-hsien, but it is doubtful whether this monk ever made the translation.

lowers) and *pratyekabuddha* (Solitary Buddha), but (eternal) is the Tathāgata's *Dharmakāya*. Pain is the way of the infidels, but joyous is nirvāna. Impure are constituted objects, but pure is the true dharma possessed by the Buddhas and bodhisattvas."[11] To the Buddhists of this period, who were familiar with the *śūnyatā* doctrine of the *Prajñā* sutras and the Lao-Chuang theory of non-being, and who believed that nirvāna was an impersonal state of emptiness, such a doctrine appeared to be heretical. Despite the opposition the sutra was widely studied and respected. It also acquired special standing, as it was looked upon as the last sermon of the Buddha, in which was contained the ultimate doctrine.

This *Mahāparinirvānasūtra* found one of its strongest supporters in Tao-sheng. Even before the Fa-hsien translation of the sutra appeared in 418, he had already evolved certain ideas of his own concerning the state of nirvāna. When he read in the Fa-hsien translation passages to the effect that *icchantikas*, or those whose primary interest was the gratification of their desires, did not possess the Buddha-nature, he felt that such an interpretation must be incorrect, that the whole tenor of the Mahāyāna teaching was against the exclusion of one group. He argued that this translation of Fa-hsien must have been incomplete, and he boldly came out with the doctrine that even *icchantikas* could achieve Buddhahood.

This was such a revolutionary doctrine that it was branded heretical by many other monks, who wanted to expel Tao-sheng from the order. Tao-sheng, however, swore that "if what I say is contrary to the meaning of the sutra, may this present body of mine be covered with sores, but if it is not contrary to the truth, then may I sit in the teacher's chair when I pass from life."[12] He felt that the Buddhist dharma supported his interpretation, and he was not to be encumbered by the text of just one sutra, which he believed was not complete. One of the fundamental Mahāyāna tenets is that all sentient beings possess the Buddha-nature in them, and that all are capable of attaining Buddhahood. By insisting that even the lowly *icchantikas* can do so, he was only carrying to its logical conclusion the Mahāyāna doctrine of universal salvation.

[11] L. Hurvitz (tr.), *Wei Shou Treatise on Buddhism and Taoism*, Kyoto, 1956, 59.
[12] *Taishō*, 50,366c.

In this connection his biographer wrote that he understood what lay beyond words. "The purpose of symbols is to gain a complete understanding of ideas, but once the ideas have been gained, the symbols may be forgotten. The purpose of words is to explain the truth, but once truth has been uttered, words may be dispensed with. Ever since the transmission of the scriptures eastward to China, their translators have encountered repeated obstacles, and many have held strictly to the text, with the result that they seldom have been able to see the complete meaning. If they were to forget the fishtrap and take the fish, then one may begin to talk with them about the way. . . ."[13]

After taking his bold and brave stand, Tao-sheng left the capital and returned to Lu-shan, arriving there in ca.430. Soon after he reached Lu-shan, the text of the Dharmakshema translation reached the southern capital of Chien-yeh, and a copy of it was made and sent to Tao-sheng. Tao-sheng read the text thoroughly and in the twenty-third chapter he found the passage that supported his stand. Here he read that the Tathāgata is eternal and unchanging, joyous, personal, and pure and never enters nirvāna, and that all living beings, even the *icchantikas*, have the Buddha-nature and are capable of attaining to the way. The monks in the capital now recalled the prophetic words of Tao-sheng and admired him all the more for his penetrating wisdom.

The last years of Tao-sheng's life were spent in Lu-shan. One day in 434 he ascended the teacher's throne, apparently in good health and spirit, and ably expounded the sutras to the delight of the audience. Then, when he was about to leave the pulpit, his monk's staff fell suddenly. He was still sitting upright, and his features were the same as before, but he had passed into nirvāna. Thus the manner of his death was a fulfillment of the oath he had made when he left the capital.

Tao-sheng was characterized by his contemporaries as one who relied on the dharma and not on people, on the meaning and not on words, on wisdom and not on knowledge.

CONCEPT OF THE TRUE SELF

According to Tao-sheng, the *Prajñā* sutras and the *Nirvānasūtra*, though different in titles, taught the same lesson, namely, that

---

[13] Fung, *op.cit.*, 2,270, with some changes.

the ultimate truth, or the Buddha-nature, is without *lakshanas* or characteristics. Being so, it transcends symbols and forms, and is not to be divided or limited. The wisdom that understands and grasps this truth must also be undifferentiated and unlimited. If one tries to conceive of this undifferentiated truth with a limited or differentiated understanding, would that not be illogical and unreasonable? Consequently, Tao-sheng taught that if one were to realize his Buddha-nature, he must do so instantly, completely, and by his own self.

To him the ultimate truth or *śūnyatā* of the *Prajñā* sutras and Buddha-nature of the *Nirvānasūtra* are the same. If living beings are able to understand that the myriads of words signify the oneness of truth, they are able to realize their Buddha-nature and attain nirvāna. This nirvāna is without characteristics—a state in which the differences between external objects and oneself are forgotten, where being and nonbeing are unified, where speech and discipline, delusions and worldly attachments are all terminated, and where the blissful and pure life is enjoyed by *chen-wo* or *shen-wo*, the true self.

To Tao-sheng this doctrine of the true self was the logical culmination of Buddhist thinking on the subject. Early Buddhist thought insisted that there is no permanent or unchanging self in an individual, only a conglomeration of the five aggregates which are constantly changing. If there is no permanent self in *samsāra*, is there a permanent self in nirvāna? Indian Buddhists never considered this question, yet one can see how it would logically arise. If there is no self, what is it that enters into nirvāna to enjoy the bliss of that state? To the credit of Tao-sheng he faced this problem fearlessly and came forth with his idea of the true self, which is in reality the Buddha-nature in each individual.

The discussion centering on the *Nirvānasūtra* indicated that it was one of the most popular sutras in the south. In a way this is understandable. Up to that time the Buddhists had been taught that there is no self in nirvāna. In this sutra, however, they are told that the Buddha possesses an immortal self, that the final state of nirvāna is one of bliss and purity enjoyed by the eternal self. *Samsāra* is thus a pilgrimage leading to this final goal of union with the Buddha, and this salvation is guaranteed by the fact that all living beings possess the Buddha-nature. All living beings from the beginning of life participated in the Buddha's eternal existence, and this gives dignity to them as children of the Buddha.

As a result of such teachings by Tao-sheng a Nirvāna School arose in the south, which was to last until it was absorbed into the T'ien-t'ai School in the latter half of the sixth century.

OTHER DOCTRINES

According to his biography Tao-sheng enunciated many strange doctrines as a result of such ideas about the Buddha-nature. Among these was his contention that there was no Pure Land of the Buddha, and that meritorious deeds brought no rewards. Since the Buddha-nature is right within us, there is no Pure Land to go to. Although the sutras speak of a Pure Land where living things would go as a result of good deeds, Tao-sheng contended that this was merely an artifice, an example of the skill-in-means of the Buddha in his teachings.

As for his other contention that good deeds entail no rewards, we do not know the full details of his position. There is a treatise by Hui-yüan that dealt with the subject, entitled *Ming-pao-ying-lun* (*Treatise on the Understanding of Retribution*), and since Hui-yüan and Tao-sheng were close companions at Lu-shan, it could be that Hui-yüan's treatise reflected Tao-sheng's ideas. The main gist of Hui-yüan's discussion is that deeds produce karma only when there is a definite mental intention behind the deed. The sage, however, is free from mental intentions; hence whatever deeds he performs produce no karma.

It is possible that Tao-sheng had other ideas in mind when he put forth his contention. During the time that he lived there was a great deal of rivalry among the populace as to who were performing more meritorious deeds. Salvation or a happy rebirth, it was thought, could be purchased by the proper amount of good deeds. The rich and the faithful vied with one another to build a more elaborate temple, stupa, or monastery, or to set up a more ornate image of the Buddha. All such deeds were motivated by the rewards to be reaped. Tao-sheng sought to expose the vanity and the ulterior motives of the Buddhists who considered the whole problem of salvation on a mercenary and competitive basis. He realized that such motives are far removed from the Buddhist ideal of performing meritorious deeds for their own sake, not for any rewards to be gained; hence his contention that good deeds entail no reward.

## SUDDEN ENLIGHTENMENT

Another doctrine that Tao-sheng advocated was that one achieved Buddhahood by a sudden and complete enlightenment. Before him Chih Tun already had the idea that truth is not to be divided, and that enlightenment is not achieved by stages. Tao-sheng, by taking a bold stand on this point, elicited strong opposition, and so the controversy of sudden versus gradual enlightenment is usually associated with him. In the ten stages of the bodhisattva's career the seventh stage is very important, for the candidate, once having achieved this stage, can no longer backslide; he is destined for enlightenment, he has left behind all attachments to the world. Chih Tun realized the importance of this seventh stage and said that there is sudden enlightenment here, but that this enlightenment is only partial, not complete. Only with the attainment of the tenth stage is enlightenment complete.

Tao-sheng's writing on sudden enlightenment is now lost, but his ideas can be gleaned from the works of others. One of the main sources of information is the *Pien-tsung-lun* (*Discussions of Essentials*), by Hsieh Ling-yun. He advocated that enlightenment must be sudden and complete, not divided and attained by stages. But he also claimed that enlightenment does not come by itself; it must be achieved by gradual training. After going through the process of religious training, the individual comes to the stage when enlightenment suddenly bursts upon him. In this emphasis on the necessity of religious discipline he agreed with Chih Tun and Tao-an, but he disagreed with them when they said that there is partial enlightenment after the seventh stage and complete enlightenment at the tenth stage. He contended that the Buddha-nature is undifferentiated and indivisible; we either have total understanding of it at once, or not at all. Hence it is not possible to get only a partial illumination of this Buddha-nature after the seventh stage. Tao-sheng thus carried to its logical conclusion the *Prajñā* teaching that the ultimate truth is without *lakshanas* or characteristics, and therefore cannot be divided.

It was said that Tao-sheng's theory of sudden enlightenment evoked a wave of discussion pro and con. The discussion spread even to court circles when Emperor Wen wrote a tract explaining sudden enlightenment. Among the opponents of Tao-sheng one of the most important was Hui-kuan, who had been his fellow student under Kumārajīva. Hui-kuan's arguments in favor of gradual enlightenment may be summarized as follows: The ultimate reality may be indivisible, but man, because of differences in faculties and abilities, is able to attain the truth at different levels. Hui-kuan said that the path to enlightenment might be compared to the ascent of a peak by a mountain climber. When the climber has reached a certain point, he can see his goal, the mountain top, in the distance. His eyes see the goal, but his feet are not yet there. From the viewpoint of his feet he is not yet at his goal, but from the viewpoint of his eyes he is there. It is the same with the understanding of truth. One can see the truth, though able to experience only a portion of it.

The lives and contributions of these three monks, Tao-an, Hui-yüan, and Tao-sheng, provide the best illustration of what Hui-chiao meant when he used the term "eminent monks." All three shone like beacons, lighting up the hidden recesses of the Indian religion for their fellow countrymen to see, they propounded new ideas that widened the intellectual horizons of their brethren, and they showed how the pure monastic life was to be lived. In their thoughts and their activities they exemplified the spirit of the Buddhism of the upper classes that developed in south China during the Eastern Chin Dynasty, and through their interpretations they made the foreign religion more palatable to the educated Chinese.

# CHAPTER V

# PROGRESS AND OPPOSITION: SOUTHERN DYNASTIES

I N 420 an ambitious general named Liu Yü deposed the Ssu-
ma family which had established the Chin Dynasty and set
up the Sung ruling house. In order to distinguish this Sung
from the later and more important Sung Dynasty (960-
1279), Chinese historians usually designate this earlier Sung as
the Liu Sung. The territory along the Yangtze Valley and south
was thus under the control of one dynasty, while north China
after 440 was unified under the Northern Wei Dynasty of non-
Chinese origin. Now began the era commonly referred to as the
Nan-Pei-Ch'ao, the Northern and Southern Dynasties, which was
to last until the country was finally unified in 589 by the Sui house.

What was known as the Southern Dynasties was really a succession of short-lived Chinese dynasties: the Liu Sung (420-479),
Ch'i (479-502), Liang (502-557), and Ch'en (557-589). While
there were breaks in the fortunes of the ruling houses, Buddhism
under the Southern Dynasties continued to develop generally along
the lines laid down during the previous period. That is to say,
monks in the south were more interested in philosophy and literature and in maintaining close relations with the Neo-Taoists. However, there were three periods during which Buddhism achieved
substantial progress: (1) during the Yüan-chia era (424-453) of
the Liu Sung Dynasty; (2) during the period when Hsiao Tzu-
liang or Prince Ching-ling was active (roughly 484-495); and
(3) during the reign of Emperor Wu of the Liang (502-549).

## THE YÜAN-CHIA PERIOD

The prevalent interest in Buddhism during the Yüan-chia era
might be reflected by the fact that in the capital alone construction of fifteen temples was recorded; the unrecorded number must
have been still greater. Another indication was the large number
of literary figures and members of the aristocracy who were actively interested in the dharma.

During the Liu Sung Dynasty some of the outstanding families in south China were diligent followers of the Buddha.[1] The most prominent literary figure connected with Buddhism was Hsieh Ling-yun (also named K'ang-lo, 385-433). At an early age he gained fame as a literary genius and calligrapher, which enabled him to have a ready entree into Sung court circles. He apparently lacked tact and diplomacy, and frequently made enemies among the courtiers. His ability as a writer won him the highest esteem among contemporary literary circles, and because of this he was asked to compose the eulogy of Hui-yüan after the latter's death. Earlier, when Hui-yüan wanted to dedicate a cave in Lu-shan, in which the Buddha shadow was painted, Hsieh Ling-yun was asked to write the inscription. During his lifetime he was engaged in various activities connected with Buddhism. When he was in the capital, he undoubtedly participated in the discussions centered on Tao-sheng's doctrine of sudden enlightenment, for he wrote the treatise *Pien-tsung-lun*, which has preserved for posterity the main ideas of Tao-sheng on this point. Together with the monks Hui-yen and Hui-kuan, he revised and polished the translation of the *Mahāparinirvāṇasūtra* made by Dharmakshema in the north.[2] Because of his literary stature he played an important

---

[1] One such family was the Chang clan, which produced some of the famous literary and political figures of the period. Chang Yü, for instance, had five sons, all talented and learned, designated by contemporaries as the five dragons of the Chang clan. Another famous clansman was Chang Jung (444-497), learned in both Buddhism and Neo-Taoism, who at death held the *Tao-te-ching* and *Hsiao-ching* in his left hand and the *Saddharma* and *Prajñāpāramitā* in his right. The Ho clan of Lu-chiang was likewise prominent in official as well as Buddhist circles. Ho Shang-chih (382-460), for instance, was the official in charge of Dark Learning, one of the four branches of learning established by the dynasty at this time, the other three being Confucianism, History, and Literature. As Dark Learning embraced both Neo-Taoism and Buddhism, one can readily see how important Buddhism had become in the minds of the literati. Still another was the Wang clan, descendants of Wang Tao and probably one of the most prominent aristocratic families engaged in the spread of Buddhism in the south. Among these descendants there were two, Wang Hsün (350-401) and Wang Min (351-398), both interested in Neo-Taoism and Buddhism, while the son of Hsün, named Wang Hung, was frequently involved in debates with Hsieh Ling-yun over partial and complete enlightenment. Another of the Wang clan was Wang Lien, who served as patron for the translation of the *Wu-fen-lü* by Buddhajīva.

[2] An example of such improvement in style is seen in the following passage. Dharmakshema's translation read, "*Shou pa chiao tao, te tao pi an*" ("With hands scrambling and feet treading, they reached the other shore"). Hsieh felt that this was too colloquial and not polished enough, so he revised it to read, "*Yun shou tung tsu, chieh liu erh tu*," which conveyed the same idea but was much more literary and refined.

role in spreading the teachings of the *Nirvānasūtra*. However, he still sought after worldly honors even though he professed Buddhism. A modern historian of Buddhism in China, T'ang Yung-t'ung, rendered the following critique of the man: Though his body was in the mountains and forests, his mind was directed to the attachments of society. His interest in Buddhism consisted mainly in using its ideas for discussion and speculation, but not as a basis for the religious life.

## PRINCE CHING-LING

The second period of progress was due mainly to the efforts of Prince Ching-ling. This prince was the second son of Emperor Wu of the Southern Ch'i Dynasty. During his lifetime he was one of the strongest supporters of Buddhism in the south. His residence at Chi-lung-shan was a meeting place for practically all the outstanding literary men and clerics of the age. It was said that every important monk of the Ch'i kingdom had visited him at one time or another. Due to his patronage the religion gained a wide following among the aristocratic and literary circles of the southern court. In his adherence to Buddhism Prince Ching-ling was most concerned with strict observance of the monastic discipline. He often assembled *Vinaya* masters to lecture on the *Shih-sung-lü* (*Vinaya of the Sarvāstivādins*). He felt that the Buddhist disciplinary rules were similar to the teachings of Confucius in that both aimed at rectifying the mind of man. He was also concerned with the practical aspects of the Buddha's teaching. To this end he convened fasting assemblies, discouraged the killing of animals, distributed alms and medicines, and even offered his person for service in the temple.

In the *Jātakas* there are numerous instances of an individual's sacrificing his own body for the sake of others, one of the most famous being that of the bodhisattva offering himself to the hungry tigress. The practice was modified somewhat when it was followed by the Chinese. During the great fasting assemblies the Chinese rulers, instead of sacrificing their own bodies, would give themselves up to a certain monastery or temple. Since the realm could not be without a ruler, it was the duty of the ministers of state and courtiers to pay a huge sum to the temple to ransom him, and the Buddhist institutions benefited. Prince Ching-ling indulged in this practice several times.

Still another aspect of the prince's activities was his propagation of the dharma. Sometimes he took part in copying the sutras, for this was before the advent of printing. He also wrote commentaries, one of which was on the *Vimalakīrtinirdeśa* in five chapters. As for his writings in disseminating the religion, these were collected during the Liang Dynasty and consisted of 116 *chüan* in all. Buddhism suffered a great loss when this benefactor and supporter died in 495, at the early age of thirty-four.

## EMPEROR WU OF THE LIANG DYNASTY

The third period of Buddhist growth was brought about mainly through the activities of Emperor Wu, founder of the Liang Dynasty, who ruled from 502-549. His family was originally Taoist, but before he ascended the throne his mind was already inclined toward Buddhism as a result of his associations with Buddhist monks at the court of Prince Ching-ling. After he became emperor, his interest in Buddhism became more and more pronounced, and by the third year of his reign, in 504, he had already become a convert. It was during this year that he uttered the earnest wish that young men would leave household life to disseminate widely the religion of the sutras and to convert sentient beings. He said too he would rather be reborn in one of the evil modes of existence under the sway of the genuine dharma than in one of the paradises under Taoism. In the same year, on the occasion of the Buddha's birthday, he issued a decree calling for the abandonment of ceremonies in honor of Lao-tzu. In 511 he adopted the practice of giving up wine and meat on the imperial table, for he believed that meat-eating would result in rebirth in one of the hells. In 517 he issued another decree, forbidding the use of living things for medicinal purposes and as sacrificial objects. For such purposes he advocated the use of flour, fruits, and vegetables. In the same year he called for the abolition of all Taoist temples and for the return of Taoist priests to the laity. Pressure on the Taoists was so great that some had to flee to the north from the Liang kingdom. He also invited well-known monks to serve as his advisers and teachers.

Under the tutelage of these Buddhist monks Emperor Wu embarked on a varied career as a Buddhist monarch, taking as his model the great Indian emperor Aśoka. One of the most obvious and concrete ways in which rulers manifested their devotion to Buddhism was in the construction of temples. Emperor Wu was no exception. Among the numerous temples that he constructed, the most famous was the T'ung-t'ai Temple, started in 521 and completed in 527. After completion it became the scene of most of the emperor's activities concerning Buddhism. He then constructed two more temples in honor of his parents: the Ta-ai Temple in memory of his father, which extended over seven li in length and consisted of thirty-six courts to house a thousand monks at all times, and the Ta-chih-tu Temple to honor his mother, where four hundred nuns were in residence at all times.

During his long reign the emperor frequently convened dharma assemblies which he personally attended, sometimes to explain a certain Buddhist sutra himself, sometimes merely to sit in the audience. At other times the emperor took advantage of these assemblies to grant general amnesty to criminals or to announce a new era. This explains why, beginning with 520, changes in the reign titles began to take place with bewildering rapidity, there being six during the years 520-549. Attendance at these assemblies must have numbered in the thousands; at the meeting held on the ninth month of 529 in the T'ung-t'ai Temple it was said that fifty thousand were present. During these assemblies, sixteen in all, there was no distinction between monks and laymen—an indication of the broadened social consciousness instilled in the emperor by Buddhism.

A special feature of these assemblies was the emperor's practice of giving himself up to a Buddhist temple to serve as a menial. He did this not once, but several times. The first instance occurred in 528, once more in 546, and a final one in 547. As a way of raising funds for the Buddhist temples this practice was without rival, and Emperor Wu undoubtedly indulged in it to show his patronage of Buddhism.

The emperor also indicated his interest in Buddhism by writing commentaries on the *Nirvānasūtra*, the *Prajñā* sutras, and the *Vimalakīrtinirdeśa*. On one occasion he wrote a preface to a commentary on the *Nirvānasūtra*, written by Pao-liang (d.509).

He frequently attended meetings where these sutras were being elucidated by the Buddhist masters, and on a number of occasions he personally ascended the platform to lecture on these texts. Once he expounded them to an audience which consisted not only of monks and officials, but also of foreign envoys from Persia, Khotan, and Korea.

Another activity pursued by the emperor was the establishment of the Inexhaustible Treasuries under imperial auspices. These treasuries, known as *wu-chin-tsang*, sometimes served as safe-deposit vaults to receive for safekeeping the wealth of the rich temple patrons, but more often they served as repositories for the donations of the faithful devotees of the religion. Such donations in turn became the capital with which the treasury administrator carried on financial transactions, the profits to be used for the benefit of the religion. Utilizing imperial authority, Emperor Wu established thirteen such Inexhaustible Treasuries throughout his realm. In 533 his donations to the treasury of T'ung-t'ai Temple consisted of 201 items valued at 10,960,000 cash; the crown prince donated 3,430,000; while the palace officials contributed a total of 2,700,000 cash.

Because of his devotion to the dharma Emperor Wu was sometimes called the Imperial Bodhisattva. Already in possession of temporal powers, he sought to assume control over the Buddhist church also. When he communicated this idea to the monks, one of them, Chih-tsang, protested the move, proclaiming that the great sea of the dharma was not to be mastered by a layman. The monk also argued that the rigid application of secular laws over the sangha would impede the progress of the monastic community.

It was this same Chih-tsang who figured in another incident involving the emperor. As a rule the emperor permitted monks to enter the imperial palaces freely; hence, in the seating arrangements for the palace lectures, there was no special order, except that one seat was usually reserved for the emperor. One day Chih-tsang occupied this chair, and when his fellow monks criticized him for his temerity, he replied that since he was the descendant of Dīpankara (the first of the twenty-four Buddhas), they should not begrudge him the seat.

On another occasion, in 535, while the emperor was lecturing in one of the palaces, the entire audience arose as a sign of respect, except for one monk. When asked to explain his behavior, the monk replied that he was the embodiment of the dharma and that if he moved, the dharma would move and there would be no peace. The emperor reportedly approved this reply. These incidents serve to illustrate that in the struggle between temporal and spiritual powers Buddhist monks were not afraid to go contrary to imperial wishes or to disobey the ruler's commands. This was in contrast to practices in the north, where the rulers expected unqualified obedience to their orders.

The imperial patronage accorded Buddhism during the Liang Dynasty inevitably resulted in some protests against the religion by native writers. Among these may be found the most vitriolic attack against Buddhism that had appeared so far, a treatise by Hsün Chi, which charged the Buddhist monks with sedition, immorality, economic liability, and hypocrisy. Another protest was presented by Kuo Tsu-shen, who charged that there was an excessive number of monks and nuns, that many of them were not leading the religious life, and that nuns were going about wearing beautiful dresses and corrupting the morals of laymen. He called upon the emperor to cleanse the sangha of these undesirable features.

During his declining years Emperor Wu turned over much of his governing powers to his followers, with the result that corrupt practices and internal confusion became more and more rampant, much to the distress of the people. Later writers have attempted to attribute this decline to his own character, especially the contradiction between his faith and his conduct. Wei Cheng of early T'ang, for instance, wrote that though the emperor was a follower of Buddhism, he still pursued fame and glory; that he preached the religion not to benefit man, but merely as an opportunity to display his knowledge. His critics also blamed him for his laxity in observing the criminal code. For instance, a certain official named Wang Hung threatened to commit suicide, but Emperor Wu restored him to office without ascertaining the nature of the offense that had led him to contemplate suicide. These critics also referred to the case of Wang Hou, who was arrogant and despotic, killing people in broad daylight and committing banditry at night, but still escaped punishment. The emperor realized that his disinclination to observe the criminal code faithfully was responsible for much miscarriage of justice and bred evil results for the dynasty, but he still persisted in following the Buddhist precept against killing and pardoned many who should have been punished. Even when it was necessary to decree execution, he delayed issuing the final order as long as possible and did so reluctantly only after burning incense and offering invocations to the Buddha. The verdict of the Confucian compilers of the dynastic history was that Emperor Wu was "immersed in the Buddhist religion, and was therefore lax in observing the criminal statutes," that he had failed to harmonize virtue with punishment, the ideal with the practical, the way of the Buddha with the way of the ruler, and that as a result the people suffered.

## THE NIRVĀNASŪTRA IN THE SOUTH

While Buddhism was making progress under the patronage of the political rulers, the monks were making their contributions to the development of the religion by concentrating on certain sutras during this period. The *Nirvānasūtra* had been introduced to the south by Tao-sheng, and his followers became very active in disseminating its teachings in that area. As the main theme in the sutra was the nature of the Buddha, many theories were advanced by various masters on this point, and numerous commentaries were also compiled to elucidate the meaning of the sutra. These commentaries became so voluminous that Emperor Wu of the Liang Dynasty commissioned some monks to gather together all existing commentaries. The resultant collection, entitled *Ta-pan nieh-p'an-ching chi-chieh* (*Collection of Commentaries on the Mahāparinirvānasūtra*), contained seventy-one in all.

One of the problems that agitated the thinkers of the period was whether or not sentient beings originally possessed, or were about to possess, the Buddha-nature. The *Nirvānasūtra* taught that all sentient beings are to attain their Buddha-nature in the future; hence, it was asked, how can it be said that sentient beings originally possess the Buddha-nature? A compromise view was developed by one of the masters, Chih-tsang of the K'ai-shan Temple, who contended that all sentient beings originally possess the nature of achieving Buddhahood in the future. Since all sentient beings can achieve Buddhahood in the future, one can say that they originally possess the Buddha-nature. But since Buddha-hood is to be achieved in the future, one can also say that they are about to possess the Buddha-nature.

One of the well-known *Nirvāna* masters of this period was Fa-yao (d.473-476, age seventy-six), who held to a doctrine of gradual enlightenment. Not only did he study and comment on the *Nirvānasūtra*, but he was also well-versed on the *Lotus* and *Prajñā* sutras. In his commentaries he developed the idea that the Buddha-nature is the spontaneous power of a Buddha who has rejected passions, acts, and misery. So long as this power is hidden, it travels through the five modes of existence; but when it is manifested, then it is integrated with the *dharmakāya*, or the Body of Essence.

Another of the famous *Nirvāna* masters was Pao-liang, who died in 509 at the age of sixty-six. A monk of good memory and extensive learning, he preached in the capital Chien-yeh to audiences of over three thousand on such sutras as the *Nirvāna*, *Satyasiddhi*, and *Vimalakīrti*. Pao-liang was very critical of the Hīnayāna doctrine of *anatta*, which he said was not suitable for the Mahāyāna. To take the place of this *anatta* doctrine, he developed the idea of a mysterious divine entity which is the Buddha-nature in all sentient beings, is eternal, immovable, nameless, without characteristics, and beyond being and nonbeing. For Pao-liang, this Buddha-nature which is immanent in all sentient beings never changes, and it is this entity that enjoys the bliss of nirvāna.

## THE SATYASIDDHI SCHOOL (THE COMPLETION OF TRUTH SCHOOL)

The main interest in Buddhist circles in south China was centered not only on the *Nirvānasūtra* but also on the *Satyasiddhi-śāstra* (*Treatise on the Completion of Truth*). This is a Hīnayāna work compiled by Harivarman (third century A.D.). He felt that the appearance of so many diverse doctrines growing out of one source was a sign of decay, and as a result he studied the canon and the writings of former masters, drawing from them what he considered to be fundamental to incorporate into his work. In this work the analysis of names and characteristics was so logical and detailed that it was extremely useful for beginners in the study of the religion. This was why Kumārajīva translated the work into Chinese in 411-412. The original text is now lost and only the Chinese version exists.

The text is considered to be Hīnayānist because it adheres to the original sacred literature as taught by the Buddha, and it accepts the Hīnayāna viewpoint concerning the analysis of the individual. However, it also taught that there are two categories of truth, the worldly or ordinary truth and the supreme truth. The former category recognizes the phenomenal existence of all the dharmas, and admits that since such dharmas are brought about by cause and effect, they enjoy only temporary existence and are constantly changing. The second category, or supreme truth, teaches that everything is unreal or empty. The self or personality is made up of five aggregates, but these aggregates have no substratum and have no abiding existence. Likewise the dharmas that comprise the external world also have no abiding existence and are empty. The text thus teaches *pudgala-śūnyatā* (nonsubstantiality of the individual) and *sarva-dharma-śūnyatā* (nonsubstantiality of all the elements of existence). Because of this feature the school which was based on this text was sometimes called Mahāyāna; but the genuine Mahāyāna adherents, such as the followers of the San-lun, attacked such a view vigorously on the grounds that its conception of emptiness was arrived at by destruction.

According to the Satyasiddhi all objects are first reduced to molecules, then atoms, then fine atoms, until finally, in one great jump, this process of division and reduction results in emptiness. From this it may be seen that the emptiness achieved by this school is one brought about by destruction or abstraction, and not the transcendental emptiness advocated by the San-lun School; hence the disapproval of the school by San-lun followers.

Since Kumārajīva translated the text late in his life, only a few of his disciples studied it. Of these, there were two who became masters of the Satyasiddhi—Seng-tao and Seng-sung.

Seng-tao was a native of Ch'ang-an, but in his later years he journeyed to the south to establish a Tung-shan Temple in Shou-ch'un (in present-day Anhui). Here he was to spend the rest of his life until he died at the ripe old age of ninety-six, although he did spend a few years at the capital, Chien-yeh, upon the invitation of Emperor Hsiao-wu (454-464) of the Sung Dynasty. His center may be called the Shou-ch'un branch, and it wielded great influence in spreading the Satyasiddhi teachings in south China.

There was another branch which was even more important, since its influence pervaded both north and south. This was the P'eng-ch'eng (in present Kiangsu) branch organized by Seng-sung. Members of this group, after serving their discipleship under the master, fanned out in different directions to carry on their activities. Besides lecturing on the Satyasiddhi, these monks from Shou-ch'un and P'eng-ch'eng also wrote commentaries; in all twenty-eight such commentaries have been counted. Such efforts resulted in the Satyasiddhi's being the most widely studied and influential text during the Southern Ch'i and Liang Dynasties in south China. It was the popularity of this text, with its discussion of emptiness, that aroused the ire and opposition of the San-lun School, who felt that a mistaken impression of emptiness was being created and fostered by the masters of the Satyasiddhi. As a result of the effort of Fa-lang and Chi-tsang in combatting the Satyasiddhi, the San-lun School finally won out, so that, with the advent of the Sui Dynasty, interest in the Satyasiddhi slowly receded.

## THE SAN-LUN SCHOOL

After Seng-chao, interest in the San-lun School appears to have declined during the early years of the Southern Dynasties, the reason undoubtedly being the dominance of the *Nirvāṇasūtra* and Satyasiddhi. There were, to be sure, some San-lun masters who carried on the traditions of the school, such as Seng-lang (died ca.615), Seng-ch'üan, and Fa-lang (507-581).

Seng-lang was a native of Korea who carried on his teachings while residing in She-shan (in modern Kiangsu). It was said that Emperor Wu of the Liang Dynasty, hearing of the fame of Seng-lang as a San-lun master, transferred his interest from the Satyasiddhi to the Mādhyamika system, and dispatched ten monks to study under Seng-lang. Nine of the ten turned out to be disappointments, but the tenth, Seng-ch'üan, proved to be a worthy disciple of the master. After mastering the system, Seng-ch'üan also remained at She-shan, where he in turn transmitted the torch to Fa-lang.

Fa-lang at first remained in the mountains, but in 558 he descended to the capital, Chien-yeh, to live in the Hsing-huang Temple, hence his title as the Great Master of the Hsing-huang Temple. As part of his efforts to revive interest in the San-lun system he boldly attacked the popular Satyasiddhi teaching, claiming that it was really Hīnayāna and that it was spreading confusion in the minds of the people concerning the meaning of emptiness. His audience in the capital numbered in the thousands, and gradually interest in the San-lun began to increase. Even Emperors Wu and Wen of the Ch'en Dynasty became interested supporters of Fa-lang. When he died in 581, at the age of seventy-five, he had reestablished the San-lun teachings on a firm footing again; this enabled his disciple Chi-tsang (549-623) to carry on where he left off.

Chi-tsang's father was Parthian, but his mother was Chinese. His ancestors had migrated from Parthia, first to south China, then to Chin-ling (modern Nanking) where he was born. Though his appearance was that of a Parthian, his education and upbringing were entirely Chinese. His father became a Buddhist monk soon after the boy's birth, and he himself at an early age (some sources say at age seven; others say at age thirteen) left the household life to join the Buddhist community as a novice. His father then took him to Hsing-huang Temple where he met Fa-lang and listened to his preaching. This led Chi-tsang to become Fa-lang's disciple, and to undertake the study of the Mādhyamika texts under the master. It was said that he possessed an exceptional memory, retaining everything that he learned. When he was ordained a monk at age twenty-one, he had already earned a high reputation as a student of the San-lun School.

During the last years of the Ch'en Dynasty the south was embroiled in confusion and turmoil, and many monks and scholars fled the region. Chi-tsang and his followers went about collecting the literature that had been hurriedly left behind, to be sorted and studied at their leisure. After the area had been pacified by the Sui armies, he then went eastward to K'uai-chi, where he settled in the Chia-hsiang Temple. It was during his sojourn in this temple that he composed the commentaries to the three treatises of the San-lun School. The best known of these commentaries is that on the *Mādhyamikaśāstra*, entitled *Chung-kuan-lun su*, in ten *chüan*. He also wrote a short treatise called *Meaning of the Double Truth* (*Erh-ti-i*), in which he elaborated on the Mādhyamika theory of contradiction. It will be recalled that the Mādhyamika School held to the theory of the double truth—the *saṁvṛtisatya* or worldly truth and the *paramārthasatya* or absolute truth. This double truth, according to Chi-tsang, exists in three levels, which may be set forth in the following scheme:

| *Worldly Truth* | *Absolute Truth* |
|---|---|
| 1. Affirmation of being | 1. Affirmation of nonbeing |
| 2. Affirmation of either being or nonbeing | 2. Denial of both being and nonbeing |
| 3. Either affirmation or denial of both being and nonbeing | 3. Neither affirmation nor denial of being and nonbeing[3] |

Thus, by a series of negations, we reach the point where nothing is affirmed or denied, and the highest level of truth is attained. Chi-tsang's fame as a San-lun master earned him the title Great Master of the Chia-hsiang Temple, and his lectures attracted thousands of listeners.

Because of his great reputation he was invited by Emperor Yang of the Sui Dynasty in 606 (variant 600) to go to Yang-chou and then to Ch'ang-an, the capital. In Ch'ang-an it was claimed that over ten thousand monks and laymen assembled to hear him preach. Among the sutras that he specialized in were the three treatises of the Mādhyamika School and the *Lotus Sutra*; he lectured on the former over a hundred times, the latter over three hundred times. In addition to his teachings he also wrote commentaries to a number of Mahāyāna sutras, such as the *Lotus, Vimalakīrti, Nirvānasūtra, Pure Land Sutra, Suvarnaprabhāsa* (*Golden Light*) and the *Prajñā* sutras. Due to his activities the tenets of the San-lun School were systematized and established on firm foundations. His contributions were so outstanding that during the Wu-te era (618-626) he was acclaimed as one of the ten great virtuous monks of the empire. With his death at the

---

[3] Fung, *op.cit.*, 2,295.

age of seventy-five the old line of San-lun transmission, starting with Kumārajīva, terminated.

## PARAMĀRTHA

Of the different translators who carried on their activities in south China during this period, the most important was undoubtedly Paramārtha or Chen-ti, a native of India, who arrived in Canton in 546, when he was already forty-eight years of age. From the southern port he made his way to the Liang capital of Chien-yeh, where he was welcomed by Emperor Wu in 548. It was the emperor's intention to install Paramārtha at the head of a translation bureau and initiate a program of large-scale translation, but a rebellion against Emperor Wu which broke out in the same year prevented this plan from materializing. The unsettled times now ushered in a period of wandering life for Paramārtha, for we find him traveling from one place to another in south China. In spite of such abnormal conditions he was still able to translate a considerable number of sutras.[4] He was not at all happy with this sort of peripatetic life, however, and several times expressed a wish to return to his native India, but was dissuaded each time by the urgent pleas of his followers. In 562 he actually boarded a ship for India, but a storm forced the boat to stop at Canton. It happened that the prefect of Canton at the time had known Paramārtha previously, and this official with his son urged him to remain in the city. Touched by such a display of hospitality and earnestness, Paramārtha decided to do so, and upon the request of the prefect completed some of the most important of his translations of sutras belonging to the Vijñānavādin or Idealistic School. These included the *Viṁśatikā* (*Treatise in Twenty Stanzas*) and the *Mahāyānasaṁgraha* (*Compendium of the Mahāyāna*). With the completion of these translations he remarked to a disciple that he was satisfied with his work and harbored no more regrets. A few years later, however, in 568, another period of depression must have occurred, for it was said that he actually was on the point of committing suicide and was

---

[4] A few of the more important translations were *Suvarnaprabhāsa* (Golden Light), finished in 552; *Madhyāntavibhāgaśāstra* (*Discourse on the Discrimination Between Middle and Extreme*), finished in 558; *Vajracchedika* (*Diamond Cutter*), finished in 562.

prevented from doing so only by the prompt action of his devoted followers. After this, some of these followers thought that a change of scenery might improve Paramārtha's outlook, and suggested he return to the capital, Chien-yeh. But this plan was thwarted by monks in the capital who were jealous of his learning and reputation. The following year he became ill and died at the age of seventy-one.

Through his translation of sutras belonging to the the Vijñāna-vādin School, such as the *Samgraha, Madhyāntavibhāga,* and the *Vimśatikā,* Paramārtha performed the very important task of introducing the idealistic teachings of the Indian masters Asanga and Vasubandhu[5] to the Chinese Buddhist world. It was unfortunate that he arrived in China and labored during a period when conditions were not conducive to the propagating of his teachings. However, the volume of his translations, over three hundred *chüan* in all, testifies to the diligence, conscientiousness, and faithfulness with which he and his disciples pursued their labors.[6] Through their efforts the way was paved for the development of the Fa-hsiang or Idealistic School during the T'ang Dynasty by Hsüan-tsang and K'uei-chi.

## ANTI-BUDDHIST PROPAGANDA DURING THE SOUTHERN DYNASTIES

With the encouragement furnished by the various rulers of the Southern Dynasties, Buddhism gradually began to win more and more converts among the Chinese. In order to take care of the

[5] Asanga and Vasubandhu were two brothers who formulated the doctrines of the Idealistic School in India. Their dates are uncertain. Some scholars assign them to the fourth century; others, to the fifth. Asanga was the elder brother and was responsible for converting Vasubandhu from Hīnayāna to Mahāyāna Buddhism. Before his conversion Vasubandhu composed the *Abhidharmakośa* (*Treasury of the Higher Subtleties*), which is the best summary of Sarvāstivādin doctrines. It is held by some scholars that there are two Vasubandhus, the earlier one being the Mahāyāna master and the later one the Hīnayāna master. The problem has not yet been satisfactorily resolved.

[6] Of Paramārtha's disciples, the one who contributed most was Hui-k'ai (518-568), who assisted him as recorder and copyist. Another outstanding disciple was Fa-t'ai (6th cent.), who followed Paramārtha from Chien-yeh to Canton and after his master's death introduced his teachings to Chien-yeh. Finally there were Ching-sung (537-614) and T'an-chien (542-607), who were instrumental in transmitting the teachings of the *Samgraha* to north China.

increased number of monks more temples were constructed throughout the region. A source of the T'ang Dynasty furnished the following figures concerning the growth of the monastic community in south China:

| Dynasty | Number of Temples | Number of Monks |
|---|---|---|
| Eastern Chin | 1,768 | 24,000 |
| Liu Sung | 1,913 | 36,000 |
| Ch'i | 2,015 | 32,500 |
| Liang | 2,846 | 82,700 |

In north China during this same period the religion was much more popular, for during the Northern Wei Dynasty the total number of clerics converted was said to be two million. The growth of this alien religion inevitably evoked opposition from the native religions, Taoism and Confucianism. It is interesting to note that this opposition took different forms in north and south China. In the north such opposition took the form of persecutions, one in 446 and another in 574-577. In the south the opposition appeared in the form of treatises attacking Buddhism on various grounds. Though the controversy was heated and forceful, it remained on the level of verbal warfare. In all likelihood this was due to the fact that the ruling dynasties in south China were generally weak, and that south China was now the center of Chinese culture, a situation brought about by the influx of scholars and gentry from north China seeking to escape the oncoming barbarians. Being steeped in the Confucian tradition of moderation, the scholars in the south did not resort to force to settle their differences of opinion with the Buddhists. For the moment attention will be directed to these anti-Buddhist attacks in the Southern Dynasties; we shall leave the discussion of the persecutions in the north for a later chapter. The discussion here will center around three individuals—Ku Huan, Fan Chen, and Hsün Chi.

Ku Huan's dates have been given as 390-453, but this appears to be incorrect, for his biography indicates that he was still alive in 483. According to this biography, his family was so poor that it could not afford to send him to school, but he overcame this handicap by standing outside the schoolhouse and memorizing what was being recited within. His treatise against Buddhism was entitled *I-hsia-lun* (*Treatise on the Barbarians and Chinese*), the main thesis of which was that since Buddhism was a foreign religion, it was inferior to the Chinese systems and hence not acceptable. Ku Huan was not the first to put forth this point against Buddhism. It had been raised in the *Mou-tzu* and also by Wang Tu in his memorial to Shih Hu. Ts'ai Mo, 312-385, had also written that Buddhism was the custom of the barbarians. Ku, however, expanded this point into a long discussion.

In his treatise Ku Huan criticized the foreign customs of cutting off the hair, wearing loose robes, squatting on the floor like a fox, and cremating the body of the deceased. In contrasting Buddhism with Taoism, he said that the former was mainly a religion to destroy evil, while the latter was one to cultivate goodness. To quote his words: "Buddhism originated in the land of the barbarians, is that not because the customs of the barbarians were originally evil? The Tao originated in China, is that not because the habits of the Chinese were originally good? . . . Buddhism is not the way for China; Taoism is not the teaching for the western barbarians."[7]

Ku's aim was to show that the Indian nature and customs were evil and different from those of the Chinese, hence Buddhism, having originated in India, was not suited to the Chinese. This idea that the Indians were evil was something new that seemed to have arisen during the Chin Dynasty, for it was not mentioned in the Han writings. Ho Ch'eng-t'ien (370-447) put this difference between the Chinese and the Indians in very graphic language: "The Chinese were by nature good and gentle, embracing benevolence and righteousness, hence the Chinese sages Chou-kung and Confucius taught them to practice their nature. The Indians on the other hand were by nature hard and unbending, indulging in the pleasures of the senses, and surly. Therefore, the Buddha had to specify the five monastic rules to restrain them."[8] In the Taoist work *San-p'o-lun* (*Treatise on the Three Destructions*) we find this argument stated in a novel manner: "The barbarians are without benevolence, unyielding, violent and without manners, and are not different from birds and beasts. . . . They are also coarse and uncivilized. Desiring to exterminate their evil progeny, Lao-tzu ordered the males not to take wives, and the females not

[7] K. Ch'en, "Anti-Buddhist Propaganda," *Harvard Journal of Asiatic Studies*, 15 (1952), 172.
[8] *Ibid.*, 172.

to take husbands. When the entire country submits to the teaching of Lao-tzu, they will be exterminated as a matter of course."[9]

## FAN CHEN

Ku Huan may be considered as the individual who relied on a nationalistic bias to attack Buddhism. Fan Chen, the Confucianist, on the other hand, based his arguments on intellectual grounds. The point of opposition between the Buddhists and Confucianists centers on the former's contention of the indestructibility of the soul—that there is a soul which does not disappear at death but continues to transmigrate through successive rebirths and to assume a new form in each rebirth. The Confucian attitude is summed up in the saying, "Not yet knowing life, how can one know about death?" From the third to the fifth centuries a spirited discussion between the Buddhists and Confucianists took place on the relation of the soul to the body.

The Buddhist viewpoint may be found as early as the third century in *Mou-tzu*, where the interrogator states his disbelief in the Buddhist teaching that a man is born again after death. The author Mou-tzu replies that even in Chinese practices, after a person dies, someone goes up to the roof to call back the soul of the departed one—a fact which indicates that though the material body has passed away, the soul still remains. He compares the body to leaves and stalks, and the soul to seeds. The leaves and stalks might wither and die in the winter, but the seeds continue to live forever to produce new life.

In the fourth century Hui-yüan wrote his treatise *Shen-pu-mieh-lun* (*On the Indestructibility of the Soul*), in which he took over the passages from *Wen-tzu* and *Chuang-tzu* to bolster the Buddhist idea of the soul. From the former he quoted approvingly: "While the body dissolves, the spirit does not change. With the unchanging spirit availing itself of the changing body, there is no end to the transformations." From *Chuang-tzu* he extracted the following: "To have attained to the human form is a source of joy. But in the infinite evolution, there are thousands of other forms that are equally good." Hui-yüan felt that these philosophers knew the truth that life is not exhausted in one in-

[9] *Ibid.*, 173, with slight changes.

carnation. To complete his argument, he referred to the favorite simile of the fire. The transmigration of the soul is like the transmitting of fire from one piece of wood to another. Although the wood is different, the fire is the same; in like manner, the body may be different, but the soul is the same. Only an ignorant person, after seeing the body decaying, would think that the soul as well as the body had perished.

The Confucian viewpoint was expressed by a former Buddhist monk named Hui-lin, who wrote a *Pai-hei-lun* (*On Black and White*), in which he severely attacked Buddhism. Hui-lin is described as one versed in Lao-Chuang philosophy and the Confucian classics, proud, haughty, and unfaithful in his adherence to his religion. He thought that Buddhism was wrong in teaching that souls live through endless transformations, for such a matter as life after death is beyond our sight and hearing, and therefore should not be discussed. Secondly, he said that Buddhism was originally a religion to suppress cravings. Now, however, the religion depicts hells to frighten people and paints rosy pictures of the paradises to attract the multitudes, so that the ignorant long for rebirth in one of them. Instead of extirpating cravings, this religion has increased them.

Closely related to this question of the soul was the Buddhist doctrine of karma. The Confucian viewpoint was that a heavenly mandate, *t'ien-ming*, controlled the fate of kingdoms and men, and that there was little that man could do about it. According to Tai An-kung of the Chin Dynasty: "Wisdom and foolishness, good and evil, longevity and early death, failure and success, all have their predestined fate, and are not brought about by the accumulation of good or bad karma. . . . When a man is born, his nature has already been determined. The meritorious ones are naturally meritorious, they are not born first and then perform good deeds to attain meritorious rewards." As evidence that there was no karma at work, he wrote, "There are some sunk deep in evil but are not punished; some have accumulated merits but have encountered misfortunes; some have acted humanely and righteously, but have lost their lives; others have been oppressive and dissolute, yet blessings have befallen them."[10]

The eminent monk Hui-yüan answered this charge with the

[10] *Ibid.*, 179.

treatise *San-pao-lun*, in which he argues that the fruits of karma are spread over many lives, so that the dissolute man who appears to be blessed in the present life will inexorably reap the consequences of his evil deeds in his future rebirths. The Confucian Ho Ch'eng-tien (370-447) joined in this controversy by writing in his *Ta-hsing-lun* (*On Apprehending the Nature*) that man should be differentiated from animals. Man has natural endowments and can attain divine intelligence, so that he should not be compared with insects and fishes. Fowls, birds, and animals are created to be used by man, and there is no evil karma attached to the killing of such living beings. Going farther, he speaks of the domestic goose swimming on a clear pond and eating only grass, rarely if ever touching the living creatures that wriggle about, but it is sooner or later taken by the cook and killed, whereas the swallows hovering above and feeding on flying insects are welcomed and loved by man. This goes to prove, he argued, that the one which kills living creatures receives no evil retribution, while the meritorious one reaps no good reward. He was answered by the Buddhist layman Liu Shao-fu, who wrote that good and evil karma are inevitably rewarded, that it is only because people are not able to see or hear what has gone on in the past or will come in the future that they oppose karma.

This brief historical review of the Buddhist-Confucianist controversy brings us to Fan Chen, a contemporary of Prince Chingling and Emperor Wu of the Liang Dynasty. It was probably during the time he was associated with the prince that he wrote his attacks against the Buddhist doctrines of karma and the indestructibility of the soul. He was undoubtedly aroused to the attack by the prevailing pro-Buddhist sentiment in the court, for he wrote that "Buddhism was detrimental to the government and the *śramanas* were corrupting the customs," that the people were "exhausting their fortunes to attend to the monks and going bankrupt in flattering the Buddha." He also felt that the Buddhist monks were "frightening people with the miseries of Avīci hell, enticing them with their empty words, and delighting them with the joys of Tushita Heaven. . . . As a result, families have abandoned their dear and beloved ones, and people have terminated their line of descendants."[11] For these reasons Fan felt that

[11] *Ibid.*, 181.

if he could disprove the fundamental tenets of karma and the soul, he would have struck a mortal blow against Buddhism.

First, with respect to karma, Fan claimed that birth and death, flourishing and withering, all followed a natural sequence, and that there was no need for the operation of karma. When Prince Ching-ling asked him how he accounted for the high and low, the rich and poor in society, he replied: "Human lives are like flowers blossoming forth from the same tree. They are blown by the wind and fall from the tree. Some brush against screens and curtains and fall on rugs and mats, some are stopped by fence and wall and fall on the manure pile. Those that fall on rugs and mats become Your Highness. Those that fall on the manure pile become my humble self. The high and low follow different paths; where does the operation of karma come in?"

His attack on the Buddhist conception of soul was presented in the *Shen-mieh-lun* (*On the Destruction of the Soul*), the central thesis of which is as follows: "The soul is the same as the body, the body as the soul. If the body exists, the soul exists, and if the body fades away, the soul disappears. The body is the substance of the soul; the soul is the functioning of the body. When we speak of the body, we mean its substance; when we speak of the soul, we emphasize its function. The two cannot be differentiated from each other. The soul is to the substance what keenness is to the knife; the body is to functioning what the knife is to keenness. The designation 'keenness' is not the knife, the designation 'knife' is not keenness. But take away keenness and there is no knife; take away the knife and there is no keenness. We have never heard of a knife disappearing and the keenness being preserved. How can the body disappear and the soul still remain?"[12]

The Buddhists lost no time in refuting Fan Chen. Hsiao Ch'en set out to prove that Fan was wrong in his analogy that the relationship of the soul to the body was like that of keenness to the knife. He argued that the keenness of the knife is due to the effects of the whetstone. If we blunt the edge of a knife, it loses its keenness, and its usefulness as a knife is destroyed, but the knife itself still remains. Therefore, it is not possible to say that when the keenness is lost, there is no knife. He also sought to disprove Fan by referring to the experiences in a dream. When

---

[12] *Ibid.*, 182.

a subject is dreaming, his body is like a piece of dead wood; it does not know when it is called, nor does it feel when it is touched. The soul, however, may be flying in the clouds or wandering in places thousands of li away. Since the body does not move, how could such a situation arise if it were not for the soul separating itself from the body?

Another Buddhist, Ts'ao Ssu-wen, sought to refute Fan by referring to the Confucian tradition. The *Book of Filial Piety*, he said, records that formerly Duke Chou sacrificed to Hou-chi, the great ancestor of the Chou people, as the correlate of heaven in the suburbs, and worshiped King Wen in the ancestral temple, as the correlate of Shang-ti. If the body and soul are both destroyed at death, then who, Ts'ao asked, are being paired with heaven and Shang-ti? Now you say that Hou-chi had no soul, and yet you have Chi paired with heaven. Would that not be deceiving heaven? Suppose, as Fan argued, there is no soul of Chi; then you would be pairing nothing with heaven, in which case you would be deceiving heaven as well as mankind. Thus the teachings of the sage would be deceitful; how could such a teaching reach the hearts of filial sons?

That Fan Chen's treatise constituted powerful propaganda against Buddhism was evidenced by the fact that even Emperor Wu felt impelled to answer it. He had the treatise circulated and solicited refutations from his ministers and officials: in all sixty-two replied, all but four opposing Fan Chen.

## HSÜN CHI

From Fan Chen we turn to Hsün Chi, who charged that Buddhism was guilty of sedition because it was undermining the imperial state. Like Fan, he was also a contemporary of Emperor Wu of the Liang Dynasty, and his animosity against Buddhism was undoubtedly aroused by the unstinting support accorded the religion by the emperor. It is also likely that this animosity was intensified by a grudge he bore against the emperor for the latter's unwillingness to appoint him to office. The highly critical memorial he wrote against Buddhism was entitled *Lun-fo-chiao-piao* (*A Memorial Discussing Buddhism*). At the outset of this memorial he criticized Buddhism for having brought about all the disorders of the period of disunity. Since the gentry fled to the eastern reaches of the Yangtze, the barbarian religion has flourished on the soil of China, causing affectionate relations between father and son to be severed, right conduct between prince and minister to be perverted, harmony between husband and wife to be neglected, and trust between friends to be broken. For over three hundred years there has been confusion within the seas.[13] He claimed that the Buddha was descended from barbarians who had been expelled from China, and that he was a perverse and violent person. Hsün based this charge on a rare meaning of the character *fo* which in a passage of the *Book of Rites* was interpreted to mean "to turn back, to oppose, to go contrary to." He likewise claimed that when Viḍūḍabha, king of Kosala, massacred the Sakyan clan, the Buddha merely stood by watching and did nothing to help. When he was alive, he was not able to help his kinsmen; after his death how could he save others?

Hsün Chi also charged that the alien religion had shortened the duration of the Liu Sung and Southern Ch'i Dynasties; that the monks and nuns were parasites, since they did not cultivate the land nor did they weave cloth; and that by their refusal to marry they were cutting off their procreative functions, a practice that was contrary to nature and deprived the country of needed man power. They were also overbearing toward their prince and contemptuous of their parents. Though they did not marry, they practiced adultery, child-killing, and abortion. They said that they valued the lives of all living creatures; yet in building temples and erecting stupas they crushed ants and worms, and they exterminated their illegal offspring without hesitation. If the Buddha were as full of love and compassion as the Buddhists claimed, then why did he permit such adultery and taking of life? If, being fully enlightened, he could merely look upon but could not prevent such deeds, then he would be of no benefit to living creatures, and the world could not be enlightened by such a one.

However, Hsün Chi's most serious charge was sedition. He listed seven specific charges that: (1) the Buddhists were imitating the imperial quarters with their monasteries and temples; (2) they were translating and circulating seditious works in dis-

13 *Ibid.*, 185.

respect of the imperial mandates; (3) they were soliciting contributions for exemption from punishment in hell, thus usurping the sovereign's power of imposing penalties and punishment; (4) the Buddhist designation of the three months for fasting each year, and six days each month, was an attempt to set up another calendar in opposition to that of the dynasty; (5) they implied the existence of hardship and suffering in the royal domain by portraying the peace and joy of the Buddha lands; (6) they regarded the great bell in the temple courtyard as a substitute for the clepsydra in the imperial palace; and (7) they hoisted banners and pennants that imitated the imperial insignias. In this manner Hsün seized upon common Buddhist practices and interpreted them in such a way that they were looked upon as seditious activities. He repeated the criticism he made at the beginning—that Buddhism was reducing the Confucian code of social relationships to a state of confusion.

This strongly worded broadside against Buddhism infuriated Emperor Wu. The emperor decided to execute Hsün, who escaped secretly, however, to the north, where eventually he was put to death for complicity in an assassination attempt. His essay was undoubtedly the most critical attack against Buddhism up to that time.

Fortunately for Buddhism, these attacks in the south were confined to words written on paper and did not result in any overt action at restricting or impeding the development of the religion. In spite of such attacks progress was achieved. The primary emphasis among the monks in the south, as indicated by the prevailing interest in the *Nirvānasūtra*, the *Satyasiddhi*, and the *Mādhyamikaśāstra*, was on the doctrines and the teachings of the religion. This heritage of religious and philosophical discussions and speculations was to be transmitted over to the T'ang Dynasty, when it was to play an important role in the flowering of the different Chinese schools of Buddhism that appealed more to the mind than to the heart of the Chinese.

# CHAPTER VI

# BARBARIAN ACCEPTANCE: NORTHERN DYNASTIES

I N north China during the period of the Northern Dynasties the most powerful state was that ruled by the Northern Wei Dynasty (386-534), founded by a T'o-pa people whose ethnological origins are still uncertain, though they are usually said to be Turkic. Under some able and vigorous rulers the Northern Wei Dynasty was able to swallow up the numerous petty kingdoms in the north, so that by 440 it controlled an empire that embraced all of north China. After unifying the north, the T'o-pa rulers began to adopt Chinese civilization and culture, and set themselves up as defenders of the Chinese way of life against the barbarians. This Northern Wei Dynasty collapsed in 534, to be divided into two states, the Eastern Wei (534-550) and the Western Wei (535-557); these in turn were succeeded by the Northern Ch'i (550-577) and then the Northern Chou (557-581), all of which were non-Chinese in origin. By 577 there were two ruling houses, the Northern Chou in the north and the Ch'en in the south. The time was ripe for reunification and this was achieved by the Sui Dynasty in 589.

## EARLY NORTHERN WEI RULERS AND BUDDHISM

The territory conquered in the beginning by the first ruler of the Northern Wei, T'ai-tsu, embraced areas where Fo-t'u-teng and his disciples had carried on their evangelical work, and hence contacts with Buddhist institutions were soon established by the T'o-pa army. T'ai-tsu was already acquainted with Buddhism, for he ordered his army not to violate or pillage Buddhist temples and monasteries. A more positive indication of his attitude toward Buddhism was his invitation to Seng-lang to become his adviser. In this respect the ruler was merely following the pattern set by many other non-Chinese rulers in the north. Lang died before he was able to accept the invitation. Another indication of the ruler's attitude was the edict issued in 398, which read: "The rise of Buddhism took place a long time ago. Its meritorious deeds of help and benefit mysteriously reach the living and the dead. The divine examples and rules which have been bequeathed can truly be relied upon. Therefore it is decreed that in the capital the officers shall erect and adorn images and prepare dwellings that the adepts of Buddhism may have a place to stay."[1]

Since Seng-lang did not live long enough to serve as imperial adviser, another monk, Fa-kuo, described as pure in conduct and versed in Buddhist literature, was chosen by T'ai-tsu as chief of monks during the period 396-398. In this post Fa-kuo exercised administrative control over the monastic community in north China, with his subordinates scattered throughout the realm to carry out the orders of the central authorities. He was thus a member of the governmental bureaucracy, whose duty it was, as with any other functionary, to reverence the ruler in the accepted fashion. But the Buddhist scriptures were emphatic on the point that monks should not bow before their parents or rulers. To solve this dilemma Fa-kuo took refuge in a bold doctrine—that the ruling emperor T'ai-tsu was the Tathāgata in person, so that when he offered his respects to T'ai-tsu, he was not reverencing the earthly ruler but the Tathāgata himself. It is likely that another factor played a part in determining this attitude of Fa-kuo. In north China the Buddhist community was in the position of a group conquered by the non-Chinese T'o-pa people; they did not enjoy independent status as did the monks in south China. Consequently, they felt that they had to rely on the power and wishes of the conquering rulers to carry out their evangelical activities. The Northern Wei ruler in the very beginning executed a brilliant maneuver in appointing Fa-kuo as an imperial official, thus circumscribing him with official barriers and removing any possibility of an organization existing side by side with the imperial state.

---

[1] J. R. Ware, "Wei Shou on Buddhism," *T'oung Pao*, 30,127-128, with many changes. Although Ware's translation suffers from a number of errors which have already been pointed out by scholars, I have found it to be much more smooth and readable in style than that of Hurvitz, and I have therefore quoted from it here, after making the necessary corrections.

# EMPEROR WU AND PERSECUTION
# OF BUDDHISM

Under the reigns of the first and second rulers, T'ai-tsu and T'ai-tsung, imperial encouragement of Buddhism resulted in widespread adoption of the religion by the T'o-pa people and their Chinese subjects. During the reign of the third ruler, Emperor Wu or Shih-tsu (424-451), however, problems began to arise. Emperor Wu considered as his main objectives the expansion of the Wei frontiers and the subjugation of dissident factions within the empire. Consequently, he was too busily engaged in military campaigns to have any time for a serious study of Buddhism. Thus when the Taoist K'ou Ch'ien-chih (d.448) and his friend the Confucian minister Ts'ui Hao (381-450) began their campaign to convert Emperor Wu to their schemes, the ruler responded with alacrity, and a stream of events began which eventually led to the anti-Buddhist persecution of 446. It is usually thought that the Taoist K'ou played the major role in instigating this persecution, but this is not entirely correct; it appears that Ts'ui Hao was even more the culprit than K'ou.

Ts'ui came from a well-known Chinese family in the north; his father had served as an official under the first two Northern Wei rulers. He was learned in the practice of politics, thoroughly versed in the Confucian classics, and a master of astronomy and astrology. His astrological studies enabled him to make prophecies and interpretations of heavenly phenomena that won him the confidence of the rulers. For instance, a bright star appeared in 415 which terrified the emperor, but Ts'ui allayed his fears by explaining that it was the omen of the death of Yao Hsing. Upon the death of T'ai-tsung in 423, Ts'ui suffered a temporary setback, as his enemies in the court forced him out of office. He returned home to seek refuge in Taoism, and it was during this period that he met K'ou Ch'ien-chih.

K'ou the Taoist entertained the lofty ambition of establishing a holy empire on earth under the auspices of Taoism, with himself as the grand Taoist pope. He considered himself very fortunate in making the acquaintance of this most astute exponent of political strategy, who could certainly assist him in achieving his goal.

Ts'ui hoped that by praising and pushing K'ou to the attention of the throne he might himself be called back to office by the new emperor. Both went to the capital, where Ts'ui boasted highly of the ability and learning of his friend K'ou. Emperor Wu already knew of Ts'ui and his talents, and obligingly followed his suggestion by appointing K'ou to an official post.

Soon afterward, in 431, Ts'ui was appointed chancellor. In this post he served as imperial adviser, and played an important role in several successful campaigns against other non-Chinese states in the north, the most prominent one being that of 439 against the Pei-Liang kingdom in the northwest. This campaign met with considerable opposition in the Wei court, but Ts'ui advocated it, advised on the strategy, and the resultant success heightened his position immensely. He now became the indispensable political and military adviser, and was ordered to compile a record of the various expeditions as well as a history of the Northern Wei people. In order to fulfill his aim he appointed fellow Chinese to serve in governmental posts in the central government and Chinese governors and magistrates in the rest of the empire, despite the opposition of Crown Prince Huang. As a means of indicating the exalted position of the Chinese, he permitted his clansmen to marry only into Chinese families of similar social standing. Such measures very naturally aroused a good deal of opposition and antagonism against him among the T'o-pa people.

While Ts'ui was advancing his political fortunes, K'ou was not idle, and his campaign to elevate Taoism to supremacy proved so successful that by 440 Emperor Wu was won over to his cause. In 444 the emperor personally conducted a Taoist service to proclaim Taoism as the dominant faith in the empire. Thus K'ou's objective, which he set out to achieve in 424, was realized.

Although Ts'ui played a prominent part in boosting K'ou and Taoism, he had an entirely different objective in mind; this was the establishment of a Confucian state to Sinicize the barbarian T'o-pa people. His method to achieve this goal was to make the Confucian literati the ruling class. To this end he appointed as many Chinese as possible to governmental offices. He wanted to recreate the ideal feudal society so highly praised by Confucius, where the literati held all the power and where the masses of people remained ignorant but pledged loyalty to the rulers. Ts'ui, therefore, opposed Buddhism, since it was the religion of the barbarians. Moreover, Buddhism taught the equality and unity of all classes, withdrawal from society, exemption from taxation, and celibacy, all of which were contrary to his Confucian ideals. One might say that Ts'ui's antagonism to Buddhism was not entirely caused by the influence of his Taoist friend but stemmed in great part from his own political philosophy. It was on the advice of Ts'ui that Emperor Wu decided on the extreme measures of 446.

In 438 a decree was issued forbidding those under fifty to join the Buddhist community of monks. When the Northern Wei armies invaded Liang-chou in 439, a considerable number of monks joined in resisting the invaders. Some three thousand monks were taken prisoners, and Emperor Wu wanted to execute them, but K'ou Ch'ien-chih interceded on their behalf and had them placed in labor battalions instead. In 444 it was decreed that no one might support monks privately; the penalty for doing so would be execution. During the same year two leading Buddhist monks, Hsüan-kao (401-444) and Hui-ch'ung were executed. These events could be interpreted as signs that the persecution was already under way and needed only a spark to make it widespread and general. Such a spark was provided in 445.

In the winter of that year a certain Ko Wu organized a revolt in Ch'ang-an. Emperor Wu immediately set out from his capital in Ta-t'ung to suppress the rebellion and arrived in Ch'ang-an during the second month of 446. It was common practice for monks to plant wheat within the monastery grounds in Ch'ang-an, and, after the imperial armies arrived there, the horses were pastured in one of these fields. When some attendants came to examine the horses, one of the men stumbled into a side building where he found to his amazement large stacks of bows, arrows, spears, and shields. Discovery of these weapons infuriated Emperor Wu, who concluded that the monks must be supporters of Ko Wu. Thereupon he condemned all the monks in that particular monastery to death. Further investigation of the monastery grounds revealed large caches of wine stored there by the wealthy families of Ch'ang-an and also subterranean apartments where monks lived and debauched with women of good families.

With the discovery of such conditions Ts'ui Hao suggested not only the execution of all the monks of Ch'ang-an, but of all the monks in the entire realm. His suggestion was accepted by the emperor, who issued in the third month of 446 the following edict: "Let those in charge issue proclamations to the generals, the armies, and the governors that all stupas, paintings, and foreign sutras are to be beaten down and burned utterly; the *śramanas* without distinction of age are to be executed." The decree also spoke of eradicating the false and restoring the true. This remarkable statement appears to reflect Ts'ui's opinion that there was really no Buddhism as such even in foreign countries, and that what was presented as Buddhism in China was actually the fabrication of some rascals.

The extreme action called for in the decree was too drastic even for K'ou, who opposed the wholesale execution of monks. Other officials, notably the crown prince-regent, likewise presented memorials in opposition. Though these memorials went unheeded, they did delay the actual promulgation of the decree, and this gave the monks an opportunity to go into hiding, with many taking the sutras and Buddha images with them. Sutras and temples were destroyed, however. How many monks were actually executed will never be known.

In 448 K'ou Ch'ien-chih died, and two years after that, Ts'ui met a violent death. It is likely that a considerable amount of racial animosity against Ts'ui had been generated by his policy of appointing only Chinese to governmental offices, a feeling that was heightened by his belittling the exploits of even such a notable T'o-pa general as Chang-sun Fei. This racial antagonism was ready to erupt at any moment into violence. Ts'ui, it will be recalled, was entrusted with the compilation of a history of the Northern Wei people. As the stone tablets on which this history was inscribed were being transported through the city streets to the Temple of Heaven outside the city walls, the populace got a glimpse of the contents. They did not like what they read, for some passages exposed the evil-doings of the early rulers. Angered by such uncomplimentary accounts of their former emperors, they reported the matter to the emperor, who immediately ordered Ts'ui and his entire clan seized and executed. In all, 128 were put to death.

To the extent that K'ou Ch'ien-chih wanted to make Taoism the supreme faith of the land and influenced Emperor Wu to take measures against Buddhism, one might maintain that the persecution of 446 was a phase in the ideological struggle between Buddhism and Taoism. However, it is clear that the chief instigator of the suppression was Ts'ui Hao, who wanted to establish the ideal Confucian state in the north. Yet his wife, as well as his brother, were followers of the Buddhist monks. In this light the persecution of 446 was not merely a Buddhist-Taoist struggle but was also an episode in the Sinicization of a non-Chinese people. Ts'ui, good Confucianist that he was, wanted to Sinicize the T'o-pa people, and to him the foreign religion Buddhism had to be suppressed.

## RESTORATION OF BUDDHISM

With the passing of Ts'ui and K'ou the grandiose schemes which they advocated also collapsed. The measures against Buddhism, though still in effect, gradually were relaxed, so that it was possible to preach and recite the sutras in private homes in the capital. The emperor was said to have regretted the action he took against the Buddhists, and when he died in 454, the stage was set for a revival of the religion.

The new emperor, Wen-ch'eng-ti, lost no time in issuing a decree in the twelfth month of the same year granting Buddhism the freedom to carry on again. The degree starts by praising the Tathāgata who supports the prohibitions and regulations of the rulers, who enriches fellow feeling and knowledge, and who banishes all errors and propagates perfect enlightenment. Then it attempts to explain away the persecution of Emperor Wu by saying that while Buddhism flourished, there were some evil elements within the monastic order which the previous emperor wanted to eliminate. His ministers, however, mistook his intentions and applied the persecution to all. The decree, therefore, seeks to pass the onus of the persecution from Emperor Wu to his ministers. It then goes on to say: "Command is now given to the provinces, prefectures, and sub-prefectures that in each place which is thickly populated, it is permitted to build one stupa. No limit is set to the amount that may be expended. As for those who love and find pleasure in the doctrine of the Way and want to become *śramanas*, without distinction of age, if they come from a good family, if their nature and conduct are normally sincere and free from doubts and indecency, and if they are known in their villages, they may be permitted to quit their homes for the monastic life; as a rule, fifty individuals from a large province and forty from a small province. . . ."[2]

During the same year that Buddhism was restored, a stone figure of the Buddha in the likeness of the emperor was set up in the capital. After the figure was completed, it was found to have black spots on the face and feet, corresponding exactly to similar marks on the emperor's face and feet. This remarkable coincidence recalled an earlier statement made by Fa-kuo, that the emperor was the present-day Tathāgata, and the populace became even more impressed. Then in 454 the emperor ordered five bronze statues of Śākyamuni constructed in memory of his five predecessors, each one to be sixteen feet high. Since these figures were to be worshiped as though they were the five previous emperors themselves, it was easy to see that the revived Buddhism had the firm support of the imperial household. Not only this, but the religion itself came under the direct supervision of the state and was conducted in close connection with state policy. This could be seen in the administration of the Buddhist sangha, first under the chief of monks Shih-hsien (d. ca.460) and then under T'an-yao.

Shih-hsien was a native of Kipin who survived the persecution by posing as a medical doctor, and after Buddhism was revived received the tonsure personally from the emperor. The governmental bureau over which he presided was the *chien-fu-ts'ao* (Office to Oversee Merits), later changed to *chao-hsüan-ssu* (Office to Illumine the Mysteries) after the capital was moved from Ta-t'ung to Lo-yang. His deputy was named *tu-wei-na*. In the various provinces branch offices were established, known as *seng-ts'ao* (Sangha Office), presided over by the *chou-sha-men-t'ung* (Regional Chief of Monks) and his assistant *wei-na*, both appointed by the chief of monks in the capital and subject to his supervision. It was thus possible for the emperor, through his appointment of the chief of monks, to maintain close supervision over the entire Buddhist community in the realm. Moreover, the chain of command established by the system of offices in the

---

[2] *Ibid.*, 144, with some changes.

capital and provinces made it possible for a strong and powerful chief of monks, enjoying the support of the emperor, to utilize the power of the central government to direct and expand the activities of the Buddhist church. The individual who took advantage of this unique situation and opportunity was T'an-yao, who became chief of monks during the period 460-464.

## T'AN-YAO AND HIS ACTIVITIES

Not much is known about the early life of T'an-yao. Even his dates of birth and death are uncertain. His early years were spent in Liang-chou, and it is possible that he was among the Buddhist monks transferred to the capital at Ta-t'ung after the Pei-Liang kingdom was absorbed by the Northern Wei in 439. During the persecution he persisted in keeping his clerical garb, although he was urged strongly by the crown prince-regent Huang to return to laity. Upon the death of Shih-hsien he was elevated to the position of chief of monks, now designated as *sha-men-t'ung* instead of *tao-jen-t'ung*, which he occupied with distinction for the next twenty to thirty years.

T'an-yao's tenure of office occurred at a time when the Northern Wei rulers were all favorably disposed toward Buddhism, as were some of the leading families of the realm. Among these may be mentioned the Feng and Kao clans. The wife of Emperor Wench'eng, who as empress dowager, held power for about twenty-five years after the death of the emperor, was a member of the Feng clan. Another was Feng Hsi, older brother of the empress dowager, husband of the sister of the crown prince-regent Huang, and probably one of the most influential political figures of the period. Although a devout Buddhist, Feng Hsi was not very humane in his administration of governmental affairs. His biography records that the stupas and temples which he erected on inaccessible mountains took, in the building, the lives of many people and animals. When Buddhist monks urged him to suspend such activities, he is reported to have replied, "When these are complete, men will only see the stupas; how would they know that men and oxen perished?" In the Kao clan the outstanding figure was Kao Yün, political adviser to Empress Dowager Feng and onetime teacher of the crown prince. The various emperors under whom T'an-yao served all manifested their devotion to the Buddha by constructing ornate temples, erecting statues of the Blessed One, and inviting monks into the imperial precincts to discuss the dharma.

## THE SANGHA AND BUDDHA HOUSEHOLDS

One of the most important steps taken by T'an-yao to encourage the spread of Buddhism was the establishment of the Sangha and Buddha Households. The story of the formation of these households has been brilliantly recounted by Tsukamoto Zenryū in his book on Buddhism under the Northern Wei Dynasty, and our information is drawn mainly from that source. In 467 the Northern Wei ruler sent an expedition into what is now Shantung to subdue the cities of Li-ch'eng and Liang-tsou. After the surrender of these cities the leading families of the region were reduced to slavery and resettled in a region near the capital of Ta-t'ung. This move was actuated by two motives—to keep these Chinese leaders under close surveillance and to increase the agricultural population in the vicinity of the capital. After the Chinese were resettled in the north, they suffered severe hardships, reduced as they were to slavery when, before, they had been free people belonging to the upper classes. Some of the aristocratic families in the north sought to alleviate the sufferings and hardships of these people, but their efforts were too puny to achieve any real results. The plight of these unhappy people was brought to the attention of T'an-yao. T'an-yao as chief of monks was mainly interested in the spread of Buddhism, and for this task he needed labor and financial resources. He felt that if he could strengthen the economic foundation of the Buddhist sangha, he could carry out the propagation of the religion on a national scale.

Such considerations prompted him to think about requesting the transfer of control over the Chinese settlers from the imperial court to his monastic organization. He therefore presented a memorial suggesting that the Chinese families be organized into Sangha and Buddha Households. The memorial was approved by the emperor, and the two households came into existence during the period 470-476.

The Sangha Household was a unit consisting of a certain

number of families that had the responsibility of paying annually to the local sangha office sixty shih of grain; the sangha office was to hold this grain in stock and to distribute it to impoverished people during periods of famine. It also had the power to sell the grain when necessary, the proceeds to be used for religious purposes. The Buddha Household consisted of a group of criminals or slaves who were to cultivate the fields belonging to the monastery, or to do the manual work within the Buddhist institutions, such as sweeping the temple grounds, carrying water, and chopping wood. The aim was to utilize the labor of criminals for productive purposes, so that they would not be an economic burden on the state; while the objective of the Sangha Household was to promote agriculture and thereby provide the means to alleviate suffering during famine years. These institutions were therefore beneficial to the state, but they also served to strengthen and to promote Buddhism under the Northern Wei Dynasty.

That the Sangha Household came into existence at a critical time may be seen in the fact that in the years 466-470, 473, and 474, famines were recorded in north China. Of interest also was the fact that in 476 the emperor went to a newly finished temple and as part of the dedicatory ceremonies granted general amnesty to all convicts; the following year he freed all criminals who were under the death sentence. These freed criminals were then incorporated into the Buddha Households, which were being organized about this time.

With the Sangha and Buddha Households functioning, it was necessary to have a census of the monks and temples in the land. Thus for the year 477 there were 100 temples and some 2,000 monks and nuns in the capital, while in the entire country the figures were 6,478 and 77,258.

It is sometimes thought that the formation of the Sangha and Buddha Households provided the human and financial resources for the construction of the Yün-kang grottoes, to be discussed later in the chapter. However, Tsukamoto thinks that there was no connection between the two, since the households were established at a time when the work on the main Yün-kang caves had already been initiated.

Strictly speaking, the sangha grain presented to the *seng-ts'ao* was considered government property, not as property legally possessed by the sangha. However, since the control and dispensing of the grain were functions exercised by the monks, it is clear that in actual practice the grain was regarded as an item belonging to the sangha. The land which produced the sangha grain came to be regarded as tax-free property owned by the members of the households, a feature which contributed materially to the rapid spread of the Sangha Household. As has already been stated, the sangha grain was to be distributed during periods of famine to relieve the sufferings of the needy; during years of bountiful harvest the grain was to be accumulated and stored in the temples for use during emergencies. Some of the monks in charge of the local sangha offices could not resist the temptation to use the accumulated grain for private gain, and cases soon arose of such monks loaning grain and charging exorbitant rates of interest, or even selling it to rich merchants in the locality. Then when famines struck, there was no grain left in stock to distribute to the needy, while the rich merchants could charge whatever prices they wanted. As the compilers of the Shih-lao-chih wrote, "They have ruined poor and humble people without limit, and the cries of sufferings of the people have increased yearly and monthly."[3] To remedy this situation the throne in 511 decreed that "when loans are made in the future, the poor and needy shall be taken care of first. The rates of payment shall conform entirely to the old provisions. The rich may be permitted to borrow freely, and if they still expose themselves to excesses, they shall be punished by law."[4] The sangha grain might also be distributed for consumption by the monks during their retreat in the rainy season.

From the standpoint of the state, the Sangha and Buddha Households were regarded as instruments to encourage agriculture, or to open up new lands for cultivation. The years of conflict in north China had resulted in a reduction in the population, and much land was left uncultivated. The main policy of the Northern Wei was to revive agriculture, so that enough food might be produced to cope with the recurring famine years. The establishment of the Sangha and Buddha Households under the auspices of the Buddhist sangha thus fitted in admirably with state

[3] Ibid., 160, with some changes.
[4] Ibid., 161, with some changes.

policy. On the part of the sangha, the households provided the economic resources necessary to develop and to expand the activities of the religion. The membership of the households also constituted a potential pool of converts. Apparently any number of families might band together to form a Sangha Household, and after each household had contributed the sixty bushels of sangha grain annually to the local sangha office, the members enjoyed exemption from taxation.

Is there any scriptural basis that permitted the Buddhist organization to administer a Sangha and Buddha Household, to sell grain, or to utilize slaves? In Indian Buddhism we often read of kings, princes, or rich householders donating houses, gardens, fields, and animals to the sangha for the upkeep of the monks. Temples were able to carry on their activities very often on the income received from their landed property. T'an-yao undoubtedly had such precedents in mind when he petitioned for the formation of the households. However, *Vinaya* rules clearly prohibited monks from working in the fields; lay peasants or serfs would be needed to cultivate the soil. In the *Vinaya* of the Sarvāstivādins (*Shih-sung-lü, chüan* 34, which was the most popular *Vinaya* in north China), it is related that Bimbisara, king of Magadha, pardoned five hundred bandits and ordered them to work for the monastic community. This was just the precedent needed for the Buddha Household. The *Vinayas* of the various schools also specified clearly that monks were not permitted to carry on commercial activities for their own gain, but if such transactions were for the advancement of the dharma, they were permissible. Since the sangha grain was administered by the entire sangha acting through its officials, and the proceeds derived from the sale of the grain were supposed to be used for the furtherance of the religion, there was no contradiction here with the *Vinaya* rules.

In the mind of T'an-yao the Sangha and Buddha Households were to serve as means of strengthening the Buddhist religion, and there is every reason to believe that his hopes were justified. Upon joining a Sangha Household, a member undertook to observe the five cardinal precepts. In the case of the Buddha Households the former criminals and slaves, since they owed their changed status to the efforts of the Buddhist sangha, were encouraged to become converts and in some cases even to be ordained. The distribution of the sangha grain also provided a convenient means of increasing the number of lay adherents. Very naturally this act fostered a feeling of thankfulness and gratitude on the part of the recipient toward the donor and also toward the religion represented by the donor. The enormous growth under the Northern Wei, according to the figures of the Buddhist historians, could be attributed, in part at least, to the influence of these households. For instance, when the census of temples and monks was taken in 477, the average number per temple was twelve monks; but at the end of the dynasty, when the count was said to be 30,000 temples and 2,000,000 monks and nuns, the average number had risen to sixty-eight.

While these households promoted the welfare of the sangha and the state, they also produced some ill effects. Through their control and distribution of the sangha grain monks in the *seng-ts'ao* acquired power far in excess of that of other officials in the different localities, and this gave rise to considerable jealousy on the part of the latter. In some instances the households became havens for lawbreakers. During the closing years of the dynasty, when the breakup of the ruling house was imminent, the labor and military service required of all able-bodied adults became very severe, and many people took refuge in the Buddhist monasteries to escape this service. Under the leadership of rebellious individuals under the guise of monks, some formed bands of religious bandits which became increasingly active during the last few decades of the dynasty. Such defects of the households probably were widespread after 510. As to when the households were finally abolished, there is no clear record, although there is no indication that they survived after the Northern Wei Dynasty.

## BUDDHISM IN LO-YANG

During the first hundred years of its rule the dynasty had its capital in what is now Ta-t'ung in Shansi. In 494 Emperor Hsiao-wen transferred the capital to Lo-yang. To the emperor, Ta-t'ung was a favorable site if military considerations were predominant, but now he felt that military campaigns were no longer necessary. He regarded himself as not merely a barbarian emperor ruling the realm by force; rather he preferred to consider himself as the successor to the long line of Chinese emperors beginning with Yao and Shun. In order to fulfill this role as a civil ruler, using Chinese ideas as the unifying factor, he decided that he had to go to a region where Chinese culture was predominant, and no city was more suitable for this purpose than Lo-yang. Some opposition arose among the conservative court circles and the non-Chinese elements at Ta-t'ung, but the emperor pushed through the transfer, and, once the change was made, the process of Sinicization of the T'o-pa Wei people in their new environment proceeded rapidly.

Buddhism, which had taken firm root in the north, was also carried over into the new capital to start a fresh growth there, for Lo-yang had already had a long history of Buddhist connections. In the beginning Emperor Hsiao-wen favored the construction of only one temple and one nunnery within Lo-yang, but said that outside the city limits other temples might be constructed. However, popular demand soon modified this plan. Furthermore, in Ta-t'ung the Northern Wei had initiated and carried out a program of cave sculpture on a gigantic scale. After the imperial palaces in Lo-yang had been completed and life became more settled, the people, with memories of the magnificent and majestic images of the Buddha in Yün-kang still fresh in their minds, again turned their attention to rock sculpture. In a later section of this chapter this aspect of Northern Wei Buddhism will be treated in greater detail, but for the present the activities of the court in Lo-yang deserves attention.

Emperor Hsiao-wen, though a Buddhist at heart, wanted to place more emphasis on Confucian institutions and practices. His successor, Emperor Hsüan-wu, however, favored Buddhism. He was fondest of the *Vimalakīrti-nirdeśa*; consequently, the sculpture carved in caves during his reign at Lung-men frequently showed Vimalakīrti conversing with Mañjuśrī. Under him some notable temples were constructed in Lo-yang—the Yung-ming Temple, the Ching-ming Temple, and the Yao-kuang Temple, just to mention a few. Of these the Ching-ming Temple, with over a thousand cells, was built like a palace among hills and ponds, amid groves of pine and bamboo; it was said that though there were four seasons outside, inside there was no summer or winter.

The Ching-ming Temple is best known as the site where the images of the Buddha in Lo-yang were assembled preparatory to being paraded through the city. This procession was an annual event held on the eighth day of the fourth month, the birthday of the Buddha. On the seventh day all the statues in the city, over a thousand in number, were assembled; then on the eighth, amid a fanfare of music, chanting, and scattering of flowers, they were carried to the gates of the imperial palaces through streets lined with multitudes.

The Yung-ming Temple was constructed to serve as headquarters for foreign monks residing in Lo-yang. At one time over three thousand foreign monks from a hundred countries were said to be living in the monastery. If this figure is to be accepted, it is indeed the best indication of how popular Lo-yang was in the Buddhist world of that period.

The Yao-kuang Temple was built as a nunnery and was the place where girls of the royal family and the nobility took refuge if they decided to join the sangha. Because of this, the temple was described in contemporary literature as a gorgeous structure, profusely decorated in the interior. It became the object of much derision later among the inhabitants of the capital because of an incident that happened in 530. The story has it that during a raid of Lo-yang handsome barbarian cavalrymen forced their way into the nunnery and despoiled the nuns. After this episode the following couplet became very popular in the capital: "Hurry up, O men of Lo-yang, and braid your hair into a chignon, lest the nuns of Yao-kuang Temple seize you to become their husbands."

It was during the reign of Su-tsung, when the governmental powers passed entirely into the hands of Empress Dowager Ling, that Buddhism reached its apex under the Northern Wei Dynasty. Fortunately for posterity, the glories of the Buddhist temples in Lo-yang during this period have been graphically portrayed by Yang Hsüan-chih in his *Lo-yang chia-lan-chi* (*Record of the Monasteries in Lo-yang*), finished in 547. Emperor Hsüan-wu died in 515 at the age of thirty-three, and his son Su-tsung was only six when he was designated emperor. Under such circumstances, power gravitated into the hands of his mother. Her clansmen were all devout Buddhists. Her father, for instance, insisted on walking with the procession of statues during the celebration of 518, even though he was eighty years old at the time. When he died, probably of overexertion, the empress dowager arranged in his memory a vegetarian feast for over ten thousand monks. As was usual in Chinese history, the dowager had as her allies the eunuchs, who became rich and powerful and served as the chief patrons of the various Buddhist activities. There is no question but that the dowager was a remarkable woman. One of the stories told about her concerned an archery contest which she arranged for her courtiers. Most of them had become weaklings through their sedentary living and therefore were unable to shoot well; whereupon the dowager herself seized the bow and hit the bull's-eye. She seemed to have been just as energetic in her amorous affairs, for her lovers succeeded one another in rapid succession, each one powerful for the moment. She even killed her own son for fear he would become too independent. Her misdeeds finally caught up with her in 528, when she was seized and drowned. Yet this same remarkable woman was a devout Buddhist, just as another strong-minded ruler of a later age, Empress Wu Tse-t'ien, was to be.

The most outstanding Buddhist activity carried out by Empress Dowager Ling was the construction of the Yung-ning Temple in Lo-yang. When the capital was still in Ta-t'ung, the Northern Wei court had already erected a Yung-ning Temple there, in which a seven-storied pagoda, soaring over three hundred feet into the sky, was the tallest structure in the kingdom. The empress dowager decided to build an even more magnificent Buddhist edifice in Lo-yang. Work was commenced at a time when the country was still enjoying unparalleled prosperity. It was recorded that the treasures presented by the surrounding countries to the Northern Wei court were so bountiful that during the period 518-524 the imperial storehouses were stocked full of them, so full, in fact, that the empress dowager in a grand gesture of generosity opened the doors and permitted her courtiers to take away whatever they could carry. The commercial classes became so opulent that even their servants wore clothing of gold and silver brocades and embroideries.

With the country living in such luxury, nothing was spared by the empress dowager in the construction of the Yung-ning Temple. It is indeed fortunate that Yang Hsüan-chih preserved for later generations an eyewitness account of the splendors of the temple. Within its precincts was a nine-storied stupa rising ninety chang above the ground (each chang consisting of ten feet). On top of the stupa was a mast which soared for another ten chang and could be seen for a distance of a hundred li from the capital. On top of the mast was a golden jar which contained twenty-five smaller jars made of rare stone. Below the mast were thirty plates of gold to receive the evening dew. All around the tower were golden bells. The tower itself had nine layers of eaves (one for each story), and at each layer golden bells were suspended, 120 in all. The stupa had four faces, each face having three doors and six windows. The doors were varnished red, and on the leaf of each door were five rows of golden nails, in all 5,400 nails. During windy nights it was said that the ringing of the bells could be heard within ten li.

North of the stupa was the Buddha hall, which was shaped like the audience hall in the Imperial Palace. Within the hall were numerous statues of the Buddha made in gold and inlaid with pearls, with the tallest one about eighteen feet in height. It was said that the artistry involved in the decoration of these Buddhas was beyond description. The beams in the hall were beautifully carved, the walls wonderfully painted and decorated. The entire temple had over a thousand cells for monks. Juniper, cypress, and pine trees brushed the eaves of the buildings with their branches, while bamboo groves and fragrant grass covered the steps and courtyards. The images and sutras presented by foreign countries were all kept there. When the temple was at the height of its glory, it was seen by Bodhidharma, first patriarch of the Ch'an School in China, who said that he had never witnessed anything like it during his travels.

The construction of the Yung-ning Temple was but the most conspicuous example of temple-building during this period. Prince Ch'eng, in a memorial presented to the empress dowager in 518, claimed that by actual investigation he had counted five hundred monasteries in Lo-yang, not to mention the numerous stupas and pagodas still under construction. Moreover, he complained that such structures had usurped more than one third of the dwelling areas within the city. "No spot is without a monastery now. Either side by side they fill the interior of the city, or close upon one another they spread over the meat and wine markets. Three or five young monks may form one monastery; Sanskrit chants and the cries of butchers unite their echoes under contiguous eaves. The statues and stupas are wrapped in odors of meat; men's nature and the spiritual powers are submerged in lust and desire."[5] Yang Hsüan-chih estimated that there were about 109,000 households in Lo-yang at this time, with a population of about 500,000 to 600,000. Within the city he counted 1,367 temples, large and small.

The extravagance of the Yung-ning Temple practically exhausted the imperial treasury. The first sign of impending economic disaster was the rising price of gold, but this storm warning was not heeded by the court, whose moral fiber must have degenerated beyond repair. Rebellions soon arose, with the capital Lo-yang itself becoming the center of disorders. In 534 disaster struck at the Yung-ning Temple. Amid thunder and lightning, fire broke out within the temple, and so huge was the institution that the fire was said to have lasted three months.

After some years of these disorders, Yang Hsüan-chih again visited Lo-yang in 547; but, instead of the stately center of religion and culture it had been only a few years before, Yang saw only heaps of ruins and ashes, the nests of foxes, and the pasture land of cows. The bells of the thousand temples in Lo-yang were stilled forever. "Impermanent are all compounded things," so said the Buddha when he was about to expire. Nothing better illustrates the truth of this statement than the fate of the Buddhist establishments in Lo-yang at the end of the Northern Wei Dynasty.

Yet these same T'o-pa people, motivated by their religious faith in the dharma, carved out of the rocks in the Yün-kang and Lung-men grottoes what they considered to be permanent symbols of their devotion to the Tathāgata, symbols which have withstood the ravages of more than a thousand years of history. The Buddha image and the imposing Buddhist rock-cut sanctuaries stand before us even today as majestic monuments to the creative spirit of these people, inspired by their religion. Not a few of the museums of the West owe some of their most treasured stone images of the Buddha to the artists of the Northern Wei Dynasty.

[5] *Ibid.*, 171, with some changes.

# THE BUDDHA IMAGE IN CHINA

The earliest literary notice concerning an image of the Buddha in China occurs in the *San-kuo-chih*, where it is recorded that Chai Jung, an official in charge of grain transportation in East China ca.193, erected a bronze statue of the Buddha and coated it with gold. If this notice is reliable, then this statue is the first of its kind in China. Nothing further, however, is known about this figure. In the *Hou-Han-shu* there are several passages referring to the sacrifices carried out by Emperor Huan to the Buddha and Huang-Lao, but it is not clear as to whether images of the Buddha were involved here.

During the same Han Dynasty images of the Buddha appeared on the ornamented backs of bronze mirrors. Such mirrors were of two types—one with designs of deities and mythical animals, and the other with designs of the phoenix. Many mirrors of the first type have been unearthed in Japan; one specimen excavated from the Shinyama tomb in the Nara prefecture consists of six sections, with each section containing an image of the Buddha seated cross-legged on a lotus throne accompanied by a tiger. Another specimen has been found in a tomb in Tatsuoka-mura in Nagano prefecture; it has four sections and each section has two images of the Buddha, sometimes seated, sometimes standing. Some of the images have the *uṣṇiṣa*, or the cranial bump, clearly indicated. These two specimens are not dated, but two other mirrors of this same type excavated in Japan bear the date A.D. 240. Of the second type of mirror a specimen may be seen in the Boston Museum of Fine Arts, where the Buddha is seen with a halo and seated on a lotus throne.

The earliest dated statue now preserved is a gilt-bronze seated Buddha about 15¾ inches in height; this figure bears the date eighth month of the fourth year of *chien-wu* (338)—a fact which indicates that the statue was made in north China under the Later Chao Dynasty, since *chien-wu* was a reign title of that dynasty. Other gilt-bronze statues which probably belong to the same century have been found in north China, although they bear no dates. A few of these figures betray some non-Chinese features, such as a bearded face, large eyes, and massive jaws, all of which point to some foreign, presumably Gandhāran, influence. The earliest dated specimen belonging to the Southern Dynasties is also a gilt-bronze seated Buddha with a face very Chinese in appearance, carrying the date first day of the fifth moon of the fourteenth year of *Yüan-chia* (437). The inscription on the statue goes on to say that Han Ch'ien reverently made this statue in the hope that his father, mother, wife, and brothers would all have the privilege of encountering the Buddha.

Before the T'o-pa people started to cut their figures out of the rocks, they also fashioned gilt-bronze images of the Buddha. One such statue, the largest of this type, dated 443, stands about 21 inches in height and represents a standing Buddha. The accompanying inscription records that Yüan Shen made the statue in Hopei and that after he completed it, he prayed that his parents and friends would be fortunate enough to listen to Maitreya when the latter appeared on earth as the future Buddha.

## THE YÜN-KANG CAVES

The statues just described are some of the known images of the Buddha created in China just before the Northern Wei Dynasty commenced its large-scale rock sculpture in Yün-kang, about thirty li west of the capital of Ta-t'ung. The village of Yün-kang is situated at the foot of an abrupt escarpment named Wu-chou-shan; this escarpment became the theater where the Northern Wei artists worked.

The persecution of Buddhism under Emperor Wu in 446 and the revival of the religion after his death have already been discussed. With the appointment of T'an-yao as chief of monks ca.460, there began an outburst of activities that vitally affected the spread of Buddhism. We have already alluded to his role in the establishment of the Sangha and Buddha Households. Even before that he conceived of a bold undertaking of chiseling out of rocky walls of the Yün-kang grottoes images of the Buddha and bodhisattvas, a project that would combine the wealth and prestige of the ruling dynasty with the talents and techniques developed by Buddhists elsewhere. From the viewpoint of the dynasty the project was to serve not only as a sort of repentance for the persecution carried on under Emperor Wu, but also as a manifestation of imperial grace and favor to the religion. For the Buddhists the project was to be a memorial for the restoration of Buddhism, for such durable works of art cut out of the rocks were to serve as concrete symbols of the permanence of the dharma, inspiring future rulers to exert efforts to protect the law. They had seen how easily images of the Buddha fashioned in wood and metal had been destroyed during the persecution of 446, and they felt that only by creating images in rock would such symbols of the religion be preserved from destruction. Through this combination of official and monastic effort the project took shape during the reign of Emperor Hsiao-wen (471-499), but even before it was completed the dynasty transferred the capital to Lo-yang. For this reason the sculpture at Yün-kang represented the first phase of Northern Wei Buddhism, the phase when Buddhist art was still influenced by the techniques of India and Central Asia.

By this time a number of channels already existed for the possible introduction of foreign influences to Yün-kang. In 439 the Northern Wei armies had captured Liang-chou in northwest China. West of Liang-chou was Tun-huang, the point where the northern and southern overland routes converged. There in Tun-huang, as early as the middle of the fourth century, caves had already been dug out in the hills, some to serve as living quarters for traveling monks and some to serve as centers of Buddhist paintings. Among the monks transferred to Ta-t'ung from Liang-chou by Emperor Wu there undoubtedly were some artisans already familiar with the work of rock sculpture. West of Tun-huang were such regions as Khotan, Karashar, Kucha, Kashgar, all flourishing Buddhist countries with which the Northern Wei rulers maintained close relationships. Respect for the military might of the Northern Wei resulted in many of these states in Central Asia sending tribute to the T'o-pa court; since these countries were Buddhist, the presents sent undoubtedly included some Buddhist images and objects. Such was the case, for example, in 455, when monks from Ceylon presented three images of the Buddha. It would not be too farfetched an idea to suggest that such objects served as models for the T'o-pa artisans as they set out to carve their images of the Buddha.

The first group of caves in Yün-kang to be cut out by the sculptors comprised Caves 16 to 20 on present-day charts. Within these caves were carved five gigantic figures of the Buddha, some standing and some sitting, with the tallest figure rising to about 70 feet in height. The five Buddhas in these caves were looked upon as representatives of the five previous emperors (T'ai-tsu, T'ai-tsung, Shih-tsu, Kung-tsung, and Kao-tsung)—an idea formulated by Fa-kuo, who said that the rulers were the present-day Tathāgatas. During this first period the main objective was to construct huge, unbreakable statues to serve as permanent symbols of the dharma.

After these five caves were completed, T'an-yao then started activities on the next group, Caves 5-10. The make-up of these caves differed from that of the previous group. Here on the face of the walls were carved numerous images of the Buddha, bodhisattvas, musicians, devas, and donors. The scenes in Caves 9 and 10 deserve special mention, for they illustrate the contents of two sutras translated by T'an-yao and a foreign monk, Kekaya. One of these sutras describes the persecution of Buddhism by a king of Kashmir and the subsequent revival of the religion; it served to remind the Chinese Buddhists of their experiences suffered under Emperor Wu.

In this group, however, the most important are Caves 5 and 6. Cave 5 measures 72 feet 4 inches east-west and 58 feet 4 inches north-south, while Cave 6 measures 40 feet 1 inch east-west and 46 feet 8 inches north-south. These two are the most elaborately carved in the entire group of caves. Here one finds the entire Buddha legend depicted: the birth of the Buddha, the seven steps and the shout of victory, the nine dragons spitting water, the tests of strength with the Magadhan youths, the life of ease and luxury in the palaces, the trips to the pleasure garden and the four signs, the great renunciation, the ride out of the city on the horse Kanthaka, the separation from Kanthaka, the life of asceticism in the forest, and finally enlightenment. It is clear that this is the historical Buddha worshiped by the Northern Wei people, the Buddha who lived in the world and went about emphasizing the religious life, urging the people to recite the sutras, erect stupas and temples, and donate alms to the monks. In some of the other caves we find scenes based on the famous Mahāyāna sutra, Vimalakīrti-nirdeśa-sutra, where the wise layman Vimalakīrti is shown in conversation with the bodhisattva Mañjuśrī.

From inscriptions carved in some of the Yün-kang caves some

idea may be gained of the motives of the patrons who supported the project. Not only the imperial household, but also the common people provided the resources for this work. In Cave 11 was found such an inscription left behind by a group who sponsored the work there. The inscription was dated 483, and its contents may be summarized as follows: A group of fifty-four persons banded together to form a society for the promotion of rock sculpture. Because they had not yet accumulated enough meritorious karma in their past lives, they still remained in the cycle of rebirths; but now in this life they had listened to the teachings of the Buddha, who had led them out of the long night of ignorance. As a result, they had developed faith in the Buddha, and were now combining their resources to carve statues in his honor. In creating these statues the group prayed for three objectives: First, they prayed for peace and prosperity for the realm, also prosperity, honor, and longevity for the ruling house. May its power be like that of the universal monarch, may it spread the three jewels to all corners of the empire, and may no shortcomings ever befall the ruling house. Second, the group prayed that their deceased ancestors and their teachers and all their relatives might be reborn in the Pure Land, and live there without blemish and be nurtured by the lotus. If these ancestors or teachers should be reborn again, may they become a deity or a human being with all their needs fulfilled. If they should meet with misfortune and be reborn in the evil modes of existence, then may they be freed from the torments of misery. Third, the group prayed that all people in the village might from that time on be more faithful and sincere in their devotion to the Buddha, that they might be more diligent in spreading the religion, and that they might practice the career of the bodhisattva, thus to convert all sentient beings.

It is very likely that the sentiments expressed in this inscription were generally held by the people at that time. For one thing, the inscription is a good indication of how closely Buddhism was identified with the fortunes of the ruling house. This close relationship was also illustrated by the popularity of a sutra translated by Dharmakshema, entitled *Chin-kuang-ming-ching* (*Suvarna-prabhāsa*). In this sutra there is one section referring to the earnest wishes of the four heavenly kings. Should a country be attacked by foes or subjected to hunger and epidemic, the four heavenly kings pledged themselves to rally to the support and relief of that kingdom if its inhabitants would only read this sutra. Again, if the ruler of a realm would encourage monks and nuns to study and to esteem this sutra, then the heavenly kings would bring peace and prosperity and security to that realm, and the ruler himself would become respected and esteemed by his fellow rulers of other lands. From this, we see that the country, ruler, and people were all protected by the teachings of the Buddha, and, in turn, the dharma was to be protected and encouraged by the ruler and the people. The contents of the inscription reflected to a certain extent the sentiments expressed in this sutra.

One of the earliest, if not the earliest, writers to notice these Yün-kang grottoes was Li Tao-yüan (d. 527), who described the scene in his *Shui-ching-chu* (*Commentary on the Water Classic*): "On the banks of the Wu-chou stream there is a Jetavana monastery in rock and also a series of habitations in the grottoes where nuns live. The river then turns east and passes south of some marvellous cliffs. . . . The people have chiselled rocks and opened the mountains, and on the rocky cliffs they have fashioned true images of such gigantic sizes and grandeur as to be rarely seen in this world. The rooms in the mountains, the palaces along the banks of the river, and the smoking temples, all gaze at each other. The woods and springs, the brocades and the bells present themselves before the eyes to create an ever changing spectacle."[6]

The Japanese scholars Mizuno and Nagahira, who visited the site and studied the rock sculpture painstakingly during the Japanese occupation of north China, have written that the Yün-kang figures betray influences stemming from Gandhāra, central India, and Central Asia. They felt that the colossal images of the Buddha in Caves 16-20 must have been modeled after the gigantic statues at Bamiyan. For example, the Buddhas in Cave 18 are clothed in thin robes which cling to the body—a feature also found in the Bamiyan Buddhas. The treatment of the hair provides a good example of various influences at work. In the case of the Gandhāran Buddhas the hair is usually represented as wavy; such a feature is found in the large standing Buddha

[6] Li Tao-yüan, *Shui-ching-chu*, 13,12a.

in Cave 16. In the Mathurā School the hair is shown in spiral locks, and such a representation is found in some of the Buddhas at Yün-kang. Furthermore, there are also some examples of Buddhas with bald heads; such Buddhas are probably modeled after images in Central Asia. It is likely that from Central Asia came another feature seen at Yün-kang—the flaming nimbus. The ornamentation in some of the caves, such as the band of floral scrolls, a capital of acanthuslike design on a storied pillar, the guardian divinities with winged headdresses, also betray foreign influences. Likewise, the presence of divinities with many heads and hands, Śiva riding on a bull, Vishnu on a bird, may be regarded as examples of Indian motifs introduced to Yün-kang.[7]

We shall leave to the art historians a detailed discussion of the technical aspects of this Yün-kang sculpture, repeating only the verdict of that eminent French savant Grousset, who wrote, "The simplified folds of drapery, the softness of the forms, . . . the slenderness of the bust, the youthful elegance of expression, the brooding peace of the whole attitude, made these figures quite a striking artistic success. A profound charm emanates from them which Chinese Buddhist art was rarely to recapture."[8]

## THE LUNG-MEN CAVES

After the Northern Wei court was transferred to Lo-yang, the first few years were spent in constructing the palaces needed for the imperial administration. As soon as this phase was completed, the people remembered the magnificent cave sculpture of Yün-kang, and they began searching for a similar site near Lo-yang. They found such a site in Lung-men, a defile twenty-five li south of the city, formed by two chains of small mountains between which flows the Yi River. Beginning with Emperor Hsüan-wu, the chiseling of the caves began in Lung-men, to continue through the rest of the dynasty. Emperors, officials, monks, and laymen, all participated in the project to cut out of the hard rock niches filled with images of the Buddha, some small and others gigantic in size. With the termination of the Northern Wei Dynasty construction activities diminished for a while, but with

---

[7] Mizuno and Nagahira, *Yun-kang Caves*, 12,75ff.
[8] R. Grousset, *Civilizations of the East*, New York, 1934, 3,186.

the advent of the Sui and T'ang Dynasties, work was resumed on a large scale. Only during the reign of Hsüan-tsung (713-755) did the cutting finally cease, although there is some evidence to indicate that it continued until the Sung. The study of the Lung-men sculpture would reveal, therefore, a picture of Buddhism in China from the final days of the Northern Wei Dynasty through the Sui and T'ang and possibly the Sung.

Numerous attempts have been made to estimate the number of Buddha figures cut out of the rock at Lung-men. One count, by a magistrate of Lo-yang in 1915-1916, arrived at the figure 97,306, while a later enumeration totaled 142,289. Most valuable for the historian, however, are the inscriptions, some dated and some not, accompanying the images of the Buddhist deities. The earliest dated inscription in Lo-yang was put up in 495, just one year after the capital had been transferred from Ta-t'ung to Lo-yang. Using such dated inscriptions as sources, the Japanese scholar Tsukamoto Zenryū has arrived at some extremely interesting observations concerning the development of Buddhism in China during the years 500-750. First he drew up a table showing when and how many images were carved:

| Date | Images | Date | Images | Date | Images |
|------|--------|------|--------|------|--------|
| 495-500 | 7 | 570-580 | 11 | 650-660 | 141 |
| 500-510 | 59 | 580-590 | 1 | 660-670 | 93 |
| 510-520 | 51 | 590-600 | 1 | 670-680 | 59 |
| 520-530 | 65 | 600-610 | 0 | 680-690 | 77 |
| 530-540 | 40 | 610-620 | 3 | 690-700 | 45 |
| 540-550 | 6 | 620-630 | 0 | 700-710 | 61 |
| 550-560 | 6 | 630-640 | 5 | 710-720 | 24 |
| 560-570 | 6 | 640-650 | 66 | 720-730 | 6 |

Such a table shows that the periods of intensive rock-cutting occurred during the years 500-530 and 650-710. The first period covered years that were prosperous for the Northern Wei people in Lo-yang, while the second era corresponded to the time when Empress Wu Tse-t'ien was bestowing all kinds of favors on Buddhism. It was also the period when the Chinese pilgrims Hsüan-tsang and I-tsing were undertaking their prodigious translation efforts, and when the eminent teachers Tao-hsüan, Fa-tsang, and Shan-tao were propagating their doctrines.

Many of the inscriptions recorded the names of the deities carved. Using such data, Tsukamoto compiled the following table:

| Deity | Dated | Undated | Total |
|---|---|---|---|
| Amitābha | 133 | 89 | 222 |
| Avalokiteśvara | 82 | 115 | 197 |
| Śākyamuni | 61 | 33 | 94 |
| Maitreya | 49 | 13 | 62 |
| Kshitigarbha | 11 | 22 | 33 |
| Bhaishajyaguru | 3 | 12 | 15 |
| Mahāsthāmaprāpta | 2 | 3 | 5 |

Here one sees that Amitābha, Avalokiteśvara, Śākyamuni, and Maitreya were the most popular deities, with the first two occupying more than half the total. Pursuing the dated inscriptions still farther, Tsukamoto then arrived at this picture:

| Date | Śākyamuni | Maitreya | Amitābha | Avalokiteśvara |
|---|---|---|---|---|
| 500 | — | 3 | — | — |
| 510 | 14 | 10 | — | 1 |
| 520 | 11 | 11 | 1 | 3 |
| 530 | 11 | 8 | 6 | 10 |
| 540 | 7 | 3 | 1 | 8 |
| 650 | — | 2 | 11 | 6 |
| 660 | 5 | 4 | 40 | 18 |
| 670 | — | 1 | 26 | 5 |
| 680 | — | 3 | 11 | 7 |
| 690 | 3 | 1 | 15 | 8 |
| 700 | — | 1 | 9 | 8 |
| 710 | 2 | — | 6 | 4 |
| 720 | — | — | 2 | 4 |

In this table one notes that under the Northern Wei Dynasty the leading deities portrayed were Śākyamuni and Maitreya, numbering 43 and 35 respectively, whereas Amitābha and Avalokiteśvara played minor roles. Under the T'ang, however, the positions were reversed. After 650 Amitābha and Avalokiteśvara became predominant, while the importance of Śākyamuni and Maitreya diminished. During the Northern Wei period Amitābha was only one fifth as popular as Śākyamuni, one fourth as popular as Maitreya; but under the T'ang, Amitābha outnumbered Śākyamuni twelve times and Maitreya ten times. Together with Amitābha, Avalokiteśvara also increased in popularity. The reason for this shift in emphasis is not difficult to understand. During the seventh century such masters as Tao-cho and Shan-tao were actively preaching the Pure Land tenets in central China, and the increased popularity of these two main deities of the Pure Land School was immediately reflected in the sculpture at Lung-men.

Besides furnishing data about the deities carved out of the rocks, the inscriptions also preserved important information about the individuals and religious organizations which acted as patrons for the sculptural activities. The inscriptions can be divided into three groups: (1) those set up by the ruling class, such as the imperial family, officialdom, and the literati; (2) those set up by religious societies under the leadership of some Buddhist monk; (3) those set up by monks and nuns who were leaders of the Lo-yang community of Buddhists.

## INSCRIPTIONS BY THE RULING CLASS

As an example of the first group there is the inscription left behind by Yang Ta-yen in honor of Emperor Hsiao-wen. Yang was one of the heroic generals of the T'o-pa Wei armies, famous for his great speed on foot. It was said that he could run faster than a horse. The hair on his head was tied with a string thirty feet long, so that when he was running or riding, his hair and the string resembled an arrow flying through the air. He frequently led expeditions against the Liang Dynasty in the south, and on his return from one of these campaigns passed by the Lung-men caves and was so impressed with the grandeur of the sculpture that he decided to set up an image of Maitreya in honor of the emperor. The inscription he left behind recorded that as he "gazed all through the night at the bright and beautiful traces of former emperors and great sages, his tears flowed freely,"[9] and he was so affected that he decided to erect a stone statue on behalf of Emperor Hsiao-wen.

There is another inscription in this category set up in 498 by one of the sons of Emperor Hsiao-wen, which reads as follows: "In the eighteenth year of T'ai-ho (495), the eleventh day of the twelfth month . . . the imperial concubine while passing by the Yi River on her way home, made a vow to construct a statue of Maitreya to be placed there. . . . On the twenty-third day of the ninth month, the twenty-second year of T'ai-ho (498) the divine statue was entirely chiselled. I arranged for a vegetarian feast, and I made an inscription on the rock to manifest my sentiments and to signal the execution of the vow of my mother. My constant desire is that my mother and I will enjoy eternally the

---

[9] Z. Tsukamoto, *Shina bukkyōshi kenkyū: Hokugi-hen*, 461.

years during which conversions will prevail, that my relatives on both paternal and maternal sides will live always in glorious epochs, and that all living beings will share in the blessings of this vow."[10]

As seen from the inscriptions, the usual motive for the ruling class or nobility in creating the images of the Buddhist deities was to honor the emperor or to perpetuate the memory of some deceased kinsmen. However, they also prayed for the prosperity of the dynasty and the empire, for the glory of the dharma, for the longevity of the present members of their clan, and for the happiness and welfare of all people.

## INSCRIPTIONS BY MONKS

The statues and inscriptions left behind by monks and nuns at Lung-men are very numerous, and of the inscriptions seventy-two bore dates of the period 498-534. The most popular deities set up by this group were Śākyamuni and Maitreya. Some personal motives were usually behind the erection of images by the nuns, such as the loss of a son or daughter or husband, which had led to the nun's departure from household life. Among the inscriptions left by monks, one of the most important was that of Hui-ch'eng, a distant cousin of Emperor Hsiao-wen. He had a statue carved in honor of his father, Duke Shih-p'ing, and in the inscription he said he wished that his father might attain rebirth in the Tushita Heaven, but that if he should be reborn on earth, he might be reborn as a high official or a famous individual. He also recorded that in gratitude for imperial favor he would commence cutting out other images in the caves. This inscription was dated the fourteenth day of the ninth month, 498.

As an example of inscriptions left by nuns, there is the following, dated the fifteenth day of the eighth month, 531: "The nuns Tao-hui and Fa-sheng respectfully made the statue of Prabhū-taratna. Having in view the benefit of their ancestors for seven generations, of their own parents, of the monks who had been their teachers, and of those related to them, they wished that these people would not fall into the three evil modes of existence, that they would be speedily delivered, that they might at present

[10] *Ibid.*, 433-434.

enjoy peace and security, and that all living beings might benefit also from this vow."[11]

## INSCRIPTIONS BY RELIGIOUS SOCIETIES

The third group of inscriptions were those set up by religious societies under the leadership of some monk or nun. Throughout Chinese history the written records concerning Buddhism have been largely compiled by those who could read and write the classical language, and these writings focused attention mainly on the religious ideas and practices held by the educated group. Buddhism appealed not only to these upper classes, however, but also to the common people. Here in these inscriptions of the religious societies one catches a glimpse of this large and important group of Buddhist devotees among the ordinary common people.

To be sure, the contents of the inscriptions do not tell much about the religious life of these people. We do know that during the Northern Wei period monks were active in traveling about and living among the people to preach the dharma. The practice became so widespread that apparently there were some abuses, for, according to edicts issued by the government, the populace was called upon to hand over to the government any monk who did not have the proper official certificate permitting him to preach. These traveling monks were instrumental in organizing religious societies among the people and serving as their advisers. When the movement to carve statues in Lung-men got under way, these societies lost no time in joining with the activities.

One inscription tells of a group of two hundred members who banded together to chisel out a statue of Śākyamuni in 502. Another inscription, dated the thirtieth day of the fifth month, 502, records the efforts of a group of thirty-two members, under the leadership of a certain Kao Shu, in carving a stone image. Thus for one fleeting moment these thirty-two individuals, whose names appear at the end of the inscription, enter onto the stage of history to perform their bit, then disappear into obscurity again.[12]

[11] E. Chavannes, *Mission Archéologique dans la Chine Septentrionale*, Tome 1, Deuxième Partie, Le Sculpture Bouddhique, 416-417.

[12] These societies were usually called *she* or *i*, with the leader of the society designated as *i-chu* and the members *i-tzu*. If the society created

On the basis of the contents of these inscriptions, the following seem to have been the purposes and motives behind the creation of the images in Yün-kang and Lung-men: (1) to acquire merits leading to rebirth in the Pure Land of Amitābha or the Tushita Heaven of Maitreya; (2) to attain bodhi or enlightenment; (3) to thank the Buddha for the fulfillment of certain wishes; (4) to obtain certain material benefits, such as wealth, position, longevity, et cetera; (5) to express gratitude for recovery from illness; (6) to assure success in a military campaign.

## THE KU-YANG AND PIN-YANG CAVES

The most important of the Lung-men caves were the Ku-yang-tung and Pin-yang-tung. In point of time the images in the former cave were chiseled out first, for the earliest inscriptions there were all dated prior to those in the latter. Of these dated inscriptions, seven were put up by members of the ruling family, eleven by officials, eleven by monks, seven by nuns, and six by religious societies. Śākyamuni and Maitreya were the chief deities portrayed here in the Ku-yang-tung, with the strong likelihood that the carving of these images was based on such sutras as the *Saddharma* and the *Vimalakīrti*. More imposing and magnificent was the sculpture in the Pin-yang cave, which was sponsored by the imperial family. Here are seen the images of emperors and empresses advancing to pay their respects to the Buddha, presented in a sitting posture flanked by two bodhisattvas, Maitreya and Prabhūtaratna, and by two monks, Ānanda and Kāśyapa. The addition of the two monks, who belonged to the Hīnayāna tradition, is significant, for it may be interpreted as the artist's attempt to show that both Hīnayāna and Mahāyāna were the teachings of the same Buddha.

Of even greater interest is the fact that the sculpture in this Pin-yang cave is based on two widely known Jātakas, the *Sudāna-jātaka* and *Mahāsattva-jātaka*. Chinese translation of the former Jātaka already existed in a number of versions. According to its contents Sudāna, out of boundless compassion, gave sixty state elephants to an enemy country. For this act he was banished from

---

a statue, then the leader was called *hsiang-chu*. This title was usually conferred upon the individual who contributed most toward the statue's construction. For instance, one inscription dated 519 stated that the leader contributed 9000 cash, while the members contributed 100 cash each.

the country for ten years by his father-king. As he traveled to the mountains with his family, he gave away first his earthly belongings, then his own children, and finally his wife to Sakka who came in the disguise of a Brahman. After these gifts had been made his meritorious karma matured, his family was restored to him, and he was recalled to take over the kingship from his father. Even his enemies were now converted by his acts of charity and compassion, so that during his reign his realm and subjects enjoyed peace and prosperity. After his death he was reborn in Tushita Heaven; then he took rebirth on earth as Śākyamuni the son of Śuddhodana. Such was the theme of the *Sudāna-jātaka*. In India, scenes from this Jātaka were illustrated in Sanchi, Amarāvatī, and Gandhāra, where they were undoubtedly witnessed by the pilgrims going back and forth between China and India. Sung Yün and Hui-sheng, who traveled to India in 516-523, wrote that they visited the spot where Sudāna gave away his children as servants to a Brahman, and reported the tradition that when the children clung to a tree, refusing to leave, the Brahman whipped them with a stick, so that blood from the wounds stained the ground. The Chinese travelers wrote that a spring now marked the spot. At Pin-yang cave the sculpture portrayed the scenes of Sudāna and his family going to the mountains.

Like the previous Jātaka, the *Mahāsattva-jātaka* also existed in a number of versions during the Northern Wei period, with the account translated by Dharmakshema in the *Suvarnaprabhāsa* as the most popular. According to this birth story the bodhisattva and two brothers were walking through a wooded area when they saw a tigress so tormented by hunger that she was about to devour her own cubs. The bodhisattva, after sending his brothers on, jumped to the ledge where the tigress was and offered his own body to satisfy her hunger, thus saving the life of the tigress as well as the cubs. In the Pin-yang cave the scene portrayed is that of the bodhisattva divesting himself of his clothes and preparing to leap.

## STATE OF BUDDHISM

What do the inscriptions and sculpture tell about the state of Buddhism under the Northern Wei Dynasty? In the first place, they tell us that the objects of veneration were Śākyamuni and Maitreya. It appears, however, that the Buddha as portrayed in Yün-kang was not conceived in the same light as the Buddha in Lo-yang. In Yün-kang the scenes portraying Śākyamuni are mainly concerned with biographical details—his conception, birth, renunciation, enlightenment, and nirvāna. This was the Buddha as the human teacher, the earthly sage who by his own efforts attained Buddhahood. As opposed to that, the Buddha in Lung-men is portrayed as supramundane or *lokottara*, and his enlightenment was attained by the accumulation of merits extending back into countless rebirths in the past, merits arising from the exercise of unlimited charity and compassion. At Yün-kang the Buddha was closely linked with the ruling emperor, in accordance with the prevailing doctrine that the earthly ruler was the Tathāgata in person, but in Lung-men the Buddha appears as the savior of all mankind, with the emphasis being placed on his dharma as the spiritual message for all ages.

The popularity of Maitreya is easy to understand. During the Northern Wei period there already existed a large number of sutras in Chinese devoted to a description of Maitreya as the future Buddha. Moreover, one of the most influential monks who ever lived in north China was Tao-an, and it is likely that the Maitreya cult which he and his followers organized was still popular among the populace in that region. Such faith in Maitreya had a twofold aspect. First there was devotion to the deity as a bodhisattva, waiting in the Tushita heaven to be reborn on earth as the next Buddha. As part of this there was the earnest wish to be reborn in that heaven so that the devotee might be able to meet Maitreya face to face. Then there was belief in Maitreya as the future Buddha here on earth. As part of this there was the earnest wish to be reborn on this earth at the time when Maitreya makes his descent, so that the individual might hear the teachings direct from him and benefit from the peace, security, and prosperity that he was to bring to earth. It was also hoped that this descent would occur during the reign of the Northern Wei Dynasty, so that Maitreya would make use of that dynasty to pacify and unify the world.

In the second place, the inscriptions and figures at Lung-men indicated definitely that the brand of Buddhism practiced by the

Northern Wei people in Lo-yang was Mahāyāna. This is seen in the stress laid upon such Mahāyāna virtues as compassion and charity in contrast to the Hīnayāna ideal of self-discipline and aloofness from society. The two Jātakas illustrated at Pin-yang cave exemplify these virtues of self-sacrifice and altruism, and they must have struck a responsive chord among the Northern Wei people. In the inscriptions, whether by nobility or commoner, there is repeated again and again the earnest wish that salvation may be attained by all living creatures. This is especially significant when it is realized that in the society of that period social cleavages between the classes were the rule rather than the exception. Such a sentiment demonstrates clearly the all-pervasiveness of the Mahāyāna message of universal salvation among the Northern Wei people.

Thirdly, the inscriptions frequently mentioned the well-being, prosperity, and longevity of the ruling emperor. These sentiments indicate the close relationship between the religion and the state; in fact, one might say that Buddhism was the state religion of the Northern Wei Dynasty. This close relationship is also indicated by the sculpture of the Pin-yang cave, sponsored entirely by the members of the ruling family, which depicts the emperor and empress paying their respects to the Buddha.

Fourthly, the frequent references to filial piety in the inscriptions testify to the change that had taken place in Buddhism after its introduction into China. Buddhism started as a religion renouncing all family and social ties; yet in the inscriptions one meets again and again with prayers for the well-being of departed ancestors, uttered even by monks and nuns. These expressions of piety indicate that although the monks and nuns had joined the monastic order, their ties to family and ancestors still remained strong and enduring. This is a specific example of how Buddhism had adapted itself to contemporary social conditions in China.

Lastly, it is perhaps justifiable to say that during the Northern Wei Dynasty Buddhism was finally able to reach large numbers of the common people and to hold their attention. For the previous Wei Chin era, there is an adequate amount of information about the acceptance of the religion among the educated circles, the gentry, and the nobility, but very little about its reception among the masses of people. This interest among the upper classes was centered on the philosophical aspects of Buddhism and was manifested by the study of the Mahāyāna sutras and discussions of their teachings concerning the absolute and its relation to phenomenal activities. Such discussions were possible only when the monks were highly educated and familiar not only with the teachings of Buddhism but also with those of Neo-Taoism and Confucianism. In the north, however, the main preoccupation was with the religious life, based on a deep and sustaining faith that the Buddha through his vast love and compassion would safely ferry all sentient creatures across the sea of misery to the other shore of salvation. During the Northern Wei period this faith, which encouraged taking refuge in the Three Jewels and living a pure religious life, was beginning to claim the attention not only of the upper classes but also of the common people. This is best illustrated by the statues which these people created in such prodigious numbers and on such a gigantic scale, and by the contents of the inscriptions in which they expressed their devotion to the Buddha and Maitreya. It is also reflected in the rapid increase in the number of monks and temples—two million and thirty thousand by the end of the dynasty. One can truly say that Buddhism had begun to take root on Chinese soil and, enjoying this wider base of support, was ready to advance into its golden age.

## BUDDHIST STUDIES IN NORTH CHINA

Even while the devotional aspects of Buddhism were being emphasized by the Northern Wei people, the literary and doctrinary aspects were not being neglected. After Dharmakshema translated the *Mahāparinirvānasūtra* in north China, interest arose in that area concerning this text with its stress on the eternal, joyous, personal, and pure nature of nirvāna.[13] This sutra was regarded by the Chinese Buddhists as embodying the final and ultimate

[13] One of the leading figures who kept this interest alive was Hui-kuang (468-537), who inspired a succession of disciples to study and to write commentaries on the sutra. For example, one of these, Fa-shang (495-580), became converted to Buddhism after having read the sutra at the age of nine, and he in turn transmitted the teachings to Hui-yüan (523-592). At the end of the Northern Dynasties, the most famous Nirvāna master in the north was T'an-yen (d.588), who composed a commentary on the sutra in 15 *chüan*, and whose disciples all became well known during the Sui and T'ang Dynasties.

doctrine of the Blessed One, since it was preached just before entry into nirvāna. Starting from this viewpoint, the Chinese developed the idea that the Buddha must have preached other doctrines earlier in his life. Such an idea led the Chinese Buddhists to undertake the task of organizing and classifying the Buddhist scriptures according to periods and doctrines. By assuming that all the sacred scriptures, Hīnayāna and Mahāyāna, were preached by the same Buddha in different periods of his life, the Chinese Buddhists attempted to bring some order of the vast and amorphous body of literature with its numerous contradictions and discrepancies. The aim was to bring the different streams of thought propounded in the various texts under a central and unifying principle. It is not known just when the practice started, but Hui-kuan (d. between 424 and 453) already had an idea of three doctrines: sudden, gradual, and indeterminate. Such classification, known as *p'an-chiao* or dividing the periods of teaching, became popular in the north during the latter part of the Northern Wei Dynasty; indeed, seven schemes in all were said to exist. To a considerable extent, the activity was stimulated by the appearance of a sutra forged in ca.460 by a certain T'an-ching, entitled *T'i-wei Po-li ching* (*Sutra on Trapuśa and Bhallika*), in two *chüan*, which elicited great interest among the common people because it prescribed a course of religious discipline for the layman written in simple popular language. According to this forged sutra the Buddha first preached it to Trapuśa and Bhallika, the two leaders of the five hundred merchants, and only afterward did he preach the rest of the sutras to his followers in the Deer Park. A certain Chinese lay convert, Liu Ch'iu (438-495), was drawn to this sutra and used it as the basis to divide the Buddha's teachings into two categories, sudden and gradual, with the latter again being subdivided into five chronological periods. The sudden doctrine, according to this view, was preached by the Blessed One immediately after enlightenment, but its contents were so abstruse and mysterious that the listeners could not understand anything. Consequently, the Buddha decided to preach his sermons in accordance with the intellectual capacity of the audience, starting with the simple sutras in the beginning and progressing to the more difficult and profound scriptures as his audience became more advanced and ready to understand and accept them. The fivefold classification according to chronology was as follows:

| Doctrine | Sutra |
|---|---|
| 1. Doctrine of men and gods | *T'i-wei Po-li ching* |
| 2. Doctrine of substantiality | *Āgamas* (Scriptures) |
| 3. Doctrine of nonsubstantiality | *Prajñā-sutras* and *Vimalakīrti* |
| 4. Doctrine of common destiny | *Saddharmapundarīka* (*Lotus Sutra*) |
| 5. Doctrine of eternity | *Nirvānasūtra* |

Another classification frequently mentioned at this time was that of the four doctrines, said to have been initiated by Hui-kuang. These were:

| Doctrine | Sutra |
|---|---|
| 1. Doctrine of cause and effect | *Abhidharma* (Higher Subtleties |
| 2. Doctrine of temporariness | *Satyasiddhi* (Completion of Truth) |
| 3. Doctrine of nonreality | *Prajñā-sūtras* |
| 4. Doctrine of reality | *Nirvānasūtra* |

These traditions were carried over to the succeeding dynasty and formed the basis of the T'ien-t'ai system of classification, which will be discussed in greater detail later.

Another equally popular work in the north at this time was the *Shih-ti ching-lun* (*Daśabhūmikasūtraśāstra, Treatise on the Sutra Concerning the Ten Stages*) of Vasubandhu, translated ca.508 by Bodhiruci and Ratnamati. This work is a commentary on the *Shih-chu ching* (*Daśabhūmikasūtra, Sutra of the Ten Stages*), a text already translated by Kumārajīva which described the ten stages through which a bodhisattva proceeded to his goal. Masters of the *Shih-ti ching-lun* (usually abbreviated as *Ti-lun*) were at the same time keen students of the *Avataṁsakasūtra* (*Garland Sutra*) since the section on the ten stages which formed the object of Vasubandhu's elucidation is to be found in the eighth *chüan* of Buddhabhadra's translation of the *Avataṁsaka*, finished in 418-420. For a century after its appearance in China the *Avataṁsaka* did not attract much attention in either south or north China, and it aroused interest only after the *Ti-lun* had become popular. Thus many of the *Ti-lun* masters were also experts on the *Avataṁsaka*. Later, when the Avataṁsaka or Hua-yen School was established in the T'ang Dynasty, those monks who belonged to the *Ti-lun* tradition quickly became affiliated with it.

It was during the latter part of the sixth century that Para-mārtha's translation of the idealistic text *Mahāyānasaṁgraha* was introduced into the north, where it soon elicited considerable interest in monastic circles. The same sixth century also witnessed the beginnings of the Pure Land and Ch'an Schools in north China. Bodhiruci, initiator of the *Ti-lun* tradition, was also a teacher of Pure Land doctrine, and it was he who in ca.530 converted T'an-luan (476-542), the first active disseminator of Pure Land tenets and practices in north China. Likewise, Bodhidharma was in north China at about the same time, transmitting his teachings to his disciple Hui-k'e.

To sum up this discussion, interest in the sangha during the latter years of the Northern Dynasties was centered mainly on the *Nirvāṇasūtra, Daśabhūmikasūtraśāstra, Avataṁsakasūtra,* and finally the *Mahāyānasaṁgraha*. Followers of the *Daśabhūmika* tradition occupied a key role, for they were the forerunners of the later Hua-yen School. The *Daśabhūmika* also belonged to the Idealist tradition, and its popularity prepared the way for the spread of the Fa-hsiang School during the T'ang Dynasty. Likewise, the various schemes for classifying the scriptures led directly to the T'ien-t'ai School with its more systematic and thorough-going arrangement of the sutras. Thus, in almost every instance, the glorious flowering of the different schools of Chinese Buddhism during the T'ang had its roots in the developments that took place under the Northern Dynasties.

## CHAPTER VII

# PERSECUTION AND TRIUMPH: NORTHERN CHOU AND SUI DYNASTIES

BEFORE Buddhism was to reach its apogee during the Sui and T'ang Dynasties, there was to be yet another attempt by a ruler to suppress the religion. For the background of the persecution of 574-577, it is necessary to go back to the fourth century, when an acrimonious debate started between the Buddhists and Taoists over the problem of priority. The Taoists claimed that after Lao-tzu disappeared beyond the western passes, he really went to India, where he converted the barbarians and became the Buddha. Such a contention would make the Buddha inferior in position and posterior in time with reference to Lao-tzu. This contention was developed very early, for it was mentioned in the memorial presented in 166 by Hsiang K'ai. At the beginning of the fourth century this Taoist contention appeared in the form of a sutra entitled *Hua-hu-ching. (Sutra on the Conversion of the Barbarians)*, by Wang Fu.

To answer the charge that Lao-tzu was anterior to the Buddha, the Buddhists began to invent their own dates concerning the birth of their master. The earliest writer to put forth a date was Hsieh Ch'eng (third century A.D.), who claimed that the Buddha was born in 687 B.C.

## BUDDHIST-TAOIST DEBATE

In the year 520 a historic debate over this question of priority, in which the antagonists were the Taoist Chiang Pin and the Buddhist T'an-wu-tsui, was held in the presence of Emperor Hsiao-ming of the Northern Wei Dynasty. Chiang opened the debate by declaring that Lao-tzu was born in 605 B.C., that he went west to convert the Buddha in 519 B.C., and that the Buddha was his attendant at the time. When asked for the source of this statement, he referred to a *Lao-tzu k'ai-t'ien ching (Sutra on the*

*Opening of Heaven by Lao-tzu*). In the present Taoist canon there is a sutra by this title, but it makes no mention of Lao-tzu's going west to convert the barbarians.

In claiming that Lao-tzu was born in 605 B.C., Chiang Pin did not go so far as another Taoist, Huang-fu Mi (215-264), who wrote that Lao-tzu was born in the twelfth century B.C. Later Taoists pushed the date even farther back, for in the *Hua-hu-ching* found in Tun-huang it is recorded that Lao-tzu was conceived during the reign of King Yang-chia of the Shang Dynasty (1408-1401 B.C.).

To answer Chiang's charge that the Buddha was born after Lao-tzu, the Buddhist T'an-wu-tsui contended that the Tathāgata was born on the eighth day of the fourth month, 1029 B.C., and entered nirvāna on the fifteenth day of the second month, 950 B.C. When asked to state his sources, he mentioned the *Chou-shu i-chi* (*Record of Anomalies in the Chou-shu*) and the *Han-fa-pen-nei-chuan* (*Esoteric Record of the Origin of the Law During the Han*). These two works are no longer extant, but quotations from them may be found scattered in various Buddhist sources. It is generally agreed that they were forged prior to 520 by the Buddhists to bolster their claims. The dates 1029-950 B.C. are so much at variance with history that a word is necessary here to explain why the Buddhists proposed them. As has been mentioned, one of the charges leveled against Buddhism after its introduction to China was that it was ill-omened and shortened the duration of dynasties. It was to counteract this charge that the Buddhists forged texts purporting to show that the Buddha lived from 1029 to 950 B.C., and that his religion was introduced to China shortly after his nirvāna. The motive for assigning the date of introduction to the early Chou was very clear, for the Chou Dynasty lasted over eight hundred years and provided just the answer needed to refute the charge of the anti-Buddhist critics.

Besides countering the Taoists' contention that Lao-tzu was anterior to the Buddha, the Buddhists also refuted the charge that their master was a disciple of Lao-tzu. They did this by forging sutras which purported to show that in reality Lao-tzu was a disciple of the Buddha. One of the earliest sources to develop this idea was the *Cheng-wu-lun* (*Treatise to Correct*

*Falsehoods*), by an unknown author. This treatise was probably compiled during the Eastern Chin Dynasty and introduced Lao-tzu as the disciple of the Buddha. Much more detailed was another forged work, the *Ch'ing-ching fa-hsing-ching* (*Sutra to Propagate the Clear and Pure Law*), which declared that "the Buddha dispatched three disciples to China to transmit the teachings and to convert the people. The bodhisattva Ju-t'ung was called K'ung Ch'iu (Confucius) by the Chinese; the bodhisattva Kuang-ching was called Yen Yüan (a disciple of Confucius); and Mahākāśyapa was called Lao-tzu."

As an aftermath of the debate of 520, the emperor appointed a committee of over 170 scholars headed by Wei Shou, compiler of the dynastic history of the Northern Wei, to examine and investigate the claims of Chiang Pin and the *K'ai-t'ien-ching* to which he referred. In its report to the emperor the committee concluded that Lao-tzu had bequeathed to posterity only the 5,000-word classic *Tao-te-ching* and no other literature, and that Chiang's assertion concerning the *K'ai-t'ien-ching* was without foundation. The emperor wanted to execute Chiang for misleading the people with his erroneous statement, but the Buddhist monk Bodhiruci interceded on the Taoist's behalf and, instead, he was banished.

## EMPEROR WU'S ATTITUDE TOWARD BUDDHISM

This defeat was not at all palatable to the Taoists, and the controversy waxed even hotter until the time of the dramatic events under Emperor Wu of the Northern Chou Dynasty, who reigned from 561-577. In the beginning it appears that Emperor Wu wanted Buddhism to carry on as usual in order that he might accumulate meritorious karma. At heart, however, he was not happy about the widespread popularity of the foreign religion. Though the Chou ruling house was of non-Chinese origin, he wanted to demonstrate that he was fully Chinese in his thinking and action, and so adopted all things Chinese. To him the foreign religion, Buddhism, was inimical to Chinese customs and institutions and should be opposed. However, he did not deem it wise to give verbal expression to this opposition to the foreign religion because of the influential power which Buddhism wielded over the minds of his subjects.

Buddhist sources inform us that Emperor Wu was opposed to Buddhism because of his fear that the Buddhists might usurp the throne. In north China at this time there was prevalent among the populace a prophecy that wearers of the black garment would occupy the throne. Rulers of the Northern Ch'i and Northern Chou were ever mindful of this prophecy. For instance, Emperor Wu once asked a leading monk who would follow him on the throne. The monk answered that he had no idea. Emperor Wu replied that, according to current rumors, wearers of black would usurp the throne and, since the Buddhist monks wore black, they were suspect. The monk vigorously denied any such designs on the part of the Buddhists. When the emperor persisted in asking who the black ones would be, the monk replied that *wu*, or crows, were black, so were *ta-tou*, black beans; could these usurp the throne? When the emperor found that there were people surnamed Wu and Tou, he had them executed on some flimsy excuse.

Such rumors about the wearers of black undoubtedly existed at the time, but the Buddhist argument that Emperor Wu turned against Buddhism because of this rumor was unfounded. In the first place, wearers of black were quite common among the people and officials. As for Emperor Wu's executing people surnamed Wu or Tou, the historical records do not support such charges. Under the Northern Chou Dynasty one of the famous families was that of Tou Ch'ih, a faithful minister whose sons and grandsons all occupied important posts in the government. Of the fourteen sons in the family, only one was known to have been executed for some crime. This certainly does not sound like the charge that the emperor exterminated people with the surname Tou. The source of Emperor Wu's antagonism and his later persecution against Buddhism must, therefore, be sought elsewhere, with the most likely culprit being someone whose activities have not been very well known, Wei Yüan-sung.

## WEI YÜAN-SUNG

Wei was a native of Szechuan. In his youth he dabbled in the occult sciences, the arts of divination, and prognostications. Being

one who had no predilection for productive work to gain a livelihood, he joined the Buddhist order as a novice, where he came
under the influence of an eccentric master named Nameless
Monk. One of the things that Nameless Monk taught him was
that if he wanted to become famous, he must act like a madman.
So Wei feigned madness whenever he came in contact with objects or persons, bursting into song or uttering some predictions
concerning the future. He soon felt that Szechuan was too remote
a place for him to exercise what he considered to be his considerable talents; so he left his native province to go to the
capital of the Northern Chou Dynasty, Ch'ang-an, in quest of
fame and fortune. At this time visitors from outlying areas had
to present a document to gain entry into the capital. Though
Wei did not possess such a document, he presented himself in
the guise of a layman at the city gate, and when he was stopped
by the guards there, he replied that he was a servant in the employ of a certain family in the city, and that he was trying to run
away. The guard obligingly returned him to that family, whom
Wei had known in Szechuan. By this clever stratagem Wei not
only gained entry into the capital but also a place where he could
stay while he plotted his future.

After a short while in Ch'ang-an, Wei found that the ranks of
the official hierarchy were not so easily breached, for they were
open only to the scions of powerful and influential families. Since
Wei came from a poor family in an obscure corner of the empire,
he could hardly expect to attract attention in the court. But, being
ambitious and arrogant, he felt that he must do something to make
a name for himself in the capital.

As he looked around, he found that Buddhism was the most
popular religion there. Ch'ang-an was and had always been one
of the main Buddhist centers in the north. Though Wei at this
time was still a member of the Buddhist community, by no
stretch of the imagination could he be called a pious and devoted
follower of the dharma. Soon in the fertile and scheming mind
of this clever individual a plan of action was beginning to take
shape. To gain a name for himself, he thought, what better way
was there than to present a memorial against the religion which
was enjoying so much support in the capital. The emperor might
not adopt some of his proposals against Buddhism, but they

would at least stir up some discussion, and his name would be on the lips of all those who counted in the government.

Once having decided on this course, Wei presented his memorial to the throne in 567. In this memorial he charged that undesirable elements had entered into the monastic community; to weed out such elements, he proposed that the community be screened and purged. He also opposed the worship of stupas and images, saying that the stupas did not increase the merits of the people or the state, and that their construction had wasted wealth and labor, and had thus impoverished the land and people. He also argued that the Buddha was not to be found in the wooden or clay images, so that there was no point in worshiping such images, which, he wrote, should be destroyed instead.

In his memorial Wei contended that the greatest fundamental virtue of Buddhism was its teaching of compassion. Instead of letting this be the special property of the Buddhist church, he proposed to extend it throughout the entire empire. To this end he put forth his most important proposal, the establishment of a great all-inclusive church to embrace everyone in the populace. "Sung proposes that a great all-inclusive church be established, which would include within it all the people in the realm. He does not advocate the establishment of a narrow prejudiced institution just for the safekeeping of the scriptures. In this all embracing church, there would be no difference between monks and laymen or between those who are proficient or ignorant of the law. Let the temples of the walls and moats be turned into the temples and stupas, and let the Chou ruler be the Tathāgata. The cities and towns shall be the quarters for the monks, harmonious husbands and wives shall be the holy congregation, the virtuous ones shall be the officials of the order, the elders shall be respected as abbots, the benevolent and wise shall serve as administrators, the brave shall serve as masters of the law. The ten meritorious deeds shall be practiced to subdue those who are not yet tranquillized, the destruction of avariciousness shall be manifested to destroy the desire for robbery and theft. Then in the entire country there shall be no cry of injustice such as that directed against Chou [the last tyrannical ruler of the Shang Dynasty], and everywhere there shall be songs praising the emperor of Chou. The birds and fishes shall rest peacefully in their nests and grottoes, while creatures on the water and land shall attain long life."[1]

Such were the chief facets presented by Wei in this memorial. Here was no scheme to suppress Buddhism; rather it was an attempt to dilute the religion by broadening the monastic community to include the entire empire. In such a scheme there would be no need for Buddhist monks and monasteries, and thus it would be possible for the Buddhist clerics to return to the laity and contribute their share of the productive labor necessary for the well-being of society.

In presenting this memorial, Wei gauged correctly the response of the emperor, who wanted to demonstrate that he was no longer a barbarian, but that he was completely Sinicized, throwing his full support behind Chinese customs and institutions. He was therefore gratified when he read Wei's memorial with its attacks against Buddhism. Here were some of the very things he wanted to say against the religion, and since they now came from a member of the Buddhist community, he felt that they justified and substantiated his own ideas. It should also be pointed out that Wei was clever enough to play on the emperor's ego by proposing that he should serve as the Tathāgata in this all-inclusive church.

To show his gratitude, the emperor bestowed upon Wei, who now left the sangha, the title of Duke of Shu (Szechuan). Wei thus achieved his objective of gaining a name for himself in the capital. Though the emperor agreed with Wei that something should be done, he felt that the time was not yet ready for definite action, for Buddhism was still too powerful and influential. He did keep Wei in the court so that the latter would be readily available for consultation. Wei now began to devote more and more time to his former interest in the occult sciences. In this revival of interest he was assisted by a Taoist priest, Chang Pin. These two individuals joined hands to stir up and increase the emperor's antagonism against Buddhism.

## THE SUPPRESSION OF 574

At this time the problem of priority also came to the attention of the emperor in a series of debates starting in 568 between the

[1] *Kuang-hung-ming-chi,* 7; *Taishō,* 52,132a.

Taoists and Buddhists. These debates, which were most acrimonious even in the imperial presence, centered, as expected, on the *Sutra on the Conversion of the Barbarians*. They were attended by hundreds of Taoists and Buddhists as well as Confucian scholars. In 573 the emperor decided that Confucianism must be ranked first, because it represented the traditional ideology of the land. Taoism was ranked next and Buddhism last, due chiefly to the machinations of Wei and Chang. The Buddhists were not satisfied with this decision, and some of them even dared to criticize the imperial opinion. This infuriated the emperor and induced him to pay more attention to the advice of Wei and Chang in favor of suppression. In the fifth month of 574 the emperor finally issued his decree proscribing Buddhism. The extent to which he was indebted to Wei Yüan-sung may be seen in the language he used; in many instances he repeated the same words and ideas that Wei used in his memorial of 567. In his decree the emperor called for the destruction of Buddhist temples, images, and scriptures; monks and nuns were to return to the laity; the treasures of the monasteries were to be confiscated and distributed to the ministers, princes, and dukes. There was one surprising and unexpected feature, however. Not only did the decree proscribe Buddhism, but it also included Taoism. In the debates before the emperor the Buddhists had so glaringly exposed the flagrant forgeries perpetrated by the Taoists that the emperor decided that Taoism was just as bad as Buddhism, for it had stolen and copied sutras from the Buddhist canon, it took money and property from the people, and it practiced magic to deceive the people. For these reasons he decreed that Taoism should be proscribed also, much to the surprise of Wei and Chang.

In 577, with the conquest of Northern Ch'i by Emperor Wu, the proscription was extended over the rest of north China. The emperor went to the capital of the conquered state, where he convened the monks of that area and read them the edict of proscription. On this occasion he declared that Buddhism must be suppressed because it practiced unfilial conduct, wasted wealth, and instigated rebellion. He also charged that since Buddhism was a foreign religion, it must be destroyed by him. The five hundred monks who were assembled listened silently in tears, with only one monk daring to protest; but Emperor Wu declared that his word was final, even though the Buddhists were to threaten him with the horrors of Avici hell.

According to Fei Ch'ang-fang of the Sui Dynasty, this persecution under Emperor Wu destroyed all the stupas, images, and shrines built by the people for several hundred years, over three million monks and nuns were returned to the laity, and over forty thousand temples were appropriated by members of the imperial family and aristocracy. The figure of three million monks and nuns is manifestly an exaggeration and not to be taken seriously.

There is no doubt but that Wei Yüan-sung was the main figure behind the action of the emperor in suppressing Buddhism. It is true that Wei in his memorial proposed only the purging of the clerical order of its undesirable elements and not the suppression of the religion. Consequently, the emperor went farther than Wei when he issued the decree ordering suppression. However, the main contributing factor which led to the suppression was Wei's memorial, which the emperor quoted to justify his action.

In view of this, what is the verdict of Buddhist historians concerning Wei Yüan-sung? The most famous of the Buddhist historians of the T'ang Dynasty was Tao-hsüan, who compiled the *Kuang-hung-ming-chi* (*Further Collection of Essays on Buddhism*), *Hsü Kao-seng-chuan* (*Further Biographies of Eminent Monks*), and *Fo-tao lun-heng* (*Essays on the Controversy Between Buddhism and Taoism*). Whenever Tao-hsüan discussed the persecution, he always mentioned Wei and Chang together and blamed the latter more than the former. In the *Fo-tao lun-heng* he wrote, "There was a Taoist priest Chang Pin, who deceived his emperor to achieve his personal schemes, and who secretly advanced Taoism in order to oppose and stamp out Buddhism."[2] Later Buddhist writers in dealing with the episode followed the lead of Tao-hsüan. Tao-shih, compiler of the *Fa-yüan chu-lin* (*Forest of Gems in the Garden of the Law*), has this passage: "In the third year of Chien-te (574) the emperor accepted the calumnious flattery of Chang Pin, who charged that Buddhism was inauspicious to the state and should be eradicated."[3] Another Buddhist writer, Chüeh-an, wrote in his *Shih-*

---

[2] *Fo-tao lun-heng*, 2; *Taishō*, 52,372a.
[3] *Fa-yüan chu-lin*, 79; *Taishō*, 53,875c.

*shih chi-ku-lüeh* (*Outline of the Ancient Records of the Sakya Clan*): "The Chou emperor at one time sincerely respected the Buddha, he constructed temples and stupas, ordained monks, and copied more than a thousand items of the sutras. Suddenly he was deceived by Chang Pin and began harboring designs to exterminate the religion."[4] In these sources no mention is made of Wei Yüan-sung.

More interesting is the way in which Buddhist writers treated the subject of the karmic effects of the persecution upon Emperor Wu and Wei Yüan-sung. In the biography of Wei in *Hsü Kao-seng-chuan*,[5] Tao-hsüan records the following episode. During the year 588 a certain Tu Ch'i was said to have died, but revived after three days. He said that during those three days he visited the nether regions, where he found Emperor Wu imprisoned in an iron chamber and wearing an iron cangue. Emperor Wu informed him that it was because he had listened to Wei Yüan-sung's advice to exterminate Buddhism that he was now enduring such torments in hell. Tu asked him why he did not report the case and have Wei summoned to hell. To this, Emperor Wu replied that he had done so, but that the officials of the nether regions had searched everywhere within the three worlds and nowhere was Wei to be found. If Tu would only return to the world and ask people to make offerings to the spirit of Wei, with the request that he go to visit Emperor Wu, then his sufferings would be relieved. Tu remembered this episode and, when he returned to the world of the living, he asked the people to do as Emperor Wu had requested.

A somewhat similar story is found in the *Fa-yüan chu-lin*,[6] where it was reported that an official, Chao Wen-ch'ang, suddenly died in 591 and descended to hell, where he met Emperor Wu with his neck heavily encased in three layers of iron chains. Wu begged Chao to return to earth to report to Emperor Wen of the Sui Dynasty that because he had listened to Wei Yüan-sung, he had persecuted Buddhism, for which crime he was now suffering heavy punishment. He had sought all over hell for Wei but found that the latter was now living beyond the limits of the three worlds and no longer subject to the effects of karma. If Em-

[4] *Taishō,* 49,804c.
[5] *Ibid.,* 50,657c-658a.
[6] *Ibid.,* 53,875c-876a.

peror Wen would offer some gifts on his behalf, his miseries would undoubtedly be lightened, and he might be released from hell. Chao did return to the world of the living and reported this episode to Emperor Wen, who called upon everyone in the Sui empire to offer one cash on behalf of Emperor Wu. It is interesting to note that in the *Li-tai san-pao-chi*[7] (*Record of the Three Jewels During Successive Dynasties*) there is a passage to the effect that this donation of one cash actually took place during a ceremony of repentance by Emperor Wen. In this ceremony Emperor Wen referred to the wholesale destruction of stupas, images, temples, and scriptures ordered by Emperor Wu, for which act the latter was now suffering in hell. In order to express repentance for the great crime against the religion, Emperor Wen called upon all his subjects to donate one cash, while he and his queen donated hundreds of thousands of bolts of silk. From this it appears that the donation was a historical fact, though the reason for the act was not to gain merit for Emperor Wu but to atone for the sins committed by the people against Buddhism.

The interesting point brought forth in these two Buddhist accounts is that Emperor Wu was made to suffer heavily in hell for his persecution of Buddhism, while the chief instigator, Wei Yüan-sung, was able to escape entirely from the karmic effects of that deed. Since Wei was a Buddhist, one would expect that his punishment would be much heavier than that of Emperor Wu; yet he was permitted to wander beyond the confines of the three worlds and thus escape from the operation of karma. Such was the way the Buddhist historians tried to cover up the activities of one of the wayward sons of the church.

## YANG CHIEN AND THE FOUNDING OF THE SUI DYNASTY

The persecutions of 574-577 instigated by Wei Yüan-sung were of short duration. As soon as Emperor Wu died in 578, a ruler more sympathetic to Buddhism succeeded him. Three years after that the Northern Chou was superseded by the Sui in 581, established by Yang Chien, one of the most remarkable figures in Chinese history. In 589 Yang conquered the Ch'en Dynasty in

[7] *Ibid.*, 49,108b.

the south, and thus achieved once more the unification of China after three centuries of disunity.

Chien had been an officer in the army of Emperor Wu, the Northern Chou ruler who had triumphed over the Northern Ch'i in 577. When Emperor Wu died on June 21, 578, power fell into the hands of his son Yü-wen Pin, a maniac who soon destroyed what his father had built up. Officially Pin abdicated in favor of his son Yü-wen Ch'an on April 1, 579, but continued to rule until June 580, when he died. Among the generals in the Northern Chou army Chien was by no means conspicuous, but he did enjoy a favored position because his eldest daughter was married to Yü-wen Pin. However, Pin became enamoured in 580 of the beautiful young wife of Yü-wen Wen, a prince of the blood, and Wen's father, unable to bear this disgrace, rebelled. The rebellion was soon quelled, and father and son were executed. With this beautiful girl in his possession, Pin then decided to eliminate Chien's daughter. He also disliked Chien, and dispatched him as an official to Yang-chou. Chien delayed his departure, and this delay proved to be his golden opportunity, for Pin soon became seriously ill and Chien's friends forged an imperial order summoning him to the imperial presence. Pin died on the very day of the audience or soon afterward, and the conspirators then urged Yang Chien to accept the regency. After doing so, Chien moved swiftly to crush all opposition, and on March 4, 581, he proclaimed himself as Emperor Wen of the new Sui Dynasty.

During the early years of his reign Chien exerted conscientious efforts to win the support of the people for his dynasty. He was punctual and diligent in his observance of the imperial audiences, he was economical in his personal habits and clothing, he rewarded liberally those who deserved rewards, he decreased the taxes and the labor services, he encouraged agriculture and weaving, and his policies soon brought prosperity to the realm. In order to justify his assumption of power he consciously fostered the practice and study of Confucianism during the early years of his reign. For example, he informed heaven of his assumption of the heavenly mandate, he exempted filial sons from taxation and the labor services, he established schools for the study of the Confucian classics at the local level and a national college in the capital. However, it was toward Buddhism that he bestowed his greatest favors. In this respect Emperor Wen stands unique among Chinese emperors, in that he definitely relied on Buddhism as an ideology to unify and to consolidate his empire.

Chinese historians, both Buddhist and Confucian, have preserved a legend that a nun arrived at the Yang household on the birth of Emperor Wen and predicted that during his lifetime there would occur a persecution of Buddhism, but that the child would grow up to be an emperor who would restore the religion. She also said that the child should not be brought up amid household life, whereupon the parents converted one portion of the house into a temple and entrusted their son to the care of the nun. Whether or not this legend is true is not known, but it does make clear two points—that Emperor Wen's parents were followers of Buddhism and that he grew up amid Buddhist surroundings. This might help to explain why, after his assumption of power, he favored Buddhism over Confucianism.

## YANG CHIEN AND THE REVIVAL OF BUDDHISM

Even before his assumption of imperial power, while still serving under the Northern Chou Dynasty, Chien began to take steps to modify the severity of the proscription against the Buddhists. He permitted one temple each to reopen in Ch'ang-an and Lo-yang. He invited a leading monk, Fa-tsang, to come down from his mountain retreat and help in the revival of the religion, and he also permitted former qualified monks to resume the practice of their religion. Through these measures it can be seen that he was making a conscious effort to win the support of those groups in the population which had been affected by the persecution of 574-577. Consequently, after his accession to the Dragon Throne in 581, he initiated a series of measures, all designed to promote Buddhism. First was the decree issued in the early part of 581 calling for the establishment of Buddhist monasteries at the foot of each of the five sacred mountains, and for the donation of landed estates for the support of each one. The five sacred mountains were T'ai-shan in Shantung, Hua-shan in Shen-si, Ho-shan in Anhui, Heng-shan in Hopei, and Sung-shan in Honan. This was indeed a significant beginning, for these sacred mountains were considered to be the habitat of the divinities of the vicinity, and the ceremonies for the propitiation of such deities were usually entrusted to Taoists. Later in the same year he ordered the construction of temples at sites where his father and he had won important battles (Hsiang-yang, Sui-chun, Chiang-

*Spread of Buddhism in the Southern and Northern Dynasties (4th–6th century* A.D.*)*

ling, and Chin-yang) and in these temples he held commemorative services for the souls of those followers who had fallen in the field of victory. It is probable that Emperor Wen was thinking of the future when he arranged for these memorial services. His long-range plans called for a military campaign to conquer the Ch'en Dynasty in the south, a campaign which would cost the lives of many of his people. He wanted to assure his followers that, though some of them would die on distant battlefields, their souls would be taken care of. In 583 he ordered the restoration of Buddhist temples destroyed during the proscription, and two years later, in 585, another edict was issued calling for the repair and reinstallation of Buddha images. A concerted effort was also initiated to repair damaged sutras, or to make new copies. It was during this year also that he promoted the construction of forty-five national Buddhist temples in the prefectures, designated as Ta-hsing-kuo Temples. Under imperial encouragement the Buddhist sutras became so popular that the Confucian historians complained that the volumes of sutras in circulation exceeded those of the Confucian classics by about a hundred times. In 585 Emperor Wen openly took upon himself the vows of a Buddhist layman, so that henceforth he was given the epithet the Bodhisattva Son of Heaven.

Learned clerics and virtuous monks were often invited into the imperial palace to lecture on the scriptures, lectures which were attended not only by the emperor but also by the ladies of the imperial family. The empress and the imperial princes were among the converts; so were a number of high officials such as Kao Chiung, Su Wei, and Yang Su.

The campaigns and battles which finally culminated in the subjugation of the Ch'en Dynasty in 589 by Emperor Wen resulted in considerable damage to Buddhist institutions in the Ch'en capital of Chien-k'ang and vicinity. For the defense of the capital the Ch'en ruler had mobilized all his resources, including Buddhist monks and Taoist priests; consequently, after the conquest of Ch'en, Emperor Wen initiated certain measures against the Buddhist sangha. Close supervision was exercised over the community of monks to prevent the development of any anti-Sui sentiment. Those sangha officials who were functionaries of the Ch'en bureaucracy were dismissed from office. Furthermore, Emperor Wen decided to limit to two the number of Buddhist temples in each department of the conquered territory. Many of the temples in the capital which were damaged or destroyed were not repaired, while those not destroyed by the fighting were requisitioned by the conquering troops. Thus the religion which flourished in the Ch'en capital suffered a period of temporary eclipse.

In spite of these measures it must be emphasized that Emperor Wen was not anti-Buddhist. As soon as conditions were settled,

one of the imperial princes, Prince Kuang of Chin, was designated as governor-general of Chiang-nan, or the area south of
the Yangtze. The emperor also dispatched in the first month of
590 a missive to Chih-i, founder of the T'ien-t'ai School and the
most respected monk in south China, soliciting his cooperation to
restore Buddhism to its former prosperous condition. Prince
Kuang likewise took steps to win the support of Chih-i, although
his motives for so doing were not entirely exemplary. While his
veneration for Chih-i was undoubtedly motivated by a desire to
win the allegiance of the Buddhist community in south China,
it was also likely that considerations of personal ambition were at
work. He knew that his father was a pious Buddhist, and, by
displaying his own devotion to the religion, he hoped to gain the
favor of his father and be designated as the heir apparent.

## BUDDHISM AS A UNIFYING IDEOLOGY

With north and south China under his sway Emperor Wen now
put into effect his campaign to unify the empire through Buddhism. He looked upon himself as a universal monarch in the
Buddhist tradition, but instead of following the Northern Wei
maxim that the ruler was the embodiment of the Tathāgata, he
declared that he owed his rise to the Buddhist dharma. He was
quoted as saying that "the Buddha had entrusted the true dharma
to the ruler of the realm. We are honored among men and we
accept the Buddha's trust." Another quotation attributed to him
was that "the *Vinaya* masters convert people to goodness. I (a
disciple of the Buddha) forbid people from committing evil. The
words are different, but the idea is the same." In an attempt to
identify Emperor Wen with the universal monarch some Buddhist writers of the dynasty quoted references from such sutras as
the *Suvarnaprabhāsa* to prove that the Buddha himself had
prophesied the appearance of this emperor in China. In an edict
of 594 the ruler called himself the Emperor, Disciple of the
Buddha, to indicate his close relationship with the Blessed One.
In that same edict he expressed the penance of a disciple over the
destruction done to Buddhist monasteries, images, and scripture
by the Northern Chou persecution, and, as an expiation for this
sin, he and the empress each pledged 120,000 bolts of silk to

repair the damage, after which he called upon his subjects to donate cash for the same purpose.

On the occasion of his birthday in 601 the emperor decided it was time to carry out his ambitious program of consolidating his vast empire through Buddhism. On that day he issued an edict proclaiming the fact that he had taken refuge in the Three Jewels, and that he was desirous of his subjects' developing the thought of enlightenment and cultivating meritorious karma. To this end he dispatched thirty monks to the various prefectural centers, carrying incense and the sacred relics of the Buddha. After arrival at the prefectural centers the monks were to select appropriate sites for the construction of stupas to enshrine the relics. Before sending forth the thirty monks, the emperor had carefully packed the relics in jars. On this initial occasion thirty stupas were constructed, and at noon of the fifteenth day of the tenth month, 601, there was a simultaneous enshrinement of the sacred relics in the stupas. All government offices declared a seven-day holiday to celebrate the occasion, and the monastic community throughout the land observed the ceremony. At the same time the emperor also held an elaborate ceremony in the palace to commemorate the historic event. He did not do this just once. The very next year fifty-one more stupas were constructed for the enshrinement of relics, and in 604 there was a third distribution of the relics to thirty more stupas throughout the land. In all, 111 stupas were erected during the years 601-604 by the ruler to manifest his patronage of Buddhism. To indicate even more clearly his support of Buddhism, in 601 he abolished the Confucian schools in the prefectures and counties, and drastically reduced the number of students in the national college.

It is safe to say that Emperor Wen, in this program of constructing stupas and enshrining the sacred relics, was but emulating the example of the famous Indian monarch Aśoka. Buddhist traditions say that the latter had 84,000 stupas constructed simultaneously throughout his realm, and that on the appointed day, Yaśas, the abbot of Kukkutārāma, covered the sun with his hand, so that the builders could work in the shade. The emperor's motive was very clear. He hoped that all classes of society would share in the merits of worshiping the sacred relics. The stupas were the symbols of the imperial support of Buddhism, and were erected in places where the scenery was especially excellent. By the ceremony of simultaneous enshrinement of the relics, with the official and clerical community participating, he sought to convey the idea that the entire empire was united in its support of Buddhism. Such an attempt to propagate Buddhism as an instrument of state policy had never been attempted by previous rulers. The repercussions of this effort were felt not only in China but also in Japan and Korea. Shōtoku Taishi in Japan was greatly impressed by this display of imperial patronage, and envoys from the three Korean kingdoms of Kokuryo, Paekche, and Silla asked for and received relics to take back to their respective countries.

As an aid to the propagation of the religion the ruler also initiated what were known as the Assemblies of Twenty-five, groups of twenty-five monks banded together for missionary purposes. The leader of each group was to remain in the capital, but the rest of the monks were to disperse throughout the empire to spread the dharma. Five kinds of study groups were also organized, each group to specialize on one fundamental scripture. In the city of Lo-yang there were at the beginning of Emperor Wen's reign sixty-four Buddhist monasteries and twenty-seven nunneries, as compared to ten Taoist temples and six nunneries. By the end of his reign the Buddhist establishments had increased to one hundred and twenty, while the number of Taoist institutions remained the same. This is one concrete example of the growth attained by the religion.[8]

## EMPEROR YANG AND THE DECLINE OF SUI

In spite of all his meritorious deeds on behalf of the dharma, Emperor Wen suffered a violent death at the hands of his own son Kuang, who ascended the throne in 604 as Emperor Yang. Confucian historians have criticized Emperor Yang as the worst type of tyrant, cruel, selfish, and extravagant. Yet he was a follower

[8] One Buddhist source written during the early years of the T'ang Dynasty (Fa-lin, *Pien-cheng lun*, 3; *Taishō*, 52,509bc) furnished some detailed information concerning this growth during Emperor Wen's reign: number of monks and nuns converted, 230,000; temples constructed, 3,792; scriptures copied, 132,086 *chüan*; sutras repaired, 3,853 items; images of statues of the Buddha erected, 106,580; old statues and images repaired, 1,508,940.

and generous supporter of Buddhism. Buddhist historians like Chih-p'an (flor. 1258-1269), who compiled the *Fo-tsu t'ung-chi* (*Record of the Lineage of the Buddha and Patriarchs*), did not castigate him, but attempted to explain away his infamous crime of patricide by saying that he had to do so because of his previous karma. By so doing, they wrote, he was but following the example of Prince Ajātasattu, who killed his father Bimbisara to obtain the throne of Magadha.

Before his accession to the throne, and while he was still governor-general of south China, Prince Kuang carried out a number of projects to indicate his zeal for Buddhism. As a result of the fighting attending the fall of the Ch'en Dynasty, extensive damage had been done to Buddhist images and sutras. Kuang ordered his troops to collect all such damaged sutras and assemble them in Yang-chou, where they could be repaired. He also established two state chapels to which he invited for residence all the prominent monks in the area. These two institutions played an important role in the restoration of the religion. After his accession to the throne he visited Yang-chou once again, on which occasion he ordered a memorial service to be held on Mt. T'ien-t'ai for the departed master Chih-i and donated a temple in his memory. By issuing a decree in 607 calling upon Buddhist monks to render homage to the emperor and imperial officials, he terminated the tradition in south China of monks not honoring their earthly rulers.

The Sui effort to use Buddhism as a unifying force was short-lived, however. The extravagance of Emperor Yang in carrying forward relentlessly the construction of canals linking the northern capitals of Ch'ang-an and Lo-yang with the Yangtze Valley demanded huge concentrations of labor and resources, which in turn wrought widespread misery and suffering among the populace. The Sui love for grandeur increased further the burdens of the people. Two capitals, Ch'ang-an and Lo-yang, were maintained by the dynasty, and the construction of palaces in each capital was carried out on a stupendous scale, requiring the services of over a million people. To climax all this, Emperor Yang dispatched three unsuccessful expeditions against Korea. The popular discontent fomented by these military reverses and by the burden of the expense of the public works finally led to revolt and assassination of the emperor in 618.

Thus ended the noble experiment of the Sui Dynasty; for, when the new T'ang ruling house inherited the ruling mandate, it again reverted to Confucianism as the official ideology. While the Sui effort expired with the demise of the dynasty, the fundamental situation concerning Buddhism remained the same. Buddhism was now the most powerful religion of the realm. It must have been; otherwise Emperor Wen would not have been so bold to use it as the official ideology to unify the empire. Thus, though the T'ang emperors did not follow the Sui example, they could not disavow the religious ethos of the people, who remained predominantly Buddhist.

## FACTORS LEADING TO GROWTH DURING THE PERIOD OF DISUNITY

When the Han Dynasty fell in 220, Buddhism was barely able to maintain a precarious existence on Chinese soil and had to seek support from Taoism to retain that foothold. By the time the country was reunited in 589, Buddhism had spread to all parts of the empire; converts had been made from all classes of society; images, statues, and temples were prevalent everywhere; and a voluminous literature had accumulated. Buddhist records present some statistics about the steady growth of temples and converts. While such statistics are not to be accepted as entirely accurate, still they are useful in giving some indication of prevailing conditions and trends. One such record of the T'ang Dynasty, the *Pien-cheng-lun* (*On the Discussion of the Correct*) of Fa-lin, showed the following growth for the Southern Dynasties: from 1,768 temples and 24,000 monks and nuns during the Eastern Chin to 2,846 and 82,700 under the Liang.

The religion was much more popular in the north, for Fa-lin estimated that during the Northern Wei Dynasty the total number of monks and nuns converted was over 2,000,000, that 47 great national temples were built, and that over 30,000 temples and shrines were erected by the common people. Wei Shou, compiler of the official history of the Northern Wei Dynasty, recorded, on the other hand, that at the end of the dynasty there were 2,000,000 monks and nuns present in north China. Fei Ch'ang-fang, compiler of the *Li-tai san-pao-chi*, stated that the number of monks and nuns returned to the laity during the persecutions of 574-577 came to 3,000,000; but Fei's work has often been criticized as being full of inaccuracies, and hence his figures are suspect. The extent of Buddhist literature translated or composed in Chinese down to the Liang Dynasty is indicated in the *Ch'u-san-tsang*, compiled ca.518, which listed 2,073 titles in 3,779 *chüan*. Moreover, the compilers of the *Sui-shu* (*History of the Sui Dynasty*) complained that the number of Buddhist texts in circulation exceeded the Confucian classics by "several tens to about a hundred times."

This growth was achieved despite a number of features in Buddhism which are opposed to Chinese culture. In the first place, the Buddhist view that life is full of suffering and is illusory and that our goal is to seek release from that life was in contrast with the Chinese view that life is good and to be enjoyed. The Buddhist practice of celibacy was opposed to the Chinese emphasis on family life and numerous offspring. The mendicant ideal of Buddhism was the opposite of the Confucian stress on productive labor by all members of society. The Buddhist advocacy of leaving the household life was contrary to the Chinese insistence on harmonious social relationships. Finally, the Buddhist concept of a monastic community not amenable to the laws of the state was not acceptable to the Confucian scholar, who held that the imperial laws should be observed by all alike.

One of the basic factors making for growth was the fact of the disunity itself. There was no strong central dynasty motivated by Confucian concepts of government to oppose the Indian religion. Thoughtful Chinese in both north and south China were looking about for a substitute; they were groping for a new way of life, a new standard of conduct, to take the place of the Confucian ideology which had been found wanting. In this quest they turned to Buddhism to see whether or not this religion could offer some satisfactory solutions to the problems they faced.

Among the Buddhist monks in north China during this period of division there were many who were proficient in the interpretation of spells and charms, or who claimed to be able to predict the future. By such powers of prognostication Buddhist monks were able to gain a wide hearing among the populace. Such feats endeared them not only to the people but also to the ruling classes. By giving advice on the outcome of a military move, or on the reliability of some ministers or friends, such monks rendered valuable service to the ruling potentates, and, in return, the state supported and patronized Buddhism to the extent of building official temples and stupas, or granted economic privileges to the monastic community. All of this also added to the growth of Buddhism.

During periods of disorder rulers of the various contending states needed man power for the armies and the labor battalions. This was especially true in north China. For those who wished to escape from such service the Buddhist monasteries offered a welcome haven. People flocked into the Buddhist institutions to become monks and nuns. Once inside, they were no longer subject to the laws of the state, and, besides being free from military and labor services, they were also exempt from taxation. Such features attracted not only the draft dodgers and the lazy, but also outlaws and undesirable elements who wanted to hide their past. This was the third factor favoring the growth of the Buddhist community.

In the chapter on Buddhism under the Eastern Chin, reference was made to the withdrawal of scholars and literati from government service and society to take refuge in Taoism or Buddhism. These men looked with disgust upon the earthly struggles going on during their times; they were sorely perplexed by the disunity of China, with non-Chinese overrunning the entire northern part of the empire; they saw little opportunity to exercise their talents and knowledge for the benefit of the state. Hence many of them sought to find tranquillity and relief within the foreign religion, Buddhism. In this religion they found satisfactory answers to many of the perplexing problems confronting them. The Buddhist doctrine of *sarvam anityam* (everything is transitory) accurately described contemporary conditions, and was like a welcome breeze which soothed those vexed by the troublesome vicissitudes of life. This prevailing temperament gave impetus, during the period of disunity, to the growth of the Neo-Taoist and Prajñā Schools. A life withdrawn from the entangling problems of society, spent in concentrated study and meditation, punctuated by sessions of brilliant conversations—such a life proved to be exceedingly attractive to scholars and aristocrats of this period. This situation also favored the growth of Buddhism, especially among the upper classes of the south.

During the period of disunity south China remained a center of Chinese culture, but north China was dominated and ruled by a series of non-Chinese dynasties. Barbarians from beyond the northern frontiers of China infiltrated into north China and mingled with the native populations. Among such non-Chinese peoples Buddhism gained a ready hearing. The very fact that Buddhism was a foreign faith was an asset in its favor. One needs only to recall the rebuttal of Shih Hu to the memorial of Wang Tu, in which he said that he was in favor of Buddhism precisely because he was a foreigner himself. Such non-Chinese peoples were not bound by conservative Confucian ideas against the foreign religion and practices, and found it much easier to accept Buddhism than would a Chinese. Being generally of inferior cultural attainments, these non-Chinese peoples were impressed and attracted by the superior levels attained in Buddhist art, literature, and thought; in their efforts to lift up their own cultural level, they embraced Buddhism. This factor was probably one of the main reasons why there were so many converts in the north during the Northern Wei Dynasty.

Among the Buddhist clergy during the Wei-Chin period the most eminent were three monks already mentioned—Tao-an, Hui-yüan, and Kumārajīva. Tao-an combined in himself the dominant trends of Buddhism of his time—*dhyāna* practices and *Prajñā* philosophy. Moreover, the activities to which he devoted his lifetime, such as preserving and systematizing the canon, commenting on the sutras, and drawing up *Vinaya* rules, all contributed to make him one of the most respected figures of his age. As for Hui-yüan, his purity of conduct and religious devotion served as a model, not only for people during his lifetime, but also for later ages. Buddhism in China, especially its Mahāyāna aspects, would have been poorer indeed if it had not been for the translations of Kumārajīva. His renditions of the *Saddharma* and *Vimalakīrti* were among the most widely read of the period, and were undoubtedly responsible for the widespread popularity of the religion, not only during the period of disunity but also during succeeding dynasties. The contribution of these three outstanding individuals was another element working for the prosperous development of Buddhism.

The inadequacy of the Confucian system to provide a satisfactory outlet for the religious aspirations of the people also contributed to the growth of Buddhism. Individuals normally desire communion with deities to find solace for their own sorrows and disappointments, or to ask for divine assistance when their earthly burdens seem too heavy to bear. Such sorrows and earthly burdens tend to become accentuated at times of uncertainty and instability. Confucianism, with its lack of emphasis on the spiritual world (one of its important doctrines advocated respect of the spirits but keeping them at a distance), was too earthbound and practical to satisfy the religious yearnings of the common people. Buddhism stepped in to fill this deficiency. It brought in a host of deities in the form of ever-compassionate and merciful bodhisattvas, always ready to lend a helping hand to those who sought their assistance. It dazzled the Chinese with a brilliant hierarchy of heavens, rebirth in which was held up as the reward for meritorious living on earth. At the same time it depicted hells where the tortures became progressively more and more tormenting and terrifying, as a deterrent to evil deeds on earth. As the Chinese philosopher Hu Shih expressed it, the Chinese were so captivated by this rich and colorful pageantry of heavens and hells that they succumbed easily to the religion. No wonder that such writers as the monk Hui-lin and the Confucian Fan Chen criticized Buddhism for increasing instead of extirpating desires, especially the desire to be reborn in heaven.

Besides these factors in the Chinese scene that favored the growth of Buddhism, there were, in addition, a number of elements within Buddhism itself which were especially efficacious during this period. Among these there was first the doctrine of karma. It was this doctrine of personal reward and retribution that buoyed up the hopes of those who were sunk in hardship and misery during the uncertainties and instability of the era, for it offered them a rational explanation of their lives. They were suffering because they were reaping the retribution for some demeritorious deeds done in the past, but by their meritorious work during their present lives they would be reborn into happier births in the future. Meanwhile, the arrogant tyrannical official who seemed to be the special object of Fortune's smiles might be living in ease and luxury now, but in his next rebirth it would be his turn to be tormented by misery. Such a rational explanation of the woes of the period won not a few converts for Buddhism and sustained them during the dark and disappointing hours of their earthly lives.

Coupled with the teaching of karma was the second element, the ideal held up by the Mahāyāna, that all creatures, no matter how lowly or humble, possessed the Buddha-nature in them and so were capable of attaining Buddhahood and salvation. Such a noble, inspiring, and glowing ideal had never been put forth before the common people until this time, and it must have acted as a powerful magnet drawing people to Buddhism. The path leading to this salvation was also made very easy by the Mahāyāna: just the repetition of the formula *namo Amitābha* or the creation of an image of the Buddha, even in the mud or sand, would be sufficient to merit deliverance.

Lastly, we might mention here the adaptability of the Buddhists in making their religion more palatable to the Chinese. A conspicuous instance of this was the Chinese Buddhists' espousal of the cardinal Confucian virtue of filial piety. Once a person joined the monastic order, he severed all relations with his family and society, so that he was no longer bound to honor the memory of his ancestors. Yet in the inscriptions found at Yün-kang and Lung-men there is repeated again and again the earnest wish of the donors that their ancestors might attain meritorious rebirths in one of the Buddhists paradises. Stupas and statues of the Buddha were often erected to perpetuate the memory of parents. Vimalakīrti, for instance, is described as teaching loyalty and filial piety to the ruling princes. Incidentally, the layman Vimalakīrti is described in such a manner that he might easily be taken as a perfect Confucian gentleman, being pure in self-discipline, obedient to all the precepts, a householder with wife and children yet learned in the dharma, a rich aristocrat always self-controlled and restrained in his desires. Such a way of life could indeed be a model for the cultivated conservative

Chinese scholar and gentleman. It was no wonder that the brilliant scholar Seng-chao became immediately converted to Buddhism after reading the *Vimalakīrtinirdeśa*. By espousing such Confucian virtues as filial piety, congenial and harmonious family life, loyalty, moderation, and self-discipline, Buddhism made itself much more acceptable to the Chinese of the age.

MATURITY AND ACCEPTANCE

# CHAPTER VIII

# THE APOGEE: T'ANG DYNASTY

BUILDING upon the Sui unification of the country, the T'ang Dynasty (618-907) established a huge empire covering the whole of China proper and extending into Central Asia. Though the imperial clan claimed descent from Lao-tzu and thus favored Taoism, the central authorities pursued a policy of religious toleration, giving each religion an opportunity to develop. Nestorian Christianity, Islam, and Manichaeism all were introduced during T'ang times, and each faith found adherents among the Chinese. The cosmopolitan ideal was upheld by the T'ang emperors because they regarded themselves as rulers not only of the Chinese but also of the barbarians. Since Buddhism was already so widespread in China, it developed to unprecedented heights under the friendly patronage of some of the T'ang rulers, so that its power and influence far exceeded those of Taoism. One might say that, during the T'ang, Buddhism finally came of age in China; it was supported by all elements of society—by the imperial household, the nobility, the great and wealthy families, and the common people. It shared in the position and influence of these great families of the realm, but it also enjoyed close relationship with the common populace through its various religious and social activities. The spacious courtyards of the Buddhist temples served as the pleasure gardens of the urban crowds, the Buddhist festivals provided entertainment and diversion to throngs in the villages and cities, the religious lectures and the vegetarian feasts were attended by huge numbers of pious laymen. In this ability to serve all classes of society lay the source of strength of the Buddhist sangha during this period.

The mass of materials translated into Chinese during the previous centuries was now digested by the Chinese, ready to emerge in the form of different schools of Buddhism. Some of these schools, such as the T'ien-t'ai and Ch'an, no longer bore the Indian imprint; they reflected peculiar Chinese characteristics, which one might interpret as the result of the Chinese genius at work. In the prosperous temples of the cities as well as in the monasteries of the remote mountain fastnesses, groups of intellectually vigorous monks discussed the prevailing sutras of these schools. In this discussion of T'ang Buddhism, first consideration will be given to the imperial attitude toward the religion, then the role played by the sangha in T'ang society, and finally the different schools which arose.

In general it is perhaps justifiable to say that Buddhism under the T'ang Dynasty assumed a more Chinese character, and be-

*Spread of Buddhism in the T'ang Dynasty (618–907)*

came more closely identified with, and under the control of, the state. Even though there were various sangha officials charged with the administration of affairs connected with the monks and monasteries, these were usually under the supervision of civil officials. Early in the dynasty there were even some attempts to require monks to reverence the rulers and parents, but these efforts were staunchly resisted by the clerical community, and the measures were allowed to lapse. Under previous dynasties monks accused of major crimes, such as murder, were tried by the state, but those guilty of minor infractions were judged by monastic law. Now, under the T'ang, all crimes committed by monks were judged by civil laws. At the beginning of the dynasty monks still called themselves *p'in-tao* (poor monk) or *sha-men* (*śramana*), but in 760 a disciple of Hui-neng, the sixth Ch'an patriarch, called himself *ch'en* (subject), and this practice became prevalent thereafter. This was a concrete indication that clerics considered themselves members of the national society.

## FU YI AND HIS MEMORIAL AGAINST BUDDHISM

Under the first T'ang emperor, Kao-tsu, a Taoist named Fu Yi (554-639), who must have been miserable through the Sui Dynasty because of that dynasty's espousal of Buddhism, presented a memorial in 621 in which he attacked Buddhism on nationalistic, intellectual, and economic grounds. He charged that the doctrines of the Buddha were full of extravagances and absurdities and that the religion was fostering disloyalty and breakdown of filial piety, for it taught that one need not show reverence to ruler or parent. By its erroneous teachings it led people to believe that by donating just one cash an individual would be able to reap rewards a hundredfold. Fu contended that matters of life and death were in the realm of nature, while justice, punishment, rewards, and virtues belonged to the realm of men. But the Buddhists taught that all these were due to karma, he said, and by so insisting they were usurping the powers of the creator. This sect of Buddhism now numbered more than a hundred thousand monks and nuns who lived in celibacy and passed their time in idleness. He advocated, therefore, that this large number of people be required to marry, so as to form a hundred thousand families and thus beget offspring to benefit the country and to swell the imperial armies.

Though the attack repeated many familiar arguments and was worded in strong language, it elicited very little support from other sources. The Buddhist clergy was powerful and enjoyed strong support from the great families of the country. Moreover, it is likely that the T'ang ruler remembered that the fall of the Northern Chou Dynasty was in part traceable to that dynasty's persecution of Buddhism; consequently, he did not want to antagonize a large segment of the population by drastic action against Buddhism. However, Kao-tsu felt that some action was necessary, and so in response to Fu Yi's memorial he issued a decree which charged that Buddhism had lost its original aim of tranquillity and purity, for its followers engaged in profit-seeking activities and in gratifying their desires. In order to separate the jade from the stones, he ordered that those monks and nuns, Buddhist as well as Taoist, who were diligent in observing the moral precepts and persevering in their cultivation of the religious life should take up residence within the temples, where all their daily needs would be supplied by the government. Those who were lax in observing the rules of discipline and lazy in their habits should be returned to the laity. In the capital three Buddhist and two Taoist establishments would be permitted, while in the departments only one each would be allowed to continue; the remainder would be destroyed.

It is clear from this decree that Kao-tsu did not intend to suppress Buddhism; he wanted to put the monks and monasteries under the control of the government. The fact that only three monasteries were allowed in the capital and one in each department did mean a drastic reduction in the number of monks and a severe restriction of religious activities. It should be noticed that the restrictions were not confined to Buddhism but also included Taoism. A few weeks after the issuance of this decree the Prince of Ch'in murdered the heir to the throne, forced his father Kao-tsu to abdicate, and proclaimed himself as Emperor T'ai-tsung. One result of this change in rulers was that the decree affecting Buddhism and Taoism was never carried out.

## T'AI-TSUNG'S ATTITUDE TOWARD BUDDHISM

During the early years of his reign T'ai-tsung was probably not much interested in Buddhism. As he had spent most of his time in military campaigns, he had had very little occasion to study the religion seriously. A good indication of his attitude is to be found in one of his early edicts, in which he said that Buddhism was not a religion that he could follow. He referred to the examples of Emperors Wu (502-549) and Chien-wen (550-551) of the Liang Dynasty, who depleted the treasury to help the sangha and exhausted the man power of the south to build stupas and temples; yet in the end their descendants were destroyed and their ancestral temples were in ruins. These results, he felt, refuted the claims of the Buddhists about the operation of karma. Instead, he began searching for ways to make himself and his clan more acceptable to the people, who were inclined to view him as a usurper of the throne.

To this end T'ai-tsung advanced the contention that the imperial family, whose surname was Li, was descended from Lao-tzu, who had the same surname. This contention was mentioned in an edict of 637, in which he further stated that the stability of the empire rested on the merits of *wu-wei* or nonactivity, and that henceforth in all ceremonial affairs and discussions Taoists were to have precedence over Buddhists. A Buddhist monk pointed out to T'ai-tsung that it was no honor to claim descent from Lao-tzu, since the latter was said to have been the bastard son of a slave woman, but the emperor apparently was not offended by this. In subsequent visits to Buddhist temples he emphasized to the monks that his policy of giving precedence to Taoism was based largely on grounds of filial piety, and that he was not unfriendly toward Buddhism.

This last assertion was not merely polite empty talk. In 629 the emperor had seven stupas and shrines constructed on battlefields where he had been victorious, in memory of those who had been killed in battle. The year before that, in 628, he ordered all the temples in the capital and main cities to observe seven days of fasting and to hold services of consolation for the dead heroes. He also decreed that monks in the temples were to pray for the ripening of grains during the first and seventh months and to recite the *Jen-wang-ching* (*Sutra on the Benevolent Kings*) and the *Ta-yün-ching* (*The Great Cloud Sutra*) for the prosperity and stability of the empire.[1]

In his policy toward Buddhism during these early years one

---

[1] The *Jen-wang-ching* was translated by Kumārajīva and the *Ta-yün-ching* by Dharmakshema and Chu Fo-nien.

might discern the emperor's desire to use the religion for the benefit and advantage of the state. Political considerations dictated that the emperor should take certain measures to gain the support of the large body of Buddhist converts. One of the measures taken was to grant support to certain important Buddhist temples, especially those on the sacred mountain, Wu-t'ai-shan, to make certain that those temples would pray for the spiritual welfare of the empire. Though the emperor professed to be a Taoist, still he was not willing to take chances in the realm of the spirits, for he wanted to make sure that the protective influences of the Buddhist deities were manifested on his behalf and that no spiritual mishap would befall the imperial administration. To this end he also held commemorative ceremonies in the Buddhist temples celebrating the birthdays and anniversaries of past and present rulers.

During the latter part of his reign T'ai-tsung appeared to have become genuinely interested in Buddhism, largely through the influence of Hsüan-tsang. The initial interview which Hsüan-tsang had with the emperor took place in 645 immediately after the pilgrim's return to China and was a short one, as the emperor was then busily occupied with a campaign against Liao-tung. The emperor asked the famous traveler why he had embarked on his journey without letting him know. Hsüan-tsang replied that he had applied for permission to leave the country, but that, since he was such an insignificant person, he received no answer from the authorities. In spite of this absence of authorization he had left the country just the same. The emperor replied that if a layman had taken such a step, it would have been a serious matter, but since he was a monk, the case was different. Anyway, he was glad that Hsüan-tsang had gone and had been able to bring back such valuable information about foreign countries. To the emperor's invitation that he become an official, Hsüan-tsang declined, stating that he wished to devote his time to translation of the texts he had brought back.

In later years the emperor displayed more and more interest in these translations, and on one occasion he remarked: "Looking at these Buddhist works is like gazing at the sky or sea. They are so lofty that one cannot measure their heights, so profound that one cannot plumb their depths. . . . I see now that there is no limit to the scope it covers. Confucianism, Taoism, and our other schools when compared with it are like mere puddles measured against a mighty ocean. It is sheer nonsense when people say that the Three Doctrines come to much the same thing."[2] He assured Hsüan-tsang that he would do his best to help spread the religion. So fond was he of the Buddhist cleric that he gave the latter a cassock made especially for the emperor by the ladies of the palace. He likewise invited this eminent monk to live with him on various occasions, so that they could spend more time discussing various points of Buddhist doctrine and the traces of the religion in India and Central Asia. After one such session the emperor sighed, "Oh why did not I meet you sooner, so that I could really do something to promote the Faith?"[3]

## KAO-TSUNG AND BUDDHISM

Under the next emperor, Kao-tsung, another significant development took place. In 666 this emperor went to T'ai-shan to sacrifice to heaven. After the ceremonies he decreed that there be established in Yen-chou (in Shantung) three Buddhists and three Taoist temples, while in each of the remaining prefectures of the realm one Taoist and one Buddhist temple be established. It is not known definitely what the names of the temples in the rest of the prefectures were, though it is probable that they were also called Kuo-fen Temple, following the designation used in Yen-chou. These Buddhist temples were officially established by the state, with the idea that the monks were to pray for the welfare and prosperity of the state and to manifest the virtue and authority of the emperor to the people. The Buddhists were so moved by this imperial action that Tao-shih, a monk in Ch'ang-an, was inspired to compile the great Buddhist encyclopedia, *Fa-yüan-chu-lin* (*Forest of Gems in the Garden of Law*), which he completed in one hundred chapters in 668.

## EMPRESS WU CHAO'S SUPPORT OF BUDDHISM

As a result of intermittent paralytic strokes which Kao-tsung suffered during the latter years of his reign, administration of

[2] A. Waley, *The Real Tripitaka*, London, 1952, 93.     [3] *Ibid.*, 98.

governmental business fell largely into the hands of the extremely ambitious and capable Empress Wu Chao. From early childhood Wu Chao had been exposed to Buddhist influences at home, for her mother was a fervent follower of Buddhism—a faith which she inherited from her father, who was a member of the Sui imperial household. As early as 672-675 Empress Wu Chao gave an indication of her intention to support Buddhism by causing the great Buddha of the Rocks to be carved out in the grottoes of Lung-men, together with the surrounding company of bodhisattvas and guardians of the world. In later years she continued to encourage such sculptural activities at Lung-men, and the large number of inscriptions and images dated during her span of power provide indubitable evidence of this encouragement.

With the death of Kao-tsung in 683, Empress Wu took over the actual administration of the government. After she had deposed and exiled the legitimate emperor Chung-tsung, she began to lay the groundwork for setting up a new dynasty to take the place of the T'ang. In these endeavors she was assisted by a crafty, arrogant, and licentious individual named Feng Hsiao-pao, a peddler of cosmetics who also possessed a smattering of technical knowledge on architecture. After he had gained the favor of the empress (because of his virility, according to the historians), he became a monk in order to facilitate his entry into the imperial palace, given the name Hsüeh Huai-i, and made the abbot of the famous White Horse Temple outside Lo-yang.

The Confucian system does not permit women to assume political control of the state. For Empress Wu to take upon herself such power was a radical departure from normal practice. She consequently had to seek justification for her acts outside the Confucian classics. For this purpose the rich mine of Buddhist literature was available. Among the Mahāyāna sutras there was one which the Buddhist supporters of Empress Wu Chao seized upon, the *Ta-yün-ching* (*The Great Cloud Sutra, Mahāmegha-sutra*), of which there were already two Chinese translations available at this time, one by Chu Fo-nien and one by Dharmakshema. Some Chinese historians have claimed this sutra was forged by Buddhist monks at the instigation of the empress, but this charge is not correct.

In Chapter four of the Dharmakshema translation there is a

passage describing a conversation between the Buddha and a female divinity named Ching-kuang. In this conversation the Buddha said that, as a result of her having heard a recital of the *Mahāparinirvānasūtra* under a previous Buddha, she was now reborn as a female divinity, but that, having heard his (the Buddha's) profound teaching, she would become reborn as a universal monarch ruling over a wide area. In chapter six of the same sutra there is another passage concerning a prediction of the Buddha to the effect that, seven hundred years after his nirvāna, in a small country in south India a girl would be chosen ruler after the death of her father the king, and that she would eventually extend her rule over all of Jambudvipa.

The monk Huai-i and his followers copied verbatim these two passages and added some comments of their own, saying that the Empress Wu Chao was the incarnation of Maitreya on earth and therefore qualified to rule as successor to the T'ang emperors. Since this was just what the empress was seeking, she immediately decreed that the *Ta-yün-ching* be circulated throughout the empire, and in the ninth month of 690 she took the fateful step of changing the name of the dynasty from T'ang to Chou and set herself up as the first empress of the new dynasty. In this same year she also proclaimed that a Ta-yün Temple be erected under official auspices in each of the two capitals and in all the prefectures of the empire. The circulation of the *Ta-yün-ching* and the establishment of the Ta-yün Temples were measures designed by Wu Chao to capture the support of the people for her usurpation of the Dragon Throne; the claim that she was an incarnation of Maitreya on earth was also directed toward this end. This fitted in with the prevailing notion during the T'ang Dynasty that Maitreya was soon to be reborn on earth as its future Buddha and bolstered even more Wu Chao's claims to imperial power.

Under the impact of this imperial patronage Buddhism flourished during the years 685-705. The sudden upsurge of activity in sculpturing at Lung-men is the best indication of the magnitude and intensity of the popular faith in Buddhism. An official of this period complained, for instance, that "present day temples surpass even the imperial palaces in design, embodying the last word in extravagance, splendor, artistry, and finesse." As for the Ta-yün Temples which the empress decreed, some were established even in Central Asia, for Hui-ch'ao, traveling during the K'ai-yüan (713-741) era, found such a temple in An-hsi or Parthia, still inhabited and managed by Chinese monks. This was concrete evidence of the prestige and power of the Chinese dynasty; it also indicated how widespread Buddhism was among the populace. The imperial favor toward Buddhism finally resulted in the decree of 691, which reversed the policy of the previous T'ang rulers and gave priority to Buddhism over Taoism. As part of this patronage palace chapels were established within the imperial precincts in Ch'ang-an and Lo-yang. Such palace chapels had already existed under previous dynasties, such as the Eastern Chin, Northern Chou, and the Sui, but not on such a large scale as under the Empress Wu and the succeeding T'ang emperors. Within these chapels were to be found images of the Buddha; monks were in attendance day and night, chanting sutras, burning incense, or preaching to the members of the imperial household. Under Su-tsung and Tai-tsung hundreds of monks were attached to the chapels, and it was said that their chanting of the sutras could be heard outside the walls of the palaces.

In 705 the aging Empress Wu was finally forced to abdicate and the Dragon Throne was handed back to Chung-tsung and the T'ang Dynasty was thus restored. As a symbol of this restoration the emperor decreed that a Buddhist and a Taoist temple be established and supported by the state in each of the prefectures of the empire, the Buddhist institution to bear the designation Chung-hsing-ssu (Mid-dynasty Restoration Temple). Immediately objections arose against the name on the ground that it implied the T'ang fortunes had been cut off during the period of the usurper. Instead, the name Lung-hsing-ssu (Dragon Restoration Temple) was suggested and adopted in 707. It must be remembered that this measure did not involve the wholesale construction of new temples; what happened was merely that the names of existing temples were changed. For example, in Ch'ang-an the P'u-kuang Temple became the Lung-hsing Temple, while in Lo-yang it was the Chung-hsiang Temple that was changed.

## HSÜAN-TSUNG

With the disappearance of Empress Wu from the stage T'ang policy toward Buddhism underwent a change. In 711 Jui-tsung decreed that in all court ceremonials Buddhism and Taoism were to be on an equal footing. With the accession of Hsüan-tsung in 712 Taoism regained imperial favor and was again given priority over Buddhism. Taoist temples were established in the two capitals and in all the prefectures, and the populace was urged to study the Taoist classics, such as the *Tao-te-ching, Chuang-tzu, Lieh-tzu,* and *Wen-tzu.*

Though Hsüan-tsung personally favored Taoism, he did not take repressive measures against Buddhism. For instance, in 738 he called for the establishment of a new set of national temples, to be designated K'ai-yüan-ssu, in all the prefectures of the empire. In some instances the former Lung-hsing Temples were converted into the K'ai-yüan Temples, but in the majority of cases other temples were so designated. The result was that in some prefectures the two official temples, the Lung-hsing Temple and the K'ai-yüan Temple, existed side by side. Of the two the latter was considered to be the more important one, for it was the scene of such national celebrations as the imperial birthday ceremonies and those on the fifteenth day of the first, seventh, and tenth months of the year. Memorial services for deceased emperors were still held in the Lung-hsing Temple. The emperor also had high respect for Buddhist monks such as Vajrabodhi, whose translation activities he encouraged. It was during Hsüan-tsung's reign also that the authoritative catalogue of Buddhist translations in China, the *Kai-yüan shih-chiao-lu,* was compiled by Chih-sheng.

However, Hsüan-tsung did initiate a number of measures to regulate or to control Buddhism. Unworthy monks, up to thirty thousand in number, were defrocked. The construction of new temples by private individuals was prohibited. If old temples needed repairs, they must first be inspected by government officials before permission was granted. Small shrines were abolished as independent units and were combined with larger temples. Lands owned by temples were also limited in size; a monastery with a hundred or more monks might possess ten *ch'ing* as its permanent property, while one with fifty monks might own only seven *ch'ing.* Monks and nuns were also prohibited from wandering about the countryside to preach, nor were they permitted to sell Buddhist scriptures and images in the public streets. Such measures greatly hampered the freedom of the Buddhist monks and nuns to carry on their religious activities. Finally, entry into the monastic order was restricted by a system of granting monk certificates, inaugurated in 747.

The attempts of Hsüan-tsung to control and regulate Buddhism probably had some effect in keeping down the number of monks and temples, but the religion was too well established and accepted by the Chinese to be affected seriously by these measures. The rich imagery, the beautiful ritualism, and the soaring metaphysical speculations of Buddhism all captured the imagination of the Chinese. For example, the magnificent festivals of the Buddhist calendar such as the Festival of the Lanterns, the Feast of the Dead, the procession of the Buddha images, the reception of the Buddha's relic into the imperial palace, were dazzling spectacles in which all, high and low, could participate. Moreover, the Buddhist temples with their shaded nooks and corners, their architectural beauty, their gilded images of the Buddhas and bodhisattvas, and their beautiful illustrations provided a welcome change for the hungry eyes of the multitudes, who had to put up with drabness, squalor, and overcrowding in everyday life. Furthermore, many members of officialdom, outwardly paying lip service to Confucianism, were inwardly relying on Buddhism for support and solace. The amazing thing was that in spite of many features within Buddhism which were opposed to Chinese culture, the religion was still able to win the attention and adherence of the Chinese.

These differences between Buddhism and Chinese culture had formed the basis of anti-Buddhist sentiment expressed from time to time during the previous centuries. They were usually behind the charges that Buddhism was a foreign religion and therefore not appropriate for the Chinese. During the T'ang Dynasty some additional considerations arose that added fuel to the anti-Buddhist sentiment. The first of these concerned the large amount of temple lands owned by the Buddhists, which were exempt from taxation. Secondly, there were vast treasures in the temples in the form of gold and bronze images, ritual implements, bells, ornaments, and so forth—wealth that was withdrawn from circulation at a time when hard metals were scarce.

# HAN YÜ'S ANTI-BUDDHIST MEMORIAL

Among the numerous memorials presented against Buddhism during the T'ang by Confucian or Taoist men of letters, the most famous by far was the one presented in 819 by Han Yü, the eminent literary figure who took upon himself the task of weakening the influence of the Buddhist sangha and of restoring Confucianism to its former position of preeminence in the minds of the people. The occasion that he chose was the emperor's annual welcoming into the palace of a relic bone of the Buddha usually kept in the Fa-men Temple of Feng-hsiang, a suburb of the capital. The procession of the relic from the suburb to the capital was a popular annual festival which attracted huge throngs of people. In this memorial Han Yü attacked Buddhism mainly because it was a foreign religion unacceptable to the Chinese and because it shortened the duration of those dynasties which embraced it. Though these points had already been stressed by previous memorialists, they took on added significance then because of the preeminent position of Han Yü as a man of letters. The main portion of the memorial reads as follows:

"Now the Buddha was of barbarian origin. His language differed from Chinese speech; his clothes were of a different cut; his mouth did not pronounce the prescribed words of the Former Kings, his body was not clad in the garments prescribed by the Former Kings. He did not recognize the relationship between prince and subject, nor the sentiments of father and son. Let us suppose him to be living today, and that he come to court at the capital as an emissary of his country. Your Majesty would receive him courteously. But only one interview in the audience chamber, one banquet in his honor, one gift of clothing, and he would be escorted under guard to the border that he might not mislead the masses.

"How much the less, now that he has long been dead, is it fitting that his decayed and rotten bones, his ill-omened and filthy remains, should be allowed to enter in the forbidden precincts of the Palace? Confucius said, 'Respect ghosts and spirits, but keep away from them.' The feudal lords of ancient times, when they went to pay a visit of condolence in their states, made it their practice to have exorcists go before with rushbrooms and peachwood branches to dispel unlucky influences. Only after such precautions did they make their visit of condolence. Now without reason you have taken up an unclean thing and examined it in person when no exorcist had gone before, when neither rush-broom nor peachwood branch had been employed. But your ministers did not speak of the wrong nor did the censors call attention to the impropriety; I am in truth ashamed of them. I pray that Your Majesty will turn this bone over to the officials that it may be cast into water or fire, cutting off for all time the root and so dispelling the suspicions of the empire and preventing the befuddlement of later generations. Thereby men may know in what manner a great sage acts who a million times surpasses ordinary men. . . . Could this be anything but a cause for rejoicing?

"If the Buddha has supernatural power and can wreak harm and evil, may any blame or retribution fittingly fall on my person. Heaven be my witness: I will not regret it. Unbearably disturbed and with the utmost sincerity I respectfully present my petition that these things may be known.

"Your servant is truly alarmed, truly afraid."[4]

## THE SUPPRESSION OF 845, OR THE HUI-CH'ANG PERSECUTION

So far as we know, there does not seem to be any direct connection between Han Yü's memorial and the suppression of Buddhism by Emperor Wu-tsung in 845. We do not even know whether or not the emperor ever read the document; at any rate, he had ample reasons of his own to suppress the Indian religion. Some historians have given the impression that the suppression was a sudden development, and that it was but another episode in the long ideological struggle between Taoism and Buddhism. It is true that Taoists were instrumental in urging a strong repressive measure against the Buddhists, but the ideological struggle is not the whole story. Factional strife within the imperial court appears to have played a role in the suppression, with the scholar-bureaucrats allied with the emperor on the one side op-

[4] E. O. Reischauer, *Ennin's Travels*, New York, 1955, 223-224.

posed to the foreign religion, and the eunuchs on the other supporting it.

Moreover, economic considerations such as the desire of the imperial court to seize and utilize the immense wealth concentrated in the Buddhist temples also entered into the picture. This is seen in the statement presented by the office of the Imperial Grand Secretariat in the seventh month, 845; "Bronze images (of Buddhist deities) and bells are to be turned over to the Salt and Iron Commissioner to be melted into coins. Iron statues will be turned over to local officials to be converted into agricultural implements. Images made of gold, silver, jade, and so on are to be turned over to the Bureau of Public Revenue. All images made of gold, silver, bronze, and iron possessed by people of wealth and position are to be handed over to the government within one month after the issuance of this decree. . . . As for images made from clay, wood, or stone, these will be permitted to remain as usual within the temples."[5] The loss of revenue to the state, brought about by the large number of tax-exempt individuals (260,000 monks and nuns, 100,000 slaves, and an army of laymen in the employ of the church estimated to be equal to the combined number of monks and nuns) and the extensive area of tax-exempt land possessed by the monasteries was another economic factor that forced the emperor to take drastic action.

The official histories of the T'ang Dynasty do not furnish much information about the various events leading to the climax of 845. Fortunately for posterity, a very observant Japanese monk, Ennin, happened to be in China during the very years of the persecution, and the diary which he kept has preserved a valuable account of this historic episode. From this diary one finds unmistakable evidence that the steps taken against Buddhism by Wu-tsung were carried on over a number of years.

As early as 841, Ennin reported the first signs of the emperor's disfavor, when on the occasion of Emperor Wu's birthday the Taoist priests present were rewarded by being granted the privilege of wearing the purple robe while the Buddhists were not so rewarded. This was repeated during the birthday celebration of 842. In the same year a Buddhist monk, Hsüan-hsüan, claimed that he could defeat the hated Uighurs (a Central Asiatic people)

[5] *Harvard Journal of Asiatic Studies*, 19 (1956), 68.

by a magic sword, but when he was put to the test, he was found to be an impostor.

Therefore the emperor issued a decree in the tenth month to the effect that all monks and nuns who practice alchemy or magic, had fled from the army, bore traces of beatings on their bodies, kept wives, or violated the rules of discipline should be forced to return to the laity. Moreover, all monetary wealth and property, such as estates and gardens, which the monks or nuns might possess were to be turned over to the government. As a consequence of this measure 1,232 monks and nuns in the eastern half of the capital and 2,259 (variant 2,219) in the western half were defrocked in the first month of 843. Then in the second month the attack was broadened to include the Manichaean temples. All property possessed by the Manichaean temples, such as fields, gardens, shops, dwelling places, money, and goods, were to be surrendered to the government, and no foreign elements were to be permitted on such property. This measure was primarily directed against the Uighurs, who were the main supporters of the Manichaean church in China at the time.

A little backtracking is necessary here to explain the presence of the Uighurs.

In order to quell the rebellion led by An Lu-shan in the middle of the eighth century, an army consisting of Persians, Arabs, and Uighurs was invited into China by the T'ang rulers. Of this army, the Uighurs were the most important element. After the rebellion was suppressed, the Persians and Arabs left, but the Uighurs remained in Ch'ang-an and Lo-yang, where they began to behave like a conquering army, looting the cities and exacting payment from the populace, thereby incurring the hatred of the Chinese. The T'ang authorities were powerless to take any action against these foreigners, especially when they were backed by a powerful Uighur Empire in Central Asia. Since these Uighurs occupied such an advantageous position, it appears that the foreign population in the two capitals placed their wealth in the Manichaean temples which enjoyed the protection of the Uighurs, very much in the manner of merchants in the treaty ports of modern China placing their wealth in British banks. When the Uighur Empire declined after 832, the T'ang authorities felt the time had come to strike down this favored position of the Manichaean church.

The decree of 843 was directed primarily against the wealth and resources stored in the Manichaean temples.

Beginning with 844, the anti-Buddhist movement began to gain momentum, spurred on in many respects by the machinations of the Taoist Chao Kuei-chen and his two cohorts, Teng Yüan-ch'ao and Liu Hsüan-ching. In the third month of that year two Confucian officials recommended that the practice of observing the Buddhist fasting periods be discontinued. According to Buddhist customs there were three months during the year (the first, fifth, and ninth months) and six, sometimes ten, days in each month (the six days would be the eighth, fourteenth, fifteenth, twenty-third, twenty-ninth, and thirtieth; the ten would be the above plus the first, eighteenth, twenty-fourth, and twenty-eighth) when a fast was to be observed. As early as 619 a decree had been issued by Kao-tsu declaring that during these periods of fasting capital punishment and killing of animals were to be prohibited in the empire. It appears that this decree, which was repeated by Empress Wu in 692, was in effect throughout T'ang history until its discontinuance in 844. In the same year the Buddhists were excluded for the first time from the imperial birthday celebrations.

Within the Hall of Longevity in the imperial precincts there had existed for a long time a chapel where images of the Buddha and sacred scriptures were kept. Attached to this chapel were monks who were permitted to enter freely and to hold services therein for the welfare and prosperity of the empire, and to celebrate the imperial birthdays. Now, following the advice of his fanatic religious preceptor Chao, Wu-tsung had the Buddha images destroyed and the scriptures burned; the monks were ordered to return to their temples. In their places he set up images of Lao-tzu and other Taoist deities, and then called upon the learned men of his court to embrace Taoism as a religion. Ennin proudly reported that not a single one did so. In this same year (844) Wu-tsung also forbade worship of the Buddha's tooth relic and decreed that, if anyone donated money for such a ceremony, he would be bambooed twenty times. On the occasion of the All-Souls Festival in 844 the inhabitants of Ch'ang-an outdid themselves in their offerings to the Buddhist temples, but the emperor seized these offerings and presented them to a Taoist temple instead—an act that incurred the wrath of the populace.

Beginning with the seventh month of 844, the anti-Buddhist movement became more repressive, for the measures now promulgated were aimed at the progressive destruction of the Buddhist sangha. First, there were the decrees calling for the closing of all small temples and shrines and the defrocking of clerics whose names were not listed on the temple registers. The images and scriptures of such small temples were removed to the larger ones, while the bells and other ornaments were delivered to Taoist establishments. According to the Japanese monk three hundred establishments in Ch'ang-an alone were destroyed at this time. Then in the third month of the following year the government prohibited monasteries from establishing landed estates and called also for an inventory of temple slaves as well as property such as money, goods, or grains owned by the monasteries.

Heretofore, measures against the sangha called chiefly for the defrocking of those who did not observe the monastic rules or carried on questionable practices such as black magic and incantations. Now the government began to initiate a program affecting all monks, regardless of character, learning, or status. First, all monks under forty were ordered to return to the laity. Soon those under fifty were laicized. The next measure called for the defrocking of those above fifty who did not possess monk certificates. Foreign monks in China were included under this decree; any foreign monk without a monk certificate from the Bureau of Sacrifices was defrocked and ordered to return to his native land.

In order to prepare for the wholesale suppression of the religion, in the fourth month of 845 the throne ordered a census of the monastic community and the number of temples; the results of this census showed 260,000 monks and nuns, 4,600 temples, and 40,000 shrines. Armed with these figures, the throne in the seventh month ordered the destructon of all the Buddhist establishments in the land with the following exceptions: in each of the major prefectures one temple was to be preserved, usually the one most beautiful and artistic, while in each of the two capitals four Buddhist temples were to be permitted, each one to have thirty monks. Following this, the Grand Secretariat memorialized on the disposition of the temple wealth. The bronze images and bells were to be converted into coins, iron statues were to be melted into agricultural implements, and images made of gold, silver, and jade were to be turned over to the Bureau of Public Revenue. Finally, in the eighth month the throne issued the edict that summed up the results of the persecution:

"We have learned that up through the three dynasties (of Hsia, Shang, and Chou) there had never been any talk of Buddhism, and only since the Han and Wei has this idolatrous religion come to flourish. In recent times its strange ways have become so customary and all pervasive as to have slowly and unconsciously corrupted the morals of our land. The hearts of our people have been seduced by it and the masses all the more led astray. From the mountains and wastes of the whole land to the walled palaces of the two capitals, the Buddhist monks daily increase in number, and their monasteries daily grow in glory. In exhausting men's strength in construction work, in robbing men for their own golden and jeweled adornments, in forsaking ruler and kin to support their teachers, in abandoning their mates for monastic rules, in flouting the laws and in harming the people, nothing is worse than this religion.

"Now, when one man does not farm, others suffer hunger, and, when one woman does not weave, others suffer from the cold. At present the monks and nuns of the empire are numberless, but they all depend on agriculture for their food and on sericulture for their clothing. The monasteries and temples are beyond count, but they all are lofty and beautifully decorated, daring to rival palaces in grandeur. None other than this was the reason for the decline in material strength and the weakening of the morals of the Chin, Sung, Ch'i, and Liang.

"Furthermore, Kao-tsu and T'ai-tsung put an end to disorders by arms and governed this fair land with literary arts. These two methods suffice for ruling the land. Why then should this insignificant Western religion compete with us? During the Chenkuan (627-650) and K'ai-yüan (713-742) periods there were also reforms, but they failed to eradicate the evil, which continued to spread and flourish.

"We have broadly considered previous statements and widely sought out general opinions and have absolutely no doubt that this evil should be reformed. Our ministers of the court and in

the provinces are in accord with our Will. It is most proper that
We regulate (the Buddhist church), and We should follow their
wishes on this. We yield to no one in chastising this source of
corruption for a thousand years, in fulfilling the laws of the
hundred kings (before Us), and in aiding the people and bene-
fitting the masses.

"More than 4,600 monasteries are being destroyed throughout
the empire; more than 260,500 monks and nuns are being returned to lay life and being subjected to the double tax; more
than 40,000 temples and shrines are being destroyed; several tens
of millions of *ch'ing* of fertile lands and fine fields are being confiscated; 150,000 slaves are being taken over to become payers of
the double tax. Monks and nuns are to be placed under the
jurisdiction of the Bureau of Guests, to indicate clearly that Buddhism is a foreign religion. We are returning more than 3,000
Nestorians and Zoroastrians to lay life, so that they will not
adulterate the customs of China."[6]

This persecution of Buddhism in 845 was undoubtedly the
most widespread of its kind in China. The earlier instances in
446 and 574-577 were largely limited to north China, in those
regions under the control of the Northern Wei and Northern
Chou, and were not responsible for any lasting bad effects on the
religion. The Buddhist communities in south China were not
touched at all. The T'ang proscription, on the other hand, was
effective throughout the empire, and because it damaged the
Buddha sangha permanently, it is one of the significant events
in the history of Buddhism in China. Even before the persecution,
Buddhism already showed signs of decay in the slackening of
faith and intellectual vigor in some areas, but the suppression of
845 supplied the crippling blow. That year is therefore a pivotal
date, marking the end of the apogee and the beginning of the
decline of the religion.

The suppression itself was of short duration. Within a year,
in the third month of 846, Wu-tsung died, his health probably
affected by the longevity potions which he had been taking, and
the imperial scepter was taken up by Hsüan-tsung, who immediately initiated action to call off the anti-Buddhist movement. To
start with, the Taoists, Chao Kuei-chen and Liu Hsüan-ching,

---

[6] Reischauer, *op.cit.*, 225-227, with some changes.

along with eleven others, were executed because they had incited the previous emperor to extreme measures against Buddhism. Imperial permission was then given to increase the number of temples in the capital from four to twelve; each prefecture was also permitted to have two, and the regional commanderie three, temples. Moreover, monks over fifty who had been defrocked the previous year were permitted to resume their monastic garb.

During the following year the emperor issued what might be considered as the go-ahead signal for the Buddhist sangha to start functioning again as usual. This edict said that though Buddhism was regarded as a foreign religion, it had not damaged the fundamental principles of the empire, and therefore should not be abolished, especially since the Chinese had practiced it for a long time. Consequently, if monks wanted to repair the temples damaged during the persecution, they should not be forbidden to do so by the authorities. Thus once again we see the 845 persecution following the pattern of its predecessors—first, violent, extreme action taken against the Indian religion by the ruler, followed soon after by his demise and the subsequent policy of revival of the religion by his successor.

## CHINESE PILGRIMS ABROAD

During this period when the religion was so widespread and influential in China, there was a noticeable increase in the number of Chinese pilgrims venturing forth to India in search of the dharma. The power of the T'ang emperors was now felt in Central Asia, and many of the small Central Asiatic states, in an attempt to be on good terms with the Chinese, facilitated the travel of Chinese monks through their territories. Buddhism had also made such deep inroads into the national life of China and converted so many pious devotees that many Chinese desired to go to the fountainhead of their religion and drink deeply of the sources there. In only one previous period, the Northern Wei, do we find the number of pilgrims remotely approaching that which left during the T'ang. At that time the Northern Wei rulers had extended their influence over Central Asia. Moreover, in India the teachings of the Mahāyāna masters Asanga and Vasubandhu were gaining prominence, serving as a powerful magnet to draw Chinese pilgrims there. These pilgrims of the fifth century brought back a mass of materials to be translated during the following century. By the seventh century the Chinese had more or less digested these materials, and, having found shortcomings and discrepancies in the body of translations, they felt the need for renewed stimulus from India. All these factors resulted in a burst of increased activity on the part of the Chinese pilgrims during the T'ang Dynasty.

While the Chinese pilgrims were traveling in India, they sometimes found lodgings in temples established for their convenience, called Chinese Temples. One such institution was located in eastern India on the lower reaches of the Ganges, another was in Kashmir, and probably still another in Rājagaha.

### HSÜAN-CHAO

Of the pilgrims who left T'ang China, one of the most intrepid was Hsüan-chao, who left ca.651. He first traversed Central Asia as far as the Iron Gate; it seems that he even crossed the Hindukush, but somewhere on his journey he either lost his way or his biographer became confused as to the geography. After having crossed the Hindukush, he seems to have retraced his steps and to have gone all the way back to Tibet. At that time the Chinese princess Wen-ch'eng, wife of the Tibetan king Srong-btsan-sgam-po, was already in Tibet, and through her friendly offices Hsüan-chao was put back on the right route to India. While in India he spent four years each at Jalandhara and Bodhgaya, and three at Nālandā, studying Sanskrit and philosophy. His return trip, which was arranged by the Chinese envoy to India, Wang Hsüan-ts'e, was by way of Nepal and Tibet, where Princess Wen-ch'eng provided him with an escort back to China. He had no sooner settled down to his translation activities when an imperial decree ordered him back to India to search for a famous Indian doctor. Once more he set out on the hazardous journey across deserts and mountains, until he came to the Indian border, where he met the physician who was the object of his search. The doctor was already on his way to China, but he requested Hsüan-chao to proceed to India for some medicinal drugs. The Chinese pilgrim took advantage of this trip to revisit the sacred sites of Buddhism, but when he was ready to start home, he found the overland route blocked by the Arabs, who were then in control of Bactria and the vicinity, and by Tibetans, who had revolted against Chinese domination and had taken over Khotan, Yarkand, Kashgar, and Kucha in 670. Hsüan-chao was therefore obliged to spend his last days in India.

## HSÜAN-TSANG

By far the most famous of these T'ang pilgrims was Hsüan-tsang (ca.596-664), to whom we are indebted for many important translations and for much valuable information concerning Central Asia and India.

Hsüan-tsang left the country stealthily in 629, for his petition to the court for permission to leave had been refused. Before his departure he was already interested in Buddhist philosophy, especially the idealism of the Vijñānavādin School, but many unsolved problems such as discrepancies in the text bothered him, and it was to search for an answer to these problems that he set out. His journey was almost terminated as soon as it began, first by an attempt of his guide to murder him—which he avoided by waking up just in time—and then by his getting lost in the trackless wastes of the desert, extricating himself only by calling upon the bodhisattva Avalokiteśvara for assistance. On his way he stopped first at Turfan, where the king, impressed by Hsüan-tsang, refused to let him leave; only the actual threat of a hunger strike by Hsüan-tsang weakened the king's will to keep him. Once the king consented to his departure, he made all the necessary arrangements to facilitate the Chinese pilgrim's travels through Central Asia. This the king did by providing letters of introduction to the various princes along the way, a measure of great help to Hsüan-tsang which practically assured the success of his journey. Hsüan-tsang then proceeded to Karashar, Tashkend, Samarkand, and on through the Iron Gate into Bactria. From Bactria he crossed the Hindukush into Kapiśa, where he started the descent from the Iranian plateau to the lower and milder region of Nagarahāra. He was so struck by the contrast between the Hindus and the mountain-dwelling Afghans that he has left behind a very graphic description of the former. "By habit the people of the country live in luxury and happiness. They also like to sing. By nature, however, they are effeminate, soft, ill-tempered, and treacherous. They treat each other with deceit and scorn and they never give way to another. They are small in stature and their movements are light and impetuous."[7]

Having entered Gandhāra, Hsüan-tsang visited Peshawar and Taxila, then went over to Kashmir to study for two years. In 633 he decided to proceed to the holy land of his faith. As he was sailing down the Ganges River, a dramatic episode took place which almost cost him his life. Bandits captured his group and wanted to offer Hsüan-tsang as a human sacrifice, since they were pleased with his appearance. The Chinese pilgrim replied: "If this dirty and contemptible body could fulfill your purpose, then indeed I would not dare to begrudge it. But I have come from afar for the purpose of paying respects to the bodhi tree, the Buddha images, and Vulture Peak, and to seek for the dharma. These purposes have not been accomplished, and if you kill me, I am afraid it may not be beneficial to you."[8] The bandits were not intimidated by this, so Hsüan-tsang asked for a few moments of calm in order to pray to Maitreya, the Future Buddha. As he was praying, he went into a trance. Suddenly a violent wind arose that terrified the bandits, and they hastily awoke Hsüan-tsang from his trance to ask his forgiveness.

After this episode Hsüan-tsang proceeded as rapidly as possible to the sacred places, starting with Śrāvastī, then Kapilavastu, Kusinara, Benares, Vaiśālī, Pātaliputra, and finally Bodhgaya. Here at the bodhi tree Hsüan-tsang saw the statue of Avalokiteśvara and recalled the old prophecy that when the statue disappeared into the ground, Buddhism would disappear also. When the pilgrim saw the statue, it had already sunk as far as the breast. After this he then went on to Nālandā to study the Vijñānavāda doctrines from the grand old abbot of the monastery, Śilabhadra, already one hundred and six years old and in the direct line of transmission from the sages Asanga and Vasubandhu. During this first sojourn at Nālandā Hsüan-tsang stayed for fifteen months, perfecting his knowledge of Buddhist philos-

[7] Ta-T'ang Hsi-yü chi, 2; Taishō, 51,878b.
[8] Ta-tz'u-en San-tsang fa-shih chuan, 3; Taishō, 50,234a.

ophy and of Sanskrit. At the end of this period he took to the
road and went down the east coast to south India, hoping to go
from there to Ceylon. However, civil strife on the island thwarted
this plan; so he started north again, this time going up the west
coast to the Gujarat peninsula. He then turned eastward to return
to Nālandā for his second stay. This time he concentrated on
Indian philosophy. As he neared the end of his stay, he expressed
a desire to return to China. His fellow Indian monks tried to
dissuade him, saying: "India is the place where the Buddha was
born, and though the great Sage has passed away, his traces still
remain here. . . . China is the land of the barbarians, the people
there scorn the monks and despise the faith. That is why the
Buddhas were not born there."[9] Hsüan-tsang defended his native
land against this charge of barbarism, pointing to the Confucian
principles of government and ethics, and to the advances made in
astronomy, music, and engineering. He said he was merely carrying out the wishes of the Buddha in returning to China.

The reputation of Hsüan-tsang was so great in India that many
rulers wanted to see and to honor him. One of these was Bhāskara
Kumāra, king of Kāmarūpa (Assam), whom Hsüan-tsang visited.
Afterward both Kumāra and the Chinese cleric traveled together
to call on Harsha, emperor of India. The emperor, having heard
of the arrival of the famous Chinese monk, hurried over to pay
his respects, which he did first by bowing to the ground and
kissing Hsüan-tsang's feet. Harsha then convened a grand assembly, over which the pilgrim presided, to dissipate the blind-
ness of the Hīnayāna and to shatter the pride of the Brahmans,
as Harsha put it. For eighteen days the contestants debated, but
in the end Hsüan-tsang emerged triumphant over all.

After this, Hsüan-tsang made preparations to return to China.
He received valuable assistance from Harsha, who provided him
with escorts and loaded him with gifts. This time he took the
southern route across Central Asia, finally arriving back in Ch'ang-
an, the T'ang capital, in 645 after an absence of sixteen years. The
tumultuous and elaborate welcome he received at the capital
must have recalled memories of the way he had sneaked across

---

[9] *Ibid.*, 5; *Taishō*, 50,246a. The Chinese had previously called the Indians
barbarous, coarse, and uncivilized, and said that the Buddha was born in
their midst to convert them.

the border of China, traveling only by night for fear of detection by the imperial guards at the passes. A few days after his arrival he had an audience with the emperor, who questioned him closely concerning the climate, products, peoples, and manners of the countries he had visited. The emperor was so pleased with the information that he wanted the pilgrim to take some official post. Hsüan-tsang preferred to remain a monk, and for the remainder of his life he dedicated himself to the task of translating the rich stores of sutras he had brought back with him. It is said he carried back to China 657 items packed in 520 cases. Of these he translated only 73 items in 1,330 *chüan*.[10] He also wrote the *Ta-T'ang Hsi-yü chi* (*Records of the Western Regions*), which has been of great value to historians and archeologists for the data it contains. When Hsüan-tsang died in 664, out of veneration and respect the emperor canceled his audiences for three days.

## I-TSING AND THE MARITIME ROUTE

The closing of the western end of the land route by the Arabs in the mid-seventh century and the eruptions of the Tibetans in Central Asia turned the attention of the Chinese pilgrims to the sea as a means of reaching India. And so, beginning with the latter half of the seventh century, more and more pilgrims followed the maritime route. The usual ports of debarkation were Canton and Hanoi in the south. At this time the coasts of Indo-China and the Indian archipelago were already Indianized; the Indian state of Śrīvijaya, established by the Śailendra Dynasty, had already set up a hegemony over the Southern Oceans. These Śailendra kings were patrons of Indian culture and were the ones responsible for the magnificent masterpiece of Buddhist sculpture, the Borobudur, in Java. As the Chinese pilgrim sailed toward India, he literally saw the Buddhist world coming to meet him all along the way.

[10] The most important of these translations are the huge *Mahāprajñāpāramitā* in 600 *chüan*; *Mahāvibhāsha* (*The Great Commentary*), 200 *chüan*; *Yogacārabhūmiśāstra* (*Treatise on the Yogacāra Stages*), 100 *chüan*; *Jñānaprasthāna*, 20 *chüan*; *Abhidharmakośa*, 30 *chüan*; *Mahāyānasaṁgraha*, 10 *chüan*; *Trimśika* (*Treatise in Thirty Stanzas*); *Viṁśatika* (*Treatise in Twenty Stanzas*); *Vijñaptimātratāsiddhi* (*The Completion of Ideation Only*), 10 *chüan*; and the *Madhyāntavibhāgatīkā*.

The first important pilgrim to take this sea route was I-tsing, who left Canton in 671 on board a Persian vessel, arriving at Tamralipti in 673. After making a tour of the holy sites, he settled at Nālandā for ten years to study the sacred scriptures in that famous monastery. In 685 he started on his return trip, again traveling by sea. During his stay in India he had collected a huge number of Sanskrit texts, which he now took to Śrīvijaya to be translated into Chinese. The task was too stupendous for him, so in 689 he returned to Canton to look for some assistants. Fortunately, he was able to find a few and together with these monks he returned to Śrīvijaya the same year to continue his translation. For five more years he remained at that outpost of Indian culture, until 695, when he finally sailed back to China. At that time the empress Wu Tse-t'ien, known for her patronage of Buddhism, was in power, and she showered honors upon the returned pilgrim. As I-tsing preferred to spend his time translating, the court assigned a group of scholars to assist him in his work. In all, he is credited with the translation of 56 works in 230 *chüan*. His most important contribution was the translation of the lengthy and detailed *Vinaya* of the Mūlasarvāstivādin School. Besides his translations, I-tsing wrote two important works, *Nan-hai-chi-kuei-nei-fa-chuan* (*A Record of the Buddhist Kingdoms in the Southern Archipelago*) and *Ta-t'ang-hsi-yü ch'iu-fa kao-seng chuan* (*Biographies of Eminent Monks of the T'ang Who Sought the Dharma in the Western Regions*), which recorded brief biographies of some fifty-six Chinese pilgrims who went abroad between the reigns of T'ai-tsung and the Empress Wu, mostly by following the maritime route.

Even among such a pious group of pilgrims could be found a rascal, namely, one Ming-yüan (latter half of the seventh century), who would have passed into oblivion but for an infamous deed that he perpetrated. When he arrived in Ceylon via the sea route, he was cordially welcomed by the Ceylonese, but this cordiality soon disappeared when the most precious Buddhist relic in Ceylon, the Buddhist's tooth, was found in his possession. After this attempted theft, the Ceylonese took the greatest precautions to guard the tooth. "They place it on a high tower, and they shut the many doors with complicated bolts. On each bolt is placed a seal and five officials put their stamp on it. If a door is opened, a resounding noise warns the town."[11]

## SERVICE TO WORLD CULTURE

By their journeys and translations these Chinese pilgrims rendered a valuable service to world culture. The records which they left behind have preserved for posterity data of inestimable value concerning India, the Indian archipelago, and Central Asia. Moreover, they helped to link India closer with China and Japan. At a time when Buddhism was slowly disappearing in its native land, being engulfed by the all-pervasive influence of Hinduism, the Chinese pilgrims of the T'ang Dynasty appeared on the scene to learn all that India had to offer. Having done this, they returned to their fatherland to play their role in the flowering of Buddhism under the glorious T'ang Dynasty. They then transmitted that learning to the Japanese monks who came to them, and after the Japanese had mastered what the Chinese had to teach, they returned to Japan to become the agents of the cultural transformation of that country.

In this chapter we have traced the attitude of the different T'ang rulers toward Buddhism and the ebb and flow of the religion in response to imperial favor or disfavor. We have also mentioned a few of the most eminent monks of the dynasty, pious and conscientious followers of the law, who braved the dangers of deserts, mountains, and oceans to get to India, in order that they might study at the feet of Indian masters and learn Sanskrit. Now that we have followed the external fortunes of Buddhism, we shall look at the religion itself, starting with an examination of the monastic community during this period of acceptance.

[11] I-tsing, *Ta-T'ang Hsi-yü ch'iu-fa Kao-seng chuan*; *Taishō*, 51,3c.

# CHAPTER IX

# THE MONASTIC ORDER

THE Buddhist sangha or monastic community was originally organized to provide the best possible conditions for the pursuit of the religious goals preached by the Buddha. In a community where the members no longer needed to worry about material sustenance or the cares and anxieties of family and society, it was felt that they could devote their whole minds and energies to the spiritual discipline demanded by the founder of their religion. As the dharma developed in India, there arose the division between the Hīnayāna and the Mahāyāna, but in the sangha no such division was to be found. For the monks and nuns in India and Ceylon, in Tibet and China, the rules of discipline which they had to observe in their daily lives were substantially the same, though there may have been differences in minor details. Thus, although the Buddhists in China were predominantly Mahāyānists, they regulated their conduct and transacted sangha business in accordance with the rules of discipline of the Sarvāstivādin and Dharmagupta Schools, both belonging to the Hīnayāna tradition.

According to the *Vinaya* rules entry into the sangha was an individual affair, dependent entirely on the wishes of the individual or his family, with the state having no say in the matter at all. As Buddhism developed during the T'ang Dynasty, however, practices arose that were not specified in the *Vinaya*, which subjected ordination to the control of the state. During previous dynasties sangha officials had been appointed by the government, such officials to exercise control over the sangha and temple activities. Not only did the T'ang court continue this, but it also assumed control over the ordination and initiated measures to limit the number of monks in the order. The freedom of individuals to join the sangha was also limited. The religion had to adapt itself to such conditions in order to exist.

## CATEGORIES OF MONKS

During the Sui Dynasty one Buddhist source recorded that 230,000 monks and nuns were converted. Just what the number was at the beginning of the T'ang Dynasty is not known, but there must have been a decrease, for the census registers showed 75,524 monks and 50,576 nuns during the K'ai-yüan era (713-741). The clerical community might be divided into three categories: (*a*) the official monks, who resided in the official temples, received their support from the state, and were entrusted with the performance of the ceremonies connected with the imperial cult; (*b*) private monks, who were ordained and supported by the rich and grand families of the empire; (*c*) monks of the people, who lived in isolated monasteries and temples in the mountains or country areas and derived their support mainly from the people. Such a division was indicated by the T'ang monk Fa-lin, who wrote that under the Northern Wei there existed 47 grand monasteries of the state, 839 monasteries of princes and eminent families, and 30,000 monasteries of the common people. Under the T'ang the number of official monks was large, since such state institutions as the Ta-yün Temple and K'ai-yüan Temple were established in all the prefectures of the realm. To the extent that the religion was orthodox and supported the legitimate powers of the state, Buddhism had its place in the religious ceremonies of the T'ang court.

## ORDINATION OF MONKS, PRIVATE AND OFFICIAL

During the first half of the T'ang, *ssu-tu* or private ordination of monks was the prevailing practice. The monasteries themselves conducted the ceremonies ordaining those who had satisfactorily passed the necessary requirements. Various members of the nobility, imperial princes and princesses, were also given the privilege of conducting ordination ceremonies, and they vied with one another in presiding over such ordinations. The number of monks thus ordained was probably large, for officials complained that in former times the revenue derived from the sale of offices went into the public coffers, while now the income from the ordination ceremonies went into private pockets. Undesirable elements also took advantage of such ordinations to become converted, for a memorial presented in 711 charged that "at present those who are able to put up wealth and to rely on their influence have all become *śramaṇas*. Those who wished to avoid the *corvée* and to practice deceit have all become converted. Only those who are poor and virtuous have not been ordained."[1] The court attempted from time to time to weed out such undesirable elements from the monastic community by forcing them to return to lay life. On one occasion during the K'ai-yüan era some 12,000 were defrocked, while on another, 30,000 were said to have been laicized. However, such periodic purges of the order appear to have been inadequate, and in 747 the court decided to inaugurate a system of official ordination, sponsored by the state, whereby the monks so ordained were to be granted a monk certificate by the Bureau of National Sacrifice. The main objective of this system was to cut down the number of ordinations. Besides prohibiting private ordination, it proposed to limit the number of clerics by refusing ordination to those whose character or intelligence was not deemed acceptable.

The purpose of the official ordination was undoubtedly a worthy one, but events on the national scene rendered it ineffective before it had a chance to operate properly. The An Lushan rebellion, which broke out in 755, required large outlays for its suppression; this left the imperial treasury virtually empty, so that the government had no funds to buy supplies for the army. Among other expedients the court resorted to the sale of monk certificates to anyone who desired to become a cleric. Large numbers of such certificates were sold in the vicinity of Ch'ang-an and Lo-yang, not only to those who wanted to join the Buddhist order, but also to prospective Taoist priests and nuns, so that the imperial treasury was enriched by over a million strings of cash. (A string consists of one thousand cash.)

This policy of the sale of monk certificates to acquire revenue was in the nature of a temporary economic expedient, and it was apparently discontinued by the state after the financial crisis was tided over. However, once started, the practice did not die so easily. Local officials began to employ the same procedure of selling certificates to increase their private income. By so doing, they revived the practice of private ordination which had been prohibited in 747.[2] Such privately ordained monks were far in

---

[1] K. Ch'en, *Harvard Journal of Asiatic Studies*, 19 (1956), 79.
[2] One well-known instance of such private ordination involved Wang

the majority in the early ninth century, for in 830, when the Bureau of National Sacrifice ordered all privately—and therefore unofficially—ordained monks to register and to receive the official certificates, the incredible number of 700,000 were reported to have registered. Probably what happened was that large numbers of people who had never been ordained took advantage of the imperial offer to register as monks in the hope of obtaining some personal benefit, in the form of exemption from taxation or the *corvée.* At any rate, it is clear that the number of privately ordained monks far outnumbered those officially ordained. During the suppression of 845 the government ordered a census of the clerical population in the empire, and the results indicated that there were 260,000 monks and nuns. This is strong evidence that the figure of 700,000 for 830 is an inflated one. However, the figure for 845 did not include novices, of which there must have been a considerable number. For instance, in the Hsi-ming Temple alone, when Hsüan-tsang was in residence there, there were 150 such novices.

## CENSUS OF MONKS

From time to time reference is made to the census of the clerical community in T'ang China. The preparation of the monk registry was started in 729. Such a registry was compiled once every three years by the local officials in the prefecture, and was recorded in three copies, one to be kept in the local prefecture, one to be sent to the Bureau of National Sacrifice, and one to the Court of State Ceremonials. This practice was continued in later dynasties, with one modification. In addition to the master registry made every three years there was to be an annual count made by the local officials after the fifteenth day of the fourth month, the figures to be sent to the Bureau of National Sacrifice, where they were checked against those in the master registry. Changes due to deaths, new ordinations; return to the laity, or removal to

---

Chih-hsing, a local official in An-hui, who established an ordination platform in his prefecture in ca.824 and began selling certificates to anyone willing to pay 2,000 cash for one. It was estimated that over one hundred people were ordained daily by this procedure, with the converts coming not only from Wang's district but also from the surrounding area.

another area were noted in the proper places. Such a close registry of the monastic order enabled the state at any year to know the exact clerical population, and this accounts for the exact figures that have been presented periodically.

## COMPOSITION OF THE SANGHA IN CHINA

As constituted in China, the monastic community consisted of eight categories, male and female postulants called *t'ung-hsing*, male and female novices, monks and nuns, laymen and laywomen. The postulant group was something new, and was established because of the belief that a candidate could not become a novice immediately but must undergo a period of training. It is not known just when this category was established, but it was already in existence during the T'ang Dynasty. From regulations drawn up during the Sung Dynasty we learn that, in order to become a postulant, the candidate first presented an application to the abbot of a temple, stating his name, age, native district, that he was free from all criminal punishments, and that he had secured parental permission to enter the monastery as a postulant. The abbot of a temple, after receiving such an application, then requested an interview with the applicant to determine whether or not he was sincere in joining the order, or whether he was merely seeking to escape from some temporal involvements. Parental permission was absolutely necessary. Other regulations specified the following grounds for turning down an applicant:

*a*) if a boy was under nineteen and a girl under fourteen years of age;

*b*) if he had joined once before and then returned to the laity;

*c*) if he had committed some crime;

*d*) if he was an escapee from justice;

*e*) if there were no adult sons or grandsons in the family.

If the applicant satisfied all requirements, he was then admitted as a postulant, and he then had to follow the five cardinal precepts of the order. In China, however, he did not shave his hair, as was the case in Japan. He had certain duties to perform. He must study the sacred scriptures, but he must also perform such tasks as attending the abbot or temple guests. Moreover, he was not exempted from the customary tax and labor services. Consequently, we read in the regulations, "The postulants keep their hair, and pay their tax through their families." It was only after they became novices that they became exempt from their tax burdens. This explains why there was such fierce competition among the postulants for ordination as novices. After completing one year of study, the postulant was eligible for an examination to determine whether or not he was qualified for the initiation ceremony.

## ORDINATION THROUGH EXAMINATION

During the T'ang Dynasty this examination usually consisted of reciting a certain number of leaves from a sutra, such as the *Lotus Sutra*, or reading and explaining a text. For instance, during the reign of Ching-tsung (825-826) a male postulant had to recite 150 leaves, a female 100 leaves. During the Period of the Five Dynasties five tests were established: (1) a lecture on the scriptures; (2) the practice of concentration; (3) memorization of a text; (4) composition of a piece of literature; (5) comment on a passage. In the Later Chou era a male *t'ung-hsing* had to recite 100 leaves and read 500 leaves, a female 70 and 300—requirements which were also adopted by the Sung authorities. Under the latter dynasty, if the candidate failed to recite the text, he was permitted to offer an excuse and to submit himself to an oral examination in which he had to pass a majority of ten questions in order to qualify. This examination of the *t'ung-hsing* was conducted not by the monks but by government officials meeting in a government office.

If the candidate were successful, he was then granted a certificate by the official in charge; then he went to his master for the tonsure and ordination. At this ceremony the candidate received the ordination rites, which signified departure from household life and entry into the monastic order. At the ordination ceremony certain fees were charged, one for the tonsure, another to cover the cost of paper and ink for printing the certificate. In 977 the fee was 100 cash, but later on, in 1073, the Japanese monk Jojin indicated that it was 1,000 cash, which was paid to the government for the certificate. This marks an important difference in practice between Japan and China. In Japan the successful candidate first went through the tonsure ceremony, then the ordination itself; whereas in China ordination came first, then the tonsure. One might say that in China the granting of the ordination certificate was an official affair, while the tonsure was a temple ceremony. The ceremony was held in the great hall of the temple, where the *t'ung-hsing* first took off his secular robes and put on his clerical garb; then he received the tonsure from his master, after which he vowed to observe the ten *silas*. He was now a *śrāmanera* or novice. Ordinarily, the next step was to proceed toward the stage of a *bhikshu* or monk, but in China the majority of the order preferred to remain as *śrāmanera*. Only those with great ambition or those who were important personalities became monks by going through the *upasampadā* or full ordination. In the Ch'an School, where meditation was preferred over observance of the rules of discipline, the *upasampadā* was reserved only for special cases. Thus in China members of the order generally remained as *śrāmanera*. Because of the higher prestige and privilege connected with being a *śrāmanera*, it was felt that some period of preparation was necessary, hence the *t'ung-hsing period*.

## ORDINATION THROUGH IMPERIAL
## FAVOR AND PURCHASE OF CERTIFICATES

Besides the examination system, ordination could be obtained by two other methods—by *en-tu* or the favor of the emperor and by *chin-na* or the purchase of the ordination certificate. In the first instance monks were ordained by the grace or favor of the emperor, usually when a tablet of recognition was granted by the emperor to a certain temple, or when a merit cloister was established. Other occasions would be the birthday of the emperor or the imperial visitation to a newly established temple. In such ordinations the procedure was that the abbot of a temple should present the names of qualified *t'ung-hsing* to the local government office for monks, with a petition for their ordination. The local official in turn presented the petition to the Bureau of National Sacrifice, and when the latter organization approved, then the ceremonies of ordination by the grace of the emperor were carried out. Usually the number of monks thus ordained depended on the number of existing monks in each district, the ratio sometimes being one for each one hundred.

Finally, there was the practice of obtaining the monk's certificate by purchase. Sale of monk certificates was carried out at the end of the An Lu-shan rebellion, but it was under the Sung that the practice was indulged in on a large scale. It is usually believed that the sale during the Sung started during the reign of Shen-tsung (1068-1075). However, as early as the reign of T'ai-tsung (976-997) there was an edict prohibiting officials from obtaining a monopoly of certificates in one district and selling them in another. Such an edict would indicate that selling of certificates was going on at that time. It is correct, however, to say that the sale of certificates as part of a national policy began with Shen-tsung.

## SOCIAL ORIGIN OF MONKS

From what groups in society did the members of the order come? If one relies merely on the information furnished by the *Biographies of Eminent Monks*, one gets the impression that they were drawn mainly from the well-to-do families who could afford to bear the cost of a literary education for their children. This could be inferred from the fact that quite a number were already well educated when they left household life and were able to read and understand the Buddhist sutras without any trouble. Such monks as Hui-yüan and Tsung-mi, the Hua-yen master, entered the order after having enjoyed a good classical education. However, it must be emphasized that since only eminent and outstanding monks were included in these biographies, the list is by no means representative. Nothing illustrates this better than the proportion of the number of monks mentioned in the biographies[3] to the total number in the order throughout the ages. In the

---

[3] The *Kao-seng-chuan*, covering the period from the Later Han to ca.520, contained biographies of 257 monks and mentioned 200 others casually. The *Hsü Kao-seng-chuan*, covering the period from the Liang Dynasty to 667, contained biographies of 485 monks and mentioned 219 others; while the *Sung Kao-seng-chuan*, covering the period 667-987, contained biographies of 532 monks and mentioned 125 others.

three standard biographies the names of 1,818 monks appeared—a mere fraction of the members in the monastic community in China down to 987.

Of the three classes of monks mentioned at the beginning of this chapter, it is safe to say that the official and private monks came from well-to-do families and were well educated. They had to be, in order to communicate on terms of equality with officialdom and the grand families. But the number of such official and private monasteries was again small compared to the total number in the realm. For example, during the Northern Wei there were only about 900 such monasteries, compared to 30,000 monasteries of the people.

So far no comprehensive studies have been made of the social origin of those monks whose names have been preserved in the numerous biographies, and even if such studies were attempted, it is doubtful whether fruitful data could be obtained, because so often the biographies do not preserve this type of information. With respect to the monks who inhabited the monasteries of the people and who must have comprised the greater majority of the monastic community, there is no question about their social origin. They came from the peasant families in the neighborhood of the institutions. Fu Yi, in his memorial against Buddhism at the beginning of the T'ang Dynasty, noted specifically that those who embraced Buddhism were mainly of peasant stock. Drawing their support from the farming families amidst whom they were located, catering to the simple religious needs of such illiterate peasant groups, these monks of the people were not likely to have been better educated than the people they served. Not very much is known about the admission and training of such monks; it is possible that the procedure described above was not adhered to strictly, so that these monks of the people may have had little or no acquaintance with the great body of Buddhist literature.

## UPKEEP OF MONKS, FOOD AND CLOTHING

One of the charges hurled against the sangha by the Confucianists was that Buddhist monks and nuns had to be fed and clothed even though they did not engage in any productive labor. How much did it cost to support one monk for one year during T'ang times? This is not an easy question to answer because of the paucity of information. For information about cost of clothing we are entirely dependent upon Ennin for data. It was indeed a far cry from the traditional simple monastic garb worn by Indian monks, said to have consisted of rags from the rubbish heap, to the elegant robes worn by T'ang monks, usually made of silk. The Chinese outfit consisted of three pieces: the undergarment, also known as the five-strip garment; the upper garment, also known as the seven-strip garment; and the great garment or cloak, which might be made of from nine to twenty-five strips. Ennin reported that while he was in Yang-chou, he needed one hundred and sixteen feet of cloth to make the three garments.[4] This was roughly equivalent to three bolts of silk, each bolt consisting of forty feet. Since each bolt of silk at the time cost 1,000 cash or one string, the price of materials amounted to about three strings of cash. The tailor's charge for his handwork was 1,700 cash. So the total cost was 4,700 cash. In the Yüan-ho period (806-820) a secretary received about 8,000 cash monthly, while in the Ta-chung era (847-859) a servant received about 500 cash as monthly wages. The secretary would have had to work nine days to earn enough to buy the silk materials; the servant would have had to work six months.

Another bit of information is furnished in a memorial presented in the year 778, when it was estimated that the total cost of food and clothing for one monk amounted to 30,000 cash or 30 strings.[5] If we estimate the census of the clerical community at the time to have been about 200,000, the total cost of maintenance so far as food and clothing were concerned would have been 6,000,000 strings of cash. The significance of this figure may be realized

[4] For the undergarment, 28 feet, 5 inches; for the upper garment, 47 feet, 5 inches; for the cloak, 40 feet.

[5] From a memorial presented by a T'ang official it is learned that a monk normally consumed one *sheng* (pint) of rice each day; for clothing he required five bolts of silk plus fifty ounces of floss each year. The price of rice per *tou* (peck) in the capital in 780 was 200 cash; that of a bolt of silk, approximately 4,000 cash. A monk consuming one *sheng* a day would eat 365 *sheng*, or about 36½ *tou*, costing 7,300 cash. The five bolts of silk would cost 20,000 cash. For rice and silk, therefore, the total would be 27,300 cash. Add to this the cost of fifty ounces of floss, and the estimate of 30,000 cash would appear to be rather conservative.

when one learns that the state's total revenue in money for 779-780 was only 12,000,000 strings of cash. It must be remembered, however, that there was a much larger revenue in kind.

Besides food and clothing, there was the problem of living quarters, and this meant temples and monasteries. The question of the cost of their construction and maintenance will be reserved for the next chapter. For the present there is the important problem of the private property of monks.

## PROPERTY OF MONKS

In T'ang China, according to the equal field regulations,[6] a monk was granted thirty mou of *k'ou-fen* or personal share fields, a nun twenty mou. This was the first instance in Chinese history that such grants were made to the clergy. It is not clear just when the grants first went into effect, for they were not mentioned until about 739. The reason for this precedent-shattering act probably will never be known, but the guess is that the measure was originally intended to favor the Taoists, and the Buddhists were included as an afterthought. Once the monks acquired land, such practices as buying and selling land arose, with the more enterprising monks gradually becoming wealthy landlords. Besides land, it seems that monks possessed other property. Numerous legal documents have been discovered in Tun-huang and Central Asia covering transactions in money and goods made by monks. One such document found in Khotan, dated 782, referred to a certain layman who borrowed seventeen shih of grain from a monk, while another document from the same locality revealed that the same monk loaned 1,000 cash to a soldier who agreed to pay ten per cent monthly on the loan. Documents discovered at Tun-huang carry notices of loans in silk or woolen materials made by monks to merchants, the latter agreeing to pay interest in most cases. For example, a certain merchant borrowed three pieces of woolen materials from a monk on the twenty-second

[6] According to the equal field system promulgated by the T'ang Dynasty in 624, all adult males received from the government 100 mou (each mou is roughly equivalent to one sixth of an acre) of land, of which 80 mou were to be personal share fields and 20 mou to be property held in perpetuity. The personal share fields were to be returned to the state after the death of the recipient. The Taoist priest and nun received the same amount of personal share fields as did their Buddhist counterparts.

day of the twelfth month, and promised to repay four pieces on the fifteenth day of the third month the following year. Another contract described a peasant who owed two shih of cereals to a monk and who ceded to the latter the usufruct of five mou of land for two years as security. The rate of interest here was exorbitant, to say the least.

The fact that monks owned property brought in its wake the problem of the disposal of such property after the monk's death. According to monastic law such property was to be divided into two categories, heavy and light. The former category included such items as fields, gardens, slaves, animals, metals, grains, carts, boats, and so forth; while the latter class included personal articles such as clothing, bedding, shoes, and religious objects used by the deceased. Sometimes the division was made between those objects which could not be divided (the heavy class) and those which could. The question might be asked as to how the monk acquired the heavy objects besides the land which was granted him by the state. Very often the answer is that the individual owned such objects before he became a monk, and when he entered the order, he was separated from but not deprived of them. Therefore such objects were still considered the property of the monk, who usually entrusted the management of them to lay administrators or to his relatives. Upon the death of the monk such heavy property passed into the possession of the sangha as a whole. However, there appeared to be some exceptions to this rule. If a monk died in the house of a layman, the latter could claim all the monk's belongings. It is conceivable that some monks who possessed heavy property would return to their family and home to die, so that their possessions would revert to the family instead of being claimed by the sangha as a whole. As for the light objects, or those which were divisible, these were usually distributed among the pupils or close followers of the deceased. A good example may be seen in the disposition of the property of Pu-k'ung, Amoghavajra. His seal, samples of his translations, some rolls of texts, and other religious objects were left to his disciples. But the most important portion of his belongings was left to the monastery as permanent property. These included two cows, a chariot, fields, copper objects, 87 ounces of gold and 220½ ounces of silver, the bulk of which went to the monasteries on Wu-t'ai-shan.

## SANGHA OFFICIALS AND
## ADMINISTRATION OF THE ORDER

In a country such as China, where the traditions of bureaucratic government were so strong and deep and where the emperor claimed homage from all his subjects, it comes as no surprise that as soon as the Buddhist community of monks became more numerous and the religion became a force to be reckoned with, the imperial government established some sort of government bureau or appointed some official to oversee the affairs of the sangha. So far as is known, the earliest government organ established to exercise such control was the *chien-fu-ts'ao* (Office to Oversee Blessings), set up by the Northern Wei ruler, probably in 396. The notice in the *Shih-lao-chih* (*Treatise on Buddhism and Taoism*) in the Wei-shu reads, "At first an Office to Oversee Blessings was established, later changed to Office to Illumine the Mysteries (*chao-hsüan-ssu*), manned by officials and charged with supervision over monks and nuns." At the head of this body was a monk appointed by the emperor and given the title Chief of Monks. The first incumbent was Fa-kuo. The *Shih-lao-chih* had this to say about the appointment: "Formerly in the period Huang-shih (396-398) there was in the prefecture of Chao a monk named Fa-kuo whose practice of the commandments was exact to the extreme, and who explained books on the doctrine. When T'ai-tsu heard of his fame, he commanded that he should be respectfully invited to the capital. Later he made him Chief of Monks, to have general charge over the monks."[7]

In his position as Chief of Monks Fa-kuo was head of the Office to Oversee Blessings. In the beginning his title in Chinese was *tao-jen-t'ung*, but later this was changed to *sha-men-t'ung* (literally, Chief of Śramanas). Next to him in rank in this central organ was the *tu-wei-na*.[8] Under the supervision of this central office there were offices established in different parts of the em-

---

[7] Ware, *op.cit.*, 128-129, with some changes.

[8] This title is untranslatable, although there is an attempt to render it as "Wei-na General." See Hurvitz (tr.), *Wei Shou, Treatise on Buddhism and Taoism*, Kyoto, 1956, 76. The term *wei-na* is usually regarded as the Chinese equivalent of the Sanskrit *karmadāna*, which refers to the monk who has charge over life in a monastery. The traditional explanation for the origin of the term is that it is a compound of the final character of the Chinese *kang-wei* (controlling regulations or principles) with the final syllable of *karmadāna*.

pire, with each branch headed by a monk appointed by the Chief of Monks in the capital and given the title Chief of Monks in such and such a prefecture or department. He was assisted by a subordinate official called *wei-na*. In some texts this subordinate official was also called *chih-shih* (One in charge of affairs) or *yüeh-chung* (One who gladdens the multitude).

Such a bureaucratic setup of the Northern Wei was taken over by the Northern Ch'i. In the Office to Illumine the Mysteries, which was under the jurisdiction of the Court of Imperial Sacrifices (*T'ai-ch'ang-ssu*) in the central government, there was one Great Chief of Monks, one Chief of Monks, and three *tu-wei-na*. The Sui Dynasty in turn followed the Northern Ch'i system, but the supervisory office was placed under the jurisdiction of the *Hung-lu-ssu* (Court of State Ceremonial).

Under the Southern Dynasties there is no mention of such a bureaucratic organ, but during the Eastern Chin Dynasty there was an office called *seng-cheng* (Monk Administrator), filled by a certain Seng-kung in Szechuan. Such an office was probably of a local nature and was established in 402 or 403. At about the same time Yao Hsing of the Later Ch'in kingdom, recognizing the need for some sort of supervision over the large congregation of monks attracted to Ch'ang-an by the magnetic name of Kumāra-jīva, set up three offices, which were *seng-chu* (Chief of Monks, filled by a monk named Seng-lüeh), *yüeh-chung* (One Who Gladdens the Multitude), and *seng-lu* (Monk Secretary). Being regular officials in the central government, they enjoyed the rank and privileges which were their due.

During the succeeding dynasties in the south the tradition started by the Eastern Chin Dynasty continued, with the chief of monks designated either as Monk Administrator or Chief of Monks, the Liu Sung and the Liang Dynasties using the former and the Ch'i the latter. The Liang Dynasty made a distinction between the central and local officials by designating the former Great Monk Administrator, while the latter was merely called Monk Administrator.

With the coming of the T'ang Dynasty important developments began to take place. The magnitude and strength of the T'ang empire gave rise to a strong national feeling that was reflected in the supremacy of the national laws over monastic laws. The supervision of the sangha was vested in positions held not by monks but by civil servants. Down to 694 monks and nuns were under the control of the Court of State Ceremonial. This government organ exercised general supervision over foreign guests, audiences, good and evil omens, and sacrifices. Since Buddhism was considered to be a foreign religion, and to be treated in accordance with ceremonies accorded to foreign guests, it was placed under the jurisdiction of this body. In 694, however, Empress Wu Tse-t'ien transferred this supervision to the *Tz'u-pu* (Bureau of National Sacrifice), one of the organs in the Ministry of Rites. This move was made by the empress to show her favor toward Buddhism and to indicate that she no longer considered Buddhism to be a foreign religion. In 737 Emperor Hsüan-tsung reaffirmed the move. Among the duties pertaining to Buddhism which the bureau had to perform were the taking of a census of the clerical community, the compilation of a monk registry, administration of the examinations to test the qualifications of candidates seeking admission into the sangha, and the issuance of monk certificates.

In the second half of the T'ang Dynasty a new office was created, entitled Commissioner of Religion (*kung-te-shih*), whose duties were concerned with activities that earn merits, such as erecting statues of the Buddha, building temples, holding vegetarian feasts, and so forth. The office was probably established during the reign of Tai-tsung (763-779), and the earliest mention of it is found in a document dated 774. Apparently there was no conflict in the beginning between the responsibilities of this office and those of the Bureau of National Sacrifice. In 779, after the death of Tai-tsung, the office was suspended, for reasons which are not clear. In 788 the office was reinstated and divided into three positions—Commissioners of Religion for the left part of Ch'ang-an, for the right part, and for the eastern capital Lo-yang. (During the T'ang Dynasty the capital of Ch'ang-an was divided into two halves, the left and the right, or the east and west, with the Chu-ch'üeh Street as the dividing line.) These Commissioners of Religion took over the supervisory powers over the monastic community formerly held by the Bureau of National Sacrifice. In 807 Taoist priests and nuns were also placed under the jurisdiction of these Commissioners of Religion.

During the reign of Wu-tsung (841-846), when Buddhism suffered from imperial disfavor, the control of the religion was transferred to the Bureau of Guests (*Chu-k'e*) in the Ministry of Rites. This bureau took care of foreign missions and embassies, and since Buddhism was then considered as a foreign religion, it was held that this bureau was the proper organ to exercise jurisdiction over it. However, this arrangement proved to be only temporary, for in 846 the clerical community was again put under the control of the Commissioners of Religion. Even after this move the Bureau of National Sacrifice still retained control over the registry of monks and the granting of monk certificates.

The holders of these important positions as Commissioners of Religion were usually not monks but powerful eunuchs, who utilized the posts to amass great fortunes for themselves. Ennin, for instance, described the wealth that was accumulated by one of the commissioners in the capital, Ch'iu Shih-liang, who was disgraced and whose fortune was confiscated. "Elephant tusks filled the rooms; jewels, gold, and silver completely filled the storehouses; and the cash, silk, and goods were beyond count. Each day thirty carts transported (the treasure) to the palace storehouses, but they did not complete transporting it within a month. The remaining treasures and rarities were (still) beyond count."[9] After the establishment of these Commissioners of Religion the office of *seng-lu* (Monk Secretary) reappeared sometime during the period 806-824, one for each division of the capital. These two positions were filled by monks, and they were responsible to the commissioner of their respective division. During the interval between 836 and 854 it appears that one monk filled both positions. In an entry in his diary dated the eighteenth day of the first month, 839, Ennin wrote that the *seng-lu* exercised control over the monasteries of the whole land.

In the rest of the empire there were local monk officials called *seng-cheng* (Monk Administrator) who exercised jurisdiction over the monasteries and clerics in a certain region under the supervision of the local civil officials, such as the governor general, regional commander, or local prefect. This is confirmed by Ennin in the same entry referred to above. Usually a virtuous and capable monk in the region was selected for the office. It seems that this

[9] Reischauer, *Ennin's Diary*, New York, 1955, 351.

office was initiated during the latter half of the T'ang Dynasty after the An Lu-shan rebellion, when the powers of the central government began to decline and local war lords and chieftains began to assume semi-independent positions. Although monks held the positions of *seng-lu* and *seng-cheng*, it is clear that the real authority over the monastic community was held by the civil officials in the central government and in the provinces.

Some interesting information emerges from this rapid survey of the sangha officials and the administration of the sangha. Some dynasties appointed monks as the chief officials of the sangha and entrusted supervision of the clerical community to them. This was the method followed by those dynasties established by non-Chinese peoples—the Northern Wei, the Northern Ch'i and the Sui. Under the T'ang, however, supervision of the clerical community was placed in the hands of civil officials. Apparently this was done to indicate that Buddhism was not to enjoy any special privilege and that it was to be subordinate to the secular laws of the land.

Also, apparently the civil bureaucracy was not sure just what organ should be entrusted with the actual administration of sangha affairs. At times Buddhism was regarded as a foreign religion and put under the control of the Court of State Ceremonial or the Bureau of Guests. At other times it was not so regarded and was placed under the Bureau of National Sacrifice. Finally, it is apparent that the Chinese clergy, after a brief assertion of independence under the leadership of Hui-yüan in the fifth century, tacitly acknowledged the supremacy of the state under the T'ang Dynasty; this was another indication of the Buddhist accommodation to the Chinese scene.

# CHAPTER X

# BUDDHIST TEMPLES AND POPULAR BUDDHISM

THE scene of the manifold activities carried on by the sangha was centered in the Buddhist temple. Such temples might be located right in the heart of the teeming metropolitan district, in the shaded luxuriant valley of the nearby hills, or on top of some famous scenic mountains far from human habitation. Some of the best-known temples in Chinese history, like the Yung-ning Temple of Lo-yang under the Northern Wei or the T'ung-t'ai Temple of the Liang rulers, are now preserved only in the memory of the faithful. But there are a few, as, for instance, some of the temples on Wu-t'ai Shan, that date back to the T'ang Dynasty. The flourishing condition of Buddhism under the T'ang was therefore reflected not only by the size and vigor of the clerical community, but also by the construction of a large number of temples, some of them of magnificent and gigantic proportions.

## NUMBER AND COST OF TEMPLES

Buddhist temples have been erected in China from the very beginning of the religion there. In the discussion of Buddhism under the Han there was already mentioned a Hsü-ch'ang Temple in Lo-yang and another one in P'eng-ch'eng erected by Chai Jung. According to Buddhist tradition an even earlier temple, the Pai-ma or White Horse Temple, associated with the dream of Emperor Ming, was erected in the western suburbs of Lo-yang. Though not much credence can be placed on this tradition, it is likely that such a temple did exist in the latter part of the Han Dynasty. During the third century it was the site of the translation activities of a number of monks—Dharmakāla, Sanghavarman, and later Dharmaraksha. In 247 the monk K'ang Seng-hui was said to have established in Chien-yeh (modern Nanking) a Chien-ch'u Temple to house a relic of the Buddha. Under the Western Chin the number of temples reached 180;

under the Eastern Chin, 1,768; Liu Sung, 1,913; Ch'i, 2,015; Liang, 2,846. In the north the figures were even more impressive. Under the Northern Wei there were 47 grand monasteries of the state, 839 temples and monasteries of princes and eminent families, and 30,000 temples of the people.

During the K'ai-yüan period a count of the Buddhist temples in the empire showed 3,245 for monks and 2,113 for nuns, making a total of 5,358. Within the city of Ch'ang-an itself there were 64 monasteries and 27 nunneries. One can get a good idea of the architectural dimensions and splendor of these temples from a number of contemporary descriptions. For instance, the Chang-ching Temple at the east gate of Ch'ang-an contained 48 courts and 4,130 *chien*. Of even greater magnitude was the Hsi-ming Temple, also in Ch'ang-an, where the pilgrim Hsüan-tsang resided and carried on a good deal of his translation work. The grounds of this temple were originally the residential area of one of the imperial princes, and at first it was proposed to build both a Buddhist and a Taoist temple there. Hsüan-tsang went to survey the premises and said that the area was too limited for two establishments. As a result only the Buddhist temple was located there. Work on the Hsi-ming Temple was completed in 656, and the finished temple had a frontage of 350 paces, with 10 courts and more than 4,000 *chien*. Trees bordered the outskirts and streams crisscrossed the grounds. Within the precincts, pavilions and halls reached toward the clouds, and the pillars covered with gold leaves dazzled the eyes. It was probably with such magnificent edifices in mind that contemporary memorialists complained: "Present day temples surpass even the imperial palaces in design, embodying the last word in extravagances, splendor, artistry, and fineness" and "At present there are innumerable Buddhist temples in the realm. One temple with its halls is twice the magnitude of the imperial palace; its splendor and beauty are extreme, and its expenditures surpass those of the latter."[1]

At this late date we shall probably never be able to find out how much was involved in the construction of these great temples. Ennin, the Japanese monk, furnished one bit of information that could serve as the basis for some calculation. While he was in

---

[1] K. Ch'en, *Harvard Journal of Asiatic Studies*, 19 (1956), 86, note 69.

Yang-chou, he and his fellow Japanese monks were called upon to donate 50 strings of cash toward a total sum of 10,000 strings needed to repair one balcony in the K'ai-yüan Temple of the city. Other foreign merchants in the city also made some contributions; Persians, 1,000 strings; people from Champa, 200 strings. There is also preserved an expense account for the construction of a pavilion in the Ta-hsing-shan Temple in Ch'ang-an, dated 775. In all, a total of 22,488 strings of cash was raised through contributions to cover the cost of construction. If 10,000 strings were needed to repair one balcony, or approximately 22,500 strings to construct one pavilion, how much would be required to build such a structure as the Ta-sheng-tz'u Temple in Ch'eng-tu, which consisted of 96 courts and 8,500 *chien*? No wonder that an official like Wei Ssu-ch'ien would charge in 709 that the large temples wasted hundreds of thousands, up to a million, strings of cash.

Within the temples there were images of Buddhist deities, bells, incense burners, and other ritual objects, usually made of gold or bronze. An inscription dated 585, found in Hopei, spoke of a golden statue of Maitreya thirty-five feet high, erected under the Northern Wei but destroyed during the persecution of 574-577. Emperor Wen of the Sui Dynasty decided to restore the statue, and the process required some 17,500 catties of cloth, 1,100 *sheng* of lacquer, and 87,000 sheets of gold. Copper was the principal metal used in the temples, and the large amounts of this metal possessed by the temples led the government to take numerous measures to regulate its use and circulation. Since copper was also used to mint coins, the government wanted to divert the whole copper output to the government mints. However, one might say that the government fought a losing battle in this policy. In order to manufacture 1,000 cash or one string, some six catties of copper were required. The same six catties, if used in the manufacture of objects or utensils, would be valued at about 36,000 cash. It is not surprising, therefore, that the repeated government decrees restricting the use of copper except for coins were flagrantly violated by artisans in central and south China, who converted the copper into images or ritual objects and reaped a comfortable profit. Government regulations banning the use of copper for utensils were issued as early as the reign of Hsüan-tsung, and repeated in subsequent years. In 825 it was specifically decreed that no copper could be used for Buddhist images. Ennin recorded in 838: "There is an imperial order prohibiting the use of copper, and throughout the land, the sale or purchase of it is not allowed. It was explained that there was such a regulation as a rule once every six years. The reason for the prohibition is that they fear that, if the people of the empire always make copper utensils, there would be no copper for minting cash."[2] These prohibitory regulations do not appear to have been very effective, for the Buddhist temples continued to hoard large amounts of the precious metal—a situation that culminated in the severe measure of 845 confiscating all the copper held in the monasteries.

## COMMERCIAL ACTIVITIES

Buddhist temples are usually considered to be institutions fulfilling a religious function, concerned with activities that revolve around the Three Jewels. This is the primary function, but during T'ang China the temples also became involved in a number of activities essentially economic in nature, such as establishing and managing water-powered stone rolling mills, oil presses, hostels, pawnshops, and the Inexhaustible Treasuries, and serving as landlords for huge estates. It must be pointed out that these economic institutions originated in the first place as a result of religious activities; faithful laymen invariably donated the rolling mills or oil presses to the temples with the idea of gaining religious merit through their acts. The profits realized by the temples in the operation of these commercial and industrial enterprises were in turn used mainly for the furtherance of the dharma in China.

### WATER-POWERED ROLLING MILLS

The rolling mills were called *nien-wei* and were used to extract the husk from the grain or to pulverize the grain into flour. Those which were used for hulling the grain were called *nien*, while those for making flour were called *wei*. However, the two words are also used as a compound word. These rolling mills were operated mainly by water power. Established by the great families as well as by the monasteries, they already existed during

---

[2] Reischauer, *Ennin's Diary*, 48.

the Sui Dynasty and were to be found near the rivers and irrigation canals in the vicinity of Ch'ang-an, the capital. The number
of such mills rose sharply during the early part of the T'ang
Dynasty, and since they depended on water power for their
operation, water was sometimes diverted from the rivers or irrigation canals to the sites of the mills. They thus became an object of controversy between their owners and the farmers in the
vicinity, who protested that the mills were depriving them
of water needed for irrigation. Such disputes led the government
to destroy some mills or to limit their operation to certain
periods when water was not needed by the farmers. An example
of the former was the decree of the emperor in 778 calling for the
destruction of eighty mills along the Po Canal in Shansi. In the
latter instance some mills were not permitted to operate from
the last month of summer to the second month of spring, while
in the Tun-huang area the installations could function only from
the end of the eighth month to the end of the year. Apparently
the period of limitation differed according to the local farming
practices or the volume of water available.

Along with members of the imperial household and the grand
families of the realm the Buddhist temples also participated in
the operation of the rolling mills. As early as the Sui Dynasty
we read of Emperor Wen's donating six such mills to the Ch'ing-
ch'an Temple in Ch'ang-an. The operation of these temple-owned
mills was usually entrusted to lay millers, called *wei-chia* or *wei-
hu,* who were probably serfs attached to the monasteries. If any
repairs to the mills were necessary, then a repairman known as
the *wei-po-shih* was summoned to do the task. These mills were
valuable economic assets to the monasteries, for they could be
rented out, or a fee could be charged for their use by people
who wanted their grain ground. Though such rolling mills were
owned and operated by the monasteries, still it appears that
they were subject to taxation, for a petition presented by monks
in Ch'ang-an in 811 asking for tax exemption on the mills was
refused by the government.

OIL PRESSES

Besides the rolling mills, the monasteries also operated oil presses
for the manufacture of oil used in copious quantities for cooking

and for religious ceremonies. Ennin met a train of fifty donkeys carrying hemp oil bound for the monasteries of Wu-t'ai-shan. These presses were usually rented to families of oil makers, and in return the temples received oil or oil cakes. The temple furnished the oil makers with the raw materials, usually hempseed, needed for the manufacture of oil. As for oil cakes made from the residue after the oil had been pressed out, these were used as fodder for animals. Besides receiving revenue from the oil makers for the operation of the presses, the monasteries also collected a charge from lay families who would make use of the presses to extract oil from their own grain.

HOSTELS

Throughout its history in China the Buddhist temple had often served as a haven for outlaws and brigands, and it was this aspect of Buddhism that repeatedly drew the ire of memorialists. In T'ang China, following practices in Central Asia, temples served as hostels not only for monks and pilgrims, but for lay travelers as well. For instance, in the rules established by Huai-hai (d. 841) it was specified that any time an important donor or functionary passed by a temple, the abbot and monks of that temple should receive him and provide him with the things he needed, such as a bed, lamp, and so forth. Ennin was able to travel extensively in north China and usually found quarters in the temples located along his route. He pointed out that in certain areas, especially along the way up Wu-t'ai-shan, there were well-organized religious hostels, called common cloisters (*p'u-t'ung-yüan*) about three to ten miles apart. These cloisters were so called, he said, because they served rice and gruel to anyone who came, regardless of whether he was a layman or a cleric. Lodgings were also provided impartially. Such cloisters must have been fairly large, for in one over a hundred travelers were taken care of. So popular were the temples as hostels that very often traveling monks themselves were not able to find lodging in them. Functionaries going to their posts, military officials on the road, or traveling merchants were the people who availed themselves of the quarters provided by the temples. Since some of the great temples in Ch'ang-an and Lo-yang enjoyed semiofficial status, candidates who went to the capital for the metropolitan examinations frequently lodged there. This practice proved very profitable to the temples, and became so widespread that imperial decrees had to be issued, in 762 and 848, forbidding functionaries from using the religious institutions as hostels, on the grounds that this destroyed the sanctity of the place. One group in society found the monasteries very convenient—the students preparing for the imperial examinations, who found in the Buddhist monasteries just the right conditions for study—quiet surroundings and writing brushes, ink slabs, lamps, and oil.

INEXHAUSTIBLE TREASURY

T'ang temples also engaged in such commercial practices as the establishment and management of the Inexhaustible Treasury (*Wu-chin-tsang*). It had already been the practice in India to set up storerooms within the precincts of the temple for the storage of sangha materials which otherwise might have been exposed to the elements. In China temple storerooms were in existence from the end of the fifth century, and were used to store articles used in the worship ceremonies or materials that had to do with the propagation of the dharma, such as manuscripts, bookcases, and writing materials. Such storerooms were used sometimes to keep foodstuffs for the residents of the temple and for the guest monks who might pass the night there. The storerooms also took care of gifts and donations which pious laymen might make to the temple.

It has been said that the economy of the Buddhist monastic community was based on the idea of exchange. The faithful layman donated alms to the clerical order or material goods to the monastery. In return the sangha made a gift of the law to the layman. Both parties were happy and satisfied with this exchange. If such goods as were presented to the sangha were not excessive and could be easily consumed, the problem of surplus did not arise. But it often happened that the contributions of the laity exceeded the needs of the sangha. To take care of this surplus, and to dispose of it, an institution known as the Inexhaustible Treasury was established in the temple.

Some T'ang monasteries owned huge landed estates from which they received a considerable amount of revenue annually. In some instances this annual revenue was also used by the monastery as the capital for the formation of the Inexhaustible Treasury.

What could the monasteries do with such large stocks of material goods? The solution was found in the *Vinayas*. In the Sarvāstivādin and Mahāsanghika *Vinayas*, both translated in the first two decades of the fifth century, it was specifically stated that if goods donated to the sangha were not used entirely by the monks and nuns, such goods could be sold or loaned, and the profits derived from these transactions could be used to defray the expenses incurred in religious activities, such as constructing or repairing temples or stupas, or in public welfare projects. Such goods were to be designated as inexhaustible articles (*wu-chin-wu*) or inexhaustible wealth (*wu-chin-ts'ai*), and it is likely that this usage was responsible for the term *wu-chin-tsang*. It has also been suggested that the origin of the term is to be sought in the Mahāyāna sutras which spoke of the inexhaustible store of merits possessed by the bodhisattva. The donation of goods to the sangha was a religious act for the purpose of gaining merit, but when these donations were accumulated, then they served as capital for commercial enterprises.

With the establishment of such Inexhaustible Treasuries in the temples the monk administrators began to broaden the scope of their commercial activities. They did not limit themselves merely to the sale of goods donated. They began to accept valuable goods for safekeeping, so that the temple storeroom served as a sort of safe-deposit vault. They also began to rent or lend objects or grains, charging interest on such loans. In some instances they engaged in the pawnbrokerage business. The most famous of such Inexhaustible Treasuries was the one established in the Hua-tu Temple of the San-chieh sect by Hsin-i during the era 618-626. Another treasury was established by a certain Tao-piao, who acquired a sufficient amount of land for his monasteries to receive an annual harvest of ten thousand shih of grain, which was deposited in the Inexhaustible Treasury to be shared by the entire community. Still another was established in the Hui-lin Temple in Lo-yang by Li Teng, who donated his entire family fortune for the purpose during the unsettled times attending the An Lu-shan rebellion.

Documents found chiefly in the Tun-huang area have given us

some indication of the nature of these commercial transactions carried on by the temples. Tun-huang is located far out in the northwest corner of China, away from the centers of Chinese civilization. One wonders whether the conditions that applied there should be extended to the rest of the country. However, in spite of its geographical location, the society in Tun-huang was definitely agrarian and Chinese in nature. Since it was the focal point of all Central Asiatic routes to China, it was not so isolated as its position would seem to indicate. Therefore the economic activities of the Buddhist temples in that region undoubtedly consisted of many features in common with those in the rest of north China. In making loans the monasteries in Tun-huang served the well-to-do and privileged families as well as the peasants. For the former group the loans were usually in money or fabrics, made for a long term, with some sort of security and payment of interest required. In the case of transactions with peasants not connected with the monastery the loans were usually in grain, made for a short period, with a rate of interest sometimes as high as fifty per cent annually, to be paid in kind. However, if the peasants were attached to the monastery, then they enjoyed special treatment and were permitted to borrow grain without any payment of interest. Such grain was classified as the permanent property of the temple, and had been entrusted to monks to earn interest. The financial reports of these monks furnish the most valuable information concerning the revenue received by the monasteries. For example, during the year 924 the receipts from the fields and gardens, fees from the oil presses, interest on loans, donations, and gifts in one temple amounted to 1,388 shih of grain.[3] In this case the total revenue was all lumped together. Of even greater interest were the reports containing data on the sources of revenue. For the year 924 the Ching-t'u Temple in Tun-huang noted that out of a total of 366.9 shih of grain received by the granary, only 44.4 shih or 12 per cent represented revenue from the temple lands; more than 200 shih or 55 per cent were taken in as interest, and the rest, 120 shih or 33 per cent, constituted donations. For the year 930 the proportions were

---

[3] This figure of 1,388 shih is broken down as follows: 378.66 shih of wheat, 390.5 shih of millet, 5.06 shih of oil, 65.03 shih of flour, 11.03 shih of coarse flour, 86.15 shih of hemp, 30.00 shih of bran, 208.89 shih of beans, 101 oil cakes, 849 feet of cloth, and 148 feet of felt.

somewhat different, but the interest on loans still constituted 45 per cent of the total, revenue from the fields 23 per cent, and donations 32 per cent. It is clear from these reports that the three main sources of revenue for the Ching-t'u Temple in Tun-huang were the interest on loans, receipts from the rolling mills and oil presses, and donations from the faithful.

Because of the operation of such commercial activities by the Buddhist monastery, it has been said that Buddhism was responsible for a very important innovation in Chinese economic history—the idea of modern capitalism, or the productive use of capital and the automatic mechanism of the accumulation of interest. It was the accepted view that objects donated to the sangha would be productive of religious merit to the donor. The Buddhist temple proceeded one step farther. It utilized the donated objects as capital for the production of further economic gain, the earning of interest to be used in the furtherance of the dharma.

## TEMPLE LANDS

It was previously indicated that one of the sources of capital for the Inexhaustible Treasury was the income from temple lands. Because the temples owned so much land, together with officialdom and the nobility they were the dominant landlords of the period. During the early part of the dynasty large tracts of land were granted outright to the officials and nobility. Or rather, it would be more correct to say that their ownership of such lands as had been acquired previously was confirmed by T'ang regulations. Members of these groups, taking advantage of their privileged position, were able to increase their holdings still more by buying land from small landowners who had been ruined by drought or famine or squeezed by heavy taxes. In this process of consolidation of land into large estates the Buddhist temples also participated.

How did the temples acquire their land? One will recall that monks and nuns were granted thirty and twenty mou of land respectively. It is possible that they pooled their holdings to make up the land held by the monastery in which they resided. However, even if all the monks and nuns had received the land to which they were legally entitled, the total area would not

have been very large, and far less than the area reportedly confiscated during the Hui-ch'ang persecution.

A second source of land was the grants made to the temples by
the emperors—a practice already in vogue before the rise of
the T'ang Dynasty. For example, when Emperor Wen of Sui
called for the establishment of Buddhist temples at the foot of
famous mountains, he donated one hundred ch'ing of land to the
Shao-lin Temple in Sung-shan. An additional forty ch'ing to the
same temple was donated by the T'ang emperor T'ai-tsung. After
Hsüan-tsang settled in the Hsi-ming Temple in Ch'ang-an, Kao-
tsung gave to this temple one hundred ch'ing of land in addition to fifty carts and two thousand bolts of silk and cotton
cloth. When the emperor Hsüan-tsung was in Ch'eng-tu after
the An Lu-shan rebellion, he donated a thousand mou to the
Ta-sheng-tz'u Temple of that city. Princess Chin-hsien, a sister
of Hsüan-tsung, donated an estate replete with orchards, wheat
fields, and woodlands to the Yün-chu Temple in Fang-shan,
Hopei, in 730.

Following the lead of the imperial household, the great and
wealthy families likewise made donations of land to the temples.
Notices of such grants are scattered throughout T'ang literature.
The famous eunuch Yü Ch'ao-en in 767 turned over a large tract
of land to the Chang-ching Temple, established in honor of
Empress Dowager Chang-ching. Likewise, Wang Wei, the famous
poet, made some land available to a temple established in memory
of his mother. The Korean merchant Chang Pogo endowed a
cloister on the Shantung coast with enough land to produce five
hundred shih of rice annually for the maintenance of the monks.
How much land was thus donated to the temples will never be
known, but the practice must have been fairly common, for Emperor Jui-tsung in a decree issued ca.710-712 prohibited officials
and common people from making such donations and warned
that if they did, such land would be taken over and distributed
to needy farmers. It is unlikely that such a decree was carried
out effectively.

With such resources available the temples were able to increase
their holdings by buying up parcels of land from others, just as
the great and powerful families of the times did. During the
T'ai-ho period (827-835) the monk Wen-chü was able to acquire

twelve ch'ing of land for the Kuo-ch'ing Temple of Mt. T'ien-t'ai. There was also the case of the monk Nan-ts'ao's buying ten ch'ing of land for the Lung-hsing Temple in Hang-chou.

How much land did the Buddhist church possess during the T'ang Dynasty? This is a difficult question to answer, for the source materials are of little help. Memorialists complained from time to time that the rich and fertile lands in the vicinity of Ch'ang-an were largely in the possession of the monasteries and that the temples controlled about 70 to 80 per cent of the wealth of the empire. The only indication in statistics of the extent of such temple lands is furnished by the suppression edict of 845, which states that several tens of millions of ch'ing of land were confiscated by the dynasty. This figure is excessively high, for it exceeds the total area of arable land in the era 742-755, said to be 14,303,862 ch'ing; it appears to be a deliberate overstatement on the part of the Confucian historians in order to portray the Buddhist church in an unfavorable light as a wealthy landowner.

Recent studies on the problem of monastic estates have indicated that many of the lands owned by the temples were not the fertile farmlands of the plains, but were, instead, marginal or undeveloped property located on mountains, forests, or pastures, and hence were not well adapted to agriculture. Such a situation is easily understandable, for the monasteries were usually located in mountain areas where land was so cheap that a large tract was easily obtainable. A concrete example may be seen in the holdings of the Ta-hsiang Temple in Lung-chou of Shensi, which consisted in 841 of 5,356 mou of wasteland and scrub-covered land, 838 mou of waste hillside land, and 4,518 mou of arable land.

### Cultivators of Temple Lands

By joining the Buddhist sangha, the monk no longer had to work in the fields, even though he often came from the peasant class. He might engage in such activities as tending the garden or orchards, but the actual cultivation of the soil was entrusted to others. There was one notable exception in the case of Zen monks, who had to do some manual labor in the fields. In general the temple lands were cultivated by *ching-jen* (pure people), free laymen in the employ of the temples, or by temple slaves.

The term *ching-jen* goes back to early Buddhist practices, when laymen called *kappiyakāraka* (Sanskrit *kalpikāra*) handled the wealth or cultivated the fields of the monasteries. They were so called because they spared the monks the necessity of committing transgressions in performing *akappiya* or impure deeds, such as handling gold and silver, trading, cooking, agriculture, and so forth. As cultivators of temple lands in China they paid to the temple a fixed share of the crops, said to vary from one half to one shih per mou. Temple slaves, however, made up the bulk of the cultivators of temple lands, and at the time of the Hui-ch'ang suppression 150,000 such slaves were manumitted. These slaves were recruited in a number of ways. Some of them had been criminals who were freed on condition that they become attached to some temples as menial workers. During the Northern Wei Dynasty the Buddha Households were made up primarily of such elements. Then there were the orphans brought up by the sangha. Before joining the order, they were sometimes treated as slaves and put to work in the fields. When they became of age, they were then permitted to become members of the sangha. A third category consisted of the tenants who were originally attached to the land when it was donated or sold to the monastery. Finally, there was the army of unemployed people who had been dispossessed of their land during the process of consolidation of the huge landed estates, when land was being bought by the rich families or by the monasteries. Not being able to earn a livelihood by other means, such people sometimes willingly accepted the status of temple slaves. Besides tilling the soil, such slaves did other menial labor, such as caring for and repairing buildings, or cleaning and sweeping temple grounds. Men and women were permitted to marry within the group, but not with peasants outside of the group. However, if such a marriage should occur between a temple slave and an outside woman, the offspring retained the status of the father. Though he was called a slave, he possessed privileges not usually enjoyed by those having a similar status in other societies. He had a plot of land to cultivate, or he served as a miller or oil presser. In exchange for the use of the land, the mill, or the oil press he paid a certain fee to the monastery. Such a temple slave was also afforded a certain protection by T'ang laws. If he were beaten to death by temple officials, the latter would be banished to another province for one year. Again, if a slave guilty of some offense were to be executed by his superiors without the civil officials' being brought into the case, such temple officials would be subject to one hundred strokes of the bamboo. On the other hand, if a slave were to beat a temple official, he would be subject to strangulation.

### Tax-exempt Status of Temple Lands

With the temples and monasteries owning such large tracts of land and controlling so much wealth, what financial responsibilities did they have to assume? Did they have to pay any tax to the state, or did they claim special privilege to escape from payment? So far as such industrial installations as the water-powered rolling mills connected with temples were concerned, it appears that in such cases the temples had to pay taxes. However, in connection with temple lands numerous passages exist in T'ang literature which indicate that the temples did enjoy special privileges, but the wording of some of these passages is such that one wonders whether there were temples which did not enjoy tax exemption. For instance, the ten temples on Wu-t'ai-shan in Shansi controlled some forty-two estates; after T'ai-tsung had subdued the Shansi area, he exempted all these estates from taxation to manifest the imperial favor. If the temples already enjoyed tax exemption, why was it necessary for T'ai-tsung to take this specific action? Since the temples on Wu-t'ai-shan were singled out, did this mean that other temples had to pay taxes on their land? Such questions are more easily raised than answered.

This problem of tax exemption was closely related to the status of the temple or monastery. During the T'ang such temples were divided into two categories, the officially recognized temples and monasteries and those not recognized. Those officially recognized enjoyed special economic privileges, usually in the form of tax exemption on the temple lands. It was this feature of the officially recognized temples that led the great families of the period to establish some sort of connection with them so as to be able to claim exemption on their holdings. Connections could be established in a number of ways. The grand families could entrust their land to the protection of the temples under the pretext that they were donating it to the Buddhist institutions. If the temple were one not officially recognized, the family would then petition the government for the preferred status, and since the family often belonged to officialdom or the nobility, its petition was usually granted.

### The Merit Cloisters

However, the most prevalent method was the establishment of *kung-te-yüan* or *kung-te-fen-ssu*, a merit cloister. The rich family constructed a Buddhist temple on its private burial grounds, petitioned for official recognition, and, if successful, then claimed tax-free privileges for the whole property on which that temple was located. In most cases, instead of constructing a new temple, the family merely attached itself to an already established and officially recognized temple, claimed that as its own, and then turned over its landed estate to that temple.

The relation of such a merit cloister to the family concerned differed from that normally existing between donor and temple. In the latter case the donor made his grant of land to the temple, with the understanding that his gift was outright and permanent. The phrase used in such proceedings was "once donated, permanently donated." With the merit cloister the family said that its property was donated to the temple, but the merit cloister itself was regarded by the family as a sort of private institution, so that what was regarded as temple land in the eyes of the public and government was still the private property of the family. In such merit cloisters the administrator of the temple property would be appointed by the donor family, and could be removed by the latter at will. This naturally made the temple administrators subservient to the donors, ready to comply with their wishes. The merit cloister thus served not only as an institution through which the rich could avoid paying taxes on their land, but also as a medium for private investments to accumulate gains with which to acquire more land. It is possible that a large portion of the land listed as temple-owned in the persecution of 845 was made up of just such pseudo grants, owned in name by the temples, but in fact by the grand families.

These cloisters, started during the T'ang Dynasty, were to flourish even more under the Sung. So beneficial were they to the parties concerned that numerous petitions were presented by officialdom and the nobility for their establishment. As a consequence, some protests against the practice were heard from monks who charged that such families took possession of everything within the temple, even to the extent of a needle or a blade of grass.

## TEMPLE CLASSIFICATION

Just as the monks in China were classified into different categories, so were the temples. The most important distinction was that between an officially recognized and nonrecognized one. The first category included the monasteries established by the grand families and by the state; their distinctive mark was a tablet inscribed with the imperial calligraphy. For instance, the grand monasteries of the state, such as the Ta-yün Temple and the K'ai-yüan Temple in the various centers of the realm, were entrusted with the duty of providing spiritual protection to the emperor and the state, and were maintained by the state. Celebrations such as the imperial birthdays and memorial days of previous emperors were observed in these state institutions. Of the more than forty monasteries in Yang-chou when Ennin was there, seven were classified as officially recognized institutions. As for the nonrecognized temples, they did not enjoy the preferred status of the recognized institutions. They were usually village temples, private hermitages, shrines, or sanctuaries, inhabited by monks who were ordained privately; they had little or no landed property or industrial installations to speak of. They were often the first ones to feel the blows of any movement directed against Buddhism, for they would be destroyed, closed, or ordered to combine with larger establishments, and their monks would be laicized first.

Besides the division discussed above, Buddhist temples in China may also be classified according to (*a*) their methods of choosing the temple administrator and (*b*) their activities. In the first classification there were the hereditary temples and the "Thickets and Groves of the Ten Directions." The hereditary temples were usually small and poor in resources and man power. Leadership was transmitted from master to disciple, generation after generation. The "Thickets and Groves of the Ten Directions," so called because they were the gathering places of monks coming from everywhere, were wealthy in resources and monk power, with scores and even hundreds of monks in residence. The abbot in charge of such a monastery was chosen by the community of monks in that particular establishment, and any properly qualified monk was eligible. The caliber of monks residing in these monasteries was often much higher than that of monks of the hereditary temples. However, certain defects existed in the method of transmission of authority. Whenever there was a change in the succession of temple administrators, the outgoing abbot would take along with him as much of the temple property as he could lay his hands on. For example, in the case of the Tz'u-yün Temple in Lin-an (Hang-chou), established during the T'ang and recognized officially during the Sung, there were eight changes in the abbotship during an interval of seventy years, and every time there was a change, wholesale looting of temple property was carried out by the deposed abbot. Finally, in 1263 this was changed into a hereditary temple. Such changes became fairly prevalent during the later Sung Dynasty.

Temples were classified according to their activities as (*a*) contemplation temples, which usually meant the Ch'an temples; (*b*) doctrinal temples, devoted to the propagation of doctrines of a particular school, such as the T'ien-tai temples; and (*c*) disciplinary temples, devoted to the study of the *Vinaya* rules.

As for the monks residing in each monastery, the number varied from time to time. The Kuo-ch'ing Temple on T'ien-t'ai Mountain normally had one hundred and fifty monks, but during the summer this number would increase to three hundred. The normal quota in Ch'an-lin Temple in the same locality was forty, but usually rose to seventy in the summer. In the K'ai-yüan Temple in Yang-chou there was a normal complement of one hundred monks.

## INTERNAL ADMINISTRATION

The internal administration of a monastery usually consisted of the *san-kang* or the three officials elected by the monks in that monastery: *shang-tso*, abbot or superior, *sthavira*; *ssu-chu*, rector, *vihārasvāmin*; *tu-wei-na*, superintendent, *karmadāna*.[4] For the

---

[4] We have come across this same title previously, where it designated an official in the Office to Oversee Blessings in the Northern Wei government. See note 8 of chap. IX.

position of abbot the monk chosen was usually one who was already advanced in age, eminent in learning and virtue, and highly respected in the clerical community. The rector had charge over the construction and administration of the monastery buildings; while the superintendent supervised the miscellaneous details concerning the daily lives of the monks, such as setting the time for the chanting of sutras, arranging for meals, supervising the making of beds, cleaning rooms, sweeping grounds, and drawing water.

Besides the three officials, there were also a number of lesser elected officers, of which the following are worthy of mention:

*a*) *tien-tso* (controller), an official who supervised the order of seats and beds for monks, the assignment of rooms, the distribution of such things as clothing, food, vegetables, fruits, and warm water, and the burning of incense.

*b*) *chih-sui* (accountant), an official who presented an annual report to the assembly of monks on the finances of the monastery. For such a report he kept a record of all income and expenditures during the year. Ennin was present in the K'ai-yüan Temple in Yang-chou when such a report was given on the twenty-ninth day of the twelfth month, 838.[5]

*c*) *k'u-ssu* (steward or keeper of the storehouse).

In Ennin's diary there is also mentioned a *chien-ssu* (monastery supervisor) who exercised jurisdiction over a single monastery. However, it is not clear just how much supervision such an official exercised in each monastery, and what his relation was to the three officials who administered the affairs of the monastery.

## TEMPLE FESTIVALS

Important though the property or the industrial and commercial activities of the temples might be, still they were by no means as significant as were the function which the institutions played in the religious lives of the people. Besides serving as the place where the devotee could worship the Buddhas and bodhisattvas,

---

[5] A good example of such a report may be seen in plate 5 of J. Gernet's book, *Les Aspects Economiques du Bouddhisme*, Saigon, 1956, which is a photographic reproduction of a manuscript found by Pelliot in Tun-huang (Pelliot mss. 3234). This was a report rendered by the accountant of the Ching-t'u monastery in Tun-huang, probably for the year 942, in which he listed the various receipts under his administration of the office.

the monasteries and temples were the scenes of numerous festivals
that meant much in the lives of the faithful. The annual calendar
of the Chinese was marked by a series of such festivals in which
all the elements of society participated. Buddhism more than
any other religion was able to bring together the emperor, the
aristocracy, the common people, rich and poor, cleric and laity,
to celebrate these religious festivities. This was due in part to
the Mahāyāna emphasis that Buddhism was a religion of salvation and compassion to all beings and in part to the lack of appeal
of both Taoism and Confucianism to all classes of society. Some
of these festivals were really imperial and official functions, such
as the celebration of the imperial birthday and the services in
commemoration of deceased emperors and empresses. There is no
better indication of the close relationship between the Buddhist
sangha and the state than in the celebration of these imperial anniversaries; here the sangha was fulfilling its function in the maintenance of the imperial cult and in protecting the country from
evil forces. These celebrations were held only in the officially
recognized and grand monasteries of the state, and in return for
the performing of such functions the monks residing in those
temples were furnished by the state with all the necessities of
life, so that there was no need for them to seek for sustenance
among the people. For example, the imperial court was the main
supporter of the monasteries in Wu-t'ai-shan, where the appearance of any auspicious sign connected with Mañjuśrī was immediately reported to the throne. Every year imperial commissioners were sent to the mountains with gifts to be bestowed
on the monks.[6]

The celebration of the imperial birthday, which was also referred to by such names as the Festival of the Thousand Autumns
or the Festival of the Imperial Longevity, was started in 730 by
Hsüan-tsung, who ordered that vegetarian feasts be arranged in
the Buddhist temples for the occasion. Later, when the K'ai-yüan

[6] When Ennin was there, he reported one such visit in which the imperial
emissary came with 500 fine robes, 500 packages of silk floss, 1,000 lengths
of cloth, Buddhist scarves, 1,000 ounces of incense, 1,000 pounds of tea,
and 1,000 handcloths. Another example of such largess might be seen in
the donation by Emperor Wen of the Sui Dynasty to the monks of Ch'ing-
ch'an temple: 14,000 pieces of satin, 5,000 pieces of cloth, 1,000 balls of
silk floss, 200 pieces of fine silk, 1,000 shih of cereals, and 5,000 strings of
cash.

temples were established throughout the empire, they became the scene of these birthday ceremonies. During the years that Ennin was in China he referred to these feasts several times. One of them took place on the eleventh day of the sixth month, 840, when he was on Wu-t'ai-shan, and he noted that all the monasteries there rang the temple bells and prepared vegetarian feasts. On another such occasion when he was in Ch'ang-an, he wrote that it was the practice to have Buddhist monks and Taoist priests from the two halves of the city gather in the imperial palace to hold a religious debate. The vegetarian feasts on Wu-t'ai-shan during these birthday celebrations were indeed gigantic events attended by ten thousand monks and laymen.

As for the commemorative services on the anniversaries of deceased emperors, the practice started as early as the first T'ang emperor, who decreed in 628 that on such occasions vegetarian feasts and the burning of incense should be carried out in the temples. A detailed description of a service held in Yang-chou in memory of Ching-tsung, assassinated in 826, was given by Ennin in 838. For this occasion the K'ai-yüan Temple received fifty strings of cash from the state to arrange for a vegetarian feast for five hundred monks. The congregation of monks gathered in the monastery very early on the appointed day. Not only monks, but also all the officials in the locality, including the minister of state, Li Te-yü, who was at the time the governor-general of Yang-chou, were present for the service. Li marched first into the great hall and worshiped the Buddha. The assembled monks then chanted Sanskrit hymns and burned incense, with Li himself taking part in the latter ceremony. A prayer was uttered by a venerable monk, and chants were intoned for the eight classes of demigods, all of which were intended to glorify the spirit of the departed emperor. After the service the officials dined in the great hall, while the monks dined in the galleries. The five hundred monks gathered together on this occasion came from various monasteries in the city, and since they could not all be accommodated at one place for the feast, they were served at different places but at the same time.

These two celebrations had nothing to do with Buddhism, but they were observed widely throughout the empire under the

T'ang Dynasty, and serve as an illustration of how closely identified the sangha was with the fortunes of the ruling house.

Besides fulfilling its role at these official festivals, the Buddhist temple also performed a function—and a much more important one at that—in organizing the grand festivals throughout the year for the edification of the local population. Through these festivals Buddhism became a religion not just for the cloistered monks and nuns, but also for the teeming multitudes in the great centers of population.

LANTERN FESTIVAL. The first of these occasions on the annual calendar was the Lantern Festival, celebrated on the evenings of the fourteenth, fifteenth, and sixteenth of the first month. In Yang-chou, according to the Japanese eyewitness Ennin, lamps were lighted along the streets and in the various temples, to be viewed by the populace who wandered around until late at night. Very often these people would cast copper coins before the lamps in each temple. The temples themselves vied with one another in constructing ingenious devices of variegated shapes that contained as many lanterns as possible. In one temple there was a spoon and bamboo structure, looking like a pagoda and holding at least a thousand lamps arranged in an amazing manner. In the capital the celebrations were even more exuberant and brilliant. The city portals were ordinarily closed between 8:00 P.M. and 4:00 A.M., with all travel on the streets restricted during those hours except for those going out on public business or on account of critical illness. At the time of the festival, however, these portals were open all night by imperial order, and the streets were illuminated by thousands of torches carried by people roaming around the city. Even the emperor would go out to view the procession of torches and lanterns, and he often permitted the inhabitants of the capitals to take a vacation from their usual duties to participate in the celebrations.

FESTIVAL OF THE BUDDHA'S BIRTHDAY. This Lantern Festival was followed by the celebration of the birthday of the Buddha, which occurred on the eighth day of the second moon (also sometimes celebrated on the eighth day of the fourth moon and the eighth day of the twelfth moon). This occasion was usually marked by two events—the procession of the Buddha images and the bathing of the Buddha. The latter ceremony was based on the tradition that as soon as the Buddha was born, he was bathed with heavenly scented water poured down by the devas. This custom apparently started as far back as the fourth century. During the T'ang Dynasty the ceremony was but rarely mentioned, and Ennin did not refer to it at all in his diary. As for the procession of the images, the practice started as early as the Northern Wei Dynasty, when images of the Buddha were paraded through the streets of Ta-t'ung in 424, with the emperor personally enjoying the spectacle. Later, after the capital was moved to Lo-yang, the occasion was celebrated with even greater enthusiasm and joy by the populace. On the previous day (the seventh) all images in the city, over a thousand in number, were first transported to the Ching-ming Temple, and on the following day were then carried through the streets of the capital in the direction of the imperial palace, where they were personally reviewed by the emperor. On this day, according to a contemporary observer, "golden flowers sparkled in the sunlight, ornamented parasols floated about like clouds, the banners and pennants formed a forest, fumes from the incense resembled the mist, music and chants resounded and shook heaven and earth. Joy and play were in full swing, with the dense crowd milling around everywhere; eminent monks and virtuous elders formed groups carrying their walking sticks while faithful laymen assembled, holding flowers in their hands. Carriages blocked all thoroughfares, causing a bewildering confusion everywhere."[7] Such a description indicates that the procession was not a solemn occasion, but one that was attended by spontaneous popular rejoicing on the part of the people.

FESTIVAL HONORING THE RELICS OF THE BUDDHA. The festival that attracted the greatest throngs in the T'ang capital of Ch'ang-an was that connected with the worship of the Buddha's relics, of which there were a number in the capital. In the Fa-men Temple of Feng-hsiang, a suburb west of the city, there was a finger bone of the Buddha, while in the capital at least four temples claimed to have specimens of the Buddha's teeth. These four teeth were put on display by the temples annually for one

[7] Yang Hsüan-chih, *Lo-yang chia-lan chi*, 3; *Taishō*, 51,1010b.

week, beginning with the eighth day of either the second or third month, and on this occasion all sorts of offerings, such as medicine and foods, rare fruits and flowers, and different kinds of incense, were presented to the Buddha. All these were spread out to be viewed by the public, who came in endless stream to worship the sacred relics. Some of the worshipers themselves made offerings—a hundred shih of rice, twenty shih of millet, or provisions enough to feed all the monks in the temple. Cash was tossed about like rain toward the hall where the tooth was enshrined.

The relic at Fa-men Temple has been immortalized by the famous memorial presented by Han Yü in 819, in which he protested vigorously against the imperial practice of welcoming the relic into the royal palace. It appears that the imperial reception of this relic was not an annual affair. The first such reception took place in 660; thereafter no mention was made of the event until the years 790, 819, and 873. Nor did the reception take place on a specific date. In 790 and 819 the bone was brought from the monastery to the palace during the first month of the year, while in 873 it occurred in the fourth month. The relic was kept in the palace for three days; then it was taken to one of the Buddhist temples in the city for public viewing. Whenever this relic was put on public display, the people in the capital and vicinity would work themselves into such a state of religious frenzy as to belie the statement that the Chinese are rational and practical in their conduct. During the 819 celebration Han Yü charged that the multitudes burned their heads and roasted their fingers, threw away their clothes and scattered their money, that old and young rushed about abandoning their work and disregarding their place in society. Other sources spoke of officialdom and the grand families' donating unlimited wealth to the monastery, while the common people vied with one another to make their offerings to the Buddha, giving up the earnings of a lifetime and fearing only that they would arrive too late.

A vivid description of the festival of 873 was given by a contemporary witness: "On the eighth day of the fourth month of 873, the bone of the Buddha was welcomed into Ch'ang-an. Starting from the An-fu Building at the K'ai-yüan gate, all along the way on both sides, cries of invocation to the Buddha shook the earth. Men and women watched the procession of the relic respectfully, while monks and nuns followed in its wake. The emperor went to the An-fu Temple, and as he personally paid his respects, tears dropped down to moisten his breast. He thereupon summoned the monks of both sides of the city to offer gifts of varying quantities to it. Moreover, to those venerable old men who had participated in welcoming the bone during the Yüan-ho era (806-820) he bestowed silver bowls, brocades, and colored silks. The prominent families of Ch'ang-an all vied with one another in ornamenting their riding carriages for this occasion. Streets in every direction were filled with people supporting the old and assisting the young. Those who came to see the spectacle all fasted beforehand in order that they might receive the blessings of the Buddha. At the time, a soldier cut off his left arm in front of the Buddha's relic, and while holding it with his hand, he reverenced the relic each time he took a step, his blood sprinkling the ground all the while. As for those who walked on their elbows and knees, biting off their fingers or cutting off their hair, their numbers could not be counted. There was also a monk who covered his head with artemisia, a practice known as disciplining the head. When the pile of artemisia was ignited, the pain caused the monk to shake his head and to cry out, but young men in the market place held him tight so that he could not move. When the pain became unbearable, he cried out and fell prostrate on the ground. With his head scorched and his deportment disorderly, he was the object of laughter of all the spectators.

"The emperor welcomed the bone into the palace chapel, where he built a comfortable couch with curtains made of golden flowers, a mat made of dragon scales, and a mattress made of phoenix feathers; he burnt incense of the most precious quality, and offered cream made of the essence of milk, all materials offered by Kalinga in 868. Immediately after welcoming the bone, the emperor decreed that in the capital and vicinity people were to pile up earth along the roadside to form incense posts to a height of ten to twenty feet. Up to about nine feet they were all decorated with gold and jade. Within the capital, there were approximately 10,000 of these posts. Legend has it that when these posts shook, rays from the Buddha and auspicious clouds lighted up the roadside, and this was regarded repeatedly as a supernatural sign by the happy people. Within the city the rich families one after another sponsored preaching assemblies, and along the streets they tied together silks to form pavilions and halls, poured mercury to form pools, set up gold and jade as trees, and competed against each other to assemble the monks or to establish Buddha images. They blew the conch-shell and struck the cymbals, they lighted lamps and candles without interruption. They also ordered several bare-footed children with jade girdles and golden headgear to sing praises and to play as they wished. Likewise they tied brocades and embroideries to form small carts to convey singers and dancers. In this fashion, they filled the imperial capital with their fun and gaiety, with the inhabitants of Yen-shou Lane putting on the most gorgeous show."[8]

ALL SOUL'S FEAST. Another Buddhist festival which became a popular celebration was the Ullambana or the All-Souls' Feast, on the fifteenth day of the seventh month. This festival was based on the Buddhist legend concerning Moggallana, who descended to the deepest hell to rescue his mother from her miseries there. After Moggallana had done this, the Buddha then suggested that a great united effort be made by faithful Buddhists to offset the miseries of hell, and, in response to this, arose the custom of offering food, clothing, and wealth for the benefit of the unfortunate denizens of purgatory. In China the offerings were made for the additional purpose of rescuing the ancestors for seven generations back from whatever misery they might be suffering; because of this connection with the virtue of filial piety, the festival became exceedingly popular. During the T'ang Dynasty it no longer was just a festival for the departed; it also became an occasion on which the temples opened their rare possessions for public display. In some instances rich laymen used the temples as exhibition halls to exhibit exquisite and rare objects. On such occasions temples took on the atmosphere of a fair, during which dramatic performances were also presented. While in T'ai-yüan in 840, Ennin visited the displays in the different temples and found the rare items dazzling in their beauty. In 844, while in Ch'ang-an, he again toured the temples at the

[8] See Su E, *Tu Yang Tsa-pien, chüan hsia.*

time of this festival and found that the people were indulging in a sort of competition in their rare possessions as well as in the ingenuity of the artificial flowers, candles, and fruit trees which they had made. These were all spread out as offerings to be viewed and admired by the visiting throngs. In becoming a competition for the display of rarities during the T'ang Dynasty, the Ullambana festival lost its original meaning and was no longer just a festival for the dead.

THE VEGETARIAN FEAST. By participating in the official ceremonies on behalf of the state, and by organizing the grand festivals on behalf of the local populace, the Buddhist temple was able to fulfill a role that identified it with the various elements of Chinese society. Such a role was strengthened by two other activities carried on by the temple—vegetarian feasts and religious lectures.

The Chinese word for vegetarian feast is *chai*. In Buddhist terminology this character is also used to denote the fasting periods observed by the monks, that is to say, periods when the monks were not supposed to eat after the noonday hour. Such fasting periods in China were regular occurrences, known as the three long months of fasting and the six fasting days.[9] During the Sui and T'ang Dynasties such fasting days assumed national importance, for during the three long fasting months and the six fasting days killing of living animals and execution of criminals were prohibited. It is difficult to see how the first prohibition could have been effectively carried out. In addition to these regular fasting days the *chai* was observed also on numerous special occasions, and here the character referred to the vegetarian banquets held at midday. Such special occasions would be the Buddha's birthday, the birthday of the reigning emperor, memorial days for deceased emperors, the date of Buddha's entry in nirvāna, memorial days in honor of deceased patriarchs of sects or eminent monks. Sometimes such vegetarian feasts would be arranged as an example of gratitude for hospitality rendered, benefits received, recovery from illness, completion

[9] The three long months of fasting referred to the first fifteen days of the first, fifth, and ninth months, and the six fasting days were the eighth, fourteenth, fifteenth, twenty-third, twenty-ninth, and thirtieth of each month. Sometimes other days in the month were added to this list, to make a total of ten.

of some meritorious project, deliverance from some calamity, or as a welcome or farewell party for visiting monks. Such feasts also might be staged as an occasion to pray for some boon or for the avoidance of some calamity, such as drought or famine. Celebration of the vegetarian feast became standard practice in the officially recognized temples throughout the T'ang Dynasty on imperial birthdays and on memorial days in honor of deceased emperors, with the state paying for the cost of such celebrations. Within the imperial precincts such a feast would be staged in the palace chapel, with laymen as well as monks included so that the numbers in attendance were often very considerable. A congregation of five hundred to a thousand was quite common, while in some instances over ten thousand were present, with the maximum of fifty thousand being recorded for a feast arranged by Liang Wu-ti in 529.

The Japanese cleric Ennin furnished detailed accounts of these vegetarian feasts as he saw them celebrated in T'ang China. All through his diary he referred to these feasts, and when he was at Wu-t'ai-shan, he wrote down a graphic picture of the banquet with all its revealing minutiae. This particular feast was sponsored by a private individual and was attended by seven hundred and fifty participants. At noon a bell was struck that was the signal for the congregation to enter the hall and take their seats. When all were seated in rows according to their ranks, the leader struck a mallet and chanted some Sanskrit verses. He then paid reverence to the Three Jewels for the sake of the lasting prosperity of the dynasty, the grandeur of the patron, and the welfare of the congregation of monks and laymen. Then came the feast, and when all had partaken of their share, they purified themselves ritually with water and then rinsed their mouths.

Ennin emphasized that the tradition in Wu-t'ai-shan was to treat equally all participants at these vegetarian feasts, whether cleric or layman, man or woman, great or small; he recounted a legend said to be responsible for this custom. Long ago, according to this story, Mañjuśrī, the patron saint of Wu-t'ai-shan, attended a feast disguised as a poor pregnant woman. When it was her turn to receive the food, she demanded another share for the unborn child. The patron, however, cursed her and refused to give the extra share, saying that even though there was a child in her belly, it did not come out to ask for food. Angered by this attitude, the woman left the hall, and, as she went out, she transformed herself into Mañjuśrī, emitting a light that illuminated the entire building. The whole assembly now besought Mañjuśrī to return to the hall, but the bodhisattva disappeared into the sky. Accordingly, the custom of the area from that time on was to have a system of equality in which each received his due share of food. If anyone requested more than his share, he would be given what he asked for.

Often at the end of a vegetarian feast there would be a ceremony in which the patron who arranged for the feast would give to each monk present a gift of some wearing apparel or cash, consisting usually of twenty to thirty coppers. This cash was one of the items of private property owned by the monks, and they used it in many different ways. Some used the cash to buy food for animals; others used it for such projects as feeding the needy or decorating the temples.

## RELIGIOUS EDUCATION

Going hand in hand with festivals and vegetarian feasts as vehicles for the propagation of the religion was the program of religious education carried on by the monasteries and monks. This program consisted of two aspects, one external, one internal. Internally there was the system of education for the religious instruction of the postulants and novices. It will be recalled that candidates for admission to the order had to pass certain tests on the sacred scriptures before they could qualify for initiation. Instruction had to be given to these candidates, and this was provided within the monasteries by qualified masters of the law. Apparently there was some specialization, for the candidates could major, so to speak, in such branches of learning as the rules of discipline, the contents of the sutras, or meditation, under the tutelage of a master in each branch of learning. At times there was probably also instruction in foreign languages in monasteries where qualified teachers were present. Here was a system of education, aimed at the training of a literate group of monks, conversant with the sacred literature of Buddhism, existing alongside of the traditional system in China, which was aimed at the training of a literary class versed in the Confucian classics. Out of such a system of monastic education arose those clerics who became leaders of the Buddhist community in China.

The second or external aspect concerned the dissemination of religious instruction to the masses. The program embraced such features as lectures and debates on the scriptures, storytelling, and drama. For purposes of disseminating knowledge concerning Buddhism there was one class of monks who traveled about lecturing on the sutras, or challenging some local masters to a debate on doctrinal points. This practice was already in vogue during the Period of Disunity, and was to become very popular during the Sui and T'ang. Hsüan-tsang, before he left for India, traveled extensively in north and central China. During the early Sui years one itinerant monk, Fa-yüan, who specialized in the rules of discipline, displayed such skill and subtlety in challenging and refuting others that he was widely known as the "Tiger of the *Vinaya.*" Another monk, Shan-chou, an expert on the *Nirvā-nasūtra,* was so successful in defeating his opponents in such open debates that three of them were said to have committed suicide rather than endure the disgrace of defeat. Such debates were held not only in temples, but also in the palaces and in homes of the aristocracy. Probably the most famous of these debates was the one held in 609 in Ch'ang-an between two venerable masters, Chi-tsang, aged sixty-six at the time, and Seng-ts'an, aged eighty-one, who argued scores of propositions back and forth, with neither one able to achieve a clear-cut victory. The audiences listening to such debates were probably small, consisting mainly of monks or highly sophisticated laymen able to appreciate the subtle discussions on the fine points of the dharma. It was also true that in some cases the itinerant monk was not so much interested in propagating the law as in achieving some sort of worldly reputation, for if he could challenge some famous local master and defeat him in debate, his own standing would be enhanced considerably.

Besides these itinerant teachers and debaters, there were those attached to particular monasteries who used these institutions as their base of operations. Such masters usually specialized on one or a few sutras, and lectured on these sutras repeatedly. The famous San-lun master Chi-tsang lectured on the *Lotus Sutra* over three hundred times during his life and on the *San-lun* over a hundred times. Shan-tao, the Pure Land master, lectured on the *Pure Land Sutra* over two hundred times. The audience listening to such lectures consisted primarily of monks residing within the monastery—about 250 to 400 in the case of the important temples in the capital, while in the important prefectures and outlying areas the number would be less. However, monks from other temples as well as devout laymen attended also, so that the audience often increased to much higher figures. Chih-i, the Tien-t'ai master, once lectured to an audience of over 5,000 in the Yü-ch'üan Temple of Ch'ing-chou; Fa-ch'in drew about 2,000 to 3,000 people in Ch'ang-an to his lectures during the K'ai-yüan era. In one instance, when Fa-min was lecturing in the I-yin Temple of Yüeh-chou, there were in attendance 1,200 local monks, 300 local nuns, and 800 clerics from other prefectures—a total of 2,300. Very often a series of such religious lectures would be sponsored by a monastery, extending over a considerable period of time and aimed primarily at reaching the community of lay followers. Lectures could also be ordered by the emperor. During the first month of 841 seven monasteries in the capital received imperial orders to hold lectures for laymen; these lectures were on the *Avataṁsakasūtra*, the *Lotus Sutra*, and the *Nirvāṇasūtra*, and lasted from the fifteenth day of the first month to the fifteenth day of the second month. Ennin has described for us in detail the procedure of these lectures which he witnessed at the Mt. Ch'ih cloister in Shantung. It is true that this was a Korean cloister, but undoubtedly the procedure followed there was similar to that in vogue elsewhere in China.

## THE PIEN-WEN OR TEXTS OF MARVELOUS EVENTS

As previously mentioned, during festival days the monasteries were usually centers of attraction for the populace, and they often took advantage of the huge crowds present to carry on some evangelical work. Since in such gatherings the poor and lowly and the uneducated were in the majority, the evangelical method could not very well be formal religious lectures on the sutras, for these probably would have been beyond the understanding of the audience. To meet the needs of such an audience the Buddhist monks resorted to storytelling, the aim of which was not so much to explain the profound ideas of the religion as to attract the attention of the common people and make them more sympathetic to Buddhism and its teachings. These stories were cast in a form of literature known as *pien-wen* (texts of marvelous events), many examples of which were preserved in the Tun-huang caves. In a *pien-wen* an episode is taken from a Buddhist sutra and retold in the vernacular in a greatly expanded form, with events and characters refurbished and elaborated. Buddhist stories told in this style became extremely popular during the T'ang Dynasty. In form they followed the Buddhist translations, being a mixture of prose and poetry. So popular was this literary form that it was soon utilized by non-Buddhist writers, wandering minstrels, and ballad singers, who went about the countryside telling stories of a secular nature mainly to amuse the people. Two of the most popular Buddhist *pien-wen* were those concerning Vimalakīrti and Moggallana. The former is considered to be a masterpiece of literature, told in a vivid, lively, and dynamic style. Several copies of the Moggallana *pien-wen* were recovered in Tun-huang, and the one preserved in London is dated 921. According to this version of the story, Moggallana ascended to one of the heavens after he became an arhat and saw his father there, but not his mother. He asked the Buddha where his mother was, and was told that she was in hell. Moggallana descended to hell to search for her. The story here describes in minute detail the horrors of hell. Finally, Moggallana found his mother in the deepest Avici hell. With the aid of the Buddha he rescued her out of purgatory. She was then reborn as a *preta* or hungry ghost. The Buddha urged Moggallana to initiate the Ullambana or All Souls' Feast to feed his mother. She soon abandoned the form of a *preta*, only to be reborn as a dog. Finally, with the help of Moggallana she was reborn in heaven.

Though this *pien-wen* is considered to be inferior in style to the Vimalakīrti story, it wielded enormous influence, as it became the prototype for the description of hell in later Chinese literature. The *pien-wen* form itself, consisting of a mixture of prose and poetry, also played an important role in the history of Chinese literature. Before the T'ang Dynasty Chinese literary pieces usually were entirely prose or entirely poetry, but after the Sung period drama and fiction containing a mixture of poetry and prose began to emerge. It is commonly held that this type of literature was influenced by the Chinese translations of Buddhist sutras. The questions that puzzled literary historians were when the practice started among the Chinese writers and what themes were covered by the early pieces. The discovery of the *pien-wen* samples at Tun-huang provided just the material to answer these questions. We now know that the themes of the *pien-wen* were the stories and tales found in the Buddhist scriptures, retold in the vernacular and enlarged with numerous interesting details designed to hold the attention of the audience. For instance, an episode in the Vimalakīrti *pien-wen*, originally consisting of about one hundred characters in the sutra, was expanded to about three to four thousand characters in length. It appears also that the *pien-wen* first emerged during the K'ai-yüan (713-741) and T'ien-pao (742-755) eras of the T'ang Dynasty.

Two other features of the *pien-wen* deserve mention. At the end of one chapter of a secular *pien-wen* there is an expression, "The narrative of events in this chapter is now finished, we now enter into the next chapter." This is an interesting forerunner of the stock passage so common in later Chinese novels, "If you want to know what comes after this, then listen to the story in the next chapter." It furnishes additional evidence that these novels were influenced by the *pien-wen* forms. Secondly, we find in the *pien-wen* some of the earliest examples of the vernacular used in literature.[10]

These *pien-wen* stories represented the Buddhist attempt to reach the Chinese masses with a religious message and to convert them. Very often the stories were built around the *pien-hsiang* or paintings and illustrations based on an episode in the life of the Buddha or his famous disciples. By telling their stories with illustrations as background, the Buddhist monks were able to transmit their message very effectively to the listening audience gathered in the monasteries.

[10] Some random examples are the use of the diminutive suffix *tzu*, the use of *li* for "inside," *che* for "this," *ni* and *t'a* as the second and third personal pronouns.

## RELIGIOUS SOCIETIES

To aid in the task of religious propagation yet another institution was developed by the monasteries—the religious society. Religious societies have always been a part of the Buddhist organization in China. In some instances these societies were secret, such as the White Lotus Society of the Yüan, Ming, and Ch'ing Dynasties, the Maitreya Society of the T'ang and Sung Dynasties, and the White Cloud Society of the Sung and Yüan Dynasties. The first two were very active in fomenting rebellion among the populace. There were also those societies founded by famous monks in connection with certain cults, such as the earlier society started by Hui-yüan to foster adoration of Amitābha and the Western Paradise, and the group formed by Tao-an to encourage worship of Maitreya. At present, however, such types of societies will not be considered; instead, we shall discuss only those groups or unions which served as instruments for the propagation of the religion in China.

Religious societies formed for the purpose of acquiring merit by the performance of some collective act had existed in China since the Period of Disunity. In Yün-kang and Lung-men numerous inscriptions have been found referring to such organizations, established mainly for the purpose of carving statues in the grottoes of those sites—an activity which was encouraged and patronized by the Northern Wei rulers. When the group was engaged in large-scale sculptural activities, the membership tended to be fairly large, ranging from a hundred to a thousand, with some society members contributing the manual work and others providing the finances. From the Northern Wei to the first half of the T'ang Dynasty those societies which concentrated on carving statues apparently were in the majority. There were also smaller groups brought together for such purposes as copying or reciting sutras, or staging vegetarian feasts. Membership in these groups usually numbered about thirty. Such a group was founded by Pao-ch'ung (d.634), who organized a society in Ch'eng-tu for the recital of the *Perfection of Wisdom in 25,000 Lines*. Once a month the group would meet for a vegetarian feast, and after the meal each member would recite a chapter of the sutra. Still another type of society was organized to furnish material support for the monks in a particular monastery, as in the case of the rice society founded by the monk Chih-tsung (550-648) in Yang-chou, which consisted of three hundred members pledged to offer annually one shih of rice each. In such societies there were usually monks serving as spiritual preceptors who looked after the spiritual life of the members.

It was once believed that beginning with the second half of the T'ang Dynasty the number of religious societies began to decline. Such a belief was based on the observation that there were few inscriptions in Lung-men dating from that period, and that societies were seldom mentioned in contemporary literature. However, the mass of documents discovered in Tun-huang indicates that such a belief was incorrect and that, on the contrary, religious societies were just as vigorous as ever.

On the basis of evidence furnished by the Tun-huang documents it is possible to divide such societies into three types: (a) Societies in the tradition of those in existence since the Period of Disunity. Instead of engaging in statue construction, these groups performed such functions as arranging for vegetarian feasts, reciting or copying sutras, or assisting in the religious lectures. (b) Societies which did not emphasize devotion to the Buddha, or non-Buddhist groups that were interested in maintaining the sacrificial ceremonies of the spring and autumn held by the populace in towns and villages, in fostering social gatherings to improve social relationships among members, and in providing economic or financial assistance to members. (c) Societies that combined the characteristics of (a) and (b). Besides the religious activities performed by the first group, this type also took over features of the second group. Consequently, the society members arranged for vegetarian feasts and recited sutras, but also provided mutual assistance to one another on such happy occasions as birthdays, weddings, and anniversary celebrations, as well as on occasions of misfortune. Such groups became in fact mutual aid societies.

Included in the Tun-huang documents are a number of notices calling for meetings of the societies. The wording of such notices is fairly uniform, and the following is a translation of one of them: "All members are requested to be present at the next meeting, due to be held on the fourth day of the coming month, at 6:00

A.M. at the entrance of the Tuan-yen Temple. The last two persons to arrive will be fined one beaker of wine, while those not attending will be fined half a jar. This notice is to be transmitted rapidly from one member to another and must not be delayed by any one. If it should be delayed, then the offending family will be fined according to the established regulations of the group. After the notice has made its round, it is to be returned to the committee to be used as a basis for levying penalties."[11] This particular notice was dated *jen-shen,* which could be either 852 or 912. Following the date, there is a list of the society members. In the Tun-huang manuscripts the societies were uniformly called *she,* an echo of the ancient reunion of the villagers at the altar of the God of Soil.

It goes without saying that these religious societies enjoyed close relations with the monasteries. The latter furnished leadership in matters pertaining to the religious life of the members, and also provided economic support for many of their activities. For their part, the society members assisted the monasteries in every way possible. They helped in the fund-raising campaigns, the missionary endeavors, the festivals and celebrations conducted by the monastery during the course of the year. By working hard for the welfare of the monastery they shared in its glory. Each society averaged about twenty-five to thirty members, sometimes up to forty; usually not just one society but frequently about ten or fifteen would be attached to one monastery. Evidence of this close relationship is found in the financial statement of the monasteries, many of which have been preserved. One such statement of the Ching-t'u Temple in Tun-huang noted that on the eighth day of the second month flour, oil, grains, and wine were used in a feast for the society members and monks; on the very next day more of the same materials were used to entertain the members of a newly organized society.[12] From these financial statements it is seen that the temples provided food and drink

[11] Naba, *Shirin,* 23,3 (1938), 522.
[12] The eighth day of the second month was a festival day for the temple, and after the celebration a temple feast was prepared for the society members who assisted in the celebration. On the very next day a new society was organized, and again a feast was prepared for the new members who had gathered to draw up regulations for the new group.

for the members on many occasions throughout the year. One might be surprised by the mention of wine in these accounts. Although the Buddhist *Vinaya* forbade the drinking of intoxicating spirits, these temples in China did not abide by that prohibition. This was another sign of the religion's adapting itself to the needs of the laymen.

Arranging for vegetarian feasts probably constituted one of the main functions of the religious societies in the temples to which they were attached. During such feasts all the societies connected with a particular monastery were present, and after the arrangements and preparation they joined with the monks in enjoying the feast, so that such occasions were in the nature of grand social gatherings to promote better relationships between clerics and laymen. Very often members of the societies donated the foodstuffs such as grains, oil, or flour used by the monastery to entertain them.

Of particular interest is one manuscript in Tun-huang which describes a society organized on February 13 in 959 to promote friendship among women. This document opens with a eulogy on friendship: "Our parents give us life, but friends enhance its value; they sustain us in time of danger, rescue us from calamity. In dealing with friends, a single word may serve as a bond of faith." As with the other religious societies this group of women had to contribute a certain amount of oil, wine, and flour on festival days and on the first of each month. However, there are some additional features about this women's organization that deserve attention. For example, discipline is emphasized: "If in the club there is anyone who disregards precedence in small things and great, in unruly fashion creates a disturbance at a feast, and will not obey the verbal instructions of her superior, then all the members shall repair to the gateway and mulct her of enough wine-syrup for a whole feast to be partaken of by the rest of the company." Once a woman joined this group, it was rather difficult to leave, for, in addition to a fine, "any member who wishes to leave the club shall be sentenced to three strokes with the bamboo." Following this were the names of fifteen club members, and at the end of the document it was stated that rules were designed to be suitable for members as water was for fishes, and that the members were to swear by them, with the sun and moon, hills and streams as witnesses.[13]

On the basis of this information one may conclude that these religious societies were a tightly knit group formed by laymen under the leadership of one or more monks connected with a local temple. The groups represented a sort of closed society, in which the members recognized in one another certain rights and duties that were permanent. For instance, each member was required to attend punctually the meetings of the society or else face the imposition of a fine. He was also expected to contribute toward the vegetarian feasts held in the temple, and such contributions were not entirely spontaneous, for neglect would result in punishment. By being a member of a society the individual was given the privilege of participating in the religious life of the monastery. He was able to use the temple grounds for meetings; he attended the feasts held there and received religious instruction from the spiritual preceptor of the society. As an individual working by himself the religious merit that he might gain was small and inconsequential, but as a member of a group composed of many others, considerable merit could be accumulated as a result of the pious activities of the group, such as carving statues or reciting and copying sutras. In addition to these religious benefits there was also the economic assistance that was available to each member of the society from the other members of the group, as well as from the temple itself.

During T'ang times such religious societies were still guided in their activities by sincere religious motives, but this was not to be the case as time went on. The existence of a number of societies in the same locality soon led to rivalry between groups. For instance, there were two groups in T'ung-chou in present Shensi devoted to P'u-hsien bodhisattva (Samantabhadra). They competed against each other in fabricating miraculous legends about the deity; one society claimed that the statue of P'u-hsien in its possession was transformed from a youth eighteen years of age, while the other claimed that its P'u-hsien image developed from a boy born on the altar. During the Southern Sung Dynasty the religious societies in Hang-chou competed with one another in the presentation of rare objects, flowers, and fruits to the

[13] L. Giles, *Six Centuries of Tunhuang*, London, 1944, 38.

temples during festival days. The motive behind such presentations was then no longer religious, for the donors were primarily interested in outdoing the others in the rarity and unique quality of their gifts, so much so that the festival on the fifteenth day of the second month became known as the meeting for the competition in rarities.

## WELFARE ACTIVITIES

In addition to the economic and educational activities just described, Buddhist monasteries during the T'ang also served as charitable institutions, performing various deeds of social welfare. This function was based on the idea of Mahāyāna Buddhism's being a religion of compassion aimed at the salvation of all living creatures. The conception of the Buddha or the sangha as a field of merit or compassion was now translated into concrete form by the *pei-t'ien* or field of compassion, which was established by the Buddhist monasteries to carry out their numerous charitable activities, such as taking care of the old and decrepit, the poor, the famished, and the sick. At first the *pei-t'ien* was administered by the monastery, but during the Hui-ch'ang suppression the institution was neglected. To remedy this situation it was suggested that the government take over the management of the *pei-t'ien*, and that the income from certain portions of land be directed solely to the support of such charitable institutions. The suggestion was accepted by the throne and put into effect; in the two capitals ten ch'ing of land were set aside, in the large prefectures seven ch'ing, and in others five ch'ing. After the suppression was lifted, management of the *pei-t'ien* reverted back to the monasteries. The proceeds from such land enabled the monasteries to establish hospitals and dispensaries for the sick, feeding stations for the hungry, and havens for the aged and decrepit. The monasteries also established bathhouses within their precincts and resthouses along the routes to famous shrines. They also sometimes engaged in such community projects as road building, bridge construction, well digging, and tree planting along the highways. Such a program of social welfare sponsored by the monastery was to continue through the ages down to modern times.

For the faithful Buddhist of the T'ang Dynasty the temple

was indeed an institution which touched on almost all aspects of his life. It sustained him with spiritual comfort, assisted him with economic aid when needed, offered him entertainment on various occasions to lighten his daily toil, provided him with opportunities for social companionship, and took care of him when he was ill, aged, or infirm. This multifold program of activities sponsored by the temple and the enthusiastic response such activities elicited from the populace reflect better than anything else the flourishing condition attained by Buddhism in China during this period.

# CHAPTER XI

# THE SCHOOLS OF BUDDHISM
# IN CHINA

T HE schools of Buddhism which emerged during the T'ang period, schools that developed out of the intense intellectual ferment engendered by the introduction of Buddhist thought in China, deserve attention at this point. Though these schools reached full bloom during the T'ang Dynasty, their roots went back to developments in north China under the Northern Dynasties. The T'ien-t'ai School, for instance, had its beginnings in the teachings of the *Mahāparinirvāna-sūtra* and the methods of dividing the Buddhist sutras into chronological periods. The Hua-yen School can be traced back to the Ti-lun group who were active during the Northern Ch'i and Northern Chou Dynasties, while teachers of the Pure Land and Ch'an were already developing their tenets and practices during the sixth century in north China. Some of these schools were the products of the Chinese response to Buddhism, and indicated how the Chinese mind took over certain basic Buddhist principles and reshaped them to suit the Chinese temperament, so that the schools were no longer Indian systems introduced into China, but were really schools of Chinese Buddhism. Such were the T'ien-t'ai, Hua-yen, Pure Land, and Ch'an. The first school to be discussed is the Sect of the Three Stages, which arose in response to the peculiar social conditions pertaining in north China prior to the Sui Dynasty.

## SECT OF THE THREE STAGES

During the Sui Dynasty a monk named Hsin-hsing (540-594) established, on the basis of the theory of the three periods, the San-chieh-chiao or Sect of the Three Stages. According to this theory, formulated from the contents of such sutras as the *Lotus Sutra* and *Avataṁsaka*, the duration of the Buddha's teachings may be divided into three periods:

1. Period of the true dharma, when the teachings of the Master were rigidly adhered to;

[ 297 ]

2. Period of the counterfeit dharma, when the true dharma was hidden, and something resembling it was then in vogue;

3. Period of the decay of the dharma, when the dharma was in disrepute, and about to disappear.

There was no agreement as to the duration of the first two periods, but in general we may distinguish four schools of thought:

1. True, 500 years; counterfeit, 500 years;
2. True, 500 years; counterfeit, 1,000 years;
3. True, 1,000 years; counterfeit, 500 years;
4. True, 1,000 years; counterfeit, 1,000 years.

Of these four the most prevalent view was the second. At the end of the counterfeit period, then the decay of the dharma would set in, to last ten thousand years.

Discussions of this theory of the three periods were already in vogue at the end of the North-South Dynasties, and one of the provoking questions was when the last period would start. This depended on the date assigned to the nirvāna of the Buddha. Chinese Buddhists during the sixth century generally accepted 949 B.C. as the date, so that fifteen hundred years after that would be A.D. 550.

According to Hsin-hsing, who was born in Honan, what was preached in the first period was the *ekayāna*, the doctrine of the one vehicle; during the second period it was the doctrine of the three vehicles (*śrāvaka-yāna*, Vehicle of the Hearers; *pratyekabuddha-yāna*, Vehicle of the Solitary Buddha; *bo-dhisattva-yāna*, Vehicle of the Bodhisattva). Both of these were considered to be limited in scope. For the third period only his own teachings, which he said were universal in scope, would be appropriate. In his system he contended that his own age was the period of the decay of the dharma. During this stage the people disobeyed all the *Vinaya* rules, believed in heresies, could not distinguish between right and wrong, good and bad, and were bound for rebirth in hell. They were ignorant of the true dharma, they had indulged in criticisms of the scriptures, and they had calumniated the Three Jewels. At such a period there was no sage in the world. The practices and beliefs which were efficacious during the first period, such as meditation and insight, or living the monastic life within the monasteries, no longer sufficed for this third period. The behavior of the followers, Hsin-hsing said, must be appropriate to the age and conditions under which they were living. The sect therefore advocated austerities as a means of purifying conduct; it also required strict adherence to monastic discipline. The members did not live in monasteries but in the courtyards or outbuildings, and spent their time mingling with the crowds in the market places. They had little respect for images and books. For salvation during such a period of decay the traditional concepts of the Buddha and dharma would not be sufficient. Consequently, this sect taught a sort of pantheism, according to which all the multitudinous objects of the phenomenal world were considered to be manifestations of the one source or unity called the Buddha-nature. This Buddha-nature pervaded everything. Because all people, regardless of sect or station in life, in fact, all living beings, were looked upon as possessors of this Buddha-nature, they were worthy of respect, to be considered as future Buddhas. To illustrate this belief the followers often prostrated themselves before strangers in the streets, or even animals—a practice that exposed them to open ridicule.

Because the sect saw the Buddha-nature in everybody and everything, it advocated all kinds of altruistic activities. The resources to carry on such activities were derived mainly from the Inexhaustible Treasury established during 618-627 in the Hua-tu Temple in Ch'ang-an. This Inexhaustible Treasury was in turn made possible by the great stress placed on almsgiving in this sect. The emphasis on almsgiving encouraged donations and contributions to the treasury on the part of the faithful followers. No matter how much was spent by the sect for its social activities, the treasury was continuously being replenished as people vied with one another to make donations. The income of the treasury was divided into three portions; one was devoted to the repair of temples and monasteries, one for the alleviation of the sick and destitute, and one for ceremonies to the Buddha. Contemporary writers said that the wealth accumulated in the treasury was so great that even the monks who managed it had no idea of the amount. People from as far away as Szechuan and east China came to the treasury to arrange for funds, and often no records were kept of the transactions. One case of embezzlement was recorded, however. A certain P'ei Hsüan-chih was first hired as a servant in the establishment. By working hard for over ten years, and observing the monastic rules strictly, he attracted the attention of the monks in the temple, who rewarded him for his good conduct and probity by appointing him caretaker of the treasury. He was not equal to the trust placed upon him, for he began to embezzle funds from time to time. However, so immense was the accumulated wealth that the monks never discovered what he was doing. One day they sent him forth on a mission from which he never returned. They then searched his room, and found a quatrain he had left behind:

> "You let a sheep loose before a wolf,
> You place a bone in front of a dog,
> Since I am not an arhat,
> How can I resist stealing?"

The teachings of the sect soon caused it to come into conflict with other groups and with the dynastic authorities. In the first place, its claim that it possessed the sole formula for salvation during the decay of the dharma did not meet with the approval of other schools. Moreover, its contention that the contemporary age was one of decay, in which people were depraved, lawless, and blinded by folly, was entirely unacceptable to the rulers, who looked upon their dynasty as responsible for the prosperity and well-being of the people. In addition, the sect further alienated the sympathies of the rulers by stating that in the age of decay no government existed which was worthy of respect of the people, and that the present dynasty was incapable of restoring the religion or leading people to salvation. It is not surprising, therefore, to find the T'ang emperors condemning the sect as inimical to the best interests of the state. Empress Wu Tse-t'ien branded the sect as heretical and ordered it to abandon all its practices save those of begging and eating once a day. In 713 the fabulous Inexhaustible Treasury of the Hua-tu Temple was ordered dissolved by Hsüan-tsung and its wealth seized and distributed. The same emperor also condemned the literature of the sect as unorthodox and ordered it proscribed. The sect appears to have clung to a precarious existence until it finally died in the persecution of 845.

## THE DISCIPLINARY SCHOOL

One of the minor schools which came into existence during the T'ang Dynasty was the Disciplinary School (Lü-tsung) founded by the famous monk Tao-hsüan (596-667). This school took its stand on the *Ssu-fen-lü* or the *Vinaya in Four Parts* translated by Buddhayaśas and Chu Fo-nien in 412. Because Tao-hsüan lived in a monastery on Chung-nan Mountain near Ch'ang-an, the school is sometimes called Nan-shan or Southern Mountain.

The emphasis of this school was on the code of discipline that governed the conduct of monks and nuns, 250 rules for the monk and 348 for the nun. These rules might be divided into two main categories: (*a*) the positive, which specify how members of the clergy should conduct themselves on such occasions as the ordination ceremonies, the fortnightly assembly, the taking of food, begging for alms, the settlement of disputes, sangha meetings and (*b*) the negative, which forbids the community of monks from committing certain crimes such as killing, stealing, lying, or adultery. Although the *Vinaya in Four Parts* belongs to the Hīnayāna tradition, it is the most widely followed *Vinaya* in China, being accepted by the Mahāyāna adherents as well. In establishing this school Tao-hsüan wanted to emphasize the fact that Buddhism meant not merely embracing a set of teachings but also strict adherence to monastic discipline, especially as it concerned the ordination regulations. From the available evidence of the period this school did not seem to have a wide following.

## THE KOŚA SCHOOL

Another minor school was the Kośa, based on the *Abhidharma-kośa* (*Treasury of the Higher Subtleties*) of Vasubandhu, translated into Chinese by Paramārtha in 563-567 and by Hsüan-tsang in 651-654. With the translation by Paramārtha this school came into existence in China. The work itself deals with the entire field of Buddhist ontology, psychology, cosmology, and ethics.

The Kośa School was called the Realistic School of Hīnayāna Buddhism because it maintained the reality of the dharmas at all times—past, present, and future. In this school the dharmas were taken as facts, things, or elements of existence, created or uncreated. In their subtle forms the dharmas always existed; it was only the objects composed of the dharmas that disintegrated. The school admitted the impermanence of all constituted objects, but it claimed that in all of them a nature of the past was transmitted to the present, and the nature of the present was in turn carried over into the future. For example, the past mango seed transmits the mangoness to the present mango, but it does not transmit its sweetness or sourness. Again, the future mango derives its mangoness from the present mango. What will be produced in the future will always be a mango, but its size, shape, or taste may not be the same. The school also attempted to prove its thesis by the example of the *sakadāgāmin* or the once-returner. In his past life the once-returner has already reduced his passions, hatred, and illusions to a minimum, and that state is carried over to the following rebirth, when the *sakadāgāmin* may be reborn as a *anāgāmin* or nonreturner.

According to this school all the dharmas in the universe may be divided into two categories, the *saṁskṛita* or created elements and the *asaṁskṛita* or uncreated elements. The created elements are in turn divided into four categories: (*a*) form, eleven dharmas, comprising all that is called matter; (*b*) consciousness or mind, one dharma; (*c*) concomitant mental functions, forty dharmas (including a wide variety of functions, such as perception, will, touch, shame, bashfulness, ignorance, idleness, anger, envy, deceit, repentance, and so forth); (*d*) elements that have no connection with mind or form, fourteen in number.

The second of the grand divisions, uncreated dharmas, are three in number: space, nirvāna, and extinction caused by the absence of a productive cause. To explain the last of the uncreated dharmas the school referred to the example of a man so intent on enjoying the setting sun that he does not hear a voice calling him, or of one so intent on one particular color that he cannot see the other colors present. The man does not perceive the voice or the colors which are present at the time because the conditions for their entry into his range of perception are not present. Thus the voice and the colors pass into extinction without entering his consciousness. This is an example of what the school meant by extinction caused by the absence of a productive cause, or cessation without consciousness.

This table enumerates all the elements in the objective world. As a matter of fact, the Realistic School was concerned with objects only; even the mind itself was not considered to be subjective, but merely a transitory state of consciousness. Thus all reality was assumed to have only transitory existence.

In China the school had only a short existence during the T'ang Dynasty, and by 793 it was registered as an appendage of the Fa-hsiang or Idealistic School, because there were no exclusive Kośa followers. From these minor schools let us now turn to those which played a more important role in T'ang Buddhism.

## THE T'IEN-T'AI SCHOOL

The T'ien-t'ai School was established by Chih-i (538-597) because it was he who systematized the doctrines of the school and brought them to their final completion. However, two predecessors of Chih-i deserve some mention—Hui-wen (fl. 550) and Hui-ssu (515-577), both of whom were born in north China. Very little is known of Hui-wen. As for Hui-ssu, it was said that he was an adept in meditation exercises, that he was twice poisoned by hostile monks who did not agree with his teachings, and that he decided to leave north China for the south when he heard a voice in the sky calling upon him to do so. After his arrival in Heng-shan in present-day Hunan his popularity as a teacher aroused antagonism from jealous monks, and they falsely accused him of being a spy sent down from the north. Happily the charge was not accepted by the emperor of the Ch'en Dynasty in the south. It was while he was preaching in the south that a gifted young monk named Chih-i came to study under him.

The biography of Chih-i is filled with those wondrous elements so dear to hagiographers. His mother was said to have conceived him when in her dream she swallowed a white mouse, which the soothsayers said was a transformation of an elephant. On his birthday a supernatural light illuminated the sky, and two monks suddenly appeared at the door of his home to announce that the newly born child would grow up to be a monk. During his youth there were many signs that he was destined for the clerical robes. Whenever he saw an image of the Buddha, he reverenced it.

At the age of seven he visited a temple and astounded the monks by remembering the text of a sutra after hearing it but once. It was said that he realized the truth of the transitoriness of life and objects when he saw a valuable library destroyed by troops, and this realization led to his decision to leave the household life to became a monk. After a period of study under Hui-ssu, he left for Chin-ling (modern Nanking), and then made his way to Mt. T'ien-t'ai in modern Chekiang, where he was to spend the greater portion of his remaining years. It was because of this residence on the mountain that the school he established was called T'ien-t'ai.

After he settled on Mt. T'ien-t'ai, Chih-i's fame as a teacher became so great that the reigning emperor of the Ch'en Dynasty decreed in 577 that the revenue from an entire district in the vicinity of the mountain be devoted to his upkeep and that of his community. Along the seashore at the foot of Mt. T'ien-t'ai fishermen had been gathering fish for ages. Now Chih-i persuaded them to adopt the doctrine of not killing any living thing. He also bought up the fishing rights along the seashore, and obtained imperial consent to a decree banning fishing in the area. Tao-hsüan, writing the biography of Chih-i in the middle of the seventh century, notes that the ban was still observed during his time. Chih-i was also invited by the Ch'en and Sui emperors to preach in the capital, and the latter bestowed upon him the title *chih-che* or Man of Wisdom. His death took place in 597 on the Mt. T'ien-t'ai that he loved so much.

As with so many famous teachers before him, Chih-i wrote very little, but his lectures were recorded by his faithful disciple Kuan-ting (561-632), also known as the master Chang-an. These lectures were concerned primarily with the basic text of the school, the *Lotus Sutra*, which teaches that the historical Śākyamuni was but an earthly manifestation of the eternal Buddha. In a later chapter on the Chinese Buddhist canon there will be a more detailed analysis of this important Mahāyāna scripture. The most important of these lectures comprise the three great works of the school:

1. *Miao-fa lien-hua ching hsüan-i* (*Profound Meaning of the Lotus Sutra*) in 20 *chüan*. This was a systematic survey of

the Buddha's teachings, with the *Lotus Sutra,* the most important text of the school, as the nucleus.

2. *Miao-fa lien-hua ching wen-chü (Textual Commentary on the Lotus Sutra)* in 20 *chüan.*

3. *Mo-ho chih-kuan (Great Concentration and Insight)* in 20 *chüan.*

CLASSIFICATION OF THE SUTRAS AND TEACHINGS

In the discussion of Buddhism under the Northern Dynasties it was already pointed out that during the latter part of the Northern Wei Dynasty there arose in north China the practice of arranging, classifying, and systematizing the enormous mass of sutras that had been translated into Chinese up to that time. The Chinese were beginning to be puzzled by this tremendous volume of literature, teaching so many diverse doctrines and ideas, and were asking how one individual could preach so many sermons during one lifetime, or how one could explain the numerous contradictions and doctrinal differences taught in the scriptures. One proposed solution at that time was to divide the Buddha's teachings into chronological periods.

Chih-i now addressed himself to a more systematic arrangement following this same idea and worked out the division in full detail—a task that was truly gigantic and one in which only a literary genius like Chih-i, who was familiar with the whole canon, could have succeeded. The system which he worked out, called *p'an-chiao* or dividing the periods of teachings, is filled with such encyclopedic details and scholarship that it fully satisfied the demands of the Buddhist scholastics and was accepted by them.

The system as formulated by Chih-i may be summarized by the words "the five periods and the eight teachings." The five periods refer to the division according to chronology, and the eight teachings refer to the division according to method and nature. The five periods are: (*a*) *Hua-yen* or *Avataṁsaka (Garland);* (*b*) *A-han* or *Āgama (Scriptures);* (*c*) *Fang-teng* or *Vāipulya* (Broad and equal, elementary Mahāyāna); (*d*) *Ta-pan-jo* or *Mahāprajñāpāramitā* (Perfection of Wisdom); (*e*) *Fa-hua nieh-p'an, Saddharma (Lotus-sutra)* and *Mahāparinirvāṇa (Great Decease).*

The T'ien-t'ai master explained that after the Buddha had attained enlightenment, he remained in a state of ecstatic beatitude, and in this frame of mind he preached the *Avataṁsakasūtra*. It was said that he preached the sutra in nine meetings in seven different places, though in reality he did not move at all from his place of meditation under the bodhi tree. However, only those of the highest intellectual capacity were able to understand the full meaning of the sutra, which teaches that the entire universe is but the revelation of the absolute spirit. The audience behaved as if they were deaf and dumb and went away discouraged. This convinced the Buddha that human beings were not yet ready for his profound teachings, and so he decided to preach the simple Hīnayāna scriptures or the *Āgamas*.

In contrast with the *Avataṁsaka* period, which lasted only three weeks, this *Āgama* period lasted twelve years. What the Buddha taught then was not the full, but accommodated truth, consisting of the four truths, the eightfold path, and dependent origination —doctrines which could be understood by beings of lower capacity. Huge crowds, including dragons, yakshas, demons, and others, came to listen and to become converted. Since the sutras preached were designed to attract the listeners, the period is sometimes called that of inducement.

Having taught these elementary doctrines which his audience understood, the Buddha then felt that he was ready to move forward. He told his audience that the *Āgamas* did not contain the final truth, that there exist higher truths in the Mahāyāna sutras that one must attain in order to gain deliverance. However, in this third period, which lasted eight years, the Buddha did not preach the Mahāyāna truths in their fullness; he was mainly interested in comparing the Hīnayāna with the Mahāyāna. In order to destroy the pride and self-satisfaction of those who believed in the Hīnayāna ideal, the arhat, he pointed out the superiority of the Mahāyāna ideal, the bodhisattva, who is mainly interested in saving others. This period is called *Vāipulya* or *fang-teng*, broad and equal—broad in the sense that the teaching is universal and equal in the sense that the sutras teach the doctrine of *samatā* or the sameness of the Buddha and man, of the absolute and the relative. Since in this period the Buddha rebuked the arhats for their wrong views, it is sometimes called the period of rebuke.

With the arrival of the fourth period, which lasted twenty-two years, the Buddha began to discuss abstract metaphysical problems. For example, in discussing the nature of the absolute, the Buddha taught in the *Prajñāpāramitā-sūtras* that the absolute is free from attributes, unconditional, undefinable, and therefore *śūnya* or void. In accordance with the doctrine of *śūnyatā*, all distinctions are artificial and are the products of our own illusions; they have no objective reality. Such dualisms as *saṁsāra* and nirvāna, subject and object, Buddha and Māra, are but figments of our imagination. Whereas during the third period the Buddha pointed out the differences between the Hīnayāna and the Mahāyāna, now in this fourth period he emphasized the unity underlying both. Because of this, the period is also called that of exploring and uniting all dharmas. The negative formulation of the absolute during the fourth was then replaced with a positive formulation in the fifth and last period.

In the fourth the Buddha pointed out the absolute nonexistence of contrasts; in the fifth he emphasized the absolute identity of the contrasts. The three vehicles, *śrāvaka, pratyekabuddha*, and *bodhisattvayāna*, are said to be only temporary; they are all united in the one vehicle, the *ekayāna*. Buddha's mission on earth is to save all creatures, and this can be done only in accordance with the *Saddharma*. Therefore the *Saddharma* is considered to be the epitome of the Buddha's teachings. This fifth period embraces the last eight years of the Buddha's life.

The classification of the *Avataṁsaka* in the first period might appear at first glance to be an anachronism, for it was a product of the idealistic trend in mature Buddhism. But the old traditions say that after Śākyamuni became enlightened, he at first hesitated to go out to preach, because he felt the truth he had attained was too profound and subtle for mankind, and that only after the intervention and entreaty of the god Brahma Sahampati did he finally consent to go forth to spread his message.

The T'ien-t'ai theory of the five periods represented the attempt to synthesize the teachings of the master chronologically. But the school also admitted that the Tathāgatha sometimes preached the teachings of the five periods simultaneously; in order to meet this contingency, the school worked out the scheme of the eight doctrines, four according to the methods of teaching and four according to the nature of the teaching itself. The first quartet consisted of:

1. Abrupt or sudden doctrine. This method is suitable for beings of the highest capacity, for though the Buddha preaches his message without any preparatory instruction, his audience is able to grasp the truth immediately. This was the method adapted in teaching the *Avataṁsaka*.

2. Gradual doctrine. In this method the audience is led to advance, step by step, from the elementary to the profound doctrines. It might be divided into three stages: the beginning, coinciding with the *Āgama* period; the middle, coinciding with the *Fang-teng*; and the end, coinciding with the *Prajñā* period. The *Saddharma* teaching of the fifth period is not included in this scheme, because the T'ien-t'ai masters considered it to be neither sudden nor gradual, but beyond all methods, since it represents the final truth of the Buddha.

3. Secret doctrine. This is the method used by the Buddha when he speaks secretly to someone, and is understood only by that one whom he addresses. There might be numerous listeners in the audience, but they are concealed from one another by the supernatural powers of the Buddha. Thus the hearers do not know one another, and the teaching is not known to all hearers in common, but each one thinks that he alone is being taught by the Blessed One.

4. Indeterminate doctrine. In this category the hearers know one another, but they hear and understand differently what the Buddha is teaching.

The last two doctrines, secret and indeterminate, were taught by the Buddha when he had to teach individuals of different capacities at the same time. These different individuals, though forming the same audience, needed different messages individually, and in order to reach such an audience, the Buddha had to isolate the listeners from one another. These methods assumed that the Buddha was endowed with the power to conceal men from one another, or to make them visible and known to one another. Such a Buddha could speak in many voices at the same time, addressing each hearer individually and conforming his speech to the requirements of each individual; or he could speak at the same time in many different places. He might be quiet in one place but speaking in another; he might preach one sutra at any given moment, but the sutra would mean different things to different people in the audience.

In opposition to those who advocated that the Buddha spoke with one voice, but that the audience understood differently, Chih-i claimed that the Blessed One purposely spoke with many voices, and that the differences in the messages were not to be ascribed to the different interpretations of the hearers, but to the Buddha's own intentions. The hearers understood differently because the Blessed One spoke to each one differently at the same time. When the Buddha used the secret method, it was for the purpose of putting everyone at ease, so that each one would not feel embarrassed with the thought that the Master was teaching him an inferior sutra.

In addition to the classification by method there is also the division according to the nature of the doctrine:

1. *Pitaka* doctrine or the *Hīnayāna* teaching intended for the *śrāvakas* and *pratyekabuddhas*.
2. Common doctrine, the teaching common to both Hīnayāna and elementary Mahāyāna, which is for *śrāvaka, pratyekabuddha*, and the inferior bodhisattva.
3. Special doctrine, preached especially for the bodhisattvas only.
4. Round or perfect doctrine, which teaches the middle path of mutual identification, that one element contains all elements.

After enumerating this theory of the eight doctrines, Chih-i then sought to connect them with the division into the five periods. The *Avataṁsaka* period involves both perfect and special; therefore it is called twofold. The *Āgama* involves only the *Pitaka* teaching; therefore it is called simple. The *Vaipulya* period teaches all four doctrines; therefore it is designated as being related to all. The teaching of the *Prajñā* period is mainly perfect, but it also involves the common and special doctrines;

hence it is called not quite complete. Only the *Saddharma* period is entirely round or completely perfect.

This T'ien-t'ai classification of Buddhism according to periods, methods, and nature represents a prodigious attempt to bring some order and system out of the mass of contradictory ideas, an endeavor to understand the evolution of Buddhist thought from its beginnings to its mature development. Putting it in another way, we may regard Chih-i's scheme as a classification of the various systems proposed by the Buddhists to solve some of the fundamental metaphysical problems of Buddhism.

The *Pitaka* teaching, for instance, represents the analytical approach. It reduces subject and object into their smallest component parts, and argues that the individual is only a series of momentary states of consciousness, one succeeding another in rapid succession, while the object is also only momentary combinations of elements or dharmas which arise and disappear ceaselessly. Therefore, according to the Hīnayānist, there is no constant subject or object, only a continuous becoming and passing away; only in nirvāna is there cessation of this process.

The common teaching emphasizes the synthetic approach. Instead of reducing the subject and object to their smallest parts, it regards them as nonexistent or void.

In the special doctrine the conception of the universe as an absolute reality comes to the fore. Each individual phenomenon is now considered a part of the whole, each part being related to the other because it is derived from the same origin. The parts still remain separate parts, however, and it is only in the perfect doctrine that they disappear to become identical with the whole; hence the T'ien-t'ai slogan, "In every particle of dust, in every moment of thought, the whole universe is contained."

The T'ien-t'ai School represented the Chinese attempt to establish a great eclectic school recognizing all forms of Buddhism. Through its comprehensive and encylopedic nature it had a place for all the Buddhist scriptures; it considered these scriptures as being gradually revealed by the master when he found that his audience was gradually beginning to understand his message better and better. The school saw no antagonism between the Hīnayāna and Mahāyāna; all sutras were to be accepted as true words of the Buddha if they were considered as being taught during a certain period. The school, however, did believe the *Saddharma* to contain the essence of all the teachings, and also taught that all men could become the Buddha, since all possessed the Buddha-nature.

## THE THREEFOLD TRUTH

The T'ien-t'ai followed Nāgārjuna in teaching that all component things are impermanent, that all dharmas are without self, and that only nirvāna is quiescence. It also taught that there is a true state or noumenon which is realizable through and manifested in phenomena. There is no noumenon besides phenomenon; the phenomenon itself is noumenon. In order to avoid thinking in terms of a dichotomy, noumenon versus phenomenon, the T'ien-t'ai School established the threefold truth: void, temporariness, and mean.

All things have no independent reality of their own; therefore they are said to be empty. This emptiness is sometimes called the truth of breaking through subjective illusions. The emptiness of the dhramas does not mean nothingness, however; if it were nothingness, how could it break illusions? Though a thing is empty, it does enjoy temporary existence as phenomenon. This is called the truth of temporary existence or the truth of establishment, since it establishes the dharma temporarily, where they can be reached by the senses. The synthesis of emptiness and phenomenal existence, of universality and particularity, is called the truth of the mean or middle. In other words the fact that every dharma is empty and temporary at the same time constitutes the middle truth. This middle does not mean something between the two; it is over and above the other two.

These three truths of the T'ien-t'ai School emphasize the idea of totality and mutual identification; the whole and its parts are identical. The whole cosmos and all the Buddhas may be present in a grain of sand or the point of a hair, or, as the T'ien-t'ai master would put it, *i-nien-san-ch'ien* (one thought is the three thousand worlds). Such an expression is intended to show the interpenetration of all the dharmas and the ultimate unity of the universe.[1] When this is applied to the religious life,

[1] According to the T'ien-t'ai scheme this universe is divided into ten realms, four saintly and six ordinary: (1) Buddha, (2) bodhisattva, (3)

it means that phenomenal life is not denied but affirmed absolutely. The everyday life of the layman is part of the life of the Buddha.

## THE ABSOLUTE MIND

The identification of phenomena with the absolute is further illustrated by the T'ien-t'ai doctrine of the absolute mind. This absolute mind embraces the universe in its entirety. All things in the world depend on this mind for their existence. This absolute mind originally and for all times contains two natures, one pure and the other impure. Its pure nature is responsible for the attributes of the Buddha, while its impure nature is responsible for the myriad things in the phenomenal world. In its substance the absolute mind is everywhere the same and undifferentiated, but in its functioning it is diverse and is therefore differentiated. But in spite of their variety all phenomenal manifestations are harmoniously integrated in the absolute mind. To illustrate this point the T'ien-t'ai scripture tells the story of a monk who asked a person to imagine just a single hair pore and then a distant large city. When the person did so, the monk drew the lesson that the hair pore and the large city are integrated in the absolute mind.

## CONCENTRATION AND INSIGHT

It follows that man's views of things in the universe as being large or small, long or short, are due to illusion, which can only

---

*pratyekabuddha*, (4) *śrāvaka*, (5) deva, (6) demon, (7) human being, (8) hungry ghost, (9) beast, and (10) depraved man. Each of these realms has the remaining nine realms—a fact which thus accounts for one hundred realms in all. Each of these hundred realms possesses ten different features —form, nature, substance, force, action, condition, effect, reward, cause, and ultimate state; so that there would be one thousand worlds in all. Furthermore, each of the thousand worlds has three separate divisions— living beings, the five aggregates, and the space we live in; this accounts for three thousand worlds. The T'ien-t'ai takes this three thousand to mean the universality of all things. The expression "One thought is the three thousand worlds" does not mean that one moment of thought produces the three thousand worlds, nor does it mean that the three thousand worlds are included in one thought. If one would say this, it would imply that there are three thousand worlds separate and distinct from the one thought. It means just what it says. "One thought is the three thousand worlds"— that a thing or being is the true state and that the true state is immanent in everything.

be destroyed by spiritual cultivation. This cultivation consists of *chih*, concentration, and *kuan*, insight. By concentration we realize that all the dharmas do not have any self-nature and hence do not enjoy real existence; they only appear to be real because of our illusions and imaginations. Once we realize this, then all erroneous thoughts cease to arise. By insight we realize that although the dharmas have no real existence, still they are created by the mind, they enjoy temporary existence, and they perform some worldly functions. Hence they seem to exist, just as dreams or a man created by magic seem to exist, though in reality they do not.

The theory that everything is a manifestation of the absolute mind leads logically to the position taken by the ninth patriarch of the school, Chan-jan (711-782), who held that the Buddha-nature is to be found even in inanimate things such as mountains, rivers, or the tiniest particle of dust.

The T'ien-t'ai tenets have been generally regarded as among the finest products of the Buddhist philosophical development in China. They are called the final and round doctrines of Buddhism—final because they synthesize all the extreme and one-sided doctrines of the other schools, and round because the school assures universal salvation by affirming the presence of the Buddha-nature in all sentient beings and because it employs all possible means to salvation.

## THE HUA-YEN SCHOOL

Another school in China that appealed to the intellect was the Hua-yen School. According to legend a sutra entitled the *Avatamsaka* or *Garland Sutra* was preached by the Blessed One immediately after his enlightenment. Because the contents of the sutra were so profound and abstruse, the audience merely sat with blank faces, unable to comprehend their philosophical ramifications. As a result the Buddha decided to change tactics and to preach, instead, the more simple Hīnayāna sutras. This *Avatamsakasūtra* became the basis of the Hua-yen School in China. There is no Indian counterpart of this school.[2]

[2] There exists three Chinese translations of this sutra: the first in 60 *chüan* by Buddhabhadra, made during the period 418-420; the second in 80 *chüan* by Sikshānanda during 695-704; and the third in 40 *chüan* by Prajñā during

## HUA-YEN MASTERS

In the discussion of Buddhism under the Northern Dynasties it was noted that the groundwork for the development of the school was already laid by the masters of the *Ti-lun*, which was a commentary on the chapter describing the ten stages of the bodhisattva, found in *chüan* 8 of Buddhabhadra's translation of the *Avataṁsaka*. Hua-yen traditions usually maintain that Fa-shun (557-640, also called Tu-shun) was the first master of the school in China and that when he commenced his teachings, the followers of the *Ti-lun* flocked to him. In his youth he had joined the service battalions of the army, doing such menial labor as carrying water and gathering firewood; but at eighteen he left household life to concentrate on *dhyāna* exercises. Because numerous miracles were said to have attended his movements, he was called the Tun-huang Bodhisattva, and his teachings proved to be so attractive that Emperor Wen of the Sui Dynasty conferred on him the honorary title Imperial Heart and bestowed on him a monthly allowance for his maintenance. The second in line of the transmission was Chih-yen (602-668), also called Yün-hua because he often used the Yün-hua Temple as the forum to preach the Hua-yen sutra. Among his disciples was Fa-tsang (643-712), usually considered to be the real founder of the school, since it was he who systematized its doctrines.

Fa-tsang's ancestors came from Sogdia, but he was born in Ch'ang-an and became thoroughly Sinicized. He is also known as the master Hsien-shou; hence the Hua-yen School is also referred to as the Hsien-shou School. In his youth he was a member of the translation bureau, assisting Hsüan-tsang; but he disagreed with the latter's view that only certain beings possessed the Buddha-nature, and that a novitiate must pass through various stages gradually to attain the final goal of salvation. It was said that he also assisted in the translation activities of I-tsing. Because he was familiar with Buddhabhadra's translation of the *Avataṁsaka*, he was asked by Empress Wu Tse-t'ien to assist Śikshānanda when the latter was working on his eighty-*chüan*

---

795-810. The last is essentially a translation of the *Gandavyūha*, or that portion of the whole sutra which describes the journey of the youth Sudhana in search for truth.

version. During his lifetime he served as preceptor for four rulers, and his written works number over a hundred *chüan*.[3]

After Fa-tsang came Ch'eng-kuan, also known as Master Ch'ing-liang. Hua-yen traditions picture him as a giant of a man, over nine feet tall, with arms extending below his knees, with forty teeth, and with eyes that glowed at night. Born in 738 (variant 737), he very early began studying the Buddhist scriptures, and at age eleven left household life, though he was not ordained a monk until he was twenty. Then followed a period of traveling through central, western, and northern China, visiting famous Buddhist centers and studying different texts under various masters. By so doing, he became acquainted with the *Vimala-kīrti*, *Mahāparinirvāna*, and *Mahāyānaśraddhotpāda* (*The Awakening of Faith in the Mahāyāna*), secular literature, mantras, Indian languages, and so forth, although his main concentration was on the *Hua-yen-sutra*. Finally, in 796 he was invited by Emperor Te-tsung to Ch'ang-an to participate in the translation of the forty *chüan Avataṁsaka* by Prajñā. After this, numerous honors were heaped on him; he was granted such titles as Master of the Purple Robe, National Preceptor, Professor Monk, and Chief of Monks, and was acknowledged as master of the law by a succession of emperors from 780 to his death in 838 (variant ca.820). His commentaries on the *Avataṁsaka* number over four hundred *chüan*, while among the disciples whom he taught, thirty-eight achieved fame as masters of the law. To a considerable extent the influence of the Hua-yen School during this period was due to his teachings and writings. Later generations of Hua-yen followers looked upon him as an incarnation of Mañjuśrī, and called him the Hua-yen Bodhisattva.[4]

[3] Of these works the most important are the following: *Chin-shih-tzu chang* (*Essay on the Golden Lion*), 1 *chüan*; *I-hai pai-men* (*Hundred Theories of the Ocean of Ideas*), 1 *chüan*; *Hua-yen ching chih-kuei* (*Essential Ideas of the Hua-yen ching*), 1 *chüan*.

[4] It was said that during his lifetime Ch'eng-kuan conducted his activities in accordance with the following ten vows:

   *a*) His body would not do anything to stain the good name of the *śramana*.
   *b*) His mind would not go contrary to the teachings of the Buddha.
   *c*) While sitting, he would not violate the norm of the dharma world.
   *d*) His nature would not be stained by passions.
   *e*) His feet would not tread on the soil of a nunnery.
   *f*) His ribs would not touch the couch of a layman's house.

Following Ch'eng-kuan, the fifth Hua-yen master was Tsung-mi (780-841). He first studied the Confucian classics and was about to take the civil service examinations in 807 when he met a Ch'an master Tao-yüan, who impressed him so much that he decided to leave household life to become a monk. He first followed the practices of the Ch'an School, but after reading a commentary on the *Hua-yen-sutra* by Ch'eng-kuan, he embraced the Hua-yen system. The next year (808) he went to Lo-yang to preach the Hua-yen tenets, and during one of his lectures an individual in the audience was so emotionally touched that he cut off his arm as a token of conversion. After this, Tsung-mi submitted himself to Ch'eng-kuan as his disciple, and learned all that the master had to offer. His reputation as a Hua-yen master became so great that he was invited by the emperor to lecture on the sutra in the palace, was given the title Master of the Purple Robe, and was designated as a Great Virtuous Monk. After his death in 841 he was given the posthumous title *Dhyāna* Master of Concentration and Insight, and his epitaph was written by the prime minister P'ei Hsiu. His writings included not only commentaries on the *Hua-yen* but also on such Mahāyāna sutras as the *Diamond Cutter* and the *Awakening of Faith.*

Shortly after Tsung-mi's death the Hui-ch'ang suppression of Buddhism set in, and this was followed by the Period of the Five Dynasties with its attendant confusion. Under such circumstances no more Hua-yen masters arose and the school declined.

HUA-YEN DOCTRINES

The basic teaching of the Hua-yen School centers around the theory of causation by the universal principle or the *dharma-dhātu*. According to this, all the dharmas in the universe arose simultaneously; in other words, it is the creation of the universe by the universe itself. The Hua-yen teaches that all these dharmas are empty. This emptiness has two aspects—the static aspect,

---

*g*) His eyes would not look at anything not in accordance with propriety.

*h*) His tongue would not taste the flavor of food after the noon hour.

*i*) His hands would not lose touch of the bright round beads of the rosary.

*j*) In sleeping, he would not be separated from his begging bowl and robes.

as principle or noumenon, and the dynamic aspect, as phenomenon. From this the school proceeds to its basic positions: first, that principle and phenomenon are interfused unimpededly with each other, and second, that all phenomena are mutually identified with one another.

It is said that in 704 Fa-tsang was summoned into the palace to explain the *Hua-yen-sutra*. When Empress Wu Tse-t'ien was puzzled by some of the profound theories of the sutra, he pointed to a golden lion and, using that as an illustration, wrote the *Essay on the Golden Lion.*

In this essay gold is the symbol of the noumenon li or principle, while the lion is the symbol of shih or phenomenon. Li or principle has no form of its own; it may assume any shih or form that conditions assign to it.

To illustrate the interpenetration and mutual identification of all the dharmas or phenomena, Fa-tsang wrote that the various organs of the lion take in the whole lion by means of the gold, so that any one organ is identified with any other organ. Thus in each of the lion's organs, such as the eye, ear, or strand of hair, there is present the whole golden lion. Similarly the golden lion of all the eyes, ears, and hairs are to be found within a single strand of hair. According to this theory, all phenomena are manifestations of li or noumenon. This being so, each individual phenomenon embraces every other phenomenon. In the *Sung Kao-seng-chuan*, chapter five, it was recorded that students listening to Fa-tsang failed to understand this point. Fa-tsang thereupon resorted to a clever experiment. He prepared ten mirrors, with eight placed at the eight points of the compass, one above, and one below, all facing one another. In the center was placed the Buddha figure, lighted by a huge torch. The disciples now saw that not only was the image reflected in the mirrors but the image in each mirror was also reflected in all the other mirrors. Not only this, but the multiple images reflected in each were also reflected in every other mirror, thus doubling and redoubling the images. This was like Indra's net, with its network of jewels that not only reflected the images in every other jewel, but also the multiple images in the others.

The second point stressed in the essay concerns li and shih, the relationship between noumenon and phenomenon. According to

Fa-tsang, the gold and lion exist simultaneously, each one inclusive of the other. This means that every event or thing in the phenomenal world represents the noumenon completely and perfectly. In such a situation every phenomenon is a manifestation of the noumenon; hence the one is the many, the many is the one. However, each phenomenon remains in its own position, distinct and dissimilar from the noumenon.

Another doctrine taught is that no dharma can exist independently, for each one possesses the sixfold nature immanently —generalness and speciality, similarity and diversity, integration and disintegration. "The lion as a whole has the quality of generalness. Its five organs, inasmuch as they each differ from the lion as a whole, have the quality of speciality. However, since they together with the lion all arise from a single cause, they have the quality of similarity. But the fact that the eyes, ears, and so forth do not overlap in their functions, gives them the quality of diversity. At the same time, these various organs all combine to make the lion, and this is their quality of integration. But the fact that each of these organs occupies its own peculiar position gives them the quality of disintegration."[5]

As with the T'ien-t'ai, the Hua-yen also has its classification of the Buddha's teachings according to their nature. Whereas the T'ien-t'ai has a fourfold division into *pitaka*, common, special, and perfect, the Hua-yen adds another category, sudden, making five in all. In this respect the Hua-yen classification is superior to that of the T'ien-t'ai. When Chih-i made his classification, such schools as the Ch'an, Fa-hsiang, and Hua-yen had not arisen, so that his scheme was not yet complete in that it did not include all the schools of Chinese Buddhism. The Hua-yen classification corrects this deficiency with its fivefold division:

1. The teaching of the *śrāvakas* or hearers. This teaching holds that the lion, being the product of causation, has no substance of its own. This refers to the Hīnayāna teachings as found in the *āgamas*, which deny the existence of the individual but admit the existence of the elements or dharmas.

2. The elementary doctrine of the Great Vehicle. This doctrine teaches that all things, having come into being by causation, have no self-nature and are therefore empty. The Fa-hsiang and

[5] Fung, *op.cit.*, 2,355.

San-lun Schools belong to this category; they are called elementary because they do not admit the presence of the Buddha-nature in all sentient beings.

3. The final doctrine of the Great Vehicle. This doctrine asserts that although there is only emptiness and that all the dharmas are illusory in nature, there is also the fact of illusory existence. This permits, therefore, the conditional existence of the lion. Such is the truth taught by the T'ien-t'ai School.

4. The abrupt doctrine of the Great Vehicle. In this doctrine enlightenment is attained at once; there is no need for studying the scriptures or practicing religious discipline. The two concepts of emptiness and being are eliminated, so that neither of them exerts any influence on the mind, which is now at rest and abides in nonattachment. Enlightenment may therefore be attained by silence, such as the silence of Vimalakīrti and the Ch'an School.

5. The round doctrine of the Great Vehicle. This doctrine teaches that the ten thousand things of the phenomenal world represent the absolute mind or the noumenon, so that the all is the one, the one is the all.

Summarizing, one may say that the epitome of Hua-yen thought consists of the following: there is a world of li or ultimate principle and a world of shih or phenomena, which are perfectly interfused with each other. At the same time each individual phenomenon is also unimpededly identified with every other phenomenon. A totalistic system is thus established, with everything leading to one point, the Buddha, in the center. It is no wonder that Empress Wu Tse-t'ien and the Japanese emperors favored the system, since it provided a religious sanction for their totalitarian schemes.

The Hua-yen differed from other Mahāyāna schools such as the T'ien-t'ai in one important respect. The latter concentrated its attention on the relationship between the noumenon and phenomenon, whereas the former elucidated the relationship between one phenomenon and another. It maintained that since all phenomena are manifestations of the one immutable noumenon, they are in perfect harmony with one another, like the different waves of the same water. From the religious point of view everything in the universe, animate and inanimate, are all representations of the same supreme mind, and can perform the work of the Blessed One. This is why the school is called the perfect teaching of the Buddha.

## THE FA-HSIANG SCHOOL

The Fa-hsiang (Characteristics of the Dharmas) School is based on the writings of two brothers, Asanga and Vasubandhu. There is a good deal of uncertainty about the dates of these brothers. Some scholars would advocate placing them in the fifth century; others, a century earlier. There is also the theory that there were two Vasubandhus, the older one born ca. A.D. 320) being the Mahāyāna master, while the younger one (born ca.400) was the compiler of the Hīnayāna text *Abhidharmakośa*. Since this school believes that only ideation exists, it was also called the Idealistic School.

In elaboration of this thesis of ideation only, Asanga wrote a treatise entitled *Mahāyānasamgraha*[6] (*Compendium of the Mahāyāna*) which became the basis of the She-lun School in China through the translation of Paramārtha in 563. The She-lun School was in turn replaced by the Fa-hsiang School started by Hsüan-tsang and his chief disciple, K'uei-chi (632-682).

One of the primary subjects discussed in the *Samgraha* is the *ālayavijñāna* or storehouse consciousness, which stores and coordinates all the ideas reflected in the mind. It is thus a storehouse where all the pure and tainted ideas are combined or intermingled. When these ideas descend to the everyday world, they manifest themselves in phenomenal existence. The storehouse is the center, while the world manifested by ideation is the environment. From the perfect enlightenment of the Buddha, pure ideation issues forth to purify the tainted portions of the ideation store, and leads it to the state of real truth in which there is no discrimination between subject and object.

Before Hsüan-tsang started on his journey to India, he had already studied the *Samgraha* doctrine, but because the opinions of his teachers varied greatly, he decided to go to India to learn the true interpretation there. In Nālandā he studied under Śīla-

---

[6] Translated into French by E. Lamotte, *La Somme du Grand Vehicule d'Asanga*, 2 vols., Louvain, 1938-1939.

bhadra, who had been a disciple of Dharmapāla; Dharmapāla in turn had studied under Dignāga, who had received the teachings directly from Vasubandhu. Upon his return to China Hsüan-tsang plunged into the task of translating the idealist texts that he brought back.[7] He had an able pupil in K'uei-chi, who systematized the teachings of his masters in two important works.[8] Because the school is concerned with the specific character of all the dharmas, it is often called the Fa-hsiang or Dharmalakshana School; but because of its idealistic emphasis it is also called Wei-shih or Ideation Only School.

FA-HSIANG DOCTRINES

The central idea of this Fa-hsiang School is taken from a passage by Vasubandhu, *idam sarvam vijñaptimātrakam*, "All this world is ideation only." It claims that the external world is but a fabrication of our consciousness, that the external world does not exist, that the internal ideation presents an appearance as if it were an outer world. The entire external world is therefore an illusion.

Because the mind occupies such an important role in the thinking of this school, it is subjected to a minute analysis. It is divided into eight consciousnesses, each one being a separate reality. There are, first, the five sense consciousnesses: sight, hearing, smell, taste, and touch. Then there is the sixth or *mano-vijñāna*, sense center, the general perceiving organ or conscious mind, which forms conceptions out of the perceptions received from the outside. The seventh is the thought center, *manas*, the self-conscious mind that thinks, wills, and reasons on a self-

[7] Among his important works is the *Ch'eng wei-shih lun* (*Treatise on the Completion of Ideation Only*), in 10 *chüan*, translated into French by L. de la Vallée Poussin, *La Siddhi de Hiuan-tsang*, 3 vols., Paris, 1928-1948. The other important texts of this school are: *Madhyāntavibhaṅga*, translated into English by Th. Stcherbatsky, *Discourse on Discrimination Between Middle and Extremes*, Leningrad, 1936; *Viṁśatikā* (*Treatise in Twenty Stanzas*), translated into English by C. H. Hamilton, *Wei Shih Erh Shih Lun*, New Haven, 1928; *Triṁśikā* (*Treatise in Thirty Stanzas*), translated into German by H. Jacobi, *Triṁśikāvijñapti des Vasubandhu*, Stuttgart, 1932; *Mahāyānaśraddhotpāda*, translated into English by D. T. Suzuki, *Aśvaghosha's Discourse on the Awakening of Faith*, Chicago, 1900.

[8] These two works are the *Fa-yüan i-lin-chang* (*Chapter on the Forest of Meanings in the Garden of Law*) and the *Ch'eng wei-shih lun shu-chi* (*Notes on the Treatise on the Completion of Ideation Only*).

centered basis. Finally, there is the *ālaya-vijñāna* or storehouse consciousness.

The storehouse consciousness is the repository where the seeds or the effects of karma performed since beginningless time are stored away. Every deed or thought generates a kind of impression, a sort of spiritual energy, which is deposited in the *ālaya*. This spiritual energy lingers on even after the thought or deed has ceased; thus it corresponds to memory in the widest sense. Such impressions, now stored in the *ālaya*, are preserved there, waiting for a favorable opportunity to manifest themselves. *Ālaya* has no active energy; it never acts by itself; it is like a mirror or smooth ocean, waiting for an agent to disturb it. This agent is *manas*, the self-conscious mind or thought center. When *ālaya* is disturbed by *manas*, then the impressions or seeds left in *ālaya* will awake from their dormant state and be responsible for the birth of individual objects, good, bad, or neutral. In other words, the principle of individuation arises.

*Manas* is therefore the particularizing or discriminating principle. This discrimination is possible only in the *ālaya*, but *ālaya* itself is neutral and is not conscious of itself. For this consciousness of itself it must depend on *manas*. *Manas* is the will, constantly asserting itself by influencing mental activities. It develops the consciousness of self, and with this consciousness the dualism of subject and object arises; it creates this dualism out of the oneness of *ālaya*.

In these discriminating activities *manas* is always working in conjunction with the mind and the five senses. As soon as *manas* brings out the dualism of subject and object, then the six senses begin to function mechanically, the whole system is set into motion, and the train of perception, cognition, and judgment follows.

The six senses have no intelligence outside their own field of activity; what they experience is reported to *manas* without interpretation. *Manas* is like a general at headquarters, gathering all the information sent in, sifting and arranging it, and then giving orders back to the six senses. At the same time *manas* is also connected with *ālaya*. The impressions or seeds of acts and thoughts committed by the subject are fed into *ālaya* by *manas*, which thus adds to the storehouse of seeds already stored there.

*Ālaya* is in this way continuously replenished with new seeds. It may be said to be in a state of continual flux, with its seeds constantly influencing external manifestations, and these manifestations in turn adding new seeds or impressions to it. This principle is illustrated by a favorite quotation of the school:

"A seed produces a manifestation,
A manifestation perfumes a seed.
The three elements (seed, manifestation, and perfume) turn on and on,
The cause and effect occur at one and the same time."[9]

Seen in this light, *manas* is the connecting link between *ālaya* and the six sense consciousnesses, the agent that sets the whole system into motion. By bringing about the idea of the ego it is responsible for the consequences of desires, passions, ignorance, belief in an external world, and so forth. In such a situation *ālaya* has become contaminated by *manas* and the six consciousnesses. However, despite this contamination *ālaya* has not lost its identity or purity; it is merely soiled. What is needed is a change in the function of *manas*. This is possible because *manas* is not blind will; it is intelligent and capable of enlightenment. The task is to get *manas* to function properly, so that it will cease to create discriminations and will feed good seeds, instead, into *ālaya*. *Manas* is the pivot around which the whole Buddhist discipline revolves. The force of this discipline is to have *manas* enlightened. This is achieved through the attainment of *prajñā* or perfect wisdom, which is the truth beyond dualism. In this state the external world is revealed as illusory and the true nature of the dharmas is understood. *Ālaya* is now transcended, and genuine thusness or *tathatā*, which is beyond causal relations and characterized by the harmony of noumenon and phenomenon, is now realized. Thusness always remains in a state of immobility and is personal, pure, and blessed. It is also everlasting, permanent, and absolute. It is the grand norm, or enlightenment. When this state is achieved, then *manas* will no longer think in terms of subject and object, and will feed good seeds that will purify *ālaya* again.

In the *Ch'eng wei-shih lun* of Hsüan-tsang there is an elaborate

---

[9] W. T. Chan, *Religious Trends in Modern China*, New York, 1953, 107.

discussion of the seeds that are stored in the *ālaya*. Such seeds are classified as those with taints and those without. Sentient beings at all times possess both the tainted and untainted seeds. Because of the action of the tainted seeds, beings remain in *saṃsāra*, but through the action of the untainted seeds, beings escape from *saṃsāra* into nirvāna. However, the Wei-shih School maintains that not all beings possess untainted seeds and hence not all beings are capable of attaining Buddhahood. In this respect the school differs from the other Mahāyāna groups.

If everything is ideation, how does the school explain such external phenomena as mountains, rivers, and lakes that everyone sees? The *Ch'eng wei-shih lun* explains that such external objects are evolved out of the universal seeds that reside in all *ālaya* consciousness in general of beings now alive or of those who will be reborn in the future. The *ālaya* consciousness of each being individually evolves its own particular mountain, river, or lake, but because this is done by the universal seeds which are common to all beings, the resulting appearances are like one another. Another question immediately arises from this. What about the differences in our bodies and sense organs? The answer is that such sense faculties and the organs in which they are lodged are evolved out of the nonuniversal seeds in one's own *ālaya* consciousness, and the sense faculties and organs of other people are evolved out of the nonuniversal seeds of those particular individuals. However, when we are looking at the body and sense organs of a particular individual, then the idea of those sense organs and body is evolved out of the universal seeds that reside in our *ālaya*. If this were not so, how would the rest of us perceive the bodies and sense organs of the other person, and have the same impression of them? But how do we know this to be the case? The answer given is that when someone is reborn into a new mode of existence or enters into nirvāna, his body, if it were the product of the particular seeds in his own *ālaya* only, would disappear and not be present. But this is not the case, for the body is still visible. From this the school concludes that our idea of the body and organs are products of the universal seeds in our *ālaya* consciousness.

Whereas the Mādhyamika School of Nāgārjuna conceives of two levels of truth, the conditional and the absolute levels, the

Wei-shih School has three levels of knowledge—*parikalpita* or sole imagination, *paratantra* or dependence on others, and *parinishpanna* or ultimate reality. The *parikalpita* view refers to the false or imagined aspect of truth and recognizes things as they appear to our senses. The *paratantra* view recognizes that all things depend on a combination and interaction of causes and conditions and have only temporary existence. The *parinishpanna* view comprises the complete and perfect understanding; it penetrates behind the veil of impermanence to attain to the absolute knowledge that transcends all conditionality and relativity.

For a time during the middle of the T'ang Dynasty the school flourished in China, but after Hsüan-tsang and K'uei-chi had gone, the school rapidly declined. One of the factors contributing to this decline was the persecution of 845. Probably another was the critical judgment of the Hua-yen School, which classified the Wei-shih School as being just a step higher than the Hīnayāna but lower than the Ch'an, T'ien-t'ai, or Hua-yen Schools. The reason for this low classification, according to the Hua-yen, was that the school did not advocate the cardinal Mahāyāna doctrine that all sentient beings possess Buddhahood, and that it did not recognize the unity of phenomenon with noumenon. Moreover, the philosophy of the school, with its hairsplitting analysis and abstruse terminology, was too difficult and abstract for the practical-minded Chinese, who preferred the direct and simple teachings of the Ch'an and Pure Land Schools. Hence these schools flourished while the Wei-shih declined.

## THE TANTRIC SCHOOL

Like the Fa-hsiang, the Tantric School was another one that flourished briefly in China. The word Tantrism is derived from the Sanskrit *Tantra*, which has the general meaning of that which spreads knowledge, and a limited meaning of an esoteric literature. It is often considered to be the third and final interpretation of the teachings of the Buddha, and is called Tantrayāna, Mantrayāna, or Vajrayāna, in contrast to the Hīnayāna and Mahāyāna—Tantrayāna because it is based on the *Tantras*, Mantrayāna because mantras or mystical formulas play a dominant role, and Vajrayāna because the *vajra* or thunderbolt is the dominant symbol. The Tantrists claim that the revelation of their teachings did not take place on this earth but on Mt. Sumeru or in Akaniṣ-ṭha, the highest of the Buddhist heavens; thus they follow the Mahāyāna in shifting the place of revelation to a sphere beyond the earth.

Tantric theories represent something new and different from those in the other revelations. According to the Tantrists man is sunk in ignorance but he still has a divine spark in him which is the Buddha-nature. For redemption from this ignorance an esoteric consecration is necessary. In this consecration the *Tantras* borrow heavily from the ancient Hindu mythologies, but these myths take on new meanings and become symbols of the powers presiding over the universe. The cosmos is conceived of as a great being, with gods and goddesses as the symbols of its function, energy, and will. Sexual symbols play an important role as a consequence of this conception. Some examples of Tantric elements present in ancient India might be: (*a*) the idea of macrocosm and microcosm, (*b*) belief in the doctrine of a divine light in man of which he is unconscious because of his ignorance, (*c*) magical formulas to invoke the gods, and (*d*) the idea that knowledge is useless unless transformed into action and experience. The presence of such elements in the *Tantras* led to the conclusion that they were indigenous to India. Even so, it is likely that they also borrowed from contemporary systems originating outside of India. This explains why the *Tantras* are usually said to have originated on the borders of India, especially in Uddiyana in the northwest and Bengal in the northeast, at some time at the end of the seventh and the beginning of the eighth centuries.

From these ancient mythologies within and without India Tantrism derives its numerous deities in the pantheon, which it inserts in the mandalas or mystic circles, as well as the practice of black magic. Thus, while many *Tantras* possess high religious values, others are purely magical formulas to increase one's prosperity or to harm one's enemy. In one text Buddha is presented as a magician who, by his power, destroys his enemies. In such *Tantras* Buddhism, the glorious religion which conquered Asia, now approaches the lowest classes, accepts their occult arts and monstrous deities, and complies with their yearning for magic and sorcery.

The invasion and spread of such ideas threatened to transform Buddhism and to consign the original doctrine to oblivion. And since both Buddhist and Hindu *Tantras* were drawing their inspiration from the common source, the line of demarcation between the two was rapidly becoming obliterated. At this juncture the Buddhist Tantric masters brought in a new concept to interpret their literature that gave it a coherent meaning acceptable to the Mahāyānists. This new concept was *śūnyatā* or emptiness. Gods and fiends do not exist in reality, but are merely creations of our fancies. In this manner Tantrism was joined to Mahāyāna speculation, and out of this conjunction arose the third vehicle, Tantrayāna or Mantrayāna.

The process of esoteric consecration as practiced in this third vehicle involves a number of props, such as the mantras, mudrās, mandalas, and *abhishekas.* Mantras are mystic syllables or formulas which form the backbone of Tantrism. They are said to be the epitome of the sutras and the short cut to enlightenment. They usually consist of a string of syllables which have lost their etymological meaning, and in some cases probably never had any meaning. Vasubandhu once remarked that the absolute meaninglessness of the mantras constitutes their real significance, for meditation on this meaninglessness will help one to realize the illusory nature of the universe. The Tantrists believe that mantras when correctly pronounced in accordance with established rules can generate enormous power for good or evil. They also claim that a mantra will be effective only if the individual uttering it has undergone the proper training and discipline, and is thoroughly familiar with its operation. For instance, mantras are often resorted to in order to drive away malignant spirits or to fend off the spells and charms of enemies. This implies that words have some special power to chase away demons or to coerce them by mobilizing some greater force against them. A good illustration of this is in the *Matanga-sūtra* of the *Divyā-vadāna (Heavenly Stories)*, where Ānanda against his wishes is led to enter the house of a Candala or outcast girl who has fallen in love with him and who induces her mother to weave a spell over him. However, the Buddha through his divine eyes sees what is happening to Ānanda and, by uttering a more powerful mantra, is able to overcome the power of the spell cast by the Candala woman, and thus frees Ānanda.

Mantras represents the first official admission of a break in the Buddhist dogma concerning karma, that miracles can take the place of the iron link between cause and effect in the moral field. By reciting a mantra sinners can avoid the consequences of evil deeds. The most famous mantra is the one uttered by every Tibetan, *oṁ mani padme huṁ*, usually translated as "O the Jewel in the Lotus." The mere utterance of this formula is sufficient to stop the cycle of rebirth, and convey one to paradise or deliverance. Hence the formula is printed everywhere—on streamers, banners, cylinders, prayer wheels, or great barrels turned round by water.[10]

Closely associated with the mantras are the mudrās or signs made by the particular position of the hands and fingers. As the mantras contain all the secrets of sounds, so the mudrās contain all the secrets of touch. Each deity has its own mudrā, to be imitated by the worshiper; thus different rites to the different deities are accompanied by different signs of the hands and fingers.

With the advent of the mantras and mudrās the door was open for the mandala, mystic circle or cosmogram, to come in. A mandala is defined in Tantrist literature as the gathering place of the saints, or the altar where the consecration ceremonies take place. It is really a diagram that shows the deities in their cosmic connections, usually painted on cloth or paper, or drawn on the ground. The deities are pictured in their visible forms or as Sanskrit letters. Some mandalas would thus present a detailed representation of the universe, with all the Buddhas, bodhisattvas, and deities in their proper places.

In T'ang China one of the prominent mandalas was the

---

[10] In this transformation of the letters into mantras, the Tantrists adopted the theory of sound held by one of the early Indian schools of thought, the Mīmāṁsa, according to which sound is held to be eternal and exists always in the form of the letters in the alphabet. The word is nothing more than the letters that compose it. The meaning of the word is independent of any human agency and by its nature belongs to the word. Words themselves also are eternal but require pronunciation to be cognizable by our consciousness. The Tantrists go farther and say that the process in the production of sound is the epitome of the process that produces the world.

*garbhadhātu* or womb-element mandala, based on the *Mahā-vairocanasūtra* (*The Great Sun Sutra*), containing thirteen divisions with four hundred and five deities. In this mandala the central figure is Mahāvairocana, the Great Brilliant One. He is shown in the center, flanked by the Buddhas of the four directions, Akshobhya in the east, Amitābha in the west, Amoghasiddhi in the north, and Ratnasambhava in the south. The origin of these five Buddhas, sometimes called the five Jinas or the Victorious Ones, may be due to the emanative conception of Buddhahood so characteristic of Mahāyāna Buddhism. As personality is said to consist of the five aggregates, so Buddhahood is said to consist of five Buddhas.

If there were this quintet of Jinas in the mandala, it was soon felt that there must be some principle transcending them, some ideal unchanging center. Thus there arose the concept of the Ādibuddha, a primordial Buddha preceding all the others and permeating and conditioning them all. Ādibuddha was the reason and the source of the five Buddhas. However, this scheme of emanation does not stop here. In Tantrism the five Buddhas are now conceived to be accompanied by their female consorts. Furthermore, from these same Buddhas also emanated five bodhisattvas. This represents an important change in the conception of the bodhisattva from that of the Mahāyāna. The close relationship between the Buddhas and their emanations is represented visibly by a small Buddha figure on the head of the bodhisattva. Now came a further increase of deities, for the five bodhisattvas must also have their female counterparts. At this point the multiplication of deities begins to run wild. The gods, male and female, are now split into their dual aspects, pacific and angry, corresponding to the functions they are called upon to perform. When called upon to repel malevolent forces, they assume their fiendish, monstrous appearances, but when called upon to assist in some beneficial functions, they assume their benign forms. The Buddhist pantheon is thus divided into male and female, peaceful and dreadful groups, all created by spontaneous emanations, portrayed by the Tantrists in their mandalas.

Entry into the mandala is called *abhisheka* or initiation into the secrets of the school. According to the Tantrists salvation is not the result of knowledge but of practice. Awareness of one's true being is not learned through books but comes as the result of progressive enlightenment attained through the sacraments. Baptism is therefore a necessary and essential part of its soteriology. One portion of the ceremony consists of baptism by water, wearing of the crown or diadem, putting the sacred band on the shoulders, touching with the bell and thunderbolt, taking the vows, bestowing the secret name, and receiving from the master the bell and thunderbolt which the neophyte could not touch until now. These seven baptisms constitute a single group and are conferred at one ceremony. After this is finished, the ceremony for the group known as Right-hand Tantrists is over, but for the Left-hand Tantrists, there is another portion for the spiritually ready in which sexo-yogic practices are carried out. Tantric Buddhism boldly attempts to transfer the drama of cosmic evolution to the body of the disciple by considering the sexual act as the symbol of universal creation. Every Buddha or bodhisattva has his female consort who is worshiped together with him. From the concept of the female consort the Tantric School draws its idea that nirvāna resides in the female organ. Union with the consort results in nirvāna or the great bliss. For this secret baptism a virgin girl under twenty-one is necessary. Since this ceremony is secret, information concerning it is scarce, and will undoubtedly remain so as the participants are sworn to secrecy.

What is the philosophical foundation of these Tantric practices? The school developed its own system of philosophy by borrowing from such Mahāyāna schools as the Mādhyamika and Vijñānavāda. Though it admits the emptiness of all phenomena, it also maintains that the phenomenal world is not to be disregarded but is to be looked upon as a vehicle for progress toward emancipation.

Mahāyāna thought always considers enlightenment as the union of wisdom and compassion. Wisdom is construed as the realization of the nonexistence of all phenomenal appearances. However, wisdom is not enough. The enlightened one must also be compassionate and imbued with the altruistic spirit to save others. When wisdom and compassion are wedded to each other, then the nirvānic state is realized. All this is good Mahāyāna theology. However, in Tantrism, these terms are not to be understood in their usual meaning but in a hidden esoteric sense intelligible only to those initiated into the secrets of the system. Wisdom is considered as female, and compassion male. The process of attaining enlightenment consequently requires the presence of a virgin who is the symbol of wisdom. The union of wisdom and compassion is represented in Tibetan iconography by the *yab-yum* or father-mother image, where the deity is locked in embrace with its consort. Such an image is not considered as vulgar or obscene, but as a symbol of cosmic creation or as a representation of the perfect union between the two aspects of the absolute, the static and the dynamic, manifested in the human world in the male and female form. It is but a ritualistic portrayal of the emancipation realized by the bodhisattva and his consort. In conformity with the doctrine of emptiness the image is merely an artifice, a temporary form with no reality at all, to be abandoned whenever we become aware of the Buddha essence within us.

For the initiated the Tantric practices and images need no justification. But since such images are open to public view, the Tantric masters feel that some justification is necessary. Two main arguments are advanced in defense of their position. Tantrism, like the Mahāyāna Idealistic School, advocates an extreme form of idealism. The external world has no objective basis, as all phenomena are merely illusory appearances created by the mind. When the yogin enters the mandala for initiation into the secret rites, his mind is already so trained and purified that he realizes the true nature or emptiness of all things. To such a person all elements of existence appear to be of the same nondual nature. When he is in the state of union with the virgin, he makes no distinction between himself and the other. In such a state of mind he does not have any mental complex of morality or immorality, virtue or vice.

Moreover, the Tantrists argue that any action by itself is neither moral nor immoral. The moral or immoral nature of an act is to be judged by the effects it produces in the general scheme of life. To be strictly ethical they argue that not the effects but the intention or the motive behind the action should be the basis of judgment. The main point of the *Tantras* is on this point of ethics. If the motive behind the action, and not the action itself, is the main criterion, then any action in the form of a religious practice leading to salvation is to be justified. From the standpoint of compassion the bodhisattva is not to be judged by the ordinary moral standards of mankind. The bodhisattva has pledged his life for the salvation of all sentient beings. As one Tantric text puts it, if a woman falls violently in love with a bodhisattva and is about to sacrifice her life for him, it is the bounden duty of the bodhisattva to save her life by satisfying all her desires. The bodhisattva never sins. For this reason it is repeatedly stated in the texts that there is nothing that the bodhisattva should not do for the salvation of others. Since the intentions and motives of the bodhisattva are noble and virtuous, whatever deeds he performs are also noble and virtuous.

Such in the briefest outline are the tenets of the Tantrayāna as they were worked out in India. In their introduction into China three names stand out, Śubhakarasiṁha, Vajrabodhi, and Amoghavajra, all of whom arrived in T'ang China during the eighth century. With their arrival the long and continuous process of introducing different aspects of Indian Buddhism to the Chinese was finally brought to completion. However, before their time vestiges of certain practices which were later incorporated into Tantrism had already been introduced into China. As early as 230 a translation of the *Matanga-sūtra* which contained mantras beginning with "om" and ending with "svaha" was made by a central Indian monk named Chu Lü-yen. The practice of magic by Buddhist monks in China was already recorded in the fourth century. Among the most accomplished of these magicians was Fo-t'u-teng, who by applying oil to his hands was said to be able to see the shape of events a thousand miles away. Another accomplishment of such monks was their ability to produce rain by uttering the proper incantations. In a text translated by T'an-yao in 462 there were instructions concerned with the making of a circle for receiving the offerings of votaries. This appears to have been a rudimentary mandala. During the early years of the T'ang Dynasty an Indian monk Punyodaya, who arrived in China in 655, tried to introduce some esoteric texts then popular in India, but was not able to elicit much response among the Chinese because of the popularity and influence of Hsüan-tsang at the time. I-tsing also evinced some interest in Tantric Buddhism, but did not pursue this interest further because of other more compelling activities.

These, then, were some of the scattered traces of esoteric Buddhism in China before the eighth century. Though this aspect of Buddhism won some backing among the Chinese, it was not established as a cult until the coming of the three Tantric masters during the eighth century. Even after Tantrism was established, it is not clear whether the secret initiation ceremonies consisting of sexo-yogic practices, in which virgins were used as part of the rites, were ever carried out to any extent. Both Maspero and Chou I-liang in their studies of Tantrism felt that sexual practices never gained any headway because they ran counter to the Confucian ritualistic principles of the separation of the sexes and moral tenets. Chou did report a story in circulation during the T'ang Dynasty which would seem to indicate that some erotic elements did exist in the cult. According to this story there was a beautiful woman of about twenty-four who lived alone in the city of Yen-Chou in Shensi and was loved by all the young men in the city. She would never refuse what the young men requested of her. She died very young and since she had no relatives, she was buried by the roadside. During the Ta-li period (766-779) a monk from Central Asia arrived in the city and offered incense at her grave. When the people asked why he honored the grave of such a voluptuous woman, he replied that she was in reality a great sage whose great compassion for all led her to grant whatever was requested of her. She was in fact, he said, the Bodhisattva of the Chained Bones. If they doubted this, he went on, all they needed to do was to open the grave and see. When the people did so, they found her bones interlocked with one another. Such a story as this might very well have been created within the environment of Tantric Buddhism.

R. H. van Gulik, the Dutch scholar, who has conducted some preliminary investigations on the erotic elements in Chinese literature and art, disagrees with Maspero and Chou, and feels that sexual practices were much more common than supposed in Chinese Tantrism. It is true, he admits, that no translation of Tantric texts dealing with such practices has been found in China, but this does not prove, he claims, that no such texts existed; it only proves that such texts have been expurgated after the rise and dominance of Chu Hsi (1120-1200) and his brand of Confucianism. To bolster his claims he points to the existence of a Tachikawa sect founded by the Japanese monk Nin-kan (1057-1123) in Japan that practised sexual union as the means of attaining Buddhahood. Very little of the literature of the Tachikawa sect is preserved, but enough fragments remain to show that they were T'ang translations introduced into Japan probably during the tenth century.

Of Śubhakarasimha or Shan-wu-wei, who arrived in 716, it was said that he was a native of central India who had mastered the three secrets of the body, speech, and mind. While he was still in India his fame as a teacher already had reached China, and when he finally arrived in that land, he was welcomed with the title of National Preceptor. After he had settled down in Ch'ang-an, the emperor repeatedly inquired about his health and also professed great interest in his translations. One of the basic texts of the Tantric School, the *Mahāvairocanasūtra*, was translated by him while he was in Lo-yang. The Sanskrit text of this sutra consisted of over a hundred thousand verses, but Shan-wu-wei translated only a summary of the essentials. One of the occult powers that he possessed which was particularly valued by the emperor was his ability to pray for rain by uttering a Sanskrit formula of several hundred syllables. In his old age he asked the emperor for permission to return to India, but this was refused, and he finally passed away in China in 735, at the ripe old age of ninety-nine. After his death the emperor conferred on him the posthumous title of Director of the Court of State Ceremonials.

Vajrabodhi or Chin-kang-chih, the second of the Tantric masters, went to China after having heard that Buddhism was prospering in that country, and arrived in Canton in 720 via the sea route. From there he was ordered by imperial decree to proceed to the capital of Ch'ang-an, where he stayed in the Tz'u-en Temple, then in the Chien-fu Temple. In both temples he ordered an altar constructed for the *abhisheka* ceremony, in which a mandala was painted. In his biography one finds the usual accounts of the extraordinary feats he performed, such as predicting beforehand that rain would fall on the day he dotted the eye of the bodhisattva he was painting, or bringing back to life one of the emperor's daughters who had lain unconscious for over ten days. However, his biography also indicates that he was untiring in his propagation of the esoteric doctrine, and made a number of important translations.[11] It was said that the mystic syllables contained in these works were most effective whenever applied, and as a result of his propagation Tantrism rose to the peak of popularity in both capitals of Ch'ang-an and Lo-yang. He was seventy-one when he died in 741.

Amoghavajra or Pu-k'ung chin-kang went to China at an early age, and it was in that country that he became a master of the esoteric tradition under the tutelage of Vajrabodhi. After the death of his master in 741 Amoghavajra left China for India and Ceylon, where he was the object of great veneration by kings and princes. In 746 he returned to China to spend the rest of his life there, performing the *abhisheka* ceremony, reciting the mystic syllables on behalf of sick members of the imperial family, praying for rain, and translating esoteric texts. He served and won the favors of three successive emperors—Hsüan-tsung (713-755), Su-tsung (756-762), and Tai-tsung (763-779). The last-named was so impressed with him that he wrote prefaces to the translations made by the monk, and also offered him imperial presents from time to time. On one occasion in 768 the emperor presented him with twelve quilts of embroidered brocade and thirty-two embroidered banners; on another occasion, for his achievement in praying successfully for rain, he received from the emperor the Purple Robe, one hundred rolls of brocade, colored cloth, and silk. As an indication of the extent of his translations Amoghavajra wrote in a memorial to the throne that up to 771 he had translated seventy-seven works in all, in one hundred and twenty odd *chüan*.

One of the magic formulas that Amoghavajra translated in 758 was presented to the emperor Su-tsung with the request that he always carry it with him on different parts of his body. Sheets of paper with this magic formula, printed with wooden blocks in 980, have been found in the Tun-huang caves. He also

---

[11] One of these was the *Yü-chia nien-sung fa* (*Method of Reciting the Yoga Formula*) which deals with the mandala and baptism in great detail, while another was an abridged translation of different chapters of the *Chin-kang-ting ching* (*Sutra on the Head of the Thunderbolt*).

translated another magic formula which he said could grant all the wishes of one reciting it. A copy of this formula was presented to Emperor Tai-tsung in 762 on the latter's birthday, and in 776 the emperor ordered it to be memorized within one month by monks and nuns in the country. From then on, they were to recite it twenty-one times each day and to report to the emperor at the beginning of each year the number of times they had recited it during the past year. This formula was extensively engraved on pillars throughout the country. The Japanese monk Ennin in his diary for 844 wrote that all the pillars inscribed with this formula were destroyed as part of the persecution against Buddhism.

Toward the end of his life, when the illustrious Amoghavajra fell ill, Emperor Tai-tsung was so solicitous of his health that he dispatched the imperial physician to minister to the monk. The emperor also bestowed upon him the title Duke of Su, with three thousand households assigned as his fief. Amoghavajra, however, refused to accept the honor, saying, "Why should I steal more titles and positions when I am dying?" When he finally died at the age of seventy, the emperor suspended his daily audience for three days; he also donated 400,000 cash for the funeral ceremonies, and 2,000,000 cash to construct a stupa in honor of the famous monk.

From these biographies one may conclude that the Tantric cult in China during the eighth century was centered in the capital of Ch'ang-an, with two temples as its base of operations—the Ta-hsing-shan Temple and the Ch'ing-lung Temple. The former was the largest temple in the city, and was located south of the imperial city. Founded by Emperor Wen of the Sui Dynasty, it occupied an entire ward. The Ch'ing-lung Temple was in the southeastern part of the capital and was also founded by Emperor Wen. Japanese monks in China during the T'ang Dynasty often stayed and studied in this temple, which they regarded as the Nālandā of China. In all probability it was better known in Japan than in China.

After the death of Amoghavajra in 774 the esoteric school declined in China. No more important teachers arrived from India. During the early part of the Sung Dynasty, Jojin, the Japanese monk, visited the imperial palace in 1073 and saw images of deities that belonged to this cult. However, as a whole the school did not flourish, and Tsan-ning, compiler of the *Sung kao-seng-chuan*, wrote: "According to the scheme of the Mandala of the Five Divisions, young men or virgins must be used as the media to summon spirits. It was once extremely easy to cure illness or exorcise evil. People in modern times, however, use this method to profit their body or mouth, therefore little result is obtained. Generally, these methods are held in contempt by the world. Alas that the deterioration of the Good Law has gone so far as this."[12]

[12] Chou I-liang, "Tantrism in China," *Harvard Journal of Asiatic Studies*, 8 (1945), 284.

# CHAPTER XII

# THE SCHOOLS OF BUDDHISM IN CHINA (*Continued*)

## THE PURE LAND SCHOOL

### CONTENTS OF THE PURE LAND SUTRA

THE Pure Land School takes as its principal text the *Sukhāvatīvyūha* or the *Pure Land Sutra*. This sutra exists in a long and a short version. The former begins with a dialogue between Śākyamuni and Ānanda concerning a monk named Dharmakara, who went to a former Buddha for a description of the ideal Buddha and Buddha land. After having received instructions from that Buddha, Dharmakara then uttered an earnest wish to be reborn as that ideal Buddha presiding over that ideal Buddha land. This earnest wish forms the nucleus of the long *Sukhāvatīvyūha*.

All this was related by Śākyamuni as having happened many kalpas or aeons ago. Ānanda then asked what had happened to Dharmakara. Śākyamuni answered that in fulfillment of his earnest wish the monk became the Buddha Amitābha, presiding over the ideal Buddha land known as Sukhāvatī. When Ānanda expressed a desire to see that ideal Buddha land, Śākyamuni sent forth rays of light from his body which illumined the whole of Sukhāvatī for all to see.

Both the long and short versions of the sutra contain a detailed description of the Pure Land, or the Western Paradise. There is one great difference between the two, however. The long version emphasizes that rebirth in the Pure Land comes as the result of meritorious deeds as well as faith and devotion to Amitābha, whereas the short version specifically states that only faith and prayer are necessary. "Beings are not born in that Buddha country of the Tathāgata Amitāyus as a reward and result of good works performed in this present life. No, whatever son or daughter of a family shall hear the name of the Blessed Amitāyus, the Tathāgata, and having heard it, shall keep it in mind, and with thoughts undisturbed shall keep it in mind, . . .

after their death, they will be reborn in the world Sukhāvatī, in the Buddha country of the same Amitāyus, the Tathāgata."[1]

The Buddha presiding over the Pure Land is designated as Amitābha, meaning Infinite Light, or Amitāyus, Infinite Life. The Pure Land is described as being rich, fertile, comfortable, filled with gods and men but with none of the evil modes of existence, such as animals, ghosts, or denizens of hell. It is adorned with fragrant trees and flowers, especially lotus, and decorated with the most beautiful and precious jewels and gems. Rivers with sweetly scented waters give forth pleasant musical sounds, and are flanked on both banks by scented jewel trees. The heavenly beings sporting in the water can cause it to be hot or cold as they wish. Everywhere they go, they can hear the dharma of the Buddha, the teachings of compassion, sympathetic joy, patience, tolerance, equanimity, and so forth. Nowhere do they hear of or meet with anything unpleasant, unwholesome, woeful, or painful. That is why the land is called Sukhāvatī, the Pure and Happy Land. Whatever the inhabitants wish, that will they obtain.

Of the two versions of the sutra it is the short one with its emphasis on faith and devotion that gained the wider acceptance and popularity among Buddhist adherents. This represented an interesting development within Buddhism. Hīnayāna Buddhism conceived of karma as being entirely personal and individual; only the doer himself could shape his future destiny through his karma. Therefore the early teachings of the Buddha were all directed toward self-reliance and self-emancipation. "Be ye lamps unto yourselves, be ye a refuge unto yourselves," runs a passage in the Pali canon. Yet in this *Pure Land Sutra* emphasis is placed not on one's own effort but on the power of Amitābha to effect salvation; the shift was from *jiriki,* self-power, to *tariki,* other-power, as the Japanese put it.

This change was but one of the many that took place in the transition from the Hīnayāna to the Mahāyāna. The Mahāyāna thinkers were not satisfied with the narrow spiritual outlook contained in the Hīnayāna concept of karma. The Buddha has attained enlightenment only after the accumulation of merits extending over long aeons of time and, in view of his great compassion and love, it

---

[1] *Sacred Books of the East,* 49, part 2, 98-99.

is inconceivable that he should restrict the karma of such meritorious deeds only to himself. Karma is therefore clothed with cosmological dressing, and the spiritual attainment of the Buddha is interpreted, not as an individual, isolated event, but as a universal episode to be shared by humanity in general. Thus was born the doctrine of *pariṇāmana* or the transfer of merits from the Buddha or bodhisattva to sentient beings. By himself each sentient being is not strong enough to cope with the problem of attaining salvation; he must depend on another power greater than his own, and in the Pure Land this other power is furnished by Amitābha.

According to the Pure Land teachings Amitābha presides over the Western Paradise, which he has created out of his boundless love for all sentient beings, and he vows that anyone who has absolute faith in him and the Pure Land will be reborn there. In that Pure Land Amitābha has as his chief minister Avalokiteśvara, the always compassionate bodhisattva who is ever ready to go anywhere to lead the faithful to the land of purity and bliss. All that is necessary to attain rebirth there is to have faith and devotion as indicated by the repeated recital of the formula *namo-amitābha* or "reverence be to Amitābha."

AVALOKITEŚVARA

The word Avalokiteśvara consists of two parts: *avalokita*, a past passive participle meaning "seen" and *īśvara* meaning "lord." It is translated in various ways—"the lord who looks down," "the lord who is seen," "the lord of compassionate glances," "the lord whom one sees." The Tibetan has *spyan-ras-gzigs*, one who sees with eyes. In Chinese the bodhisattva is usually called Kuan-yin, one who hears sounds, or Kuan-shih-yin, one who hears the sounds (prayers) of the world. At first glance this would appear to be a wrong rendering of the Sanskrit, as if the translator had read Avalokitasvara instead, for *svara* means "voice" or "sound." However, the problem is not so simple, for in a manuscript of the *Lotus Sutra* dated the fifth century A.D. and discovered in Eastern Turkestan the name Avalokitasvara appears five times on one page. This makes it rather improbable that the name was a copyist's error. In fact, all the early translators in China used Kuan-yin or Kuan-shih-yin, and it was not until Hsüan-tsang that the expression Kuan-tzu-tsai, the Onlooking Lord, a correct translation of Avalokiteśvara, was first used.

In Chinese Buddhism there are two main traditions concerning Avalokiteśvara. One is to be found in chapter 24 of the *Lotus Sutra*, where he is given the epithet Samantamukha, He who looks in every direction. In this tradition, the merciful character of Kuan-yin is fully developed. He manifests himself everywhere in the world to save people from suffering, and assumes various forms to carry out his mission. While ready to offer assistance to all, he is especially interested in those who are facing dangers caused by the sword, fetters, fire, demons, and water. Also, in the same chapter of the sutra is to be found a significant passage which reads, "If there is a woman who desires to have a son, then she should pray to Kuan-yin with reverence and respect, and in due time she will give birth to a son endowed with blessings, virtues, and wisdom."

The other tradition is that found in the *Pure Land Sutra*.

These sutras bearing information about Kuan-yin had already been translated into Chinese from the time of the third century, and after the fifth century the deity had become fairly well known. For instance, figures of Kuan-yin were already being carved in the Yün-kang caves, and with the spread of the Pure Land School after the sixth century the bodhisattva became even more popular. Through the T'ang and early Sung Dynasties it appears that Kuan-yin was still looked upon as a male figure. The paintings recovered from Tun-huang give the best evidence of this, for in these representations Kuan-yin is frequently portrayed with a moustache.[2] Because he bears the epithet Samantamukha, he is sometimes depicted with eight or eleven heads, and with a thousand eyes and hands, the better to see and to save all suffering creatures.

During the T'ang Dynasty a new element which brought a change in the form of the bodhisattva entered the picture. This was the introduction in a Tantric sutra in the eighth century of the concept of a female Kuan-yin clad in white, and from the tenth century on, the painters began to paint this figure, which

[2] Such paintings may be found scattered in Matsumoto, *Tonkōga no kenkyū*, especially the following: pl.216, dated 864; pl.98b, dated 943; pl.222, dated 968—all with the moustache prominently displayed.

was called Pai-i Kuan-yin. The French Sinologist H. Maspero has provided what appears to be a reasonable explanation of this change. Mahāyāna Buddhism has always conceived of enlightenment as the conjunction of wisdom and compassion. In Tantric Buddhism these two are symbolized by the male and female. With the introduction of the female element all the Buddhas and bodhisattvas are provided with female consorts. Thus the female consort of Avalokiteśvara in Tibetan Buddhism was called the White Tara (in Sanskrit, Pāndaravāsinī), meaning "clad in white." The Chinese Pai-i Kuan-yin is a literal translation of this term.

This Kuan-yin clad in white, introduced into China from Tibet, was soon appropriated from Buddhism by the popular religion in China, and a new figure, Sung-tzu Kuan-yin (Kuan-yin, giver of children), was developed. In this popular form so little remains of the deity Pāndaravāsinī that the connection between the two is not easily apparent. However, Maspero thinks there is a connection. In Tantric Buddhism Pāndaravāsinī belongs to the mandala or cosmogram entitled Garbhakośadhātu, the World of the Womb-treasury. What probably happened was that the Chinese popular religion interpreted this symbolical expression of the womb world literally, and Pāndaravāsinī was converted into "the giver of children." This evolution was entirely in the realm of popular religion, and did not penetrate into Buddhism itself. Still it is possible to justify such a change within Buddhism, for the Mahāyāna sutras teach that a bodhisattva could assume any form and shape to assist mankind. Moreover, there is also that passage in the *Lotus Sutra* to the effect that Kuan-yin has the power to grant children to any woman who prays to him.

In China the long *Sukhāvatīvyuha* was translated as many as ten times, with five translations still preserved in the Chinese Tripitaka, while the only extant translation of the short version was made by Kumārajīva. Besides the above two versions, there is a third sutra belonging to this school that is revered just as highly by the Chinese, the *Kuan-wu-liang-shou-fo ching* (*Sutra on Meditation Concerning Amitāyus*).

### THE PURE LAND SCHOOL AND MASTERS IN CHINA

Probably the earliest Pure Land devotees in China were Ch'üeh Kung-tse (d. 265-274), his disciple Wei Shih-tu, and Wei's mother, all of whom lived in Lo-yang. Contemporary with Wei was a monk in central China named Seng-hsien who in his old age appeared to have engaged in contemplation about the Western Paradise. During the Eastern Chin Dynasty more monks became interested in the Pure Land, and among these was the well-known Chih Tun. In one of his works Chih Tun described the Pure Land presided over by Amitāyus as a region without prince, ministers, or officials, but ruled over by the Buddha, where people were reborn in the calyx of the lotus flower and therefore not stained by the impurities of the womb. It appears that Chih Tun made an image of Amitābha and before it uttered a vow to be reborn in the Western Paradise. However, it must be remembered that Chih Tun was a follower of the Prajñā and Neo-Taoist systems of thought; his interest was mainly in the similarities between Buddhism and Lao-Chuang philosophy, and he was not interested in the teachings and practices of the Pure Land cult as a means of salvation for himself or for the masses.

One of the most important figures in the early history of the cult in China was Hui-yüan, who is usually associated with the founding of a Pure Land Society in 402. There is no question but that Hui-yüan was the leader of a group who met regularly to meditate and to utter the vow to be reborn in the Western Paradise. Though he might have been a fervent follower of Amitābha, Hui-yüan never went out into society to preach the Pure Land doctrines, for he and his group were mainly hermits, recluses, retired scholars, and gentlemen whose main purpose was to escape from the world. Yet Hui-yüan is generally regarded as the first patriarch of the Pure Land School in China, mainly because he and his group served as an inspiration and model for later groups of Pure Land adherents who were attracted by his virtues, learning, and strict code of discipline.

### T'an-luan

After Hui-yüan the next important figure in the movement was T'an-luan (476-542), whose home was near Wu-t'ai-shan in the north. For over a century north China had become infiltrated with non-Chinese peoples and the cultural level in that area had declined. Inhabitants there were more inclined to a brand of Buddhism that emphasized magic, omens, mystic formulas, and prophecies, and many Buddhists sutras were forged in that area to satisfy this tendency within the religion. It was amidst such surroundings that T'an-luan was born.

The biography of T'an-luan states that on one occasion he recovered from a serious illness when he suddenly saw a heavenly gate open before him. With this experience he decided to search for an elixir that would bring about everlasting life. When he heard that a Taoist master in the south, T'ao Hung-ching (452-536), possessed such a formula, he proceeded to that area and obtained the *Hsien-ching* (*Sutra on Immortals*) in ten *chüan* from the Taoist. On his way back to the north he met the Buddhist monk Bodhiruci, who told him that in Buddhism there was a formula for attaining everlasting life that was superior to that of the Taoist. Upon being asked to reveal the formula, Bodhiruci taught him the texts of the Pure Land School, whereupon T'an-luan became so convinced that he discarded the Taoist text which he had obtained and concentrated on the attainment of the Western Paradise. This conversion took place ca.530, and for the remainder of his life he devoted his time to the propagation of the Pure Land tenets.

T'an-luan's place in Buddhist history is based mainly on his efforts to spread the Pure Land teachings and practices among the whole of society. In this respect he differed from Hui-yüan. The practice of reciting and meditating on the name of the Buddha Amitābha probably originated with him. In one of his works he wrote about meditating on various attributes of the Buddha—his name, characteristics, extraordinary faculties, merits, wisdom, and so forth. The oral invocation of the name Amitābha was deliberately fostered by him in societies that he organized in the north. His biographer wrote that as he neared death, his disciples, who numbered about three hundred, gathered about him to chant, "Amitābha." That his efforts did succeed in spreading the Pure Land tenets in north China might be seen in the nature of the figures carved in the Lung-men caves. In 520 only one figure of Amitābha and three of Avalokiteśvara were to be found in Lung-men, but for the decade 530-540 there were six figures of Amitābha and ten of Avalokiteśvara.

During the years after the passing of T'an-luan an interesting theory concerning the duration of the Buddhist dharma on earth began to spread in China. According to this theory there would be three periods in the duration of the law—that of the true dharma, that of the counterfeit dharma, and, lastly, that of the decay of the law. Something has already been said about this theory of the three periods, and about the Sect of the Three Stages organized to cope with the decay of the dharma. During the early T'ang period the Pure Land School also entered the picture to compete with the Sect of the Three Stages for the attention of the people. The main question asked was, During this final period of the decay of the dharma (which was thought to commence from 550 A.D.) how was one to save oneself and society from the sins and vices so rampant during the age? Both the Pure Land and the Sect of the Three Stages accepted the thesis that they were then living in the last period, but the ideas formulated by each to meet the needs of society were entirely different. Hsin-hsing of the Sect of the Three Stages taught that to be effective in this last stage the methods and teachings must be different from those of the other periods. He enunciated a sort of pantheism in which everyone was a potential Buddha and worthy of being worshiped; he felt that this was the only way to overcome the impurities of the age. The leader of the Pure Land School at this time, Tao-cho (562-645), took his stand on one sole deity, Amitābha, who had vowed to save all sentient creatures from sins and depravities. He taught that all one needed to do to escape from the evils of the period was to take refuge in Amitābha. During the seventh century these two teachings were in opposition, and gave rise to intense Buddhist activities in north China. Because the Sect of the Three Stages claimed that it was the only true faith, and that during the period of decay no government existed that was worthy of the respect of the people, it incurred the opposition of both the other schools of Buddhism and the ruling authorities, with the result that it was suppressed by the throne. This left the field clear for the teachers of the Pure Land School, and they proceeded to make the most of their opportunities. They were also assisted by the favorable attitude of the throne and the people.

### Tao-cho

The leaders mainly instrumental in the spread of the school were Tao-cho and his disciple Shan-tao (613-681). The principal work of Tao-cho was the *An-lo-chi* (*Collection of Essays on the Western Paradise*). In this work the main theme treated was the question of how during the period of decay ignorant people could enter the Pure Land. His answer, unqualifiedly, was practice of *nien-fo*, invoking the Buddha, or *k'ou-ch'eng nien-fo*, uttering the name of the Buddha. If one were to do this with an undivided mind, all evil would be overcome, all sins eradicated, and one would certainly be reborn in the Western Paradise. It was Tao-cho who urged his followers to use beans as an aid in counting the number of times they repeated the name of the Buddha. One of his disciples, Tao-sheng, uttered the name a record-breaking million times during a seven-day period. In the case of a female disciple the beans she counted while practicing *nien-fo* filled fifty-seven shih, another nun filled eighty shih.

### Shan-tao

Shan-tao, the other important Pure Land teacher, is looked upon by Jōdō followers in Japan as an incarnation of Amitābha, and his works are accepted as having scriptural authority. His principal work was the *Kuan-ching-su* (*Commentary to the Sutra on Concentration*). Here he wrote that the five main activities that could lead to rebirth in the Western Paradise were: (*a*) uttering the name of the Buddha, (*b*) chanting the sutras, (*c*) meditating on the Buddha, (*d*) worshiping images of the Buddha, and (*e*) singing praises to the Buddha. He divided these five activities into two categories—the primary, consisting of uttering the name of the Buddha, and the auxiliary, comprising the remaining four. From this division one can see the importance placed on *nien-fo* by Shan-tao; he wrote that this *nien-fo* practiced with an undivided and unruffled mind could wash away the sins accumulated during eighty kalpas. Because of the simplicity of this approach to rebirth in the Pure Land, it was welcomed by the common people.

However, it appears that Shan-tao did not dispense entirely with the auxiliary activities as aids to gain the goal. He insisted that both aids should be encouraged and he himself practiced both. There is a story that one of his disciples, Tao-chüan, once underwent a ninety-day period of *nien-fo*, worship and confession. During that period he had a dream in which he saw two paths leading to paradise, one smooth and one rocky. He also saw a monk who pointed out that those who practiced only *nien-fo*, with no worship or confession, would have to take the rocky path, but those who practiced all three would be taken along the smooth path.

One of the auxiliary activities encouraged by Shan-tao was chanting the sutras. In this chanting, not only the three basic texts of the Pure Land School, but also the *Saddharma, Vajracchedika*, the *Nirvāna*, and *Prajñā* sutras were included as being specially efficacious for rebirth in the Pure Land.

While he was in the capital, Shan-tao was said to have made several ten thousand copies of the *Pure Land Sutra* to be circulated among his disciples, who were countless in number. These masters of the Pure Land would convene their followers in large assemblies where they would utter the name of the Buddha as though they were singing. One Pure Land master named Shao-k'ang (d. 805) got street urchins to utter the formula by offering them one cash each for each utterance, and his biography noted that he became so famous that his mere presence in the street would be a signal for everyone to shout, "Amitābha."

### Tz'u-min

After Shan-tao, the most important Pure Land masters during the T'ang were Tz'u-min and Fa-chao. Tz'u-min, also named Hui-jih, was born in 680. In his youth he decided to emulate the example of I-tsing in going to India—a desire which he realized in 702. He reached India by the sea route in 704 and remained there until 716, when he commenced his return trip. While in India he was inspired by the stories about Amitābha and Avalokiteśvara and decided to dedicate his life to the propagation of the Pure Land tenets. After his return to China he devoted himself not to translations of the sacred scriptures but to the task of spreading the practice of *nien-fo* among the masses, for which contribution he was granted the posthumous title of Tz'u-min, Compassionate and Benevolent, by Emperor Hsüan-tsung.

During Tz'u-min's lifetime the teachings of the Ch'an master Hui-neng and his school were gaining wider and wider audience among the populace, and this aspect of Buddhism, with its de-emphasis of the sutras and pietistic activities, served as the main obstacle to the propagation of Pure Land teachings and practices. Tz'u-min strove to overcome the prejudices of the Ch'an School, whose followers he claimed were lazy, not practicing the moral precepts, and teaching people that the world was unreal, that there was no evil to be avoided and no good or pious deeds to be performed. Instead, he maintained that the tripod on which Buddhism rested—learning and meditation and moral conduct— must all be followed with equal force; no one discipline was to be neglected. He did not object to Ch'an meditation; he merely insisted that one should not be exclusively devoted to it, as in the case of the Ch'an adherents. The antisutra and antidiscipline tendencies of the school, he argued, were fostering undesirable effects, and he sought to counteract them by emphasizing his three principal tenets: (*a*) harmonious practice of meditation and scholarship, (*b*) sympathetic practice of *nien-fo* and meditation, (*c*) practice of *nien-fo* accompanied by morality. Because he was a man of action, Tz'u-min has left behind only a few works and no translations or commentaries. One of his works, *Ching-t'u tz'u-pei chi* (*Collected Essays on Pure Land Compassion*), was reprinted during the Sung Dynasty, but because it severely attacked the ideas and practices of the Ch'an School, the latter persuaded the civil authorities to ban the book from circulation and to destroy the printing blocks.

Tz'u-min died in 748 at the age of sixty-nine. Because he advocated the sympathetic practice of *nien-fo* and Ch'an meditation, he is considered by some to be the first individual who sought to harmonize the Pure Land and Ch'an teachings. Some of the monks in later years who looked to him as their spiritual master, such as the Ch'an monk Yen-shou (904-975), were to become active proponents of this movement.

### Fa-chao

One of Tz'u-min's disciples of the second generation was Fa-chao, whose master Ch'eng-yüan (712-804) had been a direct pupil of Tz'u-min. Fa-chao was active in Ch'ang-an during the reigns of Tai-tsung (763-779) and Te-tsung (780-804), the periods when the dynasty was exerting itself to restore the glories of the T'ang imperial line after the disastrous An Lu-shan rebellion. Contemporaneous with him in the capital were the famous masters of some of the other Buddhist schools—the Tantric master Amoghavajra, the T'ien-t'ai master Chan-jan, and the Hua-yen master Ch'eng-kuan. So great was his achievement in spreading the Pure Land practices even against this competition that Fa-chao was sometimes called by his contemporaries the Later Shan-tao. He claimed that he had received revelations from Amitābha and that he had performed miracles under the inspiration of that deity. It was Fa-chao who initiated the practice of invoking the name of Amitābha in five tunes, which he said was taught to him by Amitābha himself. During the reign of Tai-tsung he was honored with the title National Preceptor.

In his teachings Fa-chao followed the doctrine of Tao-cho and Shan-tao. However, since he first studied T'ien-t'ai teachings before turning to the Pure Land, he was also interested in the movement to harmonize the tenets and practices of the different schools. In this respect he was following the example of his master Tz'u-min.

In view of such fervent activities by so many masters one can easily understand why the Pure Land soon became one of the most popular movements in north China during the T'ang Dynasty. This popularity was concretely illustrated in the shift of emphasis from Śākyamuni and Maitreya to Amitābha and Avalokiteśvara in the Lung-men statues. This increased popularity of Amitābha was also attended by a standardization in the designation of that deity. In the earlier translations a number of terms were used by the Chinese to designate him: A-mi-t'o fo, a transliteration of Amitābha; Wu-liang-shou, a translation of Amitāyus, Infinite Life; and Wu-liang-kuang, a translation of Amitābha, Infinite Light. By the middle of the T'ang Dynasty the name had definitely become standardized to A-mi-t'o-fo, and this designation appears most often in the Lung-men statues. Probably one of the factors bringing this about was the increasing tendency of the Taoists to use the term *wu-liang-shou* in line with their quest for immortality, and it was with the idea of moving away from this Taoist connotation that the Buddhists turned to A-mi-t'o-fo.

The propagation of the Pure Land tenets was also assisted by paintings and illustrations of the joys of Western Paradise and the miseries of hell. In fact, these were the most popular themes of the painters of the period, and such paintings are often mentioned by the historians of art of the T'ang and Sung Dynasties. Li Po and Tu Fu likewise refer to them in their poems. Such paintings were to be found on temple walls and corridors, on the sides of caves, as well as on silks and brocades. Fine examples of such paintings preserved in the Tun-huang caves and dating back to the T'ang may be seen in any collection of Tun-huang paintings. As the ignorant crowds saw the tortures of hell, on one hand, and the blessings and happiness of the Western Paradise, on the other, it is no wonder that their minds were attracted to the teachings of the Pure Land School.

## THE CH'AN SCHOOL IN CHINA

The Chinese are generally considered to be a practical, earth-bound people not given to speculations about such religious problems as the nature of the universe, the afterlife, and so forth. When the Chinese were first brought face to face with Indian Buddhism with its rich and elaborate imagery, concepts, and modes of thinking, they were fascinated at first and finally overwhelmed and conquered. After a few centuries, however, the practical nature of the Chinese began asserting itself; it began to search for certain features within Buddhism which it could understand and practice, and in this search it soon picked on the *dhyāna* exercise as the essence of Buddhist discipline. *Dhyāna*, or *ch'an* in Chinese, refers to the religious discipline aimed at tranquilizing the mind and getting the practitioner to devote himself to a quiet introspection into his own inner consciousness. He is made to feel an interest in things above the senses and to discover the presence of a spiritual faculty that bridges the gap between the finite and the infinite. When he is thoroughly disciplined in *dhyāna*, he can keep a serenity of mind and cheerfulness of disposition even amid the world of turbulent activity. He may start the *dhyāna* exercises by controlling the breath or by concentrating the mind on some object. Various objects are proposed to help the practitioner get rid of certain undesirable elements. If a person is addicted to lust or passion, he is told to repair to the cemetery to concentrate on the horrors of the corpse in various stages of decomposition; by so doing he will no longer feel any attachment for sensual pleasures. If he is disturbed by anger, then he is told to concentrate on *metta* or infinite love for all sentient beings. Continuous practice of *dhyāna* exercises enables him to attain to the higher ecstatic trances or to the blissful state of equanimity and wisdom.

In China, Tao-an (312-385) and Hui-yüan (334-416) were among the earliest Chinese monks to emphasize the importance of *dhyāna* exercises. Tao-an went to great lengths to collect *dhyāna* sutras and to comment on them. As for Hui-yüan, he once wrote, "I regret very much that since the introduction of the great religion into the East, so little is known of the practices of *dhyāna* that the whole structure is in danger of collapse because of lack of the solid foundation of meditation."[3] One of Hui-yüan's close collaborators, Buddhabhadra, was a famous *dhyāna* master who had trained some well-known Chinese *dhyāna* practitioners in the north. Another Indian master was Buddhasanta, whose most prominent disciple was Seng-ch'ou (d. 560, aged eighty-one), a Chinese monk so proficient in *dhyāna* exercises that he was proclaimed the greatest expert east of the Himalayas.

### BODHIDHARMA

However, it was with Bodhidharma that the Dhyāna or Ch'an School usually dated its beginning in China. According to the standard Ch'an version, *The Record of the Transmission of the Lamp*, compiled in 1004 by Tao-yüan, this worthy arrived in China in 520 (variant 526) and, after a fruitless interview with Liang Wu-ti, crossed the Yangtze and went to the Northern Wei kingdom. There he practiced what was known as wall contemplation, sitting in front of a wall, for nine years. While he was thus engaged, a monk named Shen-kuang came and asked him to teach the truth of Ch'an. Bodhidharma paid no attention to him until the monk cut off his arm to prove his sincerity. After this, Bodhidharma instructed him, and changed his name from Shenkuang to Hui-k'e.

Modern scholarship has cast a good deal of doubt on this version. The earliest source concerning Bodhidharma is undoubtedly the *Lo-yang chia-lan-chi* by Yang Hsüan-chih, finished in 547.

---

[3] Hu Shih, "Development of Zen Buddhism in China," *Chinese Social and Political Science Review*, 15 (1932), 480.

In this work Yang, while describing the fabulous Yung-ning Temple in Lo-yang, reported that a Persian monk named Bodhidharma was so impressed with the magnificence of the structure that he declared it was superior to everything he had seen thus far. This Yung-ning Temple was built in 516. In 526 a sacred vessel on the mast above the temple was blown down by the wind. In 528 and 529 troops were quartered in the temple precincts and in 534 the whole edifice was burned down by fire. For Bodhidharma to have heaped such praise on the magnificence of the temple, he must have seen it during the height of its glory, between 516 and 526. If this were the case, it would break down the Ch'an version that he arrived in Canton in 526.

Next to the *Lo-yang chia-lan-chi* in importance is the *Hsü-Kao-seng-chuan* by Tao-hsüan, who died in 667. In this source it is recorded that Bodhidharma first reached Sung territory, and then went north to the Northern Wei kingdom. Such a notice would indicate that he arrived when the Liu Sung Dynasty (420-479) was still in power in south China, and that in 520 he was already in Lo-yang admiring the beauties of the Yung-ning Temple. Data found in the biography of Seng-fu in the *Hsü-Kao-seng-chuan* would seem to verify this. Seng-fu, a native of T'ai-yüan in north China, joined the sangha under the tutelage of Bodhidharma. During the period 494-497 he left the north to travel in south China and died there in 524 at the age of sixty-one. According to monastic rules Seng-fu must have been at least twenty when he was ordained by Bodhidharma. If he were sixty-one in 524, he would have been twenty in ca.483. This would seem to indicate that Bodhidharma was already in north China at that time to ordain him. Nowhere in the *Hsü-Kao-seng-chuan* or the *Lo-yang chia-lan chi* is there any mention of Bodhidharma's meeting with Emperor Wu of the Liang Dynasty.

Bodhidharma is generally acknowledged as the first patriarch of the Ch'an School in China, with his disciple Hui-k'e the second. Instead of the usual Ch'an story that the latter cut off his arm to prove his sincerity, a more reliable account indicated that it was cut off by some robbers. One of the main texts transmitted by Bodhidharma to Hui-k'e was the *Lankāvatārasūtra* (*Descent to the Island of Lanka*), which emphasizes the doctrine of inner enlightenment. One who has realized this inner enlightenment no longer sees any duality, for he has transcended mental discriminations. This realization is made possible by the presence of the Tathāgata-womb in all of us. The *Lankāvatāra* also teaches that words are not necessary for the communication of ideas. In some Buddha lands teachings are transmitted by gazing, moving of facial muscles, raising of eyebrows, frowning, smiling, and twinkling of eyes. Here one sees a definite affinity between the *Lankāvatāra* and later Ch'an practices. Moreover, the tradition of gradual enlightenment followed by Shen-hsiu and his adherents might also be traced to this sutra.

### SHEN-HSIU AS SIXTH PATRIARCH

After Hui-k'e the Ch'an patriarchate was transmitted to Seng-ts'an (d. 606), Tao-hsin (580-651), Hung-jen[4] (602-675), and then to Shen-hsiu (600-706). This was the genealogy in vogue during the early part of the eighth century. Shen-hsiu was thus the sixth in line. From all accounts he was a powerful and attractive preacher, whose reputation was so great that he was invited to the capital of Lo-yang in 700, even though he was close to a hundred years of age at the time. A contemporary writer recorded that faithful laymen traveled over a thousand li just to hear him. He was hailed as the master of the law in the capital, the preceptor of emperors, and the acknowledged leader of the group usually referred to as the Northern Ch'an School.

### SHEN-HUI'S ATTACK AGAINST THE POSITION OF SHEN-HSIU

In 734 a southern monk named Shen-hui (670-762) suddenly attacked this line of transmission. He accepted the first five patriarchs, but he contended that the sixth was not Shen-hsiu but

---

[4] Hung-jen's biography is found in the *Sung-Kao-seng chuan*, finished by Tsan-ning in 988, but the information found there is not very reliable, as the account was influenced by the partisan works of the Ch'an writers of the ninth century. More reliable is the account in *Leng-chia jen-fa chih* (*Record of the Masters and the Law of the Lanka School*) by Hsüan-tse, finished ca.708-710. One interesting item of information furnished by Hsüan-tse was that among the disciples of Hung-jen there were eleven considered worthy of transmitting the teachings, and among the eleven were the names Shen-hsiu and Hui-neng. This would seem to indicate that Hui-neng was not the unknown illiterate rice pounder that later Ch'an accounts make him. There is, however, no mention of the famous episode of Shen-hsiu and Hui-neng's composing stanzas to vie for the patriarchate, nor of the legend that Hung-jen passed the patriarchal robe to Hui-neng in the middle of the night.

was Hui-neng (638-713), who received the patriarchal robe from Hung-jen.[5] He also attacked the doctrine of gradual enlightenment held by Shen-hsiu and put forth his own position in favor of complete instantaneous enlightenment, contending that pure wisdom is indivisible and undifferentiated, to be realized completely and instantly or not at all.

After firing these shots against Shen-hsiu, Shen-hui rapidly became well known and the Southern Ch'an School that he represented grew stronger and stronger. The Northern School under the leadership of Shen-hsiu's disciples could either stop him or ignore him. Some were in favor of ignoring him, but others could not endure the spectacle of their master's being criticized. The attacks by Shen-hui became even more fierce after 745, when he was called to a monastery in Lo-yang, from which rostrum he gained a much wider audience. The followers of Shen-hsiu now decided to take positive action. In 753 they charged Shen-hui with the crime of collecting a mob to disturb the peace and conspiring against the interests of the state. Shen-hui was arrested and banished from Lo-yang to Kiangsi. At this time he was over eighty years of age, and the spectacle of this venerable old man wandering from one place to another, all because of some sectarian controversy, must have elicited a good deal of public sympathy. By alienating the public through its highhanded treatment of Shen-hui, the Northern School was doomed to lose the struggle.

During the third year of Shen-hui's exile new developments suddenly arose. In 755 An Lu-shan rebelled and captured Lo-yang and Ch'ang-an in 756. The next year the two cities were recaptured, but the government was faced with lack of funds to feed the army. One of the schemes seized upon by the government was the sale of ordination certificates to those who desired to enter the Buddhist or Taoist orders, each certificate selling for one hundred strings of cash, the proceeds to be donated to the government.

With the recovery of Lo-yang, Shen-hui suddenly reappeared

---

[5] Shen-hui further claimed that this patriarchal robe was still in south China and that a disciple of Shen-hsiu attempted to steal it in 709. At the same meeting one of the monks present asked Shen-hui who were the patriarchs before Bodhidharma in India. This was a surprising question, for it had never before been raised in China. However, Shen-hui rose to the occasion and boldly asserted that Bodhidharma was the eighth patriarch. When pressed for the source of this information, he named a sutra where

in the city and was promptly selected by the people to head the campaign to raise funds by pushing the sale of monk certificates. Meanwhile, his opponents had been scattered to the winds during the fighting in Lo-yang. Victory thus rested with Shen-hui in his fight to dethrone Shen-hsiu as the sixth patriarch and to elevate Hui-neng in his place.

HUI-NENG

According to the standard Ch'an history of the eleventh century Hui-neng was a native of Hsin-chou in south China. One day while he was selling fuelwood, he heard some people reciting the *Diamond Cutter* and was so attracted by it that he journeyed all the way to Hupei to receive instructions from Hung-jen. In the initial interview Hung-jen tried to discourage him by saying that southerners did not possess the Buddha-nature. Hui-neng replied that so far as the Buddha-nature was concerned, there was no distinction between northerners and southerners—an answer that so pleased the master that the latter immediately gave him a position as rice pounder. When Hung-jen wanted to select his spiritual successor, he announced that anyone who could demonstrate his knowledge of the religion in the form of a poem would be given the patriarchal robe. Of all the disciples of Hung-jen, Shen-hsiu was considered the most learned, and everyone expected him to be selected. As a demonstration of his qualification he submitted the flowering stanza:

> "The body is the tree of enlightenment,
> And the mind is like a bright mirror stand,
> Always cleanse them diligently, and not let
> dust fall on them."

A few days later the following stanza was posted next to it:

> "Enlightenment is not a tree to begin with,
> Nor is the mind a mirror stand,
> Since originally there was nothing, whereon would
> the dust fall?"[6]

---

the names of seven patriarchs do appear; but the eighth was not Bodhidharma but Dharmatrata. Fortunately for Shen-hui, the monks present were all ignorant of history, and no one pointed out his grave error.

[6] *Liu-tsu t'an-ching; Taishō,* 48,348b,349a. However, in the Tun-huang copy of the sutra the third line of Hui-neng's poem reads, "Buddha-nature is forever clear and pure." See W. T. Chan (tr.), *The Platform Sutra,* New York, 1963, 41.

The composer of this stanza was none other than the unpretentious rice pounder Hui-neng, whom no one had noticed, but whose genius expressed through this stanza was instantly recognized by Hung-jen. The latter hesitated to announce his selection of Hui-neng openly for fear of antagonizing the monks; so one midnight he invited Hui-neng to his room and secretly handed over to him the patriarchal robe, the symbol of the transmission.

Hui-neng lived in seclusion for some years after this, and only when he was thirty-nine, in 676, did he go out to preach. It was said that he first came upon two monks arguing about a pennant flapping in the breeze. The first contended that the pennant was an inanimate object, and only the wind made it flap. The second argued that there was no flapping pennant, only the wind was moving. Hui-neng broke in and stopped the argument by saying that it was neither the pennant nor the wind that was flapping, only their minds. This was the beginning of Hui-neng's career as a Ch'an master.

Such a version depicting Hui-neng's choice as the sixth patriarch makes very interesting reading, but there is a strong possibility that it is not all reliable history. For one thing, the absence of any reference to the composition of stanzas and the passing of robes in the eighth-century work of Hsüan-tse, entitled *Record of the Masters and the Law of the Lanka School*, makes it doubtful that these episodes actually took place. For another thing, the standard Ch'an history, *Record of the Transmission of the Lamp*, was written almost four centuries after the events, and during that interval numerous Ch'an legends must have been fabricated and inserted into the account.

## HUI-NENG AND THE NEW CH'AN

With the triumph of the Southern School of Hui-neng and Shen-hui very little more is heard about the Northern School. The subsequent history of Ch'an is primarily the history of the Southern School, which is sometimes referred to by historians as the new Ch'an because of its emphasis on complete and instantaneous enlightenment, its iconoclastic attitude toward the Buddhas and bodhisattvas, and its disregard for literature and rituals. Liang Su (753-793), one of the foremost prose masters of the period, has left behind a good summary of this new tendency: "Nowadays, few men have the true faith. Those who travel the path of Ch'an go so far as to teach the people that there is neither Buddha nor law, and that neither sin nor goodness has any significance. When they preach these doctrines to the average man, or men below the average, they are believed by all those who live their lives of worldly desires. Such ideas are accepted as great truths which sound so pleasing to the ear. And the people are attracted to them just as moths in the night are drawn to their burning death by the candle light. . . . Such doctrines are as injurious and dangerous as the devil (Mara) and the ancient heretics."[7]

In the years following Hui-neng and Shen-hui a succession of famous Ch'an masters arose who established the different branches of Ch'an in the T'ang Dynasty—Lin-chi, Ts'ao-tung, Kuei-yang, Yün-men, and Fa-yen. Of these the first two were the most important, while the remaining three never enjoyed a large following and soon disappeared from the scene. The Lin-chi branch was founded by I-hsüan (d. 867, variant 866), while the Ts'ao-tung was established by Liang-chieh (807-869) and Pen-Chi (840-901). The centers of this branch were on Mts. Ts'ao and Tung, hence the name.

WHAT IS CH'AN?

Ch'an has been described as an intuitive method of spiritual training aimed at the discovery of a reality in the innermost recesses of the soul, a reality that is the fundamental unity which pervades all the differences and particulars of the world. This reality is called the mind, or the Buddha-nature that is present in all sentient beings. In common with other Mahāyāna systems Ch'an teaches that this reality is śūnya, empty or void, inexpressible in words and inconceivable in thought. To illustrate this the Ch'an masters often resorted to silence or negation to express the truth. Being inexpressible and inconceivable, this reality or the Buddha-nature can only be apprehended by intuition directly, completely, and instantly. Intellectual analysis can only divide and describe and scratch the surface but cannot apprehend the fundamental reality. In order to apprehend

[7] Hu Shih, "Ch'an Buddhism in China," Philosophy East and West, 3,1 (1953), 13.

it one must calm the mind and have no conscious thought. In any conscious thought there is the ego at work, making for the distinction between subject and object. Conscious thought also begets karma, which ties one down to the endless cycle of birth and death and breeds attachment to external objects. Such conscious efforts as heeding the teachings of the Buddha, reciting the sutras, worshiping the Buddha images, or performing the rituals are really of no avail and should be abandoned. Instead, one should allow the mind to operate freely, spontaneously, and naturally.

It was in accordance with this emphasis on freedom and spontaneity that the Ch'an master I-hsüan called upon his disciples to "kill everything that stands in your way. If you should meet the Buddha, kill the Buddha. If you should meet the Patriarchs, kill the Patriarchs. If you should meet the arhats on your way, kill them too."[8] Another Ch'an master Hsüan-chien (782-865) called upon his followers to do just the ordinary things in life—to drink when thirsty, to eat when hungry, to pass water and move the bowels, and, when tired, to take a rest. "There are neither Buddhas nor Patriarchs; Bodhidharma was only an old bearded barbarian. Śākyamuni and Kāśyapa, Mañjuśrī and Samantabhadra, are only dungheap coolies. . . . Nirvāna and bodhi are dead stumps to tie your donkeys. The twelve divisions of the sacred teachings are only lists of ghosts, sheets of paper fit only for wiping the pus from your boils."[9]

When the Ch'an follower apprehends the Buddha-nature within himself, he experiences an awakening or enlightenment called *wu* in Chinese, *satori* in Japanese, an awareness of the undifferentiated unity of all existence. He is now one with the whole universe, he sees all particulars and differences merged into one fundamental unity, and he is no longer troubled by problems and incidents. The Ch'an masters assert, however, that this apprehension does not mean the acquisition of something new; it means only the realization of something that is always present in him. The only trouble is that he is not aware of this because of his ignorance and folly. In this state of awakening, when the

---

[8] *Lin-chi ch'an-shih yü-lu*; *Taishō*, 47,500b.
[9] P'u-chi, *Wu-teng hui-yüan*, 7,7ab, translated in Hu Shih, *op.cit.*, 3,1,19.

mind is calm and tranquil, when the conscious self is eliminated, the mysterious inner mind takes over, and the actor performs his action automatically and spontaneously. Such a state of awakening can be repeated many times.

Though all the Ch'an branches have the same aim, the realization of this innermost mind, the methods and techniques devised by each to reach that end differ. The Lin-chi branch, for instance, follows what may be called the shock therapy, the purpose of which is to jolt the student out of his analytical and conceptual way of thinking and lead him back to his natural and spontaneous faculty. To achieve this the master shouts at his disciple or administers a physical beating to him. Or, in response to a question put by the student, he replies with an answer seemingly unrelated to the question. An example of this was the answer, "three pounds of flax," given in response to the question, "Who is the Buddha?" At times the master may pose a riddle or conundrum to the student, as, for example, "What is the sound of one hand clapping?" or, "How do you get the goose out of the bottle without breaking the bottle?" There is really no intellectual solution to such a riddle, which is called *kung-an* (literally, a case or a problem). The *kung-an* is meant to stimulate the student to the realization that logic, reason, and conceptualization are stumbling blocks to his awakening and to induce him to resort to resources other than logic and reason, resources that he has hitherto not utilized. The Lin-chi branch also accepts the idea in the *Lankāvatāra* that words are not necessary to express the truth, and regards such acts as the snapping of fingers or the raising of eyebrows as manifestations of the Buddha's message.

Instead of the shout, stick, and *kung-an* of the Lin-chi, the Ts'ao-tung branch follows the method of silent introspection or sitting in meditation under the guidance of a master, a form of meditation aimed at observing the innermost mind or nature in tranquility. In this method the master teaches his disciple directly, tangibly, and secretly. Verbal instructions are resorted to, with proper emphasis on arguments and reason. Such a method is favored by those whose temperament is not suitable for the bewildering, enigmatic, and sometimes violent approach of the Lin-chi branch.

## INTELLECTUAL ATMOSPHERE FAVORING THE RISE OF CH'AN

The emphasis of the Southern Ch'an School of Hui-neng on complete, instantaneous enlightenment would appear to point to some historical connection between this school and Tao-sheng. Though Tao-sheng enunciated his thesis of sudden enlightenment back in the fifth century, the idea was not seized upon by Chinese Buddhists until a few centuries later. During those centuries the popularity of such schools as the T'ien-t'ai and Wei-shih probably contributed toward the neglect of this doctrine. However, by the end of the seventh century the Chinese Buddhists were ready for something different. The whole body of Buddhist teachings introduced into China had been successfully digested by that time, and the Chinese mind was now ready to put forth its own interpretation of Buddhism. No longer were the Chinese to be held in bondage by Indian ideas and practices; they were now in a position to go forward with fresh ideas and new practices. One of the ideas that attracted the Chinese Ch'an Buddhists was this doctrine of instantaneous enlightenment.

By the end of the seventh and the beginning of the eighth centuries intellectual conditions in China were ready for the development of Ch'an Buddhism. For over one hundred and thirty years, from 625 to 755, the T'ang Dynasty had enjoyed tranquility, security, and prosperity without any internal rebellion or external invasion to mar the orderly march of events. During this era all phases of Chinese culture, religion, art, and literature enjoyed a long period of free growth and development. This development reached its highest level during the eighth century, during the reign of Ming-huang, which started in 713 and moved on an even, prosperous keel until 755, when the peace of the empire was rudely shattered by the An Lu-shan rebellion.

The prevailing tendency of the period was one of freedom of expression and naturalism. In poetry, for instance, the greatest names of the age were Li Po (701-762), whose poems are noted for their spontaneity of sentiment, abandoned, carefree romanticism, and revolt against conventional restraints, and Tu Fu (712-770), famous for his "daring innovations in subject matter, in form, and in diction" and for his readiness "to challenge the right of the dead classical usage to shackle living moods and creative thoughts."[10] This prevalent mood was reflected in Tu Fu's poem on the Eight Immortals of the Wine Cup, in which he describes in vivid and colorful language the propensities of this group for the cup. For instance, one of the members of the group was Ho Chih-chang, a famous literary figure. In his old age, when he was no longer feeling well, he petitioned the throne to become a Taoist priest and to return to his native village. The emperor consented, and in addition composed a poem as a farewell present to him. Such a figure, carefree, nonconformist, yet still capable of winning the respect of the emperor, is a good example of the spirit of the age. The best illustration, however, is the poet Li Po, who would be summoned into the imperial presence drowned in wine and have his shoes taken off by a famous eunuch. At times living in the forest as a hermit, at times drunk in the market place, at times taking cinnabar pills to attain longevity, at times floating on lakes and rivers, he exemplifies better than anyone else the naturalism and freedom so highly valued by the poets of the eighth century.

In art the most famous painter was Wu Tao-tzu, born in ca.700, whose great natural genius found expression in numerous murals on the walls of Buddhist temples in Ch'ang-an and Lo-yang. Besides his creative imagination and technical skill, he also displayed in his brushwork a looser, freer, and more personal style than had been previously encountered in any artist.

The Ch'an movement is but one aspect of the whole liberating tendency that characterized the age. This is one of the reasons why it became so popular in China. The school was not so speculative as the T'ien-t'ai, Hua-yen, and Wei-shih Schools, and hence appealed more to the practical tendency in Chinese thought. It did not antagonize Confucian thought, and it bore a close affinity with Taoism in its philosophical ramifications.

## CH'AN AND TAOISM

Certain aspects of philosophic Taoism unquestionably played some part in the development of the movement. Ch'an writers and artists emphasized spontaneity and naturalness as against

[10] William Hung, *Tu Fu*, Cambridge, 1952, 2.

artificiality. The exhortations of the masters to their followers to live natural lives, to eat, drink, pass water, and sleep whenever they wished, and to answer their teachers promptly and unhesitatingly, all illustrate this characteristic. Likewise, the Ch'an artist executed his work with the brush in swift, spontaneous movements without any forethought. In this emphasis on naturalness and spontaneity the Ch'an is closely akin to philosophic Taoism, for there are in *Lao-tzu* and *Chuang-tzu* many passages protesting against the artificial restraints of society against the natural development of man. This philosophy is inherent in the world, the Taoists argue, for the seasons come and go, flowers bloom and wither, the sun rises and sets, without anyone's doing anything. Likewise, they argue that the ideal state is one in which man is free to do as he pleases without having to conform to laws and institutions invented by man.

The Ch'an emphasis that the essence of the Buddha may be found in everyone and everything also finds a close parallel in the Taoist emphasis on the immanence of the Tao. Illustrative of this is the following passage from *Chuang-tzu*:

"Tungkuo Shun-tzu asked Chuang-tzu, 'Where is what you call the Tao to be found?' Chuang-tzu replied, 'Everywhere.' The other said, 'Specify an instance of it. That would be more satisfactory.' 'It is here in this ant.' 'Give a lower instance.' 'It is in this panic grass.' 'Give me a still lower instance.' 'It is in this earthenware tile.' 'Surely that is the lowest instance.' 'It is in that excrement.' "[11]

Both Taoism and Ch'an stress the idea of the wordless doctrine. Parallel to the Ch'an slogan that the truth is "not expressed in words or written in letters" are the Taoist assertions that "the Tao that can be told is not the absolute Tao" and that "he who knows does not talk, and he who talks does not know." Moreover, in both Taoism and Ch'an there is the harmony of contrasts and the leveling of opposites, the lack of attachment to worldly things and the mystic appreciation of nature. In their pedagogical method both attempt to surprise and stimulate the student by paradoxes and enigmas.

In consonance with this spirit of freedom and creativity, the Ch'an masters in China broke away from the Indian dependence

[11] J. Legge, *The Texts of Taoism*, Oxford, 1891, 2,66.

upon the sacred scriptures, objects of worship, rituals, and metaphysical speculation to build up a school of Buddhism which favored a plain, direct, concrete, and practical approach to enlightenment. These Ch'an masters spoke, not in the abstract language of the Mahāyāna treatises, but in the everyday colloquial language which could be understood by any Chinese listener. One needs only to look directly at the inner essence of oneself; there one will find the Buddha.

## IS CH'AN BUDDHIST?

If Ch'an has no place for the sacred scriptures, the images, and even the Buddha himself, then could Ch'an still be considered a part of Buddhism? The Ch'an masters answer this question unequivocally in the affirmative. They state that the main feature of Buddhism is the realization of enlightenment, which is a direct, personal experience. All the external paraphernalia of the religion, such as the sacred scriptures, the images, and the rituals, are but props and aids to realize this enlightenment; they are not enlightenment itself. Since the Ch'an masters claim that they can realize this enlightenment by looking directly into one's own nature, then there is no need for all the accoutrements of the religion. They claim that they are the genuine Buddhists, since they, like the Buddha, apprehend the ultimate reality without resorting to such externalities as literature and images.

## SURVIVAL AFTER THE PERSECUTION OF 845

Though Buddhism in general began to decline during and after the T'ang Dynasty, the Ch'an School continued to flourish. It managed to survive the persecution of 845 and to emerge during the succeeding Sung Dynasty as a vigorous movement. Its survival might be attributed to two features. In the first place, its lack of dependence on the external paraphernalia of the religion, such as the scriptures, images, and so forth, enabled it to function and carry on even after the destruction of such externals. In the second place, it escaped the charge of being a parasite on society, for one of the cardinal rules of the school was that every monk must perform some productive labor each day. The Ch'an master responsible for this rule was Huai-hai (720-814), who even in his old age insisted on working in the fields. When his disciples took away his tools so that he could conserve his energy, he refused to eat until they were restored to him. This emphasis on productive activity was the Ch'an answer to the prevailing criticism of Buddhist monks' being parasites, and it enabled the Ch'an to survive when many other schools were to suffer.

# CHAPTER XIII

# THE CHINESE TRIPITAKA

BY the end of the T'ang Dynasty the composition of the Chinese Buddhist canon was practically completed. Almost all the important sutras had been introduced to China and translated into Chinese by foreign and Chinese monks working singly or in groups. It is true that a few scattered translations were made during the following Sung Dynasty, but these were of little significance and did not add anything new. Since this is the case, this chapter on the Chinese canon will close the discussion of Buddhism under the T'ang.

The end product of over a millennium of literary and translation efforts by Chinese and foreign monks is the Chinese Tripitaka, which in its latest edition, the *Taishō*, printed in 1922-1933 in Japan, consists of fifty-five volumes, each one approximately a thousand pages in length. As was to be expected, the translation of the sutras posed problems of technique, form, and principle.

## TRANSLATION TECHNIQUES

In the beginning the process of translation was often an individual affair, with one or more monks collaborating in the work. Some foreign monks attempted the translation themselves, but more often they solicited the assistance of the Chinese. As an example of the former, there was the *Fa-chü-ching* (*Scriptural Texts, Dhammapada*) made in 224 by two Indian monks, Wei-chi-nan and Chu Lü-yen, both of whom knew but little Chinese. In the second case, the foreign monk explained the text in Chinese, and the collaborator wrote down what he heard. This was the prevailing technique during the third and fourth centuries. For instance, Dharmaraksha (fl. 265-313) had the father and son Nieh Ch'eng-yüan and Nieh Tao-chen as his assistants. This technique obviously was subject to serious flaws. In some cases the foreign monk did not understand the written Chinese language and perhaps possessed only a smattering of the spoken language. The foreign monk would explain the text with his limited knowledge of the spoken tongue, but he had no idea of what the Chinese was writing down. The latter merely wrote what he heard, but knew nothing of what was in the original text. Thus a yawning gap existed between the two; the foreign monk could not compare what the Chinese wrote against the original to test the accuracy of the translation, nor could the Chinese check his written words against the foreign language of the text. Room for misunderstanding was therefore present at every step.

There were some variations in this technique in that more than two monks were sometimes involved in the process. For example, in the translation of the *Ssu-a-han-mu-ch'ao-chieh* (*Explanation of Extracts from the Four Āgamas*) during the reign of Emperor Hsiao-wu of the Chin Dynasty (373-396), Kumārabodhi recited the text, Buddharaksha and Chu Fo-nien translated it into Chinese, and Seng-tao with the help of Seng-jui wrote it down in Chinese. An even more elaborate case was the translation of the *Abhidharma-vibhāsha* in 383, when Sanghabhuti dictated the Sanskrit text, Dharmanandi wrote down the dictation, Buddharaksha translated the Sanskrit into Chinese, and the Chinese monk Min-chih copied it. For the *P'o-hsü-mi-lun* (*Treatise by Vasumitra*) Sanghabhuti, Dharmanandi, and Sanghadeva held the Sanskrit text and recited it, Chu Fo-nien translated the Sanskrit into Chinese, and Hui-sung wrote it down. In this last case, instead of a foreign monk, a Chinese did the translating. This presupposed a knowledge of Sanskrit on the part of the Chinese monk. When this was the case there was greater accuracy in the translation, for at least one of the collaborators could compare the Chinese translation with the original text.

With the early translations it very often happened that the foreign monk recited the text from memory. This oral transmission of the text was the accepted method of instruction in India. As late as the fifth century Fa-hsien indicated that the Indian masters usually transmitted the sutras orally, with no written texts. In general the Indian masters proved equal to the task of repeating from memory even long sutras. However, there were known cases of lapses of memory. While translating the *Jñānaprasthāna* (*On the Source of Knowledge*) Sanghadeva forgot one section and required help from another monk to complete it. While translating the *Ching-lü-ching* (*Sutra on the*

*Pure Rules*) Dharmaraksha forgot several sections and only after the written text was obtained was the translation completed. It was probably an awareness of the frailties of human memory that to some extent induced the Chinese monks to go abroad in search of written texts.

Toward the end of the fourth century, when preparations were being made for the translation of the Sarvāstivādin canon, the Chinese cleric Tao-an (312-385) began assembling monks to form translation bureaus. With the arrival of Kumārajīva in 401 the translation bureau became the accepted organ to carry out the task of large-scale translations. Such bureaus were organized under the auspices of the ruling princes, and were usually furnished with spacious quarters within the royal precincts or in some famous temple.[1]

The activities of Tao-an and Kumārajīva ushered in the second period of translation (fifth and sixth centuries), characterized by greater accuracy and improved techniques. The foreign monks were now becoming acquainted with the Chinese language, while Chinese Buddhists were also acquiring a better knowledge of Buddhism and of the foreign language as well. Kumārajīva, for instance, during his long sojourn in Liang-chou, must have become very proficient in his knowledge of Chinese, while his collaborators, such as Seng-chao (384-414) and Seng-jui (fl. fifth century) were themselves masters of Chinese. Seng-jui has left behind an account of the thoroughness with which Kumārajīva pursued his task. The master held the text in his hands and proclaimed its meaning in Chinese. He would explain the foreign text twice, taking great pains to select the exact phraseology to convey the meaning in the original. If some passages were missing from the text he was using, he tried to obtain another copy of the

---

[1] Examples of such bureaus were the Hsi-ming Pavilion and Hsiao-yao Garden in Ch'ang-an, established with Kumārajīva as the head by the Yao Ch'in Dynasty; the Jetavana Monastery in Nanking under Gunabhadra, established by the Liang Dynasty; the Yung-ning Temple under Bodhiruci, established by the Northern Wei Dynasty; the Hsien-yü Palace in Ku-tsang under Dharmakshema, established by the Northern Liang Dynasty; the T'ien-p'ing Temple under Narendrayaśas, established by the Northern Ch'i; the Ta-hsing-shan Temple in Ch'ang-an under Jñānagupta and the Shang-lin Garden in Lo-yang under Yen-tsung, established by the Sui Dynasty; the Hung-fu Temple, Tz'u-en Temple, and the Yü-hua Palace, all under Hsüan-tsang, the Chien-fu Temple under I-tsing, and the Hsing-shan Translation Center under Amoghavajra, all established by the T'ang rulers.

same text to supply the missing portions. In the meantime the audience of monks was discussing the meaning of the passages and passing judgment on the literary style. If there were any doubtful points in the Chinese reading, Kumārajīva checked them with the original. When no more changes were to be made, he then had the translation written in its final form.[2]

With the organization of the translation bureaus it was now possible to have an elaborate division of labor among the various participants, especially when lengthy sutras were being translated. During the Sui and T'ang Dynasties the following divisions were to be found: chief of translation, translator who recited the foreign text and translated it into Chinese, verifier of the meaning in the Sanskrit text, scribe who wrote the translation down in Chinese, verifier of the meaning of the written Chinese, polisher of style, proofreader, and corrector of the Chinese characters.

In the setting up of periods generally followed by Japanese and Chinese writers on Buddhism, the Sui and T'ang Dynasties comprised the third period of translation. Hsüan-tsang and I-tsing were the main figures in this period, and their uniqueness lies in the fact that, in both, the streams of Indian and Chinese cultures merged. Being equally at home with Sanskrit and Chinese, steeped in the religious lore of their faith, deeply pious and humble, they became competent translators. We can clearly see the superiority of Hsüan-tsang as a translator when his translation of the *Madhyāntavibhāga* (*Discourse on Discrimination Between Middle and Extremes*) is compared with that of the same text done by Paramārtha. Hsüan-tsang was the superior stylist, for his translation reads more smoothly, and indicates that he was equally at home in both languages. In Paramārtha's

[2] One example of the tireless quest for the proper translation and style may be seen in Kumārajīva's treatment of a passage found in the *Lotus Sutra, chüan* 8. The Sanskrit reading was rendered literally into Chinese by Dharmaraksha in his version to read, "*T'ien shang shih shih chien, shih chien te chien t'ien shang*" (The gods see men, the men also see the gods). When Kumārajīva came to this passage, he exclaimed that its meaning was in accord with the original but that its expression was excessively plain and uncouth. Seng-jui immediately suggested changing the sentence to read, "*Jen t'ien chiao chieh, liang te hsiang chien*" (Men and gods meet mutually and see each other); whereupon Kumārajīva nodded his vigorous approval.

translation the text is sometimes clumsy and not Chinese in character.[3]

The detailed precision of Hsüan-tsang's translations may also be seen when his translation of the *Vimalakīrti* is compared with Chih Ch'ien's and Kumārajīva's translations of the same sutra. From such comparisons it is clear that the translations of Chih Ch'ien and Kumārajīva preserved chiefly the main gist of the original, whereas Hsüan-tsang's version went into greater detail.

## PROBLEMS IN TRANSLATIONS

As is inevitable whenever translations are made from one language into another, certain problems were faced by the foreign and Chinese translators. One was, of course, the problem of form; was it to be a free or a faithful translation? Secondly, how were the Indian names and terms to be handled; should they be translated or transliterated? From the beginning there was a difference of opinion on the first problem. An Shih-kao and Chih-ch'an favored direct translations which were faithful to the original. Two translators of the third century, Chih Ch'ien and Dharmaraksha, were interested mainly in translating the dominant ideas of the sutras in beautiful and readable style. Style was to be preferred even at the sacrifice of accuracy. This practice of Chih Ch'ien in preserving only the meaning in beautiful style came under attack from Seng-jui, one of the followers of Kumārajīva, who wrote that, though the translations of Kung-

---

[3] Hsüan-tsang's superiority is also seen in his choice of Chinese words to translate technical terms. Here are some examples:

a) *parikalpita*, which means constructing imaginary natures everywhere. Hsüan-tsang uses *pien chi so chih* (*Taishō*, 31,468c); Paramārtha uses *fen-pieh* (*Taishō*, 31,455b). The term used by Hsüan-tsang avoids ambiguity, whereas Paramārtha's term may be used for both *parikalpita* and *vikalpita*, which means mental discriminations.

b) *parinishpanna*, meaning the complete perfect reality of the dharmas. Hsüan-tsang has *yüan ch'eng shih* (*Taishō*, 31,468c); Paramārtha has *chen shih* (*Taishō*, 31,455b). This term *chen shih* is also used to translate the Sanskrit *tattva* (reality). Hsüan-tsang's translation conveys the idea of complete with the character *yüan*, and here again, because of its precision, his term is to be preferred to that of Paramārtha.

c) *samalāmala* (impurity and purity). Hsüan-tsang has *kou ching* (*Taishō*, 31,469a); this is much better than the clumsy expression of Paramārtha, *yu kou wu kou* (*Taishō*, 31,455c).

ming (another name for Chih Ch'ien) were beautiful in style, they were confused as to the main theme, with the result that the glorious objectives were lost in erroneous language, and the real taste rendered insipid by the flowery style.

Serious discussion of the form and style of translations began with Tao-an, who, although not versed in any foreign language, was so familiar with Buddhist doctrines that his commentaries on the sutras were acclaimed even by Kumārajīva. Tao-an felt that one of the greatest weaknesses of the free translation, or translation of only the meaning of the sutra, was that the translators often permitted their own subjective ideas to color the meaning of the text. Consequently, the translations were too often influenced by non-Buddhist concepts. Tao-an therefore advocated that the translator follow the original text as closely as possible. In his opinion there were five points in which the translators deviated from the original, which he called the *wu-shih-pen* or five points in which the meaning of the original was lost: (1) The translators had often reversed the order of sentences in the Indian original in order to conform to Chinese practices. (2) To attract the attention of the Chinese they had frequently preferred a polished literary style to the simple, unadorned substance of the original. (3) They sometimes omitted the repetitions, the chanted verses, and the exclamatory phrases. (4) At times they overlooked the long explanations and commentaries in the middle of a passage. (5) They often neglected a later paragraph which repeated what had been discussed in a former passage.

He also warned, however, that there were three things not easy to accomplish. In translating Buddhist texts, he said, one must strive for faithfulness to the original, but one must also translate in such a way as to render the profound truths in the original understandable to the laity of the present age. This was the first difficult task. The difference between the wisdom of the Buddha and the ignorance of the common people was vast, so that it was not easy to make the subtle words of the sage who lived a thousand years before understandable to the ignorant people of the present. This was the second difficult task. When Ānanda, the personal attendant of the Buddha, recited the sutras at the First Council held soon after the death of the

Buddha, it was still close to the Buddha in point of time; yet Kāśyapa, the monk presiding over the council, asked the five hundred arhats to check over the sutras carefully to ascertain whether any errors had been committed. Now, with the lapse of over a thousand years since that occasion, he asked, how could we ordinary people hope to ascertain and verify the true words of the Buddha? This was the third difficult task. Should one not be careful, concluded Tao-an, when one was translating from the foreign to the Chinese language?

In the hands of Kumārajīva the principles guiding translations took another turn. The illustrious foreign monk felt that translations never could capture the flavor of the original; it was like a person's being fed with food already masticated by another in that not only was the taste lost, but it might even cause nausea. Consequently, Kumārajīva was not in favor of faithful adherence to the original, as was Tao-an; instead, he advocated a process of selecting and shortening the texts and was interested only in retaining the meaning of the original. For him the main goal of the translation was to get at the central theme of the sutra. Although he did not follow the original literally, he was extremely careful in his technique to ensure against errors in translation, making textual emendations and comparisons whenever the occasion required them. At times, however, he would take the liberty of substituting for the benefit of the reader a more widely known proper name for one that was not so familiar, i.e., Mt. Sumeru for the Mandara or Vindhya Mountains, which were not known to the Chinese.

The problem of form was to occupy the attention of yet another Buddhist, Yen Tsung (557-610), a Chinese who had acquired a thorough knowledge of Indian languages. He declared that he would place more value on simple unadorned language if it were close to the truth than on a polished style that went contrary to the meaning of the original. He also listed eight qualifications that a translator must possess: (1) He should be patient, faithful and devoted to the dharma, and committed to a life of service to mankind. (2) He should be disciplined in the rules of moral conduct as he approached the sacred task. (3) He should be thoroughly learned in the Tripitaka and the two vehicles. (4) He should be well read in secular literature and conversant with the classics and poetry. (5) He should be tolerant, impartial, and catholic in his temperament. (6) He should be deeply immersed in the arts and practices of the religion, dispassionate about fame and gain, and disdainful of bragging. (7) He should be versed in Sanskrit, so that he would not be led astray from the meaning in the original text. (8) He should be acquainted with philology, etymology, and lexicography.

Such qualifications might well apply not only to translators of the Buddhist texts, but also to all those who desire to render the literature of one culture into the language of another.

In regard to the question of form the principles advocated by Kumārajīva finally won supremacy. The immense prestige he enjoyed undoubtedly was a deciding factor. Knowledge of this nature of the Chinese Buddhist canon—that it preserves primarily only the meaning of the important portions of sutras—should warn us of its limitations. For instance, if certain portions of a sutra in Sanskrit were lost, it would not be easy to reconstruct that lost portion on the basis of the Chinese translation. Nor would it be easy to use the Chinese to correct variant readings in different versions of the Sanskrit text. For such purposes recourse would have to be had to the Tibetan translations of the canon, which follow the original text almost word for word.

As for the problem of translating or transliterating foreign or proper names, the translators have veered more toward the practice of preserving the original terms and making Chinese transcriptions of them.[4]

---

[4] The early translators of the Han Dynasty had used Taoist terms to translate Buddhist ideas, such as *wu-wei* for nirvāna, *chen-jen* for arhat, *shou-i* for *dhyāna*. Chih Ch'ien also translated *prajñāpāramitā* as *ming-tu*, and Subhuti, a proper name, as *Shan-yeh*. When it was realized that these Chinese terms did not convey the subtle meaning of the original Sanskrit word, the translators decided it would be better to retain the foreign words and transcribe them into Chinese. Thus *prajñāpāramitā* became *pan-jo po-lo-mi-to*, nibbana became *nieh-pan*, arhat or arahan became *a-lo-han*, *dhyāna* became *ch'an*, bodhisattva became *p'u-sa*. In this respect Hsüan-tsang wrote that he left untranslated five types of terms: (a) terms having to do with esoterism, such as *dhāraṇī* or *mandala*; (b) terms pregnant with all sorts of meanings, such as *pao-chia-fan* for *bhagavan*; (c) things which do not exist in China, such as the Jambudvipa tree; (d) terms where one should follow the ancients, such as *anuttara-samyak-sambodhi*; (e) terms productive of merits, such as *prajñāpāramitā*.

## CATALOGUES OF SUTRAS

All these efforts of the Buddhist translators in searching for the proper form and style, the correct phraseology and word, were directed toward the objective of making the Buddhist sutras more understandable and popular among the Chinese. As the number of translations increased, the Chinese monks created another device to assist their reading public in finding their way through the voluminous mass of literature. They began to compile catalogues, giving the names of the translators and the titles of their translations. The first and one of the most important of such catalogues was the *An-lu* (*An's Catalogue*), complete title *Tsung-li-chung-ching-mu-lu* (*Comprehensive Catalogue of Sutras*), compiled by Tao-an in 374. A good deal of our knowledge concerning this catalogue is based on data preserved in the *Ch'u-san-tsang-chi-chi* (*Collection of Records Concerning the Tripitaka*) of Seng-yu, finished ca.518. This work by Seng-yu is the oldest extant catalogue and is a valuable source of information concerning not only Buddhist literature, but also history, for it contains prefaces to the various translations as well as biographies of the early translators. After Seng-yu a succession of catalogues appeared, and eighteen such catalogues are still extant. During the T'ang Dynasty alone nine were compiled. Of these probably the most important is the *K'ai-yüan-shih-chiao-lu* (*Catalogue of the K'ai-yüan Era on Buddhism*), in 20 *chüan*, by Chih-sheng, finished in 730. Being a compendium of all existing titles, it was the starting point for all succeeding compilations. In this work translators were arranged chronologically together with the titles and the number of chapters in their translations. If a sutra had been translated more than once, then the different translations and translators as well as the dates and places of translation were noted. Titles of sutras which were already lost by Chih-sheng's time were also given. Other valuable features were the short biographies of each translator and the division of the sutras into different categories.

Up to the present only translations made from a foreign language into Chinese have been mentioned. To the credit of the Chinese Buddhists two of their works were of such quality that they merited translation into a foreign language. One was the

*Ta-ch'eng-i-chang* (*A Chapter on the Meaning of the Mahāyāna*), by T'an-wu-tsui of the Northern Wei Dynasty, which was admired so much by Bodhiruci that he translated it into a foreign language to be circulated in Central Asia. The other was a Chinese version of the *Mahāparinirvānasūtra* which was rendered into a Turkic language by Liu Shih-ch'ing of the Northern Ch'i Dynasty by orders of the emperor. Liu was said to be the foremost student of foreign languages during his time.

## EDITIONS OF THE CHINESE TRIPITAKA

Before the advent of printing the Buddhist sutras were usually copied by hand and circulated in the form of long paper rolls called *chüan*, which is the word commonly used now to designate a chapter or section. These rolls were made by pasting sheets of paper together. The rich treasure of Buddhist manuscripts found in Tun-huang in northwest China by a Taoist priest at the end of the nineteenth century consisted mainly of such rolls. For example, a *Vinaya* text dated 406, now in the British Museum, runs to twenty-three feet in length. The longest roll measured ninety-nine feet.[5] Even after block printing was started, the sutras still continued to take the form of rolls. In due time, however, an advance was made, with the continuous piece of paper, printed on one side, folded up in leaves to form a book that could be opened conveniently.[6] The next step was to stitch or paste one edge of the folded leaves to form the modern Chinese book. The bulk of the Buddhist sutras in China and Japan are printed and folded in this fashion.

With the advent of block printing during the eighth century the Buddhists who were the pioneers in this development were quick to take advantage of this new medium to spread their literature. For instance, the oldest extant book printed by this new process, the Tun-huang book of 868, now kept in the British Museum, was made by order of one Wang Chieh who wanted to have copies for free distribution for the purpose of reverencing and perpetuating the memory of his parents. It contained ex-

[5] L. Giles, *Descriptive Catalogue of the Manuscripts from Tunhuang in the British Museum*, London, 1957, cat. no. 4523.

[6] A good example of this is cat. no. 5591 of the Tun-huang manuscripts in London, a commentary on the *Lankāvatāra* in 211 leaves.

cerpts from the *Chin-kang-ching* (*Diamond Sutra, Vajrac-chedika*). Before long it was decided to undertake the stupendous task of block printing the entire Chinese Tripitaka. In 972, orders were given by the first emperor of the Sung Dynasty that the huge task of cutting the blocks be started in Ch'eng-tu. In all it is said that 130,000 blocks were cut. By 983 the work of printing the Tripitaka was completed. This first edition of the Tripitaka, commonly designated as the *Shu-pen* (Szechuan edition), consisted of 1,076 items, 480 cases, in 5,048 *chüan*. Following this Szechuan edition, four others were made during the Sung Dynasty.[7]

Meanwhile, the non-Chinese dynasties in the north were also active in printing the Tripitaka. During the years 1031-1064 a complete edition of the Tripitaka in 579 cases was prepared by order of the Liao ruler. The succeeding Chin Dynasty had its edition printed in Shansi during the years 1148-1173; this edition consisted of 682 cases and some 7,000 *chüan*, of which over 4,900 still exist today. Under the Yüan Dynasty several more editions appeared.[8] Besides the above editions of the Chinese canon the Mongols also put one out in the Hsi-hsia or Tangut script, printed in the Ta-wan-shou Temple of Hang-chou under imperial auspices and completed in 1302. One hundred copies of this Tangut

[7] *a*) *Ch'ung-ning wan-shou ta-tsang*, also called *Tung-ch'an Temple Edition*, started in 1080 and completed in 1176. 595 cases in 6,434 *chüan*. Printing done in Fu-chou. The first private printing of the canon.

*b*) *P'i-lu ta-tsang*, also called *Fu-chou K'ai-yüan Temple Edition*, started in 1112, completed 1172. 567 cases in 6,117 *chüan*. Printing also done in Fu-chou.

*c*) *Ssu-ch'i yüan-chüeh tsang*, also called *Nan-Sung Hu-chou Edition*, started in 1132, date of completion uncertain. 1,421 items, 548 cases, 5,918 (var. 5,480) *chüan*. Printing done in Hu-chou, Chekiang. Commonly referred to by Japanese scholars as the Sung canon.

*d*) *Ssu-ch'i tzu-fu tsang*, printed during period 1237-1252 in Hu-chou, Chekiang. 599 cases in 5,740 *chüan*. (There is some question about this edition. Some scholars are inclined to think this is the same as the *Yüan-chüeh tsang*.)

[8] The Mongol editions are called:

*a*) *P'u-ning tsang*, printed in the P'u-ning Temple of Hang-chou during the years 1278-1294. 1,422 items, 587 cases, 6,010 *chüan*. Based on the Hu-chou edition and considered as the Yüan edition by Japanese scholars.

*b*) *Chi-sha tsang*, printed in P'ing-chiang-fu in Kiangsu. Work started as early as 1231 under the Sung and not finished until about 1322 under the Yüan. 1,532 items, 591 cases, 6,362 *chüan*.

*c*) *Hung-fa tsang*, apparently printed in the Hung-fa Temple in Peking. Date of printing 1277-1294. 1,654 items, 7,182 *chüan*.

canon, which consisted of 3,620 *chüan,* were distributed to Buddhist monasteries in the Tangut area. Many copies of this canon are still extant; the Library of Congress in Washington possesses one volume, while the Metropolitan Library in Peking has sixty-three volumes.

Two editions of the canon were printed under the Ming Dynasty, one in Nanking known as the Southern Ming edition and the other in Peking known as the Northern Ming edition. Under the Manchus there were also two editions, one completed in 1677 and the other in 1738. Printing by movable type was started in 1909 on a third edition by the P'in-chia Vihāra in Shanghai and was completed in 1914.

Printing of the Chinese canon was not confined to China alone. Copies of the Sung edition soon found their way to Korea, and in 1011 work commenced on the printing of the first Korean edition, with the Sung version as its basis. This edition was completed during the reign of Wen-tsung (1074-1082) and consisted of 570 boxes, 5,924 *chüan.* Because the wood blocks of this edition were destroyed by the Mongols in 1232, another edition was started in 1236 and completed in 1251. This was the second Korean edition. As the basis of this issue, which consisted of 639 boxes, 6,557 (var. 6,589) *chüan,* the first Sung and Korean and the Liao editions were used.

As a result of Hideyoshi's campaign in Korea at the end of the sixteenth century movable type was brought to Japan, and this led to the printing of the first complete edition of the Chinese canon in Japan by the monk Tenkai during the years 1633-1645. A few years later, in 1681, Tetsugen completed another edition, with one of the Ming versions as the basis.

## MODERN EDITIONS

Modern editions of the canon, however, began with the Tokyo Tripitaka, printed during the years 1880-1885 by the Kōkyō Shoin of Tokyo. This represented a considerable improvement over all previous editions, based as it was on the Korean edition, with the various Chinese and Japanese editions for comparative purposes. The entire work, which was printed with movable type and punctuated, consists of 1,916 items in 8,534 *chüan,* enclosed in 40 cases, 318 stitched volumes. This edition is also called the *Shukusatsu-zōkyō*. At the turn of the century, during the years 1902-1905, the Zōkyō Shoin of Kyoto put out another edition, 36 cases, 347 volumes, commonly referred to as the Kyoto Tripitaka. The text is not punctuated as in the Tokyo edition, but it has the *kaeriten* or punctuation marks, which made it very useful for Japanese scholars. Apparently the Korean and the Tetsugen editions were used as the basis. It is also designated as the *Manji Zōkyō*. From 1905 to 1912 a supplementary section was added in 150 cases, 750 volumes, which comprised materials written by Chinese monks, many of which were not printed in any other edition of the Tripitaka. This supplement was reprinted by the Commercial Press in Shanghai in 1923.

The latest and most critical of all the Japanese editions is the *Taishō Daizōkyō* in 85 volumes, 3,053 items, printed during the years 1922-1933 under the editorship of some of the leading Japanese Buddhist scholars. In the preparation of this edition the Japanese editors had recourse to all the previous Chinese and Korean editions as well as to the Sanskrit, Pali, and Tibetan canons. At present this Taishō Tripitaka is the one most widely used, although the punctuation is sometimes inferior to that of the Tokyo edition. Volumes 1 to 55 consist of the translations and works of foreign and Chinese monks; volumes 56 to 84 comprise works by Japanese monks; while volume 85 contains a miscellaneous body of works, and manuscripts of doubtful texts. Besides the text, this edition also has twelve volumes of illustrations published during the years 1932-1934.

Especially noteworthy were the pious devotion and the generosity of the monks and their loyal supporters, who by their contributions and labor made possible the printing of these voluminous editions. Some of the Chinese and the two Korean editions were prepared under imperial auspices, but in the majority of cases the printing was financed by private contributions from pious laymen anxious to accumulate meritorious karma. The loyal support of these laymen was most strikingly illustrated by the experience of the Japanese monk Tetsugen, who, after soliciting enough funds to pay for the printing, used the money, instead, for the more pressing needs of alleviating famine. This happened not once, but twice, and only after the third time did he finally succeed in using the solicited funds for the avowed purpose of printing the canon.

The Chinese Tripitaka as it is now constituted consists of both Hīnayāna and Mahāyāna texts.[9] On the whole it is justifiable to say that the popularity and influence of the Hīnayāna sutras in China were not so great as those of the Mahāyāna sutras, especially the *Lotus Sutra* and *Vimalakīrti*. The former is sometimes referred to as the Bible of the Buddhists in China and Japan, while the immense popularity of the latter was due to its emphasis on the proper behavior of the Buddhist layman and its doctrine that one could remain in society and still be a good Buddhist.

## THE LOTUS SUTRA

The *Saddharmapuṇḍarīka* or *Lotus of the Good Law* strives to reveal the true and eternal Buddha in the person of Śākyamuni, who appeared on earth for the salvation of mankind. This main thesis is illustrated in similes and parables, visions and prophecies, warnings and assurances. The sutra has its setting on Vulture Peak, where the Buddha is seated immersed in contemplation, surrounded by an immense concourse of gods and men as well as bodhisattvas and demons. The peak itself is illuminated by rays emitted by the Buddha and is strewn with heavenly flowers thrown by the gods.

The Buddha arises from his contemplation to preach that the dharma is beyond the comprehension of ordinary beings, that only those with faith can grasp it. His aim is to disclose the methods by which beings can become enlightened. Though the truth is one, the means to attain it are varied, because the beings to be converted are different in character, temperament,

[9] In the *Taishō* edition the division of the canon is as follows:
Vols.  1-21—Translations of the discourses of the Buddha
Vols. 22-24—Translations of the *Vinaya*
Vols. 25-29—Translations of the *Abhidharma*
Vols. 30-31—Translations of Mādhyamika and Vijñānavāda texts
Vol. 32    —Translations of *śāstras* or treatises
Vols. 33-43—Commentaries written by Chinese masters
Vols. 44-48—The literature of the various Chinese schools of Buddhism
Vols. 49-52—Historical records, such as biographies, annals, travel accounts, Chinese polemical literature
Vols. 53-54—Encyclopedias and glossaries
Vol. 55    —Buddhist catalogues of sutras.

and inclination. He opens three paths: the path of the hearers, for those who delight in listening to the discourse of the Buddha; the path of the Solitary Buddha, for those who are inclined to seclusion and meditation; and the path of the bodhisattva for those who wish to save and enlighten all sentient beings before entering nirvāna themselves. The opening of these three ways to the one goal is the *upāyakauśalya* or the skill-in-means of the Buddha. This doctrine of the skill-in-means gave the Buddhist philosophers the clue to explain the diversity that exists within Buddhism.

To explain this doctrine the Buddha resorts to numerous parables, the most famous of which is that of the burning house. In a house inhabited by a father and his numerous children a fire arises. All the children are playing in the house, and so cannot hear the cries of the father outside. He cannot carry them out one by one, for this will take too long, and, besides, there is only one door in the house. The father suddenly remembers that the children love carts, so he shouts that there are all kinds of carts outside—bullock carts, goat carts, antelope carts. When the children hear this, they all rush out of the burning house and so are saved. They now ask their father for the carts, and are each given a golden decorated bullock cart. In this parable the father is the Buddha, who by the promise of the three carts is able to lure people out of the world of lust and passion, so that he can teach them the one true path to the truth.

This parable of the burning house seems like justification for deceit, but the Buddha denies this specifically. In various passages of the *Lotus Sutra* we read: "Believe me, Śāriputra, I speak what is real, I speak what is truthful, I speak what is right. It is difficult to understand the exposition of the mystery of the Tathāgata, Śāriputra, for in elucidating the law, Śāriputra, I use hundred thousands of various skillful means, such as different interpretations, indications, explanations, illustrations." "In respect to these things, believe my words, Śāriputra, value them, take them to heart, for there is no falsehood in the Tathāgata, Śāriputra." "Such, young men of good family, is the Tathāgata's manner of teaching; when the Tathāgata speaks in this way, there is from his part no falsehood."[10]

[10] *Sacred Books of the East*, 21,39,43,304. There is a remarkable resem-

After the parable of the burning house the Buddha Śākyamuni proceeds to assure his followers of their future destiny—that they will all become Buddhas and bodhisattvas in the future and that these rewards are the result of causes extending to the remote past. He tells them that the essence of bodhisattvahood consists of adoration of the *Lotus Sutra* through ceremonies and recitations and of preaching its truths to others. After he exhorts the followers to revere the truth revealed in this holy work and to preach it to others and after he gives practical instructions as to how to spread the truths, the first part of the sutra comes to a close at the end of the fourteenth chapter.

Beginning with the fifteenth chapter the second half of the sutra opens, and here the true eternal personality of the Buddha is portrayed. We are told that so long as Buddhists believe that their master achieved Buddhahood in Bodhgaya at a certain time, they fail to comprehend the true nature of the Buddha, who has become enlightened from eternity, and they fail to realize their own true being, which is also eternal as the Buddha is eternal. To help convey this message a host of saints appear from out of the earth, all acknowledging the Buddha as their master. When asked who these saints are, Buddha replies that they have been his disciples since the eternal past. This reply surprises and puzzles his listeners, who wonder how one who had attained enlightenment only a short while ago could have converted these saints from the eternal past.

To remove the bewilderment of his followers the Buddha now reveals his true identity; he declares to the multitude that the master who lived and passed away was but a corporeal manifestation of the eternal Buddha on earth. The true Tathāgata, the embodiment of cosmic truth, neither is born nor dies, but lives

blance between these passages and one in the *Contra Celsum* of Origen, where he wrote: "God transforms the power of the Logos, who is made to feed the human soul, according to the condition of each separate person. To one, as Scripture says, the Logos becomes 'reasonable milk, without admixture'; to another, still weak in the Faith, He becomes a strengthening oil; to the perfect, He is solid food. And yet the Logos never deceives as to His true nature by thus feeding each person according to his needs. There is in Him neither lying nor deceit." See H. de Lubac, *Aspects of Buddhism*, New York, 1954, 108. Here Origen contends that the Logos is always truth, even though He may seem to be indulging in deceit temporarily. He therefore developed the theory of the "economy of the lie," very much like the skill-in-means of the Buddha.

and works from eternity to eternity. Those who become Buddhists also share in the eternal life of the Buddha. Having revealed the eternal past, the Buddha now assures his followers of an everlasting future also.

The *Lotus Sutra* thus teaches a gospel of universal salvation, with the Buddha as the manifestation of the eternal truth, leading all into the path of enlightenment. His power of salvation is compared to that of rain, which is uniform in essence but enables all kinds of plants to grow and flourish. It also teaches the doctrine of the eternal Buddha and the doctrine that this eternity is shared by those who have faith and are devoted to him.

Another idea stressed is the concept of the bodhisattva, that compassionate being destined for bodhi or enlightenment, who postpones his own entry into nirvāna until he has saved all sentient beings. Of these bodhisattvas the most famous is Avalokiteśvara, to whom a whole chapter in the *Lotus Sutra* is dedicated. In this chapter it is taught that when a person is faced with the dangers of fire, water, or banditry, all he needs to do is to invoke the name of Avalokiteśvara, and the bodhisattva will immediately come to his aid. Furthermore, such Mahāyāna teachings as the doctrine of the skill-in-means and the gospel of the one vehicle are also stressed in the sutra.

It is not known just when the *Lotus Sutra* was compiled and by whom. In all probability it was already in existence at the beginning of the Christian era. The first partial translation into Chinese, made about the middle of the third century, is now lost, but the one by Dharmaraksha, finished in 286, is still extant. However, the most popular and authoritative Chinese translation is that done by Kumārajīva in 406, and it is this version that was the basic text of the T'ien-t'ai School in China and Japan. Nichiren in Japan found in the teachings of the sutra the consolation that sustained him and the incentive that inspired him throughout his life.

To summarize, the *Lotus Sutra* was the most popular sutra in China because it was studied and recited by practically all the Buddhist schools there, because it contained the most comprehensive statement of the revolutionary Mahāyāna doctrines of the eternal Buddha and universal salvation, and because it had been the inspiration for Buddhist art and practices during the past millennium and a half in China. It has been likened to a powerful drama or a marvelous symphony, attracting and keeping the attention of people by its sheer imagery, pageantry, vision, similes, and parables.[11]

## THE VIMALAKĪRTI-NIRDEŚA SUTRA

Besides the *Lotus Sutra*, another Mahāyāna text, the *Vimalakīrti*, has been the source of inspiration and strength to the Chinese Buddhist. Seven Chinese translations were made of this sutra, of which three are still extant: the Chih Ch'ien translation of the third century, the Kumārajīva translation of 406, and that by Hsüan-tsang in the seventh century. Since the earliest Chinese translation, now lost, was done ca. A.D. 188, it is likely that the original text was in existence before then, for it requires some time for a sutra to become authoritative. Moreover, the sutra was frequently quoted by the eminent philosopher Nāgārjuna (second century A.D.). It must be classified as Mahāyāna since it stresses such ideas as skill-in-means, the perfections, and great compassion. The emphasis of the sutra is on the conduct and practice of a bodhisattva as against those of the hearer or solitary Buddha; it places great import on the life of the layman as against the ascetic life of the monastery. No longer mentioned are the four truths, eightfold path, or the chain of causation; in their place are stressed kindly beneficent deeds, compassion, equanimity, and the ten perfections. The Buddha as the manifestation of the eternal truth takes the place of historical Śākyamuni.

The sutra probably arose out of the dissatisfaction of laymen with the corruption and inactivity of the monks who shut themselves up within the walls of the monasteries without looking after the needs of the laity. This dissatisfaction is expressed in the glorification of the layman Vimalakīrti and the despisal heaped on such Hīnayāna arhats as Sariputta, Ānanda, and Kassapa, who are depicted here as ignoramuses.

Briefly, the contents of the sutra may be summarized as follows:

[11] The Sanskrit text of the *Lotus Sutra* has been translated into English by H. Kern and published in vol. 21 of the *Sacred Books of the East*, while the Chinese version of Kumārajīva has been rendered into English by W. E. Soothill and entitled *The Lotus of the Wonderful Law*. There is also a French translation made from the Sanskrit by E. Burnouf entitled *La Lotus de la Bonne Loi*.

Vimalakīrti the layman is sick in bed, and the Buddha wants to send his disciples to inquire about his health. Śāriputra, Moggallana, Kāśyapa, and Ānanda are all asked to go, but they refuse on the grounds that they are not worthy. For instance, Ānanda gives the following reason for his refusal, "I remember formerly my Lord had been somewhat indisposed. Some milk was required to restore him to health. Therefore holding a bowl in my hand, I stood at the door of a wealthy brahman. Then Vimala came to me and said, 'Well, O Ānanda, why dost thou stand here so early in the morning with a bowl in thy hand?' I replied, 'O sir, our Lord is somewhat indisposed. Some milk is required to restore his health. Therefore I am here with a bowl in my hand.' Vimala said, 'Stay, stay, Ānanda, never utter such words; the body of Tathāgata possesses the nature of adamant, as in him all wickedness is exterminated, and all goodness is combined together. What illness, what suffering can he suffer? Go thou away in silence. O Ānanda, thou should not insult the Tathāgata, thou should not let strangers hear these coarse words. . . . If the heretical teachers hear this, they might think thus, "Could he be a teacher who is incapable of curing his own illness, while pretending to cure the disease of others?" Go thou away in haste and in silence, never again be heard by anybody. O Ānanda, thou should know that the body of the Tathāgata is the body of the law. It is not the body of desire. Buddha is the world-honored one above the three states of existence. The body of the Tathāgata is without impurities, for all impurities have been destroyed. The body of the Tathāgata is uncreated, and does not descend into individual destinies. What illness can such a body suffer?' "[12]

After all the other arhats have given similar reasons for refusing to go to call on Vimala, the Buddha finally beckons to Mañjuśrī, the bodhisattva of wisdom. Mañjuśrī answers, "It is difficult to discuss with that excellent man; he has attained to such profound knowledge of the true nature of things; he is able to preach the essence of the law; he is in possession of unique eloquence and unimpeded wisdom; he is well acquainted with the exemplary manner of a bodhisattva; he has unravelled all the secrets of the Buddhas; he has subdued all evil ones; he plays

[12] *Taishō*, 14,542a, translated in *Eastern Buddhist*, 3,2,151-152, with numerous changes.

with all the supernatural powers; he is perfect in wisdom and the necessary means; yet in compliance with the order of the Buddha, I will go to inquire about his health."[13]

When the throng hears that Mañjuśrī is going to visit Vimala, they anticipate some excellent discourses between the two; so they all follow him. The two immediately plunge into a conversation on what constitutes the sickness of a bodhisattva. In the midst of the conversation Śāriputra enters, looking around for a seat. Not finding any, he says to himself, "Where can the assembly sit?" Vimala reads his thoughts, and so he asks Śāriputra whether he has come to hear the law or to look for seats. Embarrassed by this, Śāriputra replies that he came to hear the law; whereupon Vimala says, "He who seeks for the law never spares either body or life, how much less should he think about seats."[14]

After this amusing interlude, in which the wisest of the Hīnayāna arhats, Śāriputra, is acutely embarrassed, Vimala and Mañjuśrī continue their conversations on such questions as the power of the Buddha, the transcendent nature of his body, abiding in the uncreated, or the doctrine of nonduality. In the midst of these discussions Vimala manifests his supernatural powers and creates a bowl of food for all those present. Seeing only the one bowl of food, some of the arhats harbor doubts as to whether it would suffice for all. Vimala immediately assures them by saying that the food prepared by one who was endowed with wisdom and liberation is never exhausted. (The Christian parallel to this episode immediately comes to mind.) Finally in the discussion on nonduality Mañjuśrī asks Vimala to give his explanation. Vimala, however, remains silent; whereupon Mañjuśrī praises him by saying, "Well done, well done, ultimately not to have any letters or words, this is indeed to enter into the doctrine of non-duality."[15] This is the "thunderous silence" of Vimala so often referred to by the Buddhists.

There is no question but that the *Vimalakīrti* is one of the most popular of Mahāyāna sutras. It is this sutra that inspired much of the sculpture in Lung-men and Yün-kang during the

---

[13] *Ibid.*, 14,544ab, translated in *ibid.*, 3,3,233, with some changes.
[14] *Eastern Buddhist*, 3,4,336.
[15] *Taishō*, 14,551c, translated in *Eastern Buddhist*, 4,2,183.

Northern Wei Dynasty. During the T'ang Dynasty episodes from the sutra were expanded into stories and ballads which were then recited before the multitudes gathered during the temple festivities. Undoubtedly the figure Vimalakīrti had much to do with this popularity of the sutra. Here was a layman rich and powerful, a brilliant conversationalist, a respected householder who surrounded himself with the pleasures of life, but was also a faithful and wise disciple of the Buddha, a man full of wisdom and thoroughly disciplined in his conduct. Indeed, the educated elite of Chinese society must have felt that here was a model that they could emulate, for though Vimala was a Buddhist, he could very easily have been taken for a Confucian gentleman.

## OTHER SUTRAS

The *Lotus Sutra* and *Vimalakīrti* have been discussed in detail primarily because of their popularity and influence in China. Besides these two, there are other sutras which have also been translated into European languages. The *Chü-she-lun* of Vasubandhu, a comprehensive compendium of Sarvāstivādin doctrine, has been translated into French by L. de la Vallee Poussin. The same scholar was responsible for rendering into French the basic text of the Idealistic School, the *Ch'eng-wei-shih-lun*, entitled *La Siddhi de Hiuan-tsang*. In both of these instances Hsüan-tsang was responsible for the Chinese translation. Three other Idealistic School texts have also been translated: *She-ta-ch'eng-lun*, rendered into French by E. Lamotte and entitled *La Somme du Grand Vehicule d'Asanga*; *Ta-ch'eng ch'i-hsin lun*, translated into English by D. T. Suzuki and entitled *Asvaghosha's Discourse on the Awakening of Faith*; *Wei-shih erh-shih lun*, translated into English by the American scholar C. H. Hamilton. In the Chinese canon there is a lengthy treatise on the doctrines of the Mādhyamika School, the *Ta-chih-tu-lun*, of 100 *chüan*, reputed to be a work of Nāgārjuna. Students of Buddhism in the Occident are indebted to Lamotte for his prodigious efforts in translating a portion of this text into French, entitled *La Traite de la Grande Sagesse de Nāgārjuna*.

These translations have initiated the western world to some of the variety and richness of this vast field of Chinese Buddhist literature. However, only the surface has been touched, and a huge terrain of virgin territory remains still to be explored. To cite just a few examples, none of the *Vinayas* in the Chinese canon has been translated, nor has the important literature of the T'ien-t'ai and Hua-yen Schools been translated in their entirety. Until this is done, we must continue humbly to acknowledge the contributions of Kumārajīva and Hsüan-tsang and our own delinquency in not furthering the task of cultural interchange which they initiated.

DECLINE

# CHAPTER XIV

# MEMORIES OF A GREAT TRADITION: SUNG DYNASTY

T H E half century of turmoil, disunity, and struggle that followed the downfall of the T'ang Dynasty was finally ended in 960 by the unification of the Chinese Empire under the Sung Dynasty. It must be emphasized, however, that the Buddhism which developed under the Sung differed from that of the Sui T'ang era in several aspects. Of all the schools that arose during the T'ang, only the Ch'an and Pure Land remained active under the new dynasty. It is true that the monastic community was probably more numerous and the economic activities of the sangha were even more extensive than under the T'ang. However, no outstanding Buddhist cleric such as Hsüan-tsang, Fa-tsang, or Chih-i emerged; no new school of Buddhist thought developed; no important Buddhist sutra was translated. The intense intellectual activity within Buddhist circles during the previous dynasty, that brought out so many diverse systems of thought, was conspicuous by its absence under the Sung. In Buddhist art and architecture it appears that the great advances were already in the past, so that the main Sung contribution was one of continuation and minor changes. After the tremendous outburst of the T'ang the religion seems to have spent itself, and the results of the persecution of 845 merely accelerated the decline in the creative impulse within the sangha. Though the religious community continued to build monasteries, to ordain monks, and to carry on its economic and religious activities under the Sung, it did so under "the slackening momentum of a faith which for all its wealth and majesty survived more as a great tradition than as a spiritual force."[1]

After each of the previous persecutions of 446 and 574 the religion was able to stage a spectacular recovery and recoup its losses within a few decades. After the persecution of 845, however, there was no such recovery. Instead, the sangha declined

[1] A. Soper, Hsiang-kuo-ssu, *Journal of the American Oriental Society*, 68,1 (1948), 36.

farther as an intellectual and spiritual force. One is compelled, therefore, to look for factors peculiar to the Sung Dynasty that were responsible for this failure of the sangha to reassert itself.

## MORAL DEGENERATION OF THE SANGHA

The first and probably the most important factor was the moral degeneration of the sangha. The sangha is the embodiment of the Buddhist dharma, and so long as the members of the monastic community remain pure and sincere in living the religious life and observing the rules of discipline, the dharma will continue to live and flourish. During the Sung Dynasty the financial distress faced by the government was such that in order to raise revenue the imperial authorities had to resort to two measures which had a deleterious effect upon the moral caliber of the monks.

The financial distress faced by the Sung Dynasty was brought about by two conditions, one external and one internal. Externally the dynasty was constantly threatened by invasions and attacks along the northern frontiers, first by the Khitans and Tanguts, and then by the Jurchen or Golden Hordes. A large standing army was therefore required to defend the northern borders.[2] In addition to the huge amount of military expenses, the Sung government also paid a large amount of indemnity annually as part of its policy of buying peace with the northern barbarians. According to the treaty of 1005 the Sung guaranteed an annual payment to the Khitans of 100,000 taels or ounces of silver and 200,000 bolts of silk; later this was increased to 200,000 taels and 300,000 bolts.

Along with these defense expenditures there was also the enormous outlay needed to support a large number of supernumeraries in the government, most of whom got on the payroll by the Sung system of official protection, by which sons and grandsons and relatives of officials were recommended for posts. In 1088, for instance, the total of government employees was said

[2] At the beginning of the dynasty there were only 378,000 troops in the army, but a century later, during the period 1064-1067, the number rose to 1,162,000. In 1065 the expense for the army was said to have totaled 50,000,000 strings of cash, whereas the total annual tax income during the era 1064-1067 was said to have been only 44,000,000 strings—far below the requirements to maintain the army.

to be four times that of the period 1004-1007; in 1109 the complaint was that the bureaucracy had increased tenfold over that of the preceding reign. Even after one discounts some tendencies toward exaggeration, it is apparent that the national treasury was severely strained by the necessity of supporting a large number of surplus officials.

Among the various schemes which the dynasty resorted to in order to cope with this continuing financial crisis, there were two that had to do with the moral fiber of monks: the sale of monk certificates and the sale of the honorary title Master of the Purple Robe.

## SALE OF MONK CERTIFICATES

Heretofore it had been the practice to grant monk certificates to those who were officially ordained, usually after they had successfully passed an examination on the sacred scriptures. Once the cleric obtained this certificate, he was exempted from taxation and the labor service required of all adults. Because of this the document possessed considerable economic value.

As the demand for revenues increased during the Sung Dynasty, the Bureau of National Sacrifice, the organ which issued the certificates, felt that considerable revenue could be derived from selling the ordination certificates to all those wanting to become monks. In 1067 the sale of certificates was adopted as an official policy of the government.[3]

---

[3] At first the number of certificates sold ran to about 3,000-4,000 annually, but in the decade after 1075 the average was around 9,000 annually. In 1083 a maximum limit of 10,000 was set, but this figure was no sooner determined than it was broken; for, in the first four months of 1084, 26,000 certificates were put on sale. With the advent of the twelfth century, the limit was set at 15,000 in 1108 and 30,000 in 1110. Demand for the document became greater and greater as time went on; in 1132 between 50,000 and 60,000 were said to have been sold, and between 1161-1170 it was estimated that over 120,000 were issued and sold.

When the certificates were first offered for sale, the selling price as established by the government was 130 strings of cash each. In 1089 it rose to 170 strings; 1101, 220 strings; 1161, 510 strings; 1185, 700 strings; 1192, 800 strings. The above figures were the official rate, but it sometimes happened that the actual selling price in the open market was less than the official price; thus in 1110, when the official rate was 220 strings, the actual selling price was only 90 strings. Unfortunately, there is no information about the income the government derived from the sale of these certificates, for it is not known in any given year how many were sold at the official rate and how many at the market rate.

According to the original idea, possession of the document was evidence that the holder was a duly ordained monk, and entitled to the privileges of one in that category. However, now that these certificates could be brought, it was no longer necessary for the possessor to shave his head and wear the clerical robe; he could remain at home and carry on his normal social and economic duties and still claim the privileges of exemption from taxation and the labor services. It was this feature that was responsible for the great demand for the certificate by the populace. Very often the rich would buy a number of certificates, not to become monks, but to enjoy the exemptions, and also to keep them as a form of wealth, a sort of government bond, so to speak, to be sold again when the selling price became favorable. There were still other types of people who benefited from the sale. These were the fugitives from justice, whose purchase of the certificates permitted them to take refuge in the monasteries, where they could not be reached by the civil laws, and the lazy, who were attracted by the prospects of being clothed and fed without doing any physical labor.

One inevitable result of such a policy was the lowering of the caliber of monks joining the sangha. Under the monk examination system the candidate for ordination had to demonstrate at least some knowledge of the sacred scriptures. Now no such requirement was necessary, for all that was needed was the proper sum of money to buy the certificate. Thus it was possible to find within the sangha monks who had no knowledge of the sacred literature or the religious discipline. Prestige of the monastic community declined under such circumstances and monks were looked upon with ridicule and disrespect. This attitude is best illustrated by some of the proverbs prevalent after the Sung Dynasty:

The monk picks up a copy of the scriptures, but he cannot even read it clearly.

When a blind man sees money, his eyes open; when a monk sees money, he will even sell the sacred scriptures.

In front of the gates of hell are many Buddhist monks and Taoist priests.

While in his mouth there is Amitābha, in his heart there is a nest of poisonous snakes.

This lowering of prestige was accentuated by the other practice, sale of the honorary title Master of the Purple Robe.

## SALE OF THE TITLE MASTER OF THE PURPLE ROBE

The practice of conferring this title was started by Empress Wu Tse-t'ien, who granted it to her favorite monk Huai-i. Possession of the title permitted the holder to wear a purple-colored clerical robe, purple being the color reserved for high-ranking officials. Being different in color from the approved clerical garment, it was not looked upon with much favor by monks in the beginning. But as succeeding emperors continued to confer the title as an honor, and as it was the highest honor the state could confer on a monk, it gradually became the object of desire of those clerics who sought after worldly favors and honors. During the early Sung Dynasty the title was granted to those monks who could correctly answer ten questions on the Tripitaka. Only those who had been ordained for five years were eligible for the title. Monks over eighty years of age automatically became recipients. Also eligible were those Chinese monks who had traveled abroad in search of the scriptures, or who had assisted in the translation of the sutras, and those foreign monks who were active in translation and missionary work. In order to indicate different gradations in honor, two, four, or six additional characters were affixed to the title—the more characters, the higher the honor. On the whole the title was not so easy to obtain during the early Sung period, and it was this very feature, coupled with the prestige attached to the title, that aroused the cupidity of those monks interested in fame and honor. Ambitious monks were now willing to pay for the privilege of having the title, and it was only a matter of time before the Sung authorities put the title up for sale. This began about the same time that the government began selling certificates. It appears that the selling price was lower for the title than for the certificate, since the buying clientele was limited only to monks. In 1130 the title with two characters sold for about a hundred strings; that with four characters, for two hundred strings. In 1129 it was estimated that five thousand titles were sold.

The Buddhist sangha as originally constituted was to be a body of monks without worldly desires, untainted by worldly gain, pure in character, and devoted to the religious life. Yet during the Sung Dynasty ordination certificates were bought and sold, honorary clerical titles became objects of commercial transactions. While these transactions benefited the national treasury to some extent,[4] they undoubtedly wrought unpleasant results in the sangha, for the sale of the monk certificates opened the floodgates to all kinds of undesirable elements, thereby contributing to the deterioration of the moral and spiritual fiber of the community of monks.

## RISE OF NEO-CONFUCIANISM

A second factor that contributed to the decline of Buddhism during the Sung Dynasty was the emergence of Neo-Confucianism as a strong intellectual movement. The forerunners of the movement, Han Yü (768-824) and Li Ao (d. ca.844), had already appeared during the T'ang Dynasty, but it was during the Sung that the movement assumed proportions which enabled it to challenge successfully the claims of Buddhism for the minds of the Chinese.

[4] In view of the need for revenue faced by the government, it may be argued that the authorities were really aggravating the situation by promoting the sale of ordination certificates. While the government derived some income from the sale, it was also increasing the number of tax-exempt adults by its policy, so that it was being deprived of the tax revenue it would normally collect from those male adults. The Sung authorities were undoubtedly aware of this, for they soon came up with another scheme to raise money from the sangha; the imposition of a tax on all monks, known as the payment for the privilege of being exempt from taxation and the labor services, or, as it was more facetiously called, a payment to enjoy leisure. Monks were divided into different categories according to their status and the type of monastery to which they were attached, and the tax to be paid varied with the category.

The categories of monks established were: ordinary monk, Master of the Purple Robe, Master with Two Characters, Master with Four Characters, Master with Six Characters, Temple officials below Abbot, Abbot. Monasteries were divided into those concentrating on the *Vinaya* and sutras, and Ch'an. An ordinary monk belonging to the former type of monastery had to pay five strings of cash as his tax, but if he belonged to a Ch'an monastery, he had to pay only two strings. A Master of the Purple Robe with Six Characters had to pay nine strings of cash and an abbot, fifteen strings if they belonged to monasteries specializing in the *Vinaya* and sutras, but only six and ten strings respectively if they were Ch'an. The favorable consideration accorded to the Ch'an monks was undoubtedly due to the fact that they engaged in productive labor in the fields and were not considered parasites on society.

During its heyday under the T'ang, Buddhism had captured the imagination of the Chinese with its religious and philosophical ideas. Chinese scholars consorted with Buddhist monks and became acquainted with their systems of thought while continuing their study of the Confucian classics to qualify for the civil service examinations. Sooner or later, however, it was bound to happen that some Chinese scholars, deeply imbued with the Confucian sense of this-worldliness and social responsibility, would arise to protest against the Buddhist emphasis on other-worldliness and the illusoriness of all phenomena. Such a development took place during the Sung Dynasty to give rise to Neo-Confucianism, which marked a return by the Chinese thinkers to their own cultural heritage. They claimed that they could find in the Confucian classics a system of ethics and metaphysics which could serve as counterarguments to the Buddhist way of life and doctrines.

One of the main points attacked by the Neo-Confucianists was the Buddhist doctrine of *śūnyatā*—that the phenomenal world is not real but only an illusion. To oppose this doctrine Chang Tsai (1020-1077) put forth a metaphysical system based on the theory that ch'i, ether or matter, existed at the beginning of the world. He held that ch'i consolidated itself into things in the beginning, and that things dissolved into ch'i in the end. Thus one could not say that things end in nothingness as the Buddhists contended. In his masterpiece entitled *Western Inscription* he applied this theory to the realm of human relations. Since all things in the universe arise from the same ch'i, then "the people of the world are our brothers; things are my companions. . . . All those who are exhausted and prone to illness, maimed and deformed, lonely and childless, widows and widowers, are our brothers and sisters who are in difficulties and have no one to appeal to. If one protects them at the proper time, this is to show the reverence of a son. If one does one's work with joy and without grudge, this exemplifies the purity of filial piety. To do the contrary is to deviate from one's moral virtue, and he who violates jen (benevolence or human-heartedness) is a robber."[5]

This essay was admired and wielded great influence on the Neo-Confucians because, first, it extended the concept of jen

[5] *Chang Heng-chü chi*, 1,1b-3a.

far beyond the usual Confucian limitations. The Confucian jen emphasized gradations beginning with the parents and family, and then reaching into the community. Now, according to Chang, it embraced all under heaven. Second, it expressed accurately the Neo-Confucian attitude toward life. One should not try to escape from life and its responsibilities, as the Buddhists advocated; rather, it was the duty of everyone to lead a normal life and to do his daily duty as a member of society. "In life I shall serve unresistingly, and when death comes, I shall be at peace."[6]

The Neo-Confucianist attack against the Buddhist *śūnyatā* took a new turn in the hands of Ch'eng Hao (1032-1085), Ch'eng Yi (1033-1107), and Chu Hsi (1130-1200). The weapon which these philosophers used was the concept of li, reason or the ultimate principle, which stipulated that everything in the world has its own reason and that all things can be understood in the light of that reason. The reason of man lies in his nature, which is made up of the four virtues: benevolence, righteousness, propriety, and wisdom. These are the essential features of man's nature. Hence Ch'eng Yi enunciated the truth that human nature is reason. He held to this view because he believed that human nature is essentially good—a belief that thus followed the ideas of the ancient Chinese philosopher Mencius—and that this goodness is exemplified by the four virtues. Convinced that reason is at the basis of all phenomena, Ch'eng Yi was intensely interested in the knowledge of the physical world, which he believed to be real and existing, not illusory and empty. One can learn about this underlying reason by thinking, studying, reading books, entering into discussions, and so forth. His method was to study one thing one day, another the next. After a long process of such investigation of things one will suddenly be awakened one day to the understanding of reason, he claimed.

Likewise, the greatest philosopher of the Sung Dynasty, Chu Hsi, also based his attack against Buddhism on li or reason. In one of his works he wrote that the greatest difference between the Confucians and the Buddhists was that what the former called reality was regarded by the latter as emptiness. This reality

6 Fung, *op.cit.*, 2,495.

of which Chu Hsi spoke was li, which he said was one, but which was shared by millions of things to acquire essence.

Like the Ch'eng brothers, Chu Hsi followed the dictum that human nature is li. Since such moral sentiments as filial piety, brotherhood, loyalty, honesty, benevolence, righteousness, propriety, and wisdom are endowments of li, the Neo-Confucianists argued that the Buddhists were ignorant of the nature of li when they followed their fallacious theory of *śūnyatā* or emptiness. The duty of man, according to them, is to comprehend this li, so that he may appreciate more fully his existence on this earth.

For Chu Hsi the method of attaining understanding of li is to investigate things. As one investigates more and more, one gradually gets closer and closer to understanding. Eventually, after sufficient effort has been expended, understanding bursts upon the individual. When this takes place, then his highest nature is realized, and he believes with Chang Tsai that all people are his brothers and sisters and all creatures his companions.

To achieve full understanding of li one must practice concentration of mind. The mind must be sincere and serious; it must get rid of all desires, excitement, and stirrings, and control all passions of joy and anger; it must be characterized by equanimity and steadfastness. As Ch'eng Yi said, the mind must be preserved in calm and peace so that it will give correct responses to all that approaches it.

This emphasis on discipline of mind turned the attention of the Neo-Confucianists inward, and mind gradually assumed more importance than things. Neo-Confucianism now passed into the second phase, in which the main figure during the Sung Dynasty was Lu Hsiang-shan (1139-1192). With the Ch'eng-Chu School knowledge begins with sensations, with the investigation of things in the world. Knowledge thus comes from the outside. With Lu, however, mind is complete in itself. He emphasizes the importance of innate knowledge which exists within the mind apart from sensation and experience, without the exercise of thought. Such innate knowledge exists without being acquired from the outside. Whereas the Ch'eng-Chu School says that human nature is li, Lu Hsiang-shan says that mind is reason.

The discussion of the Neo-Confucianists brought about a resurgence of interest in the Confucian classics. Instead of emptiness, impermanence, and the Buddha-nature, the concepts which engaged the attention of the Chinese were now li or reason, ch'i or matter, mind, and the nature of man. The educated Chinese now had a system based, not on the Buddhist denial of the world, but on the Confucian acceptance of his social responsibilities. Consequently, Confucianism was restored to its position of intellectual eminence, and since the best minds of the land were no longer interested in Buddhism, the religion inevitably suffered from intellectual decadence.

## THE EXAMINATION SYSTEM

The process of intellectual decadence was accentuated by yet another development under the Sung. The civil service examination system, initiated during the Han Dynasty, improved and expanded under the T'ang, reached the peak of its development under the Sung. Held every three years, these examinations provided an avenue whereby the most learned and talented scholars of the empire could rise to positions of highest honor and authority in the imperial bureaucracy. Since prestige and power were practically assured to those who successfully passed the examinations, the outstanding men of the times very naturally devoted their time and energy to the study of the Confucian classics which formed the subject matter of the examinations. Again, this resulted in a decrease in the number of first-rate men who found refuge in Buddhism.

## POPULARITY OF THE CH'AN AND PURE LAND SCHOOLS

Another factor that contributed to the decline of Buddhism was the popularity of the Ch'an and Pure Land Schools during the Sung Dynasty. Chinese Ch'an was iconoclastic; it had no reverence for literature, images, or rituals; it discouraged the study of the texts and the exercises of the intellect. Instead, it advocated intuition, quickness of mind, keenness of wit, and lightning decisions. Likewise, the Pure Land School also discouraged study and learning, emphasizing only faith and the mechanical repetition of formulas. Such features might make Buddhism fascinating and attractive, but they did not enrich the religious life nor were they conducive to lively discussion on points of doctrine, so necessary for intellectual stimulation. It therefore comes as no surprise that with the supremacy of these two schools, with their antitextual and antischolastic tendencies, there has not emerged any writer or thinker within Buddhism since the Sung Dynasty comparable in stature to such figures as Tao-sheng and Hsüan-tsang. For, after all, the strength and vigor of Buddhism rested on the principle of equal emphasis on all three aspects of the Buddhist discipline—moral conduct, concentration, and wisdom. Special attention to one, to the neglect of the other two, would certainly result in the deterioration of the dharma.

## DECLINE OF BUDDHISM IN INDIA

Finally, an indirect contributing cause of Buddhism's decline in China was its general decline in India, which reached a climactic stage during the eleventh and twelfth centuries, a period corresponding to the Sung Dynasty in China. The glorious flowering of Buddhism in China during the first half of the T'ang Dynasty (seventh and eighth centuries) was in no small measure due to the continual stimulus from the fountain-head of Buddhism, brought to China by Indian missionaries and Chinese pilgrims. We need mention only the names of Hsüan-tsang, I-tsing, Śikshānanda, and Amoghavajra to realize the extent and depth of this stimulus. With the passing of Candrakīrti, the Mādhyamika master, and Śilabhadra, the Vijñānavāda master, both of whom lived during the seventh century, Buddhism in India was slowly beginning to be engulfed by the relentless tide of Hinduism. As a matter of fact, this process of the absorption of Buddhism into Hinduism had already started before the seventh century. During the Gupta period (fourth to sixth centuries) in India Mahāyāna Buddhism began to take over many of the Hindu deities into its pantheon in an effort to gain adherents among the populace. From the viewpoint of the Buddhists this accommodation with Hinduism was necessary if the religion were to survive, but the result was not as they expected; in fact, it was just the opposite. The Hindus now looked upon Buddhism as just another sect of Hinduism, and the Buddha was recognized as one of the numerous incarnations of Vishnu, the protector and sustainer of the world. This view was apparently accepted by the Buddhists, for in one of the frescoes at Ajanta, in the depiction of the marriage scene of the Buddha he is holding Vishnu's blue lotus, while the divine lovers of Hinduism, Shiva and Pārvatī, watch with great interest. This process of Hinduizing Buddhism meant the slow, inexorable death of Buddhism in India during the eighth and ninth centuries. By that time the line of demarcation between Buddhism and Hinduism was practically obliterated. The final blow was administered by the Moslem invasion.

The initial invasion overran northwest India in 1001, with the Moslems carrying out wholesale destruction of Buddhist institutions, including their valuable libraries, manuscripts, and iconography. A few years after the invasion the Arab scholar Alberuni traveled over northwest India, and in a book which he wrote he put together considerable information concerning Indian religions, science, and philosophy. There was hardly any mention of Buddhism, however. In 1193 the Moslems attacked and conquered Magadha, the heartland of Buddhism, and with the destruction of the Buddhist monasteries in that area Buddhism was wiped out.

With the disappearence of Buddhism as a vital religious and intellectual force in India, the flow of Indian missionaries to China and Chinese pilgrims to India practically came to a standstill. Deprived of this religious and intellectual inspiration, Buddhism in China failed to maintain its position of eminence and excellence.

## THE SANGHA UNDER THE SUNG

As soon as Sung T'ai-tsu ascended the throne in 960, he ordered the ordination of 8,000 monks on the anniversary of his birthday. During his reign he frequently invited virtuous monks of the empire into the palace and conferred on them the honor of wearing the purple robe. In his efforts to encourage the religion he dispatched a large mission of over one hundred and fifty monks to the west in search of the law, established a translation bureau under imperial patronage, and ordered the first printing of the Tripitaka in Ch'eng-tu. Moreover, he personally undertook the layman's vows, one of the few Chinese emperors to do so. On

national commemoration days, for instance, he called upon officials to assemble in the Buddhist temples to offer incense. Succeeding Sung emperors were just as friendly to Buddhism, with
the result that ordination of monks increased until in 1221 there
were 397,615 monks, 61,240 nuns, and 40,000 temples.

In the realm of economic development the monasteries continued the activities started during the T'ang, such as the operation of oil presses, water-powered mills, pawnshops, hostels, and
Inexhaustible Treasuries. So far as temple lands were concerned,
it is probable that the acreage equaled or exceeded that of the
T'ang. Individual temple holdings were sometimes larger, as may
be seen in the case of one temple whose annual income in grain
amounted to 30,000 shih, and another, 35,000 shih. As in previous
eras such temple lands were donated in the main by members
of the imperial household, the nobility, and the great families
of the realm, and the machinery for such donations was in many
instances the establishment of a merit cloister by the family, then
the donation of land to that cloister. Frequently the family did
not establish a new cloister but merely appropriated an existing
temple for the purpose, usually one that was officially recognized.
In some instances several such temples were seized by one
family.[7]

This practice became so widespread that the government felt
compelled to take some action. In 1109 a decree was issued forbidding the great families from appropriating the officially recognized temples to serve as their merit cloisters; four years later
tax-exemption privileges were taken away from such cloisters.

---

[7] The protest against the merit cloisters by the monk Ssu-lien, written
about 1250, is of interest here: "The laws of the dynasty permit the
important ministers to construct with their family fortunes temples in
memory of their ancestors and to petition for the tablet signifying recognition. This is for the purpose of conferring blessings on deceased ancestors.
At present, however, this is no longer the case as practiced by the un-
enlightened. Despite the preciousness of the ancestral remains, these
people fail to spend the money to buy an appropriate site. Instead, they
forcibly seize temple lands to serve as burial grounds, and they occupy
temples and convert them into merit cloisters. They take possession of
everything within the temples. One day the temple must present rice, the
next day tea and bamboo shoots, the next day firewood and charcoal, and
after that bamboo and lumber. . . . I once overheard one of these contemporary worthies say, 'When a temple is converted into a merit cloister, then
even a needle or a blade of grass in it belongs to my family.'" Cf. K. Ch'en,
*Harvard Journal,* 19,99-100, with slight changes.

However, when the Sung Dynasty was forced to move south of the Yangtze as a result of the barbarian invasions in the north, the shortage of housing facilities in the south led the throne to give permission to the nobility and aristocracy to live in Buddhist temples in the area. In this manner close connections were again established between the great families and the Buddhist institutions—a fact which inevitably resulted in the families taking over the temples. Once more the evils connected with merit cloisters emerged, and during the reign of Kao-tsung (1127-1162) the seizure of officially recognized temples was banned, while under Ning-tsung (1195-1224) the tax-exempt status of such cloisters was abolished. However, these decrees proved to be ineffective, and the practice continued as usual. In some instances the Buddhists sought to have their temples converted into merit cloisters under some prominent family, hoping by so doing to increase the economic holdings and prestige of the temples.

## BUDDHIST SCHOOLS UNDER THE SUNG

Two Buddhist schools managed to survive the persecution of 845 and maintain active existence under the Sung—the Pure Land and the Ch'an. The popularity of the Pure Land School was most strikingly illustrated by the increase in the number and size of the Lotus or Pure Land Societies organized among the people. Contemporary records spoke of these societies springing up everywhere, with the voices dinning the name of Amitābha into the ears of the populace. It was noted previously that the societies connected with the temples in Tun-huang were relatively small, having an average of thirty to fifty members. Now these Sung societies claimed hundreds and even thousands of members, with one going up to ten thousand and another up to twenty thousand. Though there seems to be some exaggeration here, there is no question but that the presence of these societies was one of the outstanding features of Sung Buddhism.[8]

[8] The society with the membership of 10,000 was established by Chih-li (960-1028). It held an annual meeting of all members on the fifteenth day of the second month. In the group were two hundred and ten captains, with each one responsible for getting forty-eight members to the meeting. In their daily lives the members were expected to repeat the name of

The Ch'an School, though still very active and popular, began to show some signs of inner retrogression. The T'ang masters had avoided the court and capital, and refused to accept imperial offers. But now under the Sung they began to dabble in politics. The Ch'an temples became centers of social and political life, and understandably the quality of the monks living in those temples degenerated. Moreover, the popularity of such temples resulted in an increase in the number of monks residing in them, and with the increase in numbers, quality again suffered. For Ch'an the truth was transmitted from master to pupil, from mind to mind, and masses and increased numbers were not conducive to such a transmission.

Another danger to the Ch'an movement was the increasing tendency toward intellectualism. Ch'an masters began to display more and more interest in the sutras of the Hua-yen and T'ien-t'ai Schools, sutras concerned with philosophical problems which the T'ang masters shunned.

It was under the Sung also that there occurred a change in Ch'an emphasis. During the T'ang the Ch'an masters placed little or no emphasis on literature and words, but during the Sung the Chinese reverence for the written word reasserted itself, and there arose what is known as literary Ch'an. One evidence of this was the collection of *kung-an* or cases in writing, entitled *Pi-yen-lu* (*Azure Cliff Records*), completed in 1125. Another was the compilation of various *Yü-lu* (*Recorded Sayings*) of the Ch'an masters. One might say that the inner development of Ch'an led in this direction. The Ch'an practitioners of the later age revered the renowned masters of the former days, and so they dedicated themselves to the study of the lives and experiences of those former masters, hoping that through such a study they too could grasp the enlightenment attained by the masters. Now the masters of old had realized enlightenment

---

Amitābha one thousand times a day. On the day of the meeting each member brought along forty-eight cash as membership dues. If there should be any decrease in membership by death, the captains were to report the names of the deceased to the general meeting, and the entire group would then invoke the name of Amitābha a thousand times for the sake of the departed, in order that their spirits might be speedily ushered into the Western Paradise. The captains were also called upon to suggest names immediately to bring the quota of membership up to the full ten thousand.

spontaneously through their own efforts. In the later period, with the deterioration in the caliber of monks, such spontaneous powers were lacking, and so the study of the written *kung-an* was resorted to as a necessary aid in realizing enlightenment. Hence the need of such a collection as the *Pi-yen-lu*. It now appears that the Ch'an discipline had become a systematized, mechanized, and formal technique, and to that extent there might be said to be deterioration in the movement.

## HARMONIZATION OF SCHOOLS

One of the interesting developments that arose during the Sung Dynasty was the tendency toward closer harmony among the existing Buddhist schools, with the Ch'an playing an active role in most of the attempts to find some common ground. This tendency was reflected in one of the popular slogans of the era, *ch'an-chiao-i-chih*, harmonization of meditation and study of the sutras. For instance, some Ch'an masters began paying more attention to the *Avataṁsakasūtra* by expounding its teachings in their speeches and writings and accepting the totalistic doctrine of the Hua-yen School. Other Ch'an masters sought to combine their teachings with T'ien-t'ai doctrines, but on the whole the latter school did not regard with favor these attempts at harmonization. It was with the Pure Land School that important links were established. The Ch'an practitioners saw some psychological affinities between their *kung-an* and the *nien-fo* of the Amitābha cult, and many Ch'an followers began to utter faithfully the invocation to Amitābha Buddha, often for the sake of some departed monk, so that the deceased might be reborn in the Western Paradise. The Ch'an master Yen-shou (904-975) was one of the most vocal advocates of this harmony of the Ch'an and Pure Land Schools, and he became a master of the teachings of both schools.

Under the slogan, "All the dharmas are but manifestations of the mind," Yen-shou attempted to unify the teachings of the two main schools of his time. He held that invocation of the Buddha's name, reciting the sutras, and observing the precepts should accompany Ch'an meditation. For the Ch'an School one of the main slogans was that "this mind is the Buddha," while for the Pure Land School it was held that "this mind is the Buddha Amitābha, this mind is the Pure Land." It was this idealistic bent that tended to draw the two schools closer together.

## THE LAUGHING BUDDHA

One more important development during the Sung Dynasty was the metamorphosis of Maitreya, the Future Buddha, into Mi-lo-fo, the Laughing Buddha. Today, in almost all Chinese Buddhist temples, the image of this jovial figure, with heavy jowls and a very pronounced paunch, greets the visitor as soon as he enters the temple. The metamorphosis of the Indian Maitreya into the Chinese Laughing Buddha is an interesting story.

A Maitreya cult had already been established in China as early as the fourth century, during the time of Tao-an. In the fifth and sixth centuries, when China was undergoing a critical and confusing era, people were convinced that the last period of the dharma was at hand. Consequently, they waited anxiously for the coming of Maitreya to purify and restore the dharma on earth. Images of Maitreya were therefore fairly common in the Yün-kang and Lung-men sculpture. In these early statues Maitreya appears as a large and heroic figure. After the seventh century the cult declined, to be replaced by the cult of Amitābha and Avalokiteśvara, and when the image of Maitreya reappeared during the Sung, it was usually in the shape and appearance of the fat, laughing creature. It was now designated as the Pot-bellied Maitreya or the Hemp-bag Bonze. To understand more fully how this metamorphosis took place, it is necessary to examine some of the legends surrounding the person represented in this quaint fashion.

The portrait of the Hemp-bag Bonze may be gleaned from a number of works in the Chinese canon, where he is always described as having a wrinkled forehead and a protruding belly left uncovered. The sources present him as a native of Chekiang who lived in the tenth century. His real name was unknown. At an early stage he became very popular with the people, mainly because of his ability to predict the weather. When he was seen wearing wet sandals and scurrying for shelter, rain was expected; but when he slept on the market bridge in a squatting posture, his head resting on his knees, then good weather was expected. One feature of his appearance singled him out—he carried a hemp bag wherever he went. Into this bag was deposited whatever he received, and for this reason the bag became an object of intense curiosity, especially among the children. They would chase him and climb all over him, and force him to open his bag. On such an occasion he would place the bag on the ground, empty the contents one by one, and just as methodically put them back into the bag.

The expressions attributed to him were all enigmatic and exhibit the characteristics of Ch'an. Once a monk asked him about his bag, to which he replied by placing it on the ground. When asked what this meant, he shouldered the bag and went away. Once he was asked how old the bag was, and he replied that it was as old as space. Was he a Ch'an master or just an illiterate monk? Some of the legends about him say that he had studied the *Mahāprajñāpāramitā*. But how did he become identified with Maitreya? Ferdinand Lessing, professor of Oriental Languages at the University of California, who studied all the legends, thought that he "fell a victim to idealization through religious fiction."[9] Because of his popularity the people were only too willing to believe the stories that he never died. All such stories pointed to the prediction that he was the Future Buddha in the flesh. Once people were amazed when they found him lying in the snow, unaffected by it. On another occasion a friend found him bathing in the river, and discovered that he possessed the third or wisdom eye on his back. Surprised by this, the friend exclaimed, "You are a Buddha!" whereupon the Hemp-bag Bonze silenced him and warned, "Do not tell anyone."

Two other developments now combined to raise him above the level of his contemporaries—poems attributed to him and pictorial representations of him. One poem attributed to him read:

> "Mi-lo, true Mi-lo
> Reborn innumerable times

[9] F. Lessing, *Yung-ho-kung*, Stockholm, 1942, 27.

From time to time manifested to men
The men of the age do not recognize you."[10]

The populace believed that in this poem he was referring to himself as the reincarnation of Maitreya. After his death a number of poems, all expressing the spirit of Ch'an, were also found and attributed to him. Then monks and laymen, especially of the Chekiang area, cognizant of his popularity in that region, began drawing his portraits, which were worshiped by the populace. Though exposed to the elements, these portraits never faded. Finally, in one of the legends about the Hemp-bag Bonze it was said that Maitreya appeared on earth and wandered about in the appearance of a fool, with his protruding belly uncovered and a smile on his face. No one knew his true identity. He appeared undignified and eccentric in his conduct. But when he spoke, his words were filled with wisdom.

Here we see the deification of the Hemp-bag Bonze as the Future Buddha. In this guise as a potbellied, laughing fool Mi-lo has wandered all over the Far East, and in recent times even to the western world, where his bizarre likeness adorns many a mantelpiece or bookcase. The following couplet, seen by Lessing in Hopei, is probably the most apt description of him:

"The big belly is capable to contain, it contains all the
    things under Heaven which are difficult to contain.
The broad face is inclined to laugh, to laugh at the
    laughable men on earth."[11]

In this potbellied figure one is able to see the representation of a number of Chinese life-ideals. The huge protruding stomach and the hemp bag denote prosperity and a wealth of material goods, for only a rich person would have enough to eat and be fat. The reclining figure is indicative of the spiritual contentment and relaxation of one who is at peace with himself and the world. Finally, the large number of children usually surrounding him are illustrative of another Chinese virtue—a large family consisting of many children. When these features are combined with the genial appearance of the figure, as if he were full of mirth and friendship, then it is easily understood why he has been so

[10] *Ibid.*
[11] *Ibid.*, 37.

enthusiastically received by the Chinese. When the Chinese look at him, they see not just a Buddhist deity but also a good representation of many of the things after which they aspire. This is another instance of the Chinese appropriating an Indian Buddhist element and adapting it to the Chinese environment.

# CHAPTER XV

## UNDER ALIEN DYNASTIES: LIAO, CHIN, AND YÜAN DYNASTIES

CHINESE historians in their discussions usually group the Sung with three alien ruling houses that were at one time or another contemporaneous with it—the Khitan Liao (907-1125), Jurchen Chin (1115-1234), and Mongol Yüan (1206-1368). It is therefore proper to devote some attention now to the development of Buddhism under these non-Chinese dynasties.

### THE LIAO DYNASTY

The importance of the Liao Dynasty lies in the fact that under its dominion Buddhism spread over those regions in Inner Asia now called Mongolia and Manchuria. This Liao Dynasty was established by a Mongol tribe called Ch'i-tan or Khitan, which even before it conquered north China already had some contact with and knowledge of Buddhism. For instance, as early as 902 a Buddhist temple was started by the Khitans in the Lung-hua prefecture in present Jehol, and in 916 the courtiers of A-pao-chi, founder of the dynasty, declared themselves as favoring Buddhism. After the subjugation of north China and the establishment of the Great Liao Dynasty in 947, the Khitans found a large number of Buddhist temples and clergy within their borders.

The attitude of the royal house toward Buddhism was, on the whole, favorable. Although the rulers paid nominal respect to Confucianism as the ruling ideology, they were cognizant of the inherent Confucian antagonism to alien peoples, and hence were emotionally more attached to Buddhism. Buddhist scriptures were used in educating the children in the imperial family and Buddhist names were adopted by some members. For instance, the childhood name of Sheng-tsung (ruled 982-1031) was Wen-hsü nu (servant of Mañjuśrī); the second daughter of Shih-tsung (ruled 947-951) and the first daughter of Ching-tsung (ruled 969-982) were both called Kuan-yin. Hsing-tsung (1031-

1055) was a convert to Buddhism and undertook to observe the five vows of a layman, while Tao-tsung (1055-1101) personally copied Buddhist texts and studied the scriptures. He also was credited with a knowledge of Sanskrit. The birthday of the Buddha, but not that of Confucius, was celebrated as a national festival. Monks were appointed to high honorary positions and even permitted to ride in the imperial carriage.

As a result of such encouragement temples and monasteries began to spring up, built by the imperial family, the nobility, and the common people. The religion probably was most popular during the reigns of Sheng-tsung, Hsing-tsung, and Tao-tsung, from 982 to 1101, the period when the dynasty itself was most powerful. The number in the monastic community must have been fairly high, for in 1078 Tao-tsung was said to have fed 360,000 monks and nuns in the empire. Sometimes imperial encouragement consisted of donations of property to temples.[1] The influence of the religion may be seen in the decline of animal sacrifice to heaven, for after the reign of Sheng-tsung, who ruled until 1031, notices of such animal sacrifices practically disappeared. The spirit of compassion was implemented by decrees forbidding the taking of lives on certain fast days, and cremation was now practiced by the Khitans.

One of the notable projects carried out by the Liao was the printing of the Liao edition of the Chinese Tripitaka during the period 1031-1064. As an indication of the close relationship with Korea, which was also interested in Buddhism, a set of this Liao edition was presented to the Koreans. In later years, when the Koreans were getting ready to print their second edition of the canon, they made comparisons between the Sung, Liao, and the first Korean edition, and found that the Khitan version was more accurate and complete than the other two. Another worth-while project undertaken by the Liao emperors was the engraving of Buddhist sutras on stone. As early as the Sui Dynasty work had already begun on this gigantic task at the Yün-chü Temple in Fang-shan in Hopei; it continued during the T'ang, and the Liao emperors carried on. It is probable that

---

[1] In 1059 the princess of Ch'in and Yüeh donated 10,000 mou of irrigated land and 100 families to the Hao-t'ien Temple, while in 1072 Lady Hsiao donated to the Ching-an Temple 300,000 mou of land, 10,000 shih of grains, 50 families, 50 heads of cattle, 40 horses, and 2,000 strings of cash.

not the entire Tripitaka but only individual sutras were engraved on stone.

Though the dynasty was alien, the roots of Liao Buddhism were entirely Chinese. This is confirmed by the discovery of numerous archeological sites containing structures of Chinese origin and of sculptural reliefs referring to Chinese Buddhist figures. However, some relationship with Buddhism in Central Asia probably existed, for there was an important Liao official, Hai-li, who was a Buddhist and an Uighur. As for the prevailing interest of the Liao Buddhists, there is not much information. Tao-tsung, the emperor, was a student of Hua-yen literature. The most famous cleric of his reign was one Chüeh-yüan, a Chinese interested in Tantrism who wrote a treatise on the *Great Sun Sutra*. From these scanty notices one may assume that the Hua-yen and Tantric Schools enjoyed some following.

## THE CHIN DYNASTY

While the Liao Dynasty was still holding sway over what is now Manchuria, a tribe in that area called Ju-chen (Jurchen), of Tungusic origin, asserted its independence under Akuta, and in 1115 that chieftain proclaimed himself emperor of a new dynasty, Chin. Akuta soon concluded an agreement with the Sung according to which he attacked Liao from the north while the Chinese attacked from the south. Liao was defeated and the central capital sacked in 1122. After taking over all of Liao's territory in north China, Mongolia, and Manchuria, the victorious Chin armies found themselves face to face with the forces of the Northern Sung Empire. They immediately took advantage of Sung weaknesses to invade the latter, capturing the capital K'ai-feng in 1126 and forcing the dynasty to move southward. The southern boundaries of the Chin Empire were finally stabilized roughly along the Huai River, and its capital was established at Peking. In 1215 Mongol pressure forced it to evacuate the capital from Peking to K'ai-feng, and in 1234 the dynasty finally succumbed.

Since Buddhism was already flourishing in the areas ruled by the Liao, it is reasonable to assume that the religion continued to prosper after the Chin took over. Some of the early Chin emperors were also favorably inclined to Buddhism. The first emperor was credited with providing annually for a feast to feed over ten thousand monks and nuns, while under the second emperor, Hsi-tsung, over a million monks were said to have been ordained. When one of Hsi-tsung's sons became ill, he took him to a Buddhist temple to pray for his recovery. At the same time, however, measures were taken to restrict and prohibit private ordination of monks. Such a policy was followed probably because in areas taken over from the Northern Sung large numbers of blank certificates must have been sold by the Sung authorities—a condition which resulted in the creation of numerous bogus monks and general laxity in the order.

In their relations with Buddhism the Chin rulers embraced a somewhat contradictory attitude. Prince Hai-ling, who ascended the throne in 1148, once had two of his officials punished with twenty strokes of bamboo because they had taken inferior positions when calling on a Buddhist monk, while the monk himself was bambooed two hundred times. Even more revealing was the attitude of Shih-tsung, who ruled from 1161 to 1189. The *History of Chin* describes him as being a nonbeliever who castigated Emperor Wu of the Liang Dynasty and Tao-tsung of the Liao for their favors to Buddhism and who wanted to preserve the racial excellence of the Chin people while ruling in accordance with the kingly way of the Confucianists. To this end he prohibited the construction of temples and the granting of exemptions to the clergy. However, in his personal attitude he revealed no such critical sentiment against Buddhism. In fact, he personally encouraged the construction of temples and donated land and money to them and was on good terms with famous monks; his mother became a nun after he ascended the throne. How is one to explain such a contradiction? Some Japanese scholars have suggested that a possible explanation might be that as emperor he felt obliged to regard the religion objectively, and that he had to take certain measures to establish order in the monastic community and rid it of undesirable elements. Thus in his official capacity as an emperor ruling in accordance with Chinese political principles he could not appear to be unduly favorable to Buddhism in his public statements. As a private individual, however, he found peace, comfort, and tranquility in Buddhism and, consequently, was friendly and receptive to the religion.

By the time Chang-tsung ascended the throne in 1189, it was believed that certain rules should be established to assure greater control over the order. Consequently, in 1190 private ordination was again prohibited; a system of examination to be held every three years was initiated to screen applicants for entry into the order. Texts such as the *Lotus Sutra* and the *Hua-yen-ching* were to be studied. In 1191 a decree was issued prohibiting monks from entering the homes of princes of the imperial family and of high officials, presumably to preclude any opportunity for collusion, bribery, favoritism, or clerical interference. Finally, in 1192 another decree was issued calling upon members of the order to reverence their parents and to observe the funeral ceremonies whenever the occasion arose. Such a decree indicated that the Chin emperor no longer considered Buddhism to be outside and above society. Earlier in the dynasty selling of monk certificates had been prohibited, but in 1197, because of financial stress faced by the government, the practice was resumed. In 1198 and again in 1212, because of famines in certain areas, certificates were sold to raise funds for relief. In the latter instance it was also possible that urgent funds were needed for military purposes, for by that time the Mongol armies were already pressing against the borders of the empire.

As for the schools of Buddhism popular under the Chin, some testimony was given by a Chinese named Hung Hao, captured by the Chin in 1129 and kept in Chin territory until 1143, when he was released under a general amnesty ordered by the emperor Hsi-tsung to celebrate the birth of a son. In a work which Hung left behind he wrote that in the capital there were thirty-six large and important monasteries, mostly belonging to the Discipline School. Later some Ch'an monks came from the south and established four Ch'an temples. If Hung's testimony is correct, then we may assume that no Ch'an School existed in Peking under the Liao, and that only during the latter half of the Chin Dynasty was it introduced. In support of this was the fact that Chang-tsung invited the most famous Ch'an cleric of the time, Hsing-hsiu of the Ts'ao-tung School, to lecture in the palace.

The Chin Dynasty likewise sponsored the printing of an edition of the Chinese Tripitaka during the period 1148-1173. Nothing was known about this edition until copies of it were found in 1934 in the Kuang-sheng Temple in Chao-ch'eng in Shansi.

Undoubtedly the greatest Buddhist scholar of the dynasty was Li-P'ing-shan (1185-1231), who in his youth had received such a good classical education that he was awarded the *chin-shih* degree and admitted into the Han-lin Academy. Later he turned to Buddhism after having read the sacred scriptures, and became the staunchest defender of the faith against the attacks of the Neo-Confucianists. As he was familiar with Confucian, Taoist, and Buddhist literature and thought, he advocated the harmonization of the three religions, basing his stand on the fundamental Hua-yen teaching that all things are interfused unimpededly with one another. From this one may also conclude that, besides the Ch'an and Discipline Schools, the Hua-yen was also studied under the Chin.

## THE YÜAN DYNASTY:
## INITIAL CONTACTS WITH BUDDHISM

The Mongols, with whom Lamaism is generally associated, did not come into definite contact with Buddhism until after their conquests of north China, and then that first contact was with a monk, Hai-yün (1201-1256) of the Lin-chi branch of the Ch'an School. In 1219 when the Mongols under Mukali overran Lan-ch'eng, a city in Shansi, Hai-yün, who was then eighteen years old, remained in the city to serve his master Chung-kuan, while the rest of the inhabitants fled in panic. Among the generals in the Mongol army were two Chinese, Shih T'ien-hsiang and Li Ch'i-ko, who found Hai-yün moving about unconcernedly in the city. They asked him who he was and he replied that he was a monk. Shih then asked him whether he belonged to that branch of Buddhism which emphasized meditation or to that which studied the doctrines. Hai-yün answered that both branches were as essential to Buddhism as the two wings were to a bird, or as the warrior and scholar were to the state. He then offered to take them to his master.

The two generals were by this time quite impressed by the demeanor and answers of Hai-yün, and so they readily went with him to call on Chung-kuan. They were so impressed by the exposition of the religion which Chung-kuan gave to them that they acknowledged him as their master and formed a firm friendship with him. The Mongol general Mukali himself was also so impressed by these two clerics that he sent a favorable report concerning them and their teachings to the great Genghis Khan. The Khan's answer to this report is couched in that peculiar Chinese style characteristic of the documents of the Mongols, which of course is lost in the following translation: "From what your messengers have told me, it appears that the Old Reverend One and the Young Reverend One are both true 'Speakers to Heaven.' Feed and clothe them well, and if you find any others of the same sort, gather them all in and let them 'speak to Heaven' as much as they will. They are not to be treated with disrespect by any one and are to rank as 'darkan' (Mongol free-man)."[2]

Once this initial contact was established between Hai-yün and the Mongol Khan, it appears that the relationship was not severed until the death of the monk in 1256. There is not much information about the activities of Hai-yün during the years immediately following the foregoing episode; scattered notices here and there seem to indicate that his advice on religious matters was sought after by Ogotai, Kuyuk, and Mangu Khan, and by Kublai before the latter ascended to the throne. For instance, Hai-yün once dissuaded the Mongols from carrying out a scheme of branding marks on people as a sign of identification. Kuyuk Khan in 1247 appointed him as chief of monks, and invited him to stay in the capital Karakorum, and in 1251 Mangu Khan re-appointed him to the same post. Kublai had Hai-yün choose a name for his oldest son, and the monk suggested Chen-chin (Pure Gold). After he became the great Khan, Kublai took on as one of his closest advisers Tzu-ts'ung (1216-1274), a disciple of Hai-yün, who, after he was given official appointment, re-turned to the laity and assumed the name Liu Ping-chung. In his capacity as imperial adviser and official this former monk

---

[2] *Taishō*, 49,703a, translated in A. Waley, *Travels of an Alchemist*, London, 1931, 7-8.

played a leading role in many of the important measures undertaken by the Mongols, such as the establishment of the new
capital in Yen-ching (Peking), the organization of the functionary system, the taking of the census, construction of rest houses
and depots along highways, and so forth.

Even while one group of Mongols was being introduced to
Buddhism through the medium of the Chinese monks, another
group was making the acquaintance of that type, Tibetan Lamaism, that was eventually to win the allegiance of all the Mongols.

## BUDDHISM IN TIBET

If we are to believe the Tibetan chroniclers, Buddhism was
introduced into Tibet during the reign of King Srong-btsan-
sgam-po (620-650) and prospered immediately, to become the
state religion under this ruler. A more objective examination of
Tibetan history would reveal that the religion made very little
progress during the first century of its existence in Tibet. The king
did introduce the rudiments of Buddhist art and literature, chose
Lhasa as the capital, and in general prepared the groundwork
for later development. The native Bon religion, however, still
enjoyed wide support among the Tibetan nobility, who seized
every pretext to discredit the newly introduced religion. They
claimed that the gods and demons of Tibet were wrathful over
the introduction of the Indian deity, and that this had led to
such calamities as lightning striking the palace, floods carrying
away human dwellings, harvests being damaged, and pestilence
arising. One of the Tibetan kings who supported Buddhism
thereupon invited a great Tantric master, Padmasambhava, to
come to Tibet to subdue and pacify the native demons. Padmasambhava arrived in 747 and by the exercise of his magic powers
soon triumphed over all local opposition. The arrival of this
worthy is usually regarded as signaling the introduction of
Tantric Buddhism into Tibet. After subduing the local gods and
demons, Padmasambhava remained in Tibet long enough to
instruct the king and to build the Samye monastery, thirty miles
from Lhasa.

The activities of Padmasambhava enabled Buddhism to gain

a foothold on Tibetan soil, but even then progress was not rapid. It seems that the Tibetans turned to Buddhism mainly to take advantage of the magic feats and sorcery that the Tantric masters were able to perform, and not through any deep appreciation of the superiority of the new doctrine. In the middle of the ninth century anti-Buddhists under King Lang-dar-ma mounted a severe persecution which drove the Buddhists under cover. A period of about seventy-five years was to elapse before a revival appeared, initiating what the Tibetans called a new phase of the religion. The most important event of this new phase was the arrival of Atisha in 1038, and as a result of his ministry the religion entered a period of development characterized by the rise of the numerous schools of Tibetan Buddhism. The religion became known as Lamaism, the religion of the lamas, and it represented an amalgamation of Buddhism with some features of the indigenous Bon faith. The word "lama" is derived from the Tibetan *bla-ma*, the superior one, and was used originally to designate the eminent monks, but it soon became popularized to include all monks.

By the twelfth century this religion began to capture the imagination of the Tibetans. The different schools which came into being in the eleventh century began to construct huge monasteries which were in reality impregnable fortresses commanding control over certain areas, inhabited by monks who were ready to take up arms and fight if necessary. The aristocracy also began to vie for the abbotship of these monasteries, which gave them not only political power over certain areas, but also spiritual power as well. Once acquired, the abbotship would pass from father to son or nephew, and would thus create what amounted to monastic dynasties. Safely protected by the massive walls of the monasteries these dynasties waged wars against one another, and by the time the Mongols appeared on the scene at the beginning of the thirteenth century, the struggle had resulted in the survival of only three great monasteries. The struggle between the monasteries was carried out for a well-defined purpose—nothing less than political paramountcy over all of Tibet. One of these was the Sa-skya monastery, administered by abbots who were not celibates and whose line of transmission was hereditary.

## THE MONGOLS AND LAMAISM

In 1239 a Mongol army in Szechuan under Koden, second son of the Khan Ogotai, attacked Tibet. The Tibetans, instead of resisting, decided to negotiate, and entrusted negotiations with the Mongols to Sa-pan, abbot of the Sa-skya monastery, probably the most powerful individual in Tibet at the time. Sa-pan began his negotiations with Koden in 1247. Tibetan historians said that the lamas effected cures for Koden's ailments that lengthened his life, and thus made him favorably disposed toward Buddhism. It was more probable that the Mongols had gotten a taste of the magic practiced by the Tibetan Tantric masters and had been awed by them. The negotiations ended with the Tibetans submitting to the Mongols; in turn the Mongols appointed the abbot of Sa-skya monastery to exercise political authority over the whole of Tibet. In this episode one sees the first instance of that peculiar practice in Tibet, the assumption of political power by a religious leader.

In order to win the support of the rest of the country to this arrangement the abbot Sa-pan wrote a letter to the abbots of the other monasteries, in which he said: "This king (Koden) is a bodhisattva, who has the greatest faith in the Buddhist teachings generally, and in the three gems in particular. He protects the universe by good laws, and particularly he has a great attachment for me far above the others. He said to me 'Preach religion with a tranquil mind, I will give you what you wish. I know that you do good, heavens knows if I do also.' Above all, he has a great attachment for hPhags-pa and his brother. Knowing how to govern freely, he has the good intention of being useful to all people."[3] By thus taking advantage of the power, authority, and prestige of the religious hierarchy, the Mongols were able to exercise effective control over the Tibetans without the necessity of invading and occupying Tibet. And once the Mongols were initiated into the practices of Lamaism, they began to adopt that aspect of Buddhism as their faith also, to take the place of their own Shamanism. The lamas were able to attract the Mongols with their superior magic; they demonstrated that

[3] G. Tucci, *Tibetan Painted Scrolls*, Rome, 1949, 10.

they were much more powerful than the native Shamans through the efficacy of their *dhāraṇis* and mantras. The Mongols, on their side, were converted, partly through fear of the mysterious powers emanating from the formulas and charms of Lamaism and partly because of the belief that Lamaism was better adapted to their temperament and habit, since both they and the Tibetans were hardy, accustomed to life in the open, and averse to agriculture.

The first indication that the Mongol Khan was more interested in Tibetan than in Chinese Buddhism was the appointment of Na-mo, presumably a Tibetan monk, as head of the Buddhist church in 1252. However, the Tibetan destined to play a much more important role was hPhags-pa, nephew of Sa-pan, who made his way into Mongolia and had begun to interest Kublai (before he became the great Khan) in Lamaism. So impressed was Kublai with this young Tibetan (who was still in his early twenties) that when he assumed the great Khanate in 1260, he named hPhags-pa his imperial preceptor and made Lamaism the national religion of the Mongols.

This position of the imperial preceptor was held in the greatest respect by the Mongol emperors and empresses. In court gatherings he sat next to the Khan, and each Khan, when ascending the throne, addressed messages of praise to him. If the imperial preceptor were to arrive in the capital from Tibet, the Khan would order his prime minister and high officials to go out to welcome him. In all the places he passed on his journey the local governments would receive him with great festivities and generous hospitality, and would provide him with the expenses for the journey. On the eighth day of the second month the Khan would receive the imperial preceptor as the symbol of the Buddha, after which there would be a reception for the people to meet him. As the imperial preceptor he became the chief of the *Tsung-chih-yüan* established in 1264 (changed to *Hsüan-cheng-yüan* in 1288), the highest office in the central government controlling all affairs connected with Buddhism, Tibet, and Lamaism. Offices of this bureau were also established in the departments, prefectures, and districts of the realm, with each office manned by sangha officials responsible to their immediate superiors. The practice of the Mongols in appointing a Tibetan as imperial preceptor and head of the bureau to supervise the religion indicated the high regard which they had for the Tibetans.

As imperial preceptor hPhags-pa was commissioned in 1269 to devise a system of writing for the Mongols. He worked at this task for about five years and brought forth a script based on the Tibetan, but after a short trial it proved unsuitable and was soon given up in favor of a system based on the Uighur script. hPhags-pa returned to Tibet in 1274 and passed away in 1280 at the age of forty-two. Probably more than anyone else he was instrumental in getting the Mongols to embrace Lamaism.

One of the things that attracted the Mongols to Lamaism was its literature, containing as it did the secrets of the magical powers wielded by the lamas. During the reign of Wu-tsung (1308-1311) the Tibetan Tripitaka was translated into Mongolian. Besides producing this Mongol version, the Yüan Dynasty also sponsored the printing of three editions of the Chinese canon, and one edition in the Tangut script for circulation in the monasteries located in Hsi-Hsia.

According to the registry of the *Hsüan-cheng yüan* there were for the year 1291 a total of 42,318 temples and 213,418 monks and nuns. As under previous dynasties, some of these temples were favored by huge grants of land from the ruling house and the nobility.[4]

With Lamaism accepted as the national religion, lamas enjoyed a special position under the Mongols. In 1309 an edict was issued stipulating that anyone guilty of striking a lama would have his hand cut off, and that anyone insulting a lama would have his tongue cut out. Enjoying such protection, inevitably the lamas became arrogant, haughty, and unreligious, and they indulged in such crimes as stealing land from the people and carrying away their daughters. The most glaring example of such misconduct was the behavior of a lama official in the Chiang-Huai area, named Chia-mu-lang-le-chih, who in 1295 opened the graves of the Sung royal family to rob the contents, murdered people,

---

[4] Kublai Khan in 1261 donated 500 ch'ing each to the Ch'ing-t'ao and Hai-yün Temples, while on another occasion he bestowed 9,000 ch'ing on the Ch'ien-yüan Temple in Karakorum. Emperor Ch'eng-tsung in 1301 donated 500 ch'ing to the Hsing-chiao Temple, and 600 ch'ing to the Wan-an Temple. However, the biggest grant was made by Emperor Wentsung in 1330—162,000 ch'ing in the Shantung area to the Ta-ch'eng t'ien-hu sheng Temple.

and carried off their daughters. He kept for himself the tax revenue from 23,000 families and accepted bribes for the release of criminals, while he said that he did so out of compassion for them. So many lamas had wives and children that in 1276 it was decreed that lamas with families were to be taxed the same as laymen. This measure and the one to tax the temple lands acquired since the Sung Dynasty were favored by the imperial house, but were opposed by the *Hsüan-cheng-yüan*, which had control over Buddhism, and it is difficult to see how the measures could have been carried out effectively without the cooperation of the latter.

# BUDDHIST-TAOIST CONTROVERSY UNDER THE MONGOLS

Perhaps one of the most interesting episodes during the Mongol Dynasty was the Buddhist-Taoist controversy before the Khan and the final decision rendered, which brought to an end a debate that had lasted over a thousand years.

Before the Mongols became acquainted with Hai-yün and the Ch'an School, they already had established good relations with Taoist masters of the Ch'üan-chen sect of Taoism, notably Ch'iu Ch'u-chi, better known as Ch'ang-ch'un chen-jen, who was invited by Genghis Khan to go on a campaign into Central Asia from 1220 to 1224. Upon his return Ch'ang-ch'un was made supreme head of the Taoist church, but in addition to this he was also entrusted with general supervision over all who had left the world to enter the religious life. This, of course, included the Buddhists, who did not like the arrangement. It was therefore not surprising that when Ch'ang-ch'un died in 1227, the Buddhists composed a derogatory poem to commemorate the event:

"A skeleton consisting of spindly bones
    The eternal spring one day changes to autumn,
    He died in the latrine, amidst urine and excrement,
    One stream flowed in, but two streams flowed away."[5]

---

[5] *Taishō*, 52,766c-767a. In view of the manner and place surrounding the death of Ch'ang-ch'un, it is likely that the "two ways" here referred to the urine and excrement that issued forth from the human body.

Taking advantage of their master's position and prestige in the Mongol court, the Taoists began to commit acts against the Buddhists that soon aroused the wrath of the latter. They began by taking over Buddhist monasteries which had been neglected because of the military campaigns, then became bolder by seizing those which were still flourishing, replacing the Buddhist images within with Taoist images. In ca.1230 they began decorating the walls of Taoist temples with paintings representing the eighty-one incarnations of Lao-tzu, in which the Buddha was portrayed as merely one of the incarnations. Later on appeared a text entitled *Pa-shih-i hua-t'u* (*Illustrations of the Eighty-one Conversions*), explaining these eighty-one incarnations which Lao-tzu was supposed to have undergone in the past. For the most part, this text consisted of borrowings from the Buddhist sutras.[6]

This was not the first time, however, that such Taoist paintings had appeared. As early as the Sui Dynasty paintings of Lao-tzu converting the barbarians into Buddhists already had been seen on the walls of Taoist temples. Now under the Mongols the Taoists began circulating the *Pa-shih-i hua-t'u* as well as the controversial *Hua-hu-ching* among the populace. These works, picturing as they did the Buddha as inferior to Lao-tzu, naturally infuriated the Buddhists, and the matter was brought to the attention of Mangu Khan in 1255.

In this initial confrontation between the Taoists and the Buddhists the main debate centered on the authenticity of the *Pa-shih-i hua-t'u* and the *Hua-hu-ching*.[7] Because the Taoists failed

---

[6] An example of such borrowing might be seen in the description of the tenth incarnation: "During the *chien-wu* month of the year *keng-yin* of King Yang-chia, the eighteenth king of the Yin dynasty, Lao-tzu entered the mouth of the Jade Maiden Hsüan-miao, and after eighty-one years, on the fifteenth day of the second month, the ninth year, *keng-yin*, of Wu-ting, the holy mother gave birth to him by splitting her left side while holding to a plum tree. As soon as he was born, he took nine steps and from each footstep a lotus flower sprang up. Nine dragons spat water to bathe him. He was complete with the seventy-two major marks and eighty-one minor physical characteristics. With his left hand pointing to heaven and right hand to earth, he said, 'In heaven and on earth, only the Way is to be revered. I shall now proclaim and propagate the doctrine without superior to bring salvation to all.'" Cf. K. Ch'en, *Harvard Journal*, 9,1,6-7, with slight changes.

[7] Li Chih-ch'ang, leader of the Ch'üan-chen sect of Taoism, represented the Taoists, while the Buddhist representative was Fu-yü, abbot of the Shao-lin Temple in the capital Karakorum. At the meeting Mangu asked

to answer the questions put to them by the Khan and the Buddhists, they were adjudged the losers. The Buddhists immediately charged that the Taoists had also illegally appropriated some five hundred Buddhist temples and destroyed numerous statues of the Buddha and Kuan-yin, and were still circulating the controversial works. In reply to these charges the Khan decreed that the texts should be collected and turned over to the Buddhists, and that the Taoists should replace whatever statues they had destroyed.

The Taoists refused to abide by the stipulations of the decree; so the Buddhists again appeared before Mangu Khan in 1256 to press their charges. The Taoists refused to attend this assembly. It was on this occasion that the Khan was reported to have made a comparison of the great religions: " 'The Hsien-sheng say that their teaching is the highest; the literati say that Confucianism is the first of the doctrines; the *Tieh-hsieh* [*tarsa*, Persian for "Christians"] who honor the Messiah believe in the celestial life; the *Ta-shih-man* [*Danishmand*, Persian for "the scholar," but here the word must refer to the Moslems] pray to heaven and thank it for its blessings. If all these religions were carefully examined as to their origins, one will see that no one of them can be compared with Buddhism.' Saying this, the Khan held up his hand to make a comparison and said, 'As the five fingers all project out from the palm, so Buddhism is the palm from which the others stem.' "[8]

As the Taoists did not show up at this meeting, no decision was handed down concerning the controversy. By this time, however, Mangu was wearying of the debate, and he handed over the entire business to his brother Kublai.

---

Li about the contents of the *Pa-shih-i hua-t'u*, but Li professed ignorance. The Buddhist thereupon demanded to know how he could be the leader of the Taoists when he did not know what was going on. Following this, the Buddhist attacked Lao-tzu, saying that a sage should aid his own country in times of stress, whereas Lao-tzu, according to his own followers, turned his back on the ills of China to go to the West. Was it not presumptuous for Lao-tzu to speak about converting the barbarians without putting his own country in order? It would be like a person trying to extinguish the fire in a neighboring yard while neglecting one in his own. Both the *Hua-hu-ching* and the *Pa-shih-i hua-t'u* were forgeries, he charged, and should be burned. To all these charges the Taoist Li remained silent, with perspiration rolling down his face.

[8] *Pien-wei-lu*; *Taishō*, 52,770c (brackets mine).

Since the controversial texts continued to circulate, in 1258 in the capital Karakorum Kublai convened a grand assembly attended by three hundred Buddhists, two hundred Taoists, and two hundred Confucianists. Under sharp questioning by the Buddhists the Taoists admitted that the only work left behind by Lao-tzu was the *Tao-te-ching*, and that in this work there was no mention of Lao-tzu's converting the barbarians.[9] When, upon the request of Kublai, the Taoists failed to manifest some of the supernatural powers they claimed to possess, they were declared the losers, and seventeen of them had to put on the Buddhist clerical robe. Kublai also specified in an order that all copies of the *Hua-hu-ching* and the *Pa-shih-i hua-t'u* must be collected and sent to the capital to be burned, and that the type for these texts was to be destroyed also. Likewise, all monuments, pillars, and steles which had the prohibited texts and paintings carved on them were to have these wiped out or erased, while a heavy penalty was to be inflicted on any Taoist hiding these books or

[9] Before opening the discussion, Kublai Khan asked what the punishment would be for the losers. While the Taoists remained silent, the Buddhists were in favor of the losers' having their heads cut off, but Kublai felt this was too severe a penalty and declared, instead, that the defeated should take on the faith of the victors. As expected, the controversy centered on the *Hua-hu-ching*. The Buddhist first asked whether Lao-tzu had spoken about converting the barbarians, and to this the Taoists answered in the affirmative. If he did, pressed the Buddhists, then he must have had some knowledge concerning the rules of ordination and the conduct of monks; so would the Taoists please explain some of these rules? The Taoist representative replied that he was not interested in such minor matters. The Buddhist then tried another tack and asked about the meaning of the term "Buddha" if Lao-tzu had become the Buddha. The Taoist replied that he was a good person of the highest degree. To this the Buddhist countered with the remark that since there had been numerous good people in the world, he wondered why they were not called the Buddha. This meant that the Taoists did not know the meaning of the term. Yes, the Taoist claimed, the term meant to realize, to realize heaven, earth, *yin*, *yang*, human-heartedness, righteousness, and knowledge. The Buddhists pointed out, however, that these were the very things taught by Confucius; why wasn't Confucius called the Buddha? To this question the Taoist had no answer.

The youthful hPhags-pa, who was only nineteen at this time, took over the questioning now and centered his attention on the *Hua-hu-ching*. By clever interrogation he elicited from the Taoists the admission that the only work left behind by Lao-tzu was the *Tao-te-ching* and that the *Hua-hu-ching* must have been forged by the Taoists themselves. Kublai broke in at this point to remark that while Lao-tzu was known only in China, the name of the Buddha was famous over the whole wide world; so how could one compare the two?

paintings. After Kublai assumed the Khanate in 1260, he confirmed these measures in an edict issued in 1261.

After the debate of 1258 about twenty years passed by in relative tranquility, but in 1280 the controversy flared up anew. Some Taoists burned one of their temples in the capital and attempted to implicate the Buddhists with the crime of starting the fire, but their machinations were unmasked and two of the Taoist ringleaders were executed, while one had his ears and nose cut off. The Buddhists now took advantage of the occasion to bring up their old grievances, charging that the Taoists were still circulating the banned texts. Investigation by the officials revealed that the actual situation was much worse than the Buddhists had charged, that types and plates were still kept hidden, and that the banned texts were still being circulated under changed titles. Upon hearing the evidence, the Khan issued his edict on the tenth month of 1281, stipulating that, with the exception of the *Tao-te-ching*, which he declared was the only work left behind by Lao-tzu, all the other controversial texts in the Taoist canon were false and forged, and that these texts as well as the blocks to print them were to be destroyed by fire.

With the issuance of the decree the Buddhist victory was complete. The acrimonious debate, which had started over a thousand years before with the appearance of the *Hua-hu-ching*, was now finally concluded, for after this the question of the conversion of the barbarians and of Lao-tzu's becoming the Buddha no longer was a subject of serious discussion. In these debates before the Mongol Khan one might say that the dice were loaded against the Taoists, since it was a foregone conclusion that the Mongols would decide in favor of the religion which they had embraced.

## APPEAL OF BUDDHISM FOR
## ALIEN DYNASTIES

On the basis of our discussion concerning Buddhism under non-Chinese dynasties and rulers, it is now possible to state what almost amounts to a truism—that Buddhism was the most acceptable religion for alien peoples ruling over China. The three dynasties just discussed, Liao, Chin, and Yüan, all supported Buddhism. In an earlier period a similar situation prevailed, for during the Period of Disunity practically all the non-Chinese ruling houses in the north—the T'o-pa family of the Northern Wei, the Shih house of Later Chao, the Fu family of Former Ch'in, the Yao family of Later Ch'in, and the Chü-ch'ü family of Pei Liang—called themselves followers of the law.

When these alien tribes conquered Chinese territory, they found a large number of Chinese living within their borders. While political power rested in their hands, cooperation with the great mass of Chinese had to be obtained before the alien dynasty could be stabilized, strengthened, and maintained. The alien rulers soon realized that adherence to Buddhism was one of the most desirable means to achieve this cooperation. They saw that they could not embrace Confucianism and Taoism, for in these indigenous systems the concept of Chinese versus barbarian was deep and fundamental. Anything connected with the Chinese was considered superior, while the ways of the barbarians were considered inferior. Such an attitude was best stated in Ku Huan's *Treatise on the Barbarians and Chinese*. No alien house would therefore embrace a religion that looked upon it as inferior. But Buddhism was different. Not only was there no distinction drawn between peoples, but the religion readily adapted itself to the habits and conditions of different peoples. Moreover, the barbarians felt that Buddhism was started by a non-Chinese, and this feeling produced a strong psychological affinity between them and the religion. Such a sentiment was expressed by Shih Hu in his reply to Wang Tu, when he said that since both he and the Buddha were non-Chinese, that was all the more reason why he should embrace Buddhism. By so doing the alien houses felt that they could gain the support of the large number of Chinese already devoted to the religion, while at the same time they could enhance their own culture by the superior art, literature, and thought of Buddhism, without facing the danger of being submerged by Confucianism.

## SECRET SOCIETIES

It was also during the Mongol Dynasty that secret societies claiming connection with Buddhism but in the main motivated by political considerations became very active. The information about them is still insufficient and rather tentative in nature. Moreover, in their later development these secret societies included not only Buddhist but also Taoist elements, so that the propriety of including this discussion in a history of Buddhism may be questioned. However, since their origins were rooted in Buddhist beliefs and practices, one might say that their existence was due to the impact of Buddhism upon Chinese society.

Much has been said previously about Buddhist religious societies in China. For the most part, these societies were taken up with activities concerned with the practice and propagation of the dharma, and as such they were considered to be assets to the sangha. However, there existed some groups which the Buddhists would not accept as assets, for these groups were usually associated with activities not religious but political, namely, fomenting and engaging in rebellions against the reigning dynasty. Such were the Maitreya Society and the White Lotus Society. These groups were called secret sects or societies, not so much because they practiced rituals known only to the initiated, but because their existence was banned by the ruling authorities from time to time.

## THE MAITREYA SOCIETY

The Maitreya Society was established on the conception of Maitreya as the future Buddha. According to Buddhist traditions Maitreya is now living in the Tushita heaven, waiting for a favorable opportunity to be reborn on earth as the next Buddha. During the interval between the passing of Śākyamuni and the coming of Maitreya the pure dharma would deteriorate progressively, so that at the end of the era of the decay of the law mankind would be drowned in misery, sin, and folly. At that time Maitreya would then descend to earth to restore the pure dharma, to save mankind from its state of wickedness and depravity, and to bring peace and prosperity to the realm. During his sojourn on earth just and virtuous rulers would again sit on the throne to rule the people. This was the utopia dangled before the eyes of the faithful.

To prepare for the coming of Maitreya and to keep alive the hope of the utopian future connected with his coming, Maitreya Societies were formed and became very popular, especially during periods of unrest and turmoil or of rampant corruption in the government. Under the T'ang and Sung, ambitious rebel leaders, intent on seizing power, capitalized on this prevailing popularity of the Maitreya cult by claiming that they were the incarnation of Maitreya himself, come to earth to restore the pure dharma to the realm and to bring tranquility and security to the people. Or they might claim that they were destined to be the just and virtuous earthly ruler who would welcome the future Buddha when the latter descended to earth. The earliest instance we have concerned a certain Sung Tzu-hsien, who called himself an incarnation of Maitreya and planned a revolt in 613. The plans leaked out to the authorities, however, and he was captured and beheaded. At about the same time a monk in Shensi named Hsiang Hai-ming also claimed to be an incarnation of Maitreya, set himself up as emperor in 613, but was also destroyed in short order by the authorities. One could easily imagine how attractive an appeal such claims would make to the unlettered masses, combining as they did popular discontent against the ruling regime with the strong and widespread religious sentiment. It was no wonder that Empress Wu Tse-t'ien tried to justify her revolution against the T'ang imperial family by claiming that she was the incarnation of Maitreya, and that another individual, Wang Huai-ku, during the K'ai-yüan period started a rebellion, claiming himself to be the future Buddha.

Perhaps the most serious of the revolts against the Northern Sung was led by a certain Wang Tse, who professed to be a follower of the Maitreya cult. Wang Tse was a minor army officer who started his rebellion in Hopei and Shantung, where Maitreya Societies were quite common. It was said that when he left home to join the army, his mother tattooed on his back the word *fu* (blessedness), hoping that the presence of this word would protect him and bring him back home. However, members of the Maitreya Societies regarded the word as a supernatural omen, and proclaimed him as their leader. By combining all the Maitreya and other rebellious societies in the area into one group, Wang started the rebellion in 1047 by occupying Pei-chou in Hopei, where he captured a considerable amount of military booty. Once in control of the city, he conscripted all males from twelve to seventy into his army, and, in order to prevent people from escaping, he organized a mutual guarantee system, in which each member of a group would stand as guarantor for the others. If any one of the group escaped, the rest would be executed. The Sung troops first tried to scale the walls of the city, but this attempt was foiled by the forewarned rebels. Then the government troops began tunneling under the walls into the city, and when the project was completed, they quickly surprised Wang and suppressed the revolt.

With the suppression of this revolt the Sung authorities decided to ban the Maitreya Societies as well as other heretical groups, and called upon the local officials to keep close watch and to seize the members of such societies if they should reappear. After the Sung very little further is heard about the Maitreya Societies, but it is likely that they continued to exist as secret underground groups, and that the chief reason for their not being mentioned in the records appears to be that they were merged with the White Lotus Society. This will become clear as we follow the fortunes of this society, probably the best known of its kind in Chinese history.

## THE WHITE LOTUS SOCIETY

At the outset it must be clearly understood that the White Lotus Society was not the same as the Lotus Societies of the Pure Land School so common during the Sung Dynasty, for the latter were not opposed by the Confucianists or the orthodox Buddhists, whereas the former was. The White Lotus Society was started during the early years of the Southern Sung Dynasty by an individual named Mao Tzu-yüan, a native of Kiangsu, who had been a disciple of Ching-fan (d. 1128), a T'ien-t'ai master also interested in the Pure Land doctrine. After ordination at the age of nineteen Mao began to concentrate on the meditation practices in the T'ien-t'ai tradition, but like his master he also dabbled in Pure Land ideas. Inspired by the example of Hui-yüan in Lu-shan, he organized a White Lotus Society consisting of monks and laymen devoted to the restraint of the passions and the encouragement of good karma. The group met regularly to utter invocations and sing praises to the Buddha and to hear confessions from the members. There were a few features peculiar to the society, namely, its membership included women and children, and the members were strict vegetarians at all times. They also abstained from wine, onion, and milk. Mao himself was called Master Guide of the White Lotus, while his followers were called transmitters of the way.

Another practice emphasized by Mao was the recitation of the penance every morning. It was held that this penance could destroy evil and remove the obstacles toward salvation. The fact that men and women mixed freely at the meetings of the society aroused the opposition of the Confucianists as well as the orthodox Buddhists, and the society was criticized as being a hotbed of debauchery. It was also criticized as being in league with demons, and as a result of these charges Mao was banished to Chiang-chou (present-day Kiukiang in Kiangsi) and the society banned. In spite of this prohibition, however, the society continued to exist and even to expand. Under the Mongol Dynasty the ban was reaffirmed by decrees in 1281 and 1308. In 1313, probably through the intercession of a layman, Hsiao Chüeh-kuei, and a Korean prince, the society was permitted to come out into the open to propagate its practices for a few years before it was banned again in 1322.

Under the Yüan one innovation took place. Whereas formerly only the image of the Buddha was worshiped at the meetings, now non-Buddhist deities made their appearance. Branches of the society were now to be found in Kiangsi and Fukien, with women from even noble families joining the group. Because of the ban by the government it appears that unlawful elements were now finding their way into the society, and from then on the White Lotus Society became involved in a number of rebellions under the Mongols. The extravagances of the Mongol court also spurred popular discontent against the alien Mongols. At any rate, a certain Pang Hu raised the banner of revolt in 1337 in Honan, claiming that he was preparing the way for Maitreya. In 1351 another individual, Han Shan-t'ung, whose forebears had been members of the White Lotus Society, stirred up another rebellion in Honan and Chiang-huai, rallying people with the slogan, "The country is in great confusion, and Maitreya is coming down to be reborn." His followers claimed that Han was the descendant in the eighth generation of the Sung emperor Hui-tsung, and therefore he should be the rightful occupant of the throne. Shan-t'ung's son, Lin-erh, was set up as the emperor of the restored Sung Dynasty in 1355. The rebels all wore a red kerchief and offered incense to Maitreya; hence they were sometimes called Incense Army or Red Kerchief Bandits. For a time the followers of Han controlled an area in north China stretching from what is now Manchuria to northwest China. Finally, in 1362 Han Lin-erh was defeated by the Mongols, but one of the members of the Red Kerchief Bandits, Chu Yüan-chang, continued the rebellion and eventually deposed the Mongols.

### THE WHITE CLOUD SOCIETY

There was also a third society, the White Cloud, which was also declared heretical and treacherous, although it was not involved in any insurrection against the throne. This society was founded by a monk named Ching-chüeh (1043-1121?), a native of Honan, said to be the fifty-second descendant of Confucius. In his youth he studied Confucianism but he soon turned to the *Lotus Sutra* and was so attracted by it that he became converted to Buddhism. His travels took him first to Mt. Omei in Szechuan, thence to the famous Ling-yin Temple in Hang-chou in 1093, where he lived in a White Cloud chapel at the back of the temple. It was here that he established the society in 1108 (taking the name from the temple in which he resided) for the express purpose of opposing the prevailing Ch'an School. It appears that the Ch'an was now merely preserving the form of their *kung-an* without realizing the religious experience connected with it, and Ching-chüeh wanted to start something that was easy to practice and more intimately connected with life. He emphasized, therefore, pure living, good works, and a strong spirit of unity among members. He traveled extensively in the Chekiang area, spreading the society and building temples wherever he went. He also did some writing, but only a few titles have been preserved. His opponents charged that one of his writings contained ideas disobedient to the throne, and for this he was banished to Kwangtung, probably in 1116. In 1121 he was pardoned, but he died soon after. His remains were buried in Hang-chou and a stupa and a temple, which later became the Ta-p'u-ning-ssu, were erected on this spot.

Because the White Cloud Society was opposed to the Ch'an School, it was criticized severely by the latter, who were able to influence the government to designate the society as heretical. Most of our knowledge concerning the society comes from the writings of the orthodox Buddhists, and one can rest assured that these writings were not complimentary. Yet in spite of this bias enough is said to give a fairly clear picture of the activities of the society. Branches of the society were found mostly in the Chekiang area, each one organized under the guidance of a group leader. Members included monks and laymen, who met mornings and evenings to observe the precepts, recite the sutras, and offer incense; they abstained from meat and wine as well as marriage. In this respect they differed from the White Lotus Society, whose members had wives and children. However, it appears that membership included women, for one of the charges against the society was that members assembled at night and dispersed at morning, with no separation of the males and females at the meetings. Just who the women were, if they were not the wives of the members, is not clear. In the various places where the founder traveled and lived temples were established which served as headquarters of the local branch. In the event of disputes involving members of the society, the whole society became a closely knit group dedicated to unified action for the protection of its members; it was willing to go to any length to influence local functionaries to render a favorable decision. The society not only carried on religious activities, but also engaged in public welfare acts such as road repair and bridge construction.

Other than the fact that the members were vegetarians, and that there was free mingling of the sexes, there was nothing here that could be classified as unorthodox, but the contemporary Buddhist and Confucian writers branded the society as being in league with demons, said that its members were traitors and that it was merely using Buddhism as a pretext to deceive the ignorant masses. The charge of treachery was unfair, however; for, so far as is known, the White Cloud Society did not engage in any rebellious activities. It appears very likely that these charges were circulated by the dominant Ch'an School, whom the society dared to oppose. In spite of this opposition the society continued to flourish during the rest of the Southern Sung Dynasty and into the Yüan period, when it was finally dissolved in 1320 by the government because of some alleged fraudulent activities by the administrator-general of the group. Before it disappeared, however, it did bequeath to posterity a noteworthy legacy in the P'u-ning-ssu edition of the Chinese Tripitaka, finished in 1289.

Although the Maitreya and White Lotus Societies based their origins in the first place on Buddhist ideas and practices, they later developed into organizations which were outright rebellious groups with no connection with Buddhism. Since they were a liability so far as Buddhism was concerned, they constituted one of the impacts upon Chinese society which the Buddhists were only too happy to forget.

# CHAPTER XVI

## RECESSION AND DECLINE: MING AND CH'ING DYNASTIES[1]

URING the closing years of its reign in China the Mongol Dynasty had to contend with widespread discontent and rebellion, caused very largely by the prevailing antagonism among the Chinese to an alien ruling regime and by the arrogant attitude of some of the lamas supported by the Mongols. In some instances the uprisings were fomented by monks or by common people in the guise of monks.[2] One of these rebel groups led by Chu Yüan-chang finally succeeded in overthrowing the Mongol Dynasty in 1368, and in its place he established the Ming (Enlightened) Dynasty.

According to the Maitreya legend an enlightened ruler (*ming-wang*) would arise in the world when the future Buddha descended to earth from the Tushita heaven. In all likelihood the term *ming-wang* was used because of the close relationship that existed between the Maitreya Societies and the followers of Manichaeism, which was called Ming-chiao by the Chinese because of its emphasis on light. There even existed a Manichaen text entitled *Ta-hsiao ming-wang ch'u-shih* (*The Appearance in the World of the Major and Minor Enlightened Rulers*). Thus Han Shan-t'ung, the leader of the White Lotus Society who rebelled against the Mongols in 1351, regarded himself as the Major Enlightened Ruler, and his son Lin-erh as the Minor Enlightened Ruler. Since Chu Yüan-chang was a member of the rebellious group that fought under the slogan of an enlightened

---

[1] We have decided to treat Buddhism during these two dynasties in one chapter, for the simple reason that events during the last five hundred years of decline do not warrant devoting one chapter to each dynasty. In this comprehensive chapter I shall emphasize only those outstanding individuals and dominant trends which tended to give some distinctive flavor to the religion.

[2] An example of such an uprising occurred in 1327, led by a monk from Kwangsi named Ch'en Ch'ing-an. The rebellion in 1338 in Yüan-chou in Kiangsi was led by rebels who had the character *fo* (Buddha) painted on their backs, in the belief that this rendered them impervious to injury by sharp weapons. In 1351 another revolt broke out in Honan, led by Han Shan-tung and his son Lin-erh, both members of the White Lotus Society.

ruler appearing in the world, he called the dynasty he established the Ming Dynasty, presumably to indicate that he considered himself to be the authentic enlightened ruler connected with the coming of Maitreya. By so doing he was able to win widespread support from the populace, who had been looking forward eagerly to the appearance of the future Buddha. However, Chu knew intimately the insurrectionist tendency of such groups as the Maitreya and White Lotus Societies, and one of the first things he did after ascending the throne was to issue a decree in 1370 banning those societies.

As the first Ming emperor had formerly been a monk in the Huang-chüeh Temple in An-hui, his attitude toward Buddhism was, on the whole, favorable, and he often convened assemblies of monks before whom he lectured on various Buddhist sutras, such as the *Prajñāpāramitā* and the *Lankāvatāra*. Ordination of the clergy was encouraged; 57,200 Buddhist and Taoist monks and nuns were ordained in 1372, and 96,328 in 1373. The number of ordinations was increasing so rapidly that measures were soon taken by the throne to limit them. In 1387 ordination was forbidden to those under twenty; examinations were also instituted to test the mental fitness of the candidates. In 1394 monks having wives were assembled in the capital to be examined on their understanding of the scriptures, and all those who failed were laicized, except those above sixty. Then in 1418 the throne decreed that in each department no more than forty were to be ordained annually; in each prefecture, thirty; and in each district, twenty.

In spite of these measures, however, the number of ordinations continued to increase, so that in 1486 200,000 were ordained. In a way this situation was assisted by the contradictory policy of the dynasty. One notes, on the one hand, the measures taken to limit the number of ordinations. On the other, the same dynasty was actively promoting the sale of ordination certificates, thus facilitating the process of ordination for those who desired it. For example, in 1414, because of a famine in Shansi and Shensi, the dynasty sold 10,000 blank certificates at a price of ten shih of grain each; the proceeds were used for relief of the needy.

Under the Ming Dynasty only the Lin-chi branch of the Ch'an and the Pure Land Schools remained active, though there were monks who continued to study the sutras. Temples were divided into three categories: (a) ch'an or temples devoted to meditation, (b) chiang, those concerned with instruction in the sutras, and (c) chiao. The last category, which was new, replaced the Vinaya temples of previous dynasties. The word chiao means "instruction," but the temples so designated included not only the Vinaya temples but also those concerned with yoga and Tantric ceremonies, rituals for the happiness and welfare of the common people, or ceremonies for the deceased. In brief, such temples catered to the welfare of the common people; hence the monks residing in them were called "monks who respond to needs."

Another distinct feature during the Ming Dynasty, initiated in 1372, was the circulation of a registry of monks to all the temples and monasteries in the realm. Whenever any traveling monk stopped at a temple, his name would be checked against the list in the registry, and if the name were not found there, then he was considered a fake and turned over to the authorities. Such a practice was undoubtedly initiated to prevent the temples from harboring lawless elements.

## THE SCHEDULE OF MERITS AND DEMERITS

It was during the Ming Dynasty that the Buddhists took over from the Taoists a feature known as the schedule of merits and demerits, according to which the fate of an individual was determined by the balancing of the merits against the demerits earned during his lifetime. Such an idea had existed for a long time in China and might be traced back to the Pao-p'u-tzu of Ko Hung of the Chin Dynasty. However, it became popular only with the advent of the Ming Dynasty, when its principles were set down in a work entitled Yin-chih-lu (Record of Silent Recompense), written by a certain Yüan Liao-fan (1533-1606), who early in his life had a Taoist foretell his future. The Taoist predicted that he would come out fourteenth in the prefectural examination, seventy-second in the district examination, and ninth in the circuit examinations; that he would never have a son; and that he would die in his fifty-third year. The very next year after this prophecy he sat for the examinations, and the results were exactly as predicted. This led him to be a fatalist, who believed that everything in his life had been preordained. Later he met a Buddhist monk who taught him the Buddhist doctrine of karma, that one's fate is created by oneself and that happiness is attained through one's own seeking. He called upon Yüan to perform meritorious deeds to build up his stock of merits, and concluded with a famous sentence, "Let all past die with yesterday, and let all future be born today." Yüan was struck by his earnestness, and decided to do something about his fate. He repented of his sins, and embarked on a career of performing meritorious deeds, in the hope that he might win a high place in the metropolitan examinations. To his joy and surprise he finished first when he finally took them, even though the Taoist had also predicted that he would finish third. Many years later, after more accumulation of merits, he was able to sire a son and thus again proved that the Taoist fortuneteller had been wrong. He did not die at the age of fifty-three but lived on for many more years after that. When he was sixty-nine, he wrote this work, the *Yin-chih-lu*, as a book of instructions for his son. In it he called upon him to perform the following meritorious services: (*a*) Encourage others to do good by one's own example, (*b*) be loving and respectful in heart, (*c*) be sympathetic and helpful toward the strivings of others, (*d*) encourage people to perform meritorious deeds, (*e*) save people when they are in danger, (*f*) encourage and promote charitable activities for the common weal, (*g*) sacrifice wealth for the blessings of the people, (*h*) uphold and protect the true dharma, (*i*) respect elders, (*j*) have compassion and protect all living beings.

While Yüan explained the theoretical aspects of the system of merits and demerits, the Buddhist monk Chu-hung of the Yün-ch'i Temple (1535-1615) seized upon it and developed its practical application in his work *Tzu-chih-lu* (*Record of Self-knowledge*). He divided all deeds into two categories, meritorious and demeritorious. Under the first he listed: (*a*) loyal and pious deeds, (*b*) altruistic and compassionate deeds, (*c*) deeds beneficial to the Three Jewels, and (*d*) miscellaneous good deeds. The opposite of these four were classified as demerits. Under each category detailed schedules were listed for assigning merits and demerits for each deed. For example, under altruistic and compassionate deeds is found the following table:

| | |
|---|---|
| To help a person recover from a serious illness | 10 merits |
| To help a person recover from a slight illness | 5 merits |
| To offer medicine to a sick person | 1 merit |
| To help a sick man on the road to return home | 20 merits |
| To rescue one person from the death penalty | 100 merits |
| To rescue one person from bambooing | 15 merits |
| To save the life of an animal that can do something in return (i.e., dog, horse, cow) | 20 merits |
| To save the life of an animal that cannot do something in return | 10 merits |
| To save a small animal | 1 merit |
| To save ten extremely small animals | 1 merit |

On the opposite side, if one does not help a person in serious illness, he is given 2 demerits; if one kills another person, 100 demerits. If the sum total of the demerits equals exactly the total for the merits, it is believed that the individual will die; if the demerits at the end of life should outnumber the merits, then the offspring of the individual will suffer. This last point is peculiar, for it runs counter to the Buddhist doctrine of karma, and appears to be an adaptation of the Taoist *ch'eng-fu* or transmission of burden, whereby the misdeeds of the ancestors are borne by the descendants.

Those who believed in this system would count their merit points at the end of each day, and add them to the sum total already accumulated. When the total reached 10,000 merit points, then they believed that all their wishes would be fulfilled.

The practical ramifications of such a system can be easily seen. It encouraged and promoted altruistic activities, such as public service, private philanthropy, generosity, respect for the lives of others, and care for the needy, all of which were beneficial to society. It ran counter to a cardinal doctrine of Mahāyāna Buddhism, however, that an individual perform a meritorious deed for the sake of the deed itself and not for any reward to be derived therefrom. One can see how, under such a system, the individual would become more interested in his accumulation of merit points than in the performance of the meritorious deed.

There was the danger that the deed would no longer be motivated by compassion but would degenerate into something mechanical, aimed primarily at the increase of merit points.

As a result of Chu-hung's advocacy and emphasis, this system of merits and demerits gained widespread following during his time, and might be considered as a good example of Buddhist-Taoist mixture.

## BUDDHISM AND CONFUCIANISM

It is likely that during this period Buddhism was accepted by a considerable number of Confucianists. For instance, among the twenty laymen listed as followers of Chu-hung, two attained such prominence in official life that they were included in the biographical section of the Ming dynastic history, while nine of them achieved the *chin-shih*, the third degree in the civil examinations which emphasized the Confucian classics. There were also some attempts by Buddhists to find some common ground in Buddhism and Confucianism. Yüan-hsien (1578-1657) considered Buddha and Confucius to be sages other-worldly and this-worldly, and the inherent nature of man stressed by Mencius and Hsun-tzu to be likened to the *chen-ju* or Genuine Thusness of the Buddhists. Another monk, Chih-hsü (1599-1655), tried to show there was no fundamental difference between Confucianism and Buddhism. Confucius wrote that the ten thousand objects are united in oneself, while the Buddhists taught that the mind, the Buddha, and all sentient beings are mutually related. Again, the concept of the commiserated heart of Mencius embraces and protects all within the four seas, while the compassion of the Buddha includes the whole of the sentient world. One of the prominent Buddhist laymen of the Ch'ing period, P'eng Ch'ih-mu, wrote that after Wang Yang-ming advocated emphasis on intuitive knowledge, the number of people who flocked to Buddhism was countless. Wang indeed wielded considerable influence on later scholars. One of his disciples, Lo Ju-fang, practiced Ch'an meditation, while another follower became a disciple of the master Chu-hung.

## BUDDHISM IN SOUTHWEST CHINA

During the Ming Dynasty there was one area in the far southwest, in Yunnan and Kueichou, where the religion appeared to have staged a revival.[3] One indication of this was the remarkable increase in the number of Buddhist temples, shrines, and study halls in that remote area. For instance, in the vicinity of just one mountain, the Chi-tsu-shan in Yunnan, one writer counted eight imposing temples, thirty-four small temples, sixty-five shrines, and over one hundred and seventy study halls. The famous Chinese traveler, Hsü Hsia-k'e (1586-1641), who visited the southwestern provinces in 1638 and 1639, also attested to the large number of such Buddhist establishments. Moreover, out of the eight large temples noted above, four were equipped with libraries containing the Chinese Tripitaka. It is obvious that these were not isolated institutions but centers of learning.[4]

Two factors were probably responsible for this revival—first, the pioneer efforts of monks in opening and developing the area and, second, the flight of many learned Chinese to that remote area to escape from the conquering Manchus.

Yunnan and Kueichou were areas not opened to development until rather late in Chinese history, and even during the Ming period large segments were still inaccessible and untouched. Buddhist monks in their peripatetic wanderings over the face of China were among the earliest to reach some of these remote areas and to establish temples and resthouses for aid to travelers. Once such facilities came into being, other people soon followed to settle. Again Hsü Hsia-k'e has provided information about these pioneer establishments in virgin localities. Often he found that places which were described as unexplored had already been reached by monks; where roads were said to be nonexistent, he would find some monk who knew where such were to be

[3] Ch'en Yüan, *Ming-chi Tien Ch'ien fo-chiao k'ao* (*Buddhism in Yunnan and Kueichou During the Ming Dynasty*), Peking, 1940, has brought together a mass of materials bearing on this revival.

[4] Because Yunnan and Kueichou were still sparsely settled during this period, the few schools which existed were usually found in the cities and towns. Under such circumstances the Buddhist temples often served as schools in the rural areas. One of the students met by Hsü Hsia-k'e in such a temple school eventually earned his *chin-shih* degree in 1640.

found; in places where people said nobody lived, he would discover Buddhist temples already established and monks living within. No wonder he made it a point to be accompanied by monks as guides in his travels in the southwest, and to stay in temples whenever he had the opportunity.

It is a common phenomenon for people to relate tales of marvelous deeds being performed in the pioneer development of their countries and regions, often by deities or remarkable individuals. In the case of the southwest of China it has been pointed out that the performers of such extraordinary deeds as building irrigation canals, channeling rivers, subduing poisonous dragons or man-eating tigers were invariably monks—another indication of their pioneer role.

As for the second factor, the migration of Chinese into the area, many educated Chinese loyal to the Ming Dynasty, including civil and military officials, forsook the household life to take refuge in the monasteries, and fled to the southwest with the approach of the Manchus. These refugees brought their religion with them, and the presence of such a considerable group of learned and active adherents of the religion undoubtedly stimulated the development of Buddhism there.

## LAMAISM UNDER THE MING DYNASTY

Meanwhile, what were the fortunes of Lamaism under the Ming? During the early Mongol period in Tibet the position of the abbots of the Sa-skya Monastery was upheld by Mongol arms and prestige. However, the Sa-skya abbots were unable to force the other monasteries to accept their authority. Dissent arose from those who were jealous of so much power concentrated in one monastery, and for the rest of the thirteenth century the history of Tibet was characterized by incessant sectarian strife. All the monks of the great monasteries had one thing in common, however. With their minds focussed on the acquisition of temporal powers, they began to pay greater attention to worldly pursuits and pleasures; they became insolent and complacent, and their religion degenerated into exorcism and sorcery.

Amid such widespread decay of the church a reformer named Tsong-kha-pa (1357-1419) arose, who advocated a return to the traditional Buddhist way of life, a clearing away of witchcraft and magic, restoration of celibacy, prohibition of meat and alcohol, a severe monastic discipline, and a strict curriculum for all monks. The sect which he organized, commonly called the Yellow Sect because the members wore yellow robes and hats, won immediate approval among the populace, who were fired by the fresh ideas and apostolic zeal displayed by his followers.

The rapid growth of the Yellow Sect inevitably evoked opposition from the most powerful of the older schools, commonly called the Red Sect. As part of its strategy to reinforce itself for the struggle against the Yellow Sect, the Red Sect began to strengthen its ties with the rulers of Gtsang in central Tibet. The Yellow Sect also made its moves for political alliances, but it went outside of Tibet, to the Ordos Mongols, for support. The leader of the Ordos Mongols at this time was Altan Khan, who acknowledged obeisance to the Ming court and was given the title Prince Shun-i. The visit of the third Grand Lama of the Yellow Sect to Altan Khan was, therefore, not only to propagate the faith among the Mongols, but was based on more worldly considerations. On the occasion of this meeting, which took place in 1578, the third lama proclaimed Lamaism and called upon the Mongols to accept it as their religion in place of their Shamanism. The lama then received from the Khan the title "Dalai-lama," "dalai" being the Mongol word for "ocean." Thus the title of Dalai-lama or the Great Ocean Lama originated with the third lama of the Yellow Sect. As a result of this meeting cordial relations were established between the Yellow Sect and the Mongols—a fact which resulted in the rapid spread of the sect among the Mongols. One might say that during the thirteenth century Lamaism was influential in the Mongol court but not among the people; now, during the sixteenth century, it captured the allegiance of the common Mongols.

This close relationship between the Mongols and the Yellow Sect alarmed the Red Sect and the king of Gtsang, and the latter undertook to uphold Tibetan independence and oppose outside interference by rallying to his support all the older sects of Tibetan Buddhism. These activities of the Gtsang king in turn led the Yellow Sect to lean even more upon its newly won converts, the Mongols. In 1641 the latter, under Gusri Khan, were invited to intervene in Tibet by the fifth Dalai-lama, who wanted to eliminate the king of Gtsang as his political rival. In the ensuing campaign the Tibetan armies were disastrously defeated, the Gtsang king himself was captured and killed, and in the next year the Yellow Sect was triumphantly installed in Lhasa. With the support of the Mongols, the Dalai-lama now added to his spiritual powers the temporal authority that went with being the ruler of the land. Such a situation, begun in 1642, was to endure to our own times.

The Ming rulers continued the policy pursued by their predecessors, the Yüan, in supporting the abbots of the great lama monasteries. This they did by conferring high honorary titles on the leaders of the different schools. Unlike the Mongols, who gave primacy to one monastery above the others, the Ming spread out their favors to several and thus assured that no one monastery or sect would become paramount in importance. While the lamas undoubtedly benefited from this imperial patronage, such benefits were not all one way. The Ming Dynasty, and later the Manchu, undoubtedly patronized Lamaism out of one primary political motive—to use the high priests of the Tibetan religion to help them maintain control over the Tibetans and Mongols. By gaining the support of these high lamas, who wielded tremendous power over their followers, the Chinese emperors hoped that they could effectively govern those border regions without the need of any costly occupying military force or civil administration. To a large extent such hopes were justified.

## MASTER CHU-HUNG

Of the outstanding clerics in the Ming Dynasty, Chu-hung united in his one person the two leading trends of Ming Buddhism—the harmonization of the different schools of Buddhism, specifically Ch'an and Pure Land, and the inauguration of a lay movement in the religion.

Chu-hung was born in 1535. After having lived the life of a householder, during which time he married twice (his first wife passed away when he was twenty-nine), he entered the monastic order at the age of thirty-two, one year following the death of his mother. His early apprenticeship was spent under famous

T'ien-t'ai, Hua-yen, and Ch'an masters. On a trip to south China he was so struck by the beauty of the mountains and streams in the Hang-chou area that he built the Yün-ch'i Temple there and remained in that temple the rest of his life. Hence he is sometimes called Chu-hung of Yün-ch'i Temple. In this temple he attached the greatest importance to strict adherence to the *Vinaya* rules; he ordered separate quarters for those monks who were zealous and energetic, for the sick and aged, and for traveling clerics. In one of his works he wrote that before the period of the Five Dynasties (907-960) observance of the rules of discipline was, on the whole, strict, but afterward, with the increasing popularity of Ch'an, laxity arose, with the result that monks and novices were either ignorant or negligent of the *Vinaya*. It was for the purpose of purifying the sangha that he decided to reemphasize the disciplinary code governing the conduct of monks.

During his lifetime the Jesuits had already secured a foothold in China, and had unerringly chosen Buddhism as their main antagonist in the battle for the souls of the Chinese. Chu-hung took cognizance of the Catholic arguments against Buddhism and wrote a treatise against Christianity entitled *T'ien-shuo ssu-p'ien* (*Four Chapters on the Explanation of Heaven*), which consisted of two main themes—criticism of Christianity and refutation of the Catholic arguments against Buddhism. On the first point he argued that the Christian conception of God and heaven was rather naïve, for, he contended, the Christian heaven was none other than the Tushita heaven of Buddhism, with the Christian God in the same category as the Tushita god. He based his contention on the Christian concept of Jesus as the son of God in heaven, who was then born on earth to serve mankind, just as the Buddha resided in the Tushita heaven before rebirth on earth. Thus the Christian God was just one step above the gods of Indra heaven, but still far below the gods of the Brahma heaven. Therefore the Christian God was but one, and an inferior one at that, among a host of superior Buddhist gods.

As for the criticism emanating from Catholic sources, the missionaries had said that the *Fan-wang-ching* (*Brahma's-net sutra*) taught that all sentient beings might possibly have parents in a different state of rebirth; hence it preached against killing, for it might conceivably be that in killing and eating an animal one might be killing and eating his own parents. If this were so, the Catholic missionaries argued, then one should go further and say that one should not marry or employ another person, for the wife or the servant might likewise be one of his parents.

Chu-hung replied that the main purpose of the discussion in the *Fan-wang-ching* is to prevent people from killing sentient beings. As for marriage, Confucius taught that it is permissible between people having different surnames; however, Chu-hung wrote that before this takes place, a soothsayer should be consulted to find out whether or not the proposed party is a parent in a different rebirth. Marriage is a common custom among mankind, he wrote, and therefore the laws governing marriage are rather lax, so that soothsayers and divination are permitted in the choice of mates. However, killing is the greatest evil, and therefore the laws governing killing are so strict that divination is not permitted.

## MOVEMENT TOWARD UNITY AMONG SCHOOLS

The outstanding feature of Ming Buddhism was the harmonization of the different schools, and in this movement Chu-hung played a leading role. Not only was he well informed on the *Vinaya*, but he was also conversant with the doctrines of Hua-yen, Ch'an, and Pure Land. Chu-hung was not the first to advocate such harmonization of all schools; he had a number of predecessors, the most important of whom was Yen-shou (904-975) of the Sung Dynasty.

Chu-hung held that, in reciting and meditating on the Buddha Amitābha, one should not only focus the mind on the name but also the ultimate reality behind the name. Outside of the mind that does the meditation on Amitābha, there is no Amitābha; outside of the Buddha Amitābha meditated upon, there is no meditating mind. Here Chu-hung was but expressing the Ch'an slogan of the mind's being the Buddha in another way. As for the ultimate reality behind the name, he called it the absolute mind, which is devoid of all passions and desire for existence, and free from illusions and disturbances. It is the function of *nien-fo* to attain to this absolute mind. This recitation and invocation of the name of the Buddha is like the intense meditation advocated by Bodhidharma and his Ch'an followers.

The necessity of an unperturbed and unified mind in practicing the *dhyāna* exercises served also as a connecting link with the T'ien-t'ai School, since the latter school greatly emphasized *chih-kuan*, concentration and insight. Moreover, the idealistic nature of both Ch'an and Pure Land thinking provided a common basis for these schools to be harmonized with both the T'ien-t'ai and Hua-yen teachings. The T'ien-t'ai taught that all things are the products of the mind, and that outside of the mind nothing exists. The Hua-yen School likewise held to the view that all events and things of the phenomenal world are merely creations of the mind and hence are without actual existence.

On the basis of these experiences and views commonly shared by the different schools of Buddhism, such Ming masters as Chu-hung, Tz'u-po Chen-k'o (1543-1603), Han-shan Te-ch'ing (1546-1623), and Ou-i Chih-hsü (1599-1655) all were active in pushing the movement of harmonizing and unifying the schools. They wrote that though Ch'an and Pure Land followed different paths, their psychological attitudes were the same. When the Pure Land advocate sat down to practice *nien-fo* or utter the name of Amitābha, his mind was concentrated entirely on that one phrase to the exclusion of all other thoughts, all literature, and all the accoutrements of institutionalized religion. In this respect his mental attitude was just like that of the Ch'an practitioner concentrating on his *kung-an*. Han-shan, the great Ch'an master, once wrote: "I concentrated on reciting the name Amitābha, day and night, without interruption. Before long Buddha Amitābha appeared before me in a dream, sitting high in the sky in the direction of the setting sun. Seeing his kind face and eyes radiant with compassion, clear and vivid, I prostrated myself at his feet with mixed feelings of love, sorrow, and happiness."[5] When he was thirty-four, he wrote that he spent a good deal of time copying the sutras, and with every stroke of the brush he uttered the name of the Buddha Amitābha. In his old age it is said that he recited the *Amitābha-sutra* every morning

[5] Chang, *The Practice of Zen*, 89.

and uttered the name of Amitābha several thousand times each day. Such practices on the part of a great Ch'an master illustrate how closely allied the Pure Land and Ch'an Schools were during this period.

In the works of Chu-hung is found his belief that the Hua-yen doctrine that the innumerable Buddha worlds may be found in one speck of dust may be equated with the Pure Land idea that the Buddha lands of the ten directions are reflected in the jewelled trees of the Western Paradise. Some Ch'an monks—for instance, Ch'u-shih Fan-ch'i (1296-1369) and Ch'u-shan Shao-ch'i (1404-1473) of the early Ming—practiced *nien-fo* diligently, and it was Chih-hsü who wrote that all three teachings, Ch'an, sutras, and *Vinaya,* could be unified under the banner of *nien-fo.* Chih-hsü is also known for his compilation *Yüeh-tsang chih-tsin* (*Knowing the Way in Examining the Canon*), in 48 *chüan,* a reference book containing notes on the Chinese canon which serves more or less as an annotated bibliography.

## LAY MOVEMENT IN BUDDHISM

The other movement in which Chu-hung was involved was the development of Buddhism among the laity. Through his influence as a Pure Land master and through his writings such as the *Tzu-chih-lu,* many people began practicing *nien-fo* as well as following the moral principles involved in the concept of merits and demerits, even though they did not join the sangha. At the same time the widespread degeneration of the sangha, which began under the Sung and continued through the Yüan, kept people from becoming monks, even though they were pious and devoted followers of the law. Besides, the system of civil service examinations, now operating smoothly and efficiently, attracted the best minds to the official service, so that there were few excellent people who cared to become monks. Under such circumstances the movement toward lay Buddhism arose during the latter part of the Ming Dynasty and was to continue through the next period, the Manchu or Ch'ing Dynasty. Such laymen embraced Buddhist principles and practices in their daily lives, they participated actively in the propagation of the dharma through their writings, they encouraged the printing and distribution of Buddhist literature, but they preferred to remain as Buddhist laymen and not monks.

During the early Ch'ing Dynasty one of the most prominent Buddhist laymen was P'eng Shao-sheng (1740-1796), also called Ch'ih-mu. In his early years he had specialized in the writings of the Sung Neo-Confucians, but after reading the works of Chu-hung and Chen-k'o, he became converted to Buddhism and spent the rest of his life serving as a pious and devoted layman. From these two monks he acquired his predilection for the doctrines and practices of the Pure Land School, especially its emphasis on *nien-fo*. For him, there is no need for a Buddhist image while invoking the name of the Buddha. The very invocation itself constitutes the Buddha, the Buddha reaches us without coming, and we reach the Buddha without going to him. He also wrote a book entitled *I-ch'eng chüeh-i lun* (*Treatise on the One Vehicle that Resolves Doubts*), in which he strongly refuted the wrong views on Buddhism entertained by such Sung scholars as Ch'eng Ming-tao and Lu Hsiang-shan. Although he was a Pure Land devotee, he advocated harmonization of all the different schools of Buddhism as well as a synthesis of the three beliefs—Buddhism, Confucianism, and Taoism.

This movement toward lay Buddhism was to reach its highest point during the closing years of the Ch'ing Dynasty, when the leading roles in the religion were enacted by such people as Yang Jen-shan (also known as Yang Wen-hui, 1837-1911) and Wang Hung-yüan.

During the T'ai-p'ing rebellion (1851-1865) Buddhism suffered one of its most crushing blows. The T'ai-p'ing leaders, in their campaign against all idolatrous worship, wrought their greatest damage to the Buddhist sangha by their wholesale destruction of Buddhist images, libraries, and temples in all the areas which they overran. The revival of the religion after that holocaust was engineered mainly through the dedicated leadership and activities of such men as Yang Jen-shan. With the destruction of the sutras the Chinese Buddhists found it difficult to obtain reading materials. To alleviate this shortage, Yang concluded an agreement with the Japanese Buddhist scholar Bunyiu Nanjio, who had just returned from Europe, through which he could obtain from the Japanese books to take back to China for publication. He organized the Chin-ling Sutra Publishing Center in Nanking to print and distribute the mass of literature he thus obtained from Japan. All in all, it is estimated that during his lifetime he distributed over a million Buddhist tracts, comprising both Hīnayāna and Mahāyāna texts. More than anyone else Yang was responsible for the revival of Buddhist literature through his publication endeavors.

Wang Hung-yüan's contribution lay in his reintroduction of Esoteric Buddhism from Japan into China. He had studied in Japan under renowned Shingon masters such as Gonda Raifu, and upon his return to China he translated into Chinese a number of Japanese books dealing with Esoteric Buddhism. The Association for the Renaissance of Esoteric Buddhism which he organized carried on an extensive educational program in south China, especially in his native place, Ch'ao-chou in Kwangtung.

This transition of leadership from the clergy to laymen was the culmination of the transformation from Hīnayāna to Mahāyāna. In China the degeneration and resultant weakness of the sangha hastened this process. Thus the role played by laymen in modern Chinese Buddhism has been much more impressive than that of the clergy. They were instrumental in the publication and dissemination of Buddhist texts, they stimulated a revival of Buddhist thought, they carried on the philanthropic and social activities of the Buddhist sangha, and they provided the leadership of the religion during the modern period of stress and strain. In some instances they even officiated at religious services, and in so doing took over some of the duties of the monks. This movement toward lay leadership in the church was one of the most significant developments within Buddhism in recent history.

## THE MANCHU EMPERORS AND BUDDHISM

While the lay movement was being pushed by the Chinese, the Manchu emperors were also establishing contacts with Buddhism, especially Lamaism.

Even before the Manchus penetrated the Great Wall to become the masters of China proper, it is likely that they already had become acquainted with Lamaism through the Mongol tribes. Like the Mongols before them, they favored this brand of Buddhism, which they felt was closer to the Shamanism they believed. A theory widely held by Japanese scholars contended that through this early contact the name of the bodhisattva Mañjuśrī was introduced to the Manchus, who were called Ju-chen at the time, and from the name of this bodhisattva the tribe derived the name *Man-chou*, Manchu. Nurhachi, founder of the dynasty, was looked upon as an incarnation of Mañjuśrī.

After their conquest of China the Manchu emperors continued to patronize Lamaism, with the added incentive that such a policy would aid them in winning the allegiance of the Mongols and Tibetans. On his part, the fifth Dalai-lama also quickly assessed the changing political picture in China, even before the Manchus penetrated the Great Wall; for as early as 1642 he had sent emissaries to the Manchu court in Mukden. After the Manchus were established in Peking, they extended a formal invitation to the Dalai-lama to visit Peking, which he did in 1652. No doubt the Ch'ing emperor did this in the full knowledge that this Dalai-lama was his most powerful ally in establishing Manchu control over Tibet and Mongolia. To manifest their support of Lamaism, the early Manchu emperors, especially K'ang-hsi, made numerous visits personally to Wu-t'ai-shan, the holy mountain of Lamaism, to pay their respects to Mañjuśrī and the temples dedicated to him. Numerous lama temples were also constructed, with the largest and finest concentrated in such areas as Feng-t'ien, Peking, and Wu-t'ai-shan. Those in Peking included such famous ones as Yung-ho-kung, Ch'ung-chu-ssu, and Huang-ssu. Prosperous lama temples such as the Pai-ling-miao in Inner Mongolia and the Kumbum in Ch'ing-hai housed over five hundred and a thousand lamas respectively. Moreover, living Buddhas also began to appear in alarming numbers; at one time over seventy-six of them were said to be living in various lama temples in north China and Mongolia.

In addition to their interest in Lamaism the early Manchu emperors Shun-chih and Yung-cheng were also favorably disposed to the Ch'an School, represented at this time by the Lin-chi branch. Shun-chih often invited Ch'an monks to the palace, and one of them, Yü-lin, kept a record of his conversations with the emperor on points of Ch'an doctrine and practices. The most deeply committed to Ch'an Buddhism, however, was Yung-cheng (1723-1735), who called himself the Perfectly-enlightened Layman. In the *Yü-hsüan yü-lu* (*Selected Imperial Sayings*), in nineteen *chüan*, which he finished in 1732, he has left behind a record of his interest in and study of Ch'an Buddhism. So high an opinion did he hold of his own competence that he even criticized the views entertained by Ch'an masters who had been highly praised by his predecessor Shun-chih. In the same collection may be found the biographies and collected sayings of famous monks, mostly Ch'an, but including one Taoist and one layman, none other than himself. He indicated that he had assembled the sayings of the masters for the purpose of popularizing them among the people. The inclusion of a Taoist in the group might be an indication that he looked with favor on the harmonizing of Taoism and Buddhism. In addition to his Ch'an leanings he was also attracted by the writings of the Ming Pure Land master Chu-hung, who, as will be recalled, was a strong advocate of harmonizing Ch'an and Pure Land teachings. To this extent one may say that Yung-cheng was also interested in the movement to bring closer together the two dominant schools of Buddhism of his time.

During the thirteenth year of Yung-cheng's reign (1735) work was started under imperial auspices on the printing of the Buddhist canon, a task which was completed in 1738. This is the *Lung-tsang* or Dragon Edition of the Chinese Tripitaka. Under the next emperor, Ch'ien-lung, was also initiated the tremendous project of translating the Buddhist canon into Manchu, an undertaking that was finally completed in 1790. During the second year of Yung-cheng, or 1724, the Peking edition of the Tibetan Tripitaka was completed with the printing of the Tanjur in that year, as the Kanjur had already been printed in 1700.

The Manchu emperors, like the Mongols before them, had to cope with a number of rebellions stirred up by the White Lotus Society. In addition to the slogan that it was preparing for the coming of Maitreya, the society added the nationalistic argument that it was aiming at the overthrow of the alien Manchus to restore the native Ming Dynasty. Its most formidable effort started in the year 1796, when it fomented a rebellion in the

mountainous areas of Hupei; within the next few years the con-
flagration flowed over into Honan, Shensi, Szechuan, and Kansu.
By arming and training the local militia, which served as self-
protection corps for their respective villages and towns, the
Manchus were finally able to suppress the rebellion in 1805.

In 1815 the Manchus found another rebellion brewing in Hopei,
led by a Wang family in Luan-chou. The Wang household circulated a tract, the contents of which carried the familiar story
of the three Buddhas of the past, present, and future. The Buddha
of the past was Dīpankara; that of the present, Śākyamuni; that
of the future, Maitreya. The tract went on to say that Maitreya
will soon be reborn in the Wang family. Wang went about
holding meetings of the people in the surrounding regions, and
soliciting contributions from them to prepare for the coming of
Maitreya. He told the people that when the future Buddha
actually descended on earth, all their contributions would be
amply rewarded. One sees in this tract and the activities of the
Wang family a good picture of the methods used by the White
Lotus Society to win followers and support for a rebellion
against the Manchus. In this instance the revolt was not able
to get under way because of the early discovery of the tract.

During the reign of K'ang-hsi (1662-1721), of the Ch'ing
Dynasty, a census of the Buddhist sangha indicated that there
were 79,622 temples and 118,907 monks and nuns.[6] While the
number of temples was the highest in history, the size of the
monastic community was rather small, and the suspicion exists
that the figures are not accurate. Statistics for the preceding
T'ang and Sung Dynasties were much higher, while during the
early years of the Republic it was estimated that there were
740,000 monks and nuns. Whatever the size of the sangha, one
point is clear: moral and spiritual decadence was universal. Too
many of the clerics entered the order not for the spiritual message
of the Buddha or for religious discipline, but mainly to gain a
livelihood. All too often they were the ones who failed to succeed

[6] Temples, officially constructed, large    6,073
    ”           ”            ”      small    6,409
    ”        privately        ”      large    8,458
    ”           ”            ”      small   58,682

                          Total           79,622
    Monks, 110,292; nuns, 8,615; total, 118,907

in society or who wanted to escape from society because of some crimes committed. No wonder, therefore, that numerous restrictions and measures against the order were issued from time to time by the Ch'ing emperors. For instance, a monk who married was punishable by eighty blows of the bamboo. Monasteries were not to expand their facilities at will; the abbot of any institution violating this rule would be bambooed one hundred times, the monks banished to the border regions, and nuns reduced to servants in government offices. In 1646 a measure was issued banning monks from living among the populace, and in 1677 temples in Peking were prohibited from preaching to mixed crowds within the temple precincts. In 1736 age limits were set up for entry into the order; boys must be at least sixteen and girls fourteen. In the eyes of the Ch'ing legal code monks and nuns were no different from the common people, for they had to reverence their parents and to participate in the ancestral funeral ceremonies; failure to do so would bring punishment by a hundred blows of the bamboo. The attitude of the Ch'ing emperors was well expressed in an edict of Ch'ien-lung, issued the sixth month of 1739:

"The ruling princes of old often issued decrees calling for the screening of monks and Taoist priests. Certainly this was because there was indiscriminate mixture of the good and bad among the Buddhists and Taoists. Those among them who shut themselves from the world to practice secretly the monastic discipline probably number but one or two in a hundred, while those who are idlers and loafers, joining the sangha under false pretenses just to seek for food and clothing, and those who are criminals and draft dodgers, fearing punishment and concealing themselves to escape the clutches of the law, are probably countless.

"If one male does not farm, some people will starve; if one female does not weave, some people will be cold. The addition of one new monk means the decrease of one farmer. This group does not farm but it still eats, it does not weave but it still wears clothes. Moreover, it consumes choice foods and wears elegant clothing shamelessly, as if these were its proper due. Therefore the income of two or three hard-working farmers is not sufficient to satisfy the needs of one monk or priest. Since these monks and priests waste the wealth of the people and contaminate the customs of the land, and since they are parasites in society and a disgrace to their religion, certainly they should not be permitted to increase in numbers without cease. However, since these religions have been transmitted for a long time and their followers very numerous, it is difficult to proscribe them at once. Therefore we command that the system of issuing monk certificates be again practiced, so that there may be an investigation and registration of the monastic order now, for the ultimate purpose of gradually decreasing their numbers in the future. This is our intention in administering this business."[7]

In this edict the emperor repeated many of the arguments previously leveled against the Buddhists. However, he was mindful enough of the lessons of history to know that proscription was not the correct policy, and, consequently, he sought to diminish the negative effects of the religion by decreasing the number in the monastic community. At the same time, for political and religious considerations involving the Tibetans and Mongols, the Manchu emperors embraced Lamaism and threw their support to this brand of Buddhism. Lacking imperial support and already in a low state, the monastic community in China during the latter half of the Ch'ing Dynasty dozed in a lethargic condition, and this situation enabled devout laymen like Yang Wen-hui to emerge and assume the leadership necessary for the propagation of the religion. Their efforts resulted in a temporary revival under T'ai-hsü during the early twentieth century.

[7] *Tung-hua hsü-lu,* Ch'ien-lung 9th year, 17b-18c.

# CHAPTER XVII

# REFORMS AND CHANGES: THE MODERN PERIOD

T H E revolution of 1911 that toppled the Manchu Dynasty and established the Republic of China also brought in its wake a number of problems for the Buddhist sangha. Following the political revolution, an intellectual climate was ushered in that was unfriendly to the interests of Buddhism. The intellectual leaders who emerged during the second and third decades of the twentieth century wanted to liberate the people from the shackles of all religions and the conservative old Chinese culture. To them, the Chinese should be freed from subservience to the old literary, religious, political, and philosophical traditions. This movement of cultural reassessment, which is commonly called the Chinese Renaissance, was led by many men who felt that science was all-powerful and all-sufficient and could solve all the problems of life. Their aversion to religion was reinforced by another development in the 1920's—the introduction and subsequent widespread popularity of Marxist ideas. The Marxist condemnation of religion very naturally included Buddhism as its target. The attack and criticism against Buddhism from these two sources resulted in a number of discriminatory measures, such as special taxes and contributions being levied on temples, monasteries being appropriated for use as barracks and police stations, tenants on temple lands being encouraged not to pay rent, or Buddhist images being destroyed. More serious was the Movement to Promote Schools with Temple Resources, promoted with great vigor at the time. Temples had been used as schools for a long time in China, but this was the first time that there was an organized movement to put the temples to this use. As a preliminary to this in 1928 the government ordered a survey of all the temple resources in the land.

## REFORMS OF T'AI-HSÜ

To combat these anti-Buddhist measures there arose from within the ranks of the decadent order a remarkable monk who was able to rally his disorganized fellow religionists and to initiate a program of reform within the church. This leader was T'ai-hsü (1889-1947), who wrote, "Aroused by the destruction of temples . . . I launched the movement to defend the religion, propagate the faith, reform the order and promote education."[1] His reforms called for a regeneration of the clergy, the rededication of Buddhist property for the benefit of the people, and the renewed study of Buddhist doctrines. On the national scale he organized a Chinese Buddhist Society in 1929, which in 1947 claimed 4,620,000 members. On the international scale he encouraged contacts with Buddhists of foreign countries. To bring this about he toured the world in 1928, and in succeeding years sent students to study in Ceylon, Siam, and Japan. This interchange undoubtedly strengthened the international character of Chinese Buddhism, and led to a new interest in Pali and Tibetan Buddhism.

In May of 1931 the proposal to promote schools with temple resources was presented at a national conference in Nanking. T'ai-hsü issued a manifesto to the delegates of the conference, calling their attention to the fact that many temples had been illegally seized and converted to barracks and schools, and asking for their return. He also emphasized the part that Buddhism with its emphasis on love and compassion could play as a unifying element in bringing together the five different ethnic groups (Chinese, Manchu, Mongol, Moslem, and Tibetan) in the national entity. As a result of this statement the Buddhists won their case; the principle of freedom of religion was reaffirmed, and an order was issued calling for the protection of all temple property and prohibiting the seizure of such for any secular purposes.

In order to effect reforms within the order it was necessary to have properly trained leaders. To achieve this objective the Buddhists established a number of institutes, of which the most famous were the Wu-ch'ang Buddhist Institute, started by T'ai-hsü in 1922, and the Institute of Inner Learning, started by Ou-yang Chien in Nanking in 1922. About the same time the Buddhist Institute of Southern Fukien in Amoy and the Institute of the Three Times in Peking were established. That these institutes achieved some measure of success may be seen in the

[1] W. T. Chan, *Religious Trends in Modern China*, New York, 1953, 56.

large number of prominent clerics and laymen who became leaders in the order during this period.

Under the inspiring leadership of T'ai-hsü and his fellow reformers the Buddhist community began to show signs of intellectual resurgence. In 1923 lay Buddhist leaders undertook the project of publishing the *Supplement to the Tripitaka*, in 750 stitched volumes, which had first appeared in Kyoto in 1905-1912. Later in 1933-1936 the Chi-sha edition of the canon was reproduced, in 1,362 *chüan* and 570 stitched volumes. Rare items in the Chin edition found in 1934 were also published as the *Sung-tsang i-chen* (*Precious Items Bequeathed from the Sung Canon*). Even more meaningful was the appearance of Buddhist periodicals in ever-increasing numbers, many of which were started to refute the anti-Buddhist literature of the period. During the years 1920-1935 there were 537 works and 58 periodicals published. Of the latter the *Hai-ch'ao-yin* (*Sound of the Tide*) was the most influential.

## REVIVAL OF THE IDEALISTIC SCHOOL

Probably the most significant development in the intellectual resurgence was the revival of interest in the Idealistic School. This revival was initiated by the publication in 1901 of the *Ch'eng-wei-shih-lun shu-chi* (*Notes on the Completion of the Idealist Doctrine*) of K'uei-chi, long lost in China but brought back from Japan. The leader of this revival was the layman Ou-yang Chien, and the Institute of Inner Learning which he organized in Nanking in 1922 was the center. In this institute was assembled an illustrious group of Buddhist scholars to lecture on Idealistic philosophy to eager young intellectuals attracted by the systematic and articulate arguments of the school. Another outstanding participant in this revival was T'ai-hsü, with his center at Wu-ch'ang, which was a strong rival to Ou-yang's center in Nanking. For more than two decades, starting with 1914, when he first became interested in Idealism, he taught and wrote on the subject. Finally, there was Hsiung Shih-li, who formulated what he called the new Idealism.

Though all these thinkers lectured and wrote under the banner of Idealism, still there were important differences in their interpretations. An example may be found in the controversy between Ou-yang and T'ai-hsü over the nature of *tathatā*, Genuine Thusness. In such an Idealistic text as the *Awakening of Faith*, Genuine Thusness is conceived to be permanent and absolute, pure and perfect in its self-nature. At the same time it is also conceived to be connected with the world of particulars. Therefore Genuine Thusness is not only the noumenon but also phenomenon. This is, of course, the logical outcome of the monistic position of Mahāyāna Buddhism with its identification of the two levels of truth. Genuine Thusness is therefore both tranquil and aroused.

Ou-yang objected to this view of Genuine Thusness. He argued that it remains always in a state of immobility, purity, and absoluteness, and cannot become involved in the world of multiplicity. To him the two worlds, noumenon and phenomenon, are separate; Genuine Thusness is absolute truth, and cannot be aroused from its tranquil state to make distinctions among things.

T'ai-hsü, on the other hand, saw no objection to the identification of noumenon with phenomenon, of Genuine Thusness and the world of things. To him the mind is Genuine Thusness. As reality it remains as Genuine Thusness, but as function it is aroused and makes distinctions, and thus creates the world of multiplicity. In the words of one of his disciples, "As principle, Reality is not created, but as facts and functions, it is created."[2] While Ou-yang considered Genuine Thusness to be absolutely transcendental, T'ai-hsü conceived of it as being both transcendental and immanent. In this view T'ai-hsü remained within the tradition of Chinese Buddhism—that of harmonization and synthesis.

Hsiung Shih-li started out with Buddhism but was soon influenced by Neo-Confucian thought to arrive at the realization that "principle and facts come from one source, and that the hidden and manifest are one thing."[3] Thus he experienced what Confucians called unity of reality and function. He followed the Idealistic School in explaining the origin of the external world. But whereas the school considered only the mind as real, and the object domain as void or empty, Hsiung declared that the

[2] *Ibid.*, 123.
[3] *Ibid.*, 127.

mind and object domain constitute one unity. While the object domain cannot be considered to be independent, still it is not illusory, and in this respect he differed from the orthodox Idealists. The latter say that everything in the phenomenal world is caused by seeds, that these seeds are real in themselves, different from consciousness, equipped with energy to produce, numerous, different, and independent from one another.

Hsiung disagreed with this theory of seeds, for he held that cause and effect (seed and manifestation) cannot be separated. He also proposed to explain how the energy in seeds can produce. This energy, he claimed, is voluntary and acts by itself; it is also real in itself. To him, therefore, energy has two states—the state of being itself as reality and the state of being expressed as function. However, these two states are basically one.

This position is different from that held by the Idealists. According to them phenomenon is the result of germination by seeds, and these seeds are to be found in the *ālaya*. Hsiung called this pluralism, and he charged that such a view fails to understand that reality and junction are one. He therefore criticized the Idealists, saying that although they conceived of Genuine Thusness as the reality of the dharmas, they do not equate Genuine Thusness with seeds, nor do they look upon the seeds as manifestations of Genuine Thusness. To the Idealists, therefore, Genuine Thusness and the seeds appear to be two unrelated things.

This constitutes the main difference between Hsiung's new Idealism and the orthodox school. For the latter all phenomena have the energy of seeds as their cause, but at the same time there is Genuine Thusness, which is the noumenon. Thus there appear to be two realities; whereas in Hsiung's system there is only one reality, for the active voluntary energy is Genuine Thusness itself. Again, in the orthodox system energy is plural, since there is a plurality of seeds in which the energy resides, whereas according to Hsiung energy is a complete unity. Finally, for the orthodox Idealists the seeds are the results of perfuming; hence they are not self-sufficient but require an external influence. Hsiung maintains that the energy acts by itself and is self-sufficient. Because of these differences Hsiung called his system the new Idealism.

# REVIVAL OF THE PURE LAND SCHOOL

While the discussions on Idealism were going on, there was also a revival within the Pure Land School that sought to restore piety and faith among its followers in place of the formalism that had developed over the centuries. Such practices as *nien-fo*, the fingering of the rosary, and the chanting of the scriptures could very easily degenerate into merely perfunctory activities performed without any spark of vitality or religious sentiment behind them. The monk mainly responsible for instilling new life and meaning into these practices was Yin-kuang (1861-1940), who after his conversion to Pure Land pietism concentrated on living a pure religious life based on faith, devotion, and holiness.

Yin-kuang carried on his teachings mainly in the provinces of Kiangsu and Chekiang, where he gained numerous followers and disciples. Endowed with great compassion, he believed and preached that salvation comes by faith alone—faith in Amitābha and faith in the realization of the Buddha-nature within oneself. According to one living witness, "To listen to him when he expounds the mysteries of the living faith, that is something one never forgets."[4]

These efforts by Yin-kuang and his followers brought about an extensive revival of the Pure Land School. Lotus Societies, Nien-fo Societies, and others of a similar nature sprang up all over China, consisting of pious men and women who came to seek new meanings in the traditional practices, to elevate themselves into higher planes of religious experience, and to satisfy their genuine religious aspirations. Of the four million or so lay devotees of Buddhism in China during the 1930's, it is estimated that sixty to seventy per cent considered themselves to be followers of the Pure Land School. This was the harvest reaped by the reforms of Yin-kuang.

# BUDDHISM UNDER THE PEOPLE'S REPUBLIC

With the occupation of the mainland by the Chinese Communists in 1949, the Buddha sangha was faced with an ideology

[4] K. L. Reichelt, *Truth and Tradition in Chinese Buddhism*, Shanghai, 1934, 311.

which was openly materialistic and atheistic, and which branded religion as an opiate and an escape from reality. The Communists charge that throughout its history in China, Buddhism was the spiritual weapon used by the ruling class to keep the oppressed classes in subjugation. They claim that Buddhism, by its teachings of the blessings and bliss of a future paradise, kept people docile in character and satisfied with their earthly status. They also attack the Buddhist emphasis on mind and consciousness, and condemn the idealistic Buddhist schools for advocating that the inequalities and iniquities of the present world, such as oppression, tyranny, and exploitation, are but creations of the mind and not connected with the evils of the existing social system. Furthermore, they criticize the Buddhist principle of harmony and integration of extremes as being contrary to the basic principle of Marxian dialectics, the law of contradiction. Instead of the idealistic interpretation of the world which practically all the Buddhist schools in China embrace, the Communists insist on a materialistic interpretation that acknowledges no existence outside of the material world.

While the Chinese Communists are opposed to religion, they also realize that such a religion as Buddhism has existed in China for a long time, and that it has exerted considerable influence in the past on many facets of Chinese culture. They know that even in their socialistic society, Buddhism still wields a pervasive influence over the actions, thoughts, and ideas of the Chinese masses. Consequently the leaders of the Communist party and government do not think it is opportune to use force to wipe out Buddhism, for fear that such a violent action might lead to serious repercussions among the people. The Communists also claim that as the educational and cultural levels of the masses are elevated, and as more scientific knowledge concerning the nature of the physical world and of society is disseminated, then belief in Buddhism will naturally decline and eventually disappear without the authorities taking any direct action against the religion.

On such grounds, the Chinese Communists proclaim their policy of freedom of religious beliefs in China. But they also emphatically point out that the converse, the freedom not to hold to any religious belief, is equally important. Some Communist writers have interpreted the latter to mean that it includes the right to oppose any religious belief. However, during the early days of the regime on the mainland, the government did not take any overt action against Buddhism, and its attitude was on the whole conciliatory. For instance, two Buddhist representatives, Chü-tsan a monk and Chao P'u-ch'u a layman, attended the first Political Consultative Assembly in 1949. It is conceivable that in the early stages of their power, the Communists had not yet formulated any definite plan of action.

In 1950, the Communist government made certain pronouncements which could be interpreted as paving the way for a new phase in its attitude toward Buddhism. On August 4, regulations were promulgated specifying that Buddhist monks, Taoist priests, fortunetellers, and soothsayers were religious workers, and hence were to be classified as parasites on society, since they did not engage in any productive work. At the same time, abbots in temples were singled out as a group and regarded in the same category as landlords, since they administered the large tracts of temple lands and lived on the sweat of the peasants. In these measures, one sees the attempt to set up class distinctions between peasants and monks, and between monks and abbots.

In 1951 the second phase began with the inauguration of the land reform movement. As early as 1947, the Communists had already decided on the principle of depriving temples and monasteries of their property-holding privileges. Now the People's Republic carried out this provision by confiscating the land held not only by the Buddhist temples but also that of the ancestral halls. Whenever this happened, the Buddhist temples were deprived of their main source of income for maintenance and the monastic order its means of livelihood. No longer would the monks be able to pursue their religious career of studying the scriptures and practicing meditation. Thus, while the stated objective of the land reform movement was not to oppose Buddhism, the final result amounted to just that, for if the temples no longer had the resources to buy incense and oil and to support the monks in their religious activities, the religion could not very well be expected to carry on. Young monks and nuns were therefore obliged to return to laity and marry, while those remaining in the order were required to engage in some productive activities and to undergo a period of reeducation to cleanse their minds of outmoded ideas concerning religion. As a result, monks turned to farming, establishing handicraft industries such as spinning, weaving, and sewing, opening vegetarian restaurants, planting tea, or teaching schools.

## FORMATION OF THE CHINESE BUDDHIST ASSOCIATION

With temple lands confiscated and the sangha reduced in size, the People's Government proceeded to the third phase, the organization of the Chinese Buddhist Association. Throughout the long history of the religion in China, the Buddhists have never been organized into a nation-wide body; instead they have always been loosely united in local units. The Communists felt that such a situation could not be permitted to continue, and for the purpose of bringing together all the Buddhist clergy and laymen in China into one organization which could be supervised by the government, the Chinese Buddhist Association was organized in 1953. In the winter of 1952, a preparatory commission met in the Kuang-chi Temple in Peking to draw up plans for the association. Over a hundred delegates representing groups from all parts of the country were present. The venerable monk Yüan-ying was chosen chairman. At this initial meeting, all plans for the formation of the association were completed, and it was agreed that the formal ceremonies for the inauguration of the association would be held in the following year.

On May 30, 1953, the Chinese Buddhist Association was officially declared to be in existence in a meeting held in the Kuang-chi Temple. Yüan-ying was chosen president of the association, but he died in September of the same year, and Shirob-jaltso, a native of Ch'ing-hai, was then designated to take his place. The layman Chao P'u-ch'u was chosen secretary-general. During the meeting, there were some unsuccessful attempts on the part of some monks to abolish the rules of ordination and discipline, so that monks could marry, eat meat, and drink spirits as they pleased. There were also some concerted efforts to pervert the teachings of the Buddha to conform to Marxian dialectics. Buddhism emphasized love and compassion for all sentient beings, and equality for all in the attainment of enlightenment. Now the supporters of the Communist ideology argued that these were not the guiding principles of Buddhism. They held that the Buddha in his lifetime was continuously involved in a struggle against the heretics, that the battle lines between friends and enemies of the Buddha were clearly delineated. According to the Marxists, the governing class in the feudalistic societies misinterpreted this fundamental nature of strife and controversy in Buddhism, and claimed instead that his guiding principles were love and compassion. The patriotic Buddhists of China should divest themselves of such feudalistic concepts and embrace the real spirit of Buddhism, that of strife and conflict.

According to the constitution, the purpose of the association is "to unite all followers of Buddhism under the leadership of the People's Government to demonstrate their love for the Fatherland and to preserve world peace." In elaborating upon this purpose, the Communist press at the close of the initial sessions of the association circulated statements that the members were not only to support the Fatherland and preserve peace, but also to differentiate between friend and foe, to recognize clearly the thoughts and actions of the enemies of the people, and to search out and eliminate all enemy agents, spies, and counter-revolutionaries. As for financial support of the association, the constitution provides that the expenses are to be met by voluntary contributions, but that if these should prove insufficient, then the association shall ask for financial assistance from the government.

The official mouthpiece of the association is the *Hsien-tai fo-hsüeh* (*Modern Buddhism*), a monthly that is the main source of our information concerning Buddhism in Communist China. The articles in it are generally of a popular nature, and only once in a while does one find an article that represents the results of serious research. A goodly portion of each issue is taken up with editorials and resolutions supporting the views and policies of the government. Very often the editorials had originally appeared in some official Communist organ such as the *Red Flag* or the *People's Daily*.

The association claims to represent 500,000 monks and 100,-000,000 Buddhist followers. There is no indication as to how these figures are arrived at. As a matter of fact, it is certain that the figure of 500,000 monks is pure guess, for it appeared as early as 1950 and as late as 1960, in spite of the number of monks who had fled the country or who had been defrocked in the interval. The activities of the association are largely in the hands of three individuals, Shirob-jaltso, the president, Chao P'u-ch'u, the secretary-general and one of the vice-presidents, and Chü-tsan, another vice-president.

According to the officers, the activities of the association consist of the following:

1. To serve as liaison between the government and the followers of Buddhism. Through the association, the government can make known to the Buddhists its plans and policies, and the Buddhists can inform the government what their views and interests are.

2. To train Buddhist personnel. As long as the government permits freedom of religious belief, the association plans to carry on its program of religious activities. To train the workers needed for such activities, a Chinese Buddhist Academy was established in Peking in 1956. The students in this academy are divided into two categories; one group would graduate after two years of study to become religious workers, while the other group would graduate after four years to become preachers and scholars of Buddhism. Just what is meant by the term religious worker is not clearly specified, but some observers in Hongkong have surmised that this category refers to administrators of temples which are permitted to exist.

3. To promote Buddhist cultural activities. To this end the association assists the government in identifying and protecting Buddhist cultural institutions and objects. Some of the famous centers of Buddhist art in China, such as Tun-huang and Mai-chi-shan in Kansu, Yün-kang in Shansi, and Lung-men in Honan, are designated as national treasures, and the government undertakes to restore and maintain the art objects found in these sites. According to the Communists, the art in these centers represents people's art, conceived and executed by the common people, and such a glorious contribution of the common people to Chinese culture must be preserved. The government has also assisted financially in the restoration of some of the famous Buddhist temples, such as the Pai-ma Temple in Lo-yang, reputed to be

the oldest in China, the Ling-yin Temple in Hang-chou, the Yung-ho-kung and Kuang-chi Temple in Peking, the Ta-tz'u-en Temple in Sian where Hsüan-tsang carried out his translation projects, and the famous Buddhist temples dedicated to Mañjuśrī on Wu-t'ai-shan. The association is also active in the work of studying and preserving the stone tablets containing Buddhist scriptures, found in Fang-shan in Hopei.

While the People's Government proclaims a policy of preserving historical relics and monuments, it often happens that the zeal of some local Communist cadres intent on opposing Buddhism led to just the opposite. A few examples of famous Buddhist structures being destroyed have been reported in the official Communist press. One concerned a pagoda in the Kuang-hui Temple in Hopei, built during the Chin dynasty and long regarded as an excellent example for the study of Chinese architecture; another was the Buddha hall in a certain Kuang-chi Temple in Hopei, constructed in the Liao dynasty in 1205; still another was the Buddha hall in a Hua-yen Temple in Ta-t'ung, also built during the Liao dynasty.

4. To encourage Buddhist international cooperation. The association makes it a point to send delegates to all Buddhist international conferences, with secretary-general Chao P'u-ch'u invariably as the chief delegate. In 1955 such delegations went to Japan and Burma; in 1956, to India and Nepal; in 1957, to Cambodia. In return, Buddhist representatives from the various Buddhist countries of southeast Asia are invited to China, where the Chinese Buddhist Association serves as their hosts.

Undoubtedly the association has carried out all these activities, but it is perhaps correct to say that these activities do not constitute the *raison d'être* for the organization. The fundamental reason for the establishment and the continued existence of the association is that it serves as the agent of the government for the control and supervision of Buddhist followers in China. By placing at the leadership of the association a few key individuals who are fervent supporters of its policies and programs, the government can wield effective control over the action of the association. From the articles of the constitution, and from the statements circulated in the Communist press at the time of its establishment, it is obvious that the members of the association are to be concerned not only with religious but also with political matters. In the eyes of the government, the Chinese Buddhist Association is to be no different from any other social action organization permitted to exist under the Communists. As long as the association fulfills its political role, it can carry on. The best evidence of this is to be found in the editorial policy of the journal, *Modern Buddhism,* and in the numerous resolutions passed by the association concerning national and international issues. In 1956, the association supported the government in protesting against the Anglo-French invasion of Egypt. In 1958, the association followed the government line in condemning the American and British landing of marines in Lebanon. In the same year, the association issued a statement supporting the government's claim to the off-shore islands, and condemning American aggression in Taiwan. In 1958 the government launched the year of the Big Leap, and throughout the year, regional offices of the association voiced their support of the program and objectives of the government. Then in 1959, the association came out in full and complete support of the government in the campaign against the Dalai Lama and the Tibetans. It echoed faithfully the charge that the Tibetans who were resisting the advancing Communist armies were instigated by Indian, American, and British agents, and that the Dalai Lama had been captured by reactionary elements and forced to leave Tibet against his will.

Besides serving as the agent of the government, the association fulfills another very useful role in the realm of international politics. To the Chinese Communists, the rich and fertile countries of southeast Asia, Vietnam, Cambodia, Laos, Burma, and Thailand, offer a most tempting area for expansion of their sphere of influence. In all these countries, Buddhism is the prevailing religion. If the impression could be created in these countries that Buddhism is not persecuted but is permitted to function as a religion in Communist China, then these Buddhist countries would not be suspicious and would be more favorably inclined toward the Communist giant to the north. To create this favorable image, the People's Government has permitted Chinese Buddhist delegations to visit the various countries of southeast Asia, ostensibly as representatives of the Chinese Buddhist Association, but in reality as semi-official emissaries, since no delegation can leave

Communist China without official approval. At the same time, the People's Government also extends a welcoming hand to visiting representatives of the Buddhist countries. Upon arrival in China, such representatives are received by officials of the Chinese Buddhist Association and taken on a tour of the temples in the metropolitan areas, in order to demonstrate that the Chinese Buddhists are enjoying freedom of religious belief.

One of the most powerful weapons used by the Chinese Buddhist Association to gain the good will of the Buddhist countries is a tooth of the Buddha, which the Communists claim was unearthed in China. This tooth was loaned to the Burmese government for display in Rangoon in 1955, and in 1961 it was exhibited in Ceylon.

These measures of the Chinese Communists have achieved some measure of success. For example, a group of Cambodian monks toured China in 1958, and on the eve of their departure from Canton, the leader of the Cambodian delegation announced to reporters that judging from what he saw, he sincerely believed that the Chinese Buddhists are enjoying freedom of religious belief. The display of the tooth in Ceylon also counteracted some of the unfavorable criticism aroused by the Communist invasion of Tibet.

The officers of the Chinese Buddhist Association insist that they are really enjoying such a freedom. They point to the temples that are still carrying on some semblance of religious services in such centers as Peking, Shanghai, Hang-chou, and Canton. Such temples and the monks living in them are to a large measure subsidized by the state. In view of what we have described, however, it would seem that this freedom is considerably circumscribed. The position of the government is that the followers of Buddhism will be left alone as long as they follow the official government line on all issues and abide by the pattern of coexistence, by which is meant that monks are not to carry on religious activities outside the temples, and the government is not to interfere with religious activities inside the temples. To the extent that the Chinese Buddhist Association is permitted to exist only if it supports the government one hundred percent, to that extent the Buddhists have lost some of their religious freedom. A most revealing instance of such limitation occurred in 1959.

In that year the government initiated its campaign against the Dalai Lama and the Tibetans, and once it did so, then all the members of the Chinese Buddhist Association had to denounce the Dalai Lama and his supporters as reactionaries, and to switch their allegiance to the Panchen Lama who had the support of the government. It would appear from this instance that the association is no longer free to speak the message of the Buddha, the message of love and compassion, tolerance and unity.

In view of the policy of the People's Government toward Buddhism, what are the prospects for the religion in the future? Some students of Buddhism boldly prophesy that the religion is now in the last stage of its existence in China and that it will not be able to survive the Communist pressures. They believe that the sangha, which has carried on for a thousand years since the end of the T'ang dynasty, the visible symbol of a great tradition on the wane, will soon disappear altogether on the mainland. For the moment, as we look at the present state of Buddhism under the Communists, we might be tempted indeed to agree with such a prediction. Yet the lessons of the past urge caution in any projection into the future. Buddhism is now subservient to the interests of the Communist state, but this is not something new in the history of the religion. Even when the religion was most powerful and most popular under the T'ang, it allowed itself to be controlled and supervised by the secular authorities. Temples and monasteries staged festivals at the imperial behest that had nothing to do with Buddhism. Monks and nuns were ordained and defrocked by the state. Temples were constructed and maintained by the state and the monks residing in them were subsidized by the imperial treasury. Even under such supervision and control, the resilience and elasticity of the religion enabled it to survive and prosper. The Chinese Communists are now doing some of the very things toward Buddhism which the emperors had done in the past.

It is well to keep in mind that even under the Communist regime, there still remain some of the outward symbols of the religion, temples, monks, the corpus of Buddhist literature, and the images of the buddhas and bodhisattvas. There is still interchange between the Buddhists in Communist China and those of other countries. It is true that some of the ideas held by the Chinese Buddhists on the mainland and the actions which they have performed might not be acceptable to the Japanese, Burmese, or other Buddhists, but cordial relations still remain between them. As long as such international exchange and such external symbols of the religion exist, even on a reduced scale, it is unlikely that the religion will be wiped out. The resilience and the endurance which have enabled the religion to survive controls and persecutions in the past may yet prove powerful enough to enable it to survive the Communist pressures of the present and to emerge in some different form in the future.

# CONCLUSION

# CHAPTER XVIII

# THE CONTRIBUTIONS OF
# BUDDHISM TO CHINESE CULTURE

A B O U T two thousand years in the life of a religion have been surveyed in this text. In such a sweeping history it has been impossible to explore all phases of the religion; only the significant movements, important episodes, and outstanding individuals involved have been discussed. We have shown the stages through which Buddhism passed in attaining growth and gaining acceptance by the Chinese. We have also depicted the role played by the religion during the period of its widest acceptance. Soon after that apogee Buddhism began to suffer from a slackening of intellectual and literary fervor; so that for the last thousand years, while the outward symbols of the religion continued to live, the inward dynamism was no longer present.

Before Buddhism declined, however, it made important contributions to Chinese culture, and even after it declined, it continued to exert an influence over many facets of Chinese life—its thought, literature, language, art, and science.

## NEO-CONFUCIANISM

As an intellectual movement Neo-Confucianism drew the attention of the educated Chinese away from Buddhism back to the Confucian classics. However, this Neo-Confucianism was influenced by Buddhism in more ways than one. The Indian religion had become so intimate a part of the intellectual make-up of the Chinese that it was impossible for the Sung thinkers to give up Buddhism entirely. While the Neo-Confucianists used terms found in the Confucian classics, they interpreted those terms in the light of the dominant Buddhist atmosphere, and the Neo-Confucian system would be incomprehensible to one not familiar with the prevailing Buddhist ideas of the age.

An example of this may be seen in Chang Tsai's extension of the meaning of jen to embrace all under heaven. It is more than likely that in this extension the Buddhist conceptions of the universality of life and the all-compassionate bodhisattva, ever ready to save all sentient beings, played a role.

Although the Neo-Confucian idealist Lu Hsiang-shan based his emphasis on the mind on the *Book of Mencius* and the *Great Learning*, one cannot escape the suspicion that he was influenced by Buddhist, especially Ch'an, tenets. Indeed, Lu and his chief disciple, Wang Yang-ming (1473-1529), of the Ming Dynasty, were accused by their opponents of being Buddhists in disguise, this in spite of the fact that in a letter to a friend Lu criticized Buddhism severely for its selfishness and negation of life. The Ch'an School, with its cardinal tenet that this mind is the Buddha and that this mind intuitively and instantly knows what is right and wrong without depending upon external sources, very likely influenced the thinking of Lu and Wang. It is interesting to note that the controversy which raged within Buddhist circles—that of gradual versus instantaneous enlightenment—found its counterpart in the discussions of the Neo-Confucians, with Chu Hsi representing the gradual rational approach and Lu Hsiang-shan the intuitive instantaneous approach.

In their advocacy of concentration of mind the Neo-Confucianists also appear to have been influenced by the Buddhists. Buddhist mental discipline emphasizes, among other things, mindfulness, meditation, and equanimity. Ch'eng Hao stressed these very things in his essay *Tranquility in Human Nature*. He wrote that tranquility means quietness in time of activity and inactivity, and that when the mind is excited, it becomes overactive and falls into uncertainty. He advocated concentrating the mind on one subject; when one does this, he said, the mind is its own master, will not fall prey to external influences, and cannot be harmed by any enemy.

From Li Ao to the Ch'eng brothers the Neo-Confucianists all had their say about what constituted sagehood. Li Ao wrote that a sage is enlightened when he is master of his emotions. Ch'eng Yi also wrote that the sage is one who controls his emotions of joy, anger, sorrow, fear, love, dislike, and greed, and adjusts his expression to the principle of the golden mean. This Confucian preoccupation with sagehood was probably a response to the Buddhist emphasis on the attainment of bodhisattvahood.

There were also particular views held by the Sung philosophers that might point to Buddhist influence. For instance, Chu Hsi held that any object contains within it the supreme undivided ultimate as well as the particularizing principle which gives the object its individual character. Such an idea is close to the Hua-yen doctrine of interpenetration and intermutuality, the all in one and the one in all. Shao Yung (1011-1077) in his cosmological speculations had a theory that at the end of an epoch, which he said spanned 129,600 years, the present world system would come to an end, to be replaced by another. Chu Hsi also shared in this view. Such an idea was alien to the Chinese and was undoubtedly influenced by the well-known Indian concept of aeons and recurring world systems.

While pointing out these influences of Buddhism upon Neo-Confucianism, we must not make the mistake of overestimating the extent of such influences. Though the Neo-Confucianists studied Buddhism and appropriated Buddhist ideas, the system which they constructed was distinctly Chinese in its emphasis on the reality of the phenomenal world, the importance of the individual, and the value of social relations and responsibilities. A fair verdict of history would therefore be that in this movement the Sung philosophers returned to their native Confucian traditions via some excursions into the path of the Buddha.

## BUDDHIST INFLUENCE ON TAOISM

Neo Confucianism was not the only system affected by Buddhism; Taoism was also subjected to its all-pervading influence. During the Han Dynasty Buddhism was able to gain a foothold on Chinese soil by allying itself closely with Taoism and borrowing from it, but in later centuries it was the Taoist turn to borrow from Buddhism.

To begin with, the Taoists never had any idea of their system as a religion consisting of a body of doctrines and beliefs left behind by a master and preserved in a corpus of literature. It was only after Buddhism had come in and gained widespread acceptance that the Taoists took over from the Buddhists the idea of a religion. Once having made this initial appropriation, the Taoists decided that they might just as well go all the way in imitating the foreign model.

First, the Taoists themselves admitted that they borrowed the practice of making statues and images from the Buddhists. The first Taoist images of their deities appeared about the middle of the fifth century under the Northern Wei Dynasty, with the deities flanked on both sides by Taoist saints.

It is in the field of literature that the Buddhist contribution to Taoism is most obvious. In the early stages of Taoism as a religion it was a relatively simple matter for the Taoists to build up a body of literature of their own. All they had to do was to group together those works branded as heterodox by the Confucians—works on alchemy, divination, hygiene, breathing exercises, and so forth—and attribute these to the founder of their religion, Lao-tzu. However, there was a limit to the supply of such literature and the Taoists would have faced a prolonged drought if no other sources had been forthcoming. Meanwhile, the Buddhist sutras were flowing into China in a never-ending stream, inciting the envy of the Taoists with their variety, scope, and imagination. To the latter this was an inexhaustible supply from which they could borrow and copy—exactly what the Taoists did from the fifth century on. So hasty and slipshod was this wholesale copying that the Taoists left behind numerous traces of their unethical practice. In general it seemed that what the Taoist did was to take over a Buddhist sutra and then substitute Lao-tzu for the word Buddha whenever it appeared, but very often the copyist was not attentive enough to make all the changes. Consequently, in some of the so-called Taoist works, we find such passages as the following:

"Of all the teachings in the world, the Buddha's teaching is foremost" (*Hsi-sheng ching, Sutra on the Western Ascent*).

"Our master is called the Buddha, who follows the incomparable teaching" (*Wen-shih-chuan, Biography of Wen-shih*).

"The host of saints and immortals have already realized the way of the Buddha" (*Tung-hsüan chen-i ching, Sutra on the True Unity Which Penetrates Mystery*).[1]

The most obvious of such borrowings may be seen in the biographies of Lao-tzu that appeared during the Sung Dynasty.[2] In

---

[1] The foregoing quotations may be found in Tokiwa, *Bukkyō to jukyō dōkyō*, 529-531.

[2] The following are the titles of the more important of these biographies:

one of these biographies, the *Yu-lung-chuan* (*Biography of the One Who Resembles a Dragon*), we read that Lao-tzu was born by issuing forth from the left rib of the Holy Mother, who was clinging to the branches of the plum tree at the time. As soon as he was born, he took nine steps and from each footprint lotus flowers sprang forth. At the time of his birth ten thousand cranes hovered above in the skies, while nine dragons spat forth water to bathe the newborn baby. After he was born, with his left hand pointing to heaven and his right hand to earth, he uttered the cry that in heaven and earth only the Tao was supreme. Nine days after birth his body became endowed with the seventy-two major and eighty-one minor characteristics. The Holy Mother, after giving birth to Lao-tzu, then mounted a jade chariot and in broad daylight ascended to heaven.

It is perfectly clear that such a biography of Lao-tzu was nothing more than a retouching of a Buddhist source, very likely the *Lalitavistara*, with some changes in proper names here and there.

Having built up their body of literature, the Taoists then organized it into a canon modeled, as one would expect, after the Buddhist Tripitaka. Consequently, the Taoist canon now consists of three sections, with each section then divided into twelve categories.[3]

---

*a*) Chia Shan-yüan (fl.1100), *Yu-lung-chuan* (*Biography of One Who Resembles a Dragon*), 6 *chüan, Tao-tsang,* 555.

*b*) Hsieh Shou-hao (d. 1193), *Hun-yüan sheng-chi* (*Record of the Primordial Sage*), 9 *chüan, Tao-tsang,* 551-553.

*c*) Ibid., *T'ai-shang Lao-chun nien-p'u yao-lüeh* (*Outline Genealogy of the Supreme Lao-chun*), 1 *chüan, Tao-tsang,* 554.

*d*) Ibid., *T'ai-shang hun-yüan Lao-tzu shih-lüeh* (*Historical Outline of the Supreme Lao-tzu's Life*), 3 *chüan, Tao-tsang,* 554.

The title of the first, *Yu-lung-chuan,* harks back to the legend of a visit supposedly made by Confucius to Lao-tzu. After the visit Confucius remarked to a friend that he knew that birds could fly, fishes could swim, animals could run, but that all these could be caught with some device. As for the dragon, however, Confucius said that he was at a loss as to what to do, for a dragon could mount a cloud and soar to the skies. Lao-tzu, he said, was like a dragon.

[3] The three sections of the Taoist canon are named *Tung-chen* (Understanding the True), *Tung-hsüan* (Understanding the Mysterious), *Tung-shen* (Understanding the Spirit). The twelve categories are fundamental texts, divine formulas, commentaries, efficacious diagrams, genealogies and traditions, rules of discipline, rituals, practices, manifold arts, histories and annals, hymns, and documents.

Certain concepts of the Buddhists were also taken over by the Taoists. An example of this was the concept of the bodies of the Buddha. During the Period of Disunity the Taoists had already developed the idea that the supreme Tao, in order to instruct deities and men in the world, from time to time would assume a human form to perform this function. The historic Lao-tzu was but one of these incarnations. Such a Taoist idea was undoubtedly based on the Buddhist doctrine of the two bodies of the Buddha, the *dharmakāya* or the body of essence, which is the only true and real body of the Lord, and the *nirmānakāya* or body of transformation, which is the manifestation of the *dharmakāya* on earth. In imitation of the bodhisattva, the all-loving and compassionate being, the Taoists brought forth a class of transcendent beings called *t'ien-tsun*, venerable celestials, conceived of chiefly as instructors and saviors. One of these celestials was said to have been eternally teaching and converting people since the beginning of time. The Buddhist concepts of karma and rebirth were likewise appropriated, as indicated in the following passage: "The Taoist saints since countless aeons in the past . . . have all depended on the merits of their past lives to attain to the Tao of the present; they have without exception reached their present state through the accumulation of merits derived from their former careers. . . ."[4] This is in contrast with the earlier Taoist doctrine of the transmission of burden, according to which the merits and demerits accrued by an individual were manifested not in his future lives but were passed on to descendants of later generations. Finally, the Buddhist concept of the three worlds—the world of desires, the world of forms, and the formless world—was taken over *in toto* by the Taoists.

This brief summary will suffice to show how much the Taoists appropriated from the Buddhists in their views on cosmology, pantheon, literature, and doctrines. Instead of Taoism's swallowing up Buddhism, as was feared at the end of the Han Dynasty, the Taoists were themselves overwhelmed by the Buddhists.

## LITERATURE

In the realm of literature the influence of the Buddhist translations, with their mixtures of prose and poetry, has already been

[4] *Fa-lun miao-ching* (*The Mysterious Sutra on the Wheel of the Law*), Tao-tsang, 177, 2a.

noted. Also mentioned was the part played by Buddhist literature in promoting the vernacular as an acceptable vehicle of
literary expression, for the Ch'an masters wrote their *Recorded
Sayings* in the simple, direct colloquial language of the day.
Much more important is the contribution of the element of
imagination to Chinese literature.

It is true that Taoist literature, such as the *Chuang-tzu*, contained passages which showed that the Chinese were not lacking
in imaginative powers, but this aspect seems to have been re-
pressed or neglected; so that the dominant Confucian literature
was, on the whole, formal, narrow, restricted, practical, and
having little to do with mythology. It emphasized the daily lives
and social duties of the individual; it was strong in the recording
of historical facts, but weak in telling a tale. Along came the
translation of the Mahāyāna sutras, where the Indians allowed
their imagination untrammeled freedom with fanciful descriptions of the glories of heaven and the torments of hell, of world
systems as numerous as the sands of the Ganges, of time and
space incomprehensible to the human mind. To the practical and
earth-bound Chinese this was indeed a staggering intellectual
experience. Such imagination may well be illustrated by a passage from the popular *Lotus Sutra*, where the Buddha sought to
convey to his disciples the idea of the interval of time which had
elapsed since his attainment of enlightenment: "Let there be the
atoms of earth of fifty hundred thousand myriads of *kotis* [a *koti*
is ten million] of worlds; let there exist some man who takes one
of these atoms of dust and then goes in an eastern direction fifty
hundred thousand myriads of *kotis* of worlds further on, there
to deposit that atom of dust; let in this manner the man carry
away from all these worlds the whole mass of earth. . . . Now,
would you think . . . that any one would be able to imagine,
weigh, count, or determine the number of these worlds? . . .
However numerous be those worlds, . . . there are not . . . so
many dust atoms as there are hundred thousand of *kotis* of aeons
since I arrived at supreme perfect enlightenment."[5]

Exposed to such types of unbridled imaginative literature, the
Chinese began to give freedom to their imagination again. The
best example of how well the Chinese learned the art of story-

---

[5] *Sacred Books of the East*, 21,299-300.

telling from the Indians may be found in the novels *Hsi-yu-chi* (*Record of a Trip to the West*) and the *Feng-shen-chuan* (*Annals of the Investiture of Deities*), both of the Ming Dynasty. The former is a fictitious account of the travel and adventures of Hsüan-tsang in his search for the law and the extraordinary exploits of his companions, the monkey and the pig, who helped him overcome all obstacles and dangers encountered during the journey. The other novel recounts the imaginary battles between the forces of the Shang and Chou peoples, in which even the gods participated, bringing with them the most ingenious weapons. So fanciful and unbelievable are these stories that the Chinese have a proverb to the effect that if one reads the *Hsi-yu-chi*, he will never amount to very much, and if one reads the *Feng-shen-chuan*, he will tell lies all his life. This freeing of the Chinese mind under the influence of Mahāyāna literature enabled the Chinese to produce the rich, romantic, and imaginative literature such as the novels and short stories of the Ming and Ch'ing Dynasties.

## LANGUAGE

In language new terms coined by the Buddhists gradually found their way into the Chinese vocabulary, and in the course of time they have been fully accepted by the Chinese, who never suspected that they originated from some foreign language. These new terms might be divided into two categories. The first comprises those which are translations of Buddhist concepts. Examples of these are *k'u-hai*, sea of misery; *hsi-t'ien*, the Western Paradise; *wu-ming*, ignorance; *chung-sheng*, sentient beings; *yin-yüan*, karma; *ch'u-chia*, leaving the household life. The second category comprises those terms which are transliterations of Sanskrit words. Examples are *ch'a-no*, an instant, from *kshana*; *t'a*, pagoda, from *thūpa*, which is a Pali word; *p'u-sa*, from bodhisattva; *lo-han*, from arhat or arahan; *mo-li*, jasmine, from *mallikā*; *seng*, a monk, from sangha.

## PHONOLOGY

The introduction of the Sanskrit alphabet into China influenced phonological studies in a number of ways. In the first place, there is the practice of the *fan-ch'ieh* system or the using of two characters to indicate the pronunciation of the third character. Traditional accounts say that this practice originated with Sun Yen of the Wei Dynasty (third century), but it is more likely that the method was already initiated during the waning years of the later Han Dynasty and that Sun merely popularized it. Heretofore the Chinese had attempted to indicate the pronunciation of a character by the use of homonyms, but in the *fan-ch'ieh* system the initial sound of the first character is combined with the final sound of the second to give the pronunciation. This method was undoubtedly influenced by the Chinese experience with the Sanskrit alphabet.

Closer acquaintance with the Sanskrit alphabet led to another innovation of great importance in phonology, namely, the formulation of the thirty *tzu-mu* or phonetic radicals by the monk Shou-wen during the latter half of the T'ang Dynasty. The thirty radicals were divided into the following categories: labials, languals, gutturals, dentals, and glottals. Such a division could have been possible only if the monk was familiar with the different divisions of the Sanskrit alphabet.

There is still another phonological contribution for which Buddhism is responsible, namely, the reconstruction of Chinese pronunciations of the past. Since the Chinese character is structural, the structure remains the same, while the pronunciation is likely to change with the passage of time. There have been attempts to reconstruct ancient Chinese pronunciations through the study of rhyme tables and phonetic compounds, but such methods only show that the ancient pronunciations were different from those of the present, but do not indicate accurately how the characters were pronounced. There are two ways to find out such pronunciations; the first is to note the transcriptions of Chinese into a foreign phonetic language, and the second is to note the phonetic transcription of some foreign language into Chinese. It is in the second category that the Buddhist texts have furnished us with considerable data of great importance. In the Buddhist sutras there are mantras or mystic syllables, the correct pronunciation of which was held to be extremely efficacious. Very often these mystic syllables have no meanings at all; so when they were turned into Chinese, the translators merely transcribed them with Chinese characters. Such texts, belonging largely to the Tantric School, were very popular during the T'ang Dynasty. While the pronunciation of the Chinese phonetic transcriptions have changed during the thousand or so years since the T'ang Dynasty, the pronunciation of the Sanskrit has not, since it is a phonetic language. By comparing the Chinese transcriptions with the original Sanskrit text, valuable data is derived to reconstruct the Chinese pronunciations of the T'ang Dynasty.

## CH'AN AND LANDSCAPE PAINTING

In the history of landscape painting the works of the Sung masters are generally acknowledged to be the best, and in this type of painting we see the finest flowering of the Ch'an spirit in Chinese culture. To the landscape artist nature is to be converted to the plane of ideals; all mountains, trees, rivers, and lakes are but creations of the mind and subject to the law of impermanence. In the Sung landscape mountains are to be seen as if floating in the distance, having no real existence. Thus the basic Mahāyāna doctrine of emptiness is illustrated. As Grousset, the French Sinologist, points out, the painting by Ma Yüan of the solitary fisherman on a boat is probably the supreme example of this art. In the middle of the lake a fisherman sits in his boat, rod in hand. The boat is lost in the lake, whose banks are not visible; the water is indicated only by a few lines along the boat. All the rest is emptiness.[6]

The Ch'an doctrine holds that Buddhahood or the spiritual essence of things may be found in man, animal, plant, flower, mountain, stream, and so on. The voice of Buddha may speak in the songs of birds, the silence of the mountains, the crashing of waterfalls, or the whisper of trees in the wind. The landscape artist spent his time in silent meditation on various aspects of nature, hoping to find the spiritual essence of things hidden under the cloak of outward forms. If the vision of this spiritual essence were to be recorded in paintings, it had to be done in the shortest time possible. Thus, in executing his paintings, the Ch'an artist manipulated his brush with the utmost freedom, speed, and spontaneity. There was no time for deliberation or hesitation; the inspiration of the artist moved his hand automatically.

[6] R. Grousset, *Chinese Art and Culture*, New York, 1959, 250.

Since the Ch'an artist saw in flowers and plants a representation of the Buddha essence, he aimed in his painting of such objects to express their spiritual significance rather than their external appearance. To accomplish this he sought to identify himself with the object by intense concentration. The mental image thus produced was then transferred to paper as rapidly as possible. A favorite theme was the bamboo, whose upward thrust symbolized rectitude and whose inner emptiness illustrated the Buddhist ideal of vacuity. So it was said that the Ch'an artist would paint bamboo for ten years, would literally become a bamboo himself; but when he started painting bamboo, he would forget that he was a bamboo and would manipulate the brush at the mercy of his inspiration.

## ASTRONOMY AND CALENDAR

In the realm of science there are a number of fields in which the Buddhist monks made contributions. In astronomy and calendrical studies, first of all, the Chinese were influenced by Indian ideas during the T'ang Dynasty. Yang Ching-fang, a pupil of Amoghavajra, wrote in 764: "Those who wish to know the positions of the five planets adopt Indian calendrical methods. One can thus predict what *Hsiu* (heavenly mansion) a planet will be traversing. So we have the three clans of Indian calendar experts, Chiayeh (Kāśyapa), Chhuthan (Gautama), and Chumolo (Kumāra), all of whom held offices in the Bureau of Astronomy."[7] This passage indicates the responsible roles played by the Indian astronomers in the Chinese court. A member of the Kāśyapa clan prepared the calendar of 665, while the first of the Gautama clan prepared the calendar systems for 697 and 698. The greatest of these Indians was undoubtedly Gautama Siddhārtha, who compiled a treatise on astrology in 729 which contained not only a translation of an Indian calendar but also the greatest collection of ancient Chinese astronomical writings. The last of the three clans, Kumāra, was associated with the most famous of all the T'ang astronomers and mathematicians, the Buddhist monk I-hsing (682-727).[8]

[7] J. Needham, *Science and Civilization in China*, 3,202.
[8] As an indication of the importance of I-hsing, three whole chapters in

The exact nature of I-hsing's mathematics is not known, for all his works in this field are lost. But it was said that he once calculated the total number of possible positions in Chinese chess, a game played on a board consisting of seventeen rows with seventeen positions in each row. It was I-hsing who organized an expedition to the Southern Seas to observe and chart the stars in the southern skies not discernible in China. From the observations and charts of the southern constellations made by the expedition, it would appear that the members went as far south as the southern tip of Sumatra. Even more significant was another project that I-hsing organized to measure the latitudes in China. He and his coworkers did this by setting up nine stations, stretching from a site near the Great Wall in Shansi to another in Indo-China, a distance of about thirty-five hundred kilometers. Along this line the shadows cast by the standard eight-foot gnomon at the summer and winter solstices were measured simultaneously; thus data of great importance in the determination of latitudes were obtained.

## MEDICINE

From the very beginning Buddhism stressed the great importance of health and paid a good deal of attention to the prevention and cure of maladies. Indeed, the Buddha called his teachings a therapy for the ills of the world, and one of the important Buddhas in the pantheon was Bhaishajyaguru, the master of medicine. Among the Buddhist monks in China there were a number noted for their proficiency in medicine. Understandably, therefore, Buddhism made some contributions to medical science.

One of the basic theories held by the Indians was that the physical body consisted of four great elements: earth, water, fire, and air. When these four elements were in proper equilibrium, health ensued, but when they were not, then maladies arose. This theory of the four great elements was introduced to China and adopted by the Chinese. This could be seen in the writings of one of the most eminent T'ang physicians, Sun Ssu-miao (601?-682), who, although a Taoist, was interested in Buddhism and

---

the *Ch'ou-jen chuan*, a biography of astronomers and mathematicians compiled in 1799 by Juan Yüan, are devoted to him.

was nicknamed by a contemporary as the "new Vimalakīrti" because of his interest in medicine. In his medical treatise *Ch'ien-chin yao-fang* (*Book of Prescriptions Worth a Thousand Gold*) there is a passage showing that he fully subscribed to the Indian theory of the four elements. More interesting, however, are some remarks found in the introduction to the work. Here he wrote that in order to be a great physician one must not only read the Confucian and Taoist works but also the medical literature of the Buddhists, for only so could one understand the virtues of love, compassion, joy, and impartiality. Then followed a passage which might be interpreted as containing clues to the Buddhist influence on medical ethics in China: "A great doctor in treating maladies should pacify his spirits and allay his ambitions, so that he is without desire or seeking. He should first develop such great love and compassion that he should yearn to alleviate the miseries of sentient beings. If someone in an emergency should seek his help, he should not ask whether this one is rich or poor, high or low, old or young, beautiful or ugly, enemy or friend, Chinese or barbarian, stupid or intelligent, but should regard him with impartiality, and accord him the same treatment as he would his dearest friend."[9]

Certain surgical techniques, such as laparotomy or removal of abdominal walls, trepanation or surgery of the skull, removal of cataracts, and inoculation for smallpox, all were influenced by Indian methods.[10]

Still under the heading of science might be mentioned physical education. According to Buddhist traditions Bodhidharma was taken aback when he saw the weak and emaciated bodies of

[9] *Ch'ien-chin yao-fang, Tao-tsang*, 800, 1,2b.

[10] In this connection probably some remarks should be devoted to the biography of the famous Hua T'o of the Han Dynasty, often referred to as the father of Chinese surgery because of his surgical exploits. These included a laparotomy with anesthesia, amputation of an infected portion of the intestines, then suturing the opening and applying some ointment to the wound. On another occasion he operated on the head of a patient. These exploits remind one of the surgical accomplishments of the Indian physician Jivaka, a contemporary of the Buddha, whose deeds were made known to the Chinese through the translations of An Shih-kao in the second century A.D. The earliest biography of Hua T'o appeared in the *Wei-chih* of Ch'en Shou (233-297), and this fact has led some scholars to conclude that the operations reputedly performed by him were but echoes of those of Jivaka, the information concerning which was introduced into China by the Buddhist missionaries.

the monks in the Shao-lin Temple of which he was the abbot. Being a firm believer in the adage of a sound mind in a sound body, he taught the monks a style of boxing for self-defense as well as for reinvigorating the body after a period of meditation. In this manner arose the Shao-lin style of boxing which became famous in later Chinese history.

## RELIGIOUS LIFE

It is in the religious life that Buddhism wrought its greatest influence. This is as it should be, since it was as a religion that Buddhism was introduced to China. Through its pantheon of compassionate Buddhas and bodhisattvas who offered refuge to those in need, its promise of salvation to all, its emphasis on piety and silent meditation, the colorful pageantry of its rituals and festivals, its restraint of the passions, its universality and its tolerance, the religious life of the Chinese has been enriched, deepened, broadened, and made more meaningful in terms of human sympathy, love, and compassion for all living creatures. Its doctrine of karma brought spiritual consolation to countless numbers. One by-product of the compassionate concern for all living beings was the establishment of charitable institutions such as hospitals, orphanages, dispensaries, resthouses, or homes for the aged. The deep emotional attachment to the religion encouraged pilgrimages to famous mountains connected with Buddhism. Such famous mountains as Miao-feng Shan, T'ien-t'ai Shan, or Wu-t'ai Shan were far away from the centers of population, but they were the goals of annual pilgrimages by devout Buddhists, for these pious journeys took the hard-working Chinese from the boredom of their everyday lives and provided them with a few days of carefree abandon on the open road, where they could enjoy the scenery and make new acquaintances from other parts of the country.

## ADAPTATION TO CHINESE ENVIRONMENT

One of the primary reasons why Buddhism was able to make so many contributions to so many different facets of Chinese life was that, after its introduction and spread in China, it gradually became more and more Sinicized; that is to say, it adjusted itself to the Chinese environment and, by so doing, ceased to be Indian. Hence we have used the term Chinese Buddhism often in the discussion.

The outstanding example of such change and adaptation might be seen in the establishment of such schools as the T'ien-t'ai, Pure Land, and Ch'an. The T'ien-t'ai arose out of the Chinese skill in classification and compromise—classification by chronological periods and compromise between Indian metaphysics and Chinese worldly thought by the doctrine of the threefold truths. Likewise, the Pure Land with its emphasis on faith and the Ch'an with its doctrine of abrupt enlightenment were the outcome of the Chinese bent for simplicity, directness, and practicality. These were definitely schools of Chinese Buddhism, not Indian schools transplanted to China.

The Buddhist sangha in China likewise underwent significant transformations. During the T'ang and Sung Dynasties the monasteries through their ownership of land and their commercial and industrial installations participated closely in the economic life of the country, and thus played a similar role to that of the native landlords and the aristocratic families. Moreover, Buddhist temples, organized and supported by the state, were entrusted with the performance of religious ceremonies for the welfare of the ruling house and the state, and as such might be considered as a sort of spiritual arm of the imperial government. This was a feature found in China but not in India. Because of this, the sangha in China was subjected to a degree of control and supervision by the state not found at all in the land of its birth. Such features as the granting of ordination certificates by the government in order to limit the size of the clerical community, the subordination of monk officials to the civil authorities, official ordination through examinations administered by the government, compilation of a registry of monks, all were distinctive of the sangha in China.

In the course of time the various bodhisattvas took on Chinese appearances. Maitreya, the future Buddha, became Pu-tai, the Hemp-bag Bonze, the well-fed genial figure who greets visitors to the temple. Avalokiteśvara was transformed into a female deity with her home in the P'u-t'o Islands off the coast of Che-kiang, while Mañjuśri became associated with Mt. Wu-t'ai in Shansi. Likewise, the stupa evolved into the pagoda in China, where it no longer was a burial mound to store the relics of the Buddha, but took the shape of a multistoried building erected at strategic sites to ensure the spiritual well-being of a family or community. Finally, the antifamily and antisocial concepts of Buddhism in India were modified by the Chinese Buddhists, so that filial piety was still a virtue to be observed, especially in the form of temples and pagodas erected and dedicated to the memory of deceased ancestors. By submerging some of its Indian characteristics and assuming certain features more congenial to the Chinese temperament and environment, Buddhism was able to make contributions to Chinese culture which no other foreign religion was able to match, and it is therefore no accident that the Indian religion, of all the foreign religions introduced into China, became the most powerful religious force in imperial China.

# GLOSSARY

| | |
|---|---|
| abhisheka | ordination, initiation |
| ācārya | religious teacher |
| āgama | scriptures |
| aggregates | constituent elements of an individual, five in number: material body, sensation, perception, predispositions, consciousness |
| Akaniṣṭha | name of the highest Buddhist heaven |
| Akshobhya | The Immovable One, name of one of the five jinas, presiding Buddha of the east |
| ālaya | storehouse |
| ālayavijñāna | storehouse consciousness |
| Amitābha | Buddha of Infinite Light, presiding Buddha of the Western Paradise |
| Amitāyus | Infinite Life, another name for Amitābha |
| Amoghasiddhi | Infallible Success, one of the five jinas, presiding Buddha of the north |
| anāgāmin | nonreturner |
| anāpāna | inhalation and exhalation |
| anatta | absence of a permanent self |
| anicca | impermanence |
| arhat | one who has put an end to rebirth and attained enlightenment. Arhatship is the religious ideal of Theravāda Buddhism. |
| asaṃskrita | unconditioned |
| Asaṅga | Mahāyāna philosopher of the fourth century, founder of the Idealistic School |
| Aṣṭasāhasrikā Prajñāpāramitā | *Perfection of Wisdom in 8,000 Lines* |
| Atma (atta) | inner essence of man |
| Avalokiteśvara | bodhisattva representing compassion; in China known as Kuan-yin; in Japan, Kannon |
| Avataṃsaka | garland, title of a highly idealistic Mahāyāna sutra |
| Bhagavad-gītā | *The Song of God*, name of one of the most important of Hindu sacred scriptures |

| | |
|---|---|
| bhikshu | monk |
| bodhi | enlightenment |
| bodhicitta | thought of enlightenment |
| bodhisattva | the Mahāyāna ideal, one who is destined to be enlightened |
| Brahma | impersonal cosmic principle pervading the entire universe |
| Candrakīrti | most famous commentator of the Mādhyamika School, lived ca. seventh century |
| cash | a copper coin, the lowest denomination in Chinese currency |
| ch'eng-fu | transmission of burden, Taoist doctrine according to which merits or demerits are transmitted from ancestors to descendants |
| ch'i | vital energy, matter |
| chih | concentration |
| chin-na | ordination by purchase of monk certificates |
| chin-shih | third and highest degree awarded to the successful candidate in the metropolitan examinations in China |
| ch'ing | unit of measure of land, consisting of one hundred mou |
| Chuang-tzu | name of a Taoist philosopher, also the title of a Taoist philosophical text |
| dhāranī | mystic formula |
| dharma | teachings of the Buddha, elements of existence, righteousness |
| dharmadhātu | the universal principle, the perfect and absolute source of all truth |
| dharmakāya | body of essence, the highest of the three bodies of the Buddha |
| dhyāna | meditation |
| Dīghanikāya | *Collection of Long Discourses* |
| Dīpankara | The Light-maker, the earliest in a line of Buddhas |
| dukkha | misery, suffering, unrest |

| | |
|---|---|
| Ekottarāgama | *Gradual Length Discourses* |
| en-tu | ordination by favor of the emperor |
| Fa-hsiang | characteristics of the dharmas, name of the Idealistic School in China |
| fan-pen | reverted to the original |
| garbhadhātu | womb-element, name of an important maṇḍala in Tantrism |
| Hīnayāna | Lesser Vehicle |
| Hsiung-nu | a non-Chinese people of Turkic origin |
| hua-hu | conversion of the barbarians |
| Hua-yen | literally means "garlands," name of a school in China, also title of Mahāyāna sutra |
| Huang-Lao | Huang-ti, the legendary Yellow Emperor, and Lao-tzu |
| icchantika | one who is interested in the gratification of the senses |
| Jātaka | birth story, an account of a previous rebirth of the Buddha |
| jina | the victorious one |
| karma | deeds, acts |
| karmadāna | superintendent of works in a monastery |
| ke-yi | matching the meaning |
| koṭi | ten million |
| k'ou-fen | personal share |
| Krishna | Indian deity, incarnation of Vishnu |
| kuan | insight |
| kung-an | a case, problem, or conundrum, posed by a Ch'an master to his pupils |
| kuo-shih | national preceptor, title given to eminent monks in China |
| lakshana | marks, characteristics |
| Lao-tzu | title of a Taoist work, also called *Tao-te-ching*; also name of a Taoist philosopher |
| li | principle, reason |
| Mādhyamika | the middle path, name of the Mahāyāna School of Buddhism |
| Mahāprajñāpāramitā | the perfection of great wisdom, title of a Mahāyāna scripture |

| | |
|---|---|
| Mahāsaṅghika | name of a Hīnayāna school, the word means "the Great Assembly" |
| Mahāsthāma | bodhisattva representing force |
| Mahāvairocana | The Great Sun Buddha, the primordial Buddha in Tantrism; chief deity of Shingon School in Japan |
| Mahāyāna | The Great Vehicle |
| manas | the thought center, or self-conscious mind |
| maṇḍala | mystic diagram |
| Mañjuśrī | bodhisattva representing wisdom |
| mano-vijñāna | the conscious mind, one of the six senses |
| mantra | mystic syllables |
| Mantrayāna | the vehicle that depends on the mantras or mystic syllables |
| Māyā | name of the mother of the Buddha |
| metta | infinite love for all sentient beings |
| Mithras | Iranian deity representing light |
| mou | unit of measure of land, roughly equivalent to one sixth of an acre |
| mudrā | gestures of the hands and fingers |
| Nāgārjuna | Buddhist philosopher, second century A.D., founder of the Mādhyamika School |
| Nālandā | famous Buddhist center of learning in India |
| nien-fo | invoking the name of the Buddha |
| nirmānakāya | body of transformation, the body in which the eternal Buddha appears among mankind |
| Pali | ancient literary language of India, the sacred language of Theravāda Buddhism |
| p'an-chiao | dividing the periods of teachings |
| Pāndaravāsinī | The One clad in white, name of female consort of the bodhisattva Avalokiteśvara |
| paññā (prajñā) | intuitive insight, wisdom |
| paramārtha-satya | absolute truth |
| paratantra | dependence upon others, second level of truth in the Idealistic School |

parikalpita — sole imagination, lowest level of truth in the Idealistic School

parināmana — transfer of merits

parinishpanna — complete, perfect knowledge; highest level of truth in the Idealistic School

Pātimokkha — the rules governing the conduct of monks

pen-t'i — essence, foundation

pien-wen — text of marvelous events

prajñā — intuitive insight, wisdom

prajñāpāramitā — the perfection of wisdom, also the designation of a body of Mahāyāna literature

pratyekabuddha — solitary Buddha, interested only in his own salvation

preta — hungry ghost

pudgala — individual

Ratnasambhava — Born of Gems, one of the five jinas, presiding Buddha of the south

saddha — faith

Saddharmapuṇḍarīka — *Lotus of the Good Law*, title of a Mahāyāna sutra

sakadāgāmin — once-returner

samādhi — mental discipline, concentration

samatā — sameness

sambodhi — omniscience of the Buddha

sambhogakāya — body of communal enjoyment, the body in which the eternal Buddha appears before the bodhisattvas

saṁsāra — endless round of rebirths

saṁskrita — conditioned

saṁvṛiti-satya — relative truth, phenomenal truth

San-chieh-chiao — Sect of the Three Stages

San-lun — The Three Treatises, name of the school in China based on these three treatises

sangha — community of monks

Sanskrit — literary language of the Hindus

Sarvāstivāda — name of a Hīnayāna school, the word means "the doctrine that all exists"

| | |
|---|---|
| Satyasiddhi | *Completion of Truth,* name of a Hīnayāna treatise and the school based on that treatise |
| seng-ts'ao | local sangha office |
| sha-men | a monk, derived from Sanskrit śramana |
| sha-men-t'ung | chief of monks |
| shen-ling | spirit, soul |
| shih | mundane events, empirical experience |
| shih | a unit of measure of quantity in China, usually taken to be the equivalent of a bushel |
| śīla | moral conduct |
| śramana | a religious recluse |
| śrāmanera | a novice |
| śrāvaka | hearer, Hīnayāna adherent |
| ssu-tu | private ordination of monks |
| sthavira | elder |
| string of cash | one thousand cash |
| stūpa | sacred structure containing Buddhist relics or commemorating a holy spot, originally a funerary mound |
| Śuddhodana | name of the father of the Buddha |
| sukhāvatī | the pure and happy land, goal of the followers of the Pure Land School |
| Sumeru | the sacred mountain of the Hindus, the center of the world and the supporter of the skies |
| śūnya | empty, relative |
| śūnyatā | emptiness, relativity, vacuity |
| sutra | a religious discourse |
| sva-bhava | own nature, self-nature |
| tael | an ounce of silver |
| tantra | esoteric literature |
| Tantrayāna | the vehicle that is based on the Tantras, the third and final interpretation of the Buddha's teachings |
| Tao-te-ching | *The Way and Its Power,* fundamental text of philosophic Taoism |

| | |
|---|---|
| Tathāgata | a title of the Buddha, meaning "He Who Has Thus Gone" |
| tathatā | truly so, genuine thusness, interpreted by the Chinese Buddhists as the absolute mind that embraces the universe in its entirety |
| Theravāda | doctrine of the Elders, name of the school of Buddhism dominant in Ceylon, Burma, and Thailand |
| t'i | unity, noumenon |
| Ti-lun | abbreviation of *Shih-ti ching-lun, Treatise on the Sutra Concerning the Ten Stages* |
| t'ien-ming | heavenly mandate |
| T'ien-t'ai | Heavenly Terrace, name of a school in Chinese Buddhism |
| T'o-pa | name of a non-Chinese people of Turkic origin who established the Northern Wei Dynasty, 386-534 |
| Tripitaka | *The Three Baskets*, collection of the Buddhists scriptures |
| t'ung-hsing | postulant, probationer |
| Tushita | name of one of the Buddhist heavens, where the Buddha lives before his last rebirth on earth |
| tzu-jan | naturalness, spontaneity |
| Upanishads | body of Hindu sacred literature that elaborate on the philosophical truth of the Vedas |
| upāsaka | layman |
| upasampadā | full ordination of monk |
| upāyakauśalya | skill-in-means, one of the ten perfections of the bodhisattva |
| Vaipulya | broad and equal, designation of a group of Mahāyāna sutras |
| Vairocana | The Brilliant One, the most important Buddha in Tantrism |
| Vajrayāna | the vehicle that has the thunderbolt as its symbol |

| | |
|---|---|
| Vasubandhu | Mahāyāna philosopher of the fourth century, possibly fifth, one of the founders of the Idealistic School |
| Veda | sacred literature of the Indians |
| vihāraswamin | rector of a monastery |
| Vimalakīrti | name of a Buddhist layman |
| Vimalakīrti-nirdésa | title of a Mahāyāna sutra, the *Sutra Spoken by Vimalakīrti* |
| Vinaya | rules of discipline |
| Vṛthragna | Iranian deity representing force |
| wu | nonbeing |
| yab-yum | father-mother in Tibetan |
| yung | diversity, phenomenon |

a-lo-han 阿羅漢
An-fu 安福
An-hsi 安息
An Hsüan 安玄
An-lo-chi 安樂集
An-lu 安錄
An-pan shou-i-ching 安般守意經
An Shih-kao 安世高

ch'a-no 刹那
chai 齋
Chai Jung 笮融
Ch'an 禪
Ch'an-chiao i-chih 禪教一致
Chan-jan 湛然
Chang Ch'ien 張騫
Chang-ching 章敬
Ch'ang-ch'un chen-jen 長春眞人
Chang Heng 張衡
Chang Heng-ch'ü chi 張橫渠集
Chang Jung 張融
Chang Lien 張連
Chang Pin 張賓
Chang-sun Fei 長孫肥
Chang Tsai 張載
Chang Yü 張裕
Chao-hsüan-ssu 昭玄司
Chao Kuei-chen 趙歸眞
Chao P'u-ch'u 趙樸初
ch'en 臣
Chen-chin 眞金
Ch'en Hui 陳惠
chen-jen 眞人
chen-ju 眞如
chen-shih 眞實
chen-ti 眞諦
chen-wo 眞我
Ch'en Yüan 陳垣
Ch'eng-chü kuang-ming-ching 成具光明經
ch'eng-fu 承負
Ch'eng Hao 程顥
Ch'eng-kuan 澄觀
Ch'eng wei-shih-lun 成唯識論
Ch'eng wei-shih-lun shu-chi 成唯識論述記
Cheng-wu-lun 正誣論
Ch'eng Yi 程頤

Ch'eng-yüan 承遠
ch'i 氣
chi-sha 磧砂
Chi-tsang 吉藏
Chi-tsu-shan 雞足山
Chia 賈
Chia-hsiang 嘉祥
Chia-mu-yang-le-chih 嘉木楊勒智
Chia-pin 嘉賓
Chia Shan-yüan 賈善淵
Chia-yeh mo-t'eng 迦葉摩騰
Chiang-Huai 江淮
Chiang Pin 姜斌
Ch'ien-chin yao-fang 千金要方
Chien-fu-ts'ao 監福曹
chien-ssu 監司
chien-wu 建武
ch'ien-yüan 乾元
Chih-hsü 智旭
Chih-i 智顗
Chih-li 知禮
Chih-lou chia-ch'an 支婁迦讖
Chih Miao-yin 支妙音
Chih Min-tu 支愍度
Chih-p'an 志磐
Chih-sheng 智昇
chih-shih 知事
chih-sui 直歲
Chih Tao-lin 支道林
Chih-tsang 智藏
Chih Tun 支遁
Chih Yao 支曜
Chih-yen 智儼
Chih-yen 智嚴
Ch'in Ching 秦景
Chin-kang-chih 金剛智
Chin-kang-ching 金剛經
Chin-kang-ting-ching 金剛頂經
Chin-kuang-ming-ching 金光明經
chin-na 進納
chin-shih 進士
Chin-shih-tzu chang 金獅子章
ch'ing 頃
Ching-an 靜安
Ch'ing-ching fa-hsing-ching 清淨法行經
Ching-chou 荊州
Ching-chüeh 淨覺
Ching-fan 淨梵

Ching-kuan 淨光
Ch'ing-liang 清涼
Ching-ling 竟陵
Ching-lu 景盧
Ching-lü-ching 淨律經
Ching-ming 景明
Ching-sung 靖嵩
Ch'ing-t'ao 慶濤
Ching-t'u tz'u-pei-chi 淨土慈悲集
Ch'iu Ch'u-chi 丘處機
Chiu-heng-ching 九橫經
Chou 周
Chou Hsü-chih 周續之
Ch'ou-jen-chuan 疇人傳
chou sha-men-t'ung 州沙門統
Chou-shu i-chi 周書異記
ch'u-chia 出家
Chu-ch'üeh 朱雀
Chu Fa-i 竺法義
Chu Fa-lan 竺法蘭
Chu Fa-t'ai 竺法汰
Chu Fa-ya 竺法雅
Chu Fo-nien 竺佛念
Chu Hsi 朱熹
chu-k'e 主客
Chu Lü-yen 竺律炎
Ch'u-san-tsang chi-chi 出三藏記集
Ch'u-shan Shao-ch'i 楚山紹琦
Chü-she-lun 俱舍論
Ch'u-shih Fan-ch'i 楚石梵琦
Chu Shuo-fo 竺朔佛
Chu Tao-ch'ien 竺道潛
Chü-tsan 巨贊
Chu Yüan-chang 朱元璋
Chuang-tzu 莊子
Chüeh-an 覺岸
Ch'üeh Kung-tse 闕公則
Chüeh-yüan 覺苑
Ch'ung-chu-ssu 崇祝寺
Chung-hsiang-ssu 衆香寺
Chung-hsing-ssu 中興寺
Chung-kuan lun-su 中觀論疏
Chung-lun 中論
Ch'ung-ning wan-shou ta-tsang 崇寧萬
　壽大藏
chung-sheng 衆生

en-tu 恩度
erh-ti-i 二諦義

Fa-chao 法照
Fa-chih-lun 發智論

Fa-ch'in 法欽
Fa-chü-ching 法句經
Fa-ho 法和
Fa-hsiang 法相
Fa-kuo 法果
Fa-lang 法朗
Fa-lin 法琳
Fa-lun miao-ching 法輪妙經
Fa-min 法敏
Fa-shang 法上
Fa-shun 法順
Fa-t'ai 法泰
Fa-tsang 法藏
Fa-yao 法瑤
Fa-yen 法眼
Fa-yüan chu-lin 法苑珠林
Fa-yüan i-lin-chang 法苑義林章
Fan Chen 范縝
fan-ch'ieh 反切
fan-pen 反本
Fan-wang-ching 梵網經
Fan Yeh 范曄
Fei Ch'ang-fang 費長房
fen-pieh 分別
Feng-fa-yao 奉法要
Feng Hsi 馮熙
Feng-shen-chuan 奉神傳
Fo-tao lun-heng 佛道論衡
Fo-tsu t'ung-chi 佛祖統紀
Fu-chou K'ai-yüan-ssu 福州開元寺
Fu Yi 傅毅 (Han Dynasty)
Fu Yi 傅奕 (T'ang Dynasty)
Fu-yü 福裕

Hai-ch'ao-yin 海潮音
Hai-li 海理
Hai-ling-wang 海陵王
Hai-yün 海雲
Han Ch'ien 韓謙
Han fa-pen nei-chuan 漢法本內傳
Han Lin 韓林
Han-shan Te-ch'ing 憨山德清
Han Shan-t'ung 韓山童
Han Yü 韓愈
Ho Ch'eng-t'ien 何承天
Ho Shang-chih 何尚之
Hou Chao 後趙
Hou Chi 后稷
Hou-Han-chi 後漢紀
Hsi Ch'ao 郗超

Hsi-ching-fu 西京賦
Hsi-sheng-ching 西昇經
hsi-t'ien 西天
Hsi Tso-ch'ih 習鑿齒
Hsi-yu-chi 西遊記
hsiang-chu 像主
Hsiang Hai-ming 向海明
Hsiao Ch'en 蕭琛
Hsiao Tzu-liang 蕭子良
Hsiao Wen 孝文
Hsieh An 謝安
Hsieh Ch'eng 謝承
Hsieh Ling-yün 謝靈運
Hsieh Shou-hao 謝守顥
Hsien-ching 仙經
Hsien-shou 賢首
Hsien-tai fo-hsüeh 現代佛學
Hsin-hsing 信行
hsing-chiao 興教
Hsing-hsiu 行秀
Hsing-huang 興皇
Hsiung Shih-li 熊十力
Hsü Ch'ang 許昌
Hsü Hsia-k'e 徐霞客
Hsü Hsün 許詢
Hsü Kao-seng-chuan 續高僧傳
Hsü-yün 虛雲
Hsüan-chao 玄照
Hsüan-cheng-yüan 宣政院
Hsüan-kao 玄高
Hsüan-tse 玄賾
Hsüan-wu 宣武
Hsün Chi 荀濟
Hua-hu-ching 化胡經
Hua-yen-ching chih-kuei 華嚴經旨歸
Huan Hsüan 桓玄
Huang-chüeh 皇覺
Huang-fu Mi 皇甫謐
Huang-Lao 黃老
Huang-ssu 黃寺
Hui-ch'eng 慧成
Hui-ch'ih 慧持
Hui-ch'ung 慧崇
Hui-jih 慧日
Hui-k'ai 慧愷
Hui-k'e 慧可
Hui-kuan 慧觀
Hui-kuang 慧光
Hui-lin 慧林
Hui-neng 慧能
Hui-ssu 慧思

Hui-sung 慧嵩
Hui-wen 慧文
Hui-yüan 慧遠
Hui-yung 慧永
Hun-yüan sheng-chi 混元聖記
Hung-fa 弘法
Hung-jen 弘忍
Hung-lu-ssu 鴻臚寺
Hung-ming-chi 弘明集

i 邑
I-ch'eng chüeh-i-lun 一乘決疑論
I-ching-lu 疑經錄
I-hai po-men 義海百門
I-hsia-lun 夷夏論
I-hsing 一行
I-hsüan 義玄
i-nien san-ch'ien 一念三千
i-yin 一音

jen-shen 壬申
jen-t'ien chiao-chieh, liang te hsiang-chien 人天交接 兩得相見
Jen-wang-ching 仁王經
Juan Yüan 阮元

K'ai-shan 開善
K'ai-yüan 開遠
K'ai-yüan shih-chiao-lu 開元釋教錄
K'ai-yüan-ssu 開元寺
K'ang-chü 康巨
K'ang Fa-ch'ang 康法暢
K'ang-lo 康樂
K'ang Meng-hsiang 康孟祥
K'ang Seng-hui 康僧會
K'ang Seng-yüan 康僧淵
kang-wei 綱維
Kao Chiung 高熲
Kao-seng-chuan 高僧傳
Kao Shu 高樹
Kao Yün 高允
ke-i 格義
Ko Hung 葛洪
Ko Wu 蓋吳
Kōkyō Shoin 弘教書院
k'ou-ch'eng nien-fo 口稱念佛
K'ou Ch'ien-chih 寇謙之
kou-ching 垢淨
k'ou-fen 口分

497

k'u-hai 苦海
Ku Huan 顧歡
k'u-ssu 庫司
Ku-yang-tung 古陽洞
Kuan-ching-su 觀經疏
Kuan-shih-yin 觀世音
Kuan-ting 灌頂
Kuan-tzu-tsai 觀自在
Kuan-yin 觀音
Kuang-chi 廣濟
Kuang-hui 廣惠
Kuang-hung-ming-chi 廣弘明集
K'uei-chi 窺基
Kuei-yang 溈仰
kung-an 公案
Kung Ch'ung 宮崇
kung-te fen-ssu 功德墳寺
kung-te-shih 功德使
kung-te-yüan 功德院
Kuo-ch'ing 國清
Kuo-fen-ssu 國分寺
Kuo Tsu-shen 郭祖深

Lan-ch'eng 嵐城
Lao-tzu 老子
Lao-tzu k'ai-t'ien-ching 老子開天經
Lei Tz'u-tsung 雷次宗
Leng-chia jen-fa-chih 楞伽人法志
li 理
Li-ch'eng 歷城
Li Chih-ch'ang 李志常
Li Ch'i-ko 李七哥
Li P'ing-shan 李屏山
Li-tai san-pao-chi 歷代三寶記
Li Tao-yüan 酈道元
Liang Ch'i-ch'ao 梁啟超
Liang-chieh 良价
Liang Su 梁肅
Liang-tsou 梁鄒
Lieh-tzu 列子
lien-she 蓮社
Lin-chi 臨濟
Liu Ch'eng-chih 劉程之
Liu Ch'iu 劉虬
Liu Chun 劉峻
Liu Hsüan-ching 劉玄靖
Liu Ping-chung 劉秉忠
Liu Shao-fu 劉少府
Liu Shih-ch'ing 劉世清
Liu Yü 劉裕

Lo-fou 羅浮
Lo Ju-fang 羅汝芳
Lo-yang chia-lan-chi 洛陽伽藍記
Lu-chiang 廬江
Lu Hsiang-shan 陸象山
Lu Hsiu-ching 陸修靜
Lü-tsung 律宗
Lun fo-chiao-piao 論佛教表
Lun-heng 論衡
Lung-hsing-ssu 龍興寺

Ma Yüan 馬遠
Man-chou 滿洲
Manji Zōkyō 卍字藏經
Mao Tzu-yüan 茅子元
Meng Fu 孟福
Mi-le ch'eng-fo-ching 彌勒成佛經
Mi-le-fo 彌勒佛
Mi-le p'u-sa pen-yüan-ching 彌勒菩薩
    本願經
Miao-fa lien-hua ching hsüan-i 妙法蓮
    華經玄義
Miao-fa lien-hua-ching wen-chü 妙法
    蓮華經文句
Min-chih 敏智
Ming-chi Tien-Ch'ien fo-chiao-k'ao 明
    季滇黔佛教攷
ming-chiao 明教
Ming-hsiang-chi 冥祥記
Ming-pao-ying-lun 明報應論
ming-seng 名僧
ming-tu 明度
ming-wang 明王
Mo-ho chih-kuan 摩訶止觀
mo-li 茉莉
mo-yu 末有
mou 敄
Mou-tzu li-huo-lun 牟子理惑論

Nan-hai chi-kuei nei-fa-chuan 南海寄
    歸內法傳
Nan-shan 南山
Nan-Sung Hu-chou 南宋湖州
Nieh Ch'eng-yüan 聶承遠
nieh-p'an 湼槃
Nieh-p'an i-su 涅槃義疏
Nieh Tao-chen 聶道眞
nien-fo 念佛
nien-wei 碾磑
Nü-chen 女眞

498

Ou-i Chih-hsü 藕益智旭
Ou-yang Chien 歐陽漸

Pa-shih-i hua-t'u 八十一化圖
Pai-hei-lun 白黑論
Pai-i kuan-yin 白衣觀音
Pai-ling-miao 百靈廟
Pai-ma 白馬
p'an-chiao 判教
pan-jo po-lo-mi-to 般若波羅蜜多
Pang Hu 棒胡
Pao-chia-fan 薄伽梵
Pao-liang 寶亮
Pao-p'u-tzu 抱朴子
Pei-chou 貝州
P'ei Hsüan-chih 裴玄智
P'ei Sung-chih 裴松之
pei-t'ien 悲田
Pen-chi 本寂
pen-ch'i 本起
pen-wu 本無
P'eng-ch'eng 彭城
P'eng Ch'ih-mu 彭尺木
P'eng Shao-sheng 彭紹升
P'i-lu ta-tsang 毗盧大藏
Pi-nai-yeh lü 鼻奈耶律
P'i Yeh 皮業
Pi-yen-lu 碧巖錄
Pien-cheng-lun 辯正論
pien-chi so-ch'ih 遍計所持
pien-hsiang 變相
Pien-i-ching 辯意經
Pien-tsung-lun 辯宗論
pien-wen 變文
P'in-chia 頻伽
p'in-tao 貧道
Pin-yang-tung 賓陽洞
P'ing-ch'i-chun 平齊郡
P'o-hsü-mi-lun 婆須蜜論
Po-lun 百論
P'u-kuang 普光
Pu-k'ung chin-kang 不空金剛
P'u-ning 普寧
p'u-sa 菩薩
Pu-tai ho-shang 布袋和尚
p'u-t'ung-yüan 普通院

san-chieh 三界
San-chieh-chiao 三階教

san-kang 三綱
San-kuo-chih 三國志
San-pao-lun 三報論
San-p'o-lun 三破論
san-pu-i 三不易
seng-cheng 僧正
Seng-ch'ou 僧稠
seng-chu 僧主
Seng-ch'üan 僧詮
Seng-fu 僧副
Seng-jui 僧叡
Seng-kung 僧恭
Seng-lang 僧朗
seng-lu 僧錄
Seng-lüeh 僧碧
Seng-sung 僧嵩
Seng-tao 僧導
Seng-ts'an 僧粲
seng-ts'ao 僧曹
Seng-yu 僧祐
Sha-mi shih-hui 沙彌十慧
Shan-chou 善冑
Shan-wu-wei 善無畏
Shan-yeh 善業
shang-tso 上座
Shao-k'ang 少康
shao-lin 少林
Shao Yung 邵雍
she 社
She-lun 攝論
She-shan 攝山
She ta-ch'eng-lun 攝大乘論
Shen-hsiu 神秀
Shen-hui 神會
Shen-kuang 神光
shen-ling 神靈
Shen-pu-mieh-lun 神不滅論
shen-wo 神我
sheng 升
shih 事
Shih 釋
shih-chieh-men 世界門
Shih-chu-ching 十住經
Shih-erh-men-lun 十二門論
Shih-hsien 師賢
Shih Hu 石虎
shih-i 失譯
Shih-lao-chih 釋老志
Shih-p'ing-kung 始平公
Shih-shih chi-ku-lüeh 釋氏稽古略
Shih-shuo hsin-yü 世說新語

Shih-sung-lü 十誦律
Shih Tao-pao 釋道寶
Shih-ti ching-lun 十地經論
Shih T'ien-hsiang 史天祥
Shou-ch'un 壽春
shou-i 守一
shou-pa chiao-tao, te-tao pi-an 手把脚
　蹈，得到彼岸
Shui-ching-chu 水經注
Shukusatsu-zōkyō 縮刷藏經
Shun-i 順義
Ssu-a-han mu-ch'ao-chieh 四阿鋡暮抄解
Ssu-ch'i tzu-fu-tsang 思溪資福藏
Ssu-ch'i yüan-chüeh-tsang 思溪圓覺藏
ssu-chu 寺主
Ssu-fen-lü 四分律
Ssu-ma 司馬
ssu-tu 私度
Su E 蘇鶚
su-ti 俗諦
Su-tsung 蕭宗
Su Wei 蘇威
Sui-shu 隋書
Sun Cho 孫綽
Sun Ssu-miao 孫思邈
Sung Kao-seng-chuan 宋高僧傳
Sung-shan 嵩山
Sung-tsang i-chen 宋藏遺珍
Sung Tzu-hsien 宋子賢
Sung-tzu Kuan-yin 送子觀音

t'a 塔
Ta-ai 大愛
Ta-ch'eng ch'i-hsin-lun 大乘起信論
Ta-ch'eng i-chang 大乘義章
Ta-ch'eng ta-i-chang 大乘大義章
Ta-ch'eng t'ien hu sheng-ssu 大承天護
　聖寺
Ta-chih-tu-lun 大智度論
ta-hsiao ming-wang ch'u-shih 大小明王
　出世
Ta-hsing-kuo 大興國
Ta-hsing-lun 達性論
Ta-pan nieh-p'an-ching chi-chieh 大般
　涅槃經集解
Ta-pan ni-yüan-ching 大般泥洹經
Ta-T'ang hsi-yü-chi 大唐西域記
Ta-T'ang hsi-yü ch'iu-fa kao-seng-
　chuan 大唐西域求法高僧傳
ta-tou 大豆
Ta-wan-shou 大萬壽

Ta-yüeh-chih 大月支
Ta-yün-ching 大雲經
T'ai-ch'ang-ssu 太常寺
T'ai-hsü 太虛
T'ai-p'ing-ching 太平經
T'ai-shan 泰山
T'ai-shang hun-yüan Lao-tzu shih-lüeh
　太上混元老子史略
T'ai-shang Lao-chun nien-p'u yao-lüeh
　太上老君年譜要略
Taishō Daizōkyō 大正大藏經
T'an-ch'ien 曇遷
T'an-ching 曇靖
T'an-luan 曇鸞
T'an-wu-tsui 曇無最
T'an-yao 曇曜
T'an-yen 曇延
Tao-cho 道綽
Tao-hsien-lun 道賢論
Tao-hsin 道信
Tao-hsüan 道宣
T'ao Hung-ching 陶宏景
tao-jen-t'ung 道人統
Tao-sheng 道生
Tao-shih 道世
tao-te 道德
Tao-te-ching 道德經
Tao-yüan 道原
te-tao 得道
Teng Yüan-ch'ao 鄧元超
t'i 體
ti-i-i-men 第一義門
T'i-wei Po-li 提謂波利
T'ien-chu 天竺
t'ien-ming 天命
t'ien-shang shih shih-chien, shih-chien
　te-chien t'ien-shang 天上視世間，世間
　得見天上
T'ien-shuo ssu-p'ien 天說四篇
T'ien-t'ai 天台
tien-tso 典座
t'ien-tsun 天尊
tou 斗
Tou Ch'ih 竇熾
Ts'ai Mo 蔡謨
Ts'ai Yin 蔡愔
Ts'ao Ssu-wen 曹思文
Ts'ao-tung 曹洞
Ts'ui Hao 崔浩
Tsun-shih 遵式
Tsung-chih-yüan 總制院

Tsung-li chung-ching mu-lu 綜理衆經目錄

Tsung-mi 宗密

Tsung Ping 宗炳

tu-wei-na 都維那

Tu-yang tsa-pien chüan-hsia 杜陽雜編卷下

tun-wu ch'eng-fo 頓悟成佛

tung-chen 洞眞

T'ung-chou 同州

t'ung-hsing 童行

tung-hsüan 洞玄

Tung-hsüan chen-i-ching 洞玄眞一經

Tung-hua hsü-lu 東華續錄

Tung-lin-ssu 東林寺

Tung-shan 東山

tung-shen 洞神

T'ung-t'ai 同泰

Tzu-chih-lu 自知錄

tzu-jan 自然

Tz'u-min 慈愍

tzu-mu 字母

Tz'u-po Chen-k'e 紫柏眞可

Tz'u-pu 祠部

Tzu-ts'ung 子聰

tz'u-yün 慈雲

Wan-an 萬安

Wang Ch'ia 王洽

Wang Ch'ung 王充

Wang Fu 王浮

Wang Hou 王侯

Wang Hsi-chih 王羲之

Wang Hsün 王洵

Wang Huai-ku 王懷古

Wang Hung 王弘

Wang Hung-yüan 王弘願

Wang Lien 王練

Wang Meng 王濛

Wang Min 王珉

Wang Tao 王導

Wang Tse 王則

Wang Tsun 王遵

Wang Tu 王度

Wang Tun 王敦

Wang Yang-ming 王陽明

Wang Yen 王琰

Wei 魏 (surname of Tao-sheng)

Wei 衛 (surname of Tao-an)

Wei Cheng 魏徵

Wei-chi-nan 維祇難

wei-chia 磑家

wei-hu 磑戶

Wei-lüeh 魏略

wei-po-shih 磑博士

wei-shih 唯識

Wei-shih erh-shih-lun 唯識二十論

Wei Shou 魏收

wei-shu 緯書

Wei Ssu-ch'ien 韋嗣謙

Wei Yüan-sung 衛元嵩

Wen-ch'eng-ti 文成帝

Wen-chü 文舉

Wen-hsü-nu 文殊奴

Wen-shih-chuan 文始傳

wu 烏

wu-chin-ts'ai 無盡財

wu-chin-tsang 無盡藏

wu-chin-wu 無盡物

Wu-chou-shan 武州山

Wu-fen-lü 五分律

wu-liang-kuang 無量光

wu-liang-shou 無量壽

wu-ming 無明

wu-shih-pen 五失本

wu-te 武德

wu-wei 無爲

Yang-ch'eng 陽城

Yang Hsüan-chih 楊衒之

Yang Jen-shan 楊仁山

Yang Su 楊素

Yang Wen-hui 楊文會

Yao-kuang 瑤光

Yeh 鄴

Yen-chou 兗州

Yen Fu-t'iao 嚴浮調

Yen-shou 延壽

Yen Tsung 彥琮

Yin-chih-lu 陰隲錄

Yin Hao 殷浩

Yin-kuang 印光

yin-yüan 因緣

Yü Chi 于吉

Yü-chia nien-sung-fa 瑜伽念誦法

yü-ch'üan 玉泉

Yü-fo 玉佛

Yü-hsüan yü-lu 御選語錄

yu-kou wu-kou 有垢無垢

Yü-lin 玉林

yü-lu 語錄

Yu-lung-chuan 猶龍傳
Yü Ping 庾冰
Yü-tao-lun 喻道論
Yüan-chao 元照
Yüan-chia 元嘉
yüan-ch'eng-shih 圓成實
Yüan-hsien 元賢
Yüan Hung 袁宏
Yüan Liao-fan 袁了凡
yüan-shen 苑申
Yüan-ying 圓瑛
Yüeh-chou 越州
yüeh-chung 悅衆

Yüeh-tsang chih-tsin 閱藏知津
Yün-ch'i Chu-hung 雲棲袾宏
Yün-chü 雲居
Yün-hua 雲華
Yün-men 雲門
yün-shou tung-tsu, chieh-liu erh-tu 運
手動足, 截流而度
yung 用
Yung-ho-kung 雍和宮
Yung-ming 永明
Yung-ning 永寧

Zōkyō Shoin 藏經書院

# BIBLIOGRAPHY

# ABBREVIATIONS

The following abbreviations for names of journals have been used in this bibliography:

| | |
|---|---|
| *BEFEO* | *Bulletin de l'École Française d'Extrême Orient* |
| *BSOAS* | *Bulletin of the School of Oriental and African Studies* |
| *CSPSR* | *Chinese Social and Political Science Review* |
| *EB* | *Eastern Buddhist* |
| *HJAS* | *Harvard Journal of Asiatic Studies* |
| *HKSC* | *Hsü Kao-seng-chuan* |
| *IHQ* | *Indian Historical Quarterly* |
| *JA* | *Journal Asiatique* |
| *JAOS* | *Journal of the American Oriental Society* |
| *JRAS* | *Journal of the Royal Asiatic Society* |
| *KSC* | *Kao-seng-chuan* |
| *MCB* | *Mélanges Chinois et Bouddhiques* |
| NS | New Series |
| *OZ* | *Ostasiatische Zeitschrift* |
| *SBE* | *Sacred Books of the East* |
| *SKSC* | *Sung Kao-seng-chuan* |
| *SZ* | *Shigaku zasshi* |
| *TP* | *T'oung Pao* |
| *ZDMG* | *Zeitschrift der Deutschen Morgenländischen Gesellschaft* |

# BIBLIOGRAPHY

## CHAPTER ONE

On the Indian background, T. W. Rhys Davids, *Buddhist India*, London, 1903, though quite old, is still very useful. Other books that provide useful data are the *Cambridge History of India*, New York, 1922, vol. 1, chaps. 7 and 8; R. C. Majumdar (ed.), *The Age of Imperial Unity* (vol. 2 of the series *History and Culture of India*), Bombay, 1951, chaps. 1 and 2; M. Hiriyanna, *The Essentials of Indian Philosophy*, London, 1949.

For a critical essay on the biographies of the Buddha see E. Lamotte, "La légende du Buddha", *Revue de l'Histoire des Religions*, 134 (1948), 37–71. In the first part of this article Lamotte reviews the early biographies of the Buddha by É. Senart, *Éssai sur la legende du Buddha*, Paris, 1875; H. Kern, *Geschiedenis van het Buddhisme in Indië*, Haarlem, 1882; H. Oldenberg, *Buddha, sein Leben, seine Lehre, seine Gemeinde*, Berlin, 1881. Among the recent books probably the most useful are E. J. Thomas, *The Life of the Buddha as Legend and History*, 3rd ed., London, 1949; A. Foucher, *La Vie du Bouddha*, Paris, 1949. Thomas drew his materials from the Pāli and Sanskrit sources, while Foucher depended not only on the literary data but also on the evidence afforded by archeology and sculpture.

Good summaries of the Buddhist *dhamma* may be found in L. de la Vallée Poussin, *The Way to Nirvana*, Cambridge, 1917; *Bouddhisme, Opinion sur l'Histoire de la Dogmatique*, Paris, 1909; E. Conze, *Buddhism*, 2nd ed., Oxford, 1953; H. C. Warren, *Buddhism in Translations*, 9th issue, Cambridge, Mass., 1947; N. Dutt, *Early Monastic Buddhism*, 2 vols., Calcutta, 1945; D. T. Suzuki, *Outlines of Mahāyāna Buddhism*, London, 1907; J. Takakusu, *The Essentials of Buddhist Philosophy*, Honolulu, 1947; N. Dutt, *Aspects of Mahāyāna Buddhism*, London, 1930; S. Dutt, *The Buddha and Five After Centuries*, 1957; Sangharakshita, *A Survey of Buddhism*, Bangalore, 1957; G. C. Pande, *Studies in the Origins of Buddhism*, Allahabad, 1957; Walpola Rahula, *What the Buddha Taught*, New York 1962. On the Hinayana arhat ideal see I. B. Horner, *Early Buddhist Theory of Man Perfected*, London, 1936. On the later development of the arhat see S. Levi and E. Chavannes, "Les Seize Arhats protecteurs de la loi," *JA*, (1916), 2, 5–50, 189–304; M. W. de Visser, "The Arhats in China and Japan," *OZ* (Apr.–Sept.

1918), 87–102; (Apr.–Sept. 1920–1921), 116–144. For the Mahāyāna bodhisattva see Har Dayal, *The Bodhisattva Doctrine in Buddhist Sanskrit Literature*, London, 1932.

Buddhist literature is discussed in M. Winternitz, *History of Indian Literature*, Calcutta, 1933, vol. 2 (English translation by Mrs. S. Ketkar and Miss H. Kohn); B. C. Law, *History of Pāli Literature*, 2 vols., London, 1933.

On the trikāya there is a very complete bibliography in L. de la Vallée Poussin, *La Siddhi de Hiuan-tsang*, Paris, 1929, 2, 762–813; see also his article, "The Three Bodies of the Buddha," *JRAS* (1906), 943–977. A very illuminating discussion is provided by Paul Mus, *Barabudur*, Hanoi, 1935, vol. 2, no. 1; Akanuma Chizen, "The Triple Body of the Buddha," *EB*, 2 (1922), 1–29, is also valuable for tracing the trikāya doctrine.

For the bodhisattva Avalokiteśvāra there is the latest monograph by Marie-Thérèse de Mallmann, *Introduction à l'Étude d'Avalokiteśvāra*, Paris, 1948.

General discussions of Buddhist thought may be found in E. J. Thomas, *History of Buddhist Thought*, London, 1933; P. Oltramare, *La Théosophie Bouddhique*, Paris, 1923; O. Rosenberg, *Die Probleme der buddhistischen Philosophie*, Heidelberg, 1924. On the meaning of *dhamma* in Pāli there is the monograph by W. and M. Geiger, *Pāli Dhamma*, Munchen, 1920. T. Stcherbatsky, *The Central Conception of Buddhism*, London, 1923, also discusses the word *dharma*, but he relies mainly on Vasubandhu's *Abhidharmakoça* for his interpretations, so that his ideas may have to be used cautiously when we apply them to the word *dhamma* in the Nikāyas.

On Central Asia the book by Hatani Ryōtai 羽溪了諦, *Seiiki no Bukkyō* 西域の佛教, Kyoto, 1914, is old but still useful. See also another article by Hatani, translated into Chinese by Hsü Tun-ku, "Hsi-yü fo-chiao chih yen-chiu" 西域佛教之研究, *Yen-ching hsüeh-pao*, 4 (1928), 653–702. On the Yavanas see Majumdar (ed.), *The Age of Imperial Unity*, chap. 7; *Cambridge History of India*, 1, 540–562. For the Scythians the latest book by J. E. van Lohuizen-de Leeuw, *The Scythian Period*, Leiden, 1949, is very useful, especially for the exhaustive bibliography it contains. Other articles that may be consulted are R. D. Bannerji, "The Scythian Period of Indian History," *Indian Antiquary*, 37 (1908), 25–75; R. Ghirshman, "Fouilles de Begram," *JA*, 234 (1943–1945), 59–71. R. Grousset, *In the Footsteps of the Buddha*,

London, 1932, although dealing primarily with the Chinese pilgrim Hsüan-tsang, contains some very good accounts of Buddhism in Turfan, Kucha, and Bactria.

## CHAPTER TWO

For the religious background in China during the Han period see Hu Shih, "The Establishment of Confucianism as a State Religion during the Han Dyansty," *Journal of the North China Branch Royal Asiatic Society*, 60 (1929), 20–41; H. Maspero, *Les Religions Chinoises*, Paris, 1950; *idem*, *Le Taoisme*, Paris, 1950; Fung Yu-lan, *A Short History of Chinese Philosophy*, New York, 1948; H. G. Creel, *Chinese Thought from Confucius to Mao Tze-tung*, Chicago, 1951; "What is Taoism," *JAOS*, 76, 3 (1956), 139–152; J. Needham, *Science and Civilization in China*, Cambridge, 1956, vol. 2.

For Han Buddhism the best general discussion in Chinese is in T'ang Yung-t'ung 湯用彤, *Han Wei Liang-Chin Nan-pei ch'ao Fo-chiao-shih* 漢魏兩晉南北朝佛教史, Shanghai, 1938, chaps. 1–5. In English there is the well-balanced account in E. Zürcher, *The Buddhist Conquest of China*, Leiden, 1959, 18–43.

Articles dealing with the introduction of Buddhism into China are very numerous, and no attempt will be made to mention them all here. We shall limit our list to the more significant discussions. On the various traditions which placed the introduction during or prior to the reign of Han Wu-ti see Otto Franke, "Zur Frage der Einführung des Buddhismus in China," *Mitteilungen des Seminars für Orientalische Sprachen*, 13 (1910), 295–305; H. Maspero's review of the above article in *BEFEO*, 10 (1910), 629–636; O. Franke, "Die Ausbreitung des Buddhismus von Indien nach Turkestan und China," *Archiv für Religionwissenschaft*, 12 (1909), 207–220; Ohashi Kaishun, "Die Spuren des Buddhismus in China vor Kaiser Ming," *EB*, 6 (1934), 247–278, 432–477; 7 (1937), 214–226 (the main emphasis in this article is on the "golden man"); H. H. Dubs, "The Golden Man of Former Han Times," *TP*, 33 (1937), 1–14; J. R. Ware, "Once more the Golden Man," *ibid.*, 34 (1938), 174–178. For a discussion of the Wei-lüeh version of the introduction, cf. Edouard Chavannes, "Les Pays d'Occident d'après le Wei Lio," *ibid.*, 6 (1905), 519–571; Paul Pelliot's review of the above article in *BEFEO*, 6 (1906), 361–400 (in which he also discussed various aspects of Han Buddhism); Sylvain Levi, "Notes sur les Indo-Scythes," *JA*, (1897), 1, 14–20; "Les Missions de Wang Hiuen Ts'e dans l'Inde," *ibid.*, (1900), 1, 466–468; O. Franke, ''Beiträge aus Chin-Quellen zur Kenntniss der Türkvolker und Skythen in Zentral Asien,'' *Abh. der konig. preuss. Ak. der Wiss. zu Berlin*, (1904), 91ff; Fujita Toyohachi 藤田豐八, ''Bukkyō denrai ni kansuru giryaku no honki ni tsuite'' 佛教傳來に關する魏略の本紀に就いて, *SZ* 史學雜誌, 37 (1926), 607–620; Shigematsu S. 重松俊章, ''Giryaku no butsuden ni kansuru ni-san no mondai to Roshi kakosetsu no yurai'' 魏略の佛傳に關する二三の問題と老子化胡說の由來, *Shien* 史淵, 18 (1938), 1–25.

On the dream of Ming-ti the pioneer article exposing the legendary character of the tradition is H. Maspero, "Le Songe et l'Ambassade de l'Empereur Ming," *BEFEO*, 10 (1910), 95–130; other discussions are in Pelliot, "Meou-tseu ou les doutes levés," *TP*, 19 (1920), 385–396; Tokiwa Daijō 常盤大定, "Kan-Min guhōsetsu no kenkyū" 漢明求法說の研究, *Tōyō gakuhō* 東洋學報, 10 (1920), 1–49; Naba Toshisada 那波利貞, "Hakubaji no enkaku ni kansuru gimon" 白馬寺の沿革に關する疑問, *Shirin* 史林, 5 (1920), 1, 45–62; Matsumoto Bunzaburō 松本文三郎, "Kan-Min guhō no kinen ni tsuite" 漢明求法の紀年に就いて, *Shukyō kenkyū* 宗教研究, NS, 4, 6 (1927), 115–133.

On the nature of Han Buddhism and the community of monks, cf. Maspero, *Les Religions Chinoises*, 65–83, 195–211; *idem, Le Taoisme*, 185–199; "Communautés et Moines Bouddhistes Chinois au II^e et III^e Siècles," *BEFEO*, 10 (1910), 222–232; "Les Origines de la Communauté Bouddhiste de Loyang," *JA*, 225 (1934), 87–107; Ishikawa Hiromichi 石川博道, "Go-kan no Bukkyō ni tsuite" 後漢の佛教に就いて, *Shigaku* 史學, 18 (1939), 43–75, 599–642 (where he has gathered together all the pertinent materials on Han Buddhism).

Studies on the *Sutra in Forty-two Sections* may be found in the above-mentioned articles of Pelliot and Maspero dealing with the introduction of Buddhism. Cf. also T'ang Yung-t'ung, "The Editions of the Ssu-shih-erh chang-ching," *HJAS*, 1 (1936), 147–155; Heinrich Hackmann, ''Die Textgestalt des Sutra der 42 Abschnitt," *Acta Orientalia*, 5 (1927), 197–237; Wang Wei-ch'eng 王維誠, "Ssu-shih-erh-chang-ching Tao-an ching-lu ch'üeh-tsai chih yüan-yin" 四十二章經道安經錄闕載之原因. *Yen-ching hsüeh-pao* 燕京學報, 18 (1935), 147–152; Liang Ch'i-ch'ao, *Liang Jen-kung chin-chu ti-i-chi* 梁任公近著第一輯, Shanghai, 1925–1926, 2, 10–13; Hu Shih 胡適, *Hu Shih lun-hsüeh chin-chu* 胡適論學近著, Shanghai, 1935, 1, 177–197; Matsumoto B., Shijunishōkyō seiritsu nendai kō" 四十二章經成立年代考, *Tōhō gakuhō* 東方學報, Kyoto, 14 (1943), 1–38. In this chapter I have used, with some modifications, the translation of D. T. Suzuki in Soyen Shaku, *Sermons of a Buddhist Abbot*, Chicago, 1906, 3–21. The views of Sakaino Kōyō 境野黄洋 on the sutra may be found in his book, *Shina Bukkyō seishi* 支那佛教精史, Tokyo, 1935, 36–57.

The most complete discussion of Mou-tzu in a European language is by P. Pelliot, "Meou-tseu ou les doutes levés," *TP*, 19, 255–433. See also the review of this article by L. Aurousseau in *BEFEO*, 22 (1922), 276–298, where he divides the contents of the work into an earlier and a later layer. In Japanese there is the exhaustive study by Fukui Kojun 福井康順, *Dōkyō no kisoteki kenkyu* 道教の基礎的研究, Tokyo, 1952, 326–436; see also his article in *Bukkyō shigaku* 佛教史學, 2, 2 (1951), 1–16; 2, 3 (1951), 1–14. Fukui concludes that the date of compilation of *Mou-tzu* was during the middle of the third century, after the translation of the *Jui-ying pen-ch'i-ching* in 222–228, from which work the compiler of *Mou-tzu* drew many of his passages. He does not believe that it is a spurious work. Other discussions may be found in Tokiwa, *Tōyō gakuhō*, 10, 16–26; *Shina ni okeru Bukkyō to Jukyō Dōkyō* 支那に於ける佛教と儒教道教, Tokyo, 1930, 89–110; *Liang Jen-kung chin-chu ti-i-chi*, 2, 21–23; Yü Chia-hsi 余嘉錫, "Mou-tzu li-huo-lun chien-t'ao" 牟子理惑論檢討, *Yen-ching hsüeh-pao*, 20 (1936), 1–23; *Hu Shih lun-hsüeh chin-chu*, 1, 151–154; Matsumoto B., "Bōshi riwaku no jutsusaku nendai kō" 牟子理惑の述作年代考, *Tōhō gakuhō*, Kyoto, 12 (1941), 1–33. The latest discussion is by Chou I-liang 周一良, "Mou-tzu li-huo-lun nien-tai-k'ao" 牟子理惑論年代考, *Yen-ching hsüeh-pao*, 36 (1949), 1–16.

CHAPTER THREE

For a general discussion of this period the following sources are useful:

1. T'ang, *Fo-chiao-shih*, 121–186.
2. Yamasaki Hiroshi 山崎宏, *Shina chūsei Bukkyō no tenkai* 支那中世佛教の展開 (hereafter cited as Yamasaki, *Shina*), Tokyo, 1942, 50–187.
3. Tsukamoto Zenryū 塚本善隆, *Shina Bukkyōshi kenkyū* 支那佛教史研究, Tokyo, 1942, 18–56.
4. Michibata Ryōshū 道端良秀, *Chūgoku Bukkyōshi* 中國佛教史, Kyoto, 1958, 14–52.

The best treatment in English is by E. Zürcher, *The Buddhist Conquest of China*, 1, 57–253.

For the Prajñā literature Edward Conze has contributed some valuable studies:

1. *Selected Sayings from the Perfection of Wisdom*, London, 1955. The introduction gives a good survey of the development of Prajñā literature.

2. *Vajracchedika Prajñāpāramitā*, edited and translated, Rome, 1957.

3. *Buddhist Wisdom Books*, London, 1958. Contains translations of the Diamond Sutra and Heart Sutra.

4. *The Prajñāpāramitā Literature*, Hague, 1960.

5. "The Ontology of the Prajñāpāramitā," *Philosophy East and West*, 3, 2 (1953), 117–130.

In Japanese the most exhaustive study to find out the original version of the *Prajñāpāramitāsutra* is by Kajiyoshi Kōun 梶芳光運, *Genshi hannyakyō no kenkyū* 原始般若經の研究, Tokyo, 1944. In the *Taishō Tripitaka* the various Chinese translations of these sutras occupy vols. 5–8.

For the Prajñā School in China the following discussions are helpful:

1. T'ang, *Fo-chiao-shih*, 229–277.

2. W. Liebenthal, *The Book of Chao*, Peking, 1948, 146–166.

3. Fung, *History of Chinese Philosophy*, Princeton, 1953, 2, 243–258.

4. Imai Usaburō 今井宇三郎, "Rokka shichishūron no seiritsu" 六家七宗論の成立, *Nihon Chūgoku gakkaihō* 日本中國學會報, 7 (1955), 53–68.

On Neo-Taoism good discussions may be found in:

1. Fung, *A Short History of Chinese Philosophy*, New York, 1959, 217–240.

2. *Idem*, *History of Chinese Philosophy*, 2, 168–236.

3. A. A. Petrov, *Wang Pi, His Place in the History of Chinese Philosophy*, Institute of Oriental Studies Monograph XIII, Moscow Academy of Science, 1936.

For Chinese studies on Neo-Taoism see:

1. Liu Ta-chieh 劉大杰, *Wei-Chin ssu-hsiang-lun* 魏晉思想論, Shanghai, 1939.

2. Fan Shou-k'ang 范壽康, *Wei-Chin chih ch'ing-t'an* 魏晉之清談, Shanghai, 1936.

3. Ho Ch'ang-ch'un 賀昌群, *Wei-Chin ch'ing-t'an ssu-hsiang ch'u-lun* 魏晉清談思想初論, Chungking, 1946.

4. Ch'en Yin-k'o 陳寅恪, *T'ao Yüan-ming chih ssu-hsiang yü ch'ing-t'an chih kuan-hsi* 陶淵明之思想與清談之關係, Chungking, 1945.

5. *Idem*, "Hsiao-yao-yu Hsiang-Kuo-i chi Chih Tun-i t'an-yüan" 逍遙遊向郭義及支遁義探源, *Tsing-hua hsüeh-pao* 清華學報, 12, 2 (1937), 309-314.

6. T'ang Yung-t'ung, "Tu Liu Shao Jen-wu-chih" 讀劉邵人物志, *T'u-shu chi-k'an* 圖書季刊, NS, 2 (1940), 4-18.

7. *Idem*, "Wang Pi chih Chou-i Lun-yü hsin-i" 王弼之周易論語新義, *T'u-shu chi-k'an*, NS, 4 (1943), 28-40.

8. Ho Ch'ang-ch'un, "Wei-Chin chih cheng yü ch'ing-t'an chih ch'i" 魏晉之政與清談之起, *She-hui k'e-hsüeh chi-k'an* 社會科學季刊, 1 (1944), 92-104.

9. Ch'en Yin-k'o, "Chih Min-tu hsüeh-shuo k'ao" 支愍度學說考, *Ch'ing-chu Ts'ai Yüan-p'ei hsien-sheng liu-shih-wu-shui wen-chi* 慶祝蔡元培先生六十五歲文集, (1933), 1-18.

The following articles in western languages are also helpful:

1. E. Balazs, "Entre révolte nihiliste et évasion mystique," *Asiatische Studien*, 2 (1948), 27-55.

2. W. Eichhorn, "Zur Chinesischen Kulturgeschichte des 3. und 4. Jahrhunderts," *ZDMG*, (1937), 451-483.

3. D. Holzman, "Les sept sages de la forêt des bambous et la société de leur temps," *TP*, 44 (1956), 317-346.

4. K. Ch'en, "Neo-Taoism and the Prajñā School," *Chinese Culture*, 1, 2 (1957), 33-46.

On the relation between the aristocracy and Buddhism see Miyakawa Hisayuki 宮川尙志, "Tōshin jidai no kizoku to Bukkyō" 東晉時代の貴族と佛教, *Shina Bukkyō shigaku*, 4, 1 (1940), 14-28; 4, 2, 58-76.

On Chih Tun see:

1. Zürcher, *Conquest*, 1, 116-130.

2. Fukunaga Kōji 福永光司, "Shiton to sono shūi" 支遁と其の周圍, *Bukkyō shigaku*, 5, 2 (1956), 12-34.

3. T'ang, *Fo-chiao-shih*, 177-180.

4. Paul Demiéville, "La pénétration du Bouddhisme dans la tradition philosophique Chinoise," *Cahiers d'Histoire Mondiale*, 3, 1 (1956), 19-38.

On ke-i see the following discussions:

1. T'ang, *Fo-chiao-shih*, 234-238.

2. Fung, *History of Chinese Philosophy*, 2, 241–243.

3. T'ang, "On Ko-yi, the earliest method by which Indian Buddhism and Chinese thought were synthesized," *Radhakrishnan: Comparative Studies in Philopsophy*, 1940, 276–286.

On Buddhism in North China under the Chin Dynasty see:

1. A. Wright, "Fo-t'u-teng," *HJAS*, 11 (1948), 322–370.

2. Yamasaki, *Shina*, 69–173.

On the controversy between Buddhism and the state see:

1. L. Hurvitz, "Render Unto Caesar in Early Chinese Buddhism," *Sino-Indian Studies*, 5, 3/4, 2–36.

2. Kubota Ryōon 久保田量遠, *Shina Ju Dō Butsu kōshōshi* 支那儒道佛交涉史, Tokyo, 1943, 78–88.

3. *Idem, Shina Ju Dō Butsu sangyō shiron* 支那儒道佛三教史論, Tokyo, 1931, 110–126.

4. Tokiwa Daijō 常盤大定, *Shina ni okeru Bukkyō to Jukyō Dōkyō* 支那に於ける佛教と儒教道教, Tokyo, 1930, 56–63.

5. Zürcher, *Conquest*, 1, 231–239.

On Kumārajīva see *KSC*, 2; *Taishō*, 50, 330a–333a; J. Nobel, *Sitzungberichte der Preussischen Academie der Wissenschaften, Phil. Hist. Klasse*, 1927, 206–233; Tomomatsu, *JA*, 219, 2 (1931), 135–174; Hatani Ryōtai, "Kumarajū no kenkyū" 鳩摩羅什の研究, *Geimon*, 1 (1910), 1141–1164; 2 (1911), 221–240. See also Tsukamoto Zenryū, "The Dates of Kumārajīva and Seng-chao Re-examined," *Silver Jubilee Volume of the Zinbun Kagaku Kenkyūsyo*, Kyoto, 1954, 568–584, where the author proposes 350–409 as the dates for Kumārajīva.

On Seng-chao see his biography in *KSC*, 6; *Taishō*, 50, 365a–366a. His main work, *Chao-lun* 肇論, is found in *Taishō*, 45, 150a–161b. The most exhaustive study of Seng-chao and the *Chao-lun* was carried out by a group of Japanese scholars at Kyoto University, under the leadership of Tsukamoto Zenryū, and published as the *Jōron kenkyū*, Kyoto, 1955. The book consists of two parts. Part I is a Japanese translation and annotation of the text of *Chao-lun*, while Part II consists of seven articles written by Japanese scholars, all touching on the life and thought of Seng-chao. See also Konami Takuichi 木南卓一, "Rikuchō shisō ni okeru sōjō no ichi" 六朝思想に於ける僧肇の位置, *Tōyō no bunka to shakai* 東洋の文化と社會, 4 (1954), 58–81. A translation of the text into English was made by W. Liebenthal, *The Book of*

*Chao*, Peking, 1948, 195 pp. Parts were also translated in Fung, *History of Chinese Philosophy*, 2, 258–270. See also T'ang, *Fo-chiao-shih*, 278–340.

For Nāgārjuna and the Mādhyamika School the following works are useful:

For a biography of the founder, Nāgārjuna, see M. Walleser, "The Life of Nāgārjuna from Tibetan and Chinese Sources," *Hirth Anniversary Volume*, 421–455. Also, V. W. Karambelkar, "The Problem of Nāgārjuna," *Journal of Indian History*, 30, 1 (1952), 21–33.

Translations of Mādhyamika literature may be found in the following:

1. M. Walleser, *Die mittlere Lehre des Nāgārjuna nach der Tibetischen Version ubertragen*, Heidelberg, 1911.

2. *Idem, Die mittlere Lehre des Nāgārjuna nach der Chinesischen Version ubertragen*, Heidelberg, 1912.

3. T. Stcherbatsky, *The Conception of Buddhist Nirvāna*, Leningrad, 1927 (translation of chaps. 1 and 25 of *Mādhyamika-kārikā* and the commentary in *Prasannapadā*).

4. S. Schayer, "Feuer und Brennstoff," *Rocznick Orjentalistyczny*, 7 (1931), 26–52 (translation of chap. 10 of *Prasannapadā*).

5. *Idem, Ausgewählte Kapitel aus der Prasannapadā*, Krakow, 1931 (translations of chaps. 5, 12–16 of *Prasannapadā*).

6. J. May, *Prasannapadā Mādhyamikavṛtti. Douze chapitres traduits du Sanskrit et du Tibetain*, 1959, 539 pp.

7. L. de la Vallée Poussin, *Mélanges Ch. de Harlez*, Leiden, 1896, 313–320 (translation of chap. 24 of *Prasannapadā*).

8. E. Lamotte, "Le traité de l'acte de Vasubandhu," *MCB*, 4 (1935–1936), 265–288 (translation of chap. 17 of *Prasannapadā*).

9. J. W. deJong, *Cinq chapitres de la Prasannapadā*, Paris, 1949 (translation of chaps. 18–22 of *Prasannapadā*).

10. G. Tucci, *Pre-Dinnaga Buddhist Texts on Logic from Chinese Sources, Gaekwad Or. Series*, 49, Baroda, 1929, 1–89 (translation of *Po-lun* into English).

11. E. Lamotte, *Le traité de la grande vertu de sagesse de Nāgārjuna*, Louvain, 1944, 1949, 2 vols. (French translation of chaps. 1–30 of the text *Ta-chih-tu-lun*).

The best discussion so far of the Mādhyamika School is found in T. R. V. Murti, *The Central Philosophy of Buddhism*, London, 1955. In

Chinese there is a good summary by Tao-an 道安, "San-lun-tsung shih-lun 三論宗史論, *Chung-kuo fo-chiao-shih lun-chi* 中國佛教史論集, Taipei, 1956, 2, 442-463.

On the Tunhuang caves and their treasures see:

1. P. Pelliot, *Les grottes de Touen-houang*, Paris, 1914-1924, 6 vols.

2. A. Stein, *The Thousand Buddhas, Ancient Buddhist Paintings from the Cave Temples of Tunhuang*, London, 1921.

3. Matsumoto Eiichi 松本榮一, *Tonkōga no kenkyū* 燉煌畫の研究, Tokyo, 1937, 2 vols.

4. A. Waley, *A Catalogue of Paintings Recovered from Tunhuang*, London, 1931.

5. Basil Gray and J. B. Vincent, *Buddhist Cave Paintings at Tunhuang*, London, 1959.

6. Lao Kan, "The Art of Tunhuang," *Chinese Culture*, 1, 2 (1957) 47-74.

7. Chiang Liang-fu 姜亮夫, *Tun-huang, wei-ta-ti wen-hua pao-tsang* 敦煌偉大的文化寶藏, Shanghai, 1958, 159 pp.

For biography of Fa-hsien see *Taishō*, 50, 337b-338b; for his description of foreign countries see *Taishō*, 51, 857a-866c. The latter has been translated by J. Legge, *Travels of Fa-hsien*, Oxford, 1886; H. A. Giles, *The Travels of Fa-hsien*, Cambridge, 1877, 1923; A. Remusat, *Foe Koue Ki*, Paris, 1836; S. Beal, *Buddhist Records of the Western World*, London, 1885, 1, introduction, 23-83.

## CHAPTER FOUR

Basic source materials in Chinese for the study of the foreign and Chinese Buddhist monks may be found in the following works of the Chinese Tripitaka:

1. *Ch'u-san-tsang-chi-chi* 出三藏記集, ch. 13-15, compiled by Seng-yu 僧祐 of the Liang Dynasty.

2. *K'ai-yüan-shih-chiao-lu* 開元釋教錄, ch. 1-9, completed in 730 by Chih-sheng 智昇 of the T'ang Dynasty.

3. *KSC* 高僧傳, 14 *chüan* by Hui-chiao 慧皎 of the Liang Dynasty. It covers the period from the Later Han Dynasty to ca. 519, and contains biographies of 257 monks, and mentions about 200 more casually. For a study of this work cf. Arthur F. Wright, "Biography and Hagiography. Hui-chiao's Lives of Eminent

Monks," *Silver Jubilee Volume of the Zinbun-Kagaku-Kenkyūsyo*, Kyoto University, 1954, 383–432, which contains an up-to-date bibliography of the published materials on the work. A name index of the *KSC* was first made by H. Hackmann, "Alphabetisches Verzeichnes zum Kao-seng-chuan," *Acta Orientalia*, 2 (1923), but a more complete one is to be found in the *Shina Bukkyō shigaku* 支那佛教史學, 1 (1937), 3 (1939), entitled "Ryō kōsō den sakuin" 梁高僧傳索引, compiled by Tsukamoto Zenryū 塚本善隆, Iwai Tairyō 岩井諦亮, and Ryūchi Kiyoshi 龍池清.

4. *HKSC* 續高僧傳, 30 *chüan*, by Tao-hsüan 道宣 of the T'ang Dynasty. In his preface Tao-hsüan wrote that the work was finished in 645, but in the content of the book events down to the year 665 were included. In chap. 4 there is also a biography of Hsüan-tsang, who died in 664. The author also indicated in his preface that the work contained biographies of 331 (or 340) monks, besides mentioning 160 others, whereas actually there were biographies of 485 people and casual mention of 219 others. These points prove that after Tao-hsüan had finished writing his preface, he kept on adding materials to his work until his death in 667. In all, therefore, this work covers the period from the beginning of the Liang Dynasty down to 665.

5. *SKSC* 宋高僧傳, 30 *chüan*, compiled in 988 by Tsan-ning 贊宁 of the Sung Dynasty. It covers the period from the death of Tao-hsüan in 667 to 987, and contains biographies of 532 individuals, besides mentioning 125 others.

On Tao-an there is the monograph by Ui Hakuju, *Shaku Dōan kenkyū* 釋道安研究, Tokyo, 1956. His biography in the *KSC*, 5; *Taishō*, 50, 351c–354a, has been translated by A. Link, "Biography of Tao-an," *TP*, 46 (1958), 1–48. See also Zürcher, *Conquest*, 1, 184–204; T'ang, *Fo-chiao-shih*, 187–277.

On Hui-yüan see:

1. Biography in *KSC*, 6; *Taishō*, 50, 357c–361b (translated into English in Zürcher, *Conquest*, 1, 204–253).
2. T'ang, *Fo-chiao-shih*, 341–373.
3. W. Liebenthal, "Shih Hui-yüan's Buddhism," *JAOS*, 70 (1950), 243–259.
4. *Idem*, "The Immortality of the Soul in China," *Monumenta Nipponica*, 8 (1952), 354–365.

5. Takamine Ryōshū 高峯了州, "Eon Chūgoku Jōdokyō no haikei" 慧遠中國淨土教の背景, *Ryūkoku Daigaku ronsō* 龍谷大學論叢, no. 243.

6. Hongō T. 本鄉恭世, "Rikuchō mombatsu kizoku shakai to Eon" 六朝門閥貴族社會と慧遠, *Ryūkoku shidan* 龍谷史壇, 4 (1956), 35-54. Valuable for historical background.

7. Itano Chōhachi, "Eon no shinfumentsuron" 慧遠の神不滅論 *Tōhō gakuhō*, Tokyo, 14, 3 (1943), 1-40.

For a critical edition of the surviving works of Hui-yüan see the latest book, Kimura Eiichi 木村英一, *Eon kenkyū* 慧遠研究, Kyoto, 1960.

On Tao-sheng see:

1. Biography in *KSC*, 7; *Taishō*, 50, 366b-367a.

2. T'ang, *Fo-chiao-shih*, 601-676.

3. Fung, *History of Chinese Philosophy*, 2, 270-284.

4. Liebenthal, "A Biography of Tao-sheng," *Monumenta Nipponica*, 11, 3 (1955), 64-96.

5. *Idem*, "The World Conception of Chu Tao-sheng," *ibid.*, 12 (1956), 65-104; 12 (1957), 241-268.

6. Itano Chōhachi 板野長八, "Dōshō no busshōron" 道生の佛性論, *Shina Bukkyō shigaku*, 2, 2 (1938), 1-26.

7. *Idem*, "Dōshō no tongosetsu seiritsu no jijō" 道生の頓悟說成立の事情, *Tōhō gakuhō* 東方學報, Tokyo, 7 (1936), 125-186.

## CHAPTER FIVE

General discussions may be found in the following works:

1. T'ang, *Fo-chiao-shih*, 415-486.

2. Miyakawa Hisayuki, *Rikuchō shūkyōshi* 六朝宗教史, Tokyo, 1948, 33-121.

3. Liebenthal, "Chinese Buddhism During the Fourth and Fifth Centuries," *Monumenta Nipponica*, 11, 1 (1955), 44-83.

4. Miyakawa H., "Rikuchō jidaijin no Bukkyō shinkō" 六朝時代人の佛教信仰, *Bukkyō shigaku*, 4, 2 (1955), 1-17. Valuable for the list of worthies during the Six Dynasties who embraced Buddhism.

5. Ogasawara Senshū 小笠原宣秀, "Shina nambokuchō jidai Bukkyō to shākai kyōka" 支那南北朝時代佛教と社會教化 *Ryūkoku shidan*, no. 4.

6. Ōchō Enichi 橫超慧日, Chūgoku nambokuchō jidai no Bukkyō gakufū" 中國南北朝時代の佛教學風, *Nihon Bukkyō Gakkai nempō*, 17 (1952), 1–26.

For Prince Ching-ling see also Ogasawara S., "Nansei Bukkyō to Shuku Shiryō" 南齊佛教と蕭子良, *Shina Bukkyō shigaku*, 3, 2 (1939), 63–76.

On Emperor Wu of the Liang Dynasty see:

1. Mori Mikisaburō 森三樹三郎, *Ryō no Butei* 梁の武帝, Kyoto, 1956.
2. Yamasaki, *Shina*, 188–236.
3. Mathias Tchang, *Tombeau des Liang, Var. Sinologiques No. 33*, Shanghai, 1912, 108 pp.

On the practice of *she-shen*, or renouncing the body, see Nabata Ōjun 名畑應順, "Shina chūsei ni okeru shashin ni tsuite" 支那中世に於ける 捨身に就いて, *Ōtani gakuhō* 大谷學報, 12, 2 (1931), 1–43.

For the controversy over Buddhism see:

1. K. Chen, "Anti-Buddhist Propaganda during the Nan-ch'ao," *HJAS*, 15 (1952), 166–192.
2. W. Liebenthal, "The Immortality of the Soul in Chinese Thought," *Monumenta Nipponica*, 8 (1952), 327–397 (where the pertinent literature on the question of the destructibility of the soul is translated).
3. Fung, *History of Chinese Philosophy*, 2, 284–292.
4. Stefan Balazs, "Der Philosoph Fan Dschen und sein Traktat gegen den Buddhismus," *Sinica*, 7 (1932), 220–234.
5. Hou Wai-lu, et cetera, 侯外廬等, *Chung-kuo ssu-hsiang t'ung-shih* 中國思想通史, Peking, 1950 (for a presentation of the debate over the immortality of the soul from the Marxist viewpoint).
6. Kubota, *Kōshōshi*, 62–115.
7. *Idem, Sangyō shiron*, 51–109, 150–172.
8. Tokiwa, *Bukkyō to Jukyō*, 65–106, 586–598.
9. Ōda Teizō 太田悌藏, "Shūhei myōbutsuron no shinfumetsusetsu oyobi sono sangyō chōwa shisō" 宗炳明佛論の神不滅說及その 三教調和思想, *Tokiwa hakase kanreki kinen Bukkyō ronsō* 常盤 博士還曆記念佛教論叢, 1933, 77–94.
10. *Idem*, "Shina rikuchō jidai no shamon fukei mondai" 支那六朝時 代の沙門不敬問題, *Shūkyō kenkyū*, 9, 5 (1932), 80–97.

11. Tsuda Sōkichi 津田左右吉, "Shimmetsu fumetsu no ronsō ni tsuite" 神滅不滅の論爭に就いて, *Tōyō gakuhō* 東洋學報, 29, 1 (1942), 1–52; 29, 2, 33–80; 30, 1 (1943), 24–95.

On the *Nirvānasūtra* in the south see T'ang, *Fo-chiao-shih*, 677–717.

On the Satyasiddhi and San-lun see:

1. *Ibid.*, 718–765.

2. Yamakami Sogen, *Systems of Buddhist Thought*, Calcutta, 1912, 172–209.

3. Kasuga Reichi 春日禮智, "Shina jōjitsu gakuha no ryūtai ni tsuite" 支那成實學派の隆替について, *Tōhō gakuhō*, Kyoto, 14, 2 (1944), 129–155.

4. Yang Pai-i 楊白衣, "Ch'eng-shih-tsung" 成實宗, *Chung-kuo fo-chiao-shih lun-chi*, 2, 714–729.

On Paramārtha see *HKSC*, 1; *Taishō*, 50, 429c–431a; J. Takakusu, *BEFEO*, 4 (1904), 60–65; P. Demiéville, *Bulletin de la Maison Franco-Japonaise*, 2, 2 (1929), 15–28.

Source materials concerning the discussion on the immortality of the soul may be found in *Hung-ming-chi* 弘明集; *Taishō*, 52.

There is a very important article dealing with the concept of nationalism in Chinese Buddhism which covers the entire period of disunity and the Sui Dynasty: Ōchō Enichi, "Shina Bukkyō ni okeru kokka ishiki" 支那佛教に於ける國家意識, *Tōhō gakuhō*, Tokyo, 11, 3 (1940), 99–152.

## CHAPTER SIX

The *Wei-shu* was the first dynastic history to devote a treatise to Buddhism, and in this treatise there is a rapid survey of Buddhism in China through the Northern Wei Dynasty. The emphasis was on the developments under the Northern Wei. It was first translated into English by J. R. Ware and published in *TP*, 30 (1933), 100–181. Since this translation was made at a time when not much work had been done in Chinese Buddhism, some errors were made which were pointed out by Chou I-Liang in *Shih-hsüeh nien-pao*, 2, 4 (1937), 183–190, and Tsukamoto Zenryū in *Asiatic Studies in honor of Tōru Haneda*, Kyoto, 1950, 635–662 (in Japanese). This has led L. Hurvitz to make another English translation, *Wei Shou on Buddhism and Taoism*, Kyoto, 1956, which made use of extensive explanations and annotations prepared by Tsukamoto on the treatise. For a review of this translation by L. S. Yang and K. Ch'en see *HJAS*, 20 (1957), 362–382.

The most authoritative treatment of Northern Wei Buddhism is to be found in Tsukamoto, *Shina Bukkyōshi kenkyū, hokugi-hen* 支那佛教史研究北魏篇, Tokyo, 1942. Here are treated in great detail such subjects as the policy of the Northern Wei rulers toward Buddhism, the persecution under Emperor Wu, the chief of monks T'an-yao and his times, the Sangha and Buddha households, the Yün-kang caves, religious bandits, Lung-men caves, and the formation of the Pure Land School. Of these, the chapter on T'an-yao has been translated into English by Galen E. Sargent, "T'an-yao and his times," *Monumenta Serica*, 16 (1957), 363–396. For a general discussion of the same period see T'ang, *Fo-chiao-shih*, 487–545.

On the persecution under Emperor Wu see also:

1. W. Eberhard, *Das Toba Reich Nord Chinas*, Leiden, 1949, 228–239.
2. Ch'en Yin-k'o, "Ts'ui Hao yü K'ou Ch'ien-chih" 崔浩與寇謙之, *Ling-nan hsüeh-pao* 嶺南學報, 11 (1950) 111–134.
3. Wang Yi-t'ung 王伊同, "Ts'ui Hao kuo-shu yü-shih-i" 崔浩國書獄釋疑, *Tsing-hua hsüeh-pao*, 1, 2 (1957), 84–101.

For the early examples of Buddha images and the Yün-kang caves see Mizuno Seiichi and Nagahiro Toshio, *Yün-kang Caves*, Kyoto, 1952–1956, 32 vols., which comprise the most complete record of the caves and their contents. For the Lung-men caves and sculpture see the volume by the same authors, *Ryūmon sekkutsu no kenkyū* 龍門石窟の研究, Tokyo, 1941, 482 pp. (103 plates and 28 inscriptions and 17 pp. of English). First there is the result of the study made by the authors of the caves, 1–140. Then follows Appendix 1, 141–242, which consists of a long article by Tsukamoto Zenryū entitled "Buddhism Under the Northern Wei Dynasty," This article was reprinted later in its entirety in the *Shina Bukkyōshi kenkyū*, 355–609. This is then followed by Appendix 2, entitled "Lungmen Epigraphy," by Tsukamoto, Mizuno, and Kasuga Reichi, which contains the texts of the inscriptions found in the caves.

Before the Japanese scholars published their works, the most important study made by a European is that of E. Chavannes, *Mission Archéologique dans la Chine Septentrionale*, Paris, 1909–1915. Tome 1, Deuxième partie (1915), 294–319, discusses Yün-kang; 320–561 discusses Lungmen. This section contains translations of many inscriptions found in Lung-men. In vol. 1 of the plates (1909), plates 105–160 cover Yün-kang; plates 161–264 cover Lung-men.

On monks and ordination under the Northern Dynasties see Abe Kuniharu 阿部國治, "Hokuchō ni okeru do no kenkyū" 北朝に於ける度の研究, *Buddhist Studies in Honor of Dr. Tokiwa Daijō* (in Japanese), (1933), 1–21.

On the Buddhist societies see:

1. Tsukamoto, *Shina Bukkyōshi kenkyū*, 489–501.
2. Takao Giken 高雄義堅, "Hokugi ni okeru Bukkyō kyōdan no seiritsu" 北魏に於ける佛教教團の成立, *Ryūdai ronsō* 龍大論叢, no. 297, 1931.
3. *Idem*, "Hokugi Bukkyō kyōdan no hattatsu" 北魏佛教教團の發達, in his book *Chūgoku Bukkyō shiron* 中國佛教史論, 24–36.
4. Ogasawara S., "Shina nambokuchō Bukkyō to shakai kyōka 支那南北朝佛教と社會教化, *Ryūkoku shidan*, no. 10.

On the influence of Indian sculpture on Chinese Buddhist sculpture see J. Hackin, et cetera, *Studies in Chinese Art and Some Indian Influences*, London, 1938, especially chap. 2, "Indian and Other Influences in Chinese Sculpture," by Oswald Siren. See also A. Soper, *Literary Evidence for Early Buddhist Art in China*, Switzerland, 1959, 296 pp., where he has collected and translated numerous passages from Chinese sources pertinent to Buddhist art.

## CHAPTER SEVEN

For the Northern Chou persecution of Buddhism see:

1. Tsukamoto, "Hokushū no haibutsu ni tsuite" 北周の廢佛に就いて, *Tōhō gakuhō*, Kyoto, 16 (1948), 29–101; 18 (1950), 78–111.
2. *Idem*, "Hokushū no shūkyō haiki seisaku no hōkai" 北周の宗教廢毀政策の崩壞, *Bukkyō shigaku* 佛教史學, 1 (1949), 3–31.
3. Yü Chia-hsi 余嘉錫, "Pei-Chou hui-fo chu-mou-che Wei Yüan-sung" 北周毀佛主謀者衛元嵩, *Fu-jen hsüeh-chih* 輔仁學誌, 2, 2 (1931), 1–25.

On the Buddhist-Taoist controversy see Wang Wei-ch'eng 王維誠, "Lao-tzu hua-hu-shuo k'ao cheng" 老子化胡說考證, *Kuo-hsüeh chi-k'an* 國學季刊, 4, 2 (1934), 44–55.

The various treatises put forth by the Buddhists in this controversy, such as the *Erh-chiao-lun* 二教論 and *Hsiao-tao-lun* 笑道論, may be found in the collection *Hung-ming-chi; Taishō*, 52. See also Tao-hsüan, "*Chi-ku-chin fo-tao lun-heng*" 集古今佛道論衡, *Taishō*, 52. Yang Hsüan-chih, *Lo-yang chia-lan-chi*, is found in *Taishō*, 51.

For the formation of the Sui Dynasty see P. Boodberg, "The Rise and Fall of the House of Yang," *HJAS*, 4 (1939), 253–270. Taking his materials mainly from the findings of Japanese scholars, A. F. Wright has written an informative article on "The Formation of the Sui Ideology," published in J. K. Fairbank (ed.), *Chinese Thought and Institutions*, Chicago, 1957, 71–104. The most important of these Japanese studies are:

1. Yamasaki Hiroshi, "Zui no Kōso Buntei no Bukkyō chikokusaku" 隋の高祖文帝の佛教治國策, in his *Shina chūsei Bukkyō no tenkai*, 274–354.

2. *Idem*, "Zuichō no Bukkyō fukkō ni tsuite" 隋朝の佛教復興について, *Bukkyō shigaku*, 1, 1 (1949), 50–58.

3. *Idem*, "Shin-ō-kō no shidōjō" 晋王廣の四道場, *Tōyō gakuhō*, 32, 3 (1950), 53–65.

4. *Idem*, "Yōtei no dōjō" 煬帝の道場, *ibid.*, 34 (1952), 22–35.

5. *Idem*, "Zui no Yōtei to tendai daishi Chigi" 隋の煬帝と天台大師智顗, *Tōyō shigaku ronshū* 東洋史學論集, Tokyo, 1953, 147–159.

6. Tsukamoto Z., "Kokubunji to Zui Tō no Bukkyō seisaku narabi ni kanji" 國分寺と隋唐の佛教政策並ごに官寺, *Nisshi Bukkyō kōshōshi no kenkyū* 日支佛教交渉史の研究, Tokyo, 1944, 1–21.

7. *Idem*, "Zui no kōnan seifuku to Bukkyō" 隋の江南征服と佛教, *Bukkyō bunka kenkyū* 佛教文化研究, 3 (1953), 1–24.

On the stupa building see also Sun Tsung-wen 孫宗文, "Jen-shou she-li t'a" 仁壽舍利塔, *Hsien-tai fo-chiao* 現代佛學, 1 (1958), 20–24.

## CHAPTERS EIGHT, NINE, TEN

Because it was during the T'ang Dynasty that Chinese culture in all its aspects was introduced into Japan, Japanese scholars have made T'ang China their foremost field of investigation. The stream of articles and books dealing with T'ang China literally became a torrent and Buddhism naturally shared in this increased interest, especially since it was Buddhism that served as the vehicle of cultural transformation. Therefore there is an enormous list of research articles on Buddhism in T'ang China; only a few of these can be selected for mention in this bibliography.

The best general discussion in English of popular Buddhism during this period may be found in E. O. Reischauer, *Ennin's Travels in T'ang China*, New York, 1955, 164–271. The materials for this book are drawn mainly from the diary kept by the Japanese monk Ennin, which was also translated and published by Reischauer, *Ennin's Diary*, New York, 1955. Useful discussions may also be found in A. Waley, *The Real Tripitaka*, New York, 1952, and R. Grousset, *In the Footsteps of the Buddha*.

On the T'ang official policy toward Buddhism see:

1. Tsukamoto Z., "Kokubunji to Zui Tō no Bukkyō seisaku," *Nisshi Bukkyō kōshōshi no kenkyū*, 21–47.

2. Lo Hsiang-lin 羅香林, "T'ang-tai san-chiao chiang-lun-k'ao" 唐代三教講論考, *Tung-fang wen-hua* 東方文化, 1, 1 (1954), 85–97.

3. Ch'en Yin-k'o, "Wu Chao yü fo-chiao" 武曌與佛教, *Li-shih yü-yen yen-chiu-so chi-k'an* 歷史語言研究所集刊, 5, 2, 137–147.

4. T'ang Yung-t'ung, "T'ang T'ai-tsung yü fo-chiao" 唐太宗與佛教, *Hsüeh-heng* 學衡, 75 (1931), 1–7.

5. Huang Sheng-fu 黃聲孚, *T'ang-tai fo-chiao tui cheng-chih chih ying-hsiang* 唐代佛教對政治之影響, Hong Kong, 1959, 145 pp.

On Fu Yi and his anti-Buddhist movement see:

1. Ogasawara S., "Tō no haibutsuronsha Fu Eki ni tsuite" 唐の排佛論者傅奕について, *Shina Bukkyō shigaku*, 1, 3 (1937), 83–93.

2. A Wright, *Journal of the History of Ideas*, 12 (1951), 33–47.

On the Hui-ch'ang suppression see:

1. Reischauer, *Ennin's Travels*, 217–271.

2. K. Ch'en, "Economic Background of the Hui-ch'ang Persecution," *HJAS*, 19 (1956), 67–105.

3. Chia Chung-yao 賈鍾堯, "T'ang Hui-ch'ang cheng-chiao ch'ung-t'u shih-liao" 唐會昌政教衝突史料, *Shih-huo*, 4, 1 (1936), 18–27. This contains all the pertinent official documents on the suppression.

4. Kamekawa Shōshin 龜川正信, "Kaishō no haibutsu ni tsuite" 會昌の廢佛に就いて, *Shina Bukkyō shigaku*, 6, 1 (1942), 47–68.

On T'ang laws and the sangha see:

1. Futaba Kenkō 二葉憲香, "Sōnirei no senkōhō to shite no dōsōkaku" 僧尼令の先行法としての道僧格, *Ryūkoku shidan*, 43 (1958), 25–41.

2. Akitsuki Kan'ei 秋月觀暎, "Tōdai shūkyō keihō ni kansuru kanken" 唐代宗教刑法に關する管見, *Tōhō shūkyō* 東方宗教, 4, 5 (1954), 137–152.

3. Takao Giken, "Chūgoku Bukkyō to kokka ishiki" 中國佛教と國家意識, in his *Chūkogu Bukkyō shiron*, 46–53.

4. Makino Tatsumi 牧野巽, "Keigen jōhō jirui no dōshakumon" 慶元條法事類の道釋門, *Shūkyō kenkyū*, NS, 9, 2 (1932), 64–84.

5. Michibata R., "Tōdai sōni fuhaikunshinron" 唐代僧尼不拜君親論, *Indogaku Bukkyōgaku kenkyū* 印度學佛教學研究, 2, 2 (1954), 54–64.

For Hsüan-tsang see *Taishō*, 50, 221b–280a (translated in Beal, *Life of Hsüan-tsang*, London, 1911); St. Julien, *Histoire de la Vie de Hiouen-thsang*, Paris, 1853; A. Waley, *The Real Tripitaka*. The *Ta-t'ang Hsi-yü-chi* is found in *Taishō*, 51, 868c–947c. Translations may be found in St. Julien, *Mémoires sur les Contrées Occidentales*, Paris, 1857–1858, 2 vols.; T. Watters, *On Yuan Chwang's Travels*, London, 1904, 2 vols.; Beal, *Buddhist Records*, London, 1884, 2 vols. Using both the biography and the *Record*, R. Grousset has written a fascinating account in *In the Footsteps of the Buddha*. An attempt has been made by Chang Chun-mai 張君勱 to put together a bibliography of Hsüan-tsang in his "Hsüan-tsang liu-hsüeh-shih chih Yin-tu yü hsi-fang kuan-yü Hsüan-tsang chu-tso chih mu-lu" 玄奘留學時之印度與西方關於玄奘著作之目錄, *Tzu-yu Chung-kuo* 自由中國, 14, 11 (1956), 348–351. The biography of I-tsing is found in *SKSC*, 1; *Taishō*, 50, 710b–711b. His *Chi-kuei nei-fa chuan* is found in *Taishō*, 54, 204c–234a; *Ch'iu-fa kao-seng-chuan*, in *Taishō*, 51, 1a–12b. These works of I-tsing have been translated by Takakusu, *Records of the Buddhist Religion*, Oxford, 1896; and Chavannes, *Mémoires sur les Religieux Eminents*, Paris, 1894.

The most complete study in a European language of the economic activities of the Buddhist church in China is by Jacques Gernet, *Les Aspects Economiques du Bouddhisme dans la Société Chinoise du V^e au X^e Siècle*, Saigon, 1956. See the reviews of this work by A. Wright in *Journal of Asian Studies*, 16, 3 (1957), 408–414; D. W. Twitchett, "The Monasteries and China's Economy in Mediaeval Times," *BSOAS* 19, 3 (1957), 526–549; K. Ch'en in *HJAS*, 20 (1957), 733–740. See also *idem*, "The Economic Background of the Hui-ch'ang Persecution," *ibid.*, 19 (1956), 67–105, and L. S. Yang, "Buddhist Monasteries and Four Money-Raising Institutions in Chinese History," *ibid.*, 13 (1950), 174–191.

The following are two very important Japanese works which contain the manuscript materials discovered in Tunhuang and other sites in Central Asia pertaining to the social and economic activities of the Buddhist monasteries:

1. Seiiki Bunka Kenkyūkai 西域文化研究會, "Tonkō Toroban shakai keizai shiryō" 敦煌吐魯番社會經濟史料, fasc. 1 (vol. 2 of *Monumenta Serindica*), Kyoto, 1959.

2. Niida Noboru 仁井田陞, *Tō Sō hōritsu bunsho no kenkyū*, 唐宋法律文書の研究, Tokyo, 1937.

In Chinese there is an important study by T'ao Hsi-sheng 陶希聖, *T'ang-tai ssu-yüan ching-chi shih-liao* 唐代寺院經濟史料, (date unknown), which unfortunately was printed only in a limited number and is extremely difficult to secure now. However, the preface to the study, which contains the conclusions of T'ao, was reprinted in *Shih-huo*, 5, 4 (1937), 33–38, under the title *T'ang-tai ssu-yüan ching-chi kai-shuo* 唐代寺院經濟概說.

Very good discussions are to be found in the following:

1. Michibata R., *Tōdai jiin no keizaiteki kenkyū* 唐代寺院の經濟的研究, Monograph No. 9 of *Bukkyō Hōsei Keizai Kenkyūjo* 佛教法政經濟研究所, 1934, 62 pp.

2. Inaba Kunzan 稻葉君山, "Keizaijō yori mitaru Shina Bukkyōto no chii" 經濟上より見たる支那佛教徒の地位 (chap. 7 of his famous work *Shina shakaishi kenkyū* 支那社會史研究, Tokyo, 1922).

3. Mishima Hajime and Suzuki Shun 三島一, 鈴木俊, "Tōdai ni okeru jiin keizai" 唐代に於ける寺院經濟, in *Sekai rekishi taikei* 世界歴史大系, Tokyo, 5 (1934), 322–351.

4. Mishima H., "Tō Sō jiin no tokkenka e no ichibetsu" 唐宋寺院の特權化への一瞥, *Rekishigaku kenkyū* 歴史學研究, 1, 4 (1934), 252–257.

5. *Idem*, "Tō Sō jidai ni okeru kizoku tai jiin no keizaiteki kōshō ni kansuru ichi kōsatsu" 唐宗時代に於ける貴族對寺院の經濟的交涉に關する一考察, *Ichimura hakase koki kinen Tōyōshi ronsō* 市村博士古稀記念東洋史論叢, 1933, 1159–1183. A very important and useful article.

6. Naba Toshisada 那波利貞, "Ryō-ko kō" 梁戸考, *Shina Bukkyō shigaku*, 2, 1 (1938), 1–40; 2, 2, 27–68; 2, 4, 30–82. Important for account of privileges enjoyed by the temples and of the oil presses operated by the monasteries.

7. Michibata R., "Shina Bukkyō shakai keizaishi no kenkyū ni tsuite" 支那佛教社會經濟史の研究に就いて, *ibid.*, 1, 2 (1937), 111–125. Good summary of the research done by Japanese scholars on economic and social history.

8. Tamai Zehaku 玉井是博, "Tō jidai no shakaishiteki kōsatsu" 唐時代の社會史的考察, *SZ*, 34 (1923), 284–304, 333–364.

On the water-powered rolling mills see:

1. *Ibid.*, 334–338.
2. Naba T., "Bantō jidai ni okeru Tonkō chihō Bukkyō jiin no tengai keiei ni tsuite" 晚唐時代に於ける燉煌地方佛教寺院の碾磑經營に就いて, *Tōa keizai ronsō* 東亞經濟論叢, 1, 3 (1941), 23–51; 1, 4, 87–114; 2, 2 (1942), 165–186.

On the commercial activities see:

1. Michibata R., "Shina Bukkyō jiin no kinyū no jigyō" 支那佛教寺院の金融の事業, *Ōtani gakuhō*, 14, 1 (1933), 91–129. A very good article concerning inexhaustible treasury.
2. Tsukamoto Z., "Shingyō no sangaikyōdan to mujinzō ni tsuite" 信行の三階教團と無盡藏に就いて, *Shūkyō kenkyū*, 3, 4 (1926), 571–586.
3. Naba T., "Tonkō hakken bunsho ni yoru chūbantō jidai no Bukkyō jiin no sen-koku fuhaku-rui taifu eiri jigyō un'ei no jikkyō" 燉煌發見文書に據る中晚唐時代の佛教寺院の錢穀布帛類貸附營利事業運營の實況, *Shinagaku* 支那學, 10, 3 (1941), 433–510.
4. Katō Shigeru 加藤繁, "Tō Sō jidai no sōko ni tsuite" 唐宋時代の倉庫に就いて, *Shigaku*, 4, 2 (1925), 69–94.
5. Mishima H., "Tōdai jiko no kinō no ichi-ni ni tsuite" 唐代寺庫の機能の一二について, *Ikeuchi hakase kanreki kinen Tōyōshi ronshū* 池內博士還曆記念東洋史論集, Tokyo, 1940, 857–875.
6. *Idem*, "Sōrin ni okeru koji no shokugyō ni kansuru ichi kōsatsu" 叢林に於ける庫司の職業に關する一考察, *Katō kakase kanreki kinen Tōyōshi shūsetsu* 加藤博士還曆記念東洋史集說, 1941, 807–820.

On temples as hostels see Michibata, R., "Shukubō to shite no Tōdai jiin" 宿坊としての唐代寺院, *Shina Bukkyō shigaku*, 2, 1 (1938), 41–62.

On temple lands the following articles are important:

1. D. C. Twitchett, "Monastic Estates in T'ang China," *Asia Major*, NS, 5 (1956), 123–146.

2. Michibata R., "Tōdai ni jiden sōden to sōni no shiyū zaisan" 唐代に寺田僧田と僧尼の私有財産, *Eizan gakuhō* 叡山學報, v, 17 (1939) 20 pp.

3. Tamai Z., "Tōdai no tochi mondai kanken" 唐代の土地問題管見, *SZ*, 33 (1922), 597-633; 687-718; 758-790. A very useful article.

4. Mori Keirai 森慶來, "Tō no kindenhō ni okeru sōni no kyūden ni tsuite" 唐の均田法に於ける僧尼の給田に就いて, *Rekishigaku kenkyū* 歷史學研究, 4, 1 (1935), 53-59. Important.

5. Fujii Kiyoshi 藤井淸, "Tōdai no jiryō ni tsuite" 唐代の寺領について, *Kambungaku* 漢文學, 2 (1953), 21-26.

6. Ho Tzu-ch'üan 何茲全, "Chung-ku ta-tsu ssu-yüan ling-hu yen-chiu" 中古大族寺院領戶研究, *Shih-huo*, 3, 4 (1936), 20-41.

On Buddhism and Chinese ethics see:

1. Michibata R., "Tōdai Bukkyō no kazoku rinri" 唐代佛教の家族倫理, *Indogaku Bukkyōgaku kenkyū*, 1, 2 (1953), 21-28.

2. Ogasawara S., "Chūgoku rinri to Tōdai Bukkyō" 中國倫理と唐代佛教, *Bukkyō shigaku*, 3, 3 (1953), 1-12.

3. Michibata R., "Tōdai sōni fuhaikunshinron" 唐代僧尼不拜君親論, *Indogaku Bukkyōgaku kenkyū*, 2, 2 (1954), 54-64.

On popular Buddhism and festivals during the T'ang Dynasty see:

1. Ōtani Kōshō 大谷光照, "*Tōdai no Bukkyō girei*" 唐代の佛教儀禮, Tokyo, 1937, 2 vols. This book is by far the most complete and best study of Buddhist ceremonies and festivals in China.

2. Makita Tairyō 牧田諦亮, "Chūgoku ni okeru minzoku Bukkyō seiritsu no ichi katei" 中國に於ける民俗佛教成立の一過程, *Kyoto Daigaku Jimbun Kagaku Kenkyūjō sōritsu ni jūgoshūnen kinen rombunshū* 京都大學人文科學研究所創立廿五周年記念論文集, 1954, 264-288.

3. Yamasaki H., "Zui Tō jidai no Butto no saie" 隋唐時代の佛徒の齋會, *Shina*, 732-764.

On the social and educational activities of the temples see:

1. Ch'üan Han-sheng 全漢昇, "Chung-ku fo-chiao ssu-yüan-ti tz'u-shan shih-yeh" 中古佛教寺院的慈善事業, *Shih-huo*, 1, 4 (1935), 1-7.

2. Naba T., "Chūbantō godai no Bukkyō jiin no zokkō no za ni okeru hembun no enshutsu hōhō ni tsuite" 中晚唐五代の佛教

寺院の俗講の座に於ける變文の演出方法に就いて, *Kōnan Daigaku Bungakkai ronshū* 甲南大學文學會論集, 2 (1955), 1-74.

3. *Idem*, "Zokkō to hembun" 俗講と變文, *Bukkyō shigaku*, 1, 2 (1950), 60-72; 1, 3, 73-91; 1, 4, 39-65. A very detailed and important study of the popular lectures.

4. Hsiang Ta 向達, "T'ang-tai su-chiang k'ao" 唐代俗講考, *Yenching hsüeh-pao* 燕京學報, 16 (1934), 119-132.

5. *Idem*, "T'ang-tai su-chiang k'ao," *Wen-shih tsa-chih* 文史雜誌, 3, 9, 10 (1944), 40-60. This article, although bearing the same title as the previous one, is in effect a new article, containing much more material drawn from the Tun-huang documents. It therefore supersedes the previous one and is much more valuable.

6. Cheng Chen-to 鄭振鐸, *Chung-kuo su-wen-hsüeh shih* 中國俗文學史, Peking, 1957, 1, 180-270. Good discussion on the form and value of the *pien-wen*.

7. Hu Shih 胡適, *Pai-hua wen-shüeh shih* 白話文學史, Shanghai, 1934, 1, 173-180.

8. Jaroslav Prusek, "Narrators of Buddhist Scriptures and Religious Tales in the Sung Period," *Archiv Orientalni*, 10 (1938), 375-389.

9. Yamasaki H., "Shina Bukkyō seiji no kōseki ni okeru kōshi chōshū tairon" 支那佛教盛時の講席に於ける講師聽衆對論, *Shina*, 694-731.

For collections of *pien-wen* in convenient forms there are the following:

1. Wang Chung-min (ed.) 王重民, *Tun-huang pien-wen chi* 敦煌變文集, Peking, 1957, 2 vols. This contains 78 items, including all the important ones. The introduction by Hsiang Ta contains a good short summary of the *pien-wen* and *su-chiang*.

2. Chou Shao-liang 周紹良, *Tun-huang pien-wen hui-lu* 敦煌變文彙錄, Shanghai, 1954, 411 pp. Contains 36 items.

3. Arthur Waley, *Ballads and Stories from Tun-huang*, New York, 1960, 273 pp. A translation of the Mu-lien *pien-wen* is on pages 216-235.

On the organized religious societies which played an influential role in the dissemination of the religion a large body of literature exists, produced in the main by the discovery of many documents in Tun-huang describing such societies. The articles by Naba Toshisada are especially worthy of mention:

1. Takao Giken, "Hokugi ni okeru Bukkyō kyōdan no hattatsu" 北魏に於ける佛教教團の發達, in his *Chūgoku Bukkyō shiron*, 24-36.

2. Ogasawara S., "Shina nambokuchō Bukkyō to shakai kyōka" 支那南北朝佛教と社會教化, *Ryūkoku shidan*, no. 10.

3. Yamasaki H., "Zui Tō jidai ni okeru giyū oyobi hōsha ni tsuite" 隋唐時代に於ける義邑及法社に就いて, *Shina*, 765-831.

4. Naba Toshisada, "Tōdai no shayū ni tsuite" 唐代の社邑に就いて, *Shirin* 史林, 23 (1938), 223-265, 495-534, 729-793.

5. *Idem*, "Bukkyō shinkō ni motozukite soshiki seraretaru chūbantō godaiji no shayū ni tsuite" 佛教信仰に基きて組織せられたる中晩唐五代時の社邑に就いて, *ibid.*, 24 (1939), 491-562, 743-784.

On sangha administration see:

1. Yamasaki H., "Kyōdan no tōsei" 教團の統制, *Shina*, 473-674.

2. Hattori Shungai 服部俊崖, "Shina sōkan no enkaku" 支那僧官の沿革, *Bukkyō shigaku*, 2 (1912), 393-409, 466-475, 622-632.

3. Takao Giken, *Chūgoku Bukkyō shiron*, 24-30.

4. *Idem*, "Sōdai ni okeru sōkan no kenkyū" 宋代に於ける僧官の研究, *Shina Bukkyō shigaku*, 4, 4 (1941), 1-17.

5. *Idem*, "Sōdai jiin seido no ichi kōsatsu" 宋代寺院制度の一考察, *ibid.*, 5, 2 (1942), 8-21.

6. Tsukamoto Z., "Tō chūki irai no Chōan no kudokushi" 唐中期以來の長安の功德使, *Tōhō gakuhō*, Kyoto, 4 (1933), 368-406.

7. Nogami Shunjō 野上俊靜, "Gendai no kudokushishi ni tsuite" 元代の功德使司に就いて, *Shina Bukkyō shigaku*, 6, 2 (1942), 1-11.

8. Ryūchi Kiyoshi 龍池清, "Mindai no sōkan" 明代の僧官, *ibid.*, 4, 3 (1940), 35-46.

9. Nogami Shunjō, "Gen no senseiin ni tsuite" 元の宣政院に就いて, *Asiatic Studies in Honor of Dr. Haneda*, Kyoto, 1950, 779-795.

10. Ogasawara S., "Shina nambokuchō jidai Bukkyō kyōdan no tōsei" 支那南北朝時代佛教教團の統制, *Ryūkoku shidan*, no. 14, 1934.

11. *Idem*, "Shina no sōkansei ni tsuite" 支那の僧官制について, *Ryūdai ronsō*, no. 297.

12. Moroto Tatsuo 諸戸立雄, "Tōsho ni okeru Bukkyō kyōdan no tōsei" 唐初に於ける佛教教團の統制, *Bunka*, 16, 6 (1952).

## CHAPTERS ELEVEN, TWELVE

On the decline of the dharma and the Sect of the Three Stages see:

1. Takao Giken, "Mappō shisō to Zui Tō shoka no taido" 末法思想と隋唐諸家の態度, in his *Chūgoku Bukkyō shiron*, 54–96. This contains a good summary of all the different views concerning the three periods of the law.

2. Yūki Reimon 結城令聞, "Zui Tō jidai ni okeru Chūgokuteki Bukkyō seiritsu no jijō ni tsuite no kōsatsu" 隋唐時代に於ける中國的佛教成立の事情についての考察, *Nihon Bukkyō Gakkai nempō* 日本佛教學會年報, 19 (1954), 79–96.

3. Yabuki Keiki 矢吹慶輝, *Sangaikyō no kenkyū* 三階教の研究, Tokyo, 1927. This is the most exhaustive and authoritative study of the sect.

4. Review of Yabuki's book by A. Waley, *BSOAS*, 5, 1, 162–169.

5. Tsukamoto, "Shingyō no sangaikyōdan to mujinzō ni tsuite" 信行の三階教團と無盡藏について, *Shūkyō kenkyū*, 3, 4 (1926), 65–80. A good discussion of the inexhaustible treasury started by the sect.

6. Tokiwa Daijō, "Sangaikyō no bōtai to shite no Kazanji" 三階教の母胎としての家山寺, *ibid.*, 4, 1 (1927), 35–56.

7. Yūki Reimon, "Shina Bukkyō no okeru mappō shisō no kōki" 支那佛教に於ける末法思想の興起, *Tōhō gakuhō*, Tokyo, 6 (1936), 205–216.

On the Kośa School see:

The basic text of this school, the *Abhidharmakośa*, by Vasubandhu, has been translated into French by L. de la Vallée Poussin, entitled *L'Abhidharmakośa de Vasubandhu*, Paris, 1923–1931, 6 vols. This translation was based on the Chinese version by Hsüan-tsang. Short summaries of the views of this school may be found in:

1. T. Stcherbatsky, *The Central Conception of Buddhism*, 2nd ed., Calcutta, 1956.

2. Yamakami, *Systems of Buddhist Thought*, 109–125, 143–165.

In Chinese there is a good article on this school by Yang Pai-i 楊白衣, "Chü-she-tsung" 俱舍宗, *Chung-kuo fo-chiao-shih lun-chi* 中國佛教史論集, Taipei, 2 (1956), 687–713.

On the T'ien-t'ai School see:

The basic text of this school, the *Saddharmapuṇḍarīka*, or the *Lotus Sutra*, has been translated into English twice, once from the Sanskrit by H. Kern in *Sacred Books of the East*, Oxford, 1884, vol. 21, and once from the Chinese by W. W. Soothill, *Lotus of the Wonderful Law*, Oxford, 1930. The best discussions in English of the doctrines of this school may be found in B. Petzold, "The Chinese Tendai Teachings," *EB*, 4, (1927–1928), 299–347, and Fung, *History of Chinese Philosophy*, 2, 360–386. See also:

1. Takakusu, *Essentials*, 126–142.
2. Yamakami, *Systems*, 270–286.
3. R. C. Armstrong, "The Doctrine of the Tendai School," *EB*, 3 (1924), 32–54.
4. W. Th. de Bary (ed.), *Sources of the Chinese Tradition*, New York, 1960, 349–368.

In Chinese there is a long and very informative article on the historical development of the school by Sun Cheng-hsin 孫正心, "T'ien-t'ai ssu-hsiang-ti yüan-yüan yü ch'i t'e-chih" 天台思想的淵源與其特質, *Chung-kuo fo-chiao-shih lun-chi*, 2, 385–441. For biographies of Hui-ssu and Chih-i see *HKSC*, 17; *Taishō*, 50, 562c–568a.

On the Pure Land School see:

The basic texts of this school, the long and short versions of the *Sukhāvatīvyūha*, have been translated from the Sanskrit into English in *SBE*, vol. 49. Included in the same volume is an English translation of the Chinese version of the *Amitāyurdhyānasūtra*, prepared by J. Takakusu. The following literature bearing on this school is worthy of mention:

1. D. T. Suzuki, "The Development of the Pure Land Doctrine," *EB*, 3, 285–327.
2. K. Reichelt, *Truth and Tradition in Chinese Buddhism*, Shanghai, 1927, 127–170.
3. Ono Gemmyō, "On the Pure Land Doctrine of Tz'u-min," *EB*, 5 (1930), 200–213.
4. D. T. Suzuki, *A Miscellany on the Shin Teachings of Buddhism*, Kyoto, 1949, 151 pp.
5. *Idem*, "Zen and Jodo, Two Types of Buddhist Experience," *EB*, 4, 2 (1927), 89–121.
6. Henri de Lubac, *Aspects du Bouddhisme, Tome 2, Amida*, Paris, 1955, 356 pp.
7. W. Th. de Bary (ed.), *Sources of Chinese Tradition*, New York, 1960, 374–386.

On Avalokiteśvara or Kuan-yin the following are suggested:

1. Marie Thérèse de Mallmann, *Introduction à l'étude d'Avalokiteśvara*, Paris, 1948. This is the most detailed study yet made of the bodhisattva in a western language. Iconography and historical origins of the deity and a linguistic analysis of the name are presented. The author argues very strongly for Iranian influence in the development of the *Sukhāvatīvyūha* and the ideas concerning Amitābha and Avalokiteśvara.

2. N. D. Mironov, "Buddhist Miscellanea," *JRAS*, 1927, 241–252. Presents the data in favor of the name "Avalokitasvara."

3. A. von Stael Holstein, "Avalokita and Apalokita," *HJAS*, 1 (1936), 350–362.

4. H. Maspero, "The Mythology of Modern China," in J. Hackin, *Asiatic Mythology*, New York, 1932 (?), 352–358.

5. D. T. Suzuki, "The Kuan-yin Cult in China," *EB*, 6 (1935), 339–353.

6. *Encyclopedia of Religion and Ethics*, 2, 256–261, by L. de la Vallée Poussin; 7, 763–765, by J. Takakusu.

7. Helen Chapin, "Yunnan Images of Avalokiteśvara," *HJAS*, 8 (1944), 131–186.

In Japanese probably the most complete discussion of this bodhisattva in all its aspects may be found in the *Kannon zenshū* 観音全集, in 8 vols., by various authors, published by the Yukosha in Tokyo. See also Tsukamoto, "Kinsei Shina taishū no nyoshin kannon shinkō" 近世支那大衆の女身観音信仰, *Yamaguchi Festschrift*, 262–280; Kobayashi Taichirō 小林太市郎, "Tōdai no daihi kannon" 唐代の大悲観音, *Bukkyō geijutsu* 佛教藝術, 1, 20, 21, 22.

The literature in Japanese on the Pure Land School in China is voluminous. The following is a highly selective list:

1. Ono Gemmyō 小野玄妙, "Jimin Sanzō no Jōdokyō" 慈愍三藏の淨土教, *Gendai Bukkyō* 現代佛教, 2 (1925), 17, 34–52; 2, 18, 22–41; 2, 19, 32–53; 2, 20, 30–53; 3 (1926), 21, 86–110; 3, 22, 18–51; 3, 23, 17–62.

2. Ogasawara Senshū, *Chūgoku Jōdokyōka no kenkyū* 中國淨土教家の研究, Kyoto, 1951. Traces careers of such Pure Land masters as Hui-yüan, T'an-luan, Tao-cho, and Shan-tao.

3. Sasaki Gesshō 佐佐木月樵, *Shina Jōdokyōshi* 支那淨土教史, 1913, 2 vols. This covers the whole field of Pure Land history in China.

4. *Shina Bukkyō shigaku* 支那佛教史學, 1939, vol. 3, no. 3/4. This entire issue is devoted to the Pure Land School in China.

Among the articles the following deal with the historical development of the school:

*a.* Tsukamoto, "Shina Jōdokyō no tenkai" 支那淨土教の展開, 1–36.

*b.* Mochizuki Shinkō 望月信亨, "Tōdai no Jōdokyō" 唐代の淨土教, 37–56.

*c.* Takao Giken, "Sō igo no Jōdokyō" 宋以後の淨土教, 57–93.

The rest of the volume deals with the Pure Land as religious experience and with the teachings of such masters as T'an-luan, Tao-cho, and Shan-tao.

5. Mochizuki, *Shina Jōdo kyōrishi* 支那淨土教理史, Kyoto, 1942, 547 pp.

6. Tsukamoto, *Tō chūki no Jōdokyō* 唐中期の淨土教, Kyoto, 1933. A very important book on Buddhism under the T'ang Dynasty, with special emphasis on the Pure Land School and the Pure Land master Fa-chao.

For biographies of the Pure Land masters see: T'an-luan, *HKSC*, 6; *Taishō*, 50, 470ab; Tao-cho, *HKSC*, 20, *Taishō*, 50, 593c–594a; Shan-tao, *Taishō*, 51, 119bc. See also the long article on Shan-tao by Iwai Hirosato 岩井大慧, "Zendō den no ichi kōsatsu" 善導傳の一考察, *SZ*, 41 (1930), 57–94, 244–257, 446–482, 528–568, 916–973.

On Amitābha see Yabuki K., *Amidabutsu no kenkyū* 阿彌陀佛の研究, Tokyo, 1937, 474 pp.

On the Pure Land School in recent times see Ogasawara S., "Chūgoku kindai Jōdokyō no ichi kōsatsu" 中國近代淨土教の一考察, *Ryūkoku shidan*, 34 (1951), 7–15; "Chūgoku kindai Jōdokyō ni okeru jissen" 中國近代淨土教に於ける實踐, *Ryūkoku shidan*, 37 (1952), 1–13.

In Chinese the following article is useful: Li Hsiao-pen 李孝本, "Chung-kuo ching-t'u-chiao shih" 中國淨土教史, *Chung-kuo fo-chiao-shih lun-chi*, 2, 552–619.

On the Vijñānavādin School see:

In Chinese the basic texts of this school are the following:

1. *She ta-ch'eng-lun* 攝大乘論, 3 chaps., Paramārtha's translation, *Taishō*, 31, 113b–132c; Hsüan-tsang's translation, *Taishō*, 31, 132c–152a.

2. Hsüan-tsang (tr.), *Ch'eng wei-shih-lun* 成唯識論, 10 chaps., *ibid.*, 31, 1a–59a.

3. *Idem, Wei-shih san-shih-lun sung* 唯識三十論頌, 1 chap., *ibid.*, 31, 60a–61b.

4. *Idem, Wei-shih erh-shih-lun* 唯識二十論, 1 chap., *ibid.*, 31, 74b–77b.

5. *Ta-ch'eng ch'i-hsin-lun* 大乘起信論, Paramārtha's translation, *ibid.*, 32, 575b–583b; Śikshānanda's translation, *ibid.*, 32, 584a–591c.

6. *Ju Leng-chia-ching* 入楞伽經, Gunabhadra's translation, *ibid.*, 16, 480a–514b; Bodhiruci's translation, *ibid.*, 16, 514c–586b; Śikshānanda's translation, *ibid.*, 16, 587b–640c.

7. Hsüan-tsang (tr.), *Pien chung-pien lun* 辯中邊論, 3 chaps., *ibid.*, 31, 464b–477b.

Translations of the basic texts of this school may be found in the following:

1. E. Lamotte, *La somme du grand véhicule*, Louvain, 1938, 2 vols. Translation of the *Mahāyānasaṁgraha*.

2. *Idem*, "L'Ālayavijñāna dans la *Mahāyānasaṁgraha*," *MCB*, 3 (1939), 169–255.

3. C. H. Hamilton, *Wei Shih Erh Shih Lun*, New Haven, 1938. Translated from the Chinese version of Hsüan-tsang.

4. L. de la Vallée Poussin, *Vijñaptimātratāsiddhi, La siddhi de Hsüan-tsang traduite et annotée*, Paris, 1928–1948, 3 vols.

5. D. T. Suzuki, *Aśvaghosha's Discourse on the Awakening of Faith in the Mahāyāna*, Chicago, 1900.

6. *Idem, The Lankāvatara-sutra*, London, 1932.

7. P. W. O'Brien, "A Chapter on Reality from the *Madhyāntavibhāga-çāstra*," *Monumenta Nipponica*, 9 (1953), 277–303.

8. T. Stcherbatsky, *Discourse on Discrimination between Middle and Extremes*, Moscow, 1936.

9. D. L. Freedmann, *Analysis of the Middle Path and the Extremes*, Utrecht, 1937.

Discussions of the doctrines may be found in:

1. S. N. Dasgupta, "Philosophy of Vasubandhu in Viṁśatika and Triṁsika," *IHQ*, 4 (1928), 36–43.

2. Fung, *History of Chinese Philosophy*, 2, 299–338.

3. Takakusu, *Essentials*, 80–95.

4. Yamakami, *Systems*, 210–217, 236–251.

5. D. T. Suzuki, *Studies in the Lankāvatara-sutra*, London, 1930.

6. *Idem*, "The Psychological School of Mahāyāna Buddhism," *EB*, 2 (1922), 105–128.

7. R. Grousset, *In the Footsteps of the Buddha*, 295–326.

Concerning Vasubandhu, one of the founders of the school, there is a good deal of literature, of which the following are the more important:

1. J. Takakusu, "The Life of Vasubandhu by Paramārtha," *TP*, 5 (1904), 269–296.

2. *Idem*, "A Study of Paramārtha's Life of Vasubandhu," *JRAS*, (1905), 33–53.

3. *Idem*, "The Date of Vasubandhu," *Indian Studies in Honor of Charles Rockwell Lanman*, 1929, 79–88.

4. N. Peri, "A propos de la date de Vasubandhu," *BEFEO*, 11 (1911), 339–390.

5. E. Frauwallner, "On the Date of the Buddhist Master of the Law Vasubandhu," *Serie Orientale Roma*, III, Rome, 1951.

For K'uei-chi, or Tz'u-en, see Stanley Weinstein, "A Biographical Study of Tz'u-en," *Monumenta Nipponica*, 15 (1959), 119–149.

In Chinese there are two articles in the collection *Chung-kuo fo-chiao-shih lun-chi*, vol. 2, which may be read: Yen-p'ei 演培, "Wei-shih ssu-hsiang yen-pien shih-lüeh" 唯識思想演變史略, 464–508; and Mo-ju 默如, "Wei-shih hsüeh kai-yao" 唯識學概要, 509–551.

On the Avataṁsaka School see:

There is still no adequate treatment of this school in a western language. A synopsis of the *Avataṁsakasūtra* may be found in *EB*, 1, 1–12, 147–155, 237–242, 282–290. General discussions may be found in:

1. Takakusu, *Essentials*, 108–125.

2. Fung, *History of Chinese Philosophy*, 2, 339–359.

3. Yamakami, *Systems*, 287–300.

4. Suzuki, *The Essence of Buddhism*, London, 1947, 41–56.

5. Nan-t'ing 南亭, "Hua-yen-tsung shih" 華嚴宗史, *Chung-kuo fo-chiao-shih lun-chi*, 2, 347–384.

On Mañjuśrī and Wu-t'ai-shan in China see Étienne Lamotte, "Mañjuśrī," *TP*, 48 (1960), 54–96.

On the Ch'an School see:

The literature on the Ch'an School is voluminous. No attempt shall be made here to assemble an exhaustive bibliography. Only the more valuable and significant contributions, especially by those scholars who consulted the original sources, are listed here. Moreover, since this is primarily a historical survey, we shall not list the numerous translations of Ch'an works. For such a list there is Ruth F. Sasaki, "A Bibliography of Translations of Zen (Ch'an) Works," *Philosophy East and West*, 10, 3/4 (1960–1961), 149–166.

The pioneer works in English on the Ch'an School are those by D. T. Suzuki, of which the following are the important ones:

1. *Essays on Zen Buddhism*, London, 1927, 1933, 1934, 3 vols.

2. *A Manual of Zen Buddhism*, Kyoto, 1935.

3. *The Training of a Zen Monk*, Kyoto, 1934.

4. *Introduction to Zen Buddhism*, New York, 1949.

In recent years the following useful books have appeared:

1. H. Dumoulin, *Zen, Geschichte und Gestalt*, Bonn, 1959; English translation by Paul Peachey, *A History of Zen Buddhism*, New York, 1963. A very good historical survey.

2. Chang Chen-chi, *The Practice of Zen*, New York, 1959. This work is especially commendable, for Chang has presented a concise and systematic discussion of the doctrines and practices of Ch'an in simple English, free from the enigmas and digressions that abound in Suzuki's works.

3. Lu K'uan-yü, *Ch'an and Zen Teachings*, London, 1960, 1961, 2 vols.

On the development of the school in China Hu Shih has written a number of articles:

1. "Development of Zen Buddhism in China," *CSPSR*, 15 (1931), 475–505.

2. "Ch'an Buddhism in China: Its History and Methods," *Philosophy East and West*, 3 (1953), 3–24.

3. "P'u-t'i-ta-mo k'ao" 菩提達摩考, *Hu Shih wen-ts'un san-chi* 胡適文存三集, Shanghai, 1930, 449–465.

4. "Leng-chia-tsung k'ao" 楞伽宗考, *Hu Shih lun-hsüeh chin-chu* 胡適論學近著, 1 (Shanghai, 1935), 198–238.

5. "Leng-chia shih-tzu-chi hsü" 楞伽師資記序, *ibid.*, 1, 239-247.

6. "Ho-tse ta-shih Shen-hui chuan" 荷澤大師神會傳, *ibid.*, 1, 248-290.

7. *Shen-hui ho-shang i-chi* 神會和尚遺集, Shanghai, 1930.

8. "Hsin-chiao-ting-ti Tun-huang hsieh-pen Shen-hui ho-shang i-chu liang-chung" 新校定的敦煌寫本神會和尚遺著兩種, *Studies Presented to Yuen Ren Chao on his Sixty-fifth Birthday*, 2 (1958), 827-882.

9. "Shen-hui ho-shang yü-lu-ti ti-san-ko Tun-huang hsieh-pen" 神會和尚語錄的第三個敦煌寫本, *Studies Presented to Tung Tso-pin on his Sixty-fifth Birthday*, 1960, 1-31.

These articles of Hu Shih are of primary importance, for they attempt to place the development of Ch'an in its proper historical setting in China, and to show that the movement was not something apart but had close connections with contemporary Chinese thought.

Other studies of Bodhidharma may be found in:

1. Hayashi Taiun 林岱雲, "Bodaidaruma den no kenkyū" 菩提達摩傳の研究, *Shūkyō kenkyū*, 9, 3 (1932), 62-76.

2. D. T. Suzuki, "Zenshū no shoso to shite no Daruma no zempō" 禪宗の初祖としての達摩の禪法, *Gendai Shina Bukkyō kenkyū* 現代支那佛教研究, 1936, 196-224.

3. H. Dumoulin, "Bodhidharma und die Anfange des Ch'an Buddhismus," *Monumenta Nipponica*, 7, (1951), 67-83.

On Shen-hui see also:

1. J. Gernet, *Entretien du Maître de Dhyāna Chen-houei, Publications de l'École Française d'Extrême Orient*, 31, 1949.

2. *Idem*, "Biographie de Maître Chen-houei du Ho-tso," *JA*, 239 (1951), 29-68.

3. W. Liebenthal, "The Sermon of Shen-hui," *Asia Major*, 3, 2 (1952), 132-155.

On Hui-neng the sixth patriarch see:

1. Erwin Rouselle, "Das Leben des Patriarchen Hui-neng," *Sinica*, 5 (1930), 174-191.

2. Wong Mou-lam, *Sutra Spoken by the Patriarch*, Shanghai, 1929. This is a translation of the *Platform Sutra* of Hui-neng.

3. C. Humphreys, *The Sutra of Wei-lang*, London, 1934.

4. E. Rouselle, *Sinica*, 5 (1930); 6 (1931); 11 (1936). A German translation of the first six chapters of the same *Platform Sutra*.

5. W. T. Chan (tr.), *The Platform Scripture*, New York, 1963. An excellent translation of the Tun-huang manuscript of the sutra.

On the development after Hui-neng there are two important articles by Dumoulin:

1. "Die Entwicklung des Chinesischen Ch'an nach Hui-neng im Lichte des Wu-men-kuan," *Monumenta Serica*, 4 (1941), 40–72.

2. "Das Wu-men-kuan," *ibid.*, 8 (1943), 41–102. This has been translated into English by R. F. Sasaki and entitled *The Development of Chinese Zen*, New York, 1953.

See also J. Blofield, *The Path to Sudden Enlightenment, A Treatise of the Ch'an School of Chinese Buddhism*, by Hui-hai of the T'ang Dynasty, London, 1948; de Bary (ed.), *Sources of Chinese Tradition*, 386-408; Fung, *History of Chinese Philosophy*, 2, 386-406.

On Tantric Buddhism see:

Probably the best general discussions at present on Tantric Buddhism are by S. B. Dasgupta, *An Introduction to Tantric Buddhism*, Calcutta, 1950; D. L. Snellgrove, *The Hevajra Tantra*, London, 1959, 1, 1–46; Snellgrove, *Buddhist Himalaya*, New York, 1957, 51–90. Other studies which are valuable for the Indian background are:

1. B. Bhattacharyya, *An Introduction to Buddhist Esoterism*, Oxford, 1932.

2. H. von Glasenapp, *Buddhistische Mysterien*, Stuttgart, 1940.

3. *Idem*, "Tantrismus und Saktimus," *OZ*, 12 (1936), 120–133.

4. *Idem*, "Die Entstehung des Vajrayana," *ZDMG*, 90 (1936), 546–572.

5. D. N. Bose, *Tantras, Their Philosophy and Occult Secrets*, Calcutta, 1946.

6. M. Eliade, "Yoga and Tantrism," chapter 6 of his work, *Yoga, Immortality, and Freedom*, New York, 1958.

7. G. Tucci, *Tibetan Painted Scrolls*, Rome, 1949, 3 vols.

See also R. H. van Gulik, *Erotic Colour Prints of the Ming Period*, Tokyo, 1951, 3 vols.

For Tantrism in China the best study in English so far is by Chou I-liang, published in *HJAS*, 8 (1945), 241–332. Here may be found translations, with copious annotations, of the biographies of the three Tantric masters, Śubhakarasiṁha, Vajrabodhi, and Amoghavajra.

## CHAPTER THIRTEEN

On the translations of the Chinese canon see Liang Ch'i-ch'ao, "Fo-tien chih fan-i" 佛典之翻譯, *Yin-ping-shih wen-chi*, 60, 11a–64a; "Fan-i wen-t'i chih t'ao-lun" 翻譯文體之討論, *ibid.*, 61, 11b–21a. The massive volume by the Japanese scholar Tokiwa Daijō, *Go-Kan yori Sō Sei ni itaru yakkyō sōroku* 後漢より宋齊に至る譯經總錄, Tokyo, 1938, 1013 pp. and 42 pp. of index, is an attempt to draw up a correct list of translations made by the foreign and Chinese monks on the basis of the numerous catalogues compiled by the Chinese. Probably the most important article on the compilation of the Chinese canon is Ono Gemmyō 小野玄妙, "Daizōkyō gaisetsu" 大藏經概說, *Bussho kaisetsu daijiten* 佛書解說大辭典, 12, 1–197.

On translation techniques see Fuchs, "Zur technischen Organisation der Übersetzungen buddhistischer Schriften ins Chinesische," *Asia Major*, 6 (1930), 84–103; K. Ch'en, "Some Problems in the Translation of the Chinese Buddhist Canon," *Tsinghua Journal of Chinese Studies*, NS, 2, 1 (1960), 178–188.

On the editions of the Tripitaka the most useful articles are Yeh Kung-cho 葉恭綽, "Li-tai tsang-ching k'ao-lüeh" 歷代藏經考略, *Chang Chü-sheng chi-nien lun-wen chi* 張菊生紀念論文集, 1937, 25–42; Tao-an 道安, "Chung-kuo tsang-ching i-yin shih" 中國藏經譯印史, *Chung-kuo fo-chiao-shih lun-chi* 中國佛教史論集, Taipei, 3 (1956), 979–1016. The discussions in the *Bukkyō daijii* 佛教大辭彙, 3, 3187–3190, and the *Encyclopedia Japonica*, 6, 559–561, are also very helpful. On the Sung and Yüan editions see Lo Chen-yü 羅振玉, *Sung-Yüan shih-tsang k'an-pen-k'ao* 宋元釋藏刊本考, 1920; P. Demiéville, "Sur les éditions imprimées du canon chinois," *BEFEO*, 24, 181–218. Cl. E. Maitre, "Une nouvelle édition du tripitaka chinois," *ibid.*, 2, 341–51, and Nanjio, *Catalogue*, XII–XXVII, have also put together valuable notes on the different editions. See also Ono Gemmyō, "Sōdai Shikei Engaku zenin oyobi dō hōbō Shifukuji shinchō nidaizōkyō zakkō" 宋代思溪圓覺禪院及同法寶資福寺新彫二大藏經雜考, *Nikka Bukkyō Kenkyūkai nempō* 日華佛教研究會年報, 3 (1938), 60 pp.; Suzuki, S. "Sōhan zōkyō no shohan to sono soshiki oyobi naiyō" 宋版藏經の諸版とその組織及內容, *Bunka* 文化, x, 10 (1943), 20 pp. The Liao or Khitan edition is discussed in detail by Tsumaki Naoyoshi 妻木直良, "Kittan ni okeru daizōkyō chōzō no jitsu o ronzu" 契旦に於る大藏經彫造の實を論ず, *Tōyō gakuhō*, 2, 3 (1912), 317–340. As for the Chin edition the authoritative discussion is by Chiang Wei-hsin 蔣唯心, "Chin-tsang

tiao-yin shih-mo-k'ao" 金藏彫印始末考, *Sung-tsang i-chen-hsü-mu* 宋藏
遺珍叙目, (1935) 1–43. See also Ōchō Enichi 横超慧日, "Shinshutsu
kinhan zōkyō o mite" 新出金版藏經を見て, *Tōhō gakuhō*, Tokyo, 5
(1935), 283–308. The Tangut edition is discussed in Wang Kuo-wei
王國維, "Yüan-k'an-pen Hsi-hsia wen hua-yen-ching ch'an-chüan-pa"
元刊本西夏文華嚴經殘卷跋, *Kuan-t'ang chi-lin* 觀堂集林 *(Hai-ning Wang
Ching-an hsien-sheng i-shu)* 海寧王靜安先生遺書, 9 (1940), 21, 22b–23b;
Wang Jing-ju 王靜如, "Ho-hsi-tzu tsang-ching tiao-pan-k'ao" 河西字藏
經彫板考, *Hsi-hsia yen-chiu* 西夏研究, 1 (1932), 1–14; Ishihama Juntarō
石濱純太郎, "Seikagoyaku daizōkyō kō" 西夏語譯大藏經考, *Ryūdai
ronsō* 龍大論叢, 287 (1929); Tokiwa Daijō, "Seika monji daizōkyō no
chōkoku ni tsukite" 西夏文字大藏經の彫刻について *Tōhō gakuhō*, Tokyo,
9 (1939), 1–32. See also K. T. Wu, "Chinese Printing under Four
Alien Dynasties," *HJAS*, 13 (1950), 451–457, 515–516; and K. Chen,
"Notes on the Sung and Yüan Tripitaka," *ibid.*, 14 (1951), 208–214. On
the Ming editions see Ryūchi Kiyoshi 龍池清, "Mindai kokuzō kō"
明代刻藏考, *Tōhō gakuhō*, Tokyo, 8 (1938), 319–346. On the Korean
editions see Ikeuchi Hiroshi 池内宏, "Kōraichō no daizōkyō" 高麗朝の
大藏經, *ibid.*, 13 (1923), 307–362; 14 (1924), 91–130, 546–558.

## CHAPTER FOURTEEN

On general accounts under the Sung Dynasty see:

1. Makita T., "Chōsō Bukkyōshi ni okeru Kaisū no tachiba" 趙宋
   佛教史に於ける契嵩の立場, in his *Chūgoku kinsei Bukkyōshi
   kenkyū*, Kyoto, 1957, 134–168.

2. *Idem*, "Sannei to sono jidai" 賛寧とその時代, *ibid.*, 96–133.

3. *Idem*, "Kunshu dokusai shakai ni okeru Bukkyō kyōdan no tachiba"
   君主獨裁社會に於ける佛教教團の立場, *Bukkyō bunka kenkyū*,
   3 (1953), 63–80; 4 (1954), 77–94.

For a good discussion of the sangha and sangha administration under
the Sung Dynasty see Takao Giken, *Chūgoku Bukkyō shiron*, Kyoto, 1952,
97–151; also Tsukamoto Z., "Sōdai no dōgyōshikyō tokudo no seido"
宋代の童行試經得度の制度, *Shina Bukkyō shigaku*, 5, 1 (1941), 42–64.

The best discussion of the financial difficulties of the Sung Dynasty
and of the measures taken to meet the crisis, especially those that have
to do with the Buddhist sangha, are to be found in two articles by
Tsukamoto Zenryū:

1. "Sō chōtei no zaiseinan to Bukkyō kyōdan" 宋朝庭の財政難と
   佛教教團, *Shukyō kenkyū*, 7, 5 (1930), 1–30.

2. "Sō no zaiseinan to Bukkyō" 宋の財政難と佛教, *Kuwabara hakase kanreki kinen Tōyōshi ronsō*, Tokyo, 1931, 549-594. Although the titles of the two articles are almost identical, the contents are not; the latter contains much data not found in the former.

For a detailed study of the financial problems of the Sung Dynasty see Sogabe Shizuo 曾我部靜雄, *Sōdai zaiseishi* 宋代財政史, 1941. The most complete discussion of monk certificates under the Sung is found in Yüan Chen 袁震, "Liang-Sung tu-tieh-k'ao" 兩宋度牒考, *Chung-kuo she-hui ching-chi-shih chi-k'an* 中國社會經濟史集刊, 7, 1 (1944), 42-101; 7, 2 (1946), 1-78. Other useful articles on the same subject are:

1. Fan Wu 范午, "Sung-tai tu-tieh shuo" 宋代度牒說, *Wen-shih tsa-chih* 文史雜誌, 2, 4 (1942), 45-52.

2. Sogabe Shizuo, "Sō no dochō zakkō" 宋の度牒雜考, *SZ*, 41, 6 (1930), 725-740.

3. Tsukamoto Z., "Dōkun Kōtei to kūmei dochō seisaku" 道君皇帝と空名度牒政策, *Shina Bukkyō shigakū*, 4, 4 (1941), 58-66.

4. For a discussion in English see K. Ch'en, "The Sale of Monk Certificates during the Sung Dynasty," *Harvard Theological Review*, 49, 4 (1956), 307-327.

On the religious societies under the Sung see Suzuki Chūsei 鈴木中正, "Sōdai Bukkyō kessha no kenkyū" 宋代佛教結社の研究, *SZ*, 52 (1941), 65-98, 205-241, 303-333.

On harmony and rivalry between the schools see Ogisu Jundō 荻須純道, "Sōdai ni okeru nembutsu-zen no chōryū" 宋代に於ける念佛禪の潮流, *Ryūkoku shidan*, 44 (1958), 131-138.

On Maitreya, the laughing Buddha, see:

1. F. Lessing, *Yung-ho-kung*, Stockholm, 1942, 21-37.

2. Suzuki, *EB*, 6, 4 (1935), 328-339.

3. Helen Chapin, *JOAS*, 53, 1, 47-52.

On Chinese monks traveling to India during the Sung Dynasty see:

1. E. Chavannes, "Les inscriptions Chinoises," *Revue de l'histoire des religions*, 34, 23-34.

2. E. Huber, "L'Itineraire de Pelerin Ki-ye dans l'Inde," *BEFEO*, (1902), 256-257.

3. E. Chavannes, "L'Itineraire de Ki-ye," *ibid.* (1904), 75-81.

So far, the best discussion of the interaction between Buddhist and Neo-Confucianist thought may be found in Carson Chang, *The Development of Neo-Confucian Thought*, New York, 1957. The material in this book is drawn largely from this discussion.

## CHAPTER FIFTEEN

On Buddhism under the Liao and Chin Dynasties see:

1. Nogami Shunjō 野上俊靜, *Ryō Kin no Bukkyō* 遼金の佛教, Kyoto, 1953.

2. Kamio Katsuharu 神尾 弌春, *Kittan Bukkyō bunkashi kō* 契丹佛教文化史考, Dairen, 1937, 185 pp.

3. K. A. Wittfogel and Feng Chia-sheng, *History of Chinese Society: Liao*, Philadelphia, 1949, 291–309.

On Buddhism under the Mongol Dynasty see:

A good general discussion of the relations between the early Mongol khans and Buddhism may be found in the following works:

1. Kunishita Hirosato 圀下大慧, "Gensho ni okeru teishitsu to zensō to no kankei ni tsuite" 元初に於ける帝室と禪僧との關係に就いて, *Tōyō gakuhō*, 11 (1921), 547–577; 12 (1922), 89–124, 245–249.

2. A. Waley, *The Travels of an Alchemist*, London, 1931, 5–33.

On the Yüan sangha administration see:

1. Nogami Shunjō, "Gen no senseiin ni tsuite" 元の宣政院に就いて, *Asiatic Studies in Honor of Dr. Haneda*, Kyoto, 1950, 779–795.

2. *Idem*, "Gen no kudokushi-shi ni tsuite" 元の功德使司に就いて, *Shina Bukkyō shigaku*, 6, 2 (1942), 1–11.

On Buddhism in the Yüan capital see Nogami S., "Gen no Jōto no Bukkyō" 元の上都の佛教, *Bukkyō shigaku*, 1, 2 (1950), 1–15.

On temple property see:

1. T'ao Hsi-sheng, "Yüan-tai ti fo-ssu t'ien-yüan chi shang-tien" 元代的佛寺田園及商店, *Shih-huo*, 1 (1935), 108–114.

2. Chü Ch'ing-yüan 鞠清遠, "Yüan-tai ti ssu-ch'an" 元代的寺產, *Shih-huo*, 1 (1935), 228–231.

On the Buddhist-Taoist controversy under the Mongols see the following:

1. E. Chavannes, "Inscriptions et pièces de chancellerie Chinoises de l'époque mongole," *TP*, 5 (1904), 366–404. This is important for the translation of the documents dealing with the controversy.

2. Wang Wei-ch'eng 王維誠, "Lao-tzu hua-hu-shuo k'ao-cheng" 老子化胡說考證, *Kuo-hsüeh chi-k'an*, 4, 2 (1934), 1–122. This is the most complete account of the famous controversy over the conversion of the barbarians. The section dealing with the Mongol period may be found on pages 94–106.

3. Kubota R., *Sangyō shiron*, 589–604.

4. *Idem, Kōshōshi*, 297–311.

5. Joseph Thiel, "Der Streit der Buddhisten und Taoisten zur Mongolenzeit," *Monumenta Serica*, 20 (1961), 1–81.

On the secret societies the following articles are important:

1. P. Pelliot, "La secte du lotus blanc et la secte du nuage blanc," *BEFEO*, (1903), 304–317; (1904), 436–440.

2. Shigematsu Shunshō 重松俊章, "Tō Sō jidai no Mirokukyō-hi" 唐宋時代の彌勒教匪, *Shien*, 3 (1931), 68–103.

3. *Idem*, "Sō Gen jidai no Byakuun shūmon" 宋元時代の白雲宗門, *ibid*., 2 (1930), 39–55.

4. T'ao Hsi-sheng, "Yüan-tai Mi-le Pai-lien chiao-hui ti pao-tung" 元代彌勒白蓮教會的暴動, *Shih-huo*, 1, 4 (1935), 36–39, 152–155.

5. Shigematsu S., "Shoki no Byakuren kyōkai ni tsuite" 初期の白蓮教會に就いて, *Ichimura hakase koki kinen Tōyōshi ronsō*, (1933), 361–394. This article was translated into Chinese by T'ao Hsi-sheng in *Shih-huo*, 1 (1935), 143–151.

6. T'ao Hsi-sheng, "Ming-tai Mi-le Pai-lien-chiao chi ch'i t'a yao-tsei" 明代彌勒白蓮教及其他妖賊, *ibid*., 1, 9 (1935), 46–52.

7. Yano Jinichi 矢野仁一, "Byakurenkyō no ran ni tsuite" 白蓮教の亂に就いて, *Naitō hakase kanreki shukuga Shinagaku ronsō* 內藤博士還曆祝賀支那學論叢, (1926), 701–729.

8. Suzuki Chūsei 鈴木中正, "Shindai ni okeru Byakurenkyō no hanran no seikaku" 清代に於ける白蓮教の叛亂の性格, *Tōyō bunka kenkyū*, 9 (1948), 36–52.

9. *Idem*, "Sōdai Bukkyō kessha no kenkyū" 宋代佛教結社の研究, *SZ*, 52 (1941), 65–98, 205–241, 303–333.

10. Chüeh-an 覺岸, "Pai-yün-tsung" 白雲宗, *Shih-shih chi-ku-lüeh*, 釋氏稽古略, ch. 4, *Taishō*, 49, no. 2037.

11. Ogawa Kan'ichi 小川貫弌, "Gendai Byakuunshū kyōdan no katsuyaku" 元代白雲宗教團の活躍, *Bukkyō shigaku*, 3, 1 (1952), 1–25.

12. Shigematsu S., "Sō Gen jidai no kō-kin-gun to Gem-matsu no Miroku Byakurenkyō-hi ni tsuite" 宋元時代の紅巾軍と元末の彌勒白蓮教匪に就いて, *Shien*, 24 (1940), 79–90; 26 (1941), 137–154; 28 (1942), 107–126; 32 (1944), 81–123.

13. Mochizuki, "Nansō Shigen no Byakurenshū to sono yotō no jasetsu" 南宋子元の白蓮宗教とその餘黨の邪說, *Jōdogaku* 淨土學, 14 (1939).

14. Ogasawara S., "Gendai Byakurenshū kyōdan no shōchō" 元代白蓮宗教團の消長, *Ryūkoku Daigaku ronshū* 龍谷大學論集, 344 (1952), 1–12.

15. Li Shou-k'ung 李守孔, "Ming-tai Pai-lien-chiao k'ao-lüeh" 明代白蓮教考略, *Wen-shih che-hsüeh pao* 文史哲學報, 4 (1952), 151–177.

## CHAPTER SIXTEEN

On the Ming Dynasty and Buddhism see:

1. Ch'en Yüan 陳垣, *Ming-chi Tien-Ch'ien fo-chiao-k'ao* 明季滇黔佛教攷, Peking, 1940.

2. Wu Han 吳晗, "Ming-chiao yü Ta-Ming ti-kuo" 明教與大明帝國, *Tsing-hua hsüeh-pao*, 13, 1 (1941), 49–85.

3. Wang Ch'ung-wu 王崇武, "Ming-ch'eng-tsu yü fo-chiao" 明成祖與佛教, *Chung-kuo she-hui ching-chi shih chi-k'an* 中國社會經濟史集刊, 8, 1 (1949), 1–11.

4. Mano Senryū 間野潜龍, "Mindai chūki no Bukkyō taisaku" 明代中期の佛教對策, *Ōtani shigaku* 大谷史學, 4 (1955), 14–23.

5. Nogami S., "Minsho no sōdōemen" 明初の僧道衙門, *Ōtani gakuhō*, 27, 1 (1948), 8–15.

6. Shimizu Taiji 清水泰次, "Mindai ni okeru Butsudō no torishimari" 明代に於ける佛道の取締, *SZ*, 40, 3 (1929), 1–48.

7. Tsukamoto, "Min Shin seiji no Bukkyō kyosei" 明清政治の佛教去勢, *Bukkyō bunka kenkyū* 佛教文化研究, 2 (1952), 1–16.

On the relations among the three religions see:

1. Mano Senryū, "Mindai ni okeru sangyō shisō" 明代に於ける三教思想, *Tōyōshi kenkyū* 東洋史研究, 12, 1 (1952), 18–34.

2. Shimizu Taiji, "Mindai ni okeru shūkyō yūgō to kōkakaku" 明代に於ける宗教融合と功過格, *Shien* 史淵, 6, 3.

On Master Han-shan see Chang Chen-chi, *The Practice of Zen*, New York, 1959, 79–103. See also *Han-shan lao-jen nien-p'u tzu-hsü shih-lu-su* 憨山老人年譜自叙實錄疏, in *Chia-hsing T'an-shih i-shu* 嘉興譚氏遺書, vols. 1 and 2.

On the monastic communities and monasteries see:

1. Ryūchi Kiyoshi, "Mindai no sōkan" 明代の僧官, *Shina Bukkyō shigaku*, 4, 3 (1940), 35–46.

2. *Idem*, "Mindai ni okeru baichō" 明代に於ける賣牒, *Tōhō gakuhō*, Tokyo, 11, 2 (1940), 279–290.

3. *Idem*, "Minsho no jiin" 明初の寺院, *Shina Bukkyō shigaku*, 2, 4 (1938), 9–29.

4. Shimizu Taiji, "Mindai no jiden" 明代の寺田, *Tōa keizai kenkyū* 東亞經濟研究, 8, 4 (1924), 46–67.

On the leading Ming cleric Chu-hung see:

1. *Yün-ch'i fa-hui* 雲棲法彙, *Chin-ling k'e-ching-ch'u* edition, 1899, 34 vols.

2. Takao Giken, "Unseiji Shukō to Min Shin Bukkyō" 雲棲寺株宏と明清佛教, in his *Chūgoku Bukkyō shiron*, 246–286.

3. Charles F. Neumann, *The Catechisms of the Shamans; or, the Laws and Regulations of the Priesthood of Buddha, in China*, London, 1831, 152 pp. This is a translation of a treatise on the Vinaya by Chu-hung, and is very likely the earliest rendering into English of a Chinese Buddhist text. The translation abounds in errors, especially in the Sanskrit and Chinese words, with the latter very often in the wrong order.

On Buddhism and Catholicism see:

1. Ōchō Enichi, "Min-matsu Bukkyō to Kirisutokyō to no sōgo hihan" 明末佛教と基督教との相互批判, *Ōtani gakuhō*, 29, 2 (1949), 1–20; 29, 3/4 (1950), 18–38. Important for Chu-hung's criticisms of Catholicism.

2. Ch'en Shou-yi 陳受頤, "Ming-mo Ch'ing-ch'u Yeh-su hui-shih ti Ju-chiao-kuan chi ch'i fan-ying" 明末清初耶蘇會士的儒教觀及其反應, *Kuo-hsüeh chi-k'an*, 5, 2, 1–64.

On the systems of merits see:

1. Takao Giken, "Mindai ni okeru taisei seru kōkakaku shisō" 明代に於ける大成せる功過格思想, in his *Chūgoku Bukkyō shiron*, 235–245.

2. Hu Shih, "Buddhistic Influence on Chinese Religious Life," *CSPSR*, 9 (1925), 145ff., for Yüan Liao-fan.

3. Yüan Liao-fan 袁了凡, *Yin-chih-lu* 陰隲錄, Tokyo, 1893.

4. Chu-hung, *Tzu-chih-lu* 自知錄, in *Yün-ch'i fa-hui*, vol. 15.

5. Nishizawa Yoshirō 西澤嘉朗, *Inshitsuroku no kenkyū* 陰隲錄の研究, Tokyo, 1946, 228 pp.

For the Ch'ing Dynasty see:

1. Fujii Sōsen 藤井草宣, "Shintei to Bukkyō" 清廷と佛教, *Ōtani gakuhō*, 16, 3 (1935), 150–172.

2. Shaku Dangen 釋談玄, "Shindai Bukkyō no gaikyō" 清代佛教の概況, *Nikka Bukkyō Kenkyūkai nempō* 日華佛教研究會年報, 6 (1943), 85–144.

3. Makita T., "Shin-matsu igo ni okeru byōsan kōgaku to Bukkyō kyōdan" 清末以後に於ける庙産興學と佛教教團, *Chūgoku kinsei Bukkyōshi kenkyū*, Kyoto, 1957, 253–284.

4. Mizuno Baigyō 水野梅曉, *Shina Bukkyō kinseishi no kenkyū* 支那佛教近世史の研究, Tokyo, 1925, 28–58.

On the role of the laity see:

1. Makita T., "Koji Bukkyō ni okeru Hō Saisei no chii" 居士佛教に於ける彭際清の地位, *Chūgoku kinsei Bukkyōshi kenkyū*, 231–252.

2. Ogawa Kan'ichi 小川貫弌, "Koji Bukkyō no kinsei hatten" 居士佛教の近世發展, *Ryūkoku Daigaku ronshū*, no. 339.

## CHAPTER SEVENTEEN

For Buddhism under the Republic see:

1. Mizuno Baigyō, *Shina Bukkyō kinseishi*, 58–91.

2. Tsukamoto Zenryū, "Chūka Minkoku no Bukkyō" 中華民國の佛教, *Tōyōgaku ronsō* 東洋學論叢, Feb. 1952, 295–330.

3. Fa-hang 法航, "Chung-kuo fo-chiao ti hsien-chuang" 中國佛教的現狀, *Hai-ch'ao-yin* 海潮音, 15, 10 (1934), 21–31.

The following are useful for the information about the Communist policy toward Buddhism:

1. Ts'en Hsüeh-lü 岑學呂, *Hsü-yün ho-shang nien-p'u* 虛雲和尚年譜, Hong Kong, 1957.

2. Yang I-fan 楊一凡, *Chung-kuo fo-chiao ti e-yün* 中國佛教的厄運, Hong Kong, 1955.

3. Nakanō Kyōtoku 中濃教篤, *Chūgoku Kyōsantō no shūkyō seisaku* 中國共產黨の宗教政策, Tokyo, 1958.

The most complete account of Buddhism in modern China is to be found in W. T. Chan, *Religious Trends in Modern China*, New York, 1953, 54–135. The copious footnotes refer to a wealth of references in Chinese and western languages for the benefit of those who are interested in further study.

## CHAPTER EIGHTEEN

For a comprehensive discussion of the impact of Buddhism upon Neo-Confucianism see Carson Chang, *The Development of Neo-Confucian Thought*, New York, 1957. Further discussions may be found in the following:

1. Carson Chang, "Buddhism as Stimulus to Neo-Confucianism," *Oriens Extremus*, 2 (1955), 157–166.

2. Fung Yu-lan, *History of Chinese Philosophy*, 2, 407–424, 496–498, 508–509, 566–571, 610–612.

3. *Idem, Short History of Chinese Philosophy*, 266–272, 278–280.

4. *Idem*, "The Rise of Neo-Confucianism and its Borrowings from Buddhism and Taoism," *HJAS*, 7 (1942), 89–125.

5. Derk Bodde, "The Chinese View of Immortality; Its Expression by Chu Hsi and its Relationship to Buddhist Thought," *Review of Religion*, 6 (1942), 369–383.

6. Galen Sargent, *Tchou Hi Contre la Bouddhisme*, Paris, 1955, 156 pp.

7. J. Needham, *Science and Civilization in China*, Cambridge, 1956, 2, 411–419.

8. Huang Hsiu-ch'i, *Lu Hsiang-shan*, New Haven, 1944, 67–74.

9. A. C. Graham, *Two Chinese Philosophers, Ch'eng Ming-tao and Ch'eng Yi-ch'uan*, London, 1958.

10. W. T. Chan, "Neo-Confucianism," in H. F. MacNair (ed.), *China*, California, 1946, 254–265.

In Japanese the standard treatments are found in:

1. Kubota Ryōon, *Shina Ju Dō Butsu kōshōshi*, 212–264.

2. *Idem, Shina Ju Dō Butsu sangyō shiron*, 460–566.

3. Tokiwa Daijō, *Shina ni okeru Bukkyō to Jukyō Dōkyō*, 139–470.

Articles in Japanese dealing with the subject may be found in:

1. Yokota Sōchoku 横田宗直, "Sōju no zengaku kenkyū ni tsuite" 宋儒の禪學研究に就いて, *SZ*, 23 (1912), 1310–1342; 24 (1913) 79–87, 213–232, 341–365, 459–479, 756–776. Very good discussion on the relations between the Zen Buddhists and the Confucianists.

2. Araki Kengo 荒木見悟, "Yōmeigaku to zengaku" 陽明學と禪學, *Shibun* 斯文, 20 (1958), 22–37.

3. Yūki Reimon, "Shushi no haibutsusetsu ni okeru kompon dōki" 朱子の排佛說に於ける根本動機, *Shina Bukkyō shigaku*, 4, 1 (1940), 1–13.

On the borrowings of Taoism from Buddhism the following references are useful:

1. Tokiwa Daijō 常盤大定, "Dōkyō gaisetsu" 道教概說, *Tōyō gakuhō* 東洋學報, 10, 3 (1920), 305–348.

2. *Idem, Shina ni okeru Bukkyō to Jukyō Dōkyō* 支那に於けろ佛教と儒教道教, Tokyo, 1930, 750 + 28 pp.

3. Maspero, H., *Le Taoisme*.

4. Chang Chun-fang 張君房, *Yün-chi ch'i-ch'ien* 雲笈七籤, in *Ssu-pu tsung-k'an* edition.

5. Chih-p'an 志磐, *Fo-tsu t'ung-chi* 佛祖統紀, *Taishō*, 49.

6. Chen Luan 甄鸞, *Hsiao-tao-lun* 笑道論, *Taishō*, 52.

7. Chia Shan-yüan 賈善淵, *Yu-lung-chuan* 猶龍傳, 6 *chüan*, *Tao-tsang*, 555.

8. Hsieh Shou-hao 謝守顥, *Hun-yüan sheng-chi* 混元聖紀, 9 *chüan*, *Tao-tsang*, 551–553.

9. *Idem, T'ai-shang Lao-chun nien-p'u yao-lüeh* 太上老君年譜要略, *Tao-tsang*, 554.

10. *Idem, T'ai-shang Hun-yüan Lao-tzu shih-lüeh* 太上混元老子史略, 3 *chüan, ibid.*

11. Fu Ch'in-chia 傅勤家, *Tao-chiao-shih kai-lun* 道教史概論, Shanghai, 1933

12. (author unknown), *Lao-tzu hua-hu-ching* 老子化胡經, *Taishō*, 54, no. 2139.

13. *Fa-lun miao-ching* 法論妙經, *Tao-tsang*, 177.

14. Kubota Ryōon 久保田量遠, *Shina Ju Dō Butsu kōshōshi*, 支那儒道佛交涉史, Tokyo, 1943, 341 pp.

15. *Idem, Shina Ju Dō Butsu sangyō shiron* 支那儒道佛三教史論, Tokyo, 1931.

16. H. G. Creel, "What is Taoism," *JAOS*, 76, 3 (1956), 139-152.

17. Chi Hsien-lin, "Lieh-tzu and Buddhist Sutras," *Studia Serica*, 9, 1 (1950), 18-32.

On the influence of Buddhism on Chinese medicine see:

1. Article on "Byo" in *Hōbōgirin*, 3, 225-265, especially 257-265.

2. Pierre Huard and Ming Wong, *La médicine chinoise au cours des siècles*, Paris, 1959, 27-32.

3. Ch'en Yin-k'o 陳寅恪, "Hua T'o Chuan" 華陀傳, *Tsing-hua hsüeh-pao*, 6, 1 (1930), 17-20.

On the influence on language see:

1. T. Watters, *Essays on the Chinese Language*, Shanghai, 1889, especially chaps. 8 and 9, "The Influence of Buddhism on the Chinese Language."

2. Lo Ch'ang-p'ei, "Indian Influence on the Study of Chinese Phonology," *Sino-Indian Studies*, 1, 3 (1944), 117-124.

3. H. Maspero, "Le dialecte de Tch'ang-ngan sous les T'ang," *BEFEO*, 20 (1920), 2, 1-124.

4. Chang Shih-lu 張世祿, *Chung-kuo yin-yün-hsüeh-shih* 中國音韻學史, Shanghai, 1938, 1, 130-163; 2, 17-32.

5. Ch'en Yin-k'o, "Ssu-sheng san-wen" 四聲三問, *Tsing-hua hsüeh-pao*, 9, 2 (1934), 275-288.

6. Chou Fa-kao 周法高, "Fo-chiao tung-ch'uan tui Chung-kuo yin-yün-hsüeh chih ying-hsiang" 佛教東傳對中國音韻學之影響, *Chungkuo fo-chiao-shih lun-chi*, 775-808.

On astronomy see:

1. E. Huber, "Termes persans dans l'astrologie bouddhique chinoise," *BEFEO*, 6 (1906), 39-43.

2. F. W. K. Muller, "Die persischen Kalendarausdrucke im chinesischen Tripitaka," *Sitzungberichte der koniglich preussischen Akademie der Wissenschaften, Phil. Hist. Kl.*, (1907), 458-465.

3. J. Needham and Wang Ling, *Science and Civilization in China*, Cambridge, 1959, vol. 3, section on "astronomy" passim.

# INDEX

## Other Titles in Mythology, Philosophy, and Religion Also Available in Princeton and Princeton/Bollingen Paperbacks

THE ANCIENT NEAR EAST: *An Anthology of Texts and Pictures*, edited by James B. Pritchard (#10), $2.95

ARCHAEOLOGY AND THE OLD TESTAMENT, by James B. Pritchard (#137), $2.95

ATTACK UPON "CHRISTENDOM," by Søren Kierkegaard, translated by Walter Lowrie (#116), $2.95

CHRISTIAN DISCOURSES, by Søren Kierkegaard, translated by Walter Lowrie (#225), $2.95

THE COGNITIVITY PARADOX: *An Inquiry Concerning the Claims of Philosophy*, by John Lange (#196), $1.95

THE CONCEPT OF DREAD, by Søren Kierkegaard, translated by Walter Lowrie (#90), $1.95

CONCLUDING UNSCIENTIFIC POSTSCRIPT, by Søren Kierkegaard, translated by David F. Swenson and Walter Lowrie (#140), $3.95

EITHER/OR (Volume I), by Søren Kierkegaard, translated by David F. Swenson and Lillian Marvin Swenson with revisions and a foreword by Howard A. Johnson (#253), $2.95

EITHER/OR (Volume II), by Søren Kierkegaard, translated by Walter Lowrie with revisions and a foreword by Howard A. Johnson (#254), $2.45

ELEUSIS AND THE ELEUSINIAN MYSTERIES, by George E. Mylonas (#155), $4.95

ESSAYS ON A SCIENCE OF MYTHOLOGY: *The Myth of the Divine Child and the Mysteries of Eleusis*, by C. G. Jung and C. Kerényi (P/B #180), $2.95

FEAR AND TREMBLING *and* THE SICKNESS UNTO DEATH, by Søren Kirkegaard, translated by Walter Lowrie (#129), $1.95

FOR SELF-EXAMINATION *and* JUDGE FOR YOURSELVES! by Søren Kierkegaard, translated by Walter Lowrie (#115), $2.45

KARL JASPERS: *An Introduction to His Philosophy*, by Charles F. Wallraff (#197), $2.95

THE KING AND THE CORPSE: *Tales of the Soul's Conquest of Evil*, by Heinrich Zimmer, edited by Joseph Campbell (P/B #257), $2.95

LIGHT FROM THE ANCIENT PAST: *The Archeological Background of the Hebrew-Christian Religion* (Volume I), by Jack Finegan (#173), $3.45